Royce's
Powerboating Illustrated
The best of all powerboating worlds.

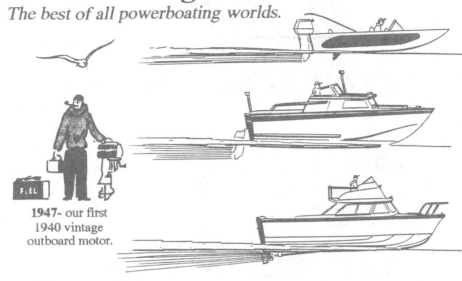

1947- our first
1940 vintage
outboard motor.

35 years of *BASIC* powerboating *CONCEPTS.*

Vocations and professions require exposure to an endless number of new unrelated ideas called **basic concepts.** Considerable study, followed by idea exchanges and "hands on" training to bring out unexpected variables, are required to pass the final exam. Such are vocational and professional standards for your recognition to officially practice that form of expertise.

27 easy ways to enter powerboating.

Powerboating Illustrated provides the ***first full nuts and bolts coverage*** in one text. The 48 page ***Workbook*** provides the key with 27 different ways for the newcomer to enter powerboating. This is a new first in powerboating education to help employees entering industry jobs, as well as boat owners.

Best korn drippins and premix in Polecat Korners.

Royce's
Powerboating Illustrated
6th edition

Copyright **1960, 1962, 1978, 1981, 1992, 1994**

by Patrick M. Royce
Much information comes from *Trailerboating Illustrated*.

other books by Patrick M. Royce-

Powerboating Illustrated
Workbook

Sailing Illustrated
Volume 1

Sailing Illustrated
Volume II

Sailing Illustrated
Workbook

Sailing Illustrated
Workbook Lectures

This manual belongs ro----

name
----

telephone
----

address
----

state, zip

Royce Publications
Box 1967
Newport Beach,
CA 92663
(714) 642-4430
FAX (714) 646- SAIL

ISBN 0-911284-02-8

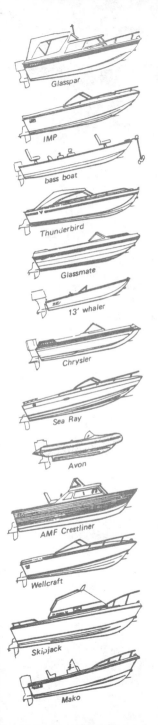

Glasspar

IMP

bass boat

Thunderbird

Glassmate

13' whaler

Chrysler

Sea Ray

Avon

AMF Crestliner

Wellcraft

Skipjack

Mako

Welcome to *Powerboating Illustrated.*

Alnico magnets. The cranky, temperamental outboard motor had been around for many years. It was necessary for the introduction of a new magnet many times more powerful, for the outboard motor to have a chance to prove itself.

Mercury took the early engineering lead to produce strong, dependable racing motors that were just as dependable for fishing, and the family cruiser. We entered this field in 1958 when the first 100 hp outboard motor was introduced with a $1000 price tag.

1960 planing hulls. They had to have clean, functional planing bottoms to easily maintain 30 mph speeds with 60 to 70 hp outboard motors and still have some degree of a soft ride compared to the very efficient hard ride of *Blunder* in any kind of wave action.

1980 planing hulls are shown at left using outboard and outdrive powerplants. As the HP had grown considerably, the boats could be larger, with gussied up lines for owner appeal little concerned with wasting some power for a soft ride at 30 to 40 mph.

3

The horsepower race. The larger dependable outboard motors in the late 1950's, spurred improved planing hulls, and long-haul trailers in the southwest. With water holes far between, it was common to tow a boat 400 miles to go fishing or water skiing. In the northeast from Minnesota thru New England with ample lakes and rivers, 50 to 70 miles towing a year was considerable at that time.

A boat performance race. When problems develop, consider checking the hull first, with the powerplant a secondary factor.

You soon find many problems blamed on outboard, outdrive, and inboard powerplants, are hull or trailer problems.

We systematically take the parts of the trailer-boating rig, define and examine them, until you run out of unexpected mechanical surprises.

Such awareness is required for efficient planing hulls and powerplants ready to serve your needs when required as dependability cannot be accidental.

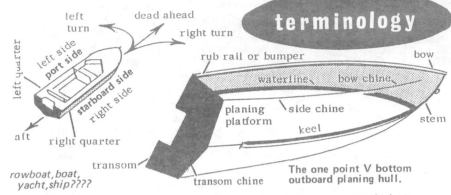

terminology

left turn · dead ahead · right turn

left quarter · left side · port side · starboard side · right side

aft · right quarter

rub rail or bumper · bow

waterline · bow chine

planing platform · side chine · keel · stem

transom

transom chine

The one point V bottom outboard planing hull.

rowboat, boat, yacht, ship????

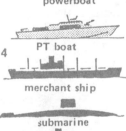

outboard boat

powerboat

4 · PT boat

merchant ship

submarine

ferry boat

motor ship

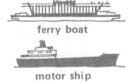

yachts

still a rowboat

Right turn or turn to starboard. It is more practical to use auto terms turn to right, or turn to left avoiding traditional terms turn to port, or starboard

Motor vs engine. Motor is the standard term for all French and German powerplants derived from the French term *moteur.*

Engine vs motor. U.S. SAE (Society of Automotive Engineers) defined *motor* as a rotating device with an electrical power source. An *engine* converts heat energy using a piston, into reciprocating mechanical power.

Outboard motor, motor car, motor oil, etc., have long been accepted by public use regardless of SAE definition. We use terms outboard motor and engine interchangeably as our interest is to communicate in a technical field with its developing language starting with a slang term foundation. This is parallel to the sailing language also growing out of slang terms that proved themselves often hundreds of years old, our everyday sailing language worldwide.

Boat vs ship. Our Navy defines a boat as less than 65' long dependant on, and capable of being carried on a larger vessel. An oceangoing *ship* has a larger cruising radius with fuel capacity for deep-water navigation.

The *PT boat* began 65' to 75' long, called a boat due to minimum cruising radius. Small *submarines* kept growing larger, are still called boats. *Ferry boats* remain boats due to limited cruising radius. **Motor ships** use diesel engines to operate electric motors. These motors turn ship propellers with minimum operating cost.

Boat vs yacht. Your dinghy becomes a yacht, a vessel used for pleasure or state occasions, while the *rowboat* remains a rowboat by legal definition. Let us all enjoy our confusing marine language.

Powerboating Illustrated

trailerboats

home port-BACKYARD
the main advantage

The term **TRAILERBOAT RIG** covers a tremendous variety of equipment with endless portable powerboat rigs finding it the exception to find two rigs that are identical.

The term refers to all general and specific applications of the trailerboat package consisting of boat, trailer, power plant, and other equipment. For the best compromise of basic elements consider the following—

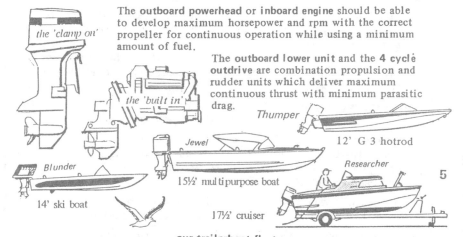

the 'clamp on'

The **outboard powerhead** or **inboard engine** should be able to develop maximum horsepower and rpm with the correct propeller for continuous operation while using a minimum amount of fuel.

the 'built in'

The **outboard lower unit** and the **4 cycle outdrive** are combination propulsion and rudder units which deliver maximum continuous thrust with minimum parasitic drag.

Thumper

Jewel

12' G 3 hotrod

Blunder

14' ski boat

15½' multipurpose boat

Researcher

17½' cruiser

5

our trailerboat fleet

The **hull design** should be able to carry the outboard motor...or inboard engine with outdrive, jet drive, or V drive, to change lower unit thrust into efficient hull movement thru, or on top of the water with minimum parasitic drag or wave action at all speeds. The bottom must be rigid and nonflexing to avoid a hook, pg. 50, at planing speeds.

The **hull interior** should have sufficient load carrying capacity, comfort, and accommodations for your kind of boating use.

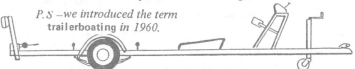

P. S —we introduced the term **trailerboating** *in 1960.*

The **trailer** is a portable dry dock providing maximum hull support with portability ease for launching, loading, trailering, and storage.

When the trailer isn't carrying your boat, will it have sufficient flexibility to provide other uses such as carrying lumber, furniture, bulky objects such as mattresses, dune buggies, motorcycles, etc.

Powerboating Illustrated

This book is designed to provide the nuts and bolts teaching and reference manual for the marine industry... and for recreational boat owners.

Individual use. It can be sufficient for many persons wanting reference ideas from this book in a hit and miss fashion.

Classroom use. Much more information can be systematically covered in a week to two weeks, five days a week, eight hours a day classroom. After students complete the terminology assigned homework, instructors can enlarge on the information the next day adding personal experiences which may differ somewhat in various U.S. areas.

Industry sponsored schools? If they can be developed nationwide in various areas, they can provide an excellent pretraining background for future mechanics in marine, and other fields. Many can then be accepted for "hands on" factory training schools including outboard motors, outdrive, inboard and diesel engines, powerboat and sailboat builders, and trailer manufacturers.

Marine stores can hire graduates to help customers with a broad foundation in metals, propellers, wiring, electrical components, etc.

Boat yards deal with considerable complexity as each boat has its own problems. The broad theoretical background can soon help solve problems beginning with the complexity of corrosion, beyond workers having a limited background.

Auto mechanics wanting to understand the marine field, can learn the new peculiarities involved, to expand their areas of expertise.

Boat owners may soon want to take the same courses to broaden their understanding of the nuts and bolts of this greatly diversified power-boating field. What better method is available than to learn it alongside with, and in the mechanics terms for easy communication and understanding when future owner problems arise.

This new manual is just another tool for the mechanic.

A well trained, quality oriented mechanic will always be in demand, especially with the present mechanic shortage.

Where do you want to be in 1, 3, and 5 years? Define your goals, and the methods to obtain them to fit your personality, needs, and desires. If you want to go fishing a couple of hours a day, your shop can be open later at night, a plus for many customers. Also, good mechanics are always needed nationwide... and in some areas, worldwide.

As for luck, forget the rabbits foot. Luck begins with good systematic planning and training to satisfy your customers needs, so you are able to make the most of your personal goals.

6

Welcome to the fascinating marine mechanic world... your NEW profession!

The story behind *Powerboating Illustrated.*

We published our first book *Sailing Illustrated* in 1956. It was followed by teaching, cruising, and racing a variety of larger sailboats, and inboard powerboats from 28' to 40' long.

The growing outboard market. had our curiosity. We bought a ski boat with a racing background, an excellent hull with a clumsy homemade trailer, we called it *Blunder.* The rig had problems confusing mechanics. The alternatives were selling the rig, or drowning... until taking a week long factory school with dealers and mechanics held by the southwest Mercury distributor.

More research was still required. *as I found most of my marine equipment operational ideas were half truths.* We spent considerable time on the ocean with our three trailerboat rigs. We systematically began exchanging ideas with dealers, owners, two and four-cycle marine mechanics.

Communications proved an interesting challenge. The traditional *Two-Stroke Cycle Engine* language of office bound engineers was impractical. We began writing in the unique, earthy, easy-going slang language of the new little-recorded trailerboating field. This paralleled the operational international sailing language developed from slang terms that were used by captains, mates, and crew... terms that are standard today.

7

Outboard motor manufacturers face a responsibility to train their new mechanics with the latest engines, tools, and concepts so their motors are dependable with happy customers. They will have an excellent background in the present generation of CDI electrical systems.

That is only part of the mechanics training. I often see half the motors in most outboard repair shops for maintenance or repair are the previous generation *PCI (points, condenser, ignition) electrical systems* plus magnetos we cover in depth in this manual.

A corrosion reporter for 35 years. Since we have found no practical text in this field, we report the fascinating basics and variables to help you with both 2 cycle and 4 cycle powerplants.

> **1960 planing hulls.** The 1960 first generation page 38 had to prove themselves using lower horsepower motors available at the time.
>
> **1980 planing hulls.** The 1980 third generation, page 39, have a wide mixture of 1960 hull basics. Larger motors made it easier for less efficient hulls to perform at their upper speeds. The extra energy needed usually shows in the wake, increased fuel consumption, and more cost.

Jewel

> *The day of the good old general mechanic,and the general store,are history.*
>
> The dilemma facing the new mechanic is to become a specialist in one area only...or have a considerable knowledge of an endless variety of subjects to be successful which is the world of a good marine mechanic.

 1. He must be a **GOOD DETECTIVE** *to identify problems affecting an outboard motor caused elsewhere... while a parts replacement operator rushes to judgment considering major mechanical surgery.*

 2. He must know how to **ASK leading QUESTIONS** *to identify the problems in simple,friendly terms without wasted time or effort.*

 3. He must be a **GOOD LISTENER** *as successful outboard mechanics have to pick up body language faster than mechanics in other fields.*

 4. He must be **PEOPLE ORIENTED** *to find normal ways within his personality to handle hostile customers making mistakes...so they will gain confidence to become his regular customers.*

 5. He must have a **SENSE of HUMOR.** *We provide the facing cartoon to help you let off steam on days when everything goes wrong,part your fault,and part,beyond control. Relax as you try to find how many people at:right are your customers...and have a good laugh.*

8

Training requires exposure to an endless variety of ideas. The *engine doctor* needs a background similar to a medical doctor who works with 'flexible plumbing'. Both require ample time, exposure, and theory to absorb endless raw, unrelated facts called *basic concepts.*

This book is a jigsaw puzzle of 416 pages of raw ideas each having its own importance. All parts must come together to complete a full picture jigsaw puzzle... with few missing parts.

Hands-on training. The MD instructor operates on an appendix with his students watching, a pattern they must follow in their first appendix operation. This is a similar pattern followed in factory school.

Diagnosis problems. Both professions soon find their texts don't have all the answers. That is the time you have to become your own detective following the five rules as your practice expands with happy customers.

Our 15th? outboard motor. I told the mechanic of its 6hp use in our sailboat. He ignored this trying to sell a 20hp motor and cases of oil. After tank testing without running the carb dry, fuel would have spilled in the auto trunk if I didn't bring this to his attention. I again questioned him when he put the motor in the trunk with the lower unit high, cooling water draining into the powerhead. He was very angry by this time pointing to his sign,"Can't you see I am a factory authorized mechanic?'

I dedicate your training manual to this anonymous mechanic who broke all five rules. My problem was beginning. After two weeks adding complex remote controls... the increased angle of the new model lower unit was too wide to fit into my motor well. I hate to see grown men cry.

Is outboarding an emotional sport? *The cartoon above grew from a question asked outboard mechanic friends, "What were your most colorful, annoying, and challenging customers?"*

"My motor is slow... does it need a tuneup?"

The parts replacement operator vs the trained detective mechanic.

The outboard motor is the portable powerplant adapted to all kinds of lake, river, and ocean fishing, water skiing, and cruising with the portable trailerboat. It is also the little praised workhorse of the world from the steaming backwaters of the Amazon jungle to the frigid Arctic for Eskimos hunting seals offshore.

● *The U.S. faces a shortage of trained marine mechanics.* This book is designed to teach a new generation of marine mechanics by simplifying the complexities of 30 years marine operation into basic ideas or concepts. Students can then put together the parts of the full package boat assembly. If one or two parts or ideas don't work, it becomes a simple matter for the mechanic detective to check and find the necessary changes... with his full analysis separating him from most parts-replacement operators.

● *HOW TO MANUALS*— most outboard manuals follow factory manual snow belt sequence *how to take apart and assemble outboard motors* in the winter months, the limitations of many parts-replacement operators.

10 The owner in the cartoon above takes his motor in complaining it is slow, "It must need a tuneup". The parts replacement operator then tunes it to factory specifications. The angry owner soon returns complaining his motor is even slower, though doing what the owner requested as the operator isn't trained to the many ways hulls can change engine performance".

● *The marine-mechanic detective must know the full story of ALL power-boating components AND the marine environment.* That is the goal of this book to analyze hulls, trailers, two and four cycle powerplants, propellers, marine metals, corrosion, electrical wiring, battery operation, etc.

Students completing this *basic training* in trade schools or junior colleges, have an excellent chance to become marine store clerks, building or repairing boats, or providing maintenance services. This basic inside foundation gives students an excellent chance to be chosen for factory training courses to become certified outboard motor, or inboard engine mechanics.

● A marine store owner asked, "Why don't you also offer this book to the boating public? It provides the first chance for boat owners to understand the mechanics inside the marine field, instead of being a spectator on the outside looking in. Owners and mechanics would have similar foundations with better understanding as they use the same language of the trade".

We agreed. We hope readers like the idea speaking to them as mechanic detectives... as well as boat owners. It will provide boat operators the best of both worlds.

It is a rather simple idea to buy a 30'to 40' sailboat since it is a fully engineered factory package. The owner can buy new sails and add a depth sounder and other installations by himself or a mechanic. The problem—find a slip or mooring for his new or used sailboat.

The outboard trailerboat rig has considerable complexity due to the numerous components of boat, trailer, motor, and equipment chosen, then assembled by the owner or mechanic. Variables are endless from well planned rigs... to others thar are accidents waiting to happen.

Another variable depends on where the mechanic lives.

● **Northeast snow belt philosophy.** The outboard motor world began in the Great Lakes area as a welcome aid to replace the oars to go to the plentiful nearby fishing holes.

Basic statistics provided by outboard motor manufacturers in the 1960's found an average outboard motor operated 25 hours a year in this area... with an 80% of all motors within a 400 mile radius of Chicago, often of a lower hp to go fishing. Portability seemed a minor factor with the rig seldom towed more than 100 miles during the four month summer boating season.

11

The motors were taken in for maintenance and overhaul in the winter season which is stressed in factory manuals with the headquarters of U.S. outboard motor manufacturers also located in this area, continually ignoring what is happening in the sun belt areas where outboard motor sales are being rapidly taken over by Japanese motor manufacturers.

● **Southwest sun belt philosophy.** The watering holes are far between from Southern California to Texas where the portable outboard rig may be operated up to 11 months a year. It was common even back in 1960 to trailer a boat 400 miles on a single weekend.

I was fortunate to be the student of Donal Graves who saw the potentials of the sunbelt trailerboating world. His emphasis began with the **entire rig** for his Mercury mechanics for their first week of school. It began with boat bottoms, trailer support, propellers, fuel, batteries, and corrosion. With this excellent troubleshooting background, the new mechanic is ready for *hands-on training* under capable supervision to maintain, take apart, and overhaul a variety of outboard motors.

This was the basic philosophy of our "TrailerBoating Illustrated" published three years later in 1960. It was the foundation for your present manual with more technical information added later.

To summarize—*we ask snow belt outboard mechanics if they could improve their income by having a better foundation in the sun belt trailerboating philosophy?*

launching

Outboard can usually be launched and recovered in shallow water without having bearings on trailer wheels get wet. Hull without skeg can be pulled up on beach without damage when camping overnight.

Inboard boat usually requires completely submerging trailer. Boat should never be anchored in less than 3 or 4 feet of water and should never be run up on shore. The inboard requires much deeper water for launching and recovery.

The outboard boat is more portable and is easier to launch and recover from a trailer.

thrust

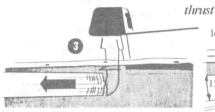

Prop is being dragged through at an angle.

level

12° to 14°

Prop delivers maximum thrust from the power available. At low speeds the outboard will kick up a smaller wake than the inboard boat will have with the same type of hull.

Some power is wasted by downward thrust of prop. Since inboard engine & hull weighs much more than the outboard, floats much lower, disturbs more water and produces a larger wake.

The outboard makes more efficient use of available hp on smaller boats and kicks up a smaller wake. Some water skiiers prefer the inboard wake which is larger and more challenging.

hitting obstructions

The outboard motor will swing up when it hits an underwater obstruction. After obstacle has been passed, motor swings down and continues operating.

Most outboard motors are vulnerable if they back into an obstruction. When in doubt as to rocks, etc., never back into shallow water.

Inboard shaft, strut, prop, and rudder, can be knocked out if it hits an underwater obstruction. The inboard should stay out of shallow water as damage to the shaft, strut, or rudder, will make it inoperative and out of control.

The inboard is vulnerable to underwater objects when going forward or reverse.

12

leaks

All wooden hulls should be fiberglassed to reduce leakage.

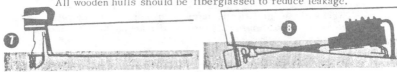

If outboard hull is well constructed, it should have few leaks since there are no through hull connections required for the outboard motor.

Inboard has many through hull fittings which may cause leaks. Since water must be constantly circulating through motor, a leaky hose connection can add to water collecting in bilge.

Never carry tanks in cabin.

fire & explosions

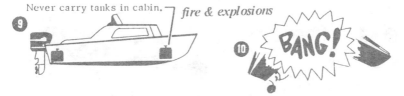

Motor is carried on transom and most fuel tanks are carried in the open. The gas fumes dissipate easily and danger of an explosion is practically nil.

Engine and gasoline are carried in sealed compartments. Gasoline fumes being heavier than air settle to the bottom of the bilge and explode when triggered by a spark.

13

cockpit space

Motor is out of boat. Tanks and battery are under seat providing maximum usable space for passengers & gear.

Engine much larger and located in middle of cockpit area which cuts down on the usable space for passengers & gear.

resale variables

What will happen if you buy a hull not to your liking?

If the inboarder is displeased with his engine OR his boat, it will usually be necessary to sell the entire rig.

If the outboarder likes his motor but chose a poorly performing hull, he can sell the hull separately. An outboard motor can be used on more than one boat.

Outboards • Inboards

In order to go 30 mph in a 16' hull for an hour - - - - -

What will the difference be in fuel consumption and weight of identical hulls made by the same manufacturer?

identical hull lines

①

②

Outboard hull with all necessary equipment but without motor may weigh approx. 750 lbs.

Inboard hull requires much heavier bracing in order to support the larger & heavier inboard engine. The inboard hull will weigh approx. 850 lbs.

powerplant weight

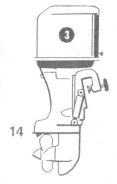

③

④

14

We have chosen a 60 hp motor which will easily put this hull over the 30 mph required. With the cooling water flowing through the motor the total weight will be approx. 200 lbs., inboard engine weighs about 800-900 lbs.

As planing speed is in proportion to wetted area, about 125 inboard hp is required to push same boat at same speed. Inboard engine weighs 800 lbs. plus another 150-250 lbs. for shaft, prop, etc.

same passengers at the same speed

⑤

⑥

The entire weight is approx. 1420 lbs. with 3 passengers, the boat, and motor. Fuel consumption of this outboard motor will be approx. 6 gallons at 30 mph.

With the same three passengers this inboard rig will weigh approx. 2100 lbs. Fuel consumption according to standard calculations will be approx. 6 gallons an hour at 30 mph.

❼ *wetted surface vs boat speed*

Speed is basically controlled by WETTED SURFACE. Reduce this friction & the speed will be increased. To push the same boat at same speed, standard inboard mounting will weigh considerably more than 2 cycle installation.

Fuel consumption comparison can never be calibrated using hp or cu. in. displacement, it is only part of story. When discussing 2 cycle vs 4 cycle fuel requirements you must use SPEED and MILES PER GALLON.

Of the two boats shown above, the gasoline consumption rate will be similar. The primary difference will be oil consumption requirements for 2 cycle operation.

Powerboating Illustrated

Outboards • Inboards

repairs and maintenance variables

Largest rig with motor on transom can be trailered to repair shop of YOUR choice.

If repair shop cannot finish your work in required time, rig can be trailered to another shop for repairs.

Service call must be made at dock by mechanic. If repairs can't be finished on boat, shaft and wiring harness must be disconnected so engine can be lifted out and hauled to shop. Mounting engine back in boat is time consuming and expensive.

propeller damage

Tilt-up feature of outboard motor protects prop from damage in most situations. If prop is damaged, the motor can be tilted up at dock permitting easy removal of prop which can be repaired or replaced. Every outboarder should carry a spare prop eliminating an expensive tow job if prop on motor is damaged.

Boat must be lifted out of water or dry docked to work on damaged prop. If prop SHAFT has been bent by hitting bottom, a rock, or a piling, the shaft must be uncoupled and removed for straightening. Relining shaft is a time consuming job. Prop failure usually means a tow job back to the nearest boat yard.

15

storage

Since most outboarders have a trailer and home parking area or garage, the storage cost when boat isn't used is reduced to minimum.

Having boat in backyard gives owner more time to work on it during the evenings and weekends.

As most inboards don't have trailers, they must be left at a mooring or in a boatyard where a watchman will watch over boats to prevent theft and vandalism.

Owner must drive to yard on weekends to work on boat.

Storage is a MAJOR boating expense.

What basic items should we consider
when shopping for our new boat?

Every trailerboat rig is a compromise...so choose the best
compromises for your boating needs.

● **SAFETY**

CONSTRUCTION vs SPEED and HP. The 25 to 40 mph
planing hull must be able to support its load, accept the
maximum thrust of the motor on the transom, then take
unexpected hazards with minimum damage.

SELF-BAILING SPLASH PAN--long shaft motors with enough
freeboard are important to prevent swamping.

●**STABILITY**...handling...controllability...buoyancy

CORNERING. Will the boat flip, dive, spin out, or reverse the
controls in tight turns at top...and at moderate speeds.

ROLLING and BROACHING. Will the hull have dangerous
tendencies when caught in rough weather wave action?

16

FLOTATION. If the boat is swamped or flipped will it sink,
float upside down, float with the stern submerged, or float
right-side up on an even keel to permit bailing?

● **SPEED vs RIDE**--the one-point planing hull

How much speed will be compromised for a soft ride?

The 2 cycle outboard motor provides its best performance
on an efficient planing hull. The minimum performance hull
may provide poor stability on a straightaway or in turns,
and it may have minimum bracing. An inefficient planing
hull will rob much of the motor's potentials to provide a
dull, lackluster ride.

MAXIMUM performance hull for smooth water. Flat and
arc bottom hulls are practical for protected lakes and rivers
with calm water. The same small hulls with low freeboard
will have a rough pounding ride in choppy water.

MEDIUM performance hull will not float as high at the
dock and will be a little slower in a similar length hull
with the same hp motor. It will ride easier in a little chop
as the hull has a less efficient bite on the water for planing.

MINIMUM performance hull is similar to an airplane which
doesn't have sufficient wing area to fly normally. AVOID
as performance is unpredictable.

● ADAPTABILITY vs SPECIALIZATION

Are you interested in a general utility open boat,a cabin cruiser,a rough water fishing boat,or a specialized racing hull.Will the boat provide the kinds of boating you desire or will it be limited to one specific use?

● COMFORT

CUSHIONS are needed to absorb the chop and ease the ride of most planing hulls.Washable naugahyde cushions are softer for use than the Approved cushions designed for flotation that are much harder to sit on.

STOWAGE SPACE. How efficiently is the stowage space designed,does it have any wasted space...and does the stowage space serve your needs.Does it have enough leg room for the cockpit,and are the bunks long enough to sleep on.

The TOP. The sunshade/spray deflector when up should not block visibility,and when down is out of the way.

The WINDSHIELD is a practical answer to protect long hair from wind and spray at planing speeds.

A large windshield may reduce top speed..while if it is too small the windshield may become a wind funnel to increase wind and spray speed going thru a passengers hair.

17

WILL THE WINDSHIELD BE SHATTERPROOF? Windshields become a hazard *if* a person is thrown into one during a flip, the reason racing drivers knowing the hazards of upsets and spinouts...may avoid windshields on their family trailerboats.

● HULL PROTECTION...design...style...durability

DURABILITY. Planing hulls must take a lot of bumps and thumps around docks and next to other boats.A wrap-around neoprene or other material bumper at deck level is required to protect the sides and the finish of your planing hull.

CORROSION. Chromed metal fittings attract attention at the boat show,but what metal is beneath the chrome plating? Avoid mixing metals when possible...our Corrosion Chapter covers this complex subject in depth.

ORIGINAL COST vs MAINTENANCE. Wooden hulls are often less expensive though they need constant care to remain in top condition.Fiberglass hulls may be more expensive,though if a good design and well built,will take more bumps and weather,yet still look **showroom fresh** with minimum effort and attention.

Almost ALL collisions...there are few accidents, ARE CAUSED by lack of knowledge of the rules, personality traits, and when both factors are involved, collision potentials rapidly increase.

Weather factors may contribute when the POSITIVE ION suddenly moves into a persons body *to diminish the brain's analytical ability for periods of 8 to 40 hours.* The positive ion replaces the negative ion as the full moon moves in. It also occurs with *devil winds* under various names such as Santanas, chinook, williwa, etc., that tumble down mountain passes to compress and warm the air.

The personality traits to analyze are those the author learned for self-protection while teaching 1600 new sailors with 8 hour lessons on the water underway

Much of this time was spent in heavy traffic to help students develop an awareness to the rules, plus the type and condition of an oncoming sailboat or powerboat to analyze the personality traits of the owner.

● A basic factor—**drivers who are accident prone on the highway, will also be accident prone when flying an airplane, or operating a boat. It is this very small percent of people who produce the major share of boating collisions, injuries, and fatalities.**

● *The accident prone person* may be a slow talker, or a fast talker. He acts on impulse, then later tries to analyze his reasoning...often when having to explain it to the USCG, the judge, or the insurance investigator.

● *The dirty, banged-up boat at right indicates, a careless, sloppy person* with little attention to details...who will always be a problem.

18

● Glib, fast talking businessmen, entertainers, and salesmen *people handlers* work long and hard to excel in their field. While their trained, instant impulses are excellent to handle people, the other side of their personality has little time or interest left to study mechanical operation...for which their boating impulses are poorly prepared.

● *Steering controls should be from the center to the right side of a powerboat so the operator has full visibility of the* **danger zone,** see pg. 78. Left hand controls on the black boat at right provide instant warning that the operator has little knowledge of the operational rules to prevent collisions, and his visibility may be limited.

● *The macho image* may be a man who tries to act masculine to cover his lack of self assurance. *Power gives him masculine self assurance,* while he collects speeding tickets on the highway. And on the water to impress himself and/or others, or with the challenge of a dare, he will go full throttle in dumb situations to impress himself.

● *A whale of a tale*—after thousands of hours teaching others to avoid collisions, we hit a whale on our sailboat at maximum speed. His tail struck our bow as he panicked to sound, sending our bow skyward at a 60° angle. He probably flipped our heavy boat clear of the water while wiping out much of our bottom paint...without structural damage. Was he an accident prone whale?

● **The negative personality traits were included for your self protection.** Do a thorough, competent job when assembling or overhauling equipment so if a collision results, it will be due to the fault of the operator, not equipment failure...as lawyers are darn expensive.

Just can't understand what happened, it looked so beautiful at the boat show.

Design Practicality

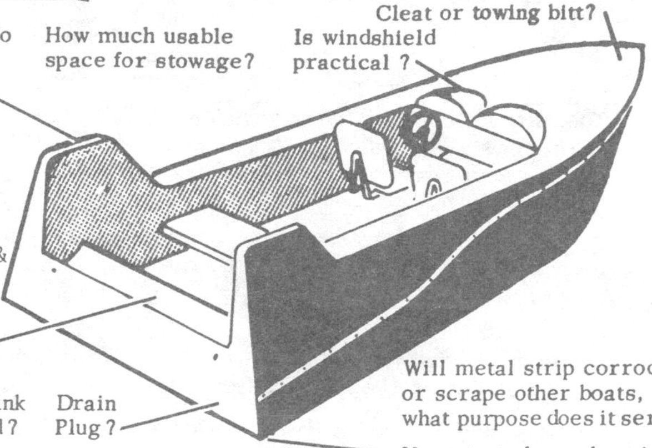

What purpose do the extreme fins serve?

How much usable space for stowage?

Is windshield practical?

Cleat or **towing bitt?**

Where are cleats for fenders?

In rough water & a following sea splash pan may not be enough protection.

Will this boat sink if it is swamped?

Drain Plug?

Will metal strip corrode or scrape other boats, what purpose does it serve?

For better visibility, steering wheel should be on other side of boat, see Pilot Rules.

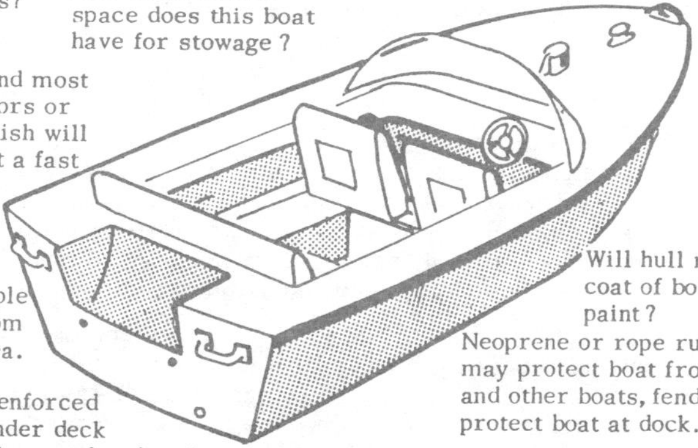

Unprotected overhanging chine can receive a lot of punishment.

19

Does boat have necessary navigational lights?

How much usable space does this boat have for stowage?

Ample cleat or towing bitt reinforced under deck.

Will boat spend most of time outdoors or indoors. Varnish will deteriorate at a fast rate under a hot sun.

Stern has ample protection from a following sea.

Will hull need a coat of bottom paint?

Neoprene or rope rub strip may protect boat from piling and other boats, fenders can protect boat at dock.

Are cleats reenforced sufficiently under deck to permit towing another boat?

Is boat too small or too large for the area in which you will do most of your boating?

If boat is to spend a lot of time around salt water, metal fittings should be at a miminum.

Fiberglassing a wooden boat may be a good idea, it also stops a lot of leaks.

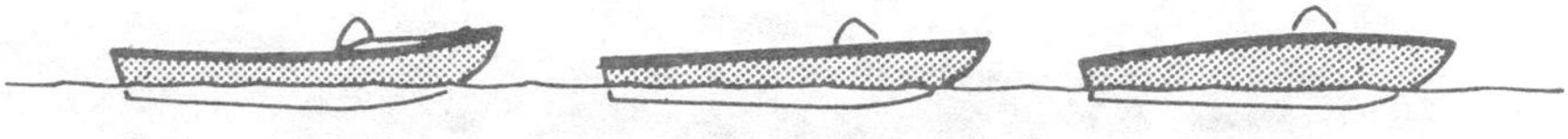

Conventional Sheer

Straight Sheer

Reverse Sheer

Powerboating Illustrated

To plane or not
to plane ——

oops...

The cartoonist illustrates impossible situations so readers may smile
or laugh, or to emphasize technical points for readers attention. The
facing page shows the extremes of planing and displacement hulls,
a foundation that will be expanded in the rest of the book.

The long lean displacement hull can perform admirably with the
correct hp for propulsion. A 7½ hp outboard motor pushes our 24'
sailboat to a little over 6 knots, while a 20 hp motor might increase
the speed a ½ knot.

The displacement hull operates in its own specialized world, pgs. 29-35,
with examples of the overpowered displacement hull shown above.

We combine the worst of both worlds at right with the long, lean
displacement hull powered by a huge, winged 7 banger. While the
powerplant weight alone would sink the boat, the cartoon, "How's
that for power?" shows the powerplant going faster than the hull.
Two years later at the New York Boat Show I was stunned to see an
almost identical hull... without the 7 banger motor. The builder
became very angry when I showed him my cartoon.

After completing the cartoon of the wide outboard planing hull, I
found several almost identical workboats carried on the stern of large
tuna boats that remain at sea for up to six months at a time. The wide
workboat performs excellently to close their nets on the open ocean.

The outboard powered ocean liner cartoon below developed while
listening to a lecture on high performance hulls. I wasn't in a serious
mood, my fingers began drawing, and my mind began drifting. Dealers
sitting around me began laughing at the cartoon, which interrupted the
lecturer. I suddenly faced the occupational hazard of a cartoonist when
confronted by my victim without a sense of humor... the lecturer.

The hydroplane cartoon was inspired by an acquaintance who enjoyed
racing hot cars and hot boats. He was very pleased with the cartoon of
his lifetime dream, the impossible goal of a flying hydroplane. I found
the cartoonist can't please everyone, the final score—2 losses and 2 wins.

20

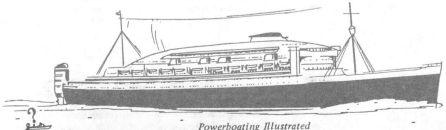

Powerboating Illustrated

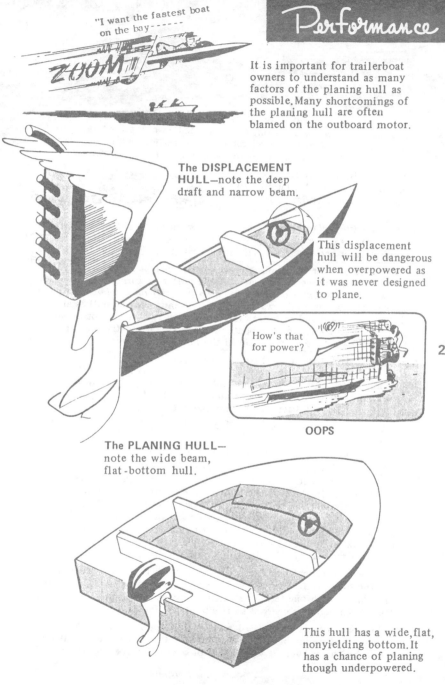

"I want the fastest boat on the bay------

ZOOM

It is important for trailerboat owners to understand as many factors of the planing hull as possible. Many shortcomings of the planing hull are often blamed on the outboard motor.

The DISPLACEMENT HULL—note the deep draft and narrow beam.

This displacement hull will be dangerous when overpowered as it was never designed to plane.

How's that for power?

OOPS

21

The PLANING HULL— note the wide beam, flat-bottom hull.

This hull has a wide, flat, nonyielding bottom. It has a chance of planing though underpowered.

Ahoy mate! Which direction is Tahiti?

The cartoon above was inspired by a West Los Angeles dealer in 1957. He was disturbed by a customer who wanted to buy a boat and motor to be the first to go to Hawaii on an outboard boat. While the dealer needed the sale, he didn't want to be responsible for a drowning.

I asked, "How many gallons of beer and outboard mix did he plan to take on his outboard cruise to Hawaii?"

● The *seaworthy planing hull* with a wide stern is a questionable term. If it operates on any large body of water the boat has to operate in good weather and reach protection *before* a storm can move in.

> When a 15',30',or 60' planing powerboat is caught in a storm in deep water and the engine or engines quit, the hull will turn sideways to the waves *as wind pressure tries to equalize itself on the bow and stern.* If the beam waves don't swamp the boat, so much of the hull is above the water surface, and so little below the sideway rolling motion will increase in intensity, and the boat roll over. The alternative is to ride to a *large parachute anchor* to hold the bow into the wind.

22

● We have a dory fishing fleet limited to 18 boats which has been operating from our local beaches for over 100 years. Most are sturdy wooden hulls designed for 35 hp motors. The 1950 present hull design is perfectly matched for this size motor with the bow riding high to provide a softer, and drier ride for normal operation.

For up to ten months a year they launch their boats thru the surf at dawn, with the first boat returning thru the surf to the beach having the best opportunity to sell his catch to waiting customers.

● Professional fishermen operating out of Oxnard and Ventura harbors use heavily constructed wooden flatbottom boats with outdrive to reach 40 mph...in the Channel Islands nearby with much more severe weather in the summer and winter. They seem to operate 12 months a year knowing every harbor or bight to use for storm protection. We've seen outdrive boats to 26' struggling at full throttle behind these work boats breaking the waves downwind with throttle eased to protect our struggling, quality fiberglass planing hulls. to reach their harbor.

● Our *Jewel* was caught in an upper force 6 storm that hit at dusk when returning from Avalon with four of us aboard the 15½' boat. We bailed with 7 hands, with one left for steering to reach our harbor to keep the battery from being submerged so it wouldn't short out.

Our boat was a mess with 8" of water still aboard when we tied up to our dock at midnight. At 4 a.m. a cloudburst sunk our *Jewel* at the dock to finish the job...it wasn't one of our better boating times.

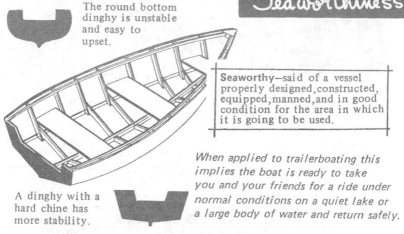

The round bottom dinghy is unstable and easy to upset.

Seaworthy—said of a vessel properly designed, constructed, equipped, manned, and in good condition for the area in which it is going to be used.

When applied to trailerboating this implies the boat is ready to take you and your friends for a ride under normal conditions on a quiet lake or a large body of water and return safely.

A dinghy with a hard chine has more stability.

The dinghy above is poorly constructed. It is possible to lose your footing and step thru the thin wooden hull as it has no floorboards to spread out your weight. The stern bracing isn't enough to support a small motor and waves can come aboard over the stern.

The *Jewel* is sturdily constructed which uses a long shaft motor was excellent for protected areas and for short trips along ocean coastal areas in good weather.

20 pt white r & g lights

23

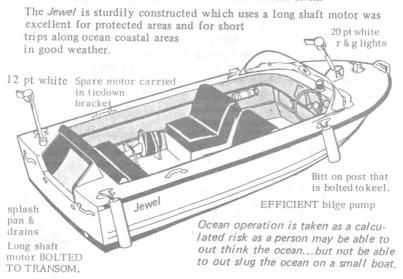

12 pt white   Spare motor carried in tiedown bracket

Bitt on post that is bolted to keel.

splash pan & drains

Jewel

EFFICIENT bilge pump

Long shaft motor BOLTED TO TRANSOM.

Ocean operation is taken as a calculated risk as a person may be able to out think the ocean...but not be able to out slug the ocean on a small boat.

The added 2 to 3 inches of freeboard are important to reduce waves coming aboard over the side in a summer squall. The windshield and convertible top prevent waves from coming aboard over the bow, and the splashpan/covered transom protects the stern in a following sea.

"Thanks for the WONDERFUL ride!!!!!"

Our 14' arc-bottom *Blunder* was a very efficient planing hull in smooth water. If it had a clean bottom, pg. 40, could easily pass 30 mph with two passengers and gear aboard.

We launched it in Long Beach Harbor with three of us aboard to watch the beginning of the sailboat race to Honolulu. The choppy water made a wet, merciless ocean ride. The next day the wife had me looking for a new boat (P.S., if the cartoon above looks like my wife...).

◈ **Planing hull extremes—one extreme produces a hard, wet ride which may be desired for high performance on protected waters...and be overcompensated for a slushy ride on the ocean.** The majority of trailerable planing hulls will be a compromise between these extremes. Some factors to consider to make your best compromise are—

◈ **Wind and spray flow** must be controlled and directed downward, outward, and aft...and by controlling these factors it increases planing efficiency. The boat will have a softer ride with minimum planing efficiency loss, and your passengers won't feel they survived a middle ages torture machine after returning to the dock. Our second boat *Jewel*, a Glasspar design shown upper right was chosen replacing *Blunder*.

Planing powerboats require a sufficient amount of **bow entry flare** to channel bow spray outward and aft instead of upward and across the deck. The windshield should be large enough to deflect the rest of the spray; if the windshield is too small it can become an air scoop to soak passengers, and if too large, will reduce the top boat speed.

◈ **The soft cushion ride.** As *Jewel* climbs up to planing trim, the flare and spray deflecting chine funnel the air and spray downwards and aft under the hull providing a cushion, with the excess curling aft and away from the hull. **If the spray curls forward**—it may be a wet boat when planing, with a performance loss.

The air and spray cushion provides lift to make a soft, comfortable ride on the ocean with 8 to 18 mph winds with air bubbles breaking the water surface tension...while the boat on a flat ocean would have a 2 to 4 mph speed loss.

The catamaran rides on a continuous air and spray cushion bubble for lift to increase top speed upwind with a softer ride...with an obvious drop in speed while going downwind with less lift as less air is flowing between the hulls.

Consider the planing hull in a controlled, hovering flight attitude on the surface of the water. *Will your boat be your friend with a controlled air and spray slipstream as the planing speed increases... or will it be a wet and miserable enemy with uncontrolled spray patterns and a rough, pounding ride?*

24

Planing hull spray and air has to be channeled into a controlled slipstream. It will improve hull speed while producing a softer ride in choppy water.

outward FLARE

Non-trip chine ❶

Jewel Spray chine ❷

❸

SPRAY DEFLECTING CHINE funnels most air and spray aft, downward, and outward. The downward and aft deflection and compression of air and spray forms a softer ride cushion when more efficient hulls will have a harder ride.

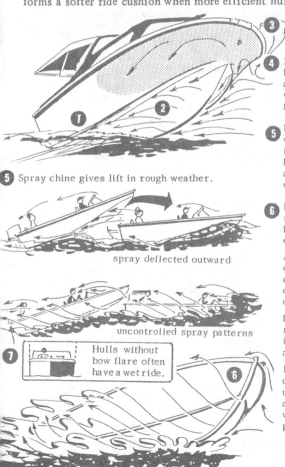

❸ FLARE helps to deflect wind and spray away from passengers.

❹ EXCESSIVE FLARE should be avoided on a light boat as bow may catch too much windage climbing onto plane, flipping over backwards.

25

❺ Illustration shows how well designed Spray Deflecting Chine provides added buoyancy in rough weather as bow resists digging in due to chine lift.

❺ Spray chine gives lift in rough weather.

❻ Round hull with small spray rails has little bow lift so bow has more tendency to dig in during chop.

spray deflected outward

As water follows least line of resistance during attempted compression, water & spray curls upward instead of outward at upper left.

uncontrolled spray patterns

Dissipation of this energy results in wet slushing ride instead of harnessing it to an efficient planing force.

❼ Hulls without bow flare often have a wet ride.

❻

Large wasteful wake and a cloud of spray indicates unnecessary disturbance as boat goes through water wasting horsepower, soaking passengers and gear.

Powerboating Illustrated

——ME, interested in speed?
All I want is something to take me
out to the fishing holes and back.
By the way what do you think
of my new boat ????

The outboard boat is called she as she must put her best profile forward...yet protect herself in the clinches.

The planing hull that has never hit an object hard or a glancing blow, has never left the dock...it goes with the territory. Let us examine the basic concepts of the factors involved in a planing boat colliding with an object...which should be a major factor for any owner to consider BEFORE buying a planing hull.

It is too late to find your boat hasn't been built to absorb the normal stresses of speed after hitting an object full throttle then trying to put the pieces together as you explain to to the USCG investigator, the insurance adjuster, or the judge.

We recommend a good, efficient planing hull should hold 30 mph easily with a top speed of 35 mph under ideal conditions...while some would rather have a top speed of 40 mph.

At first glance many boat owners may feel, *"If a boat goes twice as fast it will only hit an object twice as hard. So if my boat held together at 20 mph, it should also absorb a 40 mph impact"*.

As the speed of a planing hull increases, the forces of SUPPORT, MASS, and VELOCITY become quite complex.

BOTTOM SUPPORT—The speed of a planing hull at planing speed is governed by the amount of wetted bottom surface area. To double the speed requires the bottom support area to be decreased by ½ without flexing. Expressed another way, the bottom must support twice as much weight per square inch without flexing.

Enforcement officers we've taught have been quite interested when told that when at planing speeds they see a log, or other object ahead that is too late to miss pg. 73, hit the object head on, If you try to turn too late the unbalanced force produces many unnecessary hazards.

The seat directly in front of an outboard motor should be empty at planing speeds. If the lower units hits an underwater object and tilts forward momentarily...it could seriously hurt anyone sitting directly in front of the tilting outboard motor.

All objects, especially behind the driver, should be bolted down during a sudden impact with the sudden deceleration. The average full tank of outboard fuel and battery may average around 40 lbs. each.

USCG standards require a battery be contained, pg. 264, so it cannot move more than an inch in a pull of twice the weight of a battery in any direction. Instead of the 90 lb. basic pull they recommend, the 40 lb. basic battery becomes a projectile moving forward with approx. 640 lbs. of kinetic energy in a sudden stop from a 40 mph impact.

How much punishment will boat be able
to take on sudden impact with rock, log, etc?

$$1/2 \text{ Mass} \times \text{Speed}^2 = \text{Impact Force}$$

5 According to the formula for Kinetic Energy of motion, the governing factors
are the MASS (weight) and VELOCITY (speed) of a moving body. Other factors
are size of impact area & rate of DECELERATION measured in G (gravity) forces.

The planing hull has to withstand terrific stresses, both from the action of the
hull friction/support discussed in the planing chapter, and from IMPACT forces
such as hitting driftwood, stumps, sandbars, etc.

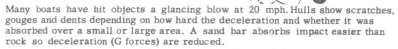

6 According to formula, boat hitting object
at 20 mph will be **FOUR** times as hard
as 10 mph; at 30 mph, **NINE** times as hard.

Many boats have hit objects a glancing blow at 20 mph. Hulls show scratches,
gouges and dents depending on how hard the deceleration and whether it was
absorbed over a small or large area. A sand bar absorbs impact easier than
rock so deceleration (G forces) are reduced.

Most hulls can take a 20 mph impact with little damage if some cushioning is
present to reduce deceleration rate. Suppose lower unit hits an immovable
object. It becomes a turning moment and pivots upward, swinging down after
obstructions is passed. Lower unit, clamp bracket & transom must be strong
to absorb sudden unbalanced force on upward and downward arc.

27

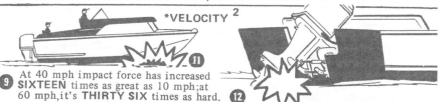

*VELOCITY ^{2}

9 At 40 mph impact force has increased
SIXTEEN times as great as 10 mph; at
60 mph, it's **THIRTY SIX** times as hard.

10 If boat travels in 40-60 mph range, forces set up may be more than boat & motor
can take. If lower unit hits immovable object, it can shear off or powerhead
may break loose from clamp bracket as tilting action cannot act fast enough to
ABSORB GRAVITY FORCES.

So think twice before you develop speed forces where racing drivers tread
gently. It is obvious there will be many variations when applying this
velocity/impact formula. Generally it isn't the impact that causes the damage
13 but the sudden DECELERATION whether in a car or boat. At 40 mph in a
sudden stop, a loose 40 lb. battery or full 6 gallon fuel tank suddenly becomes
an aimed projectile with approx. 640 lbs. of kinetic energy hurtling it through
the air or boat. SHOCK CORDS are very important to contain heavy objects
in place during a sudden stop or impact.

*Batteries and portable fuel tanks MUST BE CONSTRAINED
during sudden deceleration or they become lethal projectiles!*

Powerboating Illustrated

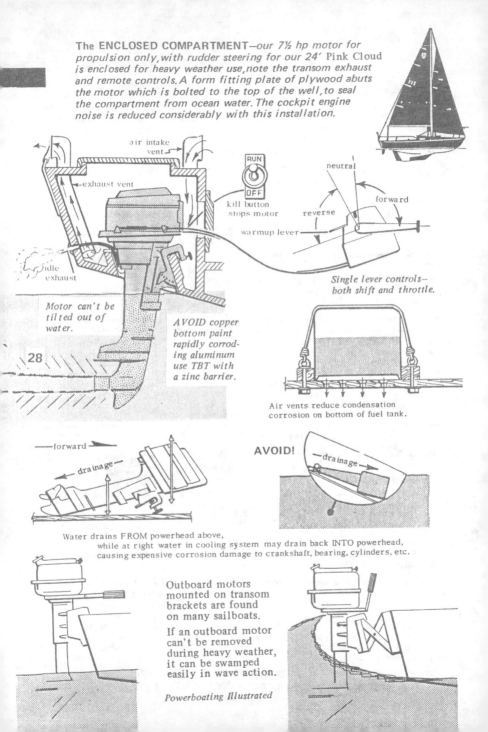

The **ENCLOSED COMPARTMENT**—*our 7½ hp motor for propulsion only, with rudder steering for our 24'* Pink Cloud *is enclosed for heavy weather use, note the transom exhaust and remote controls. A form fitting plate of plywood abuts the motor which is bolted to the top of the well, to seal the compartment from ocean water. The cockpit engine noise is reduced considerably with this installation.*

air intake vent

exhaust vent

RUN
OFF

kill button
stops motor

neutral

forward

reverse

warmup lever

idle exhaust

*Single lever controls—
both shift and throttle.*

Motor can't be tilted out of water.

AVOID copper bottom paint rapidly corroding aluminum use TBT with a zinc barrier.

28

Air vents reduce condensation corrosion on bottom of fuel tank.

forward

drainage

AVOID!

drainage

Water drains FROM powerhead above,
while at right water in cooling system may drain back INTO powerhead,
causing expensive corrosion damage to crankshaft, bearing, cylinders, etc.

Outboard motors mounted on transom brackets are found on many sailboats.

If an outboard motor can't be removed during heavy weather, it can be swamped easily in wave action.

Powerboating Illustrated

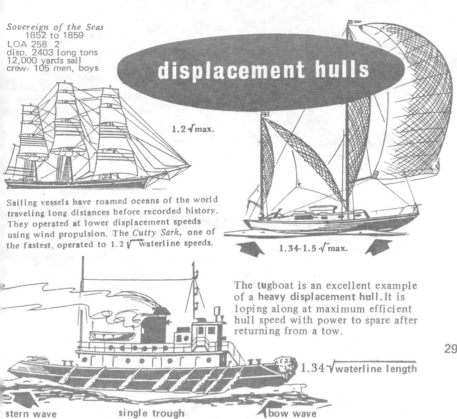

Sovereign of the Seas
1852 to 1859
LOA 258 2'
disp. 2403 long tons
12,000 yards sail
crew- 105 men, boys

displacement hulls

1.2 √ max.

Sailing vessels have roamed oceans of the world traveling long distances before recorded history. They operated at lower displacement speeds using wind propulsion. The *Cutty Sark*, one of the fastest, operated to 1.2 √ waterline speeds.

1.34-1.5 √ max.

The tugboat is an excellent example of a **heavy displacement hull**. It is loping along at maximum efficient hull speed with power to spare after returning from a tow.

1.34 √waterline length

stern wave   single trough   bow wave

The **HEAVY DISPLACEMENT HULL** is designed to plow thru the water as effortlessly and efficiently as possible such as the sailboat above up to the 1.34/maximum displacement hull speed ratio. The limiting factor is the waterline length with the self-generating bow and stern waves which coincide with the equal peaks of **ocean generated trochoidal waves.** Considerable power is required to exceed this limit on heavy displacement powerboats and sailboats.

The **LIGHT PLANING HULL** is a *surface skimmer* that is designed to skim across the water's surface as efficiently and effortlessly as possible after displacement and surfing speeds are exceeded.

Planing speeds are limited by weight, hull design, the amount of efficient bottom wing or lift area for support and stability, with ample hp propulsion. Tunnels on multihulls provide air lift to increase planing speed upwind by reducing wetted surface, with a comparable speed loss while planing downwind.

3.4 to 4.0 √   *Powerboating Illustrated*   3.4 to 4.0 √

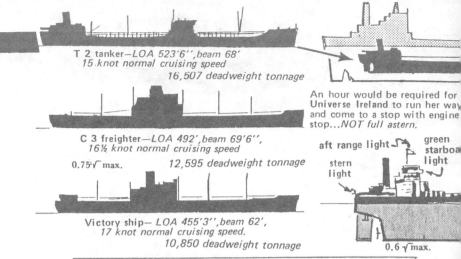

T 2 tanker—LOA 523'6'', beam 68'
15 knot normal cruising speed
16,507 deadweight tonnage

An hour would be required for
Universe Ireland to run her way
and come to a stop with engine
stop...*NOT full astern.*

C 3 freighter—LOA 492', beam 69'6'',
16½ knot normal cruising speed
0.75'√ max.   12,595 deadweight tonnage

aft range light ⤴   green
                       starboa
stern   light
light

Victory ship— LOA 455'3'', beam 62',
17 knot normal cruising speed.
10,850 deadweight tonnage

0.6 √ max.

A naval architect's analysis of displacement and planing hulls—
the hull speed-length ratio   vs   water and wavemaking resistance.

(1) **FRICTIONAL RESISTANCE.** The 200,000 ton and larger supertankers
gain speed slowly until reaching 14 to 15 knots. It is an efficient
0.6 ratio speed with 3 lbs. frictional resistance per ton of displacement.

30

(2) The bulk of world trade such as the Victory ship which is smaller, will
operate under an 0.8 ratio (see scale below) with approx. 4 lbs. of
frictional resistance per ton with minimum hull stress & conserve fuel.

(3) **WAVE MAKING.** High speed shipping begins on a 0.7 to 1.0 ratio
with 10 to 15 lbs. of frictional resistance. Fine ends are required to
maintain these speeds on large vessels with over 50% of the resistance
caused by wave making. This group includes some warships, smaller
coastal passenger vessels, and large passenger liners.

(4) From 1.0 to 1.25 ratios with water resistance increasing to 30 lbs.
of frictional resistance per ton, requires vessels with fine lines. They
also require considerable power to maintain these ocean speeds for
special vessels, and the faster classes of large warships...that do not
operate for profit.

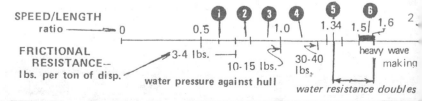

SPEED/LENGTH
ratio ———➤ 0   0.5   **1** **2** **3** **4**   **5**   **6**
                                            1.0   1.34 1.5 1.6   2

FRICTIONAL
RESISTANCE—
lbs. per ton of disp.   3-4 lbs. ——| 30-40   heavy wave
                                     10-15 lbs.   lbs.   making
                            water pressure against hull
                                                    water resistance doubles

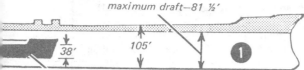

Bantry Bay Class Supertanker

maximum draft—81 ½'

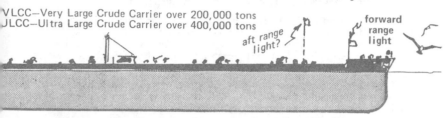

A T 2 tanker is shown for size comparison.

38' 105' **1**

Universe Ireland—
a Bantry Bay Class

LOA 1135' beam 174'

*326,000 tons with a
capacity of 2,513,588
barrels of oil*

Deadweight tonnage—*is the carrying capacity of a vessel, the
difference between being fully loaded, then without cargo.*

VLCC—Very Large Crude Carrier over 200,000 tons
ULCC—Ultra Large Crude Carrier over 400,000 tons

aft range
light?

forward
range
light

$1.34\sqrt{\text{waterline length}}$ = max. efficient displacement hull speed

5 The 90' tugboat at right is operating
at 12 knots with a ratio of 1.34 /WL
pushing over 50 lbs. of frictional
resistance per ton of displacement. The
tugboat waterline length and the **bow to
stern wave crest lengths** are equal.

31

6 The 1.55 ratio is the maximum
speed of some vessels which
cannot be exceeded with a
reasonable power increase. If the tugboat above reaches the 1.6 ratio,
it may capsize, water pressure may crush the hull, or erratic steering
may develop as fore and aft stability has been lost.

7 **SURFING.** The small planing hull easily passes this barrier with the
stern wave moving aft to cause the stern to sink, and the bow to rise
at 2.5 ratio with considerable pressure against the hull.

8 **PLANING.** The stern begins to rise and the bow drop at a 3.5 ratio
with decreasing wave-making resistance. The light planing hull skims
across the water surface due to lift from water resistance which is
14 times the pressure of the 1.0 ratio.

Powerboating Illustrated

7 see pages 36, 42 **8**

2.5 3.0 3.5 4.0

surfing begins all-out planing

**TREMENDOUS
WATER PRESSURE
PLANING LIFT**

1.0

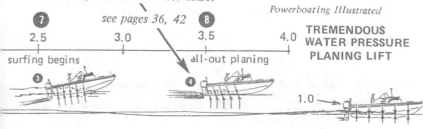

Maximum efficient speed & hp for light displacement hulls						
10'	4 3/4 knots	5 hp	25'	7 1/2	knots	25 hp
15'	5 3/4 knots	10 hp	30'	8 1/4	knots	30 hp
20'	6 3/4 knots	15 hp	35'	8.8	knots	35 hp
			40'	9 1/2 knots		40 hp

not possible

To convert *Land Miles to Nautical Miles...* divide by 0.87
To convert *Nautical Miles to Land Miles...* multiply by 1.15

The old fashioned rowboat with a narrow transom and rocker bottom is designed to slide as efficiently and effortlessly as practical thru the water with minimal wake or turbulence for rowing. When an adequate hp motor is used, the rowboat will reach maximum displacement hull speed with the hull, upper left, caught between bow and stern waves.

If the rowboat uses too large a motor, more throttle will cause the narrow stern to begin to sink due to minimum water support, while the bow wants to go skyward. If more throttle is applied the stern may go beneath the water swamping the boat and motor.

32

BOATS FOR RENT

FUEL

LENGTH	MOTOR	SPEED
8'	3 hp	4 1/2 mph
10'	5 hp	5 1/2 mph
12'	5 to 7 hp	6 mph
15'	8 to 10 hp	6 1/2 mph

propulsion only

2 *steering AND propulsion*

Outboard motors provide **thrust and rudder action** for steering. The good old 5 hp motor should easily take a 10' to 12' rowboat to maximum displacement hull speed. It also provides efficient steering control when it is necessary to throttle down in rough weather wave action, with the boat still under control.

Underpowered- smaller outboard motors may be used on the same size or larger rowboats in calm weather with the bow weaving from side to side **as they don't provide enough rudder action for efficient steering.** The same boat will be completely out of control in rough weather.

Propulsion only- our 24' sailboat has a 7½ hp outboard motor locked in position to provide **thrust** moving our heavy sailboat to hull speed. The large sailboat rudder **provides excellent steering control** with the keel providing directional stability to steer a straight course.

USS America—1047' long, 79,724 tons, 252' wide deck

speed 30 knots   four 22' dia. props   *Powerboating Illustrated*

The displacement hull **displaces a volume of water that is equal to the weight of the vessel.**

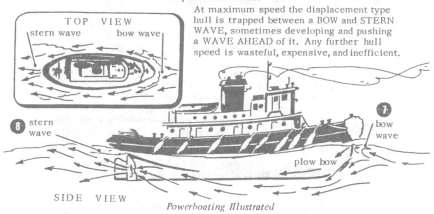

These vessels have displacement hulls.

At maximum speed the displacement type hull is trapped between a BOW and STERN WAVE, sometimes developing and pushing a WAVE AHEAD of it. Any further hull speed is wasteful, expensive, and inefficient.

TOP VIEW
stern wave   bow wave

SIDE VIEW

8 stern wave

bow wave

plow bow

Powerboating Illustrated

33

Tugboat has typical displacement hull which plows or pushes its way THROUGH the water as efficiently as possible. Water displaced by hull must regroup or replace itself at the stern of the boat. As water can't be compressed, tremendous horsepower is required to exceed maximum efficient hull speed.

*In the past 50 years, speed of the world's fastest ocean liners has increased by only 10 knots. The liner United States had average of 35.59 knots in the record Atlantic run which seems near maximum for conventional displacement hull.

Flat bottom skiffs, rowboats, punts, and cabin cruisers with a narrow transom and an upward curve on the bottom of the boat from a point amidship to the bottom of the stern are classed as displacement hulls. They are designed to slide efficiently through the water at low speeds.

10 minimum wake

EDDIES
EDDIES

Narrow-transom rowboat with upward curve at stern is easy to row since it slides efficiently through water without creating turbulence under transom.

Wide stern of planing hull develops eddy currents if rowed. It is slow, awkward, and very clumsy when handled under oars.

Where will the daytime signals be displayed on this supertanker?

We've enjoyed operating many adequately powered rowboats. AVOID overpowered AND underpowered rowboats as they can become hazardous.

Disp. characteristics

The most efficient rowboat hull has a rocker profile with a narrow transom to produce a minimum wake at displacement hull speed.

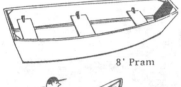

8' Pram

The traditional rowboat has a narrow transom with a rocker bottom...while a pram has a wider stern with a rocker bottom. The overpowered pram is unpredictable as it doesn't know whether to plow or plane.

The motor thrust will pull the stern down and the bow up. If more throttle is applied the bow might go skyward and make a loop, just kidding.

34

If the pram is on a crippled plane at 15 mph going into a 20 mph wind, and the bow goes up, the sudden pressure on the bottom of the boat will be similar to carrying a 4 x 8 sheet of plywood in a 35 mph wind...anything can happen to the pram.

Balance the pram with your weight to keep the bow down, use the forward motor tilt pin and throttle down.

Hand propulsion is needed for planing hulls if the motor quits...with oars and paddles impractical to use, and they will become a clumsy storage problem.

The only practical method we've seen is a stern mounted SCULLING OAR with an underwater blade moving back and forth like the tail of a fish. When disassembled it takes minimum storage room.

May we recommend a race with competitors having to row or paddle their planing hulls for 100 yards.

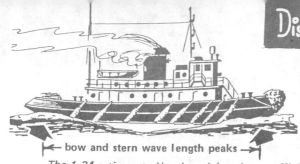

This ratio is based on the dynamic moving waterline of bow and stern wave length peaks.

These coincide with equal peaks of tro-choidal ocean waves.

← bow and stern wave length peaks →

The 1.34 ratio waterline length/maximum efficient speed for displace-ment hulls is not an absolute due to numerous variables, especially on displacement hulls under 100'. The ratio was chosen by naval architects as it was the average factor for most displacement hulls.

SEMI-PLANING HULLS. We have 10,000 sail and powerboats in our local harbor with many larger powerboats able to exceed the 1.34 ratio...that are underpowered. While they can reach 2.5 to 3.0 ratios with bow high and stern squatting, tremendous strain is put on the hull, hull fittings, with maximum fuel consumption. We've seen many dangerous to hazardous semi-planing hulls thru the years.

Choose a good displacement hull...OR a powerboat with a good planing hull and ample power to pass the surfing 3.0 ratio and plane easily with a top speed around 35 mph for normal operation.

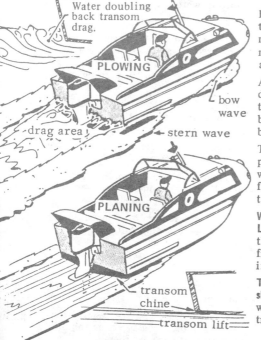

Water doubling back transom drag.

PLOWING

bow wave

drag area

stern wave

PLANING

transom chine

transom lift

35

Large wake and wasteful transom drag produces maximum wetted surface, maximum fuel consumption at displacement speed.

As throttle is applied the drag rapidly increases until the hull breaks out of the bow/stern wave trap to begin planing operation.

The same hull when planing has **minimum drag** which is noticed in the flat wake/minimum turbulence behind the boat.

Water drag changes to LIFT when planing as the water breaks cleanly from the transom chine instead of doubling back.

Transom chine should be sharp as possible so water won't double back on transom while planing.

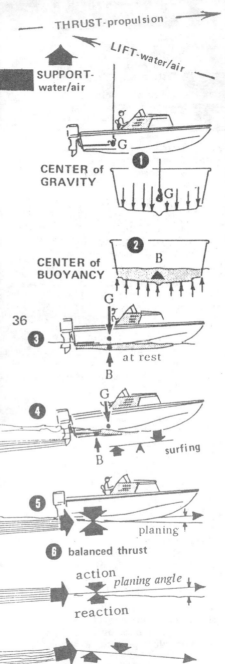

THRUST-propulsion

LIFT-water/air

SUPPORT-water/air

CENTER of GRAVITY ❶

CENTER of BUOYANCY ❷ B

36

❸ at rest
B

❹ surfing
B A

❺ planing

❻ balanced thrust

action
planing angle
reaction

❼ unbalanced thrust

The forces of nature acting on a planing hull are balance and lift... to provide stability and control for maximum planing performance.

CENTER of GRAVITY (G) is the resultant of all downward forces from the pull of gravity.

G is the point a boat may be suspended from a single cable without tipping. G should remain stationary with correct weight trim including all gear and passengers.

CENTER of BUOYANCY (B) is the resultant of all upward forces of a hull's buoyancy. After launching a boat will sink into the water until the upward buoyancy force equals the downward force of gravity.

At surfing speed— B moves aft to remain in center of the decreasing bottom wetted surface area.

DYNAMIC LIFT

After surfing speed is exceeded— the separated forces of B and G come together again to force the stern up and the bow down for planing trim.

The hull at planing speed becomes a manned projectile requiring balanced force vectors for stability.

Planing hull balance depends on the law of action vs reaction, the resultant of thrust vs lift.

Compare the planing forces with the simplified diagrams lower left showing the balanced force vectors.

If these forces aren't balanced due to wrong weight distribution, wrong thrust angle, a rocker or secondary rocker, or overpowered hull exceeds wing *lift area—*

The unbalanced forces produce a wet, uncomfortable ride with lost performance...

As the unbalanced forces acting on the hull fight each other.

Powerboating Illustrated

THRUST (propulsion)

LIFT (air/water)

8

SUPPORT (air/water)

Me, interested in speed?
What ever gave you that idea—

planing hulls

The planing hull is designed to perform efficiently at planing speeds.
The degree of planing efficiency is usually determined by the wake
or disturbance left being a planing hull...which is the resultant of
effort or energy involved.

*If all factors are equal—the greater the disturbance or wake left behind
the planing hull, the greater will be the fuel consumption.*

There are varying degress of planing efficiency to analyze for your
boating choice. If your boating area is a relatively protected inland
lake or river, you may choose a highly efficient planing hull using a
smaller motor to adequately maintain your hull at the desired
planing speed of 30 to 35 mph maximum.

9 • MINIMUM WAKE—
MAXIMUM planing efficiency

Is wake ripple or tidal wave?

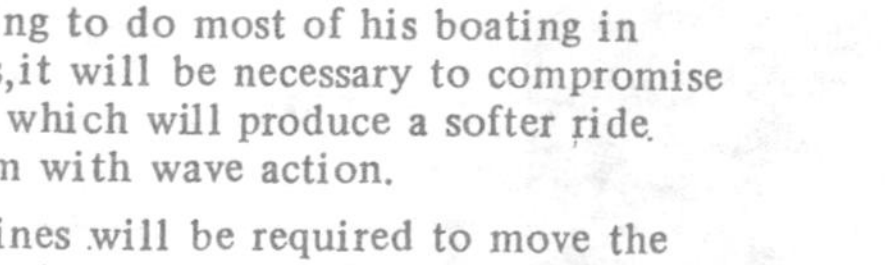

Wake thrust is aft, downwards, ⌐ outwards.   air/spray lift

For the trailerboat owner expecting to do most of his boating in
coastal areas or large inland lakes, it will be necessary to compromise
with a less efficient planing hull which will produce a softer ride.
especially if caught out in a storm with wave action.

As larger 2 cycle and 4 cycle engines will be required to move the
hull at the same 30 to 35 mph maximum, you must expect higher fuel
consumption due to the large wake left behind a less efficient hull...
to provide for that more comfortable ride.

Powerboating Illustrated

10 • MAXIMUM WAKE—
MINIMUM planing efficiency
Excessive wake shows
wasted energy.

Spray curling upwards.

the extremes----good or poor compromise?

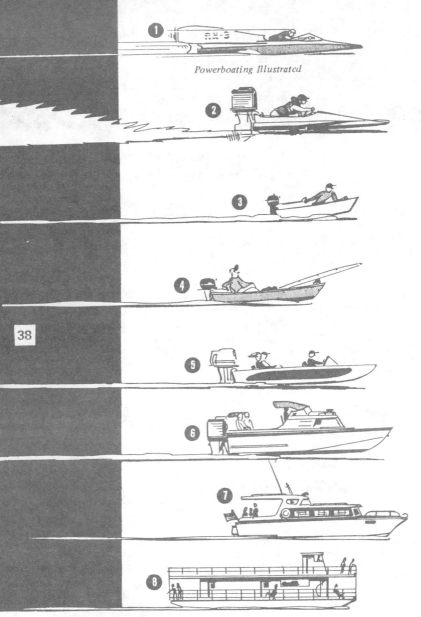

Powerboating Illustrated

38

First generation planing hulls are covered as they had to be basic and efficient in the 1957 to 1960 period with outboard motors large enough to plane the runabout and small cabin cruisers, and ample power for the fishermen. The last two examples operated at displacement speeds, the advantage, their motors were portable to be taken to the shop for servicing.

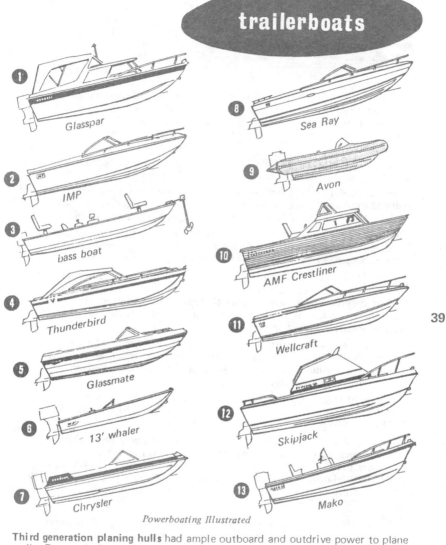

trailerboats

1. Glasspar
2. IMP
3. bass boat
4. Thunderbird
5. Glassmate
6. 13' whaler
7. Chrysler
8. Sea Ray
9. Avon
10. AMF Crestliner
11. Wellcraft
12. Skipjack
13. Mako

Powerboating Illustrated

39

Third generation planing hulls had ample outboard and outdrive power to plane easily. Fore and aft strakes were added to several hulls providing a softer ride and better directional stability. For the following ten years hull designs seem to merge together with endless 'almost' look alikes.

The planing inflatable surfaced in the late 1970's with many advantages especially for dinghies on larger powerboats as they were lighter than hard dinghies. If the large boat sunk, the soft dinghy could carry several passengers and still be seaworthy.

The bass boat started a new trend with large motors for competitors to race to the fishing grounds with the goal the largest prize for the biggest fish.

14' ski boat at 30 mph

Total weight of *Blunder* with boat, motor, battery, passengers, gear, etc., is approximately 1400 pounds at left.

The 1400 pound boat load of *Blunder* is supported by an upward force equal to the total weight of the hull and its contents at displacement speeds. The water displaced at the bow...flows around the sides and beneath the hull to fill the void developing at the stern.

As throttle is appled, the **DRAG** increases until the hull is able to climb up on the water surface to reach **PLANING TRIM.**

Since the weight of the hull remains constant but is supported by a reduced wetted bottom area, the remaining bottom surface or **PLANING PLATFORM** must be able to support more pounds per square inch.

The faster the speed of the planing hull, the higher it will be on the water surface. *As the wetted support area decreases, the remaining wetted surface must support the total weight without flexing.*

On the 14' arc-bottom *Blunder*, approx. a third of the bottom surface will be in contact with the water at 23 mph. The planing platform or wetted surface area must support **three times the amount of weight per square inch** that it would have to support without flexing when moving at displacement speed.

At 30 mph the wetted surface contact area has been reduced to a quarter, which means the planing platform bottom area must support **four times the amount of weight per square inch** without flexing to maintain normal steering control.

We show *Blunder* on page 43, maintaining approx 60 mph being very close to running out of planing platform support due to the **WATER-PLANE LENGTH being considerably shortened.**

The planing platform which is similar to the wing area of an airplane, must support the load of the boat and contents at planing speeds. The water must be cut cleanly along both transom and side chines. The faster a planing hull is moving, the more critical a slight irregularity becomes which results in a speed loss... while a larger irregularity may cause a loss of control.

A slight hull defect that is hardly noticeable at 20 mph, may become very obvious at 30 to 40 mph on the highly efficient arc bottom planing hull. If *Blunder* had an excellent planing hull and could carry unlimited hp in smooth water it would run out of fore and aft support or **WATERPLANE LENGTH,** the speed limit of one-point planing hulls.

If a softer ride is desired you may choose a hull that will sacrifice 2 to 6 mph from the maximum planing speed for larger lakes or coastal areas to compensate for wave action.

40

1 Illus. at right shows WATERPLANE of ski boat with 1400 lbs. load while at rest, or at displacement hull speeds.

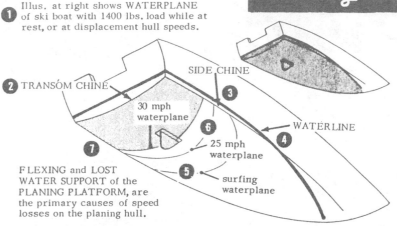

2 TRANSOM CHINE

SIDE CHINE

3

30 mph waterplane

6

7

4

WATERLINE

25 mph waterplane

5 · surfing waterplane

FLEXING and LOST WATER SUPPORT of the PLANING PLATFORM, are the primary causes of speed losses on the planing hull.

FLEXING must not be permitted at any hull speed.

8 As speed increases, wetted support area is reduced. Planing platform must support following pressures per square foot without flexing—

not moving	60 lbs.
surfing	120 lbs.
25 mph	180 lbs.
30 mph	240 lbs.
45 mph	360 lbs.

Will bottom be able to take ROUGH WATER POUNDING which can be two or three times amount shown on table. The impact force of boat hitting water after being airborne is tremendous in a chop at top speed. Throttle down in rough water!

41

The planing platform should develop MAXIMUM SUPPORT from water it is exerting a force against. The greater its efficiency, the higher the boat planes, & the greater its top speed will be.

radius   secondary rocker   sharp edge

9 The faster the planing hull goes, the greater the opposite force directed upon it by the water. If it is cut clean at the TRANSOM CHINE, maximum lift reduces wetted planing platform resulting in top speed. A slight radius on the transom chine reduces the **10** amount of lift and top speed as wetted surface area increases.

minimum efficiency ←——————————→ maximum efficiency **11**

The faster the planing hull goes, the greater the water pressure will be against it. A SLIGHT ROUND on the SIDE CHINE permits a little water to escape, while a LARGE ROUND permits a lot of water support to escape out from under the planing platform. The more water that leaks out, the lower the boat floats. This will increase the hull drag and lower the top speed.

Powerboating Illustrated

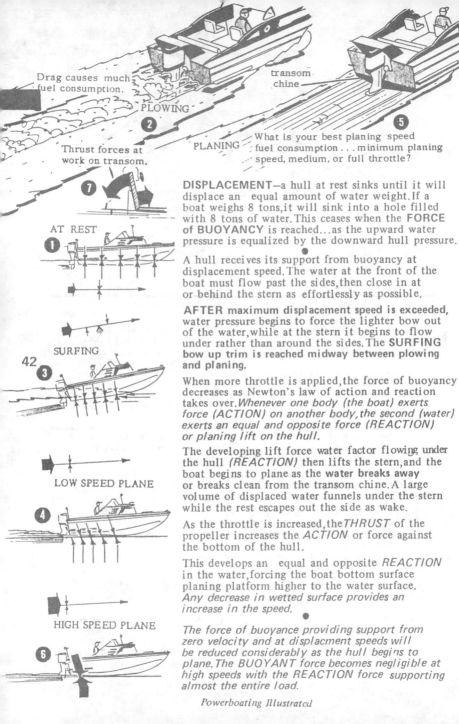

Drag causes much fuel consumption.

PLOWING ②

Thrust forces at work on transom.

transom chine

PLANING ⑤

What is your best planing speed fuel consumption ... minimum planing speed, medium, or full throttle?

⑦

AT REST ①

SURFING ③

42

LOW SPEED PLANE ④

HIGH SPEED PLANE ⑥

DISPLACEMENT—a hull at rest sinks until it will displace an equal amount of water weight. If a boat weighs 8 tons, it will sink into a hole filled with 8 tons of water. This ceases when the **FORCE of BUOYANCY** is reached...as the upward water pressure is equalized by the downward hull pressure.

A hull receives its support from buoyancy at displacement speed. The water at the front of the boat must flow past the sides, then close in at or behind the stern as effortlessly as possible.

AFTER maximum displacement speed is exceeded, water pressure begins to force the lighter bow out of the water, while at the stern it begins to flow under rather than around the sides. The **SURFING bow up trim is reached midway between plowing and planing.**

When more throttle is applied, the force of buoyancy decreases as Newton's law of action and reaction takes over. *Whenever one body (the boat) exerts force (ACTION) on another body, the second (water) exerts an equal and opposite force (REACTION) or planing lift on the hull.*

The developing lift force water factor flowing under the hull *(REACTION)* then lifts the stern, and the boat begins to plane as the **water breaks away** or breaks clean from the transom chine. A large volume of displaced water funnels under the stern while the rest escapes out the side as wake.

As the throttle is increased, the *THRUST* of the propeller increases the *ACTION* or force against the bottom of the hull.

This develops an equal and opposite *REACTION* in the water, forcing the boat bottom surface planing platform higher to the water surface. *Any decrease in wetted surface provides an increase in the speed.*

The force of buoyance providing support from zero velocity and at displacment speeds will be reduced considerably as the hull begins to plane. The BUOYANT force becomes negligible at high speeds with the REACTION force supporting almost the entire load.

Powerboating Illustrated

Speed-wetted surface

While the maximum efficient DISPLACEMENT HULL SPEED is determined by LENGTH...the PLANING HULL SPEED is governed by the amount of WETTED SUPPORT AREA dragged across the water.

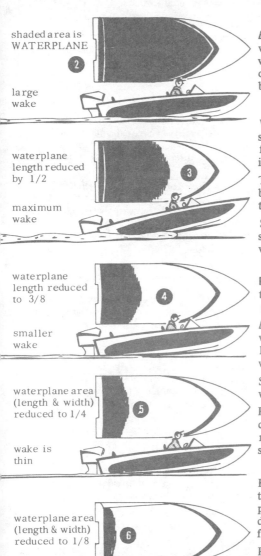

shaded area is WATERPLANE

(2)

large wake

waterplane length reduced by 1/2

(3)

maximum wake

waterplane length reduced to 3/8

(4)

smaller wake

waterplane area (length & width) reduced to 1/4

(5)

wake is thin

waterplane area (length & width) reduced to 1/8

(6)

wake almost disappears

Blunder is **PLOWING** thru the water at 8 mph kicking up a wake that disturbs nearby boat owners...note the long wetted bottom surface **WATERPLANE**.

●

When the bow is high and the stern is low with spray coming from mid point on *Blunder*... it is **SURFING**.

The arc-bottom hull is surfing between 14 to 16 mph...note the MAXIMUM WAKE.

Steering controls in the back seat are dangerous due to limited visibility when surfing.

●   43

PLANING trim is reached when the stern rises and the bow levels off as more throttle is applied.

Blunder is traveling at 25 mph with less wetted surface and less fuel consumption than when surfing.

Spray and wake are becoming very thin at 30 mph.

Planing factors become very critical at this speed and above requiring a firm planing platform, sharp stern and side chines.

●

Except for a roostertail behind the stern caused by a surface prop, the wake at 60 mph almost disappears as the hull wants to fly but the wings are missing.

Regardless of the motor hp, it is the amount of wetted bottom surface that becomes the major factor determining planing speed.

A boat is a mass. When it starts moving it has to overcome opposite force or reaction called **INERTIA of the MASS.** That is the reason a smaller, lighter boat can reach hull speed earlier than a heavy hull.. and run out of inertia earlier than a heavy boat. The basic formula—

BOAT (mass) x **THRUST** (acceleration)= **ACTION** vs **REACTION** (force)

As the throttle is advanced—the *thrust* produces the *action* that pulls the water aft of the transom. This thrust develops an equal and opposite *reaction* against the bottom of the hull. This reaction is proportional to the acceleration *against the supporting water* which has *800 times the density of air.*

The sum of the separate *action* and *reaction* forces is the *lift of the hull* that has to be equal to the total boat load on the water. As the propeller *thrust* is increased, the *reaction* force of the water will lift the planing hull to the water surface so that at 30 mph ¼ of the bottom planing platform must support the entire boat and load.

If a loaded boat at the dock displaces 1500 pounds—*the wetted bottom planing platform must support the 1500 pounds identical load at 20, 30, and 40 mph without a pressure hook* due to bottom flexing.

The **one point** family planing outboard hull if an excellent design may reach 35 to 40 mph. It reaches a speed barrier as the *waterplane length has been considerably reduced* with the boat falling off a plane which considerably reduces the boat speed.

While racing records of highly complex and tremendously over complex drag boats continually exceed these speeds —our interest is the family performance hull at the upper end of recreational purposes. While an excellent one-point hull may reach 40 mph…*stability becomes so critical that moving an arm or turning a head* may throw a planing hull out of balance above this speed.

Many planing hulls have minor to major problems covered in the next two chapters with different speed barrier limits, with two examples of the *secondary rocker,* pg. 41. One was an excellent wooden boat that was stable while planing in the 30 to 40 mph range. After the bottom was fiberglassed, a wild careening porpoise action developed as it tried to plane due to a radius added to the transom chine.

After a specialized drag boat was clocked at 72 mph thru the traps, it had a new owner. It developed a high speed porpoise with two aboard, also when towing a water skiier…for which it wasn't designed. Many hundreds of dollars were required to remove the 1/64'' rocker, and a secondary rocker so small it couldn't be measured to make it stable above 70 mph, after which the owner could no longer afford the boat.

44

We use the term one, two, and three point planing suspension to replace hydroplane (water lift).

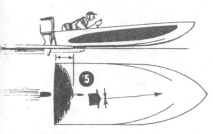

TWO POINT suspension with water support, spray/air lift. (STEP hydro has two point suspension without air/spray lift.)

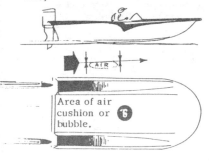

Area of air cushion or bubble.

THREE POINT hydroplane with THREE POINT suspension when planing.

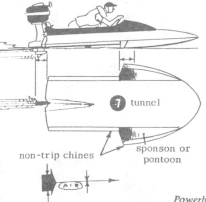

non-trip chines

tunnel

sponson or pontoon

One point (stepless) hull gains most of its lift support from the water. It will have a rougher ride with only a thin cushion of air and spray trapped under the hull.

The one point hull runs out of its waterplane stability at upper planing speeds. Any minor defect becomes critical at upper speeds with the hull falling back into the water. Increased wetted surface reduces hull speed until it can climb back out of the water to again be on a plane.

The older **step hydro** had better stability than a one-point hull, though the speed was limited without air support.

●

Two point catamaran divides the load and wetted bottom support into two hull areas for better stability.

45

The two point hull has a softer ride with less water friction plus higher speeds *due to an air bubble or an air and spray cushion between the hulls...* it isn't limited to water support.

The forward deck area between the hulls was removed as the upper speeds rapidly increased to reduce the hull tendency from flipping over backwards at full throttle.

●

Three point hydro. It uses water, air, spray, and propeller support with excellent high speed racing stability for protected areas.

The entire hull at upper speed is flying just above the water surface on a cushion of air and spray trapped in its tunnel, with the prop supporting some weight.

When the hull loses stability, it drops till the after ends of the sponsons momentarily touch the water to regain balance with a slight speed loss, then continue the hovering action on the water.

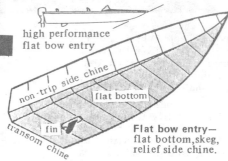

high performance
flat bow entry

non-trip side chine

flat bottom

transom chine

fin

Flat bow entry—
flat bottom, skeg,
relief side chine.

● **FLAT BOW ENTRY**—used on maximum performance hulls with smaller motors.

The hull is designed for protected areas, a smaller size hull with minimum freeboard. It will pound in rough water and will be easy to swamp.

Some of these planing hulls have a slight built-in rocker, the slight jumping motion in flat water increasing the speed a mile or two which in a race is enough to move from 4th to 1st place.

Medium bow entry—
small keel replaces
fin. It floats lower,
is larger, needs
more hp for
same top
speed.

flare

bow chine

46

side chine

slight keel

medium bow entry

transom chine

● **MEDIUM BOW ENTRY**—a good utility hull which may take some rough water. It is the most popular design that will be larger, have more freeboard, and be partially decked over.

The hull may have an arc or V bottom with a slight keel for directional stability. It will take a larger hp motor and require more time to plane to produce a softer ride than the flat bottom hull.

The slight keel replaces the fin, the keel also acting as a skid when the hull is pulled up on a beach.

Deep bow entry is used on
heavier, longer outdrive boats.
It is questionable on
light, fast outboard
hulls, pg. 37.

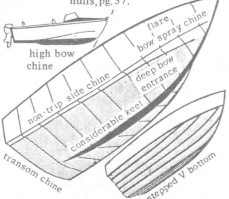

flare

bow spray chine

high bow
chine

deep bow
entrance

non-trip side chine

considerable keel

transom chine

stepped V bottom

● **DEEP or DEEPER BOW ENTRY**—is used on larger hulls, with larger, long-shaft outboard motors and more freeboard for rougher water. A self draining splash pan with enclosed transom reduces swamping if a wave breaks over the stern.

Performance will differ considerably whether the deep V hull uses outboard or outdrive propulsion units.

The BOW ENTRY ANGLE is critical on light outboard performance hulls for planing requiring a compromise for weight, length, beam, and hp.

Light, high performance flat-bow entry hulls require more bow angle to avoid bow from digging into a wave than a heavier hull. **Analyze hazardous bow entry hull extremes,** see pgs. 71,76,77.

★ Choose the hull compromises that will best serve your type of boating needs. Consider the following requirements when shopping for your next boat.

① MAXIMUM PERFORMANCE—*you must become performance conscious as no person likes a dull razor...or a dull boat.*

② SOFT or HARD RIDE—*how much performance do you want to compromise for a softer ride on a good performing planing hull without overcompensating your planing efficiency.*

③ Your BOATING AREA—*the high performance rig is an excellent choice for smooth protected water but dangerous in rough water... while the seaworthy rough water hull is a dull performer in small protected boating areas.*

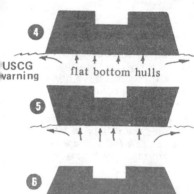

④

USCG warning   flat bottom hulls

⑤

⑥

relief chines

⑦

⑧

● The FLAT BOTTOM planing hull will provide maximum speed *in the straightaway.*

The flat bottom hull floats higher at the dock and planes more easily providing the highest top speed with available thrust. The stern should be as wide OR wider than the rest of the hull for maximum lift. A FIN or SKEG is needed to reduce weaving tendency on the straightaway...and to minimize skidding in turns.

47

SLOW DOWN WHEN TURNING. If you don't on a flat bottom hull, it may skid until the LOW SIDE CHINE digs in. It becomes a fulcrum to flip the boat and its occupants outward, see page 75.

● The non-trip SIDE CHINE or relief chine. The side chine is cut at an angle so a flat bottom racing boat can maintain top speed in a turn, a fin is still required.

With less bottom support the hull will float lower and take longer to plane.

The water is cut cleanly by the side chines. In a turn the hull should bank normally with sufficient drifting or skidding to provide a safety valve. This reduces forces which are the major factors in reversed controls, flips, and spin outs.

Powerboating Illustrated

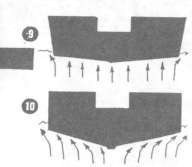

- The shallow V BOTTOM hull with SHARP side chine —floats lower in the water than flat bottom hulls. The planing platform at planing speeds provides solid lift with spray cut and flung outward and aft to help boat speed.

The slight keel eliminates a skeg to provide enough steering stability to eliminate weaving. Our *Jewel*, pg. 12, is a good example of the shallow V bottom hull with a relief chine.

The shallow V bottom hull is a good utility design for outboard boats under 20' long.

- The ARC BOTTOM with SHARP side chines— see *Blunder*, pg. 40, requires a SKEG for directional stability, provides better performance with less hp. It requires a slot on the aft trailer crosswise support for the skeg which will simplify launching and loading.

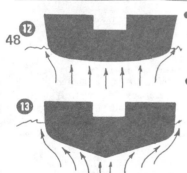

48

- The ARC BOTTOM hull with ROUNDED side chines is deeper in the water than the arc bottom hull above. It requires more hp, takes longer to plane, produces a mushy ride with a lot more wake and spray.

- The side chine with a SMALL RADIUS on a hull has a softer ride plus the ability to take sharper turns. *Any increase in the side chine radius becomes counterproductive.* It may produce a wet, sloppy ride. While it may turn on a dime, excessive drift with inertia may cause it to roll outward to flip the boat and its passengers, see page 75.

- AFT SPRAY RAILS, pg. 50, are added to large inboard powerboats with a round chine. This increases the planing platform area for lift while cutting the water clean on the sides when planing.

- WINE GLASS shaped hulls with ROUNDED SIDE CHINES are excellent for oceangoing cabin sailboats which are controlled by the displacement *speed/length ratio*, pg. 29. Powerboats with a large side chine should follow the speed limitations of displacement hulls since overpowering will develop unpredictable control problems with excess wasted fuel.

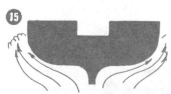

Powerboating Illustrated

Hull Efficiency

flat bottom lapstrake

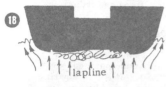

round bottom lapstrake

lapline

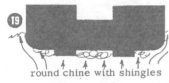

round chine with shingles

stern   stepped
deep V
inboard
hull

bow

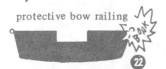

Avoid tumblehome!

protective bow railing

● **The LAPSTRAKE planing hull** has a small advantage over a smooth bottom hull for racing on flat water. It is able to break the large surface adhesion into smaller areas. Expect a variety of planing differences with lapstrake hulls.

The flat bottom, shallow bow lapstrake hull will plane earlier than one with a medium bow entrance, especially if it has a slight rounded side chine. It will have more wetted bottom water friction due to extra lifting surfaces than a smooth bottom hull.

● **The LAPLINE planing hull** may have a small side chine radius for easy turning. For a softer ride the bottom tunnel will provide an air/spray cushion. The downward pointing laplines provide lift and directional stability or steering. The lapline hull is efficient in turns, while it becomes a medium straightaway performer.

● **Early planing hulls** with a slight rounded side chine for turning, used shingles, pg. 50, to help flat water racing ability.

● **The one point DEEP V STEPPED HULL—** is a low performance hull that was able to use unlimited horsepower, an interesting combination.

49

It provides a soft riding seaworthy hull in average ocean conditions with excellent tracking to hold a straight course...at the expense of considerable fuel consumption. The deep V stepped hull due to beam, weight, length, and hp will have tremendous variables. Throttle down before making a tight turn to avoid reversed controls showing up in USCG records, see page 261.

—Stern TUMBLEHOME is questionable—

● Tumblehome—*the inward curve of a vessels side above the water.* Pirates were a hazard in the days of square rig sailing vessels. Many of them such as slow cargo vessels were built wider at the waterline than at the deck to make it difficult for pirates to board these vessels.

The **tumblehome** on *Blunder*, pg. 41, required constant attention with fenders, otherwise the sharp side chines would bang into the dock.

● **The wrap-around DECK BUMPER railing** provides excellent protection for dinghies and outboard planing hulls to absorb unexpected bumps dockside or next to other boats.

Powerboating Illustrated

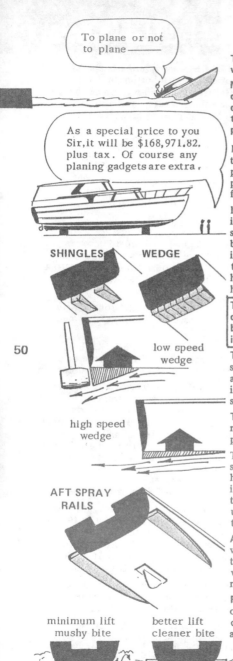

To plane or not to plane——

As a special price to you Sir, it will be $168,971.82. plus tax. Of course any planing gadgets are extra.

SHINGLES　　**WEDGE**

50

low speed wedge

high speed wedge

AFT SPRAY RAILS

minimum lift
mushy bite

better lift
cleaner bite

The outboard cruiser for many decades was an unreachable dream.

Much experimentation was required during this period to develop the clean lines we see on planing hulls today, with engines that are able to put them on an adequate plane.

Many crutches were tested during this trial and error period. the goal was to put underpowered hulls on a minimum plane to increase speed and reduce fuel consumption.

It is interesting how many of these ideas developed on the small and sensitive outboard hull were used by builders for larger, underpowered inboard powerboats. It is still amazing to find how few of these boat owners have any knowledge of a good planing hull...and the reason for planing aids.

Two important ideas that developed during this testing period were the built-in HOOK, and increasing or improving the PLANING AREA.

The SHINGLES were added to break smooth water adhesion into three areas to increase racing speed. While it may resemble the wedge the shingle serves a considerably different purpose.

The WEDGE is a built-in hook to raise the stern earlier from a surfing position to a low speed plane.

The deeper wedge will provide earlier stern lift to help underpowered inboard hulls to reach a low speed plane to increase speed and reduce fuel consumption...while a faster inboard hull will use a shallower wedge to accomplish the same purpose.

AFT SPRAY RAILS provide added wing area, pg. 48, as well as cutting the water clean on the sides of a hull with a large side chine radius. These rails are underwater at disp. speeds.

FORWARD SPRAY RAILS are used on large powerboats to reduce spray coming aboard in rough weather for a hull without bow flare, page 25.

Powerboating Illustrated

oops...

~ fantail

FIXED AFTERPLANE
additional planing area

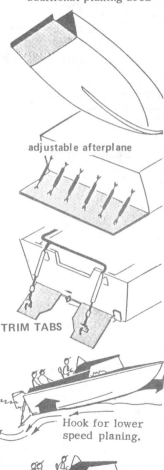

adjustable afterplane

TRIM TABS

Hook for lower
speed planing.

Trim tabs level out
with speed increase.

Is it easier to climb out of the water on wide
water skis, or on narrow ones? This situation
also applies to planing hulls with wide transoms...and those with narrow transoms.

Many navy vessels are overpowered displacement
hulls that don't operate for profit. When you
meet an atomic sub on the surface, a cruiser
or aircraft carrier operating at full speed..keep
your distance and prepare for a HUGE wake.

The first of a new class of destroyers was on
a speed trial shortly after WW 1. Everyone on
the bridge was pleased as it began to pass
30 knots, but...

A chief on the bridge at the time told me he
began to feel uncomfortable...so he looked aft
to see the fantail disappearing beneath the
wake. It was basically an overpowered displacement hull, a double ender without planing lift.

If planing hulls are correctly designed using
enough hp, and properly loaded, planing aids
would not be needed. Such is NOT the normal
planing trailerboating situation.

51

The FIXED AFTERPLANE. Around 1960 one
was introduced for outboard boats to reduce
cockpit noise...with battery, fuel tanks, and the
outboard motor carried aft of the transom. A
slight problem developed while surfing as fuel
tanks, battery, and occasionally the motor might
be submerged during the surfing angle.

Before race time outboard racers could make
ONE adjustment of the turnbuckles on the
afterplane at left to make a hook for sticky
smooth water, or level it out if enough wind
existed to break the water adhesion.

TRIM TABS aee remotely operated adjustable
afterplanes with a variety of trade names.

Drag boats use trim tabs to force a hook so they
can plane earlier to increase speed, reducing
their time thru a speed trap.

Underpowered, heavily loaded, and/or incorrectly
loaded planing hulls with weight, hp, or balance
problems, use trim tabs as a hook to raise the
stern earlier from the surfing position. After
planing is reached the trim tabs are raised part
or all the way to reduce trim tab drag.

Powerboating Illustrated

soft ride,
HEAP speed!

air scoop

Air Lift

As the wind comes up increasing the air lift between the hulls, the catamaran's advantage of speed, soft ride, and easier steering becomes apparent while the harder riding one point hull has to throttle back to reduce pounding action. *Due to the cat's ability to ride on a bubble,* it will ride higher and faster upwind with more wind lift flowing thru the tunnel...and less wind and less speed, downwind.

Due to tunnel cavitation and awkward handling with one motor, twin motors, double batteries, controls, fuel tanks, etc., will be required for normal catamaration operation.

full length sponsons

bow entry

shorter wings

air scoop

sponson

V hull

tunnel

52

shallow V bottom

tunnel

The tri hull under a variety of names, *is designed to use air lift while operating on one motor or engine.*

There are a variety of tri hull designs from shallow, to medium, to deep V center hull with sponsons on both sides.

The outer sponsons may be almost as long as the center hull. It may have slender sponsons with sharp bottoms, or shallower, shorter, and wider sponson wings to control the air and spray lift support of the tri hull.

The tri configuration has generally been quite successful. It has a softer ride, with better tracking ability to steer a straighter course than many one-point hulls. At the dock or at anchor the tri has more usable cockpit space plus better stability than the one-point hull. The *bowrider tri* is popular for protected areas while ocean use may be hazardous as a wave breaking over the bow could easily swamp the large forward cockpit with several gallons of water.

Some tri hull designs are more efficient with lower hp motors to produce adequate planing speeds. Others with a deeper V bow hull and a softer ride require more hp to reach the same planing speeds.

The *sea sled* was the first outboard hull to use the air lift ability to ride on a minimal bubble, note the tunnel or bow air scoop which extends about half the length of the hull.

While sea sled air and spray lift may provide a softer ride with one motor, the motor cavitation plate must be mounted an inch or so below the transom chine to avoid cavitation. This produces tremendous strain and drag on the motor bracket and transom. at planing speeds.

Powerboating Illustrated

The top speed of a one-point planing hull is limited by the amount of bottom planing platform stability...regardless how much hp is used. Let us eliminate this water friction by lifting the hull totally out of the water.....

The term foil is the shape of a wing that provides lift in the air and in the water. The airplane uses an *air wing airfoil ...while the water wing or hydrofoil* will lift a vessel clear of the water.

Water density is approximately 800 times the density of air. Less than a square foot of *water wings* are required to lift the 14½' boat above clear of the water. The boat then develops its own limitations due to the air drag hull shape...which should be aerodynamically designed.

strut

Water resists compression. Movement of the *water wing* thru the water develops a thrusting pressure action against the bottom surface, with a low pressure lift reaction on the top surface. The combination thrust and lift forces due to water density lifts a vessel clear of the water.

53

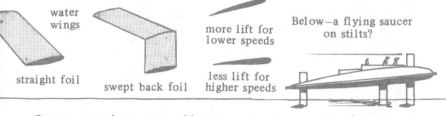

water wings

straight foil

swept back foil

more lift for lower speeds

less lift for higher speeds

Below—a flying saucer on stilts?

Some *water wings* are movable to permit a steeper angle of attack during acceleration and climbing, which are leveled off when cruising speed is reached. Slower craft will require more wing area and more foil angle of attack...while faster craft will require smaller foils with less angle of attack. Straight foils and swept back foils have been successfully tested, the latter having less tendency to catch seaweed.

I was watching the early USN hydrofoil craft above successfully planing on its awkward stilts. It came down rapidly off La Jolla to hit the water...possibly tripping on a patch of kelp.

The propeller has to pass its own speed barrier... when cavitation begins as water flow is no longer able to follow the blades. This is the reason for the *supercavitating prop* for the hydrofoil craft so the bubbles caused by cavitation will collapse behind the propeller instead of on the blades...see page 224.

How would you discuss the following hull problems affecting outboard motor performance with customers seeking your expertise?

1. How would you explain the differences between displacement and planing hulls?

2. What are the two basic design factors that differ between the rowing dinghy and the planing dinghy? What is a pram?

3 What are the risks faced by a person operating an overpowered rowboat...and an underpowered rowboat?

4. Why is a planing hull difficult to row or paddle?

5. What are the two functions an outboard motor provides for a rowboat and a planing hull? What is the single function required of an outboard motor on a 25' displacement sailing hull?

6. What are the basic factors to consider when choosing a one point planing hull? What are the best compromises to consider for outboard planing hulls in your area?

7. What type of bow entry, and for what reason...would you recommend to most of your customers?

8. If a new boat develops a roostertail at planing speed, what does it indicate...and how can it be eliminated?

9. What type of a hull needs a rocker...and on what kind of a hull will a rocker become hazardous?

10. What is a secondary rocker...and how does it produce a careening, porpoising ride? Can it be owner caused?

11. How does a hook affect the performance of a planing hull? How can you determine if a boat has a permanent hook? What is a major way a hook can be owner caused?

12. What is the cause of a temporary pressure hook?

13. Why is a semi-planing hull dangerous...what factors do you look for?

14. The owner was happy with the 30 to 35mph speed of his new boat...which can only produce 20 mph two weeks later. What would be the first factor to check for the speed loss?

15. How do flare, spray chine, and a non-trip chine on a planing hull produce a more comfortable ride?

16. Why should left-hand controls be avoided?

17. What type hulls should be throttled down at planing speeds to avoid a flip, a spinout, and reversed controls?

18. What is a broach...and what type of an outboard hull will have the most tendency to broach?

Powerboating Illustrated

54

Friction.... friend or foe?
Unnecessary spray and wake represent wasted power and money.

Minimum wake shows planing hull has efficient support and stability from friction/lift of water.

Minimum wetted surface needed to support and balance planing hull.

planing problems

Parasitic drag of underwater garden produces unnecessary turbulence.

Ever try to slide on coarse sandpaper?

Lower unit drag, marine growth, bait tank scoops, exposed screw heads must be kept to minimum.

Wasted energy is expensive — would you drive a car with the brakes on?

Prop thrust fights lifting action of hull, producing unnecessary strain & wave-making resistance.

Inefficiently designed hull, incorrect thrust angle & load incorrectly balanced.

Powerboating

Illustrated

Will air provide lift or drag? How deep a hole will an over-loaded planing hull have to pull behind it?

H.M.S. AFTERTHOUGHT

Overloaded hull has too much wave-making resistance and excessive air drag.

Disturbed air flow patterns, boat is overloaded & topheavy with excessive superstructure.

The Side Chine
SHOULD be sharp;
the Transom Chine
MUST be sharp.

A propeller provides thrust to put an efficient hull on a plane using water for a running balancing medium. The next factor to consider— *is to release the water pressure lift with as little fuss as possible to maintain efficient planing speeds.*

> *The transom chine, similar to a sharp razor, must cut the water cleanly and efficiently after use.* The side chine should also be razor sharp for maximum performamce, though a small side chine radius will produce a softer ride with a considerable loss in performance (speed).

20 or so high performance boat builders display their boats yearly in a separate hall at the L.A Convention Center. I like to make the rounds of these craft to test the sharpness of their chines. If even one tiny transom chine radius is found which may produce a high speed porpoise ...it may be the builders last boat show.

For another field—*if a dinghy sailor wants to win races, his light, planing dinghy will also need an almost razor sharp transom chine.*

A major builder produced a 12' planing hull in 1960 with a problem, it wouldn't plane. After a 3/8" transom chine was changed to a sharp one, the boat planed without hesitation.

A nearby outboard motor distributor was testing motor performance on an excellent, predictable wooden hull. Minor repairs were eventually needed, at which time they also wanted the bottom fiberglassed. Afterwards it was able to climb up on a plane, but as throttle was increased it produced a wild, uncontrollable porpoising ride.

The craftsman doing the fiberglassing had an excellent background... with displacement hulls. He sanded a radius on the transom chine to provide a better surface for the cloth to adhere to. The radius also reduced the chance of the fiberglass being cut when the boat was pulled up on a sandy or gravel beach.

After the boat reached a plane, the transom chine radius became a pressure release valve. This pulled the water support out from under the boat bottom and tripping it as throttle was applied. The release valve radius produced a wild hull with minimum steering control.

An inquisitive marine mechanic can soon spot a transom chine radius that will limit a hull speed to 25 mph, to 35 mph, to 50 mph, and to 70 mph and above.

When outboard boat races are being held in your area, take time to check transom and side chines of the various competitors... who will be fully aware what you are looking for. A poor planing hull can be compared to a dull razor. Even though it will cost almost as much as a sharp razor, who wants to use a dull razor?

After water supporting the hull at planing speed has done its job, the transom chine must cut the water cleanly with as little fuss as possible to keep the hull on an efficient plane.

3 √ SHARP TRANSOM CHINE

full hydraulic lift

As planing speeds increase, greater will be the tendency for the force of the supporting water to leak up around the chine, with the radius a relief valve. Lost lift, lost speed, and lost support results from the *secondary rocker turbulence.*

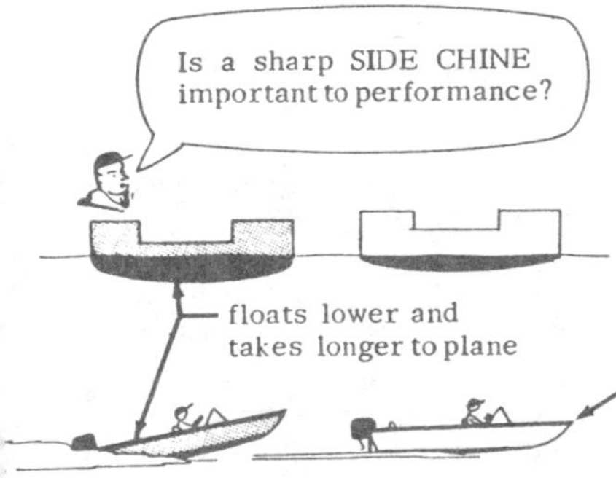

4 SECONDARY ROCKER

partial hydraulic lift

Is a sharp SIDE CHINE important to performance?

57

floats lower and takes longer to plane

The hull with a small side chine will be slower with a less efficient planing hull and more wetted bottom area. As the side chine radius increases, so will be the speed loss.

The hull with a sharp side chine will float higher, and climb onto a plane earlier with less hp and less rpm.

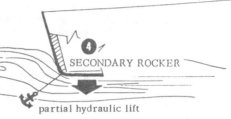

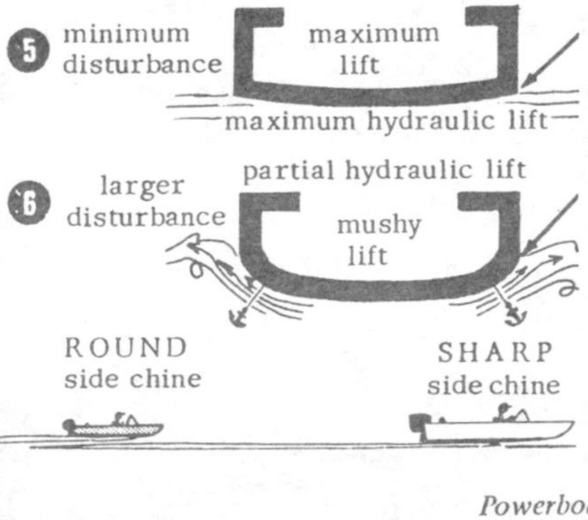

5 minimum disturbance — maximum lift

maximum hydraulic lift

The hull with a sharp side chine will have a more positive bite on the water...with a rougher ride in wave action, *Blunder,* page 43.

6 larger disturbance — partial hydraulic lift — mushy lift

The hull with a considerable side chine radius and more wetted area will have a mushier ride in a chop.

ROUND side chine

SHARP side chine

The speed difference between two identical hulls if all factors are equal except the side chine radius...can range from 3 to 10 mph.

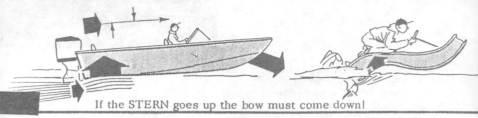

If the STERN goes up the bow must come down!

The planing platform must be firm, clean, and nonflexing *at all speeds.*
Any flexing will *increase the wetted surface... which decreases the
planing speed,* which may also reduce steering control.

> *A HOOK is an upward curve in the planing platform of a hull.* The
> *PERMANENT HOOK* is caused by inefficient planing platform
> bracing, or poor trailering support, see below.
>
> The permanent hook may be small, medium, or large, which will appear
> at all times. *A boat with a flexible bottom will develop a PRESSURE
> HOOK after it begins moving.* As the planing speed increases, the
> larger will be the flexing pressure hook.

A hook may be hardly noticeable though it extends the full length
of the bottom on a slow moving, underpowered displacement hull,
with the flying mattress above being the exception.

The hook on a planing hull with a 40 hp motor is getting the speed
or performance of a 30 hp motor, with the 3 to 5 mph speed loss is
something you have paid for which you didn't get. The owner not
aware he has a boat problem soon feels the motor he bought was
considerably overrated.

58

- *If the stern goes up and the bow goes down*—it seems normal to cure
  it by moving the lower unit away from the transom. This increases
  the hull trim angle, it increases wetted bottom area, in addition to
  dragging the lower unit thru the water at an inefficient angle. In order
  to *cure the hook,* a power robbing, wave-making resistance develops.

- *If the bow rises heavily—*the normal tendency is to move the lower
  unit away from the transom. If all outboard motor tilt angles are
  tested unsuccessfully... a large permanent hook is indicated.

- If a boat has a hook—it will be necessary to increase the bottom
  support of the planing platform. It will be necessary to use heavier
  frame members, or by boxing in to reduce the size of the areas
  without full support to produce a firm, non-yielding planing platform.

  After you have determined your boat has a hook when testing the
  various ideas above, the best idea for the most of us is to consider
  trading your boat for a new one *without* a hook.

- We show two examples of a hook caused by incorrect trailer support,
  one which is obvious, the other which develops slowly.

Powerboating Illustrated

Is it a permanent hook,
or a flexing pressure hook?

PLOP

SPLASH!

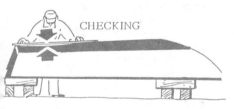

CHECKING

The boat with a hook planes faster than normal. If the hook is large the bow will fall from a low speed plane. This reduces speed momentarily until it repeats the cycle.

The worst hook offenders were early fiberglass boats without stiffeners. Their bottoms wobbled and flexed until the bottoms dropped off.

The hook defect should be avoided in planing hulls as a large hook may cause a low speed porpoise above 20 mph.

For a 60 mph racing boat a 1/32'' hook may mean the difference between 5th and 1st place in the race. At 70 mph a high speed porpoise will produce a wild ride with loss of steering control which may cause a serious collision.

A permanent hook can be checked by placing a straight edge across the planing platform while the *flexing pressure hook* develops when a boat is underway.

Powerboating Illustrated

59

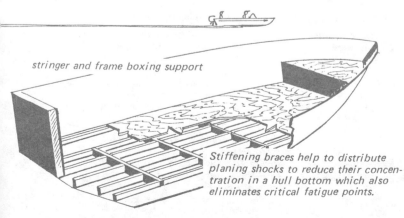

stringer and frame boxing support

Stiffening braces help to distribute planing shocks to reduce their concentration in a hull bottom which also eliminates critical fatigue points.

"Porpoising ain't habit forming!"

If the STERN goes down the bow must go up!

The upward curve of the planing platform is called a ROCKER, pg. 34. It is excellent to help rowboats, prams, plus larger sailboats and powerboats to move easily thru the water at displacement speeds.

The semi-planing hull – if a displacement hull is overpowered, yet it doesn t have sufficient bottom support to maintain a plane...it is similar to an airplane with enough horsepower, yet not enough wing area to takeoff and fly normally.

When a hull with a rocker and a wide transom is overpowered, the bow will climb skyward as throttle is increased. *When the planing platform runs out of support, the bow drops back into the water with a loud splash..* while attempting to climb back on a plane. This galloping, leapfrogging cycle affecting steering control of a boat that doesn't know whether to plow or plane *is called PORPOISING.* If you add more throttle the cycle becomes wilder and more hazardous.

What goes up must come down (oops, moon shot excepted) ...with a lot of wear and tear on occupants in the front seat.

The bow is stopped from going skyward --by changing the motor tilt pin moving the lower unit towards the transom. While reducing the porpoising action, it increases the wetted surface drag area. The boat performance has been killed to eliminate the porpoising action.

60

The HIGH SPEED PORPOISE --develops on one point quality planing hulls for family use. It will occur between 35 to 50 mph and above when the *waterplane* becomes so short the hull loses stability. The boat falls back into the water with varying degrees of porpoising before the hull can again climb up on an efficient plane.

A boat may have sufficient *planing platform WIDTH* for 25 to 30 mph speeds...above which the planing platform may not be wide enough to support its load. The boat falls back into the water with a loud splash to follow the porpoising cycle as it tries to plane again.

This pattern is common to older hulls that planed adequately until larger motors were added to go beyond their hull speed limit.

Powerboating Illustrated

We discussed a galloping, porposing pram with a 15 hp motor on page 34. The water was calm in a protected San Pedro channel with a happy dad watching his son enjoy his birthday present.

The wide plane provided enough lift to start planing, while at 15 to 18 mph the rocker tripped the boat to splash back into the water with minimum steering control. What motor hp would you recommend for an 8' pram?

Powerboating Illustrated

Porpoising develops when a hull wants to plane, but due to an inadequate planing platform, falls back into the water producing a wet, pounding ride.

correct trim

INCORRECT TRIM

PLOP

ROCKER BOTTOM with NARROW TRANSOM will not usually support itself on a plane.

PLOP

FLAT BOTTOM

HOOK

WHAM

Porpoising can develop on a small planing hull with a narrow transom that can handle a light load easily, but develops when overloaded.

The overloaded or incorrectly loaded boat may not climb up to a plane which is similar to an overloaded light airplane.

If passenger or weight is moved forward to trim the hull, it may be able to climb up to a plane.

●

The traditional rowboat with a narrow stern which is not designed for planing will be easy to recognize.

The problem—some rowboats with a wider transom and less rocker may climb onto a low speed plane.

Take enough time so you are able to recognize both rowboat extremes to avoid an overpowered porpoising ride. The second hull will be more difficult to row as the wider transom disturbs more water, pg. 33.

●

An extreme hook will make a V bottom boat plane earlier, with the bow also digging in earlier to start the porpoising cycle.

Our fun begins when we combine a hook, a small secondary rocker, a flat bottom and narrow transom.

The hull will climb out of the water faster than normal and the bow splashing back like a wounded porpoise. Instead of the more comfortable V bottom digging in, *the wide midship flat bottom* part of the hull will hit hard and bounce upwards.

The combination of hull defects is an expensive way to mix martinis.

Powerboating Illustrated

61

Tilt angle
is wrong—
what's that?

There are many ways a planing hull can waste outboard motor power. A primary offender is the *wrong tilt or thrust angle*, will cause a speed loss and unnecessary strain on the transom and motor clamp bracket. It is comparable to driving a car with the hand brake on.

•

The outboard motor is designed to push a hull straight ahead with minimum effort and minimum resistance. Incorrect tilting in either direction fore or aft will change the angle of attack. The result is increased wetted surface that produces a speed loss.

1 Place the motor on the transom when the boat is on the trailer...not in the water. Line the *anti-cavitation or ventilation plate* parallel to the transom chine. Raise or lower the motor on the transom according to the manufacturer's specifications.

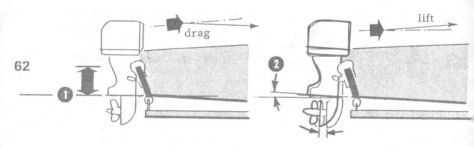

2 Raise the outboard motor tilt pin so the centerline of the gear case housing will be parallel to the bottom planing platform...*then move it one additional pin hole farther aft.*

3 Maximum thrust is delivered from the power available when the prop shaft is parallel to the water at planing speeds. IF hull flare, etc., will provide a slight air lift, AND the prop thrust is 3-6° further aft of the transom...the extra tilt pin aft can give the bow extra lift for better planing efficiency in smooth water.

The extra tilt pin hole aft advantage is obvious on some hulls, and less on others. We found it worked excellently on our 3 outboard boats in smooth water, while in rougher water the tilt pin had to be moved one hole forward for better thrust and less cavitation potentials.

Powerboating Illustrated

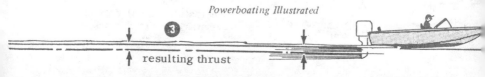

• *The motor is mounted the correct height and adjusted to the best thrust angle. The boat should plane easily with minimum support area, reaching top speed with normal effort.*

Thrust forces are efficiently used eliminating steering problems.

Anti-cavitation plate presents minimum drag or disturbance.

3-5° attack

• Thrust angle is too far aft—*increasing windage and wetted surface drag. The cavitation plate is dragged thru the water at an angle producing a wave action... while developing unnecessary drag with wasteful forces on the motor clamp bracket and transom.*

The stern squats as the prop digs a hole under the transom. Handling becomes unpredictable.

too far AFT

• The prop is too far forward—*it is biting into semi-disturbed water with the prop CAVITATING excessively.*

The resulting downward bow thrust will cause the bow to dig in and swamp the bow, or the stern will pivot around the bow causing a broach with the boat flipping or spinning out.

63

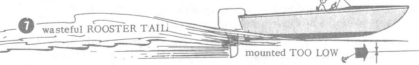

big STERN WAVE   big BOW WAVE

• The best designed gear housing has tremendous PARASITIC DRAG. The top speed can be increased if the motor can be raised ½'' above normal without cavitating. *Mounting the motor lower than normal will increase parasitic drag. This increases wasteful forces on the clamp bracket and transom reducing boat speed. Water may go into powerhead.*

wasteful ROOSTER TAIL

mounted TOO LOW

• If the motor is carried too high—*the prop not having sufficient bite in the water begins to CAVITATE. Few forces are as damaging as cavitation erosion on the prop... with an expensive companion, excess powerhead rpm.*

WHEEEEEE

mounted TOO HIGH

Powerboating Illustrated

Outboard motor manufacturers thru continuous experimentation have arrived at an average mounting height for outboard motors on outboard hulls. After understanding the basics you will be able to know whether a deviation from the standards may help the performance of a boat... or cause unnecessary expenses.

● *Lower unit drag*—regardless how much engineering is used to streamline the outboard lower unit, since it delivers THRUST without lift it has considerable parasitic drag which increases with speed.

● *The waterpump*—the top speed can be improved if the motor can be carried higher on the transom reducing lower unit parasitic drag without cavitation, and the waterpump has an ample water supply.

● *Experimentation*—motor height can be adjusted by raising it with thin wooden strips used as shims. After the motor has been raised sufficiently, a wooden block is substituted which is equal to the height of the strips, then the motor is *bolted to the transom.*

64

● *Transom angle*—is another factor with the 20° transom permitting the motor to be mounted a little higher so the water flowing under the transom has a chance to regroup before hitting the prop while operating as efficiently as possible. This and the correct *tilt pin angle* are major factors in racing which can also improve performance of the family outboard boat.

● *The tilt pin angle*—as discussed on page 62, proved that the difference with one tilt pin hole on *Jewel* and *Researcher* could change the prop thrust angle enough to improve smooth water performance, then moved one hole forward, could provide a better bite in rougher water for maximum performance. If the lower unit wasn't moved one hole forward, the prop would begin to occasionally cavitate when biting into a mixture of air and water in wave action.

If the tilt pin angle was so important on our boats, it should be one of the first items a mechanic detective checks when an owner asks for a tuneup as the motor isn't producing enough performance.

If a mechanic overlooks this thrust angle which is incorrect due to the wrong pin hole angle, and provides a motor tuneup, his problems are just beginning.

The owner takes his boat out again, but the performance hasn't changed. Back at the launching ramp he tells friends, "After spending $38 at J-----'s shop for a tuneup, my boat runs slower. If I were you...."

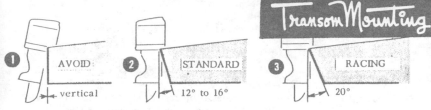

① AVOID: ── vertical

② |STANDARD| 12° to 16°

③ | RACING | 20°

The outboard boat is basically a *bottom* with a motor board or *transom*.
The transom in the early days was standardized from 12° to 16°. The
20° transom angle introduced later improved performance as it put
the prop farther away from the transom. The lower unit could be
carried a little higher to reduce drag without causing cavitation.

The vertical transom doesn't permit proper motor mounting. The
alternative is to carry a motor on a bracket behind the stern inviting
corrosion and swamping problems.

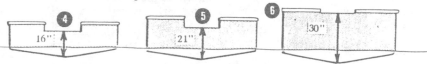

④ 16"   ⑤ 21"   ⑥ 30"

The 16'' transom seemed sufficient in the early days for small lakes
with ample weather protection. For larger lakes and rougher water
small waves were able to swamp many 16'' transom hulls.

We feel the 21'' transom with a self draining well or splash pan should
be standard for coastal AND inland use, the exception...small, protected
lakes.

65

All of our outboard research was done on the ocean except for a few
days on Lake Mead. *Blunder*, 14' long, had a short shaft with water
continually ¼ to ½'' from coming over the transom. Both *Jewel* and
Researcher required long shaft motors and splashpans. Even with this
protection we occasionally had to do a lot of bailing, see pg. 22.

A review on motor transom height—

The outboard lower unit should be carried as high as practical
due to parasitic drag. The three basic factors are—

1. How high can cavitation plate be carried yet maintain an
efficient water flow without air entering prop stream.

2. How high can the intake inlet be carried yet have the water
pump still work efficiently.

3. How high can the prop be carried without cavitating.

⑦ tion

A neighbor bought a wide, heavy planing hull yet it could
barely plane following standard mounting spec's. I soon noticed
a *roostertail*, pg. 63, indicating the motor was mounted too
low. After the motor was raised 1½'' the boat was 8 mph faster.

⑧

Water flow may *bend upward* on a wide, heavy hull when
planing, instead of flowing straight back from the transom
chine, which is normal for many planing hulls.

Powerboating Illustrated

Can't understand why it isn't planing with full throttle!

The speed of a planing hull is increased *by reducing the wetted bottom surface area and drag...while providing efficient fore and aft stability support at maximum speed.* While this is an excellent basic theory,let's consider some unpleasant factors in the complex trailerboating field.

● It is a common practice for a person buying his first portable boat to overlook adding bottom paint before their boat goes into salt water where it will be tied up at a dock or float.The top speed will drop slowly,and then rapidly with a puzzled boat owner.

Our *Blunder* had a white bottom paint as the previous owner had used it for racing...which was not resistant to marine growth.In a week the speed dropped to 30 mph,two weeks later it could barely reach 20 mph.Around ten days later no matter how the 40 hp motor growled and groaned,*Blunder* could only surf,not plane.

Barnacles,grass,shellfish and endless kinds of marine growth cannot distinguish from fiberglass,wooden,and metal boats...they love them all. Check pages 394-5 for bottom paint variables which are considerable. Study page 354 for painting aluminum lower units and aluminum hulls.

66

● Ski boats such as *Blunder* have wide sterns and sometimes tumblehome so they can plane earlier using larger motors for upper planing speeds.

The cartoon at right is somewhat exaggerated to illustrate an incident that a competent dealer or mechanic could have avoided if they had enough answers.The boat owner enjoyed racing autos.He became interested in racing outboard boats,buying an excellent choice for his first rig with an excellent racing record...but he wasn't satisfied.

He complained bitterly after buying a larger motor,that his top speed had been considerably reduced proving money can't buy everything. His well balanced rig now had too much weight on the stern,similar to an overpowered airplane with undersize wings.

●Frank bought a used boat for $700.He was very pleased with the 20 mph performance until one of his fishing buddies enjoying the new sport, bought a sleek $10,000 inboard cruiser,the year,1950.

Frank's fishing boat suddenly looked like a tub,but bankers wouldn't loan him with enough money to buy a better boat.When we met Frank he had rebuilt his old boat to look like $10,000.The damage had been completed with FOUR major speed losses.

The boat floated lower increasing the wetted hull area...the windage increased considerably,and the overloaded boat could barely creep along at displacement speed.Due to the topheavy flying bridge,the boat wanted to roll over in the slightest chop.When we last saw Frank he was painting a sign,"Buy my customized powerboat...a REAL bargain".

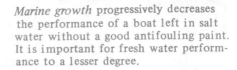

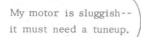

My motor is sluggish-- it must need a tuneup.

Marine growth progressively decreases the performance of a boat left in salt water without a good antifouling paint. It is important for fresh water performance to a lesser degree.

A hard bottom antifouling paint will be required if left in ocean water for more than three weeks. The bottom will need a hand rubbing at least weekly for shorter periods to remove beginning marine growth.

Outboard and outdrive lower units need TBT antifouling paint, page 354, as the high content copper bottom paint will corrode aluminum.

The big motors are lemons. Double the horsepower like I did----and the boat goes SLOWER!

The boat at left had reached optimum planing speed before being sold to the new owner. After adding a larger motor, the narrow transom increased the load and wetted bottom dragged thru the water.

67

The rig was soon for sale after the new owner realized he was lucky to have a speed loss and not a boat loss due to swamping, or the boat disintegrating in a race.

Before buying a used *high speed dream boat,* check bargains closely.

My motor is slow.

Ϝrank was one of those sweet, innocent boat owners you would do everything to help, but—*consult the naval architect or builder before CUSTOMIZING* an outboard boat, inboard boat, or sailboat.

Random customized improvements can be wasteful and expensive.

Planing hull balance is a major factor. When all of the mistakes were added together, the topheavy boat could roll over in mimimum wave action.

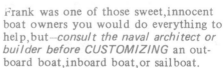

> I give the motor full throttle but it just won't take off---
> the carb must not be getting enough air!

The engineering philosophy-- *bumblees shouldn't be able to fly...* has fascinated me. We loaned *Blunder* to a group of aircraft engineers for a weekend at Catalina, to be towed by a large sailboat.

I soon found some of the greatest powerboating bloopers came from those who should know better. They returned starting with,"Why don t motor manufacturers let more air into the carb. It choked so much that the boat barely moved!''

Another enterprising engineer said he tried every tilt pin, but the motor was still a dead duck. A third volunteered,''Why don't they put enough power into those engines so the boat can reach a plane?''

The day before I loaned *Blunder,* it was in top condition, purring along easily just above 30 mph. After analyzing their *improvements* with endless adjustments, our motor was a mess. *Score one for the bumblee.*

Questioning revealed that instead of 3 passengers expected, 10 were aboard weighing approximately 1750 pounds, plus 200 lbs. of gear. I asked, "Supposed ten of you loaded aircraft engineer heavyweights were in a three passenger airplane... would it take off and fly at the end of the runway?" Can't understand why they haven't spoken to me since their boat ride.

I slowly began to understand a remark made by a favorite mechanic–
"How can you tell your small percentage of problem customer the truth, then be able to still keep them as happy customers?'

> STAND BACK!

These cartoons happened. The cabin cruiser incident above came from a dealer with a hostile customer claiming his motor was slow. When the dealer asked to see the boat horribly overloaded, you see the reply.

It was moving day. A dinghy passed us at 60 mph on the highway. We soon found the owner, a new neighbor. When asking where his Irish Setter was, he replied, ''What Irish Setter? We don't have a dog''.

ZOOM

The new boat... then six months later.

Keep it on a diet!

The cartoon above is a classic repeated endless times in the last 30
years with boat owners not exposed to flying basics. Small airplanes
and planing hulls have to stay within their weight limits so an airplane can takeoff and begin flying... and a hull reach planing speeds.

*Sometimes overloading is obvious... and at other times on cabin
cruisers it grows with little awareness until an unusual event occurs.*
This happened in 1959 when testing one of the first boat trim tabs.

A 17½' Sunliner, an excellent planing hull, was chosen, using ample
hp. With the company rep, the mechanic, the boat designer Bill Tritt,
and myself aboard the boat, it went thru a speed trap from start to
planing using the trim tabs once, the second without trim tabs.

Bill and I agreed the tabs worked. Yet if a person buys a good planing
hull with ample hp, and loads it properly, the trim tabs wouldn't be
worth the extra cost. Eventually I found *we were 10% right* with 90%
of cabin cruisers needing trim tabs due to poor design, poor loading, etc.

How many mpg does your cabin cruiser require, what is the maximum load so it will plane, and who designs and builds custom fuel tanks for outboard cruisers in your area?	*custom fuel tanks*  69

The name *Researcher* developed normally in 1959 as we faced endless
decisions without standards including battery tiedowns, electrical
wiring... AND extending the fuel range beyond the limit of portable
6 gallon tanks. Larger tanks were available that would corrode rapidly
on the ocean, the shapes were awkward, and they had other problems.

We ordered probably the first 18 gallon built-in fuel tanks in outboard
history. Our Glasspar designer Bill Tritt said *boat balance on the
water and on the trailer required the tank weight centered over the
trailer axle, pg. 276.* The tank builder measured then made the tanks we
installed which when full would hold 36 gallons of premix.

The test came soon with friends on a 43' powerboat we were to meet
for a New Years party at Cherry Cove on Catalina Island. As it was
a 70 mile round trip without refueling, we were close to our maximum
weight for the *Researcher* to reach planing trim.

The boat climbed on a cranky plane for an economical endurance
speed reaching the island between storms... with a force 8 storm
hitting us New Years eve that lasted for two days. We returned as the
storm eased to avoid another storm moving in... with our built-in fuel
tanks running dry 100 yards inside our jetty. Two gallons from a spare
fuel can took us to the fuel dock. It was a sloppy trip both ways with
the spinning compass almost useless, but we had good visibility to
steer as straight a course as possible.   *Powerboating Illustrated*

Nothing is more fun than to hear stories of mechanics favorite customers, this one involving an elderly fisherman who owned a V bottom low performance boat with a long keel...which with his trusty 5 hp motor could turn on a dime.

When his buddies passed him up in newer rigs, it was time for Alvin to buy a new boat. He bought a considerably larger motor, and a flat bottom hull similar in size to his old boat. The important item...the boat was green, as Al believed only green boats can catch fish.

He enjoyed his new boating world having the time of his life breezing thru his old haunts. That was until he made a sharp right turn to enter a narrow crooked side channel leading to a favorite fishing hole. The motor turned but the flat bottom boat didn't with Al going up a gently sloping bank at 20 mph, to dump him in the middle of some porkers enjoying their mudhole on a hot summer afternoon.

The dealer had forgotten to tell him that his new boat had a flat, very fast bottom without the fin which was still on order. All Al could say, "But they were both green, what was the difference?"

> *The effect of a keel on the handling and turning ability is very important to a high performance outboard, outdrive, or hot rod boat.*
>
> On the straightaway or with a beam wind the keel gives directional stability as the boat wants to steer a straight line. The keel also determines how high the motor can be raised, and which tilt pin angle to be used. The keel also acts as a rubbing strake to protect the bottom when the boat is dragged up on the beach or on a trailer.

A fin gives directional stability to the flat and arc bottom boats without a keel so the boat without one especially at displacement speeds would wander instead of steering a straight line.

The fin we found on *Blunder* was troublesome when launching or loading on a trailer...and the boat with a fin should never be beached. Some owners prefer the fin bolted thru the hull so it will take greater shocks while permitting leaks. Others prefer it to break away under stress when hitting a submerged rock or piling at high speed.

One of the funniest and most disturbing moments with *Blunder* was when taking a sailing friend out for his first exposure to a planing hull...in a strong breeze. It almost spun out in a turn, and I banged into the dock on the return with my companion razzing me saying I should have stayed with sailboats. The reason, I somehow lost the fin, finding the loss the hard way.   *Powerboating Illustrated*

● *displacement speed steering stability*

The Tahiti Ketch cruising sailboat is designed for
long distance ocean operation from ½ to 7 knots
with a long keel to stay on course requiring minimum
steering effort at low speeds. The boat is difficult
to turn in a small radius due to the long keel.

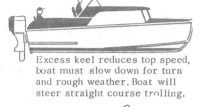

Excess keel reduces top speed,
boat must slow down for turn
and rough weather. Boat will
steer straight course trolling.

Flat bottom boat with-
out directional stability
is unpredictable when
planing, clumsy at a
trolling speed.

Fin gives good stability
for planing and turning at
high speeds, steering is
sluggish when trolling.

Outboard planing hull with
vertical stem is hazardous!

BOW RUDDER

insufficient momentum

UNBALANCED force

Dumbo sufficient momentum

Boat plows through wave.

A *long keel* with excess directional stability is good for trolling to stay on
course at low speed. The same hull will
resist a tight turn at planing speed as it
may spin out... or broach and flip.

●

The flat bottom boat without a keel has
NO steering response at low speed. Since
it has no bite on the water, it will resist
banking and wants to skid the direction
the boat *was going...* even if it has to
go sideways to prove the point.

*The flat-bottom hull at 30 mph may take
an acre for a 180° turn if it doesn't flip.
If it does flip...* can you swim?

71

●

The arc-bottom hull with fin designed
for planing speeds handles very sloppy
at 3 to 5 mph. The fin may permit high-
speed turns with sufficient bite, while
banking and skidding at full throttle.

●

*The straight stem, hatchet bow with little
flare* is common for large craft designed
for displacement speed steering.

The 30' *Dumbo* easily cruised from 25 to
30 mph. While it almost had a vertical
bow, the *momentum* with enough *inertia/
mass* to keep the boat moving and under
control if the bow temporarily digs into
a wave. ●

If the same bow entry is used on a light
outboard planing hull, and the bow digs
into a wave without the *inertia/mass
momentum*—

The bow may stop to become a pivot for
stern to turn on causing a broach and flip.
*The light planing hull requires a shallow
bow entry,* also see page 76.

Developing failures are obvious—

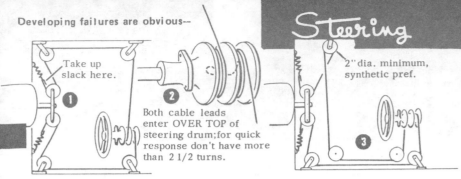

Take up slack here. ①

② Both cable leads enter OVER TOP of steering drum; for quick response don't have more than 2 1/2 turns.

2" dia. minimum, synthetic pref.

③

Two pulley/cable lead methods are shown. As corrosion and chafe are always at work, keep moving parts well lubricated, and continually check the system to remove trouble potentials in the developing stage. Cables must run freely without touching bulkheads. Can motor be tilted without undue strain or cable chafing?

Developing failure is NOT obvious—

④ RACK and PINION single rod steering

1. Rack & pinion (inside)
2. Movable arm
3. Pivot point
4. Locknut
5. Zerk fittings

72

USCG-pg. 261.

When the steering wheel turns it engages the gear rack 1. to move the arm 2. that is shortened or lengthened by pulling or pushing on a fixed motor pivot.

Locknut 4. must be tight, and keep zerk fittings 5. well lubricated. Movable arm 2. needs to be covered with silicone grease for lubrication and rust protection.

Carry cable above floorboard to avoid stepping on; also avoid tight cable turns.

Check steering controls constantly!

chafe ⑤ jamming

Avoid controls in back seat. ⑥

Other boat has R't-of-Way.

⑦

Steering controls should be in front seat for visibility while back seat controls may block operator visibility while surfing.

Steering controls must be on the *right side of the boat* so the operator continually has *full visibility* of the DANGER ZONE especially on high performance craft used for fishing and cruising.

Left hand steering controls should be limited to rescue boats, and for closed course racing where all turns are to the left.

flip, broach

The annual USCG Boating Statistics, COMDTINST M16754.1C—*lists yearly boating accidents, injuries, and fatalities.* Major 1981 listings are: capsizing-467; falls overboard-288; flooding-94; collision with fixed objects-90; collision with another vessel-48.

How fast can it safely take a turn?

● *Capsizing and falls overboard-*begin with tight turns. which cause forces under your control to be overwhelmed by those out of your control. We cover the wide range of factors so you will be able to analyze hull design features in a high speed turn that may cause *broaches, flips, reversed controls, spin outs, and others that may change course so fast it may flip the passengers overboard.*

● Low speed and high speed causes of *porpoising* , pages. 34, 44, and 60, with careening rides and minimum steering response are also involved with capsizing, falling overboard, and collisions.

● *The barrel roll* can occur with a boat having a narrow hull/round side chine while paralleling the wake of another boat, may do a barrel roll in a straightaway...while a boat with a wide stern/sharp side chine may broach and flip. *Slow down, keep weight low, and head into or take the wake at an angle.*

73

the barrel roll

Powerboating Illustrated

● *Collision with fixed objects—*if a log, sandbar, or underwater object looms up ahead and it is too late to miss...*consider hitting the object head on!* The outboard or outdrive lower unit will swing up on impact to clear the object, then swing down after the object has been passed.

If you turn too late, the lower unit suddenly becomes a pivot as it hits the object at an angle. The *unbalanced force resulting* may shear off the lower unit or put a boat into a spin, throw passengers overboard, lose steering control, broach, and/or flip...or the outboard motor may be ripped from its bracket if it can't tilt normally going overboard, or flying forward into the cockpit. Maintaining a continuous lookout will eliminate most out-of-control unbalanced forces from *colliding with fixed objects* by maintaining a continuous lookout.

● Will the powerhead be able to tilt freely forward when hitting an underwater object without hitting a passenger in the back seat?

balanced force

hit object head on

the unbalanced force

turning too late!!!

CRACK

After buying that performance trailerboat, the first wish of many owners...is to find how sharp of a turn their boat can take at full throttle.

USCG accident reports list many owners who found the answer the expensive way.

The chance of finding a round chine on a racing boat is zilch. The flatter the bottom and the sharper the transom and side chines, the faster the boat will be in a straightaway...*and the more dangerous it becomes in a fast sharp turn, or in rough water maneuvering.*

Approximately a quarter of the bottom surface of a flat bottom boat will be in the water at 30 mph. When a tight turn is made *the hull will bank and the low side chine will dig in deep with minimum DRIFT or skidding.* When the inertia moving the boat forward exceeds the resistance to turn...*the low side chine becomes the pivot point for the boat which then rolls outward.* Man aimed the boat one way, but nature with the final answer decided it would go another way.

If we cut the side transom off a flat bottom boat as shown at right, it will float lower and take longer to plane in the straightaway. Without the sharp side chine angle, it will not have as solid a bite in a turn, and be able to drift thru it at or near top speed in a race.

The other extreme, the bottom with round side chines and an arc bottom may turn on a dime when planing...*then roll outward.* The flat bottom hull with round side chines may bank efficiently in a planing turn as it has just enough drift to compensate for the inertia.

The planing flip happens so fast that few people involved can explain it with any accuracy. USCG boating inspectors with many years in the field of accident reporting told me when reviewing this chapter that it was the first time they realized that the boats rolled **outward.**

Unusual conditions will cause even the best of boats to flip...beginning with bilge water weighing 8 ¼ lbs. per gallon.

Our 14' *Blunder* could make a full throttle turn with enough banking and skidding in ideal conditions...with a small safety margin. Add five gallons of bilge water weighing approximately 40 lbs., then take the same full throttle turn. The movable bilge water wanting to *go in the direction the boat WAS going* could be enough to unbalance and flip the boat...which could also happen with a battery or full fuel tank that was not bolted down.

Are there any other articles that may break loose and cause a weight shift during a high speed planing turn?

Every planing hull is made with specific design compromises with limitations that if exceeded mean trouble. Many boat upsets today are bought specifically due to top speed in a straightaway that are very tender in tight curves. Slow down before making a tight turn as a flip can hurt your passengers and/or you, repairs may be expensive, and you may suddenly be involved in an expensive and unnecessary lawsuit.

The planing hull enters a tight turn at full throttle. The aft chine digs deep, with the hull becoming an *unbalanced force* that flips outward.

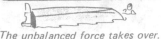

The unbalanced force takes over.

When a boat goes into a high speed planing turn, it must bank with the low side chine aft, and the outside bow forward, much higher. A slight normal skid will be felt. *Throttle down if it isn't as a FLIP is developing.*

As the low bow side rides high on a wave, it will ride higher than normal using the wave as a cushion. *Without this lift... BEWARE as the bow may dig into the bow wave and flip.*

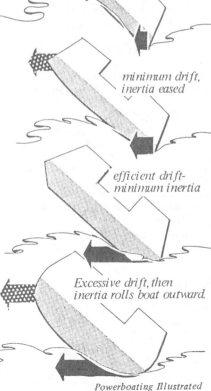

Boat has no drift as chine digs in. Inertia increasing turns chine into a fulcrum

minimum drift, inertia eased

efficient drift-minimum inertia

Excessive drift, then inertia rolls boat outward

Powerboating Illustrated

> The FLIP. When the *inertia or force to resist a direction turn OVERCOMES the boat tendency to change direction, an UNBALANCED FORCE takes over...* and the boat rolls or flips outward.

The unbalanced force... let us define it in other terms. A polevaulter starts running (to begin the first law of inertia vs mass). When one end of the pole digs in and stops, it becomes a fulcrum, and the pole a lever.

The inertia or motion started has been acted on by an unbalanced force. The direction of the force has been changed and the inertia/mass, the polevaulter... *becomes a TURNING MOMENT as he flies up and over the standard.*

- *Flat bottom hulls* plane faster, carry a bigger load, with the highest speed on the straightaway. Ease the throttle in a turn to keep the forces under your control... still under your control.

- The *arc bottom hull with fin* has more drift in a full throttle high speed turn. The hull may be on the ragged edge... with such turns left to the racers.

- The *non-trip chine* hull has sharp side chines for the straightaway, *yet banks and drifts easily thru a full throttle turn.* Full throttle turns should be discouraged for pleasure boating as drift wood, etc., can cause a turn upset.

- The *round chine, round bottom boat* will turn on a dime then rapidly reverse itself and roll outwards.

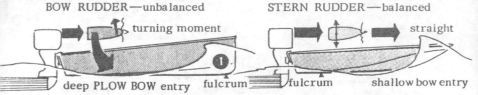

BOW RUDDER—unbalanced   STERN RUDDER—balanced

turning moment   straight

deep PLOW BOW entry   fulcrum   fulcrum   shallow bow entry

The little reported information on hull operation was developed from three sources. Donal Graves was testing his Mercury motors on a variety of boats, who taught high performance boat operation to his mechanics, spent considerable time checking ideas in our book. The second was Bill Tritt, a neighbor, who began building boats in his garage. That was the start of Glasspar which three years later was the largest builder of outboard planing hulls in the U.S. The third source was a curious author who enjoyed testing new ideas.

Bill was a rare genius without formal training in boat design. While some builders were trying to shrink large inboard boat designs to make outboard planing hulls, the origin of the plow bow at right which could broach and flip... Bill produced beautiful high bow entry planing hulls above right, with flare and spray deflecting chines, page 25.

> We had four Glasspar boats with our 12' G3 hotrod *Thumper, Jewel, Researcher,* and the 10' planing dinghy above that we exchanged for a Newporter displacement dinghy we still use.
>
> We were able to have 11 months yearly operation in our harbor and on the ocean during the testing period of our outboard book from 1957 to 1960. *Jewel* and *Researcher* were the best designs available on the market for our testing at the time. They had excellent compromises with stable planing bottoms in the 30 to 35 mph range. They were also quite seaworthy for good weather ocean operation.

Unusual opportunities presented themselves with the full exchange of ideas with Bill and Don, and my sailing background. Three times we were able to take *Researcher* 2 to 5 miles downwind in 25 to 40 mph winds jumping off the top of the waves, and sometimes digging the bow in up to the deck. While we were on the ragged edge a few times, the shallow bow entry and ample flare kept the stern the boss. If the plow bow hull without flare and the low bow chine were in the same rough and tumble wave action, it would broach and roll immediately.

We sold our outboard rigs after publishing our *TrailerBoating Illustrated* in 1960 becoming fully involved with our sailing books and teaching sailing. We rented a 26' RV for 3 weeks in 1979 to check the trailerboating field. We visited launching ramps, lakes, rivers, harbors, etc., from California, to Oregon and Washington, plus beautiful Victoria. We were amazed to find many of the planing hull and trailer problems we provided answers to in our 1960 book... still existed. The real surprise was the $25,000 to $35,000 outboard and outdrive fishing rigs at Hoodsport on the Hood Canal in Washington.

Enjoy studying the boat and trailer chapters so you know the endless variables involved to help your customers help themselves.

76

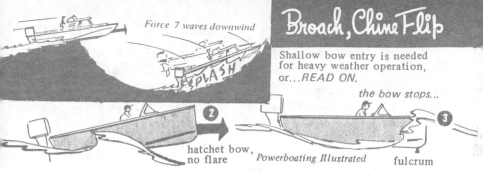

Force 7 waves downwind

SPLASH

Broach, Chine Flip

Shallow bow entry is needed for heavy weather operation, or...*READ ON.*

the bow stops...

hatchet bow, no flare

Powerboating Illustrated

fulcrum

The overpowered hull is coming too fast off the top of a wave.

The deep bow entry without flare digs deep into the next wave.

the stern keeps going...

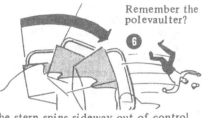

Remember the polevaulter?

fulcrum

The bow becoms a fulcrum as it suddenly stops, but the stern keeps going. *The stern thrust energy now becomes a TURNING MOMENT.*

The stern spins sideway out of control, while the low side dips under to become a new fulcrum. The inertia or energy of the high side completes the flip throwing passengers, anchors, and equipment overboard.

77

The bow chine flip—

Low bow chine flips boat easily.

Higher bow chine reduces flip tendency.

High soft bow chine has least chine flip tendency.

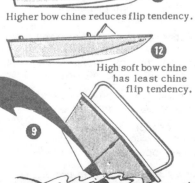

the temporary, misguided keel

Examine closely the bow chine on a planing hull. *Does it raise slightly or considerably...and does it have a sharp or soft high bow entry?*

When a hull at planing speed with a low, sharp chine entry comes off the top of a wave at an angle, the bow chine may dig into the next wave to become *a temporarily curved keel.*

The lower and sharper the bow chine, and the faster a boat is going, the more vicious and rapid may be the resulting *bow chine ROLL and FLIP.*

The best way to avoid injuries and fatalities, is to plan ahead. Would you drive an auto at high speed with bare tires...is the best way to consider a boat with the low bow chine. It can reverse controls, flip suddenly in wave action...or produce a wild barrel roll when crossing the wake of another boat.

Powerboating Illustrated

At top of page, illustration with captions:

Visibility problems?

decksweeping jennie

"Enemy sighted—launch torpedoes!"

Have you seen the video *Boatnicks?* It was taken in our harbor showing local operation in an average day*... visitors don't always agree.

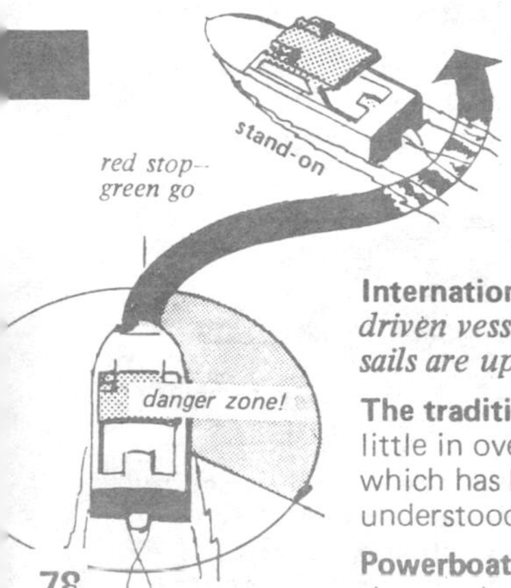

red stop—green go

stand-on

danger zone!

78

Rule 15(a), Crossing situation *Right-of-Way*.

When two power-driven vessels are crossing so as to involve risk of collision the vessel which has the other on her starboard side shall keep out of the way and shall... avoid crossing ahead of the other vessel.

International Rule 25 (e). *A sailboat becomes a power-driven vessel when her engine is turned on even if the sails are up.*

The traditional legal language. These rules have changed little in over 150 years between steamboats. This language which has been time-tested in Admiralty Courts, must be understood by todays operators though confusing at first.

Powerboating and sailing Right-of-Way. We offer 8½ x 11 three color charts that are laminated, as a handy reference on a boat underway, an excellent method to show to friends and family.

This chart shows the situations, the applicable rule numbers, exposing users to their new international legal marine language.

Knowing the rules are just a part of the problem. *If you can't see the other operator, can he see you?* The sailboat with jib blocking visibility has a crew member ignoring his responsibility. The dinghy operating at 5 mph and the outboard boat at right above also operating at harbor speed with the driver near the stern... also having limited visiblity.

Inside powerboat left-hand controls. A passenger or fathometer is blocking view of the operators danger zone, with zero visibility aft.

Right hand or center console steering and operational controls are required for full visibility of the danger zone to avoid collisions at 5 mph... and 50 mph. **Left-hand controls** should be restricted to single purpose racing craft turning counterclockwise racing courses, putting his weight on the low side.

Left-hand controls should be limited to *rescue boats, harbor master, police, and USCG.*

It makes it easier for them to speak to operators of other boats if they have left hand, or center console steering and operational controls.

* 1991—Newport Beach, CA. Our harbor has 10,367 dock and slip berths, 113 moorings, and 2,328 open, dry-storage spots on three story racks.

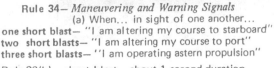

regulations, lights

Rule 34– *Maneuvering and Warning Signals*
       (a) When... in sight of one another...
one short blast— "I am altering my course to starboard"
two short blasts— "I am altering my course to port"
three short blasts— "I am operating astern propulsion"

Rule 32(b)... short blast... about 1 second duration
Rule 32(c)... prolonged blast... 4 to 6 seconds duration

Head-on Situation, Rule 14(a). When two power-driven
vessels are meeting... so as to involve risk of collision,
each shall alter her course to starboard (turn to right)
so that each shall pass on the port side of each other.

Exceptions— Inland Rule 9(a)(ii)— *a power-driven vessel*
... with a following current shall have the right-of-way
over an upbound vessel, shall... initiate... signals.

Inland Rule 15(b).... *a vessel crossing a river shall keep*
out of the way of a power-driven vessel ascending or
descending the river.

Overtaking Rule 13(a). Any vessel overtaking... shall
keep out of the way of the vessel being overtaken.

79

USCG 1989 types of boating accidents		
1. Collision with another vessel	3995	60
2. Collision with fixed object	797	60
3. Capsizing	576	330
4. Other	517	47
5. Falls overboard	428	217
6. Grounding	386	13
7. Fuel fire/explosion	303	7
8. Swamping/flooding	228	70
9. Sinking	219	31
10. Falls within boat	119	0

(vessels involved / fatalities)

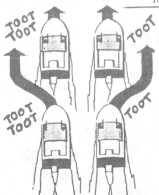

These signals are used in a developing
situation when action of the other vessel
isn't clear.

**Prompt action must be taken in time to
maneuver out of a misunderstanding.**

Take the initiative using these signals
usually with a Freon horn, with other
vessel replying with the same signal.

If crossed signals result, the danger signal
may be considered.

Powerboating Illustrated

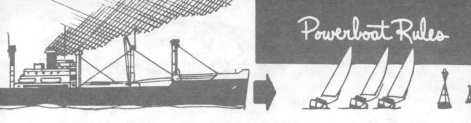

Powerboat Rules

- **Sailboats and powerboats must give way to large vessels with highly limited maneuverability** —

  ▲ *Rule 9 (b) A vessel of less than 20 meters in length (65.6') or a sailing vessel shall not impede the passage of a vessel that can safely navigate only within a narrow channel or fairway.*

  ▲ *Rule 9 (c) A vessel engaged in fishing shall not impede the passage of any other vessel navigating within a narrow channel or fairway.*

  ▲ *Rule 9 (d) A vessel shall not cross a narrow channel or fairway if such crossing impedes the passage of a vessel which can safely navigate only within that channel or fairway. The latter vessel may use the danger signal prescribed in Rule 34 (d) if in·doubt as to the intention of the crossing vessel...*see right page.

- **River currents and tidal currents.** The rules governing a vessel under power are a vast improvement over the previous CG-169 rulebook, as the obligations of vessels operating in tidal currents are now defined. While not covered in the previous rules...they were still applied in little publicized court decisions.

- **Narrow channels.** *Rule 9 (a) (ii) Inland—...a powerdriven vessel operating in narrow channels...and proceeding downbound with a following current shall have the right-of-way over an upbound vessel, shall propose the manner and place of passage, and shall initiate the maneuvering signals...The vessel proceeding upbound against the current shall hold as necessary to permit safe passage.*

- **Crossing situation.** *Rule 15 (b) Inland— ...a vessel crossing a river shall keep out of the way of a power-driven vessel ascending or descending the river.*

- **Power and sails.** *International Rule 25 (e) A vessel proceeding under sail when also being propelled by machinery shall exhibit forward where it can best be seen a conical shape, apex downwards.*

  Rule 25 (e) Inland—...A vessel of less than 12 meters in length (39.4') is not required to exhibit this shape, but may do so.

  The first black cone I remember was more than 20 years after the rule was introduced that was torn and nailed to the spreader of an old motorsailer with the engine horribly out of tune. The boat was rolling miserably as it limped out our jetty belching a smoke cloud out the exhaust.

- **Sailboat engine controls should be mounted on the starboard side of the cockpit.** This permits the operator when his vessel is under power, to have better visibility of his danger zone to reduce chances of a collision. For night operation under power remember the idea, **red—STOP....green—go.**

  Sailing Illustrated

ENJOY POWERBOATING

Since a collision at sea can disturb one's whole afternoon, study, then follow the International and Inland Rules closely.

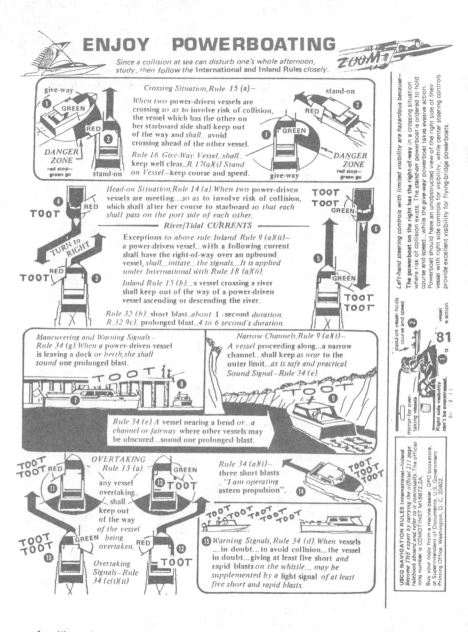

Crossing Situation, Rule 15 (a)—

When two power-driven vessels are crossing so as to involve risk of collision, the vessel which has the other on her starboard side shall keep out of the way and shall...avoid crossing ahead of the other vessel.

Rule 16. Give-Way Vessel...shall... keep well clear...R. 17(a)(i) Stand on Vessel—keep course and speed.

give-way

GREEN

RED

DANGER ZONE
red stop—
green go
stand-on

stand-on

RED

GREEN

DANGER ZONE
red stop—
green go
give-way

Head-on Situation, Rule 14 (a). When two power-driven vessels are meeting...so as to involve risk of collision, which shall alter her course to starboard so that each shall pass on the port side of each other.

TOOT

RED

TURN to RIGHT

RED

TOOT

TOOT
TOOT
GREEN

GREEN

TOOT
TOOT

River/Tidal CURRENTS

Exceptions to above rule: Inland Rule 9 (a)(ii)— a power-driven vessel...with a following current shall have the right-of-way over an upbound vessel, shall...initate...the signals...It is applied under International with Rule 18 (a)(ii).

Inland Rule 15 (b)...a vessel crossing a river shall keep out of the way of a power-driven vessel ascending the river.

Rule 32 (b)...short blast...about 1 : second duration. R. 32 9c)...prolonged blast...4 to 6 second's duration.

Maneuvering and Warning Signals—
Rule 34 (g). When a power-driven vessel is leaving a dock or berth, she shall sound one prolonged blast.

TOOT

Narrow Channels, Rule 9 (a)(i)—
A vessel proceeding along...a narrow channel...shall keep as near to the outer limit...as is safe and practical. Sound Signal—Rule 34 (e).

TOOT

Rule 34 (e). A vessel nearing a bend or...a channel or fairway where other vessels may be obscured...sound one prolonged blast.

TOOT
TOOT
RED

OVERTAKING
Rule 13 (a). any vessel overtaking... shall keep out of the way of the vessel being overtaken.

GREEN
TOOT

Rule 34 (a)(i)—
three short blasts
.."I am operating astern propulsion".

TOOT
TOOT
TOOT

TOOT
TOOT

GREEN

RED

TOOT

Overtaking Signals—Rule 34 (c)(i)(ii)

TOOT
TOOT TOOT
TOOT TOOT

Warning Signals, Rule 34 (d). When vessels ...in doubt...to avoid collision...the vessel in doubt...giving at least five short and rapid blasts on the whistle... may be supplemented by a light signal of at least five short and rapid blasts.

Left-hand steering controls with limited visibility are hazardous because—

The powerboat on the right has the right-of-way in a crossing situation where risk of collision exists. The stand-on powerboat is ordered to hold course and speed...while the give-way powerboat takes evasive action. Powerboat should have an unobstructed view of the right side of their vessel with right side controls for visibility, while center steering controls provide excellent visibility for flying-bridge powerboats.

stand-on vessel holds course and speed

vessel in action

'81

mirror for over-taking vessels

Right side visibility can't be overstressed.

USCG NAVIGATION RULES International—Inland
Become THE expert by carrying the official 211 page rulebook aboard and refer to it continually. The official long number is COMTINST M16672.2A.

Buy your copy from a marine dealer, GPO bookstore, or Superintendent of Documents, U.S. Government Printing Office, Washington, D. C. 20402.

A sailboat becomes a powerboat when its outboard or inboard engine is turned on requiring sailors to operate on powerboat rules.

Powerboating Illustrated

Annex V— 88.05-Copy of Rules. After 1/1/83, the operator of each self-propelled vessel 12 meters (39.4 ft.) or more in length shall carry on board and maintain for ready reference a copy of the Inland Navigation Rules.

While the rulebook is mandatory to be carried on sailboats 39.4' and longer, it is also an excellent idea to be carried aboard cabin sailboats and power-boats 20' to 25' and longer...for your own protection.

We have taught sailboat and powerboat operation going back to 1958 in Newport Harbor more as a personal test to understand problems faced by new boat owners, to develop methods to help them adapt to their new sailing and powerboating worlds.

Local boating traffic was heavy even in those early days, the reason we developed the sailboat and powerboat right-of-way rules, illustrating the basic regulations, with the rule numbers if further information was needed.

Powerboat rules are just as important to sailboat owners because if their sailboat operates with an outboard motor, or an inboard engine, it becomes a powerboat even if the sails are up. The operator then has to follow the powerboat rules, making it obvious so nearby powerboat operators know it is no longer following the sailboat rules.

82   We prepared laminated all-weather charts of the sailboat and powerboat rules that can be used for instant reference so you can show to family, crew, and visitors the unique world of Admiralty Law. It has a long history, being probably the first kind of international law to prevent collisions, with one vessel ordered to maintain course called the *stand-on vessel,* while the other *give-way vessel* must use methods to avoid the stand-on vessel.

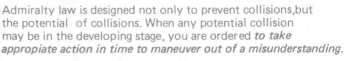

poor visibility

Admiralty law is designed not only to prevent collisions, but the potential of collisions. When any potential collision may be in the developing stage, you are ordered *to take appropiate action in time to maneuver out of a misunderstanding.*

If an unusual situation develops where you have to break all the rules to prevent a collision, you begin to understand Admiralty Law, which is a unique world of its own. If you operate your sailboat in any high-density traffic area, take ample time to study the thinking of this type of law which is very strict that is designed for your self protection.

good visibility

Deck-sweeper genoa jibs. This is a chronic problem we have faced for over 30 years as it blocks a large area of the operators visibility. When an owner uses this large size jib, he must take the responsibility to *maintain a proper lookout by sight and hearing* to prevent collision potentials. We recommend a jib to be raised at least 7'' off the deck when not racing to provide much better visibility for the cabin sailboat owner.

Powerboating Illustrated

ENJOY SAILING

It is cheaper to buy a sailor a friendly drink at the bar, than spend a week in court while the judge explains the term "port tack" to the newcomer. Can you think of a better reason to know the sailing regulations thoroughly?

"I suppose youse gentlemen know the rules regarding my sailboat right-of-way!"

Rule 12 (a). When two sailing vessels are approaching one another, so as to involve risk of collision, one of them shall keep out of the way of the other as follows:—

Sailboat International AND Inland right-of-way Rules are identical.

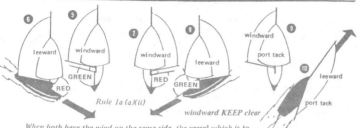

WIND

port tack ❶ ❷ starboard tack

GREEN RED

port tack ❹

❸ starboard tack

Rule 12 (a)(i) port tack KEEP clear

Rule 12 (b)...the windward side shall be...the side opposite to...which the mainsail is carried.

When each has the wind on a different side, the vessel which has the wind on the port side shall keep out of the way of the other.

❻ ❺ leeward windward ❼ windward ❽ leeward ❾ windward port tack

GREEN RED RED GREEN ❿ leeward port tack

Rule 1a (a)(ii)

windward KEEP clear

When both have the wind on the same side, the vessel which is to windward shall keep out of the way of the vessel which is to leeward.

Responsibilities Between Vessels—Rule 18 (a): A power-driven vessel underway shall keep out of the way of: (iv) a sailing vessel. *Exceptions are—* Rule 9—Narrow Channels? Rule 10—Traffic Separation Schemes? Rule 13—Overtaking.

Overtaking, Rule 13 (b). A vessel shall be deemed to be overtaking when coming up... *from a direction more than 22.5 degrees abaft* her beam...to the vessel she is overtaking.

Rule 13 (d)...keeping clear of the overtaken vessel until she is finally past and clear.

meeting ⓫ powerboat keep clear ⓬ overtaking vessel keep clear ⓭ overtaking

sailboat OR powerboat 135° ⓮

Rule 9 (b), Large Vessels, Narrow Channels— A vessel of less than 20 meters in length (65.7 feet) or a sailboat shall not impede the passage of a vessel that can safely navigate only within a narrow channel.

Overtaking, Rule 13 (a). Notwithstanding anything contained in the Rules...any vessel overtaking... shall keep out of the way of the vessel being overtaken.

Rule 2 (a)—Nothing in these rules....shall exonerate any....master or crew... from the consequence of the neglect to comply with these Rules. If your vessel is involved in a collision and you didn't know the rules, ignorance becomes a questionable defense. If your vessel has the right-of-way, and you want to be a nice guy giving the right-of-way to another vessel and a results...you are in trouble for breaking Rule 2 (a).

83

Admiralty law exists for a single purpose—to prevent collisions. You have strict regulations to follow to avoid collisions, yet when a collision is inevitable, you are ordered to break some or all the rules to prevent a collision. You then begin to realize the basic concept in an unclear situation, is **to initiate action so both vessels will have time to maneuver out of a misunderstanding.**

© 1985 by Patrick M. Royce, from *Sailing Illustrated Homestudy Guide*

Less than 9% of collisions occur in open waters!

8½ x 11 all-weather charts are available for these sailboat and powerboat rules for instant on-board reference.

Powerboating Illustrated

360° anchor light   emergency strobe light

Combination all-round white running light can also substitute as an anchor light for powerboats under 39.4 feet long, which surely covers all practical portable trailerboats. When buying one, if possible have it also include a separate strobe light.

The strobe light is finding increasing use in boating, though its official use is clouded, our latest information, it isn't illegal. Use a strobe light only in an emergency or to avoid collisions.

Boat operation at night causes problems of its own since many people buy running lights being satisfied their boat meets the MINIMUM USCG requirements.

You should instead approach running lights for your SELF PROTECTION, hoping owners of approaching boats will have the same interest in the running lights on their boats.

We've started many debates stating probably 70% of the running lights are illegal as they are improperly mounted as they are too low being momentarily blocked behind waves in wave action. Many are incorrectly used being blocked by persons sitting in front of them, or on a sailboat, by sails.

We also see numerous boats operating without any running lights, weak lights, and a few times, red and green lenses which were reversed. We also see people adding stronger red and green lights with stronger bulbs added to the lenses which overpower the red and green color lenses.

Then a light can go out underway with the bulb not possible to replace except dockside and/or you forget to take along a spare bulb. These are all situations that can contribute to unnecessary collisions.

nautical miles	
	feet
1.0	0.8
1.5	1.5
2.0	3.0
2,5	5.0
3.0	7.5
3.5	9.0
4.0	12.0
4.5	15.5
5.0	19.0

While the new regulations require stronger lights, the higher a light is carried, the less chance it has to be momentarily blocked, also increasing its visibility . . . see table at left.

The masthead light requires a dodger below it so the light does not shine down nor into the operators eyes, partially blinding him.

Red and green running lights on smaller planing hulls may be temporarily blocked when climbing onto a plane, momentarily riding bow high, also when coming down from a plane.

84

International Rule numbers are listed.

Rule 25(d)(ii). A vessel under OARS...show white light in...time to prevent collision.

Rule 23(c), POWER-DRIVEN vessel less than 7 meters(23 feet)whose maximum speed(underway) doesn't exceed 7 knots (though it can go faster) may.. exhibit all-round light...if practicable, also exhibit sidelights (shown on vessel under 39.4' long. Outboard powered rowboats and dinghies are included in this rule.)

— lengths —	
meters	feet
7	23
12	39.4
20	65.6
50	164
100	328
150	492
200	656

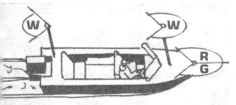

Rule 22(b)(c)	less than 12 meters (to 39.4 feet)	12 to 20 meters (to 65.6 feet)	less than 50 meters (to 164 feet)	
R/G 112.5° each	comb. or separate 1 mile vis.	comb. or separate 2 mile vis.	separate 2 mile vis.	Rule 21(b)
masthead 225°	2 mile vis. 3.3' above R/G	3 mile vis. 8.2' above gunwale	5 mile vis. ◄— (Annex 1)	Rule 21(a)
stern light 135°	2 mile vis.	2 mile vis.	2 mile vis.	Rule 21(c) 85

A POWER-DRIVEN VESSEL THAT EXCEEDS 7 KNOTS—

navigation light definitions Rule 21 (a)(b)(c)
navigation light visibility Rule 22(b) 12. meters to under 50 meters:
(c) vessels less than 12 meters (39.4 feet long)

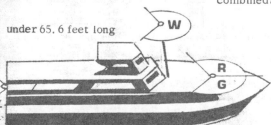

All powerboat lights are covered in Rule 23(a)----
(i) masthead light (225°)
(iii) sidelights (112.5° each)
(iv) sternlight (135°)

(International Rules require SEPARATE masthead and stern lights...they may NOT be combined as with Inland Rules).

under 39.4 feet long

under 65.6 feet long

Int'l/Inland R.21(b) .. a vessel less than 20 meters(65.6 feet) ... sidelights may be combined into one lantern.

Powerboating Illustrated

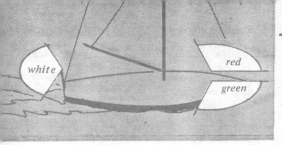

Rule 25(a)..shall exhibit
(1)sidelights;(ii)sternlight.

Def.;Rule 21(b)sidelights..
green light on the starboard
side,and red..on the port
side showing an unbroken
light...of 112.5° (each).

Int'l/Inland Rule 21(b)continues..In a vessel of less than 20 meters
(65.6')the side lights may be combined in one lantern carried *on*
the fore and aft centerline of a vessel.

Inland only Rule 21(b)continues...a vessel of less than 12 meters
(39.4')...the sidelights when combined in one lantern shall be placed
as *nearly as practical* to the fore and aft centerline of the vessel.

Int'l/Inland Rule 25(a)(ii) sternlight-Def. Rule 21(c)...a white
light placed as nearly as practical at the stern showing an
unbroken light over an arc...of 135 degrees...

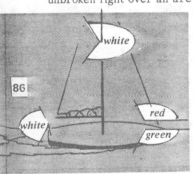

86

───── *Power Driven Vessel Underway* ■■■■■■■

Int'l/Inland Rule 23(a)..shall exhibit:

(i)a masthead (engine) light forward..
(iii) sidelights; and (iv)a sternlight.

Int'l/Inland Def.;Rule 21(a) "Masthead light" (engine light)..a white
light...showing...over an arc...
of 225 degrees.

Sternlight variables Under Power—

Int'l Rule 21(c)...a white light...
of 135 degrees...

Inland-Rule 23(c) A power-driven vessel of less than 12 meters
(39.4')..may..exhibit an all-round 360° white light and sidelights.

Int'l-Rule 23(c) A power-driven vessel of less than 7 meters (23')
..whose maximum speed does not exceed 7 knots may...exhibit
an all-round white light... if practical,also exhibit sidelights.

─────── *Anchored Vessels and Vessels Aground* ■■■■■■■■

Int'l/Inland Rule 30 (a)...shall exhibit.....
(i) in the fore part,an all-round white light...
Def.;Rule 21(e)..an unbroken light..of 360 degrees.

Inland (only)Rule 30(g) A vessel of less than
20 meters(65.6'). when...in a special anchorage
area..shall not be required to exhibit anchor lights...

Inland(only)Rule 30(e)...less than 7 meters (23')
at anchor, not in or near a channel...where other vessels normally
navigate..shall not be required to exhibit..(an all-round white light).

*NOTE: the original 1977 (COLREGS) Navigation Rules list
20 meters as 65.7 feet... while the 1982 rules,list it as 65.6 feet.
Did the meter expand,or did our foot measurement shrink?*

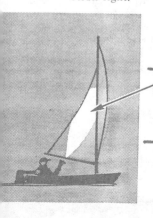

tricolor light   anchor light   strobe light

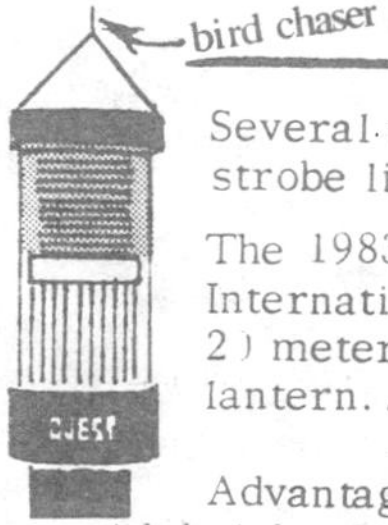

bird chaser

Sailing Vessel Underway-Sail ONLY

Several manufacturers combine the running, anchor, and strobe lights shown above into one unit (at left).

The 1983 USCG Navigation Rules are now identical for International and Inland Rules 25(b)... sailboats less than 2) meters (65. 6').. . the lights. . . may be combined in one lantern. . . at top of mast where it can best be seen.

Advantages of tricolor running light . . . visibility increases with height above water surface . . . while its visibility cannot be blocked with the jib.

Tricolor running light uses one bulb with less drain than pulpit mounted sidelights/stern light requiring two or three bulbs. A 10 watt bulb may have a mile visibility . . . while a 25 watt bulb may double its visibility, with an increased battery drain.

If your sailboat has both running light systems, pulpit mounted sidelights and sternlight at eye level are easier to see in close quarter harbor maneuvering situations.

When a sailboat becomes a powerboat, the tricolor MUST be turned off . . . replaced by the engine light, side lights, and the stern light.

Tricolor light disadvantage . . does your mast have a tabernacle to lower your mast in order to replace a burned out tricolor bulb?

STROBE light (pg. 232) should only be turned on *when a vessel is in distress and requires assistance.*

Int'l/Inland Rule 25(d)(i) A sailing vessel of less than 7 meters (23').. (if she doesn't show other lights covered).. shall have .. a white light which shall be exhibited in sufficient time to prevent collison (see left).

Marine Strobe Light— *for emergency use only.* We use it for vessels in distress requiring assistance. The original purpose in heavily traveled European waters was a warning in addition to the horn for large vessels underway to keep clear of each other.

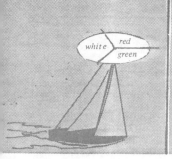

[Left margin, rotated text:] ... Some of us would like it used as a KEEP CLEAR warning to a vessel on a collision course with our vessel. Inland Rule 27 states instead—When a vessel is in distress and requires assistance she shall use or exhibit... A high intensity white flashing light at regular intervals from 50 to 70 times per minute.

87

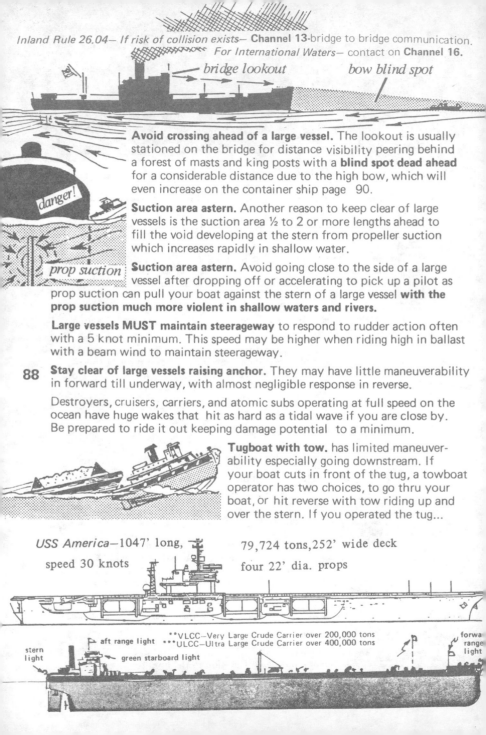

bridge lookout   *bow blind spot*

danger!

prop suction

Avoid crossing ahead of a large vessel. The lookout is usually stationed on the bridge for distance visibility peering behind a forest of masts and king posts with a **blind spot dead ahead** for a considerable distance due to the high bow, which will even increase on the container ship page 90.

Suction area astern. Another reason to keep clear of large vessels is the suction area ½ to 2 or more lengths ahead to fill the void developing at the stern from propeller suction which increases rapidly in shallow water.

Suction area astern. Avoid going close to the side of a large vessel after dropping off or accelerating to pick up a pilot as prop suction can pull your boat against the stern of a large vessel **with the prop suction much more violent in shallow waters and rivers.**

Large vessels MUST maintain steerageway to respond to rudder action often with a 5 knot minimum. This speed may be higher when riding high in ballast with a beam wind to maintain steerageway.

88 **Stay clear of large vessels raising anchor.** They may have little maneuverability in forward till underway, with almost negligible response in reverse.

Destroyers, cruisers, carriers, and atomic subs operating at full speed on the ocean have huge wakes that hit as hard as a tidal wave if you are close by. Be prepared to ride it out keeping damage potential to a minimum.

Tugboat with tow. has limited maneuverability especially going downstream. If your boat cuts in front of the tug, a towboat operator has two choices, to go thru your boat, or hit reverse with tow riding up and over the stern. If you operated the tug...

USS America—1047' long,   79,724 tons, 252' wide deck

speed 30 knots   four 22' dia. props

stern light   **VLCC—Very Large Crude Carrier over 200,000 tons   forward range light
aft range light   ***ULCC—Ultra Large Crude Carrier over 400,000 tons
green starboard light

> Do everything possible to avoid collision courses with large vessels on the ocean and in narrow channels as you are placing yourself in a difficult position, and you may not be around afterwards to argue your case.

- The WW II T-2 **17,000 ton tanker** below, 523' long, 68' beam, requires ½ mile and 5 minutes to come to a *crash stop* from 15k cruising speed.

- The **Very Large Crude Carrier 200,00 tonner** *Idemitsu Maru* requires from 10 to 15 ship lengths, or 2½ miles and 21 minutes for a *crash stop*.

- The **326,000 ton** *Universe Ireland below, engines put on stop* not full astern will take an hour to run her way off and come to a stop.

- A **400,000 ton Ultra Large Crude Carrier** requires 4 to 5 miles and 30 minutes backing full to come to a *crash stop.* During this time she will be unable to respond to her rudder or regulate her speed.

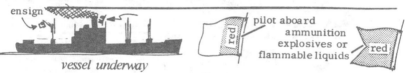

ensign

vessel underway

pilot aboard
ammunition
explosives or
flammable liquids

red · red

- **Is a large vessel underway**...docked, or anchored and out of control? When the black anchor ball forward, and the Union Jack (on U.S. military and other vessels under our government control) are coming down, and the national ensign is being removed from the stern staff...**Stay clear as the vessel is out of control while preparing to get underway.**   89

ensign

vessel not under control

black anchor ball
in rigging
Union Jack
on bow

blue

- **How large is large?????** The carrier *J.F. Kennedy,* a **83,000 tonner,** is 1050' long, 270' beam, with a crew of 5000, while the *Queen Elizabeth II* is a **67,000 tonner** 963' long and 13 stories high.

The 1968 Bantry Bay Class tanker *Universe Ireland* is a **326,000 tonner** 1136' long, 174' beam, carrying 2,513,588 barrels of oil, with largest tankers **1,000,000 tonners** 2000' long, with a 300' beam. Our LA/ Long Beach Harbor is one of 20 ports in the world...with a maximum 65' high tide draft, the only U.S. port able to handle smaller supertankers.

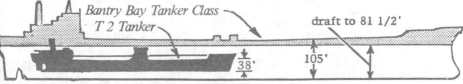

Bantry Bay Tanker Class ·
T 2 Tanker

draft to 81 1/2'

38'   105'

Do you know these warnings?

"Instead of taking the long way around the barge, the shortcut will save us thirty seconds".

A shortcut across a towing hawser may disturb more than just one's afternoon.

aft bridge lookout

blind spot dead ahead

If you can't see the lookout, can he see you? A huge blind spot exists on most large vessels, with the poorest lookout potentials on containerships averaging 20 to 25 knots.

Oops.

Inland—Annex V, Rule 88.05...the operator of each self-propelled vessel 12 meters or more...shall carry on board and maintain...a copy of the Inland Navigation Rules.

submarine underway ❶

intermittent amber flashing beacon
PART A—Rule 1 (c)

Rule 24 (e) (i) (ii)

GR ❸

Aft masthead light is optional for vessel less than 50 meters in length.
Rule 24 (a) (i) (ii) (iii) (iv)

❷ GREEN

Length of tow is 200 meters or less.
Rule 24 (e) (i) (ii) (iii)

The length of tow exceeds 200 meters. ❺
GREEN

All towing vessels are under 50 meters in length.
Rule 24 (a) (i) (ii) (iii) (iv) (v)
Rule 24 (a) (iv)
yellow towing light ❹ GREEN

vessel being towed
GREEN ❻
Rule 24 (f)

towing vessel
Special flashing light—Inland-Rule 24 (f) (i) ❼ GR

Vessels are being towed alongside, or pushed ahead.
Rule 24 (g) (iv) ❾
Rule 24 (g) (i)
Rule 24 (a) (i) (ii) (iii) ❽ GREEN

The tow is a partially submerged vessel or object.

❿ A vessel is engaged in towing operation which severely restricts the towing vessel and her tow in their ability to deviate from their course.
Rule 27 (c)
RED
GREEN RED

Searchlight— International Rule 24 (h)
Inland—Rule 24 (g) (v), 24 (h)

A searchlight in direction of the tow indicates its presence.

⓫ RED RED Both vessels shown are not under control
Rule 27 (a) (i) (ii) (iii)
GREEN

⓬ RED RED
Rule 29 (a) (i) (ii)
The pilot vessel is underway.
GREEN

⓭ RED GREEN

not making way ⓮
Rule 23 (a) (i) (ii) (iii) (iv)
GREEN
displacement mode

making way ⓯
Rule 23 (b)
air-cushion vehicles
all-round flashing yellow light
GREEN
non-displacement mode

Many thanks go to the Port of Los Angeles harbor pilots, and to Chief Pilot Jackson Pearson, for patience with the final review of this chart.

metric conversion	
1 m—3.3 ft	5 m—16.4 ft.	50 m—164.0 ft.
1.5 m—4.9 ft.	6 m—19.7 ft.	75 m—246.1 ft.
2.0 m—6.6 ft.	7 m—23.0 ft.	100 m—328.1 ft.
2.5 m—8.2 ft.	8 m—26.2 ft.	150 m—492.1 ft.
3.5 m—11.5 ft.	10 m—32.8 ft.	200 m—656.2 ft.
4.0 m—13.1 ft.	12 m—39.4 ft.	500 m—1640.4 ft.
4.5 m—14.8 ft.	20 m—65.8 ft.	1000 m—3280.8 ft.
	25 m—82.0 ft.	

This chart was prepared for the author's personal use.

While teaching commercial vessel light recognition for over 30 years, after being wet, cold, and fatigued with too many operational hours on the water...the memory of red over white and white over red becomes fuzzy.

Commercial vessel operator friends grinned saying the chart could also help their judgment when fatigued for rapid identification...*in time to maneuver out of a misunderstanding* as the reason for Admiralty Law is to avoid collisions AND collision potentials.

These lights and signals are used worldwide. They are basic theories...which in application have variables that are endless. To this we add careless operators, plus tired or fatigued operators on the approaching vessel.

❶ Naval vessels due to unusual construction often have difficult to display normal running lights. A submarine on the surface displays an intermittant flashing beacon with one flash each second for three seconds on, three seconds off.

Avoid taking a shortcut BETWEEN tugboats and tows. The lethal hawser can upset and sink many vessels going between tugboat and tow.

❷❸ The tug has a **tow 200 meters long or less.** Will the tow have strong running and stern lights, or will the last barge have a weak kerosene lamp?

❹❺ The tug has a tow that **exceeds a length of 200 meters.** The **yellow towing light** is an aid when helmsman is steering the towed vessel.

❻❼ The tugboat is pushing barges ahead. A special **flashing light** is added as a special warning on a long string of barges for Inland.

❽❾❿ These are difficult towing situations. Can you see the light or diamond on a partially submerged object? Can you recognize a tug with a submerged tow which can't deviate from course?

⓫ The two vertical lights indicate a vessel **not under command** and not underway.

⓬ The vessel is underway though not able to respond to steering controls.

⓭ These lights show a pilot vessel on **pilotage duty underway** at night...with pilot vessel painted on the side for daytime identification.

⓮ A strange shaped vessel is operating at displacement speed.

⓯ The all-round **flashing yellow light** indicates an air-cushion vehicle operating above displacement speed. The light also provides a warning to avoid trying to follow the vehicle to port as it can operate in shallow water, and operate on dry land.

© 1987 by Patrick M. Royce

If you collide with a submarine...please don't sink a friendly one.

Containership lookout visibility is highly restricted producing a major hazard for any vessel crossing under its bow in the blind spot dead ahead.

Tugboat with tow. Hazards of the tow line between cannot be overstressed since outboard boats to large cruisers are lost yearly by operators blundering thru, taking a shortcut across the lethal tow line.

Powerboating Illustrated

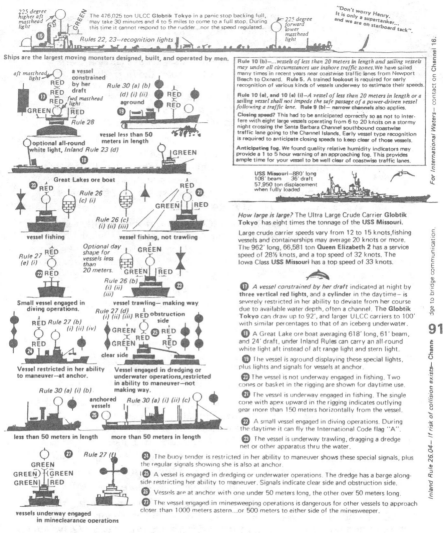

225 degree masthead higher aft light

The 476,025 ton ULCC **Globtik Tokyo** in a panic stop backing full, may take 30 minutes and 4 to 5 miles to come to a full stop. During this time it cannot respond to the rudder...nor the speed regulated.

225 degree forward lower masthead light

"Don't worry Henry. It is only a supertanker... and we are on starboard tack".

Rules 22, 23—recognition lights

Ships are the largest moving monsters designed, built, and operated by men.

aft masthead light

a vessel constrained by her draft

Rule 30 (a) (b) (d) (i) (ii) aground

fwd masthead light

Rule 28

optional all-round white light, *Inland Rule 23 (d)*

vessel less than 50 meters in length

Great Lakes ore boat

RED *Rule 26 (c) (i)*

GREEN RED

Rule 26 (c) (i) (ii) (iii)

vessel fishing

Optional day shape for vessels less than 20 meters.

Rule 27 (e) (i) RED

RED

GREEN RED *Rule 26 (b) (i) (ii) (iii)*

vessel fishing, not trawling

Small vessel engaged in diving operations.

GREEN

vessel trawling— making way

RED *Rule 27 (b) (i) (ii) (iv)*

Rule 27 (d) (i) (ii) (iii) RED obstruction side

GREEN RED

GREEN RED clear side

Vessel restricted in her ability to maneuver—at anchor.

Vessel engaged in dredging or underwater operations, restricted in ability to maneuver—not making way.

Rule 30 (a) (i) (b)

anchored vessels

Rule 30 (a) (i) (ii) (c)

less than 50 meters in length

more than 50 meters in length

GREEN

GREEN) (GREEN

GREEN) (RED

vessels underway engaged in mineclearance operations

Rule 27 (f)

Rule 10 (b)—...*vessels of less than 20 meters in length and sailing vessels may under all circumstances use inshore traffic zones.* We have sailed many times in recent years near coastwise traffic lanes from Newport Beach to Oxnard. **Rule 5.** A trained lookout is required for early recognition of various kinds of vessels underway to estimate their speeds.

Rule 10 (e), and 10 (i)—*A vessel of less than 20 meters in length or a sailing vessel shall not impede the safe passage of a power-driven vessel following a traffic lane.* **Rule 9 (b)**— narrow channels also applies.

Closing speed? This had to be anticipated correctly so as not to interfere with eight large vessels operating from 6 to 20 knots on a stormy night crossing the Santa Barbara Channel southbound coastwise traffic lane going to the Channel Islands. Early vessel type recognition is required to anticipate closing speeds to keep clear of those vessels.

Anticipating fog. We found quality relative humidity indicators may provide a 1 to 5 hour warning of an approaching fog. This provides ample time for your vessel to be well clear of coastwise traffic lanes.

USS **Missouri**—880' long 108' beam 36' draft 57,950 ton displacement when fully loaded

How large is large? The Ultra Large Crude Carrier **Globtik Tokyo** has eight times the tonnage of the **USS Missouri**.

Large crude carrier speeds vary from 12 to 15 knots, fishing vessels and containerships may average 20 knots or more. The 962' long, 66,581 ton **Queen Elizabeth 2** has a service speed of 28½ knots, and a top speed of 32 knots. The Iowa Class **USS Missouri** has a top speed of 33 knots.

⑰ *A vessel constrained by her draft* indicated at night by three vertical red lights, and a cylinder in the daytime – is severely restricted in her ability to deviate from her course due to available water depth, often a channel. The Globtik Tokyo can draw up to 92', and larger ULCC carriers to 100' with similar percentages to that of an iceberg underwater.

⑱ A Great Lake ore boat averaging 618' long, 61' beam, and 24' draft, under Inland Rules can carry an all-round white light aft instead of aft range light and stern light.

⑲ The vessel is aground displaying these special lights, plus lights and signals for vessels at anchor.

⑳ The vessel is not underway engaged in fishing. Two cones or basket in the rigging are shown for daytime use.

㉑ The vessel is underway engaged in fishing. The single cone with apex upward in the rigging indicates outlying gear more than 150 meters horizontally from the vessel.

㉒ A small vessel engaged in diving operations. During the daytime it can fly the International Code flag "A".

㉓ The vessel is underway trawling, dragging a dredge net or other apparatus thru the water.

㉔ The buoy tender is restricted in her ability to maneuver shows these special signals, plus the regular signals showing she is also at anchor.

㉕ A vessel is engaged in dredging or underwater operations. The dredge has a barge alongside restricting her ability to maneuver. Signals indicate clear side and obstruction side.

㉖ Vessels are at anchor with one under 50 meters long, the other over 50 meters long.

㉗ The vessel engaged in minesweeping operations is dangerous for other vessels to approach closer than 1000 meters astern...or 500 meters to either side of the minesweeper.

bridge to bridge communication.

91

Inland Rule 26.04— If risk of collision exists— Channel

We have enjoyed operating near large vessels for over 30 years, requiring us to know the lights and signals to keep out of their way. We planned to have several pages in this major revision covering these lights and signals.

After considerable day and night testing on the water, the full size 8½ x 11 charts we were also testing proved more practical for your use. These facing pages show greatly reduced identical reproductions of this chart,

Powerboating Illustrated

Rule 35— *Sound Signals...In or near an area of restricted visibility, whether by day or night...*will include sandstorms, fog, heavy rain or snow.

Freon horns are excellent for boating use, always carry a spare full tank aboard. AVOID weak, mouth-operated horn devices.

Use your autopilot as much as possible for a more predictable course in fog than steering by hand as the helmsman tends to under, then overcompensate. You must be able to disengage the pilot immediately if required for a course change to avoid a collision.

● **Most collisions occur on the edge of a fog.** We were underway at night from Catalina to San Pedro on a Newporter ketch. We entered a light fog that rapidly became a peasouper. One of the crew was on the bow making fog signals with a freon horn, with another lookout stationed between us as I could barely see the forward mast from the cockpit.

I told the owner to call Long Beach USCG to find if their weather was clear. The answer,"That is restricted information", provoked my reply which was unprintable as we were close to the steamer lane. We suddenly broke out of the fog bank in clear visibility...on a collision course with a freighter 200 yards or so from us NOT in the fog and NOT making signals,breaking Rule 35—...*In or near an area of restricted visibility...*

● **Portable RDF.** We were returning to San Diego after a disasterous sea trial on the 97' schooner *Estrilita* when entering a fog bank. One of my crew had taken along his RDF, using it as a homing device standing next to me on the bow while I was operating an old hand pump fog signal. We tangled with a large outbound navy vessel we couldn't see,but we could hear the bow wave. We suddenly came out into bright sunshine to find we were missing the partially submerged south jetty by a few adequate feet.

● **17' outboard cruiser.** We were swallowed up in a fog bank in 1960 on the way to Catalina as we entered the steamer lane. The ocean was very flat and it was difficult to hold an adequate course at displacement speed. I cut the engine hearing a swissshing sound with a tow line dead ahead.

Fog can play strange sound tricks. Neither of us heard fog signals, nor saw the towing or towed vessel, with the tow line too close for comfort. Even the traditional four-legged fog warning, a barking dog, would have helped.

● **My mistake.** I had a sailing lesson the next day in San Pedro with a thick fog outside our jetty. I waited for it to lift until midafternoon. I left under autopilot and power knowing that *if a collision occurred I would have a hard time defending my action.* I soon picked up the sounds of a very large vessel at anchor,getting my curiosity.

Suddenly I saw the anchor chain and bow but not the deck line above which was lost in the fog. I turned 180 degrees heading back to the harbor using RDF and depth sounder, disoriented and horribly scared,to postpone the lesson. The large vessel was a USN transport that had just returned from Korea, anchoring probably an hour or so earlier. The crew was preparing it for an open house for local residents the next day. *Powerboating Illustrated*

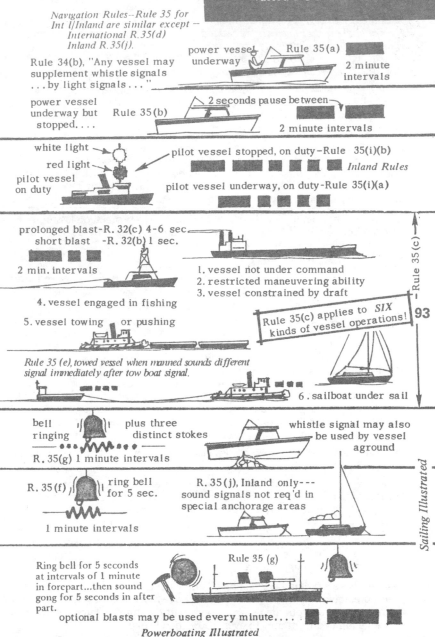

*Navigation Rules–Rule 35 for
Int'l/Inland are similar except –
International R.35(d)
Inland R.35(j).*

Rule 34(b), "Any vessel may
supplement whistle signals
...by light signals..."

power vessel
underway   Rule 35(a)

2 minute
intervals

power vessel
underway but   Rule 35(b)   2 seconds pause between
stopped....

2 minute intervals

white light

red light

pilot vessel
on duty

pilot vessel stopped, on duty–Rule 35(i)(b)

Inland Rules

pilot vessel underway, on duty–Rule 35(i)(a)

prolonged blast-R.32(c) 4-6 sec.
short blast -R.32(b) 1 sec.

2 min. intervals

1. vessel not under command
2. restricted maneuvering ability
3. vessel constrained by draft

4. vessel engaged in fishing

5. vessel towing   or pushing

Rule 35(c) applies to *SIX*
kinds of vessel operations!

– Rule 35 (c) –

93

*Rule 35 (e), towed vessel when manned sounds different
signal immediately after tow boat signal.*

6. sailboat under sail

bell
ringing   plus three
        distinct stokes
R.35(g) 1 minute intervals

whistle signal may also
be used by vessel
aground

R.35(f)   ring bell
      for 5 sec.

1 minute intervals

R.35(j), Inland only---
sound signals not req'd in
special anchorage areas

Sailing Illustrated

Ring bell for 5 seconds
at intervals of 1 minute
in forepart...then sound
gong for 5 seconds in after
part.

Rule 35 (g)

optional blasts may be used every minute....

Powerboating Illustrated

● **Limited visibility.** *Fog signals must be given by all vessels underway, adrift, or at anchor, that need to be started before a vessel enters a fog bank, or area of restricted visibility including a sandstorm. Speed must be reduced so a vessel can theoretically stop in half the visibility distance. A lookout is required, especially in low visibility, with no other duties at the time.*

While the low visibility operational rules are well defined, their application may be poorly applied on recreational craft...though the rules are made to protect the same people.

> **Consider air a sponge** that will soak up a lot of water vapor on a warm day. The air sponge volume is reduced during the evening when the temperature drops. *Saturation begins* as temperature drops, the sponge not able to hold the water vapor. The *dew point is reached* with fog potentials. The problem becomes finding an instrument which will indicate when the *dew point* is reached...with ample time to warn you of an incoming fog.

● **Sling psychrometer.** The theory sounds good in a protected classroom. How many boat owners though will swing one around their heads two or three times an hour to anticipate a fog moving in?

A better answer was required when we were caught out on the ocean with sailing students aboard as a thick fog moved in. We tested a **relative humidity indicator** for three years. The time lag required three years to understand its patterns before the idea was ready to recommend to readers.

● **Time lag patterns.** The indicator predicted approaching fogs often 3 to 5 hours hours in advance ...AND the two types of fog expected. A **medium to dense fog** was indicated with the humidity between 88 to 93% for daytime displacement operation, NOT for sailing at night. A **peasoup fog** was indicated during the day or night if visibility was clear, and the relative humidity 100% or above. If a light fog developed in your area, the peasouper was over the hill or a couple of miles away. A medium fog could lift at night. If visibility was suddenly above normal, a peasouper would soon move in, with the short visibility period nicknamed *the kiss of death.*Without the fog warning indicator it seemed an excellent time to go sailing.

● **Outgoing fog** also involves the time lag with the humidity dropping to 60% or 50%....though the fog may lift three hours later.

Mount a relative humidity indicator topside where it has a continuous air flow, easy to see from the cockpit. A shroud is needed on the top and sides to provide a more accurate reading when raining.

A new inexpensive humidity indicator designed for inside use has to be replaced yearly, preferably in the fall when our fog season begins. If used for a longer period, a loss of 5% accuracy will no longer be sufficient to predict a fog moving in, or a fog moving out.

● After 3 years preliminary testing to understand the time lag, the first fog not predicted was 6 years later when a huge black fog moved in at over 40 knots blanketing our area with zero visibility. A minute later the indicator needle jumped from 55% to over 100% then broke!

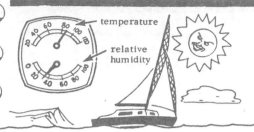

- **Moisture particles in suspension** →

  Air contains water vapor which is invisible below the saturation or dew point.

  Much is written about fogs. The object is to predict a fog to avoid it, or keep your problems to a minimum by staying clear of shipping lanes.

temperature

relative humidity

- **Heavy falling moisture particles**

  A light fog results with an inflow of moist air, or a temperature drop. It will be indicated up to 5 hours in advance when humidity increases to 87-93%.

  Light daytime fogs have sufficient visibility for sailboats to operate at displacement speeds...*but NOT enough visibility for night operation.*

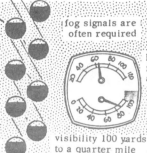

fog signals are often required

light to medium fog

Displacement speeds for daytime operation, avoid nighttime operation.

visibility 100 yards to a quarter mile

95

Fog is visible moisture.

- **Heavy blanket of moisture particles**

  If a light fog exists and the humidity climbs to 100%, a peasouper can follow.

- *WARNING*—a light fog can lift with excellent visibility as humidity increases, with a peasouper moving in.

- *Time lag proved confusing* with early testing.,,before a fog moved out.

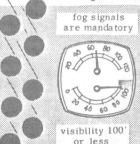

fog signals are mandatory

heavy fog or 'peasouper'

Any boat movement may be hazardous.

DEW POINT is 100% humidity

visibility 100' or less

Humidity can drop to 50% in a fog, lifting 3 to 5 hours later... be patient!

Powerboating Illustrated

The single-purpose drag boat evolved around 1960. The purpose, record official time thru the ¼ mile drag course at 70 to 80 mph.

They were stripped down to bare essentials eliminating the waterpump. Engines with direct drive were underway when starting as the transmission was eliminated to reduce weight eliminating neutral and reverse.

Hot rods evolving usually attract first time 'accidental' boat owners. The low freeboard, high-performance craft are a prestige symbol expensive to buy, operate, and maintain. Owners should take a specialized course before buying such craft to understand the capabilities, limitations and variables of such craft and their engine needs. Operational rule training has to be thorough as little time is left in a meeting or crossing situation with two 60 mile an hour craft blundering thru a misunderstanding.

Smaller ones are often swamped or sunk by their own wake throttling down too rapidly, the engine suddenly quits, a line wraps around the prop or is pulled into the water jet intake, or a ski tow line fouls the fan belt.

We see many 50' and longer monohull racers in our harbor operating at 5 mph

sight seeing, going to lunch and supper at local restaurants. What fun it must be for passengers as the engines gulp, choke, and wheeze as they cough along to stay at harbor speed limit.

96

The inland Sacramento delta records more collisions, injuries and fatalities than on our ocean, with only Alaska having a longer coastline than California. The delta is a huge, triangular, protected inland waterway with fishermen in small boats and full-throttle hot rodders. Give me the ocean anytime.

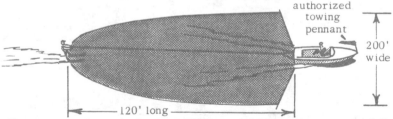

authorized towing pennant

200' wide

120' long

You are operating a planing boat 120' long and 200' wide, not under full control, while towing a skier on a 100' tow line.

Specialized training and awareness are required for tow operators in rapidly developing traffic or other situations. You have to continually remember you are operating a planing hull that large to anticipate and make allowances in time to avoid a collision if the other operator is confused or panics.

Water ski associations could set up standards, test new tow operators, to provide a card and bow pennant indicating the tow boat is under control of a trained, aware operator.

Powerboating Illustrated

 **operation**

Boating is a sport which by definition means some risk is involved. How much of a risk exists in powerboating?

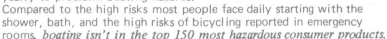

National Safe Boating Week occurs yearly to proclaim boating hazards. Compared to the high risks most people face daily starting with the shower, bath, and the high risks of bicycling reported in emergency rooms, *boating isn't in the top 150 most hazardous consumer products.*

We don't go boating to be safe, but to accomplish individual goals. Many go for pure pleasure from cruising with a weekend floating bungalow, to water skiing. For others the boat is secondary such as transportation for fishing, SCUBA diving, etc.

Powerboat seaworthiness is the definition of a vessel properly designed, constructed, equipped, manned, and in good condition for the area it will be used... includes the 12' fishing boat to the 80' ocean racer.

Planing powerboat operation is similar to a small airplane. The engine must start normally, the craft take off and fly on the water or in the air, both hostile environments for a limited period, then make a good landing. Both operators must know the capabilities and limitations of their craft, then stay within these operation limits.

97

Maintenance... would you park an airplane on a cloud to change a fouled spark plug? Maintenance is continuous in both craft so only minor equipment failures develop   that are easy to compensate for.

This unique book is designed for marine mechanics AND boat owners   to bring them together using the same shirtsleeve language... and the same basic reference point to start with whether to agree, or disagree.

Southern Californians are raised in autos. Many drive 7 days a week. The subconscious mind has been programmed since early childhood to stay alive and learn rapidly in heavy freeway traffic at 65 mph. As we are often a second from instant disaster, poor drivers are rapidly weeded out.

Survival teaches them to give room to problem drivers changing lanes rapidly with minimum clearance. Banged up fenders indicate a hazard to stay away from, followed by a car with an engine running ragged that may also have faulty brakes. *Accident prone operators* make a lot of headlines, the same ones being hazards on the road, water, and in the air.

Welcome to powerboating! We provide a yardstick you are familiar with, to also recognize and avoid trouble in a developing situation on the water.

Hands-on operator/mechanic? Operators must know an awesome number of operational boat, engine, and trailer concepts to communicate efficiently with mechanics. While teaching carburetion to many mechanics, I explain the problem to my mechanic to work on. That is his expertise I pay for with his many years *hands-on experience* to help operators.

12½ —average length   10' to 14'— 68% of U.S. boats

The high-risk inland fleet of car-top boats. The first statistics came out in 1972. "USCG has new figures... *average length* for all boats of only *12½'*... *68%* of them are *between 10' and 14'*... *with 70%... deaths* (1971). CG-357 statistics for the same year lists only 1099 fatalities on boats under 26', with 119 on larger craft, 219 unknown.

The broad base of car top boats... *"According to USCG Admiral Wagner, Sears sold 300,000 of this type of boat".*

The smaller the boat, the closer occupants are to the water increasing chance of upset, falling overboard, injuring and/or drowning occupants. *USCG Boating Statistics 1989* list the following statistics in weather and water coditions as **Type of Body of Water.**

totals	vessels involved	fatalities
1. Lakes, ponds, reservoirs, dams, gravel pits	3823	465
2. Rivers, streams, creeks	1936	254
3. Bays, inlets, sounds, harbors, intercoastal waterways	1210	105
4. Ocean/ Gulf	545	49
5. Other	375	0
6. Great Lakes (not tributaries)	89	20
7. Unknown	42	3

Ten years of boating fatalities. 1400 were listed in 1979, reduced to 896 in 1989. Expressed another way, fatality rate per 100,000 estimated boats has dropped from 10.1 to 5.0 in 1989.

1989 types of accidents by state, statistics page 14. *Florida— 1208; California— 903; Michigan—420; New Jersey—412; New York— 392; Texas—295; Missouri—267; Wisconsin—266; Minnesota—216; Washington and and North Carolina—203; Ohio—202; and Arizona— 191* the leaders.

Sunbelt vs snowbelt hours exposure (author's opinion). Take another look at the state statistics above with roughly *4 months snowbelt exposure... compared to a good 11 months locally.* We can operate almost three times as many hours if desired, compared to snow belt operators. While we prefer harbor and ocean operation with a long coastline... the highest number of collision and other statistics is the inland Delta area of protected waterways from San Francisco, to Stockton, and Sacramento.

Defining the high risk boating potentials follow starting with the highest statistics,and the highest risk potentials being— *June... Sunday... 2:30 to 4:30 pm... water calm... wind light...visibility good.*

USCG Boating Statistics 1989, published yearly, can be obtained by writing to USCG Commandant (G-NAB) Washington, DC 20593-0001 Request *Commandant Publication P16754.3*

Powerboating Illustrated

Leading months— *June... August... July... May... September... April.*

Day of week— *Sunday... Saturday... Friday... Monday... Thursday.*

Time of day— *2:30 to 4:30 pm... 12:30 to 2:30 pm... 4:30 to 6:30 pm...*
10:30 to 12:30 pm... 6:30 to 8: 30 pm... 8:30 to 10:30 pm

Wind— *light... moderate... none... strong... unknown... storm*

Water conditions— *calm... choppy... rough... unknown...strong current*

Visibility— *good... dark... fair... unknown... poor*

Water temperature— *70-79F... unknown... 60-69F... 80-89F... 50-59F...*
40-49F... below 40 degrees F

Persons on board— *two... one... three... four... over ten... five... none???*

Environment— *strong current, rough water... submerged object... wake or*
wave striking vessel... poor visibility... slippery surface or deck

Operational problems— *improper lookout... inattention or carelessness...*
navigation error... speeding... high speed maneuver...
view obstructed

Equipment problems— *steering, throttle, or other non-power equipment*   99
had tremendous failure numbers... improper nav-
igation lights... fuel system... electrical system...
auxiliary power or heat equipment

Loading— *overloading... leaning over edge of boat, moving or standing...*
improper weight distribution... sitting on gunwale, transom,
bow, or back of seat... movement of passengers

Life preservers— *Approved, accessible, not used... Approved, accessible,*
used... unknown ... Approved, not accessible...
none, or not enough on board

Age of operator— *26 to 50 years... 19 to 25 years... over 50 years...*
unknown... 12 to 18 years... no operator?????

operator's experience— *over 500 hours... unknown... 100 to 500 hours...*
20 to 100 hours... less than 20 hours

Formal instruction— *none... unknown... other?... CGA... no operator?...*
USPS... state... American Red Cross

Powerboating Illustrated

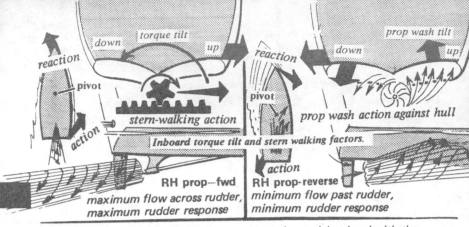

Single-engine powerboat. While an auto tracks straight ahead with the steering wheel straight ahead, powerboating steering factors are quite different, especially when accelerating.

Accelerating forward. Prop blast passes rudder flowing aft of transom. *Thrust action* is maximum, the difference between prop thrust and hull speed. *Stern walks to right.* Torque reaction lifts right or starboard side of boat... with the bow turning the other way to port.

Reverse acceleration. *Rudder neutralized.* Rotary prop thrust blasts upward against right side the *lifting hull action,* pushing port or left side down. The *depressed port hull reaction* pulls stern to port, bow to starboard.

Stern action is normally stressed. While it is the action, the *reaction* is just as important pulling the bow the opposite direction.

Sailboat steers with rudder. Outboard motor in our sailboat with RH prop, is locked in position so it won't turn. It follows stern-walking acceleration pattern shown above.

Single screw prop has maneuvering problems leaving dock in adverse conditions requiring spring, bow, or stern pivots.

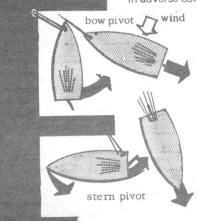

bow pivot · wind

stern pivot

Bow pivot— *rudder over, prop reverse.* Boat pivots out from dock on bow line. When boat has steerage way far enough from dock, bow line is slipped and taken in. *Warning—* does bow line have a knot on the dock end to hang up on the cleat?

Off-center stern pivot— *rudder over, prop reverse.* Stern pivots around dock until clear, then pull in stern line without wrapping around prop. Forward spurts are used to clear dock. *With wind on beam—* let it blow bow out, slip stern line, apply throttle.

100

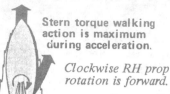

Stern torque walking action is maximum during acceleration.

Clockwise RH prop rotation is forward.

PROP TORQUE IDEAS

RH prop is shown

water

Stern walking is shown during acceleration in fwd.

boat going forward

rudder in center

prop in reverse

Normal port side docking method.

boat is backing

rudder in center

prop in forward

Stern may swing to starboard if it isn't affected by wind or current.

boat going fwd

rudder to port

prop in reverse

Stern pulls to stbd then pulls rapidly to port.

boat is backing

rudder to port

prop in forward

Stern swings to stbd rapidly bow may hit dock. 101

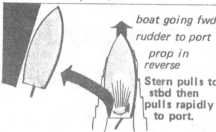

Approach slowly with less angle to dock.

boat going fwd

prop reverse

Stern to port, straighten out with short bursts of forward throttle.

boat is backing

prop in forward then reverse

Stern rapidly turns to port. Will bow hit the dock?

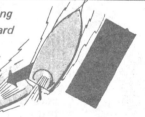

boat is backing

prop in reverse

Stern walks rapidly to port as bow swings rapidly to starboard.

boat is backing

rudder to starboard

prop in reverse

Stern turns slowly to port.
Examples are exaggerated to show the peculiar action of prop torque.

Sailing Illustrated

Powerboating Illustrated

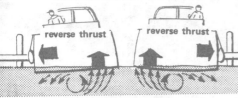

discharge current reacting on hulls

reverse thrust   reverse thrust

RH prop torque   *LH prop torque*

Many single-engine powerboats in the 1930's had RH rotation props. It was a special art to dock these clumsy, underpowered displacement-hull craft with considerable windage in strong winds, and/or current conditions.

Left-hand controls, RH prop. Traffic was minimal, a special occasion to meet other powerboats underway at displacement speed. When the owner came alongside his dock in slow forward, the engine would be put in reverse with torque and prop wash pulling the port side to the dock. LH controls were normal for visibility docking single engine with RH prop.

RH controls, LH prop. should be standard for single-engine powerboats without center pedestal, or midship flying bridge, as full visibility of danger zone is of major importance in heavy traffic. Note how LH prop wash and torque in reverse pulls stbd side of powerboat into dock.

Single-purpose outboard and inboard racing craft and water ski tow boats using *traditional counterclockwise closed course racing patterns* require left-hand steering and throttle controls, with RH prop.

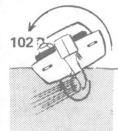

102

Racer is more comfortable at full throttle on the low side in a left-hand turn with his left-hand steering and throttle controls and RH prop torque minimizing an upset roll.

Right-side steering and throttle controls. Racer would feel uncomfortable at full throttle on high side in a tight left turn increasing the chance of a flip or rolling outward.

Torque/tilt proved hilarious mystery after outboard motors passed the 50 hp barrier, page 221. The larger engine torque permanently tilted the hull... while fighting back on the steering system that had to be compensated for.

The LH vs RH control battle has been underway a long time. When we bought our 70 hp Merc in 1958, we ordered a RH rotation prop with RH controls. The traditional LH steering concept was so prevalent at the time, that when the engine was fired up dockside, the boat went forward as the single lever control moved aft, and aft when it went forward... which had to be reversed by rereversing controls.

Turn/ stop powerboat signals. Friends tell us they are used on crowded European rivers and canals in heavy traffic when a mistake could involve several vessels. Was it a good idea to also reduce collisions in the U.S.?

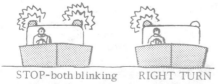

STOP-both blinking   RIGHT TURN

When testing this concept in a magazine article, the only opposition to this idea to reduce collisions... came from our U.S. Coast Guard. Oh, well.....

Powerboating Illustrated

spring lines

Bow line is secured to bow of boat; **stern line** is secured to stern of powerboat.

Spring lines reduce fore and aft movement of boat at dock. The *stern spring* leads forward from the stern and the *bow spring* leads aft from the bow. **Spring line pivots** are efficient to undock powerboats.

Twin screw powerboat operation

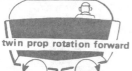

twin prop rotation forward

Opposite rotation props are used to neutralize stern-walking tendency when accelerating., and *back a straight line* with engines at same rpm.

Backing— unfavorable conditions. Twin props are adjusted to different rpm's with prop pulling/ steering action compensating for clumsy conditions involving wind and/or current.

twin prop rotation reverse

Backing out of the slip below left combines both forward and reverse pulling/ steering action of the twin propellers.

Left prop neutral, right prop reverse. 1. This pulls stern left 90 degrees. 2. Left prop in forward and right prop still in reverse spins boat in its own length.**103** 3. Both engines are in forward with prop blast across rudders provides normal steering response.

Face aft when backing with hands on throttles to visualize stern pulling/ turning prop action.

Advantage– is excellent maneuvering in dock areas under good *and* bad conditions when adequately powered with correct props. *Disadvantages—* additional space, weight, and installation cost... plus *double* engine fuel operating cost.

Safety factor of twin engines is questionable as I've seen several double engine failures ...IF operator always depends on his other engine.

Port engine quits with wind on stern as boat enters tight dock area at 4. with right engine put in reverse to stop boat.

By stopping, then letting wind swing boat sideway at 5 and 6... the right engine is slowly accelerated in forward with enough speed at 7 to dock the boat in its own slip.

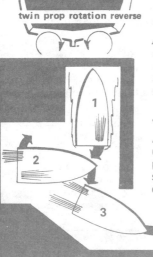

Powerboating Illustrated

Our U.S. Buoyage System is numbered proceeding from the sea. The best way to remember the correct side to pass buoys is *RRR or Red Right Returning* to stay in the channel. When buoys can be passed on either side, the one preferred is indicated by the color of the topmost band.

- **Thirty major buoy systems** were used worldwide in 1976. Major collisions resulted especially in European waters with heavy ship traffic due to the variety of buoyage systems often in complete contradiction with each other. Buoyage systems are undergoing worldwide standardization.

- **Two basic patterns** evolved from the 30 systems. *Region A—red buoys to port,* and **Region B— red buoys to starboard** which was adopted by the Western Hemisphere nations, Japan, Korea, and the Phillipines*.

- **Revised U.S. Buoyage system.** It is to reach full compliance to meet the Region B buoyage system by 1989. Basic changes are the black buoys on the facing page being painted green. This is a change I question finding it difficult to spot green spar buoys in the Sacramento Slough area with green foliage in the background.

- **Mid-channel marker.** It is a round, white buoy with vertical red stripes which is also a landfall indicator. It is added to our system replacing the previous mid-channel buoy with black and white vertical stripes. Some lights have been made stronger for better identification in low visibility.

- **Isolated danger mark** is a continuing problem for an example, to indicate submerged pilings existing on Chart 1210 TR. Another, two systems meet and terminate with a rock between. A third, an unmarked hazard between two buoyage systems which can be an underwater obstruction or sunken vessel (recent?) not visible on the surface.

- **Hazard buoy—** a barber-pole buoy with red stripes curling up a black buoy could easily perform this function. USCG seems to have little interest to consider a hazard buoy until after 1989 though few are required.

- **After a storm—** question the location of floating buoys for your own protection...are lights out, and have they drifted off course? If such is the case, notify the closest USCG unit soon as possible to eliminate the hazard to help other sailors. If the buoys are state installed, contact your appropiate state officials.

Water depths on the east coast are charted *from Mean Low Water...*while **west coast depths** are charted from *Mean Lower, Low Water.*

The latest chart corrections in past years were added to the charts with the latest changes dated on the bottom of U.S charts. Most of the updating on our charts are now left to boat owners. The charts are produced by—

- **National Ocean Survey, NOOA—** Rockville, MD 20852
- **Defense Mapping Agency Hydrographic Center—** Washington, DC 20390

IALA Maritime Buoyage Systems were developed by the International Association of Lighthouse Authorities. Their headquarters are— 13 Rue Yvon Villarceau 75116 Paris, France.

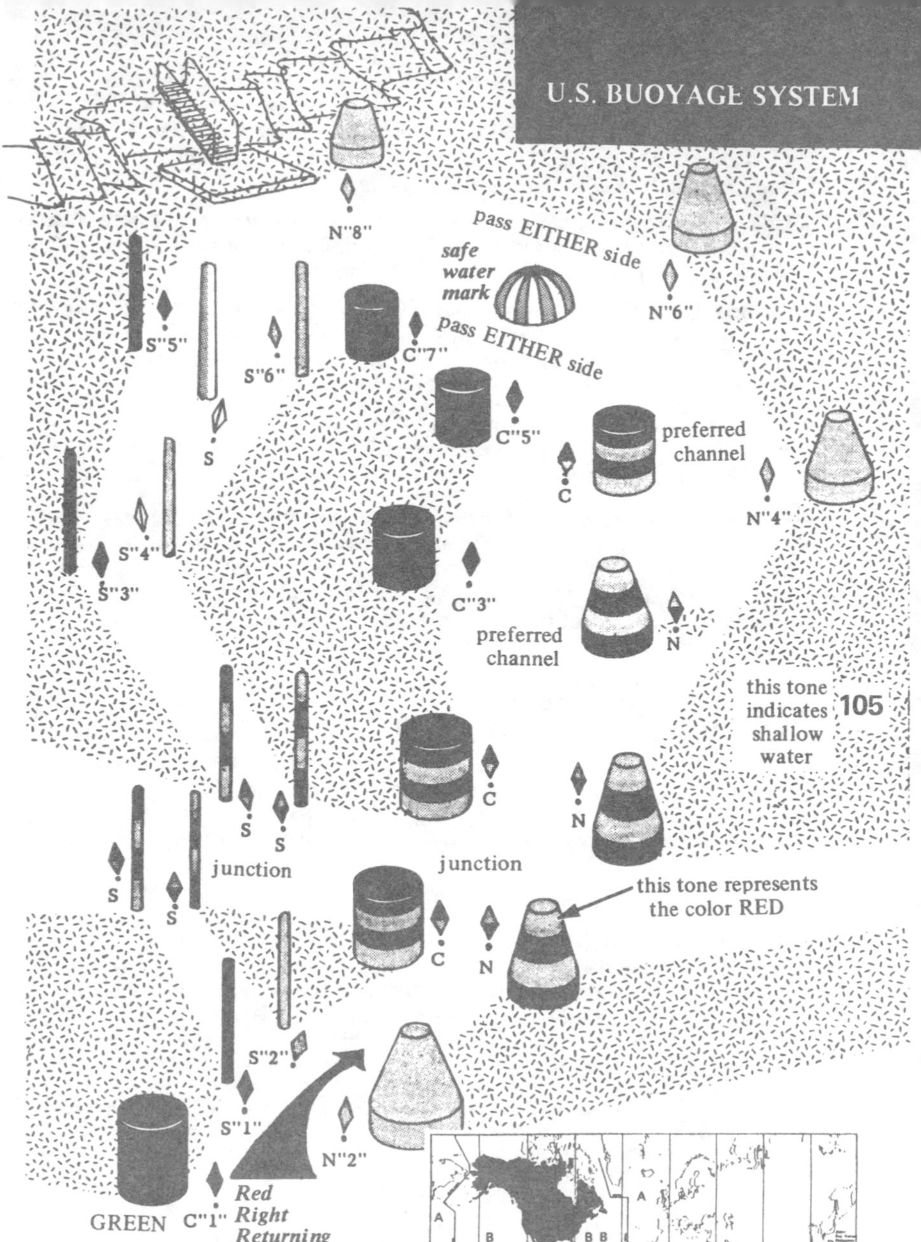

N"8"

*safe
water
mark*

Pass EITHER side

N"6"

S"5"

S"6"

C"7"

Pass EITHER side

C"5"

preferred
channel

N"4"

C

S

S"4"

S"3"

C"3"

preferred
channel

N

this tone
indicates **105**
shallow
water

C

S S

junction

junction

C N

this tone represents
the color RED

S

S

N

S

S"2"

S"1"

N"2"

GREEN C"1" *Red
Right
Returning*

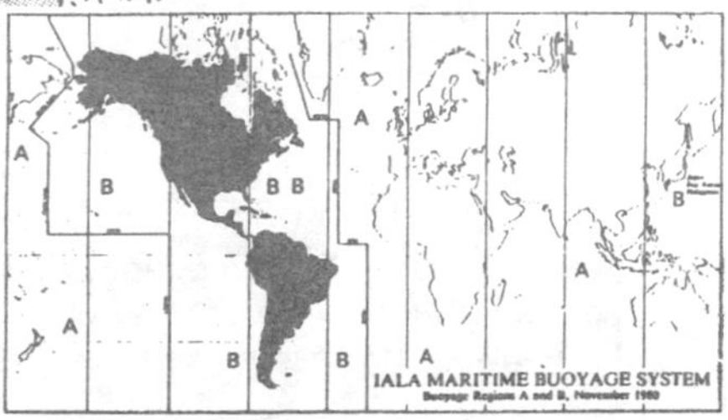

Powerboating Illustrated

All black buoys will
be changed to green
by 1989.

IALA MARITIME BUOYAGE SYSTEM
Buoyage Regions A and B, November 1980

- **Our tidal day.** *The moon averages approximately 24 hours and 50 minutes to go around the earth. This corresponds to the two highs and lows on the facing page which complete a full tidal day.*

- **Tide** results on the ocean and in a glass of water, from the alternate vertical rise and fall of water caused by the gravitational pull of the moon and the sun, with a month required to go thru the four tidal stages.

- **Spring tide** has the greatest normal tide range occurring twice a month when the sun, moon, and earth work as a team to provide the maximum gravitatational pull; while a **neap tide** occurs when moon and sun gravitational forces are in conflict and nullify each other.

- **Perigee and apogee.** Additional tide variables result due to the *elliptical course* of the moon with a maximum pull when it is closer to **perigee,** and a weak pull at **apogee** when it is farther away as shown on facing page.

- **Tidal surges occur during a hurricane** producing more extreme tidal ranges than found in spring tides. A large mushroom anchor is a pivot for the mooring chain, with the chain weight providing the holding power even in a storm with spring tides. During a hurricane tidal surge the scope may disappear with a direct pull on the mushroom anchor. This may pull the mushroom loose setting the boat adrift.

Depths listed on our navigational charts are charted on the east coast at **mean low tide**...while it is a **mean lower low tide** on our west coast.

As we sail farther south the tides begin to follow different rhythms.We recommend *The Sea Around Us* by Rachel Carson. While we find one type of rhythm in our area, the tides around Tahiti without the 50 minutes advance each day may find high tide at noon and midnight, plus low tide at 0600 and 1800.

- **Current** is a horizontal flow of water such as a river current gravity flow.

- **A tidal current** results when a tide change causes a directional change in flow in the current which reverses itself with the next tidal change. A good example is the Hudson or North River tidal current with the flow going farther north during the fall with minimal rain, and with the tidal current farther downstream with the spring snow thaw and rains with a much stronger outer ebb tidal river current.

- **Tsunamis** or **tidal waves** are caused by earthquake activity under the water making their own rules. They will pass on the open ocean surface with jet plane speed. Their wave peaks are so far apart they are seldom noticed.

As the tsunamis approaches the shore at right angles, the ocean can receed a half mile, then return a similar distance past the high tide mark with waves 60' to 100' high. Waves may have peaks to 200' high in narrow fiords.

When a tsunamis warning indicates one is coming straight into your harbor entrance in 3 to 4 hours, consider taking your boat out as far as practical into deep water for protection. If it is expected to pass at right angles to the harbor entrance, expect wild tidal surges without high,damaging wave action.

New Moon—Spring Tides

First Quarter—
Neap Tides

moon

The tidal day—

HIGH

0.00 hours
ebb tide begins

LOW

6.12 hours
flood tide begins

Full Moon—
Spring Tides

HIGH

12.25 hours
ebb tide begins

Third Quarter—
Neap Tides

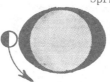

LOW **107**

18.37 hours
flood tide
begins

moon

HIGH

0.50 hours on
the following day

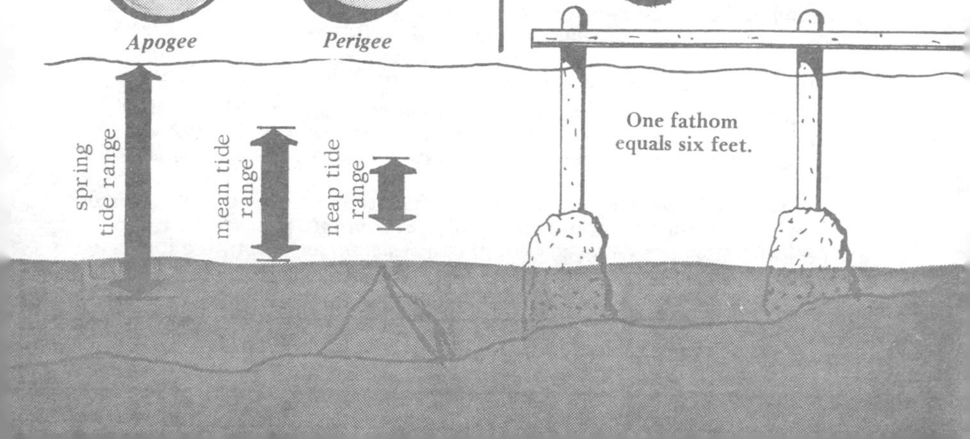

Apogee *Perigee*

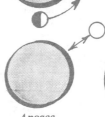

spring
tide range

mean tide
range

neap tide
range

One fathom
equals six feet.

Chinese
S land compass

Viking
lodestone compass

True, magnetic, compass course heading. Magnets on the underside of the compass card align in a north-south direction with the magnetic poles. The card is stationary while the boat changes course by turning around the compass card. The *lubber's line reference mark* shows the new magnetic heading of the vessels course.

The mariner's navigation compass has complexity with simplicity. Since many **how-to courses** are available to teach mathematical complexity of variation and deviation, we concentrated on *how* the compass operates.

The magical rock called lodestone. Man first came in contact with Magnesia in Asia Minor centuries ago. An iron ore was found with magnetism, the popular name of the mineral today, is called lodestone.

2000 years ago Chinese envoys used land compasses on their wagons to guide them around their huge country. They used the *south magnetic pole* for reference, while Europeans chose the *north magnetic pole.* Both of the concepts are correct as like poles repel, and unlike poles attract.

A permanent magnet is induced with an electrical current thru a bar of *hardened steel,* while the same current flowing thru a *soft iron bar* rapidly develops, then loses magnetism in a solenoid, pages 306 and 317.

The floating compass with a magnetized needle mounted on a pivot, or thru a piece of wood floating on water, emerged around 1100 A.D. During the next 150 years it was used by Arabs, Europeans, and Scandinavians.

It was marked with 4 cardinal points eventually— north, south, east, and west. The compass card was later subdivided into 32 points called *boxing the compass.* It was called the merchant marine compass card used in WWII.

108

The 360 degree circle measurement introduced by ancient Babylonians followed, being easier to understand by recreational boat operators. Choose a black or red compass card with white numbers for night operation.

The earth's weak magnetic field is strongest at the equator where it only has a horizontal pull on the compass card. *A vertical pull* also develops when going north or south of the equator. This weakens the horizontal pull, eventually cancelling it out... but who is interested in north, or south pole powerboating?

Why do trailerboat and powerboat compasses become sluggish and stop responding while crude compasses on Greek sailing vessels sunk centuries ago and still underwater still accurately point to the magnetic north?

Planing hull pounding and engine vibration affect the compass card floating in its water and alcohol dampener liquid. Friction wear on the bearings, and the tiny hammering vibrations of the card, dulls the pivot point it is mounted on, with rapid deterioration on large ocean racing machines.

Dampening methods are required to extend compass life using rubber and spring shock cords to reduce aging by pounding and vibration, and the compass spinning in rough water. *Also carry a spare compass replacement.*

Compass bubbles? The sealed dampening liquid is under slight pressure to reduce contraction and expansion... and *bubble potentials.* Bubbles develop earlier in average priced compasses that rely on tilting for readability. An indication of compass quality is the amount of gimballing to maintain a horizontal card within the sphere of dampening liquid, with a bottom pendulum weight to steady the compass card.

Powerboating Illustrated

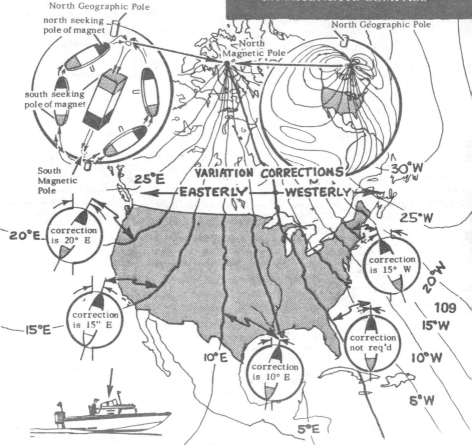

North Geographic Pole

north seeking pole of magnet

North Geographic Pole

North Magnetic Pole

south seeking pole of magnet

South Magnetic Pole

VARIATION CORRECTIONS

EASTERLY — WESTERLY

25°E

30°W

25°W

20°E correction is 20° E

20°W

109

15°E correction is 15" E

15°W

correction is 15° W

10°E correction is 10° E

correction not req'd

10°W

5°W

5°E

Variation. North and south magnetic pole magnetic meridians, do not coincide with our north and south geographic poles. *Variation angle* between true north and magnetic meridians are compensated as shown above from Nova Scotia, to New Orleans, and Western Canada.

Variation is a fact of nature we can't change. Columbus seems to be the first sailor to notice and question this problem reaching the new world. He carried compasses on the second voyage that could be altered.

Deviation is the pecularity influence of your boats own magnetic field that must be calibrated thru trial and error that goes with the territory.

At the last moment powerboat compasses are located on top of, or in the middle of a large instrument panel using how many different kinds of metals? Magnetic tugs, permanent, or intermittant come from steel steering wheel spokes plastic covered, windshield wiper motors, loudspeaker magnets, screwdrivers or knives in the pocket, bottle openers, etc.

Powerboating Illustrated

Our weather bureau reports wind speed in miles per hour which is of little use as wind speed is invisible. Sailors need some kind of a visual measurement.

Wind speed produces visual ocean wave patterns that can be calibrated into wind pressure driving your sailboat. These wave patterns can be translated into existing wind pressure for use on all kinds of sailboats.

The wind force scale is easy to memorize— forces 1-2, ripples...forces 3-4, small waves...force 5, a few whitecaps...force 6, many whitecaps...force 7, *small craft warning,* tremendous wind pressure with whitecaps AND swells.

●Your wind force or pressure scale was developed by Admiral Beaufort in 1806 for the British navy. It recorded square rigger rudder action in light winds trying to develop steerageway, to force 5, reaching hull speed. Above that it indicated sail reductions patterns to force 12, after which vessels were under bare poles out of control, no longer able to carry sails.

We have slightly altered the traditional wind force scale to make it easier to remember and apply for recreational sailors.

110

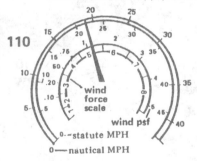

We show wind speed in statute miles and nautical miles per hour using a masthead wind gage cockpit dial...adding a dial for comparison with wind force or pressure.

We wish new wind speed dials showing speed in miles per hour could add a wind force scale so owners could know how much sail area to add or reef as the wind changes.

Meanwhile you can pick up wave patterns to estimate wind pressure, to know whether to reef for best efficiency, or increase sail area.

●**Variables are involved.** When a force 7 suddenly starts to blow over a flat ocean, time is required to catch up with the force 7 wave pattern. When the force 7 suddenly quits blowing, time is required for the wave patterns to fall out of sequence...then the waves flatten out. If you know this scale you will have your sails reefed the correct amount before the storm hits, while other sailboats are floundering around trying to reef their sails **after the storm hit**...for which they weren't prepared.

●**Currents.** When wind blows against the current, waves will be higher with the crests closer together. When wind blows with the current, waves will be shorter and crests farther apart...though having the same wind pressure.

▲ **Inland lakes.** The wind force or pressure scale was developed for ocean use over unobstructed stretches of water. While inland lakes don't have the area to develop ocean wave patterns, add 1, 2, or 3 forces to the wave action that is visible to compute the existing wind pressure on your sails and hull.

▲**Wind funnels** can double,and even triple the overall wind pressure, pages 158 and 159, on inland lakes and hills next to the ocean...with predictable results using the water color and wave action.   *Powerboating Illustrated*

WIND PRESSURE
or force   mph   lbs. pressure
                          per square foot

Force	mph	lbs. pressure per square foot		Description
1	1-4 mph (1-3)knots	.003- .03	flat bottom boat	water sticky smooth slightly reducing top planing speed
				ripple patches
2	4-7 (4-6)	.05- .12		air pockets on water help to break adhesion increasing speed
				overall ripple pattern
3	8-12 (7-10)	.16- .33		same as above, more fun
				small waves
4	13-18 (11-16)	.40- .85	V-bottom	more spirited, sloppy for small V-bottom boats
				longer waves
5	18-24 (17-21)	.96- 1.4		quite spirited, larger V-bottom boats begin reducing throttle
				some whitecaps
6	25-31 (22-27)	1.6- 2.4		trouble .. overall whitecap patterns mean stay in port
				many whitecaps

111

Force	mph	lbs. pressure			
7	32-38 (28-32)	2.6- 3.6		whitecaps and swells	Small Craft Advisory
8 9	39-54 (34-47)	3.8- 7.3			Gale Warning
10 11	55-73 (48-63)	7.6- 13.2			Storm Warning
12	OVER 63 knots	OVER 13.2 lbs. per sq.ft.		red	Hurricane Warning

stay ashore

flags and pennants by day, watch for lights at night

- *Powerboat operators can out think... but not try to out slug the ocean.*
  Wind pressure action is invisible... but wave pattern reaction is obvious.
- The *Beaufort Wind Pressure Scale* above was designed for open ocean use. It can also be applied for inland lakes adding 1, 2, or 3 pressures, since the water expanse is too short to develop ocean wave patterns.

3 Above force 3— flat bottom hot boats should head for protected areas.

5 Force 5 with a few whitecaps— larger V-bottom boats may find the wave action fun and spirited... yet hang close to port.

6 Force 6 with many whitecaps— with higher waves and deeper troughs is the time all recreational planing hulls to be in protected areas, as even a minor equipment failure can be hazardous.

Powerboating Illustrated

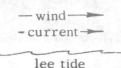

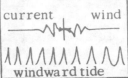

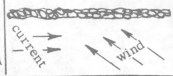

current   wind

lee tide

windward tide

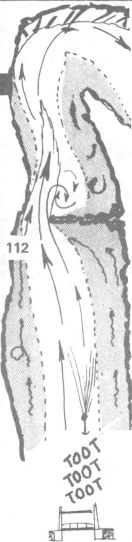

TOOT
TOOT
TOOT

- **River current** flows downstream due to gravity, while **tidal current** flow changes direction with the change of tide. The upper stretches of rivers flow downstream, while the lower stretches may also have a tidal current. River current pushes the tidal current farther downstream with the spring thaw and rains, a tidal current extends farther upstream in the fall dry season.

- **Wave action** is minimal when wind and current flow the same direction, with maximum wave action when wind and current directions oppose each other.

  When a strong outgoing tidal current is opposed by the strong wind at an angle above fighting against a concrete jetty, vicious haystack random waves out of sequence may develop. If you sail in a similar tidal current area with a similar jetty, plan ahead to avoid losing steering control when these three elements fight each other.

- **Manhattan tidal currents.** Our first craft was a Folbot kayak. It provided a rapid exposure to the Hudson River tidal currents. It was possible to drift upstream one weekend, and down towards the Battery the next weekend with little effort. A person can use the tidal currents to circumnavigate Manhattan.

- **Reading the river** is the term used to analyze and make the most of river currents. *Current flow* will be faster and smoother in the center, while slower and more disturbed in shallow water next to the bank. If a *V points upstream,* it indicates an underwater obstruction or funnel. A *V pointing downstream* in a straight stretch indicates the greatest depth. *The greatest depth in a bend* is on the outside near the river bank. *Eddies and whirlpools* on the downstream side at the end of a dike is a hazard to be avoided.

  Shooting the rapids in our Folbot in the spring when rivers peak provides thrills. A sharp bend with a strong current sent us charging into a herd of cows cooling off in the river causing a mass panic. To put it tastefully, we couldn't dodge the sudden bombardment as they ran tails high for the river bank.

- **Drawbridge.** If your boat doesn t have enough clearance, the normal signal is **three long blasts** to open. It may only open on scheduled times operator didn't hear your signal, is asleep, having lunch or ....

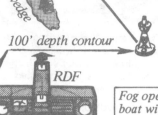

to wedge

335°M

100' depth contour

RDF

weak   strong   overpowered

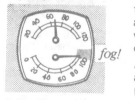

BRRWNGG

fog!

*Fog operation becomes a spirited challenge for a sail-
boat with an accurate compass after adding 3 basic
instruments. Practice with these instruments entering
harbors in your area to eliminate surprises and easy
to make mistakes without such familiarity.*

The panic a new sailor faces suddenly caught in a
peasoup fog on his new boat can be considerable. In
time he realizes he can operate normally in an open
cockpit, steering accurate compass courses on a
sensitive displacement hull under sail or power.

The situation is much worse on a planing powerboat
that has to throttle down becoming clumsy to steer
accurate compass courses at displacement speed, and
with inside controls, the windshield continually fogs
over.

A displacement hull powerboat may operate almost
as efficiently as a sailboat in fog conditions. The
planing powerboat owner should avoid going to sea
and stay dockside even if it is a light fog.

113

● **A humidity indicator** pages 94-5, is required to provide ample warning of
a fog moving in to prepare for it...and also when moving out.

● **Depth sounders** should be standard equipment on ocean-going sailboats to
learn underwater contours to avoid shoals and entering harbors, see page 158.

● **Radio Direction Finder (RDF)** is an excellent homing instrument to help
you outwit a peasoup fog, though the less expensive ones may have an
180 degree error which is easy to compensate for. The problem, few owners
ever seem to use them for familiarity even in good weather.

The basic RDF above could pick up our low-powered radiobeacon six miles
from our local jetty which was excellent for student practice. They would
steer on the NULL as the signal grew louder, and was finally overpowered.
We were leaving deep water with the bottom shallowing rapidly. The preset
depth sounder alarm went off indicating a 100' depth.

A sharp right turn on the 100' depth contour takes the boat to the entrance
buoy, followed by a hard left turn to enter the jetty into the harbor. For
entering harbors in heavy fogs, *use magnetic courses only* on your charts
to eliminate juggling the differences between true and magnetic courses
when maneuvering is tight, and critical.

                                             Powerboating Illustrated

Severe spring storm, Long Island, late 1940's. A Daily News photographer friend, in shock without sleep for over 40 hours, told the following story. "A fishing boat with 30 passengers had engine failure. Another vessel in heavy wave action tried to pass a tow line without success. The disabled boat rolling sideways to wind and wave action upset, and all drowned.

"I had to photograph the boat and bodies as it was hauled out for the official records, and our newspaper. I usually go fishing on the boat that upset... changing to another fishing vessel at the last minute".

If one person thinks while others panic, *many disasters can be avoided, or damage limited.* A fisherman can cast a sinker to 200' downwind, to go across the disabled boat from the rescue boat. A light tow line can be tied to the fishing line... followed by a heavy tow line. The tow can soon be underway with the line secured from the stern of the rescue vessel, and bow of the disabled vessel without hull damage banging into each other.

Above, a small boat hard aground on a lee shore. Your boat must stay at least 100' upwind due to ground swells and shallow water. Anchor your boat, cast sinker downwind across grounded boat, to pull tow line across.

Anchor leverage required. The next idea is to protect your prop. Secure tow line to anchor line, and move out. Disabled boat can be kedged off lee shore by its operator to await tow, repair engine, or.....

114

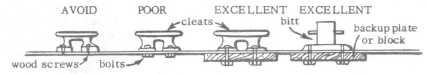

AVOID   POOR   EXCELLENT EXCELLENT

cleats   bitt   backup plate or block

wood screws   bolts

Double braided tow line only. "During an attempt to refloat a grounded cruiser with a nylon towing line... the towing cleat on the cruiser suddenly pulled free and became a lethal projectile under the impetus of the violent recoiling line. The cleat struck a man... death was instantaneous"... *Proceedings of the Merchant Marine Council, May, 1964.*

The *3 strand rubber band stretch* of nylon rope for towing, can be a hazard best defined by the official release above. The flexibility surges also make it clumsy and difficult to maintain speed towing a straight line.

How are cleats mounted on tow and towing boats? Are they secured with short wood screws on wooden and fiberglass boats that may pull loose with minimum tension? Are cleats too small made of inexpensive metals for land use only? Bitts are lighter, carrying larger diameter line bolted thru deck, with wooden or metal backup plates below deck.

Tow ski bridle secured to twin stern eyes provide stable directional towing operation you can easily splice page 200. It should be short and snug enough to stay above cavitation plate to not wrap around prop when not under tension. *Powerboating Illustrated*

retrieving line   towing bridle

Basic equipment failure. District 11, Long Beach. USCG officers indicated ¾ or more tows or assists were due to running out of fuel, dead batteries, electrical shorts, items which should have been taken care of before leaving the dock.

75-80% of boat tows could and should have been prevented. District 7— Florida, Georgia, Southern Carolina, Pureto Rico. USCG listed these assistance cases in a similar period due to *basic equipment failures.*

Fuel tank capacity vs Miles Per Gallon. What is your powerboats most economical speed in miles covered... the planing hull usually does much better when not operating at displacement speeds. *How much reserve fuel* do you carry if headwinds or an assist reduces your mileage?

Are fuel tanks exposed to hot summer weather with rapid condensation at night aging and destroying the fuel? Fresh, clean gasoline with sufficient octane is your engines best friend.

The mysterious black box. That was also our idea when starting this book in 1957. Watching endless snafu's due to the black box proved boat owners had to thoroughly know battery operation to have a dependable engine. The battery chapter may prove dull reading at first, then....

Electrical system failures. We've witnessed endless failures on small, medium, and large boats. While some are obvious, others are difficult to trace. Most **115** failures are due to poorly maintained, crude installations, often with under-size wiring. Vibration, chafe, poor and/or loose connections are major sources of electrical failure.

New or used boats. One of the first jobs after survey every owner should take, is to check and understand, and trace every electrical wire thruout the boat looking for chafe and poor connections, study our wiring chapter.Become familiar with *every engine wiring lead.*

Water pump failures on outboard motors, and inboard engines with outside cooling water *should be replaced yearly* as barnacles have wiped out possibly five impellers caught just in time ... at a minimum replacement cost. Four-cycle engines with closed cooling systems should replace impeller every 3 years. *Operating an engine in a dry condition even momentarily will chafe impeller.*

All shear pins are a major hazard *as they fail, or corrode AND fail at the most unlikely moment. Replacement is always a hazard if adrift.*

Weight is as important to a planing hull as a small airplane. Memorize these approximate numbers to keep your powerboat on a continuous diet.

- **Fresh water—** 8.3 lbs. per gallon
- **Regular gasoline—** 6.6 lbs. per gallon, Premium weighs less
- **Diesel fuel—** 7.3 lbs. per gallon, is rarely listed

What is the weight of 20 gallons of water and 30 gallons of gasoline?

Powerboating Illustrated

We were aboard a new 31' sailboat on sea trials. A conversation was started by a physician owner, "Is drinking a problem on boats?"

"It is a person problem, not a boat problem. It is that very small part of a percent of accident-prone troublemakers that cause dumb headlines on the highway, in the air, and water. They blunder into situations, or try to show off their macho image, going beyond their potentials"

Responsibility. For 35 years I've spent as much time on the water as possible. more on large sailboats than powerboats. We may have a beer or two underway, and a drink at the end of the day. These are stable owners and crew with well-insured boats. I can't remember seeing a sailor underway having too much to drink. On the other hand, did the author forget to look in the mirror a couple of times?

The death report concludes, open zipper. It is amazing the amount of beer fishermen can load into small, tippy boats... *a person problem!*

Hot-rod misfits. I was aboard the 68' Sea Scout *Argus,* sailing as far east into the Sacramento Delta as possible, anchoring near Stockton. The next afternoon the ship's dinghy took us to a nearby open bar/cafe where a beer bust had been underway for a long time.

Lining the docks were 16 or more *tinsel toy* 40 to 60 mph thrill craft. Few knew capabilities or limitations of these craft. How many carried liability insurance, where was responsibility for their heavy drinking?

116

More collisions, injuries, and fatalities occur in this protected delta area than along our coast and in harbors with opportunists after dumb thrills. Are responsible owners to share blame for these misfits?

1960- our week long power and sail classes for professionals. At days end we often exchanged ideas over a drink. Officers were concerned with drinking problems... my answer little changed in 30 years.

A couple of weeks later we had a knock at the door. It was the first Redondo Beach Harbormaster, an ex student. "I am involved in a court case. Two men passed our dock at 15 mph, they wouldn't slow down with our warning. We had to board their boat, then forcibly take it over to reach the controls. Both were staggering, and their breath was horrible. The judge will call in 15 minutes asking for your advice" My phone reply without hesitation, "Throw the books at them!"

The judge called back ten minutes later laughing so hard it was difficult for him to tell the story. "I followed your advice. I hit the gavel... the fine is $500... next case".

"But judge, when I was arrested two weeks ago by the highway patrol for drunk driving, my fine was only $200!"

"One more outburst and your fine is $700". The silence that followed was deafening. *If such fines could be awarded 30 years ago,* why must we face all kinds of new redundant regulations by nonboating politicians? Is it to increase their campaign funds by twisting distillers arms?

Capsize, USCG 1972— 613 vessels 432 fatalities
Capsize, USCG 1989— 576 vessels 330 fatalities

When USCG was trasferred to DOT in 1967, the new big boss demanded more tax revenues with boat operator licensing (sound familiar?). The new Commandant in 1972 demanded it before the Boating Industry Association. *"We are willing to give voluntary education one last chance".*

The statement by Admiral Wagner that 68 % of boats were 10' to 14' long came at the right time to make USCG licensing leaders uncomfortable. We prepared a 24 page booklet challenging USCG licensing, with over 370 copies hand delivered to Wash., D.C. Headquarters Dec. 7, 1972.

40% of Californian1972 statistics involved the high risk *accidental boater fisherman/ duck hunter* with 52 vessels, 41 fatalities, and 32 injuries. Our booklet well defined USCG was the problem. Their answer was the 1976 *Nationwide Boating Survey* proved the accidental boater hazard much higher than anticipated. The bottom line,... *fishermen and duck hunters are licensed!*

Car top transportation boats must serve a purpose. Most are cheap, portable, hard or soft boats, minimum size, narrow, tippy, with little freeboard that are often department store 'weekend specials'.

Most fishermen have to stand up to cast (why?). They seldom check the weather, often wearing heavy, bulky clothing that rapidly soaks up water in a capsize. Many are *nonswimmers* as they panic immediately, hollering for help underwater.

117

Pants fly unzipped? Many single occupant capsize drowning victims seem to answer the call of nature, probably standing up on the side of their tiny, tippy boat before capsize, especially after a couple of beers.

A plastic jug/ boat bailer (Approved?). It needs to be carried aboard all small tippy boats to eliminate   the high-risk open zipper hazard.

After USCG licensing push came to a screeching halt in 1973, we were invited to a closed conference in Alameda with officers representing the retired Commandant. Was it to reduce drownings? Our comments—

"The troublemakers are licensed... fishermen and duck hunters. They need to produce a certificate they could swim 100' under normal conditions, tested by Red Cross, YMCA, school systems, etc., *before being able to apply for their next license".* This would eliminate the major share of capsize, nonswimmer drownings in so shallow water they can walk ashore".

"Second, Approval of a quality ski belt, the most practical answer for this high-risk field". As their new tax source disappeared, their minimum interest dropped to zilch for an answer to help recreational boating.

Mandated Boating Course? USCG began a quiet end run in 1976 to again raise taxes with little in return for boat owners. It was a pleasure to stop it in 1977 in a 3 day USCG seminar. Present USCG plan in the works started by present USCG Commandant Admiral William Kime in 1981, is a yearly *$25 duck stamp user fee* for registered boats. Will it support their *no tolerance, no intelligence, no responsibility* boarding policy?

Powerboating Illustrated

dock line / slippery deck

Falls within the boat— *California not USCG.* This potential faces boat owners and passengers dockside, at anchor, and underway in *user friendly* powerboats and sailboats. *User-hostile performance boats?* Will the high gloss, slippery deck boats require more evaluation and better hardware, to reduce your chance of falls dockside, at anchor, or underway?

1974-80	California records all-year operation on lakes, Sacramento
1975-82	delta, rivers, and ocean. California personal casualty reports,
1976-104	injuries and fatalities at left. Years chosen were when the
1977-144	new performance boats were gaining popularity.

Avoid that first mistake. We have been involved full time since 1958 in the boating field under sail and power, spending as much time on the water as practical. I've had eight bad falls on various boats without reportable injury. Luck is involved, and excellent judo training in early years to relax if a fall is unavoidable. *As we grow older and the body is less flexible,* we must be more careful to avoid that first mistake.

Plan each step systematically avoiding any urge to suddenly move by impulse. The *screw driver* is a major hazard when it flips, or drops out of your hand while working on your boat. *Freeze instantly* instead of grabbing for it to avoid a bad fall overboard, or in your boat. Buy two sets of screw drivers at a time for replacement as they are cheaper than hospital bills.

118

Round all sharp corners is standard practice for USN on boats under 70' capable of being carried on larger ocean-going vessels. Only in a bad storm will you realize how many sharp corners your boat has above and below. In a pitching, tossing boat, best protection we find to reduce body impact is Stern's preservers. You soon learn the metal and wooden corners to round off the next time you want to work on your boat.

Helmsmans seat may be hazardous. The seat suddenly collapsed under me in smooth water just before giving a new boat full throttle. One collapsed under another operator at full speed. As he started to fall, he grabbed the steering wheel for support with one hand. This turned his boat into a large boat which he hit broadside at top planing speed.

Handholds. If you fall or trip on your boat at the dock or underway, what can you grab onto to steady yourself... and will the part be bolted securely? What permanently mounted handholds do you have in your cockpit, on the bow, and below deck, to avoid a bad fall?

Companionway stairs. Many are easy to walk up, some sideways, but are necessary to go down backwards. USN practice is to add *monkey bars* to the overhead. Sailors can swing below to avoid falling down steep stairs.

Permanently mounted dockline on bow not long enough to wrap around prop, avoids the need to walk on a slippery deck when docking.

Rear-view mirror. It is easy for a powerboat suddenly turning, to collide with an overtaking boat the operator didn't realize that was overtaking. A mirror plus turn signals by arm...could reduce this hazard considerably.

It could warn operator of other boats following too closely, to avoid throttling down rapidly with the overtaking boat hitting your stern. Even though you have the required *lookout facing aft when towing water skiiers,* the mirror helps operator avoid sudden surprises. Does this sound like an auto accident report?

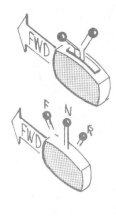

Double lever *throttle and shift controls* are dangerous. One launching ramp had nine drownings in three weeks with boat operators backing from ramp, hitting full throttle forgetting to shift pulling stern under, sinking the boats.

As the stern went under rapidly, the cushions shot forward lodging under the bow. Occupants could almost walk ashore, but being nonswimmers drowned rapidly.

Single lever combination *shift and throttle control* is easy to understand and operate. Start engine in neutral with lever vertical, then move throttle forward to go forward, and aft for reverse. As lever is moved farther either direction it increases engine rpm.

119

Throttle sticking suddenly *while turning or docking shows in accident reports.* It happened to us at 33 mph full throttle when a thin carburetor pin vibrated loose locking the carb butterfly to lock in open position. We had maneuvering room making a 180 degree sharp turn in smooth water to present bow to stern wave when turning off ignition.

Jackrabbit starts before passengers are ready, cause many dumb unnecessary injuries and fatalities.

Tight bends in narrow channels especially in Northern California caused many collisions, injuries, and fatalities. They occurred both during the day and at night when hot rodders barreled around blind tight curves running into and over boats at anchor or drifting.

Narrow channels *Rule 9(a)— A vessel shall keep as near to the outer limit of the channel... on her starboard side as is safe and practicable. Rule 34(e)— A vessel nearing a bend... where other vessels may be obscured...sound* **one prolonged blast.** They apply to boats & ships!

Head-on collisions with fatalities occur when speeding around blind corners on the *left or WRONG side of narrow channels.*

Boat operation rules are complex... but ignorance becomes a weak defense if wrong, for the person trying to justify his actions in court.

Carbon monoxide (CO) poisoning produces approx. 3800 US deaths yearly.

Home hazards— natural gas stove or heater, inside barbecue grill, and fireplaces with faulty mixture adjustments producing inadequate oxygen burning ventilation, become major carbon monoxide hazards.

The smoker— after finishing a cigar or cigarette, may have a 10% to 15% CO level absorbed into the blood hemoglobin, sometimes with minor toxicity symptoms. An ongoing debate is the amount by nearby non-smokers inhaling secondary smoke with carbon monoxide potentials.

The diesel engine— produces unpleasant exhaust fumes. Only diesel engines not deemed a health hazard, are used in deep mine confined areas. While using large quantities of oxygen, they don't produce CO. Before CO detectors, mice or canaries were taken into the shafts by miners. Due to smaller size and higher metabolic rates, they died rapidly when exposed to even low carbon monoxide levels.

Carbon monoxide potentials in boating **are predictable** when you know what to look for. The culprit is partially burned exhaust hydrocarbons, a part of the combustion process in all gasoline engines. These partially burned byproducts must be exhausted and dissipated into air or water. Volume is reduced by a lean carb mixture, increased by a rich mixture.

We start by challenging high school physics teaching **CO is tasteless, colorless, and odorless.** *Any time you can smell gasoline engine partially burned exhaust fumes...* **carbon monoxide is also present.**

120

Be continually aware of any gasoline exhaust fumes on a boat as the awareness will only last a short period. CO poisoning soon puts smelling factors to sleep. As carbon monoxide is a **deoxidizer,** it is absorbed into the blood stream 240 times faster than oxygen. CO bonds with hemoglobin in the blood to prevent oxygen going to the muscles and vital organs

A child, or small active adult will use up oxygen in the body faster, and succumb to CO poisoning earlier than a larger, slow-moving adult.

Symptoms are firsthand. The author was asleep on a sailboat under power returning from the 1964 Ensenada Race when a hairline crack developed in the exhaust manifold while I was asleep with a cold and sinus condition. When awakened for my watch at dawn, I had a heart pumping wildly, and a splitting, 5 double martini hangover.

I rolled over to go back to sleep, when realizing I had one bottle of beer for breakfast the previous morning. The realization of the only answer, CO poisoning began to wake me to get out of the cabin.

I next realized I had vertigo with the balance factors of what is up and down, were missing.

The subconscious training on many boats in rough weather, and it was a rough tumbling sea, helped me grab the right handholds to climb topside into the fresh air... as smoke began coming from the engine. A good mechanic crew member found and fixed the problem, a starter motor that partially hung up and overheated.

Also see page 266.

Over four years were needed to wear down the neurological complications, waking up depressed, the mind going one way, the body the other way. It was the miserable effects of the 30-40% COHb level, while a 40-50% COHb level of poisoning might cause irreversible changes.

Physicians today question the duration of the tour year nervous system upset, indicating complex side problems may also have been involved that may be diagnosed today, but not in the mid 1960s.

100% oxygen CO poison treatment. Victim needs a tight-fitting, non-rebreathing mask to take the COHb level below 5% while monitoring heart patients closely.

AVOID smoking on gasoline-powered boats. It dulls your smelling sensitivity of smoker and nonsmokers nearby in the cockpit and below.

CO fumes may be found on most gasoline powered boats underway. Hull contours topside, below, and outside, can play all kinds of tricks. Avoid buying powerboats with inside controls, and stay topside in the cockpit when underway.

Develop an alertness to that *sweet, sickly exhaust smell.* Engine exhaust can be pulled over the transom into the cockpit, some more than others going upwind, and others downwind. Awareness is self protection as much of the time it may be weak, probably less than we face daily in our autos.

upwind

boat cover

downwind

121

Reverse the flow. A new flying-bridge cruiser was sucking fumes into cabin below. I warned the owners wife of the problem that boat would always have. open a window or hatch below. The air flow would eliminate the CO trap potentials.

Periodic inspection is important. Check all exhaust system clamps, hoses, and manifolds. Replace any part showing potential failure before it fails.

Trolling downwind under power is an efficient way to pull CO fumes into the cockpit and cabin.

Boat covers? USCG boarded a pilotless boat going in circles with one of seven passengers still conscious. A boat cover pulled in and trapped exhaust fumes.

Mild to moderate CO poisoning contributes to accidents reducing the thinking process. A woman partially overcome on the boat at left with inside controls, fell overboard when a door opened.

The operator should have turned the bow towards her as shown. He turned the wrong way with his CO exposure. She was killed by the prop blades.

Powerboating Illustrated

Motion sickness. The small percentage of people who experience it in autos, trains, and airplanes, will also face it on boats requiring medication.

Seasickness potential is almost always a temporary situation with one in four sailing students facing the problem to some degree. Time and exposure are needed for the subconscious mind to accept a new type of motion.

The first symptom begins when a person looks down instead of out at the horizon. He has an uneasy feeling as his confused subconscious mind says, "Hey boss, something is wrong!" Disorientation begins as the victim looks down. His subconscious mind panics as a one foot wave grows to three, seven, then fifteen feet high. The disorientation process speeds up when going below. The mind panics with the stomach out of control.

Sailboat motion is easy to adjust to in normal conditions at displacement speed, operating with the normal motion of the ocean. The abnormal motion of powerboats, plus diesel exhaust, will require much more time for the subconscious mind to adapt to, especially on a fishing boat.

● **Fight back** without medication is the best answer while the subconscious mind analyzes, accepts, and adjusts to the new motion. Watch the horizon, keep busy, and enjoy a spirited discussion or argument to ignore the early stomach symptoms.

Medical doctors and their wives were the most seasickness prone students, as they are continually monitoring their body actions. While prescribing medication to patients, it is the first time many doctors have faced this new sensation. They unwittingly talk themselves into becoming seasick, a pattern repeating itself many times.

● Their minds had to be kept very busy to overlook the stomach symptoms for the adjustment period lasting up to an hour or so. After the minds have adjusted to the new sensation, I disclose my secret method to fight this monster with a good laugh as they know how to fight back.

It backfired twice with overmedicated medical doctors as their confused subconscious minds speeded the panic process. They were taken ashore to prescribe more drugs...with results worse than a 15 martini hangover!

● The best advice— **keep seasickness problems to a minimum.** Have ample sleep, then begin the day with a good breakfast even if you are on a diet. If you are on a race or cruise for a few days, avoid greasy foods such as sausage, pork chops, and fried chicken for the first day or so. *Seasickness will be assured for a person with little sleep, having donuts and coffee for breakfast, after a wine and pizza party the previous night.*

Our USN and USCG recruited many professional seamen at the beginning of WW II. A top secret conference was called as the majority had chronic seasick problems. Each person had to comment starting with a long list of admirals down to the lowest in rank, enlisted man Fred Kissner who said, "The answer is simple as they aren't accustomed to the slow roll of 300' to 400' vessels. Return them to the small rapidly moving craft they had been operating". The admirals groaned as the answer was so simple.

All sailboats and powerboats underway must carry at least one USCG Approved preserver for every person on board or the operator will be subject to a stiff fine.

- **Before 1970.** If your boat was swamped or sunk and you had to rely on the Approved cushion, you would spend considerable time and effort to just hang onto it...instead of being able to have it become a part of your body as a swim aid to go to shore.

Type 4
- **AK-1 Approved jacket.** The theory was to hold the head of an unconscious person above water, a rare occurrence. When exposed to spray and humidity the metals corroded rapidly, and the organic cloth was mildew prone. Due to the basic design theory, it proved almost impossible for use as a swim aid.

- **Ski belts** proved the most practical swim aid and on more than a a couple of occasions we used them to make rescues of persons drowning. Guess they were too practical for Approval.

Type 2   *Four major life-preserver factors for you to consider—*

- A comfortable swim aid with practical flotation that becomes a part of the body.
- Comfortable enough to wear for long periods without inner condensation.
- Tough synthetic cloth with corrosion-resistant metals.
- Storage—size is important and it must be ready for instant use.

123

- **Stearns Mfg. Co.** was the pioneer in the new preserver field in the late 1960's, producing new jackets fitting the factors above before Approval. We put endless hours testing on two of them in four years, finding them practical, efficient swim aids.

We preferred the next smaller size to fit comfortably under jackets, windbreakers, and foul weather gear, providing protection by padding *Type 3* the body in a sloppy sea to protect it from sharp objects.

- **Condensation** built up in other jackets we tested at the time. They became hot and uncomfortable in a half an hour in humid weather. On a cold winter night the condensation would soon drain body heat providing chills, As they interrupted your concentration span they became hazardous.

The Sterns inner mesh minimized condensation buildup on inner surfaces being comfortable to wear in a hot summer squall with high humidity. I wore one continually in a three day cold weather sail in heavy weather. It protected my body when below, and was warm to wear while sleeping.

The preserver picture is confusing to many new sailors due to regulations, price...and the purpose for which we have provided the history above.

- Swim with preservers at least 100 yards, then wear them topside and below to know their strengths and weaknesses. Do this under ideal conditions as you may have no more testing time when you and your friends suddenly have to use them as a last resort.

Powerboating Illustrated

We are **warm-blooded creatures.** Our body functions produce enormous heat energy from digesting food to exercise. Our self protection begins with the continuous release of body heat called **metabolism.**

Comfort-zone limits. Our inner-core body furnace regulates at 98.6° .F. The core temperature must be protected in hot areas with loose clothing for sun protection, with ample drinking water allowing prespiration to evaporate easily cooling the skin surface.*In cold air and water*— clothing must retain body heat for comfort and survival. While we have endless energy, *cold-blooded sharks and fish* with body temp. a few degrees above the water with limited energy, must be protective using energy wisely.

Heat dehydration— *our army normal fresh water daily need in the Arabian desert, is 6 gallons each.* Three motorcyclists ran out of fuel taking a shortcut across a nearby Mexican desert, one survived. He was in critical condition losing 30 pounds ... losing 4½ gallons of water.

Ocean dehydration— survival conditions adrift without drinking water to cool the core, no shade, comfortable air temperature seems limited to 3 or 4 days depending on age and physical condition.

Our furnace. Our inner body core distributes heat from the inner body core, to the outer skin layer tissues evenly throughout your body with a network of blood vessels to maintain inner body core heat of 98.6° F.

124 **A hot day.** The body must increase its release of heat energy. Blood vessels near the skin surface enlarge for a more rapid blood flow to keep you cool, while maintaining the inner core 98.6F body temperature.

Sun's rays are transferred without direct contact by radiation, with the body core becoming a radiator having to increase heat release. The best answer is thru prespiration.

Perspiration. The sweat glands release excess heat with moisture and body salts collecting on the skin surface. The body heat is released as perspiration evaporates, a comfortable cooling effect on a hot day.

Cold temperature body core protection. A person adrift on a liferaft finds the blood vessels shrink or constrict on the skin surface in cold weather. This keeps valuable body heat from being lost too rapidly.

Hypothermia. 1968-72 Great Lakes USCG statistics list 73 cases of immersion in cold water... with 40 deaths.

Cold weather temperature variables— *still air, wind, immersion.* If adrift, a *wind chill factor* will rob and transfer body heat far more rapidly than in still air. Can you cover the body with a tarp to reduce wind factor?

When the body is fully submerged in cold water the same temperature as the air, body core heat is transferred by direct contact with cold water *25 times faster than in cold air.*

EXPOSURE VARIABLES

water temp. temp F	exhaustion or unconsciousness	expected survival time
over 80	indefinitely	indefinitely
70-80	3-12 hrs	indefinitely
60-70	2-7 hrs	2-40 hrs
50-60	1-2 hrs	1-6 hrs
40-50	30-60 min	1-3 hrs
32½-40	15-30 min	30-60 min
32½	under 15 min	less 15-45 min

Cold water boating... who need it?

1912 Titanic sinking— no wind water 32° F. None of 1489 persons immersed were alive an hour and fifty minutes later when rescue vessels arrived.

USCG— *A Pocket Guide to Cold Water Survival*, Oct. 1980, states that at 40° F, calm water, body heat loss is a gradual process. A normally dressed person has a 50% chance after an hour exposure. This time can be extended to three hours beginning with wearing a *lifevest*.

The body core temperature must remain constant. During immersion the preserver keeps you afloat conserving energy. *Thermal clothing and underwear* should be worn beneath to retain body heat, to reduce conductivity rate of body heat going to the water with a lower temperature.

Trapped air insulation. Body heat must be trapped between the skin and clothing with an insulating air layer. If this layer of warm air is lost, the skin temperature will drop. as your insulation is lost. The inner body core will try to maintain its normal body heat as it panics with body core temperature dropping rapidly... *the greatest survival at sea hazard.*

Shivering. Early in the heat loss process the body constricts the surface **125** blood vessels. This reduces heat transfer by blood to skin surface, while shivering helps produce more body heat. During a severe exposure when the body can't produce sufficient heat, the body core temperature drops.

Hypothermia— *body core drops to 95° F.* As the body panics, temperature begins to fall even faster. Unconsciousness follows when the body core temperature drops below 90 degrees. The starved muscles become stiff, the skin veins collapse as skin turns blue, and the pupils enlarge.

Body core temp. below 90° F. Pulse is barely detectable, the heart beat becomes irregular, and death may occur. **Below body core temp. 85° F—** is the victim dead or alive? Death will be defined as failure to revive on rewarming.

Ship sinkings often take 15 to 30 minutes to fully submerge. Take time to wear as much warm clothing as possible covering head, neck, hands, and feet... wear as much wool as possible. Add an exposure suit over clothing, add lifejacket. Avoid entering water if at all possible.

Seasickness is a major mental and physical hazard. Vomiting removes precious body fluids, reducing survival chances as victim becomes more prone to hypothermia. USCG booklet recommends tablets or medicine to combat seasickness.

My experience indicates that if seasickness can be avoided normally, it is much better as I've seen medicines may produce side effects sometimes confusing thinking process, and balance factors.

Swimming is an excellent exercise, the perfect way to cool off after a hot day, and/or strenuous sail. But how far can you normally swim?

 The *Sea Temp indicator* is excellent to find warm spots in the ocean for snorkeling, swimming, and fishing, as a temperature drop of one degree finds fish losing their appetite...also to recognize hypothermia potentials with water below 70 degrees.

● **It is easy to fall overboard.** The nonswimmer will panic instantly while hollering for help underwater. Rescue must begin immediately which will always be hazardous. I've seen a 100 lb. weakling in a drowning trauma I rescued with the momentary strength of an angry professional wrestler.

● **Ski belt or horseshoe preserver.** Throw one to the victim to hang onto to stop the panic. My choice is usually a quality, correct size ski belt.

● **The heaving line,** page 194, with a boat fender tied onto the other end is excellent. Pull panicky victim slowly to the boat. Let nonswimmers come aboard on their own power as they are still dangerous.

● **Minimum swimming standards?** A medical survey listed ¾ of all drownings occur within 60' of shore. While many of these drownings occur on the beach...*it makes good sense for all sailors to easily swim 100' in normal conditions.* During a fall overboard, or a sailboat capsize, they will be comfortable in the water and easy to rescue.

● **Take swimming lessons** if you can't easily swim this distance...yet what happens to the person who claims he can't be taught to swim? We took a new approach to help a few nonswimmers with this claim.

We took a different approach than swimming pool lessons. They used flippers and ski belts, joining us for an hour or so swim around the bay for ten days. Their reaction was laughter when I suddenly removed the ski belts in deep water. They knew they had positive flotation in ocean water as the mental hangups had disappeared, and the flippers gave them good propulsion.

Scuba diving instruction is the next major requirement so you can enjoy the additional benefits of snorkeling, tank, and free diving.

During the winter months take the time to invest in Scuba diving lessons. A warning is necessary as the pool has to be at least 13' to 15' deep to continually practice clearing your ears until it becomes second nature. Little did I realize I was a poor swimmer before taking these lessons in 1958. Though seldom using tanks afterwards, they taught me competency in the water to retrieve items dropped overboard, to check anchor holding, and snorkling to enjoy underwater scenery. While having positive flotation in salt water, I found many people also have negative buoyancy in fresh water, the author included.

● *Underwater Christmas?* The first televised underwater Christmas was held in Avalon Harbor at a depth of 30' in 1960. We found it difficult to have neutral buoyancy long enough to tie decorations on the Christmas tree, while schools of confused fish tried to fathom what the strange black land animals were doing.

Young children are frequent drowning victims. On the plus side they are *the best candidates for resuscitation* because of the **diving reflex.** A University of Michigan research program found 2/3 of cold water drowning victims successfully revived were up to 3½ years old.

The younger the victim— and the colder the water, the better will be the chance for the young victim to survive.

The **primeval mammalian diving reflex** is started by the sudden contact with cold water. It shuts off the blood and oxygen circulation to most parts of the body except heart, lungs , and brain.

Scientists have known about this mechanism in seals, whales, and porpoises to survive for long periods underwater. Yet it was found about ten years ago to also apply to people.

Drowning victims have all the symptoms of being dead without heart beat or breathing. Their eyes are dilated and fixed with no other vital signs life.

If the water is cold the victim still has a good chance of survival. Much depends on age of victim, how cold the water is, how long the person was under, state of the victims health... and how well rescuers do their job.

cartoid artery

lungs

heart

127

After four quick initial breaths covered on the last pages. it is time to check if the heart has stopped , and begin external heart massage..

The heartbeat often starts functioning on its own after artificial respiration has started.

Check for pulse at the cartoid artery lying close to the neck on either side of the adam's apple. Can you find it on your neck?

Check pupils. If pupils do not get smaller or dilate in brighter light, the blood and oxygen flow to the brain is insufficient.

CPR should begin immediately in addition to artificial respiration without pulse nor dilated pupils. While one rescuer may be sufficient, two are preferable to help each other.

We don't cover CPR. It needs to be taught 'hands on' under guidance of experts in this field.

We were surprised to find may heart attack victims could have been saved and returned to an active, useful life IF CPR was more widely known and practiced.

Who teaches CPR regularly in your area?   *Phone*

   Dates—

   Location—

Powerboating Illustrated

If no preserver is available and you are overboard, treading water can waste too much energy. Relax and try this drownproofing method.

Adapted from Coronet, July '52
© Esquire, Inc.

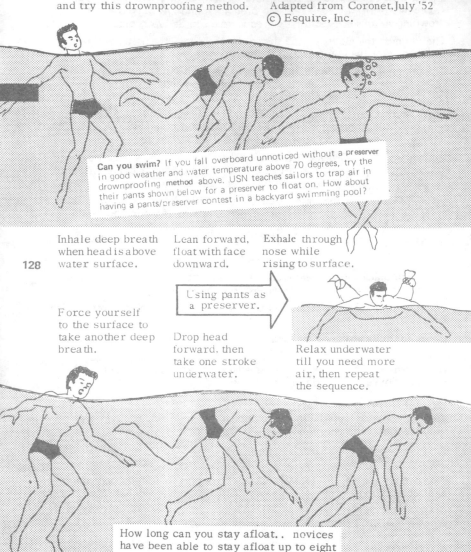

Can you swim? If you fall overboard unnoticed without a preserver in good weather and water temperature above 70 degrees, try the drownproofing method above. USN teaches sailors to trap air in their pants shown below for a preserver to float on. How about having a pants/preserver contest in a backyard swimming pool?

128

Inhale deep breath when head is above water surface.

Lean forward, float with face downward.

Exhale through nose while rising to surface.

Force yourself to the surface to take another deep breath.

Using pants as a preserver.

Drop head forward, then take one stroke underwater.

Relax underwater till you need more air, then repeat the sequence.

How long can you stay afloat.. novices have been able to stay afloat up to eight hours under ideal conditions using this method. Survival time rapidly drops in cold water.

Every dinghy, car topper, trailerboat, and large boat needs a practical, built-in method to climb aboard especially if you are alone without assistance.

The basic idea– *climbing up on a horse.* A bowline stirrup is basic and practical, especially when many ladders are weak and require much storage space.. It can be secured to a cleat on the side of the boat so it can't wrap around prop if it falls overboard underway.

The nylon webbing strap at right marketed in the early 1960's could be permanently bolted to the boat. It was more comfortable on the foot than a 3 strand bowline stirrup. It is always ready to take you aboard after a swim or if you fall overboard. Children and persons of average height could easily reach the nylon stirrup from the water to come aboard.

The smaller the boat the more important tt becomes to have a person on the other side for balance to help a swimmer come aboard. Coming aboard over bow or stern in a small boat flirts with disaster.

Time permitting we try to spend as much time as practical on the ocean in the winter on sailboats when sane people and their boats stay ashore. Those winter days on the ocean especially after a storm, provides a high few people realize in a lifetime, and many new ideas are learned to help readers. **129**

Approved vests and float coats comfort? The smooth nonbreathing inner lining rapidly collect moisture in less than an hour. As the perspiration increases, it begins to drain body heat. Your concentration is reduced as the discomfort grows. *This potential can trigger a series of mistakes.*

Stern's vests with net webbing. As perspiration is released, they are comfortable in a summer thunderstorm. In heavy weather winter sailing they can be worn continually under parkas or jackets. I sleep with it on for warmth, and protects the body from sharp points reducing impact.

Float coats. We soon found during testing, an interesting surprise as it can come up around your neck if you go in feet first. An uncomfortable *tail strap* will prevent this surprise.

Tow jobs are always hazardous. Move upwind, stay clear of other boat, send a heaving line across. Operator on other boat can tie line for towing to heaving line that can be pulled back to rescue boat. It can then be page 194 secured to bow of rescued boat, and stern of rescue boat.

We cannot stress how important it is for tow line to be secured to strong, well-anchored cleats. Discussing of nylon *three-strand rubber band stretch* is questionable... especially with weak anchored cleats used for towing and being towed, see pages 114 and 192.

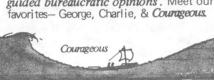

Boating safety is a term we have been trying to understand for over 30 years.

Major contributions come from highly motivated individuals challenging misguided bureaucratic opinions. Meet our favorites— George, Charlie, & *Courageous.*

Courageous

George

Charlie

Boating safety????? **If you had time to choose your boat and equipment—** what products would be of most use in a *short time situation* where rescue was apparent. If that fails, prepare for a *long time survival situation* with rescue and survival preparation and equipment worlds apart.

Survival techniques for ocean recreational boating? George Sigler, was an ex USN fighter pilot highly trained in the art of survival with many combat hours. He bought a 23' sailboat after returning to civilian life. He was amazed to find many USCG Approved survival equipment and ideas little changed since WW II, leaving boat owners to rely on their own resources.

Survival equipment provides something to eat (fish hooks?) **and** solar stills with a continual supply of fresh water, instead of limited usage canned water.

The Japanese Current. Suppose you were operating a powerboat from San Francisco to Los Angeles, having joint electrical and engine failure 30 miles from shore, a trailerboat out for the big ones in a similar situation, or a dismasted sailboat with engine failure . They may begin drifting in a clockwise direction with the current, then pushed SW by the trades with the craft if still afloat, heading roughly for Hawaii, easy to miss.

Survival raft? George eliminated the round Approved inflatable raft with canopy drifting helplessly to the whims of wind and current.

Soft dinghy— George bought a 15' 5'' long Zodiac Mark III. It was light and strong, producing a seaworthy smooth ride in a rough sea. The riding efficiency wasn't fully appreciated until picked up by a USCG cutter, ordered by the USN, 80 miles out from Oahu, Hawaii. They had trouble adjusting to the violent, uncomfortable cutter movement.

Singlehanded exposure? "You need a partner", argued Judy, Georges wife. He picked another USN fighter pilot Charlie Gore, the most important decision in any survival trip. Two persons confined to a 15' boat for 56 days... *is rough on ANY kind of even the best friendships.*

Wind power maneuverability. *Courageous* carried a small nylon square sail supported by mop handles, parts that might be available in most of the survival situations. Prevailing winds provided downwind maneuverability thru an arc of approximately 90 degrees.

This meant the difference between changing course sufficiently to go ashore on an island, instead of drifting helplessly past in the round inflatable raft to see trees and beaches, drifting helplessly back to the vast empty ocean.

Afternoon July 4, 1974. *Courageous* was towed under the Golden Gate Bridge and set adrift 30 miles out at sea. While George and Charlie seemed cheerful to those aboard the rapidly disappearing tow boat, both were well aware of the huge Pacific Ocean water world before them.

Wind power. They hoisted their small, stout nylon square sail supported by mop handles. The boat started moving downwind in a good breeze that kept increasing thru the night.

The next morning as they started to surf down the slope of a steep wave, the 8 foot steering oar would temporarily lose its bite and steering ability. This was due to bubbles flowing under the boat from barnacles... as the boat was in the water three weeks before departure.

Upset. A series of three converging waves suddenly peaked, causing their boat to broach and flip in 53 degree water off Monterey. 2½ hours were required in rough seas to disassemble the boat, get it upright, and assemble the boat again, during which most backup equipment was lost.

If the upset had occurred at night, all equipment would have been lost, and they would have died rapidly of exposure. It would be impossible at night to right the boat in the same force 7 to 8 high wave action.

Hypothermia. George and Charlie were out of energy as they climbed back into the Zodiac. They were in the early stages of hypothermia as their body heat was below 95 degrees.   131

They rested the next 20 hours huddled together in their one, thin sleeping bag, continually in ten inches of sloshing water. When their bodies began to warm slowly, the pains resulting as the numbness disappeared, felt like nails driven thru their shoulder blades and hip bones.

Storm anchor. The storm lasted 3 days along the Southern California coast. They rode to a storm anchor stabilizing the craft, as it twisted rapidly underwater with a strong swivel. They had learned the limits of *Courageous*, knowing when to sail... and when to use the storm anchor.

Five body heat areas to be protected   *head, armpits hands, groin, feet.* They covered their heads with wool caps, the most effective material to retain body heat, drying more rapidly in open air than cotton or synthetics. Wool is resistant to wear, and doesn't deteriorate as fast as cotton. Even when wet *wool fibers will retain 70% to 80% of your body heat*, while cotton and synthetic fibers release most body heat.

Sunburn screen protection (1974). Creams and lotions were analyzed with Zinc Oxide chosen for nose and cheek protection.

After growing beards, their whiskers protected their cheeks, and wool caps, their heads. Zinc Oxide was limited to protecting the nose.

Navy pilots not seamen. If they did their homework they could make up in preparation what they lacked in seamanship. The result is many ideas which may also be of use to you in everyday boating situations.

Their basic philosophy carried them thru many bad storms, to develop new ideas covering survival AND rescue situations we report.

The unexpected— *it didn't rain once in their 56 days on the ocean.* Storms lasted three days to a week, with good weather only on Sundays. They were becalmed for only three days.

Existing on raw fish and birds. This was their plan to live comfortably on the open ocean, free of parasites and sewage disposal areas along the coast. It was 54 days before they speared the first fish on a Hawaiian sling, a mahi-mahi, not catching it on a hook. George even tried using his tennis shoes for bait... promptly swallowed by a ten to twelve foot long shark.

They were damp every night. Thin, light nylon sleeping bags were chosen which could dry rapidly in sunny weather. The first one off watch could sleep soundly for an hour or two before a wave broke over the boat, having to bail the boat. Then they'd have to lay long enough in the remaining water to become warm enough again for the important body heat.

The boat wasn't long enough so they had to sleep in the fetal position. They couldn't stretch out due to their equipment. When both were off watch they'd have catnaps in one position for about 45 minutes, then become uncomfortable with the sleeping area 32" wide and 6' long. Both had to turn over together *sleeping like two spoons* to prevent hypothermia.

132

The fetal position became a growing problem. The discomfort increased as they lost weight, with less fat protection for their more exposed bones.

Low blood pressure *caused by weight loss, dehydration or hypothermia* **requires caution to avoid that first mistake.**

Take blood pressure, pulse rate, and temperature often as possible. Their blood pressure dropped considerably from a normal 120 over 80. They felt good physically, but they became weak. With diastolic pressure down, they would feel dizzy any time they stood up as blood would drain from the brain.

They stood up slowly and moved slowly being lightheaded with low blood pressure. In a survival situation if you become frustrated or in a hurry, one wrong movement is the difference between life or death.

The clothes they were wearing... were another self imposed limitation for realism.

George lost his socks in the upset the second day. From that time on his dreams at night were a pair of new, dry socks... then food.

Position plotting. He used a Timex quartz watch, an accurate timepiece to plot daily positions according to time of sunset and sunrise.

Amazing 56-day survival on raft

Sunglasses for protection from glare and ultraviolet rays. They were a luxury not all castaways may have. As their primary income was being pilots, they had to protect their eyes from glare, avoid dryness, etc.
Night vision drops rapidly after the 4th and 5th days in strong light on the ocean especially if you don't use sunglasses during the day. If you don t have any, cut slits in paper or cloth as temporary protection.

Body protective compensating mechanisms are fascinating. Both men had extensive briefings by USN medical doctors that are seldom reported,that we discuss as they are all important.

For the first 54 daystheyexisted on water from solar stills, and a few small sugar pills, being able to metabolize body fats and proteins before harpooning a mahi-mahi. They ate only 3 oz. of the fish. Since they hadn't eaten for so many days, they were afraid they might become sick with diarrhea.

Fish jerky? They dried the mahi-mahi to avoid spoilage as they didn't know if they would be adrift another 10 to 12, or even 30 days. Since the body has to provide moisture to eat and swallow dried fish removing precious body moisture, it became self defeating. Fish stench was so great USCG seamen stayed upwind of the boat as it came aboard the cutter.

Old seamen usually do rather well under survival conditions if they remain emotionally stable. Age factor and normal deterioration of the body must be taken into account, with a person in good health having rather good survival chances. Children metabolize their energy a lot faster, reducing their chance to survive as long under survival conditions.

133

Success depends on your state of health and mental attitude. Metabolism rate is very important in an ocean survival situation. Charlie was 27, and George 29 two days out, both emotionally stable individuals.

Involuntary castaways— the Baileys were adrift for 118 days, and the Robinsons adrift 38 days, were older couples. They moved very slowly to metabolize at a slower rate, also not to lose weight as fast.

You can drain your body fluids and worry yourself to death. USN doctors predicted urine would become darker, heavier, and purple, almost the same amount ingested. *Don't expect a bm if you don't eat...* which provided a major worry among many castaways.

Laxatives and enemas. They are unnecessary and hazardous *as the lost body fluids place a tremendous shock on the body.*

After you begin eating the bm will again resume its normal function. Your body computer has been programmed going back hundreds of centuries, to compensate for itself under survival conditions... and then return to normal body functions after the crises is over. If you try to outsmart Mother Nature in survival conditions, you may be dead right.

Large commercial vessels are castaway hazards. George and Charlie studied many accounts of castaways almost run over by ships they were trying to signal for help. Aboard *Courageous* they signalled several tankers for 4 to 5 minutes... *never receiving a response. WHY?*

International Rule 5— look-out. *Every vessel shall at all times maintain a proper look-out by sight and hearing as well as by all available means appropiate in the prevailing circumstances and conditions so as to make a full appraisal of the situation and the risk of collision.*

Rule 5 is obvious, yet many problems develop in application. **Boredom** is a major factor on the open ocean with nothing in sight but water for days on end. Then we have the lookout location on the ocean bridge usually trying to peer thru masts and cables with the huge blind spot dead ahead, page 88. Lookouts on supertanker bridges may be 1000 feet aft of the bow.

We have met more than our share of fishing vessels underway, operating under autopilot with the operator/ lookout asleep in his chair day and night. A large fishing boat was on a converging course with us for two hours... on our port side. I finally honked the FREON HORN six or seven times, causing much action on the fishing boat.

134

Professional friends soon found the answer. The captain was sleeping below with his alarm clock soon to ring. The boat was going faster than planned, and he forgot to assign a lookout, it was under autopilot. My friends gave him unexpected publicity in their own circle of friends.

A student called,"I was on a 200 passenger ferry last night easily making 16 knots. I walked to the bridge to watch the professionals. I found the captain was watching TV, no lookout, it was operating on autopilot". Call the USCG I advised. The TV was removed from the bridge while the captain was put on a year probation with his license. As for his boss........

10,000 to 20,000 candle-power flare is almost useless in the daytime. Their flares were used only for signalling. They could have been used to chase sharks nibbling on the raft, or start a fire after making landfall.

Flare guns and Very pistols. They are limited to *rescue equipment* hoping someone is visually looking for you to make a rescue.

Carry a signalling mirror. Use the seven million candlepower sun's rays when conditions are right. A USCG chief working on a tanker fire 40 miles off the coast of Baja, Mexico saw a mirror flash in his helicopter, later returning and landing on the shore finding two castaways in serious condition after a boat sinking, They used **half a broken signal mirror.**

An emergency hand held, hand-operated alarm... inventors start thinking. Design one to trigger an electronic emergency alarm on a nearby large vessel. Another idea is *a launcher for shredded aluminum particles* to trigger an alarm on the nearby vessels radar. *Powerboating Illustrated*

dead zone

A boat is barely a speck on the water to planes flying at 40,000 feet. Many people at boat shows felt that with all the transatlantic flying, airliners would always have boats in sight on the water below. Add a force 5 ocean, and any speck is lost in whitecap wave action.

George and Charlie used their 1974 EPIRB with talkback to contact commercial aircraft pilots overhead, one 230 miles away.

Coastwise use– *line-of-sight VHF marine radio.* If you can't shine a light to another vessel, you can't talk to it. As signals couldn't curve over the horizon, they couldn't communicate with a vessel 8 miles away. Consider waterproof, handheld short range VHF to take with you in a sinking.

EPIRB– *Emergency Position Indicating Radio Beacon.* Rapid changes are taking place as complaints to FCC forced more stringent rules.

Class B 121.5/243 MHz EPIRB is used by offshore racers. It can be picked up by commercial aircraft if monitoring 121.5 MHz emergency channel, then relayed to USCG Rescue Coordination Center, Scott AFB, Illinois. It is the first 'hit'. USCG sits on report waiting for a second 'hit' before launching a helicopter or notifying the closest vessel.

Signal picked up by Cospas/Sarsat satellites can't be stored. Satellite has to relay signal directly to ground station if both are in radio sight at the same time. Three day battery potential is low after two days. Satellite determines 25 mile radius location. Advantage, lower cost. **135**

Class 406 (406 MHz) EPIRB replaced commercial vessel Class A EPIRB at greatly increased cost with seven times the battery power of Class B, also used on long distance cruising boats. Each has its own digital code system register with country of origin, and type of vessel, on file.

A 406 distress signal is picked up and recorded by satellite then relayed to LUTs ground station at next pass. 406 also broadcasts on 121.5 MHz emergency channel monitored by commercial aircraft as time permits. The 406 signal pinpoints within a 3 to 5 mile radius, approximately 4% of the search pattern of the less expensive Class B EPIRB.

LUTs—local user terminals. Fifteen ground stations operate 24 hours a day in seven countries tracking 406 MHz signals on land and sea., with more recorded on land. West coast signals are forwarded to Kodiak, Point Reyes, a 3rd to Scott Airforce Base, Illinois.

97% of EPIRB signals are false, the reason USCG wants multiple hits for confirmation. Was one accidentally activated when carried to a boat, or self-activated when righted for storage. Is it turned off before sending thru the mail to have the battery periodically replaced in an EPIRB center.

Whitbread Round the World Race. Two EPIRBs continually sent false signals when not supposed to; two had no signal overboard; four worked. EPIRB is an insurance policy, not a good-luck rabbits-foot charm. What is battery condition. Was it turned on before being activated?

Powerboating Illustrated

Drinking seawater—reverse osmosis. *

seawater intake

brine return

piston

semi-permeable membrane barrier

drinking water recovery tank

90% seawater intake under pressure, is returned... with 10% drinking water.

The vast Pacific— it didn't rain once during the 56 days underway on *Courageous*, providing the need for thorough planning with the fickle patterns of nature. George and Charlie used surplus USN solar stills to provide drinking water from sea water, no longer available.

* **Present answer**— William and Simonne Butler spent 66 days in a liferaft when their 38' sloop was sunk 6/15/90 by whales in the Pacific... "Without the *Survivor 35* T.M., we would have not survived".

Sigler summarizes, "This system has been proven as you see, but it is expensive... cheap if you are on a life raft 1000 miles from nowhere".

While the manufacturer has various models, the one chosen by Butler was designed to USN specifications, producing 1.4 gallons of purified fresh water average per hour output. It weighs less than 7 pounds, is 22 inches long.

136 If life raft emergency equipment carries canned water, or a desalting kit producing hardly palatable water... *both are limited and not reusable, wasting much precious space aboard.*

A continuous supply of fresh water becomes the major need for survival conditions. **Three quarts of liquid daily** are used in normal conditions, average consumption for most people in one form or another.

A pint of fresh water is recommended minimum every 24 hours for survival when NOT eating. *Drinking water requirements are doubled* when air temperature increases from 70 to 90 degrees F.

Readers may have heard of half authenticated accounts of survivors living by drinking sea water... but how much, and for how long?

Dr. Alan Bombard, MD, was one of the first to test answers in 1952 as he drifted across the Atlantic from the Canaries to the Barbados on his raft *L'Heretique*... **drinking lots of rainwater.** He used a fruit press to squeeze juice from fish he caught containing some fresh water. In between he was reported to have drank sparingly of sea water.

"Do not drink sea water"— is summarized in U.S. Air Force Manual 64 carried in all Air Force survival kits, and on many commercial aircraft.

Drinking sea water. Dehydration begins with loss of weight. Thirst will increase as discomfort grows. It follows with loss of appetite, sleepiness, nausea, inability to walk develops as the senses fail. Victim becomes silent, his eyes are glassy, he has bad breath, followed by delirium. He may die quietly, become violent, and/or jump overboard to drown.

* **Recovery Engineering, Inc., Minneapolis, MN   phone 1-800-548 0406**

The hot-air lifeboat. A large powerboat bound for Cape San Lucas at the tip of the Baha Peninsula, sunk without survivors. I was supposed to help take a 65' powerboat from the Cape to Newport,when a printing deadline intervened. It unknowingly went thru the sinking area a few hours later. The water temperature was 56 degrees.

I passed the word thru the grapevine for information. A transient professional seamen said, ''You are looking for me as I was offered a job on that boat. I checked below finding the condition was terrible. Glad I turned down the job''. That was the only time I saw him.

I asked trailerboating columnist Norm Phillips for ideas.

''Hard dinghies for survival are a waste of time. Most will be swamped, upset, and/or sink in any wave action with 2 or 3 persons aboard... and in 56 degree water, survival wearing a preserver will be limited.

''The French are ahead of us as almost all their dinghies hanging from davits are planing inflatables for ship-to-shore, and survival use.

Soft dinghy. ''Your Mark I 10½' inflatable is excellent for a survival condition. If one had been aboard, four could have survived even in sloppy weather. With discipline and ropes along its side, two more could be in the water, trading off with others. The 65' boat may have been able to pick up 4 to 6 survivors several hours later in that area''

137

What better lifesaving potentials can we include than the 65 day trip of George and Charlie sailing a Mark III Zodiac to Hawaii. When we were in Papeete, all rescue boats for the Hobie Worlds Competition were inflatables. Large sailboats were being positioned to tie stern to the quay, with inflatables used as *push boats* against their hulls, so with limited maneuverability, sailboats could back in with precision.

Inflatables aren't a work of art. After hanging on stern davits for a few weeks without being pumped up, they resemble a very dead shark.

They are workhorses serving endless purposes. Our kids spent endless hours at Catalina with ours exploring nearby beaches, and other boats. The exception... no fishing, as inflatables don't enjoy sharp hooks.

Armies and navies use inflatables worldwide. The best planing rescue boats for rough water are made in Vancouver and Victoria, B.C.

The rascals are collapsible for storage in small areas. Let us consider new names such as a *soft, soft dinghy* for small motors operating at low speeds, and *hard-bottom soft dinghies* for planing. If you think you can row either kind... start a contest.

We named our little Zodiac the *politician.* While it may be full of promises and hot air, it can explode with a lot of noise when stuck with a sharp pin.

Powerboating Illustrated

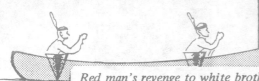

Red man's revenge to white brother? While Americans try to identify the canoe with our heritage, USCG listed 502 fatalities from 1972 to 1975, in canoes.

UNSTABLE cone

Upset cone canoeist is on seat almost to the upper edge of the open canoe shell that is not decked over. The canoe can be upset easily in wave action, The upset cone canoeist has an increased upset risk, also of falling overboard. As canoeists sit far apart, the balance problem increases in rough water.

STABLE cone

138

Stable cone kayaker provides excellent stability resistance to upset. Kayak sides and ends are covered to prevent swamping. Balance is stable in white water rivers, and in wave action on lakes with paddlers sitting on bottom in center of kayak.

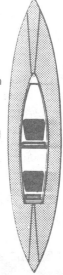

Brooklyn, 1947. We wanted to buy a canoe. We soon found many canoe fatalities... and how could we carry a rigid canoe on a busy subway?

Portable Folbot kayak. It provided endless happy surprises. We carried the two bags of parts on the subway to Dykeman Street in upper Manhattan, riding the Hudson tidal current south one week, and north, the next. We rode the subway to Jamaica Bay to camp out on weekends... in the middle of Brooklyn.

Folbot inventor, founder Jack Kissner, was a close friend for many years. We enjoyed working long hours together on his first outboard boat design and its advertising art, while he continually urged me to start my own business.

After buying a car, we shot the Housatonic rapids in the spring, finding the Wyoming Platte River more challenging at high water. Our 15 year old Folbot veteran was finally given to the Newport Beach Sea Scouts.

While we own 5 boats at present, if we chose one more it would be a new, versatile Folbot. For more information—

Folbot Inc., PO Box 70877, Charleston, SC 29415

The first 15-20 minutes exposure to heavy weather is terrorizing to most boat owners. It then becomes spirited if he is prepared with a good, well maintained boat. Otherwise it becomes a dumb statistic.

Our powerboat and sailboat operation has been on the ocean, with few exceptions. A dusty sign greets new USN plebes— *You must be on the defensive to outthink the ocean, as few boats are able to outslug the ocean.*

Sailboat downwind steering motion *forces 7 thru 9.* The author has many hours under bare poles on ocean sailboats with keel ballast using wind and wave pressure on hull. It can be a wet, wild, exciting exposure under control with waves to 20' in a trough. Sailboats have to be well designed and well maintained before entering bad weather.

Disabled powerboat pendulum action— *force 6 and above.* Many powerboats have tremendous hull and cabin windage above the water, and little below for steerage and hull stability. When engine power fails, the *vessel often turns beam to the wind and wave action, as pressures try to equalize on bow and stern.* The rolling pendulum action can become progressively violent as wind force increases, especially with planing hulls.

Pendulum action caused the Long Island fishing vessel page 114, to roll over in an increasing upper force 6 with steep, violent, short wave action in shallow water. If the skipper headed for port 15 minutes earlier...

Force 6 powerboat operation. I was a passenger on a 40' plus twin-screw **139** powerboat with wind increasing on the ocean in long, easy swells. Operator had little feel of inside controls I continually question with little feel of outside weather. The more he tried to compensate with dual engine controls to hold upwind course, the more steering became erratic. When turning the helm to me, I equalized, then ignored the engine throttle controls.

Wind pressure is the boss at force 6. It is the primary powerboating operating force against the hull for compensation. Steering action eased, with a more comfortable ride and steadier course. 'Hands-on exposure' was the answer. The owner behind me studying my actions, eventually took over.

The unexpected storm at dusk. Page 22 discusses our 15½' outboard boat returning downwind from Avalon. When we switched to our second tank, our 6 cylinder motor quit, then operated on 2 to 4 cylinders grudgingly. The cause, water in the gasoline we bought. It was a wet miserable ride for survival with the boat still half full of water when entering the jetty. *The encore—* a cloudburst sunk our boat at the dock three hours later.

The *two-pennant storm anchor* was so efficient we gave it this name. We tested the rugged, heavy mesh underwater parachute designed for USN on seven powerboats 14' to 57', folding to a pillow when not in use. It is our contribution to powerboating, the product of a wet scared author. I don't remember sending a bill for my testing. The knowledge it could save us and many other powerboat owners, was ample payment.

bow cleat

retrieving. line

Many falls occur when anchoring, or taking in an anchor when standing on a tippy, slippery deck of a small boat.

The four-power *Anchor-Krank* out of Provo, Utah. The small boat above is at anchor. The braided anchor line is easily cranked in from inside the boat, the line automatically falling into the anchor bucket or bag.

The *Anchor-Krank* can pull in a 30 pound anchor with its winch leverage. **Warning–** if anchor is stuck under rock, think twice before you pull the bow of your boat under water.

Anchor retriever line. is secured with a loop around anchor line leading to other side of boat. When chain or anchor breaks water, the retrieving line pulls anchor into other side of boat without operator leaving cockpit. **Locking bow chock** is required to keep anchor line lead on bow.

Anchor-Krank is removable so winch and anchor-line bucket can be stowed out of the way when not in use. We have found no better method to eliminate many injuries and falls inboard and overboard for trailerboats and car top boats than this simple anchoring method.

grommet drains

140

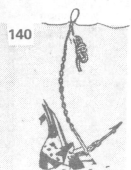

Anchor stuck on stump or rock that normally cannot be pulled out. Pull anchor line snug, then secure line to a float. Tie bowline loop around anchor line, letting it slide down line. Pull from the opposite direction shown to break out stuck anchor.

Paint anchors white. We anchored a 40' sailboat to go SCUBA diving, finding it had drifted slightly when returning. While we thought it was dug in correctly, the water was so clear we could see the anchor fouled around the chain. A check on the depth sounder showed the water over 80' deep.

It is important to put on mask, snorkel and fins to check your anchor. We anchored a 43' trimaran in a tight Todos Santos bay with many boats almost hull to hull. Water was murky. We spotted our white anchors 20' away with galvanized anchors often seen 3' away.

Two-pennant storm anchor. While we designed it as a storm anchor to protect smaller powerboats, it has other uses such as being folded to the size of a pillow for sleeping. It is an excellent method to maintain your position for deep-water fishing... in water 20 feet or deeper.

Powerboating Illustrated

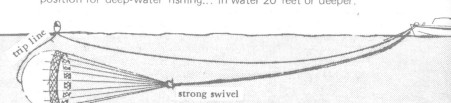

trip line

strong swivel

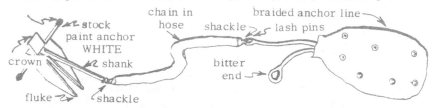

light breeze — puffy breeze — hurricane

2/1 scope   4/1 scope   8/1 scope

Anchor line scope? 7 to 1 is recommended for major storms in shallow water with vicious wave action with waves cresting close together. 3 to 1 is ample in calm water, increased as wind and/or current becomes stronger.

14' to 20' trailerboating anchoring needs may be simple, or more complex than larger boats due to trailer mobility, variety of uses and boating areas.

chain in hose — braided anchor line

stock
paint anchor
WHITE
crown   shank
fluke   shackle

shackle — lash pins

bitter end

150' 3/8" double braid line and anchor used on our last two outboard boats with storage space minimum, is shown. Heavy chain is in a soft fire hose to reduce paint and varnish damage. Whipping secures hose to shackles on both ends. Sharpen tips of 2½ lb. High Tensile Danforth, Grind sharp edges off stock ends. Nylon sail bag is used, add grommets for water drainage and ventilation.

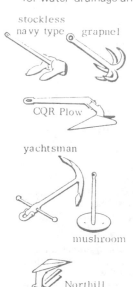

stockless
navy type   grapnel

CQR Plow

yachtsman

mushroom

Northill

Double-braided nylon is more chafe resistant, **141** drops into sail bag or bucket for stowage, paying out normally without kinks. 3 strand nylon chafes more rapidly, has more *rubber-band stretch.*

Junk sold to fishermen and trailerboaters as anchors defy reasoning. A San Pedro store sold all anchors, selling buckets as anchors to 30 or so trailerboats coming to Avalon July 4th continually banging into moored boats... especially ours, but why us?

Stockless is poor and heavy, avoid. **Yachtsman** has poor holding in small size. Anchor with the **grapnel** only on rocky bottoms, also recovering anchor line or outboard motor overboard. **Northill** type folds, is second choice with less storage space. **Mushroom** 150 lbs. or heavier with heavy chain makes a permanent mooring in mud bottom after it has dug deep. For small boats rocks may be as good as a mushroom, and cost less. **Plow** is best for powerboats over 30' as it is heavier than a Danforth. Plow has a wider swing before breaking out, then digs in rapidly when current reverses without fouling, seldom fouling in kelp.

Cow or earth anchor is an excellent land anchor for car top boats, trailerboats, big boat dinghies.

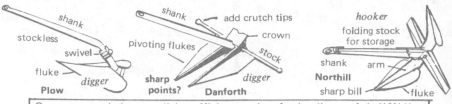

Plow: stockless, shank, swivel, fluke, digger

Danforth: shank, add crutch tips, crown, stock, pivoting flukes, sharp points?, digger

Northill: hooker, folding stock for storage, shank, arm, sharp bill, fluke

Kissner bought our first anchor, a 16 lb. Danforth. We pulled into a small cove near Jones Beach Inlet on Long Island on 6/4/48 in the afternoon with wall to wall large powerboats and our sailboat bow into the beach, plus a tahiti ketch in the middle with 6 anchors out. The stuffy gent next door peered down at me over the railing of his 54' powerboat with grinning servants on either side holding his dainty liqueur glass,"I say chap, why are you using an anchor twice the size of mine?"

A squall hit at 0200 recorded at 98 knots at the nearby USCG base. Only 4 out of 54 powerboats held...while our anchor dug in a couple more inches. The last I saw of my glassy-eyed neighbor, his nightshirt was wrapped around his neck. He was trying to hang onto his red night cap while hollering at his terrified servants clinging to him. His 54' boat was drifting backwards into the tahiti ketch, its owner trying to hang onto his night cap with his red nightshirt wrapped around his neck. My anchor interest was no longer passive.

142

● **Paint mud-hook anchors white.** When returning to a Newporter ketch after a September dive at Catalina I could see the anchor had broken loose, the water was clear, at a depth of 84'. We no longer kidded the owner who had painted the anchor white, it saved his boat. I've dived many times to check anchors which disappear rapidly and are hard to find if not painted white.

● **Imported anchor imitations—** who makes them? After an Ensenada Race a new 46' ketch was anchoring at nearby Todo Santos Island near us in an upper force 6 wind. One of the flukes bent double on the new anchor with the boat drifting thru shoal water with a rocky bottom; was it a bargain?

● **Plow anchors** were introduced in England. Their popularity came much later in the U.S. Cruising sailors from Mexico reported the heavier plow had a better bite, it broke out later, and set more rapidly without fouling.

Our testing with the lighter Danforth found it gaining lift at 3 to 4 knots planing above the bottom, becoming helpless when catching seaweed. We tested the plow at similar speeds finding it digging in due to the negative angle. Kelp didn't seem a problem when drifting thru kelp beds.

   ● **Bruce anchor—** a good basic design with no moving parts. Though not using one at time of writing, reports indicate it is an efficient design.

   ● **Anchor shackle bolt.** We prefer monofilament fishing line as a locking method, others choose noncorroding wire. Use a hammer and punch if you want to lock the shackle threads permanently.

   *Digger vs mud hook. Traditional *mud hooks* used one fluke to hook into the bottom. Plow, Danforth, and Bruce, are *diggers* that can be fully submerged and still dig deeper for a solid bite. *Weight* instead of efficient holding power is preferred for many large power vessels.

Action– boat, wind, wave action pull against. **Reaction–** digging angle, anchor holding power.

A mud hook can be overpowered, while a digger anchor digs deeper.

Anchor line can foul on exposed mud-hook fluke as wind, current, or both change direction.

- **Normal practice–** drop anchor slowly to avoid hitches in the line, as well as anchor fouling on its own line.

- **Scope–** is ratio of anchor rode paid out with water depth with tidal changes. Tidal changes are extreme in periods of Hurricane high and low water.

fluke *Yachtsman* shank

The Danforth can also foul on one of its flukes.

2:1 scope– ¼ holding power

4:1 scope– ½ holding power

8:1 scope– maximum holding power in shallow water. chafe

good weather strong wind major storm

nylon chain nylon chain nylon chain

Use sufficient chain to improve anchor rode digging angle. Tape 3' or so of nylon anchor line and thimble exposed on bottom to chafe from rocks, etc.

143

- *Traditional terms–* anchor line is called a **cable** usually 100 fathoms, 720', or 1/10th of a mile. **Sheet anchor** is heaviest bower in reserve for emergency. Two **bower anchors** were carried on port and starboard bows. **Stream anchor** at stern is about 1/3 weight of bower, may also be used for *kedging off.*

- **Rocky bottoms–** use a buoyed trip line secured to your anchor. Your anchor will be easier to locate if caught under a rock, see page 140.

- **Shorter scope, better catenary?** Use as much chain as possible. Send a *weight** down the line to improve the anchor digging angle. This will also improve shock loads on the hull fittings and nylon anchor line in wave action, pg. 188.

- **Alarm** indicates the sailboat is drifting and the anchor is dragging.

- **Chafe** is major problem for nylon anchor line in wave action. Wrap towels around line where it goes thru bow chock.

Periodically change the nip of the line where it goes thru the chock to also reduce chafe potentials.

float or plastic bottle BRRRRING

better catenary

light line

rocks

*Traditional weight term was *killick* or *sentinel*. The best weight pulling angle is a little more than halfway down the rode.

Square riggers followed prevailing winds, the trades and westerlies from a beam reach to run, sometimes facing contrary headwinds when approaching land. The goal was to make profit by carrying cargo to a port, then pick up a new cargo for the return trip.

Clippers were the first square riggers with smaller holds, designed for and making profit from speed for light or perishable cargoes ranging from tea, opium, and the wool trade from Australia to England.

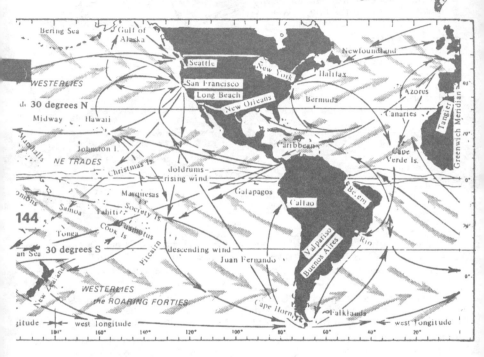

The year is 1850 as our square rigger leaves Manhattan with the ebb tide. It sails to mid Atlantic slowly turning south for Rio covering 4 to 5 times the distance of the rhumb line, with the shorter distance requiring twice the time. It picks up new cargo going 100 miles offshore to pick up the steady prevailing winds. The destination is Cape Horn in the roaring forties facing strong headwinds for 2 to 3 weeks.

After breaking loose it heads roughly to Kodiak, Alaska holding a steady course for 30 North, slowly turning east for San Francisco. Her new cargo can take her to Australia and New Zealand. Or she can sail to Hawaii, and the Marquesas, to round Cape Horn downwind. After she heads NNE her next destinations can be the Caribbean, New Orleans, Florida, Carolinas, the Chesapeake, New York, New England, and/or Halifax.

from Sailing Illustrated

Wind machines. *Cutty Sark* is the only surviving clipper ship, square rigged on all three masts. She was launched in 1869 sailing the oceans of the world for over fifty years using the prevailing winds shown at left. We provide considerable information of square rigger days in our *Sailing Illustrated*.

She was fully rebuilt and is preserved by *the "Cutty Sark" Maritime Trust*, individuals contributing their time and money to preserve their sailing heritage for future generations. You can board, and walk her decks near London in her drydock at Greenwich, S.E., England.

145

from Sailing Illustrated

Cutty Sark figurehead, witch *"Nannie"* in her short chamise with a horse tail, graced her bow.

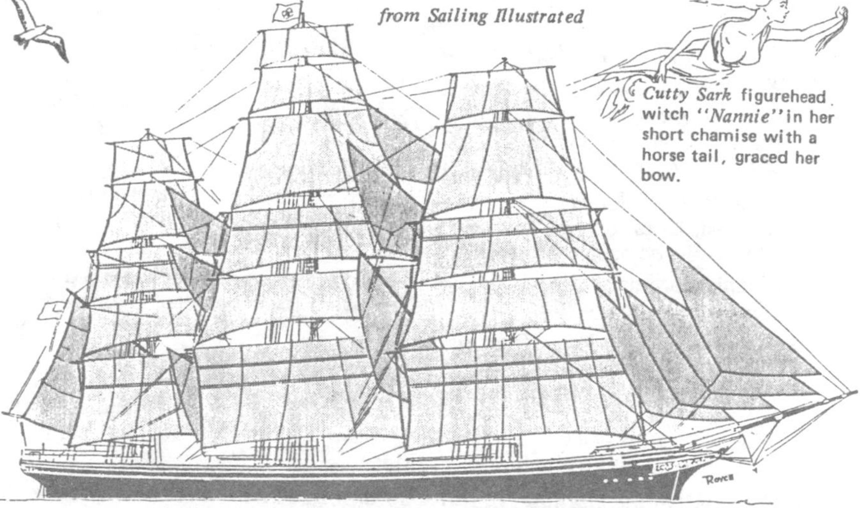

Length Overall— 280 feet   waterline length— 212'5'' beam— 36 feet 921 net tons
wool cargo draft— 20 feet   tea cargo draft— 17' 6'' 29 sails, approx. 32,000 sq. ft.
maximum crew— 28; minimum crew— 19.   maximum speed— 17½ knots

⟨••• CUTTY   SARK •••⟩

*Weather proverbs, rhymes, and reasons, may be of more use
to powerboat operators than they may realize.*

Sailors have gone down to sea in small sailing vessels since before
recorded history, before newspaper and TV weather reports, and way
before the barometer. These seamen developed a primitive, practical
weather wisdom to survive, while using the forces of nature to drive
their vessels sometimes for weeks out of sight of land.

Ancient sailors had to be continually alert to changing weather applicable
today in proverb form. It involved temperature changes, different colors
of the sky with rising or setting sun, the moon with its halo, changing
cloud patterns, plus the erratic action of porpoises, fish, and sea birds.

● *Mackerel sky and mare's tails, make lofty ships carry low sails.*

● *When wind shifts against the sun, trust it not, for back it will run.*

● *When clouds appear like rocks and towers, the earth is refreshed by
frequent showers.*

● *If clouds look as though scratched by a hen, get ready to reef your
tops'ls then!* Mare's tails develop, followed by a scratchy mackerel sky,
with a white cirrostratus film produces a *lunar halo,* soon to follow is a
backing wind. A storm is indicated in 12, 24, to 48 hours. As barometer
drops, wind flowing from the W and SW may ease, then blow hard.

● *At sea with low and falling glass, the greenhorn sleeps like a careless
jackass.*

● *But when the glass is high and rising, may soundly sleep the careful
wise one.*

● *Short warning, soon past.* Shorter the warning and change, shorter will be
the disturbance. It defines the 20 minute thunderstorm that may have winds
of hurricane force, rapidly changing directions plus downdrafts.

● *Long foretold, long last!* Longer the warning, the longer the disturbance
will last. Duration and intensity of bad weather depends on size and speed
of the advancing low pressure cyclonic storm in our northwesterlies.

A rapid barometer drop indicates rain and stormy weather. Severe N and NW
gales often occur AFTER a barometer is very low, then begins to rise—

● *Quick rise after a low... foretells a stronger blow.*

● *While rise begins after a low... squalls expect and a clear blow.*

If barometer is erratic or rises rapidly, it indicates unsettled weather. When
a barometer rises slowly and steadily, it can indicate fair weather... but
still be prepared for the few exceptions.

● *A red sky in the morning is a sailor's warning; but a red sky at night is a
sailors delight.*

● *A light blue sky clap on all sails, yet think twice with a dark, gloomy blue
sky.*   *from Sailing Illustrated*

● *A pale yellow sky brings rain... while a bright yellow sky at sunset presages wind.*

Light color tints with soft delicate cloud forms indicate light winds... while ragged, oily, to greasy looking clouds with hard edges and/or bright colors, indicate strong winds.

● *The moon, governess of the floods (high tides)... pale in her anger, washes all the air.*

Positive ion behavior disturbances. Expect such occurances worldwide... also— *when the desert winds are howling.* As the positive ion moves into our bodies greatly restricting our analytical ability, unanticipated brawls and riots increase with intensity. .. while horses stumble, and cats trying to jump up on a high fence, miss and go over the top. When maximum tides and **devil winds** peak at the same time, avoid making decisions for at least 24 hours until the body recovers from the positive ion.

● *Wooly fleeces deck the heavenly way... make sure no rain will mar a summer day (on the open ocean?).*

Beware on land– if it is a hot, humid, inland afernoon. The wooly fleeces can grow skyward into unstable air masses. This provides short duration thunderstorms, with possible winds of hurricane intensity that also include strong downdrafts.

Thunderstorms are predictable. with static from an inexpensive AM radio!

● *Seagull, seagull, sit on the land......... it's never good weather when you are on the land (sand).*

A low pressure grounds many birds, especially my favorite the heavy cormorant built like a heavy bomber, is barely able to take off and fly. It is fun chasing them perched on mooring cans, barely able to gain any altitude for 200 feet or more.

Then we have other reasons such as no minnows are around. Civilization has also made its contribution in the last fifty years when we see rows of gulls sitting on our beaches in the mid afternoon. I soon found they had returned with a full stomach after their gourmet feast at the local garbage dump five miles away. So... expect variables.

● *When the sea hog jumps... stand by your pumps.*

While we've seen propoises and fish jumping before a few large storms, erratic bird behavior was more obvious. As Lin and Larry Pardee bullt their own 24'7" *Seraffyn,* spending ten years sailing it around the world without an outboard motor or engine, I asked Lin to review these proverbs.

We were both stumped with the *sea hog jumps.*

Two years later I met a deliverly skipper who suddenly had the answer. He was taking a well-found sailboat from Hawaii to the U.S. He was caught in an **El Nino** with tremendous wind, wave action violence. Porpoises were jumping erratically, running into the sailboat, while birds were ramming into the rigging and hull. Glad I didn't do THAT research.

from Sailing Illustrated

● **The clouds above.** Nature sends advance physical warnings of storms in the every changing world of clouds. While well known to most farmers, much effort is required by us city folks living in air-conditioned homes and offices to understand these storm patterns.

Most radio and TV forecasts are of secondary importance to sailors as they cover large areas. You have to become your own weather expert to predict wind patterns in your immediate area to power your sailboat. Will the water surface action be stronger, or weaker than predicted?

● **Cirrus--** (ringlet) is thin, stringy Mares tails that make beautiful sunrises and sunsets due to light refraction thru ice crystals.

● **Cirrocumulus--** (ringlet-heap) is called Mackerel sky as it resembles fish scales. It has no cloud shadows...indicating a weather change.

● **Cirrostratus--** (ringlet-layer) is white, frozen, cobwebby fog which often predicts rain.

● **Ringlet?** These high clouds make a halo or ringlet around the sun and moon predicting a weather change in a day or two.

● **Altocumulus--** (middle-heap) form lumpy patterns producing flattened globular masses as shown at right.

● **Altostratus-** (middle-flat) may thicken to nimbostratus. It does NOT produce a halo around the sun or moon.

● **Stratus--** (layer) is low, indefinite, with a dry bottom giving water a hazy appearance...becoming **fog** down on the water surface.

● **Nimbostratus--** (storm-layer) cloud is flat, gray, ragged, with a wet looking bottom. It usually indicates steady rain over a large area.

● **Cumulus--** (heap) clouds are clean, fluffy, and dome shaped on the upper surface. If one grows tall enough to reach the high cloud ice crystal area where temperature is below freezing, it becomes the—

● **Cumulonimbus--** (heap storm) results when cumulus clouds develop into **clouds 2 to 5 miles tall.** When it reaches the freezing area, the cumulonimbus top flattens. *An anvil top* results with thin, wispy Mares tails indicating the direction of the thunderhead producing strong winds in a short duration storm.

● **Stratocumulus--** (flat layer) may resemble altocumulus though they may appear darker, lower, and larger, sometimes covering most of the sky. They can develop from altostratus, or flattened cumulus clouds.

upper clouds — *middle* — *low clouds*

148

Weather proverb accuracy? Sailors went down to the sea long before recorded history, while weather forecasts are a few decades old. These seamen developed their own weather prediction methods in proverb form to drive their sailing vessels hundreds and thousands of miles, reported on page 56 of our *Homestudy Guide.*

I wish we made a tape of our discussion with Lin Pardey while testing the proverb page. Many held up, while a few were inconclusive. Word interpretation may be involved with some proverbs hundreds of years old such as *when the sea hog jumps...stand by your pumps.* Sea hogs?

basic CLOUD FORMATIONS

ringlet

cirrus

high clouds are
ice particles

anvil top

cirrostratus

cirrocumulus

- - - - - - - - 20,000 feet - - - - - - - -

medium clouds

altostratus

altocumulus

- - - - - - - 6,500 feet - - - - - - -

low clouds

stratocumulus

149

cumulonimbus,
thunderstorm,
thunderhead

roll cloud

cumulus

nimbostratus

stratus

catspaw

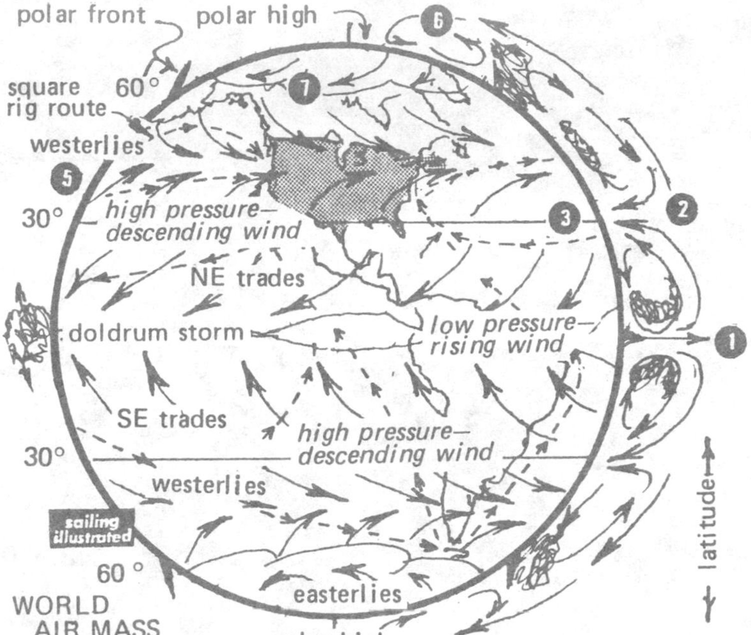

polar front — polar high

square rig route

westerlies

5

60°

30° *high pressure— descending wind*

NE trades

: doldrum storm

SE trades

30°

westerlies

60°

150 WORLD AIR MASS PATTERNS

6

7

3

2

1

low pressure— rising wind

high pressure— descending wind

easterlies

polar high—

← longitude →

latitude →

sailing illustrated

Our continually changing weather is a product of varying degrees of heat from the sun producing rising masses of warm air, and descending masses of cold air. To this we add rotation of the earth varying from a thousand miles an hour at the equator...to zero, at the poles.

The interaction of these factors produces complex tug-of-wars and collisions of worldwide air masses eternally on the move from the surface of the earth and ocean to the stratosphere.

Six surface wind patterns result with updraft and downdraft separation barriers caused by rising masses of warm air and descending cold air masses.

- **Doldrum barrier** at the equator has the most heat and high humidity. It has weak, changing surface winds due to rising masses of warm air.

- **30 degree north and south barriers,** *the horse latitudes,* result from the warm air doldrum masses bumping into cold polar air masses. Both mingle and descend producing a vertical barrier of weak surface winds. This separates the trades from the westerlies to the north influencing most U.S. weather

- **Our prevailing westerlies** in the northern latitude belt of 30 to 60 degrees flowing from south, southwest, west, and northwest, produce the best and most varied climates in the world. They range from the dry, balmy latin weather conditions in our local buffer zone, to the rapidly changing seasonal conditions in our eastern wind funnel producing lush vegitation with ample moisture with more predictability than elsewhere in the world.

from Sailing Illustrated

from Sailing Illustrated

Birth, life, and death of a storm. We provide a brief review of a low pressure storm in our westerlies as a quick on-board reference for readers in rapidly changing weather conditions. Sailors should spend considerable time studying the details and variables on pages 60 to 63 of our *Homestudy Guide* with a continuation on the following page.

Major air masses affecting our weather.

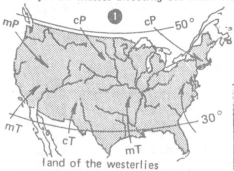

land of the westerlies

A low pressure area begins at left when polar air bumps into tropical air on a frontal surface

2 A ripple begins...

cP-cold,dry air mass

mT-warm,humid air mass

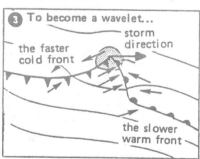

3 To become a wavelet...

the faster cold front

storm direction

the slower warm front

Disturbance is more intense as circulation increases around apex.

5 The wave becomes unstable...

The low deepens as the warm sector shrinks in size.

151

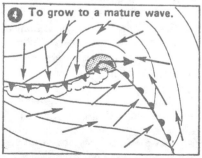

4 To grow to a mature wave.

A mature cyclone has developed around an intense low.

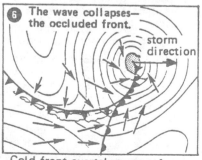

6 The wave collapses— the occluded front.

storm direction

Cold front overtakes warm front forcing the warm air aloft.

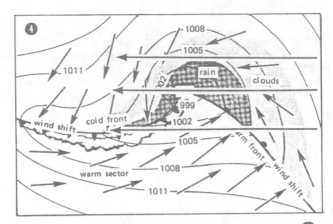

- **A mature low-pressure storm** is shown above, an enlargement of ④ on the previous page. Owners of the three sailboats above if exchanging ideas of the storm afterwards may seem to be discussing three very different storms. The differences increase if the hulls vary considerably.

> *Wind direction is reported in the direction it comes from...with a westerly flowing from the west toward the east.*

152   Basic flow of high and low pressures move from west to east in our **prevailing westerlies.** Local winds vary due to location of high and low pressure areas.

- **Barometers** measure relative air pressures in inches or millibars with *isobars* showing lines of equal pressure.

- **Wind direction** in our northern hemisphere flows in a *clockwise direction* from a high or hill of air...into a *counterclockwise direction* to a low. The warm moist air rises, cools, condenses, and precipitates, with a storm beginning.

  Due to earth rotation our westerlies move lows an average of 300 miles in the summer, and 700 miles in the winter every 24 hours.

- We in Southern California live in a **buffer zone** midway between the westerlies and moist tropic southern area beginning at Point Conception west of Santa Barbara, to 20 miles SW of Ensenada, Mexico, seldom going 50 miles inland.

  Sailors on the east coast from Cape Hatteras northward thru New England live in a wind or storm funnel with rapidly changing weather conditions.

- **Wind funnel sailors** on the east coast must be their own forecasters for rapidly changing weather which in your small local area may be weaker or much stronger than predicted.

  Draw a 500 mile radius on a map to the west, then north, and south. You can anticipate storms flowing thru Canada, to Chicago, and southward to the Carolinas that may funnel thru your area the following day affecting your sailing...AND at anchor overnight. *New England storm lows don't affect Chicago* due to our northern hemisphere prevailing westerlies.

from Sailing Illustrated

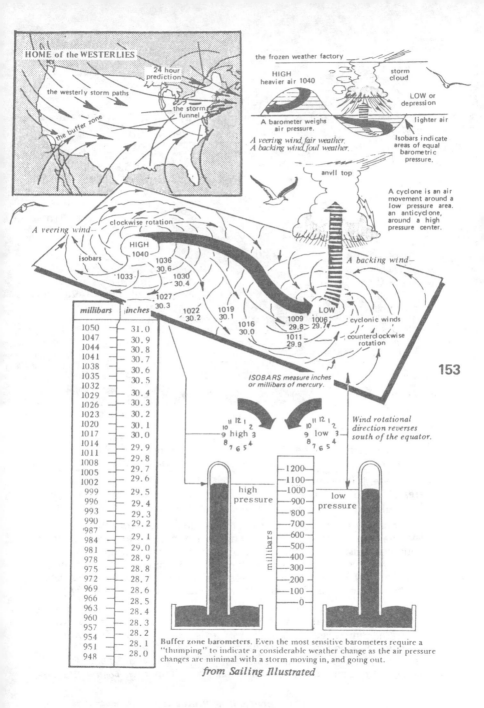

HOME of the WESTERLIES

24 hour prediction

the westerly storm paths

the buffer zone

the storm funnel

the frozen weather factory

HIGH
heavier air 1040

storm cloud

LOW or depression

lighter air

A barometer weighs air pressure.

A veering wind, fair weather.
A backing wind, foul weather.

Isobars indicate areas of equal barometric pressure.

anvil top

A cyclone is an air movement around a low pressure area. an anticyclone, around a high pressure center.

A veering wind—

clockwise rotation

isobars

HIGH
1040

1036
30.6

1033

1030
30.4

1027
30.3

1022
30.2

1019
30.1

1016
30.0

1011
29.9

1009
29.8

1006
29.7

LOW

A backing wind—

cyclonic winds

counterclockwise rotation

millibars	inches
1050	31.0
1047	30.9
1044	30.8
1041	30.7
1038	30.6
1035	30.5
1032	
1029	30.4
1026	30.3
1023	30.2
1020	30.1
1017	30.0
1014	29.9
1011	29.8
1008	29.7
1005	29.6
1002	29.5
999	29.4
996	29.3
993	29.2
990	29.1
987	29.0
984	28.9
981	28.8
978	28.7
975	28.6
972	28.5
969	28.4
966	28.3
963	28.2
960	28.1
957	28.0
954	
951	
948	

ISOBARS measure inches or millibars of mercury.

153

Wind rotational direction reverses south of the equator.

high

low

high pressure

low pressure

1200
1100
1000
900
800
700
600
500
400
300
200
100
0

millibars

Buffer zone barometers. Even the most sensitive barometers require a "thumping" to indicate a considerable weather change as the air pressure changes are minimal with a storm moving in, and going out.

from Sailing Illustrated

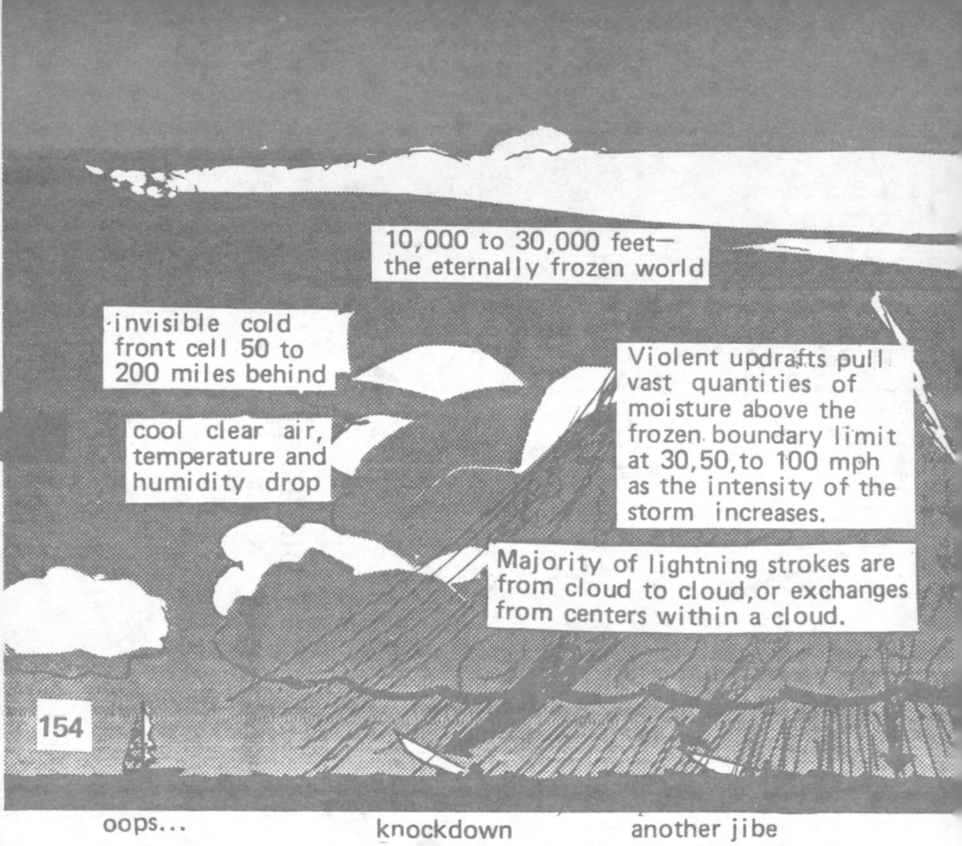

10,000 to 30,000 feet—
the eternally frozen world

·invisible cold
front cell 50 to
200 miles behind

cool clear air,
temperature and
humidity drop

Violent updrafts pull
vast quantities of
moisture above the
frozen boundary limit
at 30,50,to 100 mph
as the intensity of the
storm increases.

Majority of lightning strokes are
from cloud to cloud,or exchanges
from centers within a cloud.

154

oops...   knockdown   another jibe

Highly complex thunderstorm lightning protection is covered on page 63 of our *Homestudy Guide.* Thunderstorms vary from one predicted yearly in our buffer zone, to 90 predicted for the west coast of Florida.

- **Hurricane.** It is a storm with winds force 12 and above, covering a large area of long duration. A thunderstorm may have violent, rapidly changing winds of hurricane strength averaging 20 minutes passing thru your area.

- **Low pressure storm areas** in our westerlies can be seen from the SW, W, to NW quadrants. They may be visible one to five hours before passing thru your area. **Dusters** occur in clear weather in our western and midwestern states which are just as violent, with dust clouds coming from the same direction. **AM radio static** which keeps increasing, *is an excellent inexpensive method to predict, and be ready for a thunderstorm or duster moving in.*

- **Thunderstorms**—a cool updraft is the beginning. The wind momentarily stops and reverses direction with strong downdrafts requiring ALL sails down. When the center passes overhead, it is vertical with downdrafts slowly changing direction. As the thunderstorm moves out, wind direction will make a sudden reverse with a strong updraft. This is your final chance to enjoy a strong accidental jibe if any sails are still up. *Powerboating Illustrated*

from Sailing Illustrated

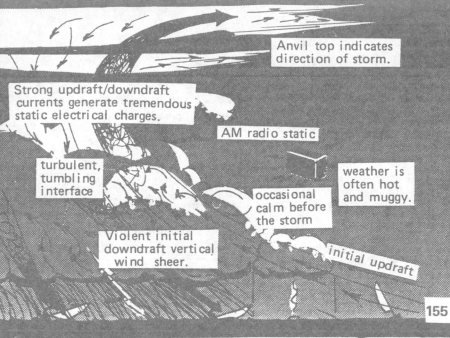

Anvil top indicates direction of storm.

Strong updraft/downdraft currents generate tremendous static electrical charges.

AM radio static

turbulent, tumbling interface

weather is often hot and muggy.

occasional calm before the storm

Violent initial downdraft vertical wind sheer.

initial updraft

155

knockdown   violent jibe | buffer   ⁱ cool updraft

Cable requires a minimum turn angle...avoiding metal objects on sailboat.

- **Permanent lightning protection** is questionable for wooden and fiberglass boats relying on metal bonding systems. Whether the surge goes up or down the mast, *vertical lightning surges require the straightest path which has the least resistance.*

- **Temporary protection.** Use a 1/16" thick sheet of copper a square foot or larger as a grounding plate. Use a copper grounding strap bolted temporarily to the mast...an aluminum strap will have 2/3 as much conductivity.

- **Sudden 25,000 degree heat** requires bolt on or crimp-on fittings as solder and insulation are instantly incinerated. Fore and aft insulated tiedowns will keep the grounding plate fully submerged in erratic wave action, as the strap must be isolated from aluminum fittings to avoid lightning flashovers.

- **Stainless has 1/50th the conductivity of copper.** An 18-8 stainless ground strap secured to stays or shrouds may cause unnecessary flashovers.

from Sailing Illustrated

A downward lightning strike releases an electronic surge thru your boat that can go skyward...or in a reverse direction,

Is your hair standing up? Charges building up in the water go skyward...colliding with a downward lightning strike.

When lightning is visible and you hear the thunder 10 seconds later, it can hit your area in two minutes traveling 5 miles in 5 seconds.

Lightning continually hits the Empire State building, surging around occupants protected inside, while flowing to ground.

The steel auto shell provides lightning protection. When lightning hits the frame, current surges around occupants, flowing thru tires to ground as *carbon black, a conductor* is added to tire during manufacture. Don't touch metal window and door handles, and the steering wheel becomes a conductor. **Convertibles and fiberglass bodies** don't afford protection.

Lightning rod. Sailboat with a wooden mast has a sharp metallic tip 6" above masthead equipment. It connects to a 6 to 8 gage copper wire coming down mast in a straight line without turns or twists, grounded to keel. Wire can't have insulation, solder, or crimp-on fittings which in the 25,000 degree heat would be incinerated. Later research to protect ammunition storage areas found the blunt metallic tip pointing skyward could have twice the conductivity as one with a sharp point.

Lightning should surge up or down the straight path at left as efficiently as possible, unhook bonding, page 363.

Many sailboats hit have considerable lightning damage as current makes a sharp turn thru cabin and engine to exit out prop. Side flashes wipe out electronice equipment Due to wave action, passengers may accidentally hit metal parts with burns of varying degrees.

Lighting flow direction? A few years ago researchers found many more surges go skyward than suspected... traveling 300 times faster skyward. If you are in the water or on a catamaran trampoline and your hair stands up... head for the shore for protection of the steel auto shell.

Examine lightning current surges on sailboats above. Wooden sailboats thru the centuries often had lightning damage. Damage was eliminated with steel hulls, metal masts and rigging as conductors for the surges.

BEWARE— *open metal powerboats.* Panama City, Florida, 8/29/91; the powerboat was underway in a thunderstorm with heavy rain, thunder, and lightning. The metal boat was a lone opportunistic target to pull in lightning injuring two, and killing the other two occupants.

We provide considerable lightning coverage in our *Homestudy Guide* for grounding protection with cabin sailboats on the ocean.

Have you ever been hit by lightning... the author was hit twice. The first time I was one of three boys in a rainstorm running to a house for protection. All we remember was being surrounded by a bright light, no sound. We were mentally frozen in motion.

The second time on a mountain in a light drizzle, I was walking towards a huge oak tree for protection (?) 200′ away when surrounded by a bright white light, no sound. I awoke 15 to 20 minutes later soaked, cold and shivering violently, staring at the smoldering tree stump. It is fair game for critics to blame my misguided ideas being hit by lightning.

Direct impact. A boat on a bay, lake, or open ocean, and/or a person with a metal object in his hand, will produce the most severe lightning injuries. **Splash** occurs when lightning hits a large metal object, then jumps to a nearby person, is another common lightning injury.

Eye damage may occur to some degree to half the lightning victims. *Skin burns* by lightning are surface burns due to the short duration... in comparison to *alternating current burns* that may go deep into muscle tissue.

Ear damage— *lightning hits a telephone line, 3/20/91.* The explosion/ expansion shock waves were so violent it ruptured his ear drum, knocking victim on the phone across the room. *Hang up when lightning moves in.* 157

Water sports are involved in many lightning injuries. Some areas where they seem most common begin with New Mexico, Arkansas, Colorado, Delaware, Connecticut, etc., but may occur anywhere.

May thru September in snowbelt areas are the months of greatest risk as local thunderstorms move thru in warm weather with a short 15 to 20 minute duration. **Thunderstorms can be predicted** one to several hours ahead with increasing static on a (cheap!) *inexpensive AM portable radio.*

Ground current is a major cause of multiple strikes especially for swimmers, water skiiers, SCUBA divers in the water... the closer the strike, the greater will be the damage with current surging thru the victims body. Immediately leave the water while a thunderstorm moves in before lightning hits your area... and don't seek protection under a tree as I did.

Treatment is immediately required **for victims APPEARING dead.** Cardiopulmonary resuscitation is needed to get oxygen rapidly to the heart and brain, often with a success rate up to 50%.

Most lightning strikes hit more than one person! Begin with apparently dead victims, delaying treatment to moving, moaning victims. Call the closest physicians as victims may have unpredictable, multisystem injuries, a major challenge to physicians for short to long range complications.

early ketch

Thomas W. Lawson

Pride of Baltimore

America

European sailors joining us for an afternoon sail continually photograph schooners, the first they've seen. Why is it a unique American design?

Land and sea breezes develop in the absence of other patterns. When land temperature is greater than the nearby ocean, sea breezes flow onshore from noon to dusk, then disappear as the temperatures are equalized. The land temperature becomes cooler than the ocean after midnight when a flow of air begins seaward, lasting to early morning when temperatures are again equalized. *Square rigged vessels had stronger, more stable winds on the west coast where prevailing westerlies combined with the coastal sea breezes.*

- **Westerly facing European coasts** have strong westerlies combining with sea breezes permitting normal square rigger operation close to shore. A parallel situation provided efficient square rigger operation on our west coast, except it is rocky and hostile with few natural harbors.

- **Our east coast** with weak shifting westerlies opposing incoming sea breezes, proved discouraging for early square rigger operation close to shore. Land breezes seldom go more than a mile offshore on our west coast, join on the east coast with the westerlies providing better sailing after midnight.

- **1700 east coast commerce.** Schooners began taking trade from square riggers with smaller crews, better maneuverability, and less time from port to port. Our only successful craft to equal the English in the Revolutionary War was a handful of privateer topsail schooners. Read *Baltimore Clippers* * by Howard Chapelle, an excellent history of its evolution from pirates and slavers to the Baltimore clippers, influencing pilot schooners such as *America,* to the fishing and racing Glousterman schooners.Schooners captured by the British had their rigs cut down being "overhatted" for European waters.

- **West coast commerce.** Prevailing westerlies greatly increase the sea breeze flowing thru the San Francisco Bay and Sacramento Slough wind funnel spawning large fleets of lumber schooners and barkentines after 1850.

East coast boatbuilders lured by our gold rush, found the real gold in endless western forests. They built tiny maneuverable schooners to pick up lumber in small dog holes along rocky coasts. Lumber was transferred to large bark-entines and schooners. The largest schooner was the 1,443 ton five masted *Crescent* launched 1904, abandoned at sea in 1918 after catching fire.

- **Wind funnels.** One coming up the Colorado River canyon is further squeezed as it rises up and over Hoover Dam into Lake Mead. Another funnel coming down a long converging canyon combines with it,tripling the overall speed of an undisturbed wind flow. These violent random winds are predictable by studying large area *USGS Topographic Maps* affecting mountain and canyon lakes and reservoirs. *from Sailing Illustrated*

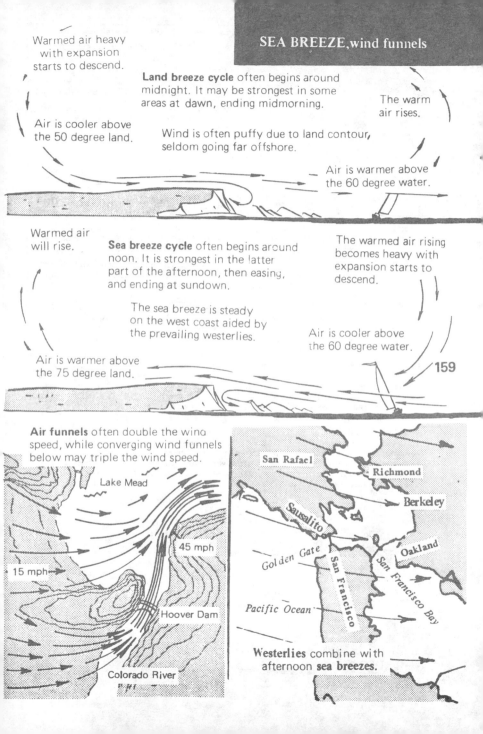

SEA BREEZE, wind funnels

Warmed air heavy with expansion starts to descend.

Land breeze cycle often begins around midnight. It may be strongest in some areas at dawn, ending midmorning.

The warm air rises.

Air is cooler above the 50 degree land.

Wind is often puffy due to land contour, seldom going far offshore.

Air is warmer above the 60 degree water.

Warmed air will rise.

Sea breeze cycle often begins around noon. It is strongest in the latter part of the afternoon, then easing, and ending at sundown.

The warmed air rising becomes heavy with expansion starts to descend.

The sea breeze is steady on the west coast aided by the prevailing westerlies.

Air is cooler above the 60 degree water.

Air is warmer above the 75 degree land.

159

Air funnels often double the wind speed, while converging wind funnels below may triple the wind speed.

Lake Mead

45 mph

15 mph

Hoover Dam

Colorado River

San Rafael

Richmond

Berkeley

Sausalito

Oakland

Golden Gate

San Francisco

San Francisco Bay

Pacific Ocean

Westerlies combine with afternoon **sea breezes**.

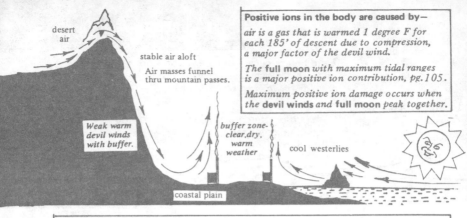

desert air

stable air aloft

Air masses funnel
thru mountain passes.

Positive ions in the body are caused by—

*air is a gas that is warmed 1 degree F for
each 185' of descent due to compression,
a major factor of the devil wind.*

*The full moon with maximum tidal ranges
is a major positive ion contribution, pg.105.*

*Maximum positive ion damage occurs when
the devil winds and full moon peak together.*

*Weak warm
devil winds
with buffer.*

buffer zone-
clear,dry,
warm
weather

cool westerlies

coastal plain

The least understood weather pattern found worldwide under a variety of names is
called *Santa Ana* by our weather bureau and TV weather forecasters.

A better descriptive term was needed for worldwide recognition. We began with the
term used by indians in the LA basin surrounded by high mountains.Their *santanta*
was shortened to *santana* for *devil wind*. After 30 years research feeling its wrath on
the land and ocean...we could find no better term than *devil wind*.

- **Warm devil winds** occur during spring, summer, and early fall with a high pressure area
  on the high Nevada plateau to the east, and a lower pressure on the ocean. The weak
  devil winds flow down the passes to be stopped by the cool incoming westerlies...with
  a warm, no wind buffer area between the opposing forces.

160 - **Cold devil winds** can become strong and vicious after Thanksgiving in our area as the
  storm tracks move south. While the winds may be weak on the high plateau, they gain
  speed as after going thru the passes they tumble down the slopes. This compresses
  and warms the air 20 to 30 degrees...while reducing the humidity. The *relative humidity
  averages 30%* as the cold devil winds move in...while the relative humidity in the warm
  devil wind buffer zone often registers *10 to 0 % relative humidity*.

- **Positive ion body charge** is developed as the devil winds move in. It blocks the analytical
  ability of the mind for 6 to 12 hours until the mind recovers its normal functions
  though the mind may produce normal mechanical operations. During this period you
  should avoid critical decisions. It is a time when auto collisions escalate,friendly arguments
  turn into dumb fights...and riots suddenly balloon out of control. Switzerland has well
  documented the escalating number of suicides as the devil winds move in.

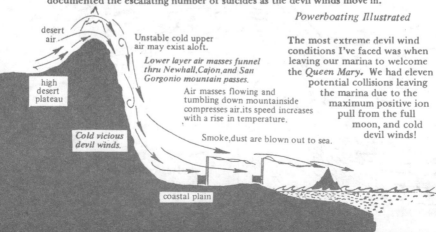

Powerboating Illustrated

desert
air

Unstable cold upper
air may exist aloft.

*Lower layer air masses funnel
thru Newhall,Cajon,and San
Gorgonio mountain passes.*

Air masses flowing and
tumbling down mountainside
compresses air.its speed increases
with a rise in temperature.

Smoke,dust are blown out to sea.

high
desert
plateau

*Cold vicious
devil winds.*

The most extreme devil wind
conditions I've faced was when
leaving our marina to welcome
the *Queen Mary.* We had eleven
potential collisions leaving
the marina due to the
maximum positive ion
pull from the full
moon, and cold
devil winds!

coastal plain

Nine drownings in 1973 in high mountain lakes, cause unknown.
One of the men involved said," My partner and I have been fishing
together for probably twelve years, and we have never seen anything
like this happen. We were fishing at one end of the lake. A violent wind
blew half of the water out of this end of the lake, lasting for around a
half hour. It upset our boat and my partner drowned".

Similar experiences listed strange, unpredictable, violent winds in other
reports which our California boating department related to me hoping for
an answer. As we explored the reports with phone calls to the officers
involved, patterns appeared. All were on high-altitude lakes *with a steep
hill on one side.* As man extends his boating horizons, he must expect
new and different experiences. Meet the **Clear Air Turbulence—** *CAT.*

Air like the ocean around us, is always on the move. High flying jets
occasionally hit a CAT without flow patterns. They drop out of control
until again reaching stable air.

Light, low-flying aircraft are very vulnerable to the CAT in mountain areas
when ground air speed exceeds 35 knots. They must gain altitude to avoid
this disturbance... which was my first clue.

That steep hill next to the high-altitude lake. This ground turbulence also
raises havoc with boating. A strong wind coming up the side of a mountain
changes too rapidly going down the other side , turns into a series of whirl- **161**
pools. The confused, tumbling air masses need time to pull together again
into a steady column of air part way down the hill... *or the confused, chaotic
tumbling air masses* may come all the way down to hit a high-altitude lake.

Strong confused, tumbling downdrafts, also common in thunderstorms
responsible for starting cyclone twisters, are comparable to few things in
nature. The CAT winds are severe and confused, hitting the lake at a variety
of angles *with wave patterns completely out of pattern.*

A thin, small, hovering wind cloud is natures warning. *If it hovers on the
lake side of the mountain continuously, get off the water immediately!*

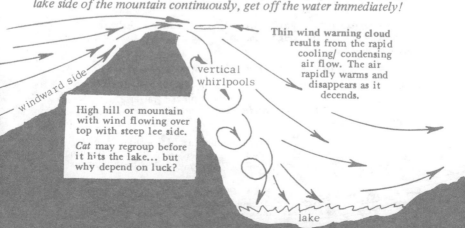

windward side

vertical
whirlpools

Thin wind warning cloud
results from the rapid
cooling/ condensing
air flow. The air
rapidly warms and
disappears as it
decends.

High hill or mountain
with wind flowing over
top with steep lee side.

Cat may regroup before
it hits the lake... but
why depend on luck?

lake

Powerboating Illustrated

● Auto,van,or truck towing vehicle terms—

Curb weight—is the weight of the towing vehicle with a full fuel tank ...yet without passengers or other payload aboard.

GAW is the *gross axle weight,* the load an axle is capable of supporting ...plus the unsprung weight of the axle itself and its components that include the tires,wheels,and brakes.

The *GAW rating should never be exceeded* which is usually equivalent to the combined left and right spring capacities at the ground.

GVW is the *gross vehicle weight* or overall weight of the fully loaded towing vehicle which includes passengers and payload.The *maximum GVW* of a truck *should never be exceeded.*

The *half ton truck* has a normal payload capacity of 1000 pounds. The term in everyday use is often applied to any short wheel base pickup or van regardless of the actual payload.

The *three-quarter ton truck* has a nominal payload capacity of 1500 pounds. The term in everyday use is often applied to any *long wheel base* pickup or van regardless of the actual payload.

The *payload* is the amount of weight a vehicle can carry safely which includes passengers and cargo. Payload *is the difference between its curb weight...and its maximum GVW rating.*

162

UNSPRUNG WEIGHT is the *weight of components including axles, brakes, wheels, and tires* not supported by the springs.

SPRING CAPACITY is *the load an individual spring is capable of supporting.* Spring capacity *at the ground* is the load a spring can support,plus all adjacent unsprung weight.

Spring capacity *at the pad* is the load a spring can support in this position on the axle.

● The boat and trailer weight terms—

GTW is the *gross trailer weight* of the boat,the trailer,and the load. This will determine the weight class of of the hitch the towing vehicle should install.

● Boat,trailer,and towing vehicle weight terms-

GCW is the *gross combination weight,* which is the combined weights of a fully loaded tow vehicle,AND the boat on the trailer.The GCW is the *sum total of the gross vehicle weight...and the gross trailer weight including the boat.*

Front bumper hitch? Consider one for launching and recovery in a tight winding ramp during daytime, and to launch and recovery after dark.

It also prevents submerging auto exhaust.

Always use a tire stop under the auto tires with a rope puller for removal easy to install and recover.

A hull is supported dockside in the water by an even pressure over the entire wetted bottom surface.

boat trailers

The portable dry dock is often the boat's home for more than 80% of its life.

The trailer is the boat's home away from the water. A trailerboat owner should understand what type of support should be used, and how best it may be utilized since the weight of your hull will be concentrated in a few areas. Even the best trailer can't provide the overall support found in the water, but the trailer has an advanatge ...the boat can't collect barnacles.

163

WEDGE ACTION coupler

lock

CAM LOCK coupler

Safety chain should prevent this from happening.

The safety chain during a coupling failure, should be able to prevent the trailer tongue from jumping off the ball and hitting the pavement.

The trailer chain should have no more slack than is needed for proper turning.

double chain

single chain

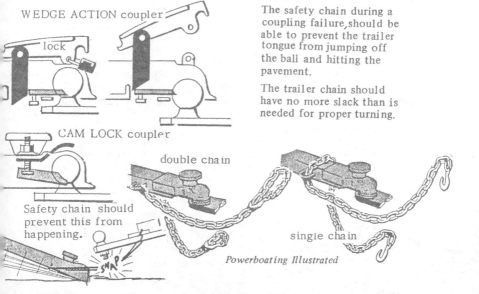

Powerboating Illustrated

> Make the trailer CHEAP AS POSSIBLE-----I've already spent a lot more than I had ever planned on!!!!!!!!!!!!!!!!

More outboard planing hulls are damaged by flimsy trailers than by any other method.

The price of trailers can be compromised by reducing the quality of the steel which increases the flexing of structural members; cheaper,smaller rollers may be used for support;and the parking wheel can be eliminated making the trailer and boat clumsy to handle on the ramp,and in the backyard.

The first requirement– all trailers must be able to support and carry their load of a given length and weight within reasonable limits.

The second requirement– is ease of handling with the boat on its trailer for loading,launching,trailering,and for storage.

The third requirement– is flexibility of use.Can it be adapted to carry furniture,lumber,etc.,when not carrying the boat?

- *Two wheel trailers* with minimum engineering are clumsy to handle for outboard boats 14' and larger,due to excess tongue weight that produces hernias and back problems.

- *A parking wheel or parking jack* eliminates the need for lifting and carrying the trailer tongue weight when moving the boat on its trailer at the launching ramp,in the backyard,garage,or storage area.

- *Tilt-bed trailers with parking wheels* are easy to handle if adjusted to your boat and well engineered,with the need for this trailer rapidly increasing for larger size hulls.

The tilt bed trailer eliminates the tug-of-war pushing and pulling of inefficient trailers when launching and loading.If the bow is raised sufficiently,the inertia takes over and the boat is able to roll or slide into the water.Planing hull recovery will be easy when using an electric winch or hand winch IF it has an ample gear ratio.

How efficient is the lock on the winch...and will the rapidly moving winch handle,especially with an ample gear ratio,become dangerous as it spins around when the boat is being launched?

- *Tongue weight–*periodically causes controversy as large,light, slab-sided house trailers require 10% to 15% tongue weight,especially when hit by strong side winds.The driver must keep moving since if he stops,the wind pressure may upset the house trailer.The trailerable boat has a much lower profile with considerably more weight.As the wind pressure is considerably reduced in an identical situation, 5% to 7% tongue weight is ample to serve the purpose.

- *Many boats and cars are submerged yearly* at launching ramps..which can be avoided using a tire stop with a rope puller.

Powerboating Illustrated

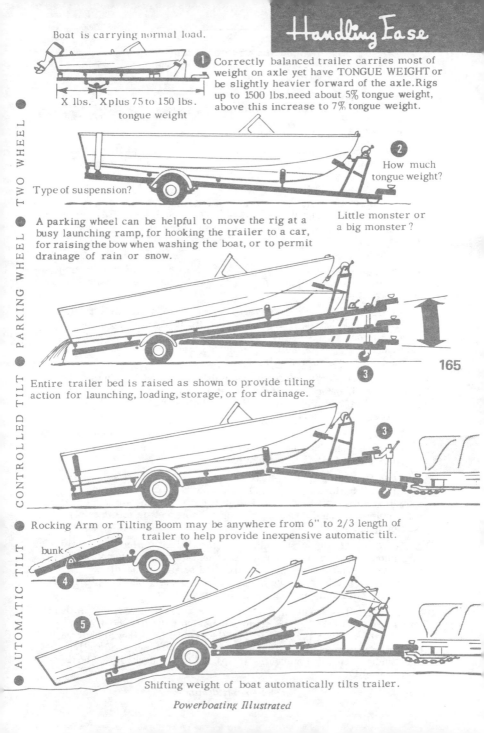

TWO WHEEL • PARKING WHEEL • CONTROLLED TILT • AUTOMATIC TILT

Boat is carrying normal load.

X lbs. X plus 75 to 150 lbs.
tongue weight

1 Correctly balanced trailer carries most of weight on axle yet have TONGUE WEIGHT or be slightly heavier forward of the axle. Rigs up to 1500 lbs. need about 5% tongue weight, above this increase to 7% tongue weight.

Type of suspension?

2 How much tongue weight?

Little monster or a big monster?

A parking wheel can be helpful to move the rig at a busy launching ramp, for hooking the trailer to a car, for raising the bow when washing the boat, or to permit drainage of rain or snow.

3

165

Entire trailer bed is raised as shown to provide tilting action for launching, loading, storage, or for drainage.

3

Rocking Arm or Tilting Boom may be anywhere from 6" to 2/3 length of trailer to help provide inexpensive automatic tilt.

bunk

4

5

Shifting weight of boat automatically tilts trailer.

> With such a variety of trailers to choose from, what are the first things to be considered?

Consider the following trailer functions--

- *Dry dock*--the trailer cradle must provide sufficient support to protect the hull without flexing when work has to be done inside a boat. The trailer wheels should be large enough so the boat is high enough to permit easy access to the bottom surface for scraping and painting.

- *Bottom support*--the trailer must give maximum, safe, and nonflexing support to the keel and transom to protect the planing platform. If the trailer doesn't provide sufficient bottom support, a hook can develop on the planing platform, see pg. 58, which in extreme cases can break the keel.

- *Trailering safety*--the boat cradle must be well braced with minimum flexing to be able to support several hundred pounds more than it will normally carry.

  The trailer must be able to support and carry your boat safely at highway speeds as well as having sufficient rigidity to take a limited amount of bouncing on rough roads without flexing which could damage the hull. The *hitch*, pg. 163, must be strong and well engineered so it won't uncouple or fail when trailering.

166

- *Launching and loading platform*--should be measured by whether the boat will be launched into the water at a ramp from its trailer...will it be lifted off the trailer using slings or hooks, pg. 180 or will the boat use two, or all three methods?

  There are countless kinds of boat trailers. Some trailers, even designed for the same boat, may have minor to major differences. Let us try to separate boat trailers into three basic groups—

- *Minimum trailering*--it is basically a dry dock for winter storage and painting the bottom of the boat. This type of trailer is common in snow-belt areas averaging under 100 miles yearly. Some are home made, clumsy to handle, have minimum support, and trailering safety may be questionable.

- *Short haul*--it is the most common, average priced trailer that provides minimum support and minimum trailering safety. *If the owner realizes the trailer limitations* he may obtain good service by handling it gently, never overloading the boat...and continually checking to see if his boat is efficiently resting on all rollers or pads.

- *Long haul* trailers are usually found in the sun-belt areas from Southern California to Texas. They are seldom bought for the first boat. After active owners realize the need to pay the extra price...it will increase the trailerboating fun with a boat that is easy to launch, load, trailer, and handle at crowded launching ramps, and in the backyard or boat storage facility.

The first trailer is often bought as an afterthought, then neglected and/or misused. Check used trailers thoroughly.

How much support will dry dock provide; with how much portability?

DRY DOCK ONLY

How much tongue weight?

How often is tire pressure checked?

Trailer above is temporary drydock providing questionable support. COVER provides partial protection against rain and snow, yet hull is level permitting water to collect instead of draining if bow were raised and drain plugs pulled. Homemade trailer is TOO SHORT requiring additional support.

Cover isn't needed on second rig as it is stored in garage except on weekends. Were small tires designed for trailering or low speed industrial and farm use? Where is spare tire ... would you drive a car without a spare tire?

SHORT HAUL

Is boat overloaded?

Equipment can fall out of boat.

Avoid removable hitch.

trailer lights?

167

motor tilted   failure at highway speeds?

Trailer has sufficient minimum support ... if boat isn't loaded. Handling ease at launching ramp depends on use of rollers or pads and tongue weight. Motor should be carried in RAISED POSITION, never on side or in down position.

Owner has quality trailer that permits maximum HULL SUPPORT with maximum PORTABILITY EASE for launching, loading, trailering and storage. Tires are same size as car eliminating need for extra trailer tire. Running light on boat is retractable to prevent whipping action. Trailer lights are of good quality with stop and turn indicators; much reflector tape and extra reflectors are used. Owner carries spare bearings and periodically checks for bearing heat buildup. Cover was tailor made just for boat and has good ventilation.

LONG HAUL

stern running light   Where is spare tire; is it same as auto tire?

Is dust cover fire resistant?

guide bracket

double bow tiedowns

parking wheel

motor support   tilt trailer   reflector tape

corrosion resistant metals?

Trailer has DOUBLE LASHINGS in case one set should fail, and HITCH was designed for and installed by people with trailer experience. Owner constantly checks roller/pad adjustments so boat has maximum use of available support.

 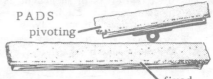

ROLLERS	PADS
MINIMUM support	MAXIMUM support
Most efficient for loading and launching because of minimum friction.	Most troublesome for loading and launching because of too much friction.

CORRECT
transom support

INCORRECT
transom support

HOOK

Transom support rollers must carry full motor weight, as well as battery, and stern fuel tanks. If transom is carried aft of roller a damaging hook or flexing will begin. Always carry the transom rollers as close to the transom chine as is practical for maximum roller support.

CORRECT tiedown   INCORRECT tiedown

resting on ALL rollers   resting on PART of rollers

The rollers were correctly adjusted for the boat at right but it was incorrectly mounted on the trailer. A broken keel and hook will result in a short space of time.

BEWARE of a SHORT TRAILER!!!
Watch trailer closely in package deals as they may have less than minimum req. support. A cheap trailer can soon become expensive.

● ROLLERS are preferred if----

      trailer is correct length
      trailer has enough good hard rubber rollers
      hull is correctly resting on ALL support rollers
      most launching will be done from the trailer
      boat is never overloaded when it is out of water

● PADS are preferred if----

      boat is always launched with slings or hooks
      used for light racing hulls launched manually

Powerboating Illustrated

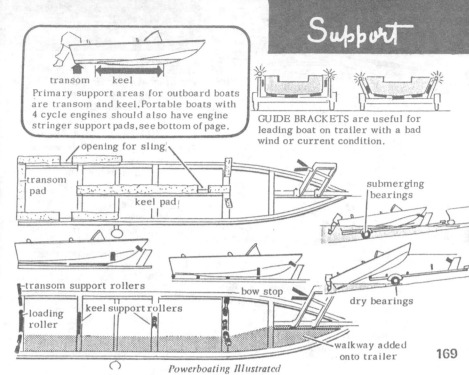

transom   keel

Primary support areas for outboard boats are transom and keel. Portable boats with 4 cycle engines should also have engine stringer support pads, see bottom of page.

GUIDE BRACKETS are useful for leading boat on trailer with a bad wind or current condition.

opening for sling

transom pad

keel pad

submerging bearings

transom support rollers

bow stop

dry bearings

loading roller

keel support rollers

walkway added onto trailer

169

Powerboating Illustrated

PADS-upper trailer uses pads for maximum support in planing areas, keel and bow. Full length TRANSOM PAD which must support maximum weight of all pads with outboard boats is sometimes overlooked though side chines have full length support. It is next to impossible to launch or load boat without submerging wheel bearings as boat is floated off or back onto trailer.

ROLLERS-provide ease in loading and launching of correctly designed boat not requiring submerged hubs. Even best rollers only give knife edge minimum support so owners must be alert to get maximum support from rollers by—
    1. Hull must be resting on ALL support rollers.
    2. Eliminate UNNECESSARY WEIGHT when trailering or in storage.
    3. Hull must ride correctly on rollers especially at TRANSOM CHINE.

COMBINATION PADS and ROLLERS are used on deep V trailer designed for jet boat. Though transom chine is still critical, it isn't nearly as critical as outboard boat with most weight on transom. Walkway on either side is very commendable especially for launching or loading on a 'submarine trailer'.

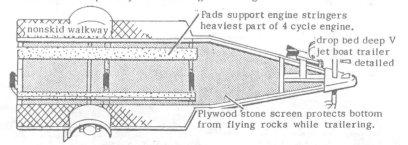

nonskid walkway

Pads support engine stringers heaviest part of 4 cycle engine.

drop bed deep V jet boat trailer detailed

Plywood stone screen protects bottom from flying rocks while trailering.

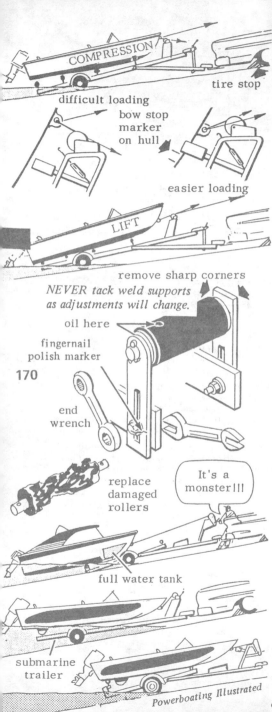

COMPRESSION

tire stop

difficult loading

bow stop
marker
on hull

easier loading

LIFT

remove sharp corners

*NEVER tack weld supports
as adjustments will change.*

oil here

fingernail
polish marker

170

end
wrench

replace
damaged
rollers

It's a
monster!!!

full water tank

submarine
trailer

If the boat *bow eye is higher
than the winch pull*, a downward compression begins
with the boat and trailer
fighting each other...it is
like trying to pull in a whale.

If the boat *bow eye is lower
than the winch pull*, the lift
leverage helps to pull the
boat much easier onto the
trailer.

•

*Are ALL the rollers turning
easy?* It is easier to pull a
boat across moving rollers
with minimum friction...than
to slide across stuck rollers.

All rollers must have EQUAL
bottom contact support. Check
all roller adjustments continually so the hull will have
MAXIMUM bottom support.

•

An owner loudly complained
his new boat was difficult
to pull back onto the trailer.

Checking found a 30 gallon
water tank the owner had
installed in the bow which
when full added 250 pounds,
the cause of his trouble.

•

Boats with skegs such as our
Blunder, may require submarine trailers as they may
have to be floated off from,
then back onto the trailer.

•

*What may happen to your boat
if your auto has to suddenly
hit the brakes?*

Our 12' *Thumper* below had
the bad habit of riding forward
off the stern rollers, wanting to
climb over the bow stop.

our 12' G 3 *Thumper*

Tiedowns

POP!

CRACK!

stainless
steel eye
AVOID
brass
eye

secondary
tiedown

primary
tiedown

winch with
large gear
ratio

Paint marker so you
can tell if adjustable
bow stop moves.

guide bracket
roller

stainless steel eye
with wood backing

Turnbuckle method
detailed is often
questioned.

Many trailer manufacturers feel that
spring action or nylon tiedowns are
preferred to ease warping, twisting
action of even the most rigid trailer
frame on bumpy roads.

Flexible tiedowns can squeeze boat
instead of holding it in place; the short
trailer is crushing the planing surface

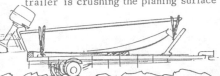

*Boat tiedown failure in traffic
will be hazardous.*

Primary bow tiedown should have
metal to metal contact, with the
winch cable as a *secondary* tiedown.

*IF failure occurs when the winch
cable is the primary tiedown,* wind
pressure on the trailered boat will
compress, bind, and stretch the cable
on the drum. The cable may fail or
the winch handle accidentally release.

Stern tiedown on a good frame will
permit the boat to be lashed down
snugly with the trailer springs
taking the road bumps. These tiedowns
must restrain back and forth, up and
down movement of boat on trailer.

Polyethelene rope, a floater, is easy
to use for dinghies. *Steel cable* with
a smaller winch drum is used on
larger boats. The steel cable should
be *a little longer than the boat.*

171

When trying to use 100' of metal
cable on our trailer winch, it caused
tremendous compression on its own
strands...also AVOID KINKS which
will shear metal strands.

The greater the WINCH RATIO, the
greater will be the pulling power...
IF it is periodically lubricated. The
electric winch is preferred for larger
and heavier boats.

The flimsy trailer is a torture rack.

It doesn't take long to recognize a
planing hull that has been bouncing
on a rough road on a flimsy and/or
short trailer as the flexing movement
of the trailer is applied to the boat.

At lower left is a light boat with a
short haul trailer for smooth roads.
The tiedowns were eased on a bumpy
road so most flexing is on the trailer,
not the boat. If eased too much, the
hull will be bouncing up and down,
back and forth on its rollers or pads.

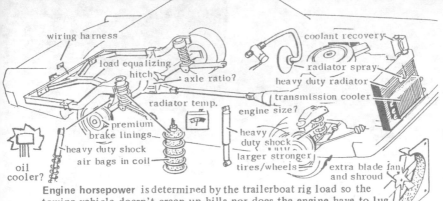

wiring harness
load equalizing hitch
axle ratio?
radiator temp.
premium brake linings
heavy duty shock
air bags in coil
oil cooler?

coolant recovery
radiator spray
heavy duty radiator
transmission cooler
engine size?
heavy duty shock
larger stronger tires/wheels
extra blade fan and shroud

Engine horsepower is determined by the trailerboat rig load so the towing vehicle doesn't creep up hills,nor does the engine have to lug at full throttle to maintain highway speeds.The average passenger car is designed just to carry people,and if it pulls more than the lightest trailerboat rigs,it needs beefing up. 150 hp provides minimum towing power,with 240 hp to be considered for mid size trailerboat rigs. Larger engines must be considered for towing mountain grades,pg 278 with at 7000 feet altitude,a 20% hp loss may be considered.

Engine cooling requires a heavy duty,high capacity radiator with *more core tubes to speed heat release*. When radiator temperature becomes critical a special fan shroud,a coolant recovery unit,and a thermostat operated unit is needed to spray cool water on the radiator core tubes.With the down sizing of autos and engines,is it time to consider oil cooling units for big rigs,for towing vehicles?

172

The transmission works harder requiring its own radiator for air to cool the hydraulic fluid.Otherwise as the heat buildup increases,the hydraulic fluid will thin down to reduce transmission efficiency.

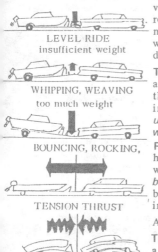

LEVEL RIDE
insufficient weight

WHIPPING, WEAVING
too much weight

BOUNCING, ROCKING,

TENSION THRUST

COMPRESSION THRUST

Standard auto brakes are designed for the towing vehicle only,plus a very light trailer...with replacement requiring heavy-duty linings for most autos or vans.*When new autos are ordered* with towing options,it may indicate oversize drums and/or heavy duty brake linings.

Tongue weight compensation may be needed as 100 pounds of tongue weight four feet from the rear axle...is the same as adding 400 pounds in the rear trunk.*Suspension has to be beefed up to avoid rear end sagging,or bottoming out when hitting bumps.*

Rear wheels require air bags in coil springs with heavy duty shocks...so the car or van rides level without the rear end sagging *which reduces braking,steering controls,*and at night the low-beam headlights angle will be higher,shining into the eyes of oncoming drivers.

A better rear axle gear ratio may be required.

Tires for all but minimum weight rigs may need a heavier load carrying capacity...and sometimes, stronger **tire rims**.

Trailer wiring detailed is for easy
removal ... use minimum wingnuts.

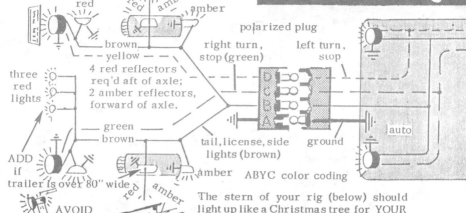

red
red amber amber

polarized plug

brown
– – yellow – –

right turn,
stop (green)

left turn,
stop

three
red
lights

4 red reflectors
req'd aft of axle;
2 amber reflectors,
forward of axle.

D
C
B
A

auto

green
brown

ADD
if
trailer is over 80" wide

tail, license, side
lights (brown)

ground

red amber

AVOID

amber

red amber

amber

ABYC color coding

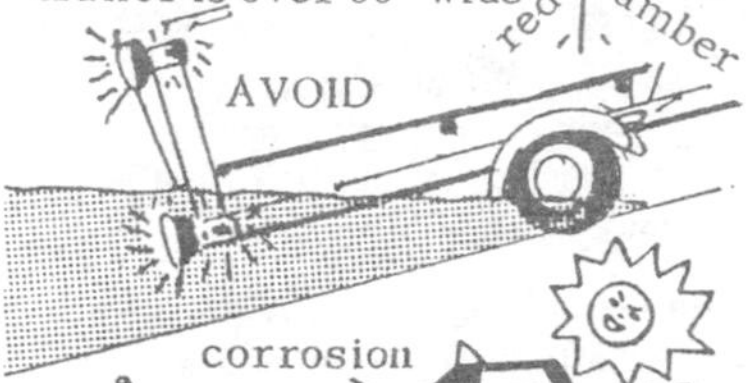

corrosion

The stern of your rig (below) should
light up like a Christmas tree for YOUR
self protection. Add extra reflector
tape and reflectors, especially for black
trailers which don't show corrosion as
rapidly as white trailers.

store
in,
garage

All trailer wiring should be stranded for
better flexibility, chafe resistance, less
vibration breakage. No single conductor
wire should be smaller than #16 AWG

173

(American Wire Gage); multi-conductor cable circuits, #18 AWG.
Secure exposed wiring at intervals 18" or less to reduce its
rubbing, chafing, and sideways movement.

Trailer lights corrode rapidly in salt water areas reducing
conductivity. The trailer ground is especially susceptible, the
reason we prefer a double wire system instead, eliminating
the trailer as a ground. If practical, have trailer lights removed
for launching/loading/storage so trailer lights will be bright
and reliable when needed. Avoid having trailer/auto plug fall
into water while launching especially when still connected. If
pulse is slow or turn signals don't flash, replace standard auto
flasher with heavy duty type such as #550. Carry extra fuses
and bulbs for use with your rig, also to help other trailerboaters.

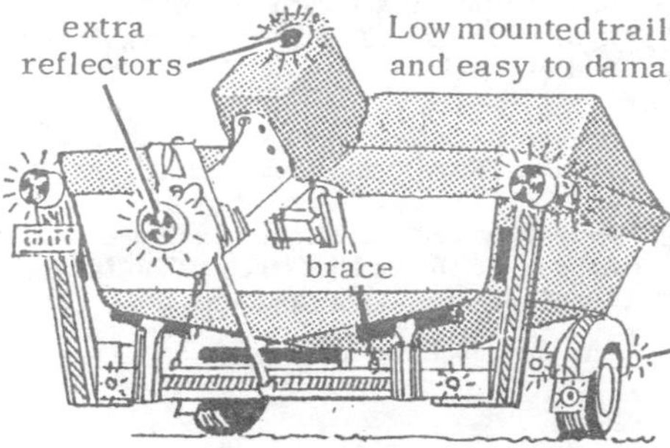

extra
reflectors

Low mounted trailer lights are usually unprotected
and easy to damage when parking. If state spec's*
permit, mount tail, license
lights higher (to 5' in Calif.),
and clearance lights just
inside fender edge to reduce
chance of breakage when
parking or when in storage.

brace

clearance light

Powerboating Illustrated

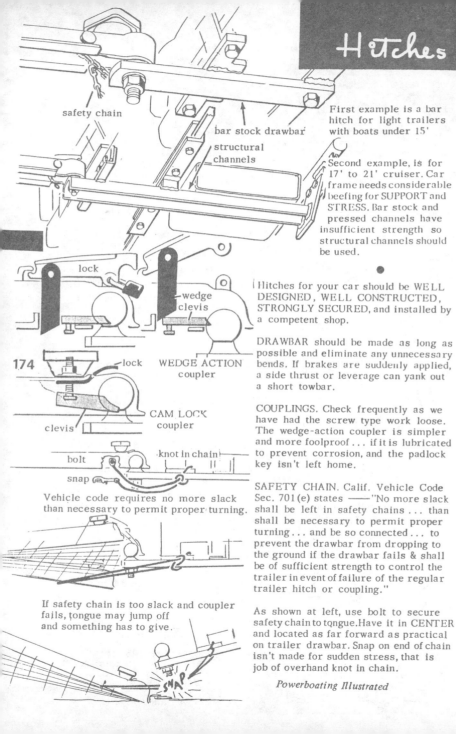

safety chain

bar stock drawbar

structural channels

lock

wedge clevis

174   lock   WEDGE ACTION coupler

CAM LOCK coupler

clevis

bolt   knot in chain

snap

Vehicle code requires no more slack than necessary to permit proper turning.

If safety chain is too slack and coupler fails, tongue may jump off and something has to give.

SNAP

First example is a bar hitch for light trailers with boats under 15'

Second example, is for 17' to 21' cruiser. Car frame needs considerable beefing for SUPPORT and STRESS. Bar stock and pressed channels have insufficient strength so structural channels should be used.

Hitches for your car should be WELL DESIGNED, WELL CONSTRUCTED, STRONGLY SECURED, and installed by a competent shop.

DRAWBAR should be made as long as possible and eliminate any unnecessary bends. If brakes are suddenly applied, a side thrust or leverage can yank out a short towbar.

COUPLINGS. Check frequently as we have had the screw type work loose. The wedge-action coupler is simpler and more foolproof ... if it is lubricated to prevent corrosion, and the padlock key isn't left home.

SAFETY CHAIN. Calif. Vehicle Code Sec. 701(e) states ——"No more slack shall be left in safety chains ... than shall be necessary to permit proper turning... and be so connected ... to prevent the drawbar from dropping to the ground if the drawbar fails & shall be of sufficient strength to control the trailer in event of failure of the regular trailer hitch or coupling."

As shown at left, use bolt to secure safety chain to tongue. Have it in CENTER and located as far forward as practical on trailer drawbar. Snap on end of chain isn't made for sudden stress, that is job of overhand knot in chain.

Powerboating Illustrated

Atwood Mobile Products Division
4750 Hiawatha Drive
Rockford, Illinois 61101

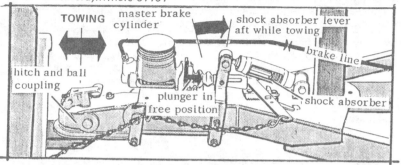

The self-contained **trailer surge brake system** is automatically coupled and self actuated by the trailer tongue pressure when the trailer tongue is secured to the ball hitch on the towing trailer. Since electrically operated trailer brakes provide an expensive repair bill if the hubs are submerged, surge brakes are more commonly used for boat trailers.

At constant speed—the plunger is in a *free position* with no pressure from the trailer master cylinder to the trailer brakes... while the shock absorber prevents the intermittent application of the brakes when towing on rough roads. If the trailer uncouples when underway, a chain pulls the breakaway lever forward applying the trailer brakes.

Before surge brakes—in the 1940's the boat we were trailering passed our car on the left on a two lane country road. Our first response... where did that boat come from as it looks familiar.

175

Powerboating Illustrated

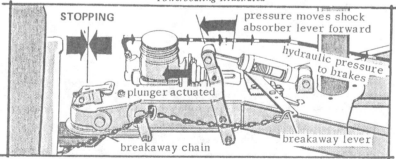

As the towing vehicle brakes are applied—the trailer tongue moves forward to apply pressure to the master cylinder, which is transferred to the trailer drums. The built-in *shock absorber* helps to provide an even, smooth application of the surge brakes.

Lubrication is needed—for the linkage to work smoothly, also wheel-bearing grease on the hitch is required for smooth towing action. As the surge brakes are energized only in forward, they permit easy backing to launch, and to load your boat... *during this time you must rely on your towing vehicle brakes,* also a **tire stop**, pages 162, 164.

How much portability do you want? Our boat trailer experience started in late 1957 while testing a variety of trailers and outboard rigs. Considerable research was necessary to be able to publish our 1960 **Trailerboating Illustrated,** the first book on the portable, planing outboard hull.

▲**How many miles will you trailer your boat yearly?** While many owners in the northeast may trailer their boats 50 or so miles yearly, we have worked with owners in the southwest that are active all year. They want efficient, ample-capacity trailers for their fully loaded boats that can move on short notice. If New Englanders also considered long-haul trailers, instead of minimum ones for short hauls, they could look forward to one or two sun-belt sailing vacations during the winter months.

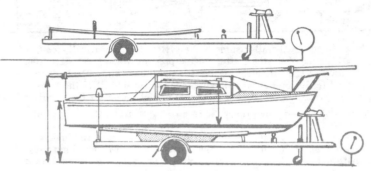

176

▲**Will the weight of the fully-loaded boat exceed the maximum capacity of the trailer which was ample for your new boat when it was empty?**

❶ **Weigh the empty trailer** on local public scales without the boat.

❷ **Weigh the trailer with the empty boat as it came from the factory.** You can subtract the trailer weight...to find the weight of your boat.

❸ **Weigh the fully-loaded sailboat on its trailer.** This includes the outboard motor, anchors and anchor line, tool kit, radio, cooking gear, food, etc. Weight of such carry-aboard items normally increase the longer you own your boat. Fill your water tanks at your destination with water at 8.3 lbs. per gallon, and gasoline at 6.8 lbs. per gallon, if possible.

▲**The 15% safe load factor** is ample for an empty boat. This capacity is often exceeded when fully loaded reducing the useful lifespan of the trailer and tires considerably. The overloaded trailer is a hazard due to unexpected metal fatigue such as springs breaking that cause steering problems. We hope you buy your first trailer with a larger safe load factor... the reason most owners choose better trailers the second time around.

▲ **Keep trailerable sailboats on a continual diet.** Your sailboat or powerboat will then be able to perform to the best of its ability on the water...and what is equally important, is on the highway.

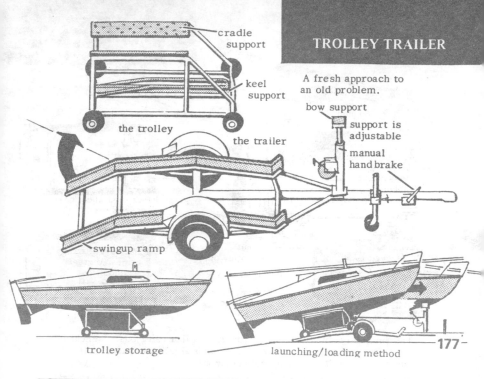

A fresh approach to an old problem.

cradle support

keel support

the trolley

the trailer

bow support

support is adjustable

manual hand brake

swingup ramp

trolley storage

launching/loading method

Combination trolley/trailer. It provides excellent flexibility for sailboat storage. Several Varianta's in the Bonn, Germany area, have their own trolleys using one trailer. Auto hubs are used and corrosion problems are reduced as the trailer and trailer lights aren't submerged.

▲**The 21'4" Varianta.** It is a cb/keel sloop, a E.B. van de Stadt design with over 3000 class sailboats throughout Europe. What makes it unique is its trolley/trailer with the boat and trolley/trailer made at the Dehler Factory in Hamburg, Germany. The *Menina,* shown above, is owned by our sailing language expert, Karl Freudenstein of Bonn, Germany.

▲**Loading the trailer.** The winch cable snap hook is secured to the underwater eye on the forward edge of the keel to pull the boat onto the fully submerged trolley. A fender tied to the front end of the trolley, its rope length a couple more inches than the boat draft, helps to position the boat keel on its submerged trolley.

Boat and trolley are winched aboard the trailer until the bow of the boat rests on its Y-shaped bow support. Then the "slipping rails" or ramps are raised and locked vertically. Tiedowns are added to secure the sailboat to the trailer, and the rig is ready to move out. While we feel the trolley/trailer has excellent potentials for portable sailboats and powerboats, none are presently made in the U.S.

Powerboating Illustrated

AVOID submerging
automotive hub bearings!

Submersion can damage
unprotected wheel bearings.

inner
seal

hub

dust cap

spindle   inner bearing

outer bearing

cone   cage

lug bolt

roller   race

nut
cotter pin

trade terms

CUP-race
CONE-cage,
rollers,cone

air inside hub

correct amount
of grease

Fiber type wheel bearing
grease is used in this
type of hub.

water flowing
past seal

water and grease
emulsifying

The automotive hub is excellent for trailers that carry boats launched
with slings or eyes...and IF the trailer hubs aren't submerged at the
launching ramp. If these hubs are submerged—

A heat buildup may result that spells trouble. *It is indicated by squeaky
trailer hubs, or hubs too hot to hold your hand against them.* If these
obvious warnings are ignored and failure occurs at highway speed, the
trailer will begin to sway. It may sideswipe other cars, or if the trailer
sways into gravel, it may becom a fulcrum, pg. 76, to flip the towing
car. The cause of automotive hub failure—

● *New trailer, fresh water.* After trailering a boat at highway speeds for
many miles, wait at least ¾ of an hour if it is necessary to submerge
the auto hubs, giving them a chance to cool off, or—

● The hot hubs cool suddenly with the air inside contracting to cause
lowered air pressure. This pulls water past the inner seals which close,
as the water mixes or *emulsifies* (similar to adding sugar to coffee)
reducing the grease heat conduction properties. *OVERPACKING* also
results as the fiber type wheel bearing grease loses much of the air
which is required to act as a coolant. The continual heat buildup will
cause *intergranular corrosion or metal fatigue failure,* pages 269, 358.

● *New trailer, salt water.* In an identical situation, *CORROSION expands
the bearing surfaces* increasing metal to metal rubbing friction contact
surfaces...*plus overpacking* to increase hub heat buildup which will
produce rapid metal fatigue intergranular corrosion failure.

● *Old Hubs.* Water coming in forces grease past inner seals to emulsify
with the rest of the grease, causing a damaging heat buildup. *Repack
wheel bearings immediately after a salt water dunking,* page 180. and
carry a spare set of wheel bearings along as standard procedure.

Powerboating Illustrated

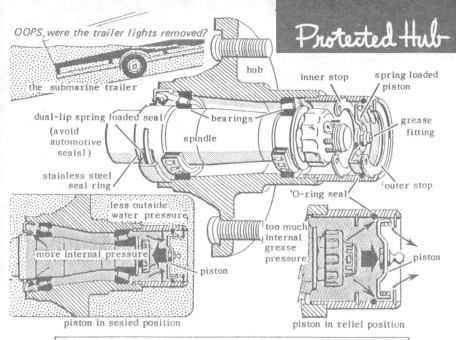

OOPS, were the trailer lights removed?

the submarine trailer

hub

inner stop

spring loaded piston

dual-lip spring loaded seal (avoid automotive seals!)

bearings

grease fitting

spindle

stainless steel seal ring

'O-ring seal'

outer stop

less outside water pressure

more internal pressure

piston

too much internal grease pressure

piston

piston in sealed position

piston in relief position

> *Grease is a coolant that dissipates heat from trailer bearings, plus reducing metal to metal contact.* The auto hub uses fiber type wheel bearing grease that requires *air* to function as a coolant...while the protected trailer hub uses grease similar to an outboard or outdrive lower unit that doesn't require air to function as a coolant.

The protected *Bearing Buddy*® hub detailed was the pioneer in this field. The basic concept...maintain more internal pressure (3 p.s.i.) in the hubs than the outside or external water pressure. This elimates water coming into the submerged hubs thru the seals.

The dust cap is replaced with a *Bearing Buddy*® having a piston with a grease fitting. Grease is added thru this spring loaded piston to fill the hub with grease. This forces the piston out, while increasing the internal pressure sufficiently in the hub to keep out the water.

The *Bearing Buddy*® has an automatic safety relief valve. This avoids overpacking which protects the inner seal as any excess internal pressure inside the hub which instead acts on the piston. This allows the extra grease to leak past an *O-ring* with the piston in the relief position...after which the piston returns to the sealed position.

WARNING—use only the dual-lip spring loaded seals made by the manufacturer. Standard automotive seals designed for less hub pressure may start to leak which reduces the internal hub pressure...look for grease puddles under the trailer axle. Periodically put your hand on the protected hubs while trailering, to check for any unnecessary heat buildup to avoid bearing failure.

Powerboating Illustrated

Bearing Buddy® —

Unique Functional Products, 135 Sunshine Lane, San Marcos, CA 92069

When were your wheel bearings last inspected and packed?

Use scissors jack to support axle/frame.

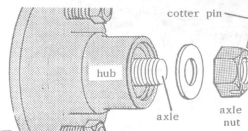

cotter pin

Removing bearings and grease seal—

force out with wooden lever if necessary.

hub

axle

axle nut

dust cap

Force grease seal into inner hub until flush with end of hub.

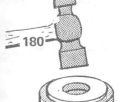

180

An auto type trailer hub should require a half hour maintenance to inspect and repack. After the cotter pin and axle nut are removed, the wheel will pull off the axle.

Remove the bearings, clean with *kerosene*, then follow with a *butyl alcohol* rinse to dissolve water and grease. Replace rollers and races showing pitting and/or rust to avoid metal expansion heat buildup corrosion failure. To reduce oxygen exposure... repack bearings soon as possible with water resistant grease, but avoid overpacking with wheel bearing grease.

Replace the inner grease seals every time the bearings are packed, forcing the seal into the inner hub as shown at left.

Add the wheel to the axle, and tighten the hub... but not too tight as the wheel must spin freely. Insert and lock the nut with the cotter pin, add the dust cap, and remove the jack.

Launching with **SLINGS** will be preferred when possible.

Launching with **hooks and eyes** off a high pier.

Jewel

SLING positions should be marked on both trailer and boat... so the boat can be rapidly lifted off the trailer, and the slings easily located when taking the boat out of the water.. The bow line permits easier handling and control.

PAD EYES should be stainless or drop forged that are secured to the strongest part of the hull... keep the boat light as possible when lifting. to reduce strains. Does your insurance cover this type of launching?

sensor lead   brake lining

return springs

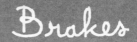

wheel cylinder   anchor pin

brake shoe

adjusting screw   parking brake

return spring

revolving brake drum

After your car, camper, or van is loaded with passengers and gear, the limit has been reached for braking ability.

> Trailer loads of 700 lbs. or more will need a separate braking system. Even our light *Jewel*, lower left and pg.25, tried to jacknife in heavy downtown San Francisco traffic when we had to brake hard to avoid a collision. Let's examine trailer brake systems—

● *Electric brakes* used on travel trailers, are excellent for boat trailers... until that first expensive dunking. An owner with a large new rig that had never been in the water, took it to a mechanic for last minute changes who submerged the brakes. When the owner arrived, it wasn't a pleasant scene as the repair bill was considerable.

● *Surge brakes,* discussed on pg. 175, are self contained. Excess moisture in surge brakes can be eliminated by slowing down, and speeding up a few times, before entering highway traffic.

● *Hydraulic brakes* are designed for automotive use to keep out dust in a protected atmosphere. A *backing plate* is used to keep out water that is splashed up from the roadway. Wet hydraulic brakes are not very efficient. Remove moisture by applying a slight pressure to the brakes while driving the car.

181

Hydraulic brakes are excellent for boat trailers IF they are properly maintained as they aren't designed for the marine environment. When they are submerged and water leaks in, the backing plate tends to retain the water which can cause rust and corrosion. Use *waterproof grease* sparingly on the inner metal surfaces, but don't let it touch the brake lining... also AVOID using automotive grease.

● *Bearing Buddy* ® hubs require especially designed dual-lip spring loaded seals. If automotive inner seals are instead used with much wider tolerances, they may permit grease to leak out of the hubs into the brake drums, and suddenly... no brakes.

When grease reaches trailer brake linings, the linings have to be replaced. The inner automotive seal, the cause of the leak, also must be replaced. *In an emergency*--some temporary braking power may result if gasoline is used to remove grease from the brake linings... yet the linings still have to be replaced as soon as possible.

● *Periodic adjustment* is required for the brake shoe to drum clearance from 2500 to 5000 miles, or earlier if much time is spent on dusty roads. Jack up the wheel being adjusted, turning the adjustment screw at the bottom (from the inside) until the shoe just touches the drum. Atwood Mobile Products pg. 175, has an excellent manual to adjust surge brakes, that also includes drum brakes. Study closely as the number of notches of the screw to back off after the shoe touches the drum, as it will vary with drum size, also for the single or tandem axle.

Balancing tires extends the life of leaf springs and the tires.

correct inflation

Excessive flexing with heat failure, tread scuffing, separation & breaking of cord & plies.

HEAT

underinflation

Excessive wear in center of tread. Tire bruises & blows with insufficient flexing.

overinflation

182

midget tires

hull
clearance,
tire
bounce
space?

auto tires

The figures are approximate—if your car has 14" wheels towing a trailer at 50 mph, its 12" tires would be turning 60 mph, 10" tires at 70 mph, and 8" trailer wheels, turning at 90 mph.

● *SHORT HAUL*—if your favorite watering hole is 20 to 30 miles from your storage area, the small tires may be sufficient, an advantage, the boat is lower and easier to climb aboard.

Since most heat is liberated out the side of the tire, the small 8" and 10" tires with small cooling areas should be avoided for extensive driving on hot roads as they are more prone to failure.

● *LONG HAUL* this trailer evolved in the southwest thru necessity where owners may drive 500 miles or more for a boating weekend on hot asphalt roads with summer surface temperatures to 135°. Trailer tires the same size as the auto are preferred to eliminate the spare. Tire heat buildup results from tire pressure, road surface temperature, and friction between the tire and the road.

TIRE PRESSURE is listed for a tire when it is COOL... which allows for an increased pressure up to 15% for heat buildup when driving on a hot road. Since filling station air hose tire gages often lose accuracy within the first month due to dropping and rough handling, buy your own tire gage to check air pressure, adding air if only a few pounds low.

Most tire failures are caused by *underinflation* that results in flexing with excessive heat buildup. This heat buildup, especially on the bias ply, causes friction between the layers that separate them, increasing the chafe and heat buildup. A blister on the tire sidewall is the first indication of delamination, with a flat tire or blowout predicted.

Large size tires last longer, and if properly inflated may be less expensive in the long run than small tires. The advantages, they have much larger sidewall surfaces to release heat. They also develop less internal friction than smaller tires which have to rotate at much higher speeds than the towing vehicle.

● *TRAILER TIRE COVERS.* If your rig is stored outside and it will be used weekly or monthly... cover the trailer tires. This will reduce the aging and checking noticed on the sidewalls caused by the ultra-violet rays of the sun. While a light colored canvas cover may do an adequate job at less cost, *Acrylic* is the best material for such use, which is also used on sailboat sails dockside to screen out these rays.

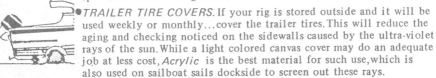

● **If you don't intend to use your rig for a month or more-- jack up your trailer. This protects the wheel bearings and eliminates flat spots on tires. Cover tires for ultra-violet ray protection. Does boat have ventilation?**

Powerboating Illustrated

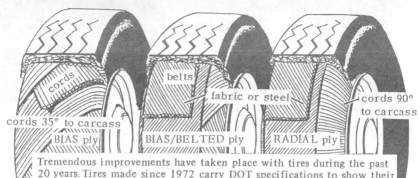

cords 35° to carcass
cords
belts
fabric or steel
cords 90° to carcass

BIAS ply | BIAS/BELTED ply | RADIAL ply

Tremendous improvements have taken place with tires during the past 20 years. Tires made since 1972 carry DOT specifications to show their capacity, pressure, ply ratings, and materials. Previous to this we had considerable confusion for trailer tires and their air pressure.

From the end of WW II until 1965 the *bias ply tire* with cords at 35° to a cars line of travel was our U.S. standard. The minimum life expectancy was extended by adding more plies, as it was a hard, high pressure tire. When the bias ply tire was *not carrying enough pressure,* the plies began chafing, working against each other and separating. A blowout often results as this is a high pressure tire.

● *The belted/bias tire* then came onto the market with the price and life expectancy about midway between bias and radial tires.

● *European radial tires* were developed to provide an answer to a very different problem without speed limits on many major highways. The answer was low pressure tires with a much better, flatter road contact for tight curves, and thin flexible sidewalls to reduce heat buildup.

We enjoyed our first auto 24 psi radials, going 39,700 miles before a tire failed without warning, which is common with radials. The low pressure radials on the boat trailer caused sway potentials on a tight curve. It disappeared on later radials which carried more pressure.

183

> Tire and axle (GAW) capacity require second thoughts. Trailer capacity may be ample and legal when a customer buys a NEW boat. The capacity should instead be considered **after the boat is fully loaded.** Capacity of the trailer which had been legal, has passed the maximum capacity with early tire, spring, axle, or structural failure to be expected. If any question develops as to overloading... where is the closest truck scale you can recommend to a customer?

Tire weight carrying capacity should be at least 15% more than that of the fully loaded boat and its trailer. Increase this to 20% for long-haul summer driving on dark, heat retaining asphalt highways.

● *Replace tire valve stems every 2 years.* A crack may develop around the stem's base letting air leak out, followed by flexing, heat buildup, and failure. Check periodically for leaky tires as valve failure may occur long before the useful life of the tire is over.

● AVOID the *auto bumper jack* as you may find with your first flat tire, it will not normally have a good bite on a trailer channel frame. The *scissors jack* at left is recommended for your auto and boat trailer... if it has the load capacity for the heavier of the two components.

Powerboating Illustrated

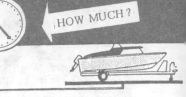

A well know boat builder was leaving
for a week vacation to the Sea of Cortez
to test the prototype of his new hull
design. At the last moment he weighed his
rig to find it 600 lbs. overweight.

⬤If trailerboat rig weight can fool an excellent craftsman, take another
look at your boat, and that of your customers. What is the maximum
capacity listed on the trailer...and what does the fully loaded rig weigh
on truck scales. If weight is close to maximum, consider—

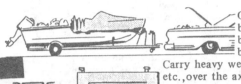

Carry light articles such as sleeping
bags in the boat cabin or under the
boat cover to prevent them from
being blown out while driving?
Carry heavy weight such as canned goods, tools,
etc., over the axle in the auto trunk.

Gasoline weight averages 6.6 lbs. per gallon with
a 6 lb. portable tank weighing an average of 43 lbs.
when full. A built-in 25 gallon fuel tank may weigh
20 lbs. when empty, and approx. 185 lbs. when full...with two full
25 gallon tanks weighing as much as two adults. Fill built-in tanks
close to launching to reduce the weight while trailering. *Diesel oil
weighs approx. 7.3 lbs.* which is information difficult to find.

184 ⬤*Fresh water weight averages 8.3 lbs. per gallon, salt water a little more.*

I was walking thru a boatyard north of San Francisco with the owner
after a heavy rainstorm the previous day when we heard two explosions.
We found it came from a 17½' boat filled to the brim with water.

⬤*A puddle formed in the boat cover. It kept growing with the weight
of the water ripping a hole in the cover which became a funnel for
the heavy rain.* The weight was too much for the small tires causing
them to blow a minute apart. This was followed as we walked toward
the boat with the rusted springs snapping, and the keel breaking.

At left is a 15' boat on its trailer caught
in a heavy summer rainstorm. If the bow
wasn't raised and the drain plugs pulled,
the open boat may collect up to 100
gallons of water weighing 830 pounds.

Large powerboats and sailboats have
built-in cockpit drains when caught dockside in a heavy rainstorm... an advantage
most trailerboats don't have.

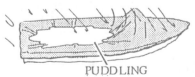

PUDDLING

Water will puddle in a poorly designed
boat cover. The water may eventually
pour into the boat to cover the battery,
and the boat become awash to sink at
the dock. We were too tired to put the
cover on *Jewel*, pg. 25, also we had no
warning a cloudburst was moving in.

Trailerboat covers should be tailored to a specific boat, to fit snug around the powerhead in tilted position, to stay in place under many conditions.

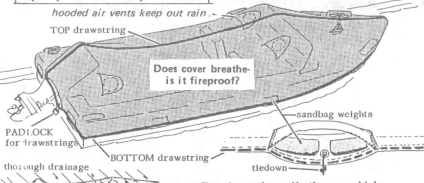

hooded air vents keep out rain

TOP drawstring

Does cover breathe—
is it fireproof?

PADLOCK
for drawstrings

BOTTOM drawstring

sandbag weights

thorough drainage

tiedown

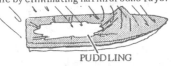

Tire cover for storage extends tire life by eliminating harmful suns rays.

PUDDLING

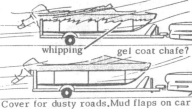

whipping   gel coat chafe?

Cover for dusty roads. Mud flaps on car will reduce water/mud splashing boat.

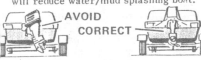

AVOID   CORRECT

- *Top drawstring* pulls the cover high enough to drain rain water, providing more headroom for camping out.

- *Bottom drawstring* (Dacron preferred) prevents the cover from excess whipping in strong winds and highway speeds. Canvas covers though much heavier, seem to last longer with less cloth chafe resistance than synthetic covers.

185

- *Tiedowns* which go under the boat, keep the boat cover snug while trailering to prevent whipping, chafing action.

- *Sandbags* or other weights sewn into pockets help to keep the boat cover snug when dockside...while sandbags and tiedowns help to keep a boat cover snug while trailering.

Outboard motor or **outdrive lower unit** while trailering *must be tilted and locked in a straight back position.* If lower unit is trailered in down position,..and on an angle, a sudden impact with the lower unit hitting the road will cause much unnecessary and expensive damage.

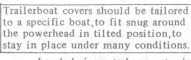

GAW

- *Springs fail* from lack of maintenance, overloading, metal fatigue aging, and corrosion. Use zinc chromate paint, grease flexing areas, check nuts periodically, hose off springs after salt water dunking. If you balance trailer tires it will extend the life of both tires and springs.

- *Is your cover fire resistant?* Carelessly flipped cigarettes landing in a boat, or on a boat cover causes serious fires on the highway...with most cigarettes coming *FROM the towing vehicle,* see page 264.

Powerboating Illustrated

Breaking strength table is for new rope in laboratory test conditions.							
diameter	mm-metric	traditional 3 strand manila	impact absorption—controlled stretch		minimum stretch—for control lines		galvanized chain
			3 strand nylon	braided Gold-N-Braid	3 strand Dacron & polypro	braided Yacht Braid	
1/4	6	600	1850	2100	1750	2300	2700
5/16	8	1000	2850	3500	2650	3450	3700
3/8	9	1350	4000	4800	3600	4950	4600
7/16	10½	1750	5500	6500	4800	6600	6200
1/2	12	2650	7100	8300	6100	8600	8200
9/16	14	3400	8350	11200	7400	11700	10200
5/8	16	4400	10500	14500	9000	15200	12500
3/4	18	5400	14200	18000	12500	19100	17700
7/8	22	7700	19000	26500	16000	28300	24000
1	24	9000	24600	31300	20000	33600	31000

Braided rope specifications are provided by *Samson Ocean Systems, Inc.*
Expect many variables with 3-strand rope specifications.

- **Marine rope** is the term commonly used by dealers, while sailors use the term **marlinspike seamanship.** It is the mark of an able seaman to care for, handle, plus being able to splice a variety of kinds and sizes of ropes.

- **Rope strength tables** list new rope being tested under laboratory conditions. American tables list the *average tension* which rope may break at any given point exclusive of damage from chafe, sharp edges, etc. European tables list the rope **minimum tension** breaking strength. **Chain breaking strength** tables follow identical American and European reporting methods.

- **Safe working load.** It is computed with a safety factor of **20% or 5 to 1,** providing maximum security where life and property are involved. A rope for example with a normal working load of 2000 pounds without chafe, should require a ratio on the table above of 10,000 or more pounds. This large safety factor ratio is recommended for unusual conditions for your boat with extreme wind and wave action, sudden jerks and strains, etc.

Splices and knots reduce rope strength.

eye splice with thimble	95%
long splice	90%
short splice	85%
two half hitches	65%
fisherman's bend	65%
fisherman's knot	65%
bowline	60%
carrick bend	55%
sheet bend	55%
square knot	50%
figure-eight knot	45%
overhand knot	45%

- **Friction** between the fibers is the force holding a knot together. This decreases with slippery synthetic fibers...and increases with rougher, coarser manila organic fibers.

  Complex friction stresses are involved with rope knot strength, which will decrease rapidly when knots are used repeatedly in the same area.

- **Rope failure.** The standing part is the major culprit where maximum stress is put on rope fibers entering the knot.

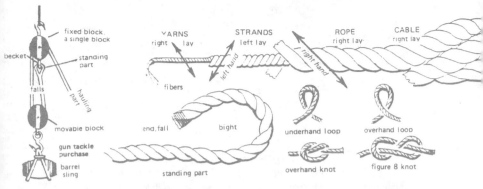

fixed block, a single block

becket — standing part

falls — hauling part

movable block

gun tackle purchase

barrel sling

YARNS right lay

fibers

end, fall

STRANDS left lay

right hand

left hand

bight

standing part

ROPE right lay

CABLE right lay

underhand loop

overhand knot

overhand loop

figure 8 knot

trolling to unwind snarls

Rope-knots, splices

- **Rope vs line**—expect variables. Our USN seamen refer to **rope** as wire rope and **line** as fiber rope. It becomes more complex with the sailing fraternity defining rope as raw material...**which becomes line when cut for specific use in boat operation.** This includes anchor line, standing, and running rigging.

Rope used to secure an object, or the sail bolt rope is still called rope. The **traditional square rigger ropes** were foot ropes, yard ropes, bell ropes, bucket ropes, back ropes, top ropes, tiller ropes, and man ropes.

- **Three-strand twisted rope** is always under its own tension, use *medium lay only.* This tension results from the alternate twisting of the individual fibers, yarns, and strands shown above to increase the internal friction of the various elements of the rope working together.

A **hockle** develops when the three rope strands are twisted out of balance. Retwist *to unkink* to eliminate the three-strand hockle before putting under load. The overstressed fibers will otherwise cause a dangerous defect in a sound line.

- **Double-braided rope** is not under tension with itself. It is a rope within a rope with a *hollow-braided cover* over a *hollow-braided core.* It is held together by the natural geometry of the interlocking cover and core sharing the load equally.

This interlocking method produces a softer and more flexible rope with less elongation and greater strength. Built-in variables can however result if the cover is made to provide extreme abrasion resistance...with the high strength core carrying 90% of the load.

Double-braided rope not under tension with itself *does not have a memory.* This lack of memory makes it excellent for heaving line use page 185, and for easy anchor line stowage free of kinks, page 188.

high-point crown chafe contact areas

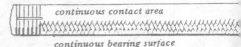

continuous contact area

continuous bearing surface

Enjoy the strong opinions for and against organic and synthetic rope variables sailors gain thru experience. Some of our ideas are...

> *Three-strand rope is easier to splice, yet the energy absorption and elasticity may be excessive and questionable. While rapid chafe of three-strand anchor line crowns mean little for a weekend sailor...the active long-distance cruiser should only use chain where the anchor line touches the bottom.*

- **Minimum bearing surface contact areas.** We tested the chafe resistance of three-strand, and braided anchor lines in 1965, fore and aft in a rough anchor anchorage with maximum tidal ranges.We had to leave on the 4th day as the boat movement was excessive. Rocks and barnacles had cut numerous high point crowns with a strength reduction on the three-strand anchor line.

- **Continuous bearing surface contact areas.** The same diameter braided line showed wear. No broken threads resulted as the impact area was spread out, rather than being concentrated in a few high point areas.

- **Three-strand nylon anchor line...will keep stretching under load.** After approx. 50% elongation, it may break and the ends snap back.We were in a poor anchorage having to leave when the wind reversed itself. The rubber band stretch in a vicious surge made the three-strand anchor line difficult to take in as I continually wondered...is it 20%, 30%, or 40% longer than normal?

188 It takes more time to know if a three-strand anchor line has the anchor dug in properly. Up north a powerboat anchor was caught under a log, the anchor line was three-strand. Tremendous windlass pressure was applied.The anchor suddenly broke loose, flying up thru the window of a flying bridge cruiser, with the window approximately 30' above the water surface.

- **Double-braided tow lines only!** "During an attempt to refloat a grounded cruiser with a nylon towing line...the towing cleat on the cruiser suddenly pulled free and became a lethal projectile under the impetus of the violent recoiling line. The cleat struck a man...Death was instantaneous". This is from *Proceedings of the Merchant Marine Council, May, 1964.*

- **Sheets and halyards.** The continuous bearing surface of double-braided Dacron or polyester is preferred with a 50% better surface area contact with the winch, it is easier on the hands, with minimum elongation for crucial settings.

After three sets of braided dock lines, we spliced a set of three-strand dock lines. Their performance seemed equal in our short slip.

- The **neutral lay** permits braided anchor lines to be stowed easily **without hitches and/or kinks.** They can be dropped into synthetic sail bags for stowage; add grommets for drainage and ventilation. They can be stored in easy to carry plastic buckets. All braided anchor lines stowed this way should pay out rapidly and easily without problems.

drains beneath

grommet drains

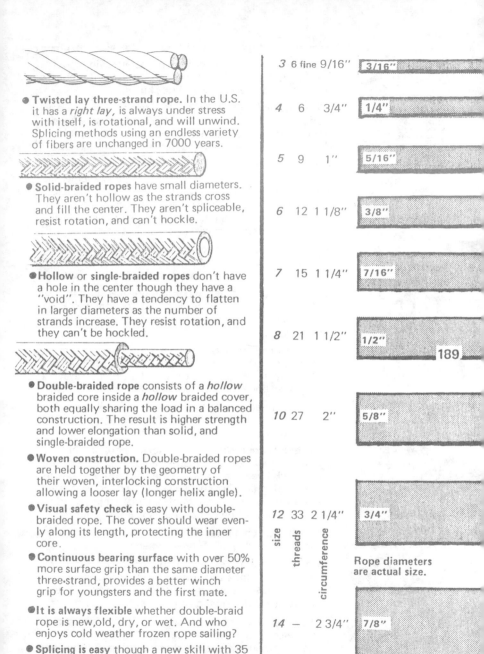

● **Twisted lay three-strand rope.** In the U.S. it has a *right lay*, is always under stress with itself, is rotational, and will unwind. Splicing methods using an endless variety of fibers are unchanged in 7000 years.

● **Solid-braided ropes** have small diameters. They aren't hollow as the strands cross and fill the center. They aren't spliceable, resist rotation, and can't hockle.

● **Hollow** or **single-braided ropes** don't have a hole in the center though they have a "void". They have a tendency to flatten in larger diameters as the number of strands increase. They resist rotation, and they can't be hockled.

● **Double-braided rope** consists of a *hollow* braided core inside a *hollow* braided cover, both equally sharing the load in a balanced construction. The result is higher strength and lower elongation than solid, and single-braided rope.

● **Woven construction.** Double-braided ropes are held together by the geometry of their woven, interlocking construction allowing a looser lay (longer helix angle).

● **Visual safety check** is easy with double-braided rope. The cover should wear evenly along its length, protecting the inner core.

● **Continuous bearing surface** with over 50% more surface grip than the same diameter three-strand, provides a better winch grip for youngsters and the first mate.

● **It is always flexible** whether double-braid rope is new, old, dry, or wet. And who enjoys cold weather frozen rope sailing?

● **Splicing is easy** though a new skill with 35 basic steps required in the correct sequence.

size	threads	circumference	
3	6 fine	9/16"	3/16"
4	6	3/4"	1/4"
5	9	1"	5/16"
6	12	1 1/8"	3/8"
7	15	1 1/4"	7/16"
8	21	1 1/2"	1/2"
10	27	2"	5/8"
12	33	2 1/4"	3/4"
14	—	2 3/4"	7/8"

189

Rope diameters are actual size.

braided rope

three strand rope

Ooooops!

the dull razor

"My new block saved two ounces!"

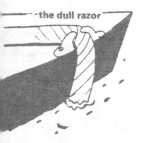

the dull razor

locking skene chock

leather chafe guard

> **A full spool of rope may average 600' long.**
>
> **Braided rope.** It is taken from a freely moving spool letting it fall into a container, page 188, so it is able to *maintain its neutral lay* without kinks.
>
> **Three-strand, right-lay rope.** It is removed from a coil by pulling the inside end, coiling it *counterclockwise.* If right-lay three-strand is coiled clockwise, it rapidly develops kinks and hockles, see hockle on page 187.

- **When three-strand kinks develop**—after the ends are whipped or fused so they can't unlay, tow a larger dia. line behind a boat for a few minutes to stabilize itself, then coil. For smaller diameter short lengths, pull thru your hand while maintaining some tension on the line. You can watch it untwist and stabilize itself.

- **Good rope is expensive.** An understanding owner may have a long, useful, and productive life...or a short, expensive, and dangerous one with his rope investment.

- Hardware catalogs list **maximum line diameter for each block.** If a larger diameter line goes thru the block, the line begins to chafe on the outside...while the tight radius starts to crush and break the inner fibers.

- **Small straight chocks** with sharp cutting edges are members of the knife and razor family. Dock lines or anchor lines can chafe at the chock in wind or wave action cutting your boat adrift at the worst moment.

  Another disadvantage of the straight chock in wave action...your dock or anchor line may jump out of the chock to chafe on nearby sharp edges, screw heads, etc.

- **Adequate size locking skene chocks** should be installed of a larger size than first considered. This reduces anchor and dock line chances of jumping out of the chock in wave action. **Leather chafe guards** of correct size are in kit form with punched holes, needle, and thread to minimize dock line chafe when going thru chocks.

- **Manila rope chafes rapidly** due to its coarse, abrasive surface, occuring much faster when wet.

  We towed our 14' outboard boat *Blunder* behind a 40' ketch. The manila tow line of top quality chafed rapidly at the outboard bow chock. We had to resplice it twice in three days during the early part of our vacation.

  The third short splice was wrapped with a hard surface vinyl electricians tape. Little chafe was evident two weeks later at the end of the vacation with thanks to the tape.

Powerboating Illustrated

The **fisherman's knot** is used to join fishline, twine, and small rope.

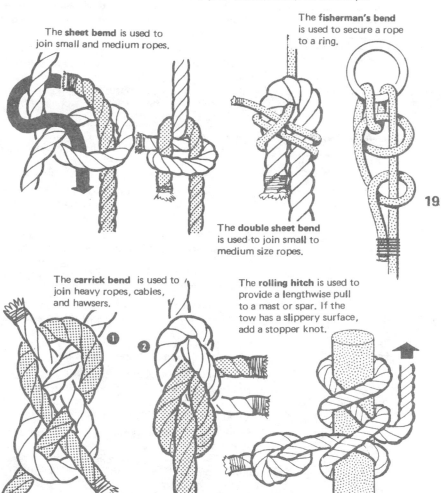

The **sheet bemd** is used to join small and medium ropes.

The **fisherman's bend** is used to secure a rope to a ring.

The **double sheet bend** is used to join small to medium size ropes.

191

The **carrick bend** is used to join heavy ropes, cables, and hawsers.

The **rolling hitch** is used to provide a lengthwise pull to a mast or spar. If the tow has a slippery surface, add a stopper knot.

Powerboating Illustrated

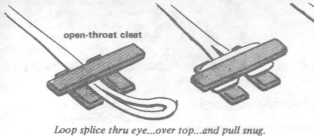

open-throat cleat

bitt

Loop splice thru eye...over top...and pull snug.   *Use two loops...then pull tight.*

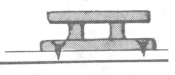

AVOID short
wood screws!

Organic vs synthetic dock lines.

Coarse surface friction. Large diameter manila dock lines with larger cleats were standard to 1960. Two locking hitches were usually sufficient.

Smooth surface, minimum friction. Nylon dock lines were stronger, with smaller diameter line ample for the purpose. Extra locking half hitches are required to prevent the nylon dock lines from slipping, and jumping off their cleats.

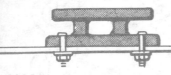

192 Cleat may still pull out
under extreme pressure.

- **Open throat cleat.** It permits an eye splice to go thru the opening, then looped over and locked tight. Two locking loops overcome the tendency for small dia. nylon dock lines to jump the bitt.

- **AVOID wood screw cleat installations** on fiberglass AND wooden boats. Wood screws may pull out with minimum stress, while the cleat becomes a hazardous projectile, see page 188.

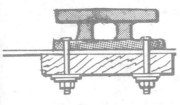

Bolt thru with backing
plate is required for
bitt and cleat.

- **Bolts and washers are better, BUT** the fiberglass may momentarily open under extreme pressure to release the small washers. The cleat can again be a hazardous projectile for anyone in its path.

- **Wood or metal backing plates** are required to spread the full tension of the cleat or bitt over a large area to prevent the part under tension from pulling loose. **Add different size washers for a good bite, use locking nuts, and don't mix metal families.**

- **Sandwich fiberglass construction.** All bolt holes require special handling to seal out moisture. If water may leak into the wood blocks, a rot action can begin, requiring expensive repairs to correct.

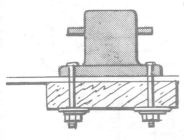

- **The bitt.** It is smaller, lighter, and easily handles a larger diameter line than the bow anchor/dock cleat commonly found on many sailboats and powerboats during the past 20 years. Will a bitt do a better job for you on your sailboat?

Powerboating Illustrated

bollard   bitt   cleat

standing part

Take the line **twice** around a cleat...add a half hitch...then as many as required.
The line can then be released without taking up on the standing part.

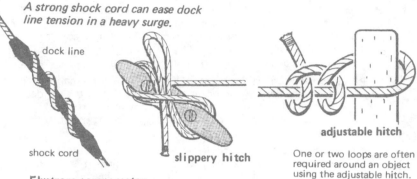

*A strong shock cord can ease dock
line tension in a heavy surge.*

dock line

shock cord

Elvstrom compensator

slippery hitch

adjustable hitch

One or two loops are often
required around an object
using the adjustable hitch.

193

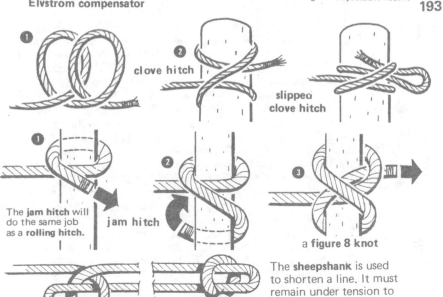

clove hitch

**slipped
clove hitch**

The **jam hitch** will
do the same job
as a **rolling hitch**.

jam hitch

a **figure 8 knot**

The **sheepshank** is used
to shorten a line. It must
remain under tension to
avoid slippage.

Powerboating Illustrated

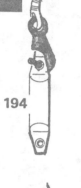

All cabin sailboats should carry a heaving line that is easy to reach and throw, preferably carried just inside the companionway. Our heaving line with over a 20-year history has pulled tired swimmers and divers to our boat, towed dinghies and rowboats, and was a means to pull across a heavier line in rough weather without having to be too close to another boat. It proved very useful at a crowded launching ramp for a variety of uses.

●**Three-strand heaving lines** are questionable. When used by professionals the heaving lines must be coiled in the morning. If they won't be used until the evening, they must be coiled again...to avoid hitches. If coiled by a right hander then given to a left hander or visa versa, expect endless hitches.

●**Braided rope** can make a practical heaving line for recreational use due to the *neutral lay, or resistance to coiling.* If the braided line is dropped into its container, it will stow itself efficiently for use without hitches for long periods, plus being used by left handers and right handers without problems.

●**Yellow braided ¼" polyethylene** has an 1100-pound breaking strength. It is easy to see, easy to handle, and since it is a **floater** it protects the propeller. Our favorite is the 50' heaving line using a "soft" softball, while a 75' one uses a small fender. Neither ball or fender can hurt a receiver as they are soft and light.

194

The best way to avoid most drownings is to stay on your boat. Whether you face a short vicious summer squall, or a storm of several days, rope yourself to and become part of your boat.

● **Shoulder harness.** While an excellent idea providing maximum protection for major storms especially during a night watch, they are clumsy and seldom worn in changing weather conditions.

● **Waist harness.** It is easy to use, and is less confining during hot summer weather in a short duration squall, but you will have to make your own. Use a 10' length of ½" three-strand nylon, and a size 3 bronze snap. Have the line go thru the bronze snap twice before starting the eye splice.

The waist harness is also a **belt.** When not being used, it is long enough to circle your waist a second time. It should be snug and out of the way when snapped onto itself when going below, though always ready for instant use. After adjusting to a snug, comfortable fit for you, cut the excess rope, burn to seal the end, then add whipping, page 200. Both harnesses are excellent for their intended purposes, to help you become a part of your sailboat.

Powerboating Illustrated

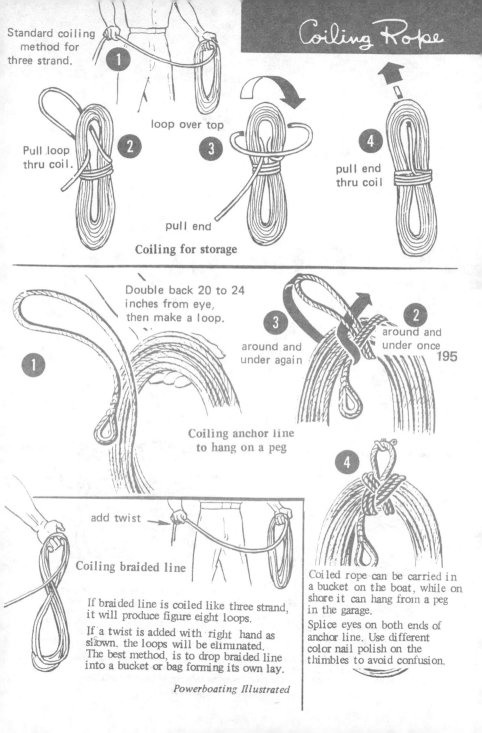

Standard coiling method for three strand.

1

loop over top

2 Pull loop thru coil.

3 pull end

4 pull end thru coil

Coiling for storage

1 Double back 20 to 24 inches from eye, then make a loop.

3 around and under again

2 around and under once

195

Coiling anchor line to hang on a peg

4

add twist →

Coiling braided line

If braided line is coiled like three strand, it will produce figure eight loops.

If a twist is added with right hand as shown, the loops will be eliminated. The best method, is to drop braided line into a bucket or bag forming its own lay.

Powerboating Illustrated

Coiled rope can be carried in a bucket on the boat, while on shore it can hang from a peg in the garage.

Splice eyes on both ends of anchor line. Use different color nail polish on the thimbles to avoid confusion.

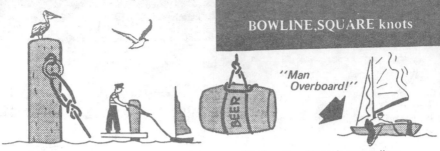

The **bowline** performs many practical purposes.

The **bowline stirrup** is an excellent method to take a person aboard a small sailboat. A bowline performs the same purpose as a saddle stirrup does to help climb aboard a horse.

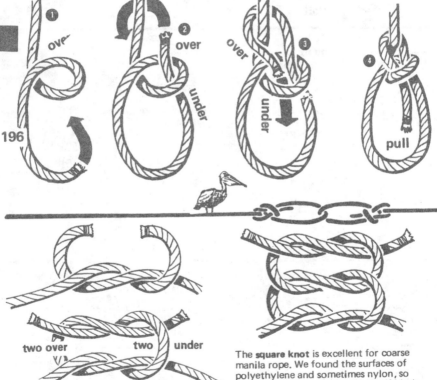

196

The **square knot** was originally called a *reef knot*.

The **square knot** is excellent for coarse manila rope. We found the surfaces of polyethylene and sometimes nylon, so slippery we had to add a third half hitch called the **double-square knot** above which hasn't failed with synthetic rope.

Lever's Young Sea Officers Sheet Anchor— *Edward W. Sweetman Co., Box 1631, Valdosta, GA 31603. It is excellently illustrated reproduced exactly from its 1819 printing from making rope to rigging square rig sailing vessels.*
Powerboating Illustrated

We have tested synthetic and organic whipping thread during the past 25 years under identical conditions.

Both kinds of thread seem to last a similar amount of time.

Permanent needle whipping is required for synthetic rope ends.

double-braided whipping.

Avoid short matches as they don't develop enough heat!

① Add tape an inch from end.

② Cut end ¼" from tape.

③ Fuse ends, rolling melted end to hold same diameter

④ Remove tape after end cools.

A **soldering iron** is excellent to fuse synthetic rope strands, while 12" **fireplace matches** also provide enough fusing heat.

197

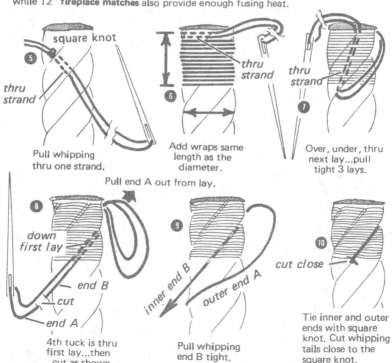

square knot

⑤ thru strand

Pull whipping thru one strand.

⑥ thru strand

Add wraps same length as the diameter.

⑦ thru strand

Over, under, thru next lay...pull tight 3 lays.

Pull end A out from lay.

⑧ down first lay

end B

cut

end A

4th tuck is thru first lay...then cut as shown.

⑨ inner end B

outer end A

Pull whipping end B tight.

⑩ cut close

Tie inner and outer ends with square knot. Cut whipping tails close to the square knot.

Powerboating Illustrated

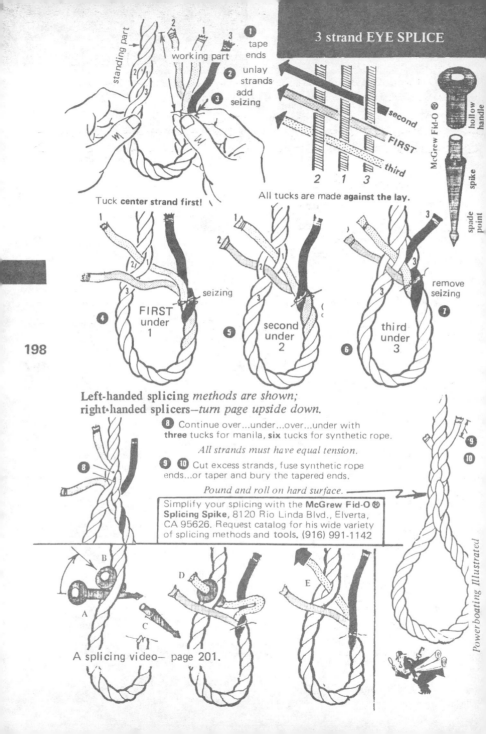

3 strand EYE SPLICE

standing part
working part

1. tape ends
2. unlay strands
3. add seizing

second
FIRST
third
2 1 3

McGrew Fid-O ®
hollow handle
spike
spade point

Tuck **center strand first!**

All tucks are made **against the lay.**

seizing

4. FIRST under 1
5. second under 2
6. third under 3
7. remove seizing

198

Left-handed splicing *methods are shown;*
right-handed splicers—*turn page upside down.*

8. Continue over...under...over...under with **three** tucks for manila, **six** tucks for synthetic rope.

All strands must have equal tension.

9. 10. Cut excess strands, fuse synthetic rope ends...or taper and bury the tapered ends.

Pound and roll on hard surface.

A B
C
D E

A splicing video— page 201.

Powerboating Illustrated

1 Tape synthetic rope ends... then fuse the strand ends.

2 Unravel desired strands for manila...with twice as many strands for synthetic rope.

3 Add outer seizings to prevent further strand unwinding.

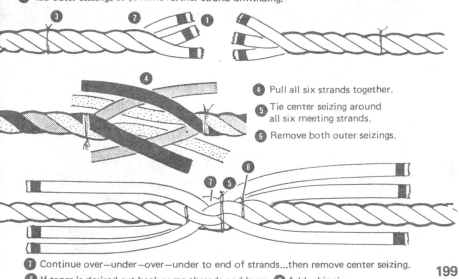

4 Pull all six strands together.

5 Tie center seizing around all six meeting strands.

6 Remove both outer seizings.

7 Continue over—under—over—under to end of strands...then remove center seizing.

8 If taper is desired cut back some threads and bury. **9** Add whipping.

10 If ends show, removed tape. **11** Roll and pound on hard surface.

199

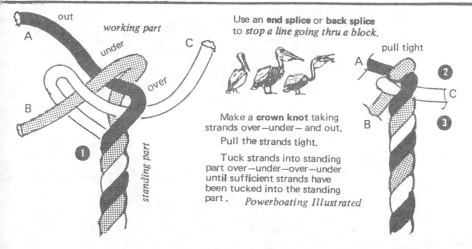

out

working part

A

under

C

B

over

standing part

1

Use an **end splice** or **back splice** to *stop a line going thru a block*.

Make a **crown knot** taking strands over—under— and out.

Pull the strands tight.

Tuck strands into standing part over—under—over—under until sufficient strands have been tucked into the standing part. *Powerboating Illustrated*

pull tight

A

2

C

B

3

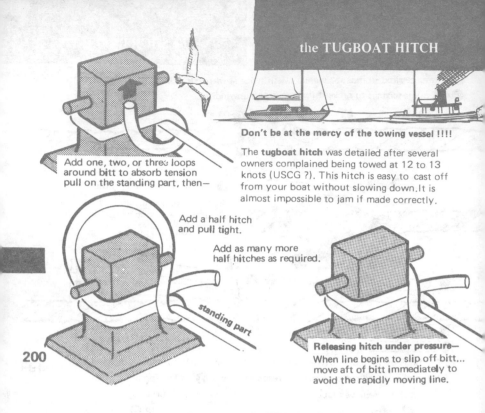

Add one, two, or three loops around bitt to absorb tension pull on the standing part, then—

Don't be at the mercy of the towing vessel !!!!

The **tugboat hitch** was detailed after several owners complained being towed at 12 to 13 knots (USCG ?). This hitch is easy to cast off from your boat without slowing down. It is almost impossible to jam if made correctly.

Add a half hitch and pull tight.

Add as many more half hitches as required.

standing part

Releasing hitch under pressure—
When line begins to slip off bitt... move aft of bitt immediately to avoid the rapidly moving line.

200

Splice your own towing bridle.

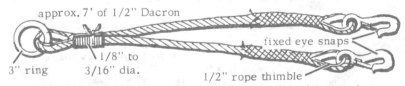

approx. 7' of 1/2" Dacron

fixed eye snaps

3" ring   1/8" to 3/16" dia.

1/2" rope thimble

You will eventually be involved in a towing job either towing, or being towed. Since tow angle pull should be from sterns center where the outboard motor or outdrive is, splice the tow bridle to make towing easier. Splice it short enough so eye will not drop below cavitation plate fouling the prop.

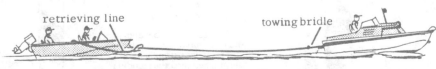

retrieving line

towing bridle

● Synthetic double-braided rope appeared in 1960. It provided a new splicing education for ALL sailors...while three-strand eye splices were found in Egyptian tombs reputed to be 7000 years old.

Our first double-braided splices were less than satisfactory. To find the answer I made 47 braided splices during the following days until running out of things that could go wrong. While the basic theory is simple...the problem seemed to be oversimplified splicing instructions.

● We tested, then prepared our sequence of 35 simple steps shown on the following four pages. **Take these steps in exact numerical sequence without shortcuts** *until* the sequence involved in this new skill becomes easy and simple to use...then make several splices at the same time.

We chose seven people at random to test our sequence who had never made a braided eye splice. All made a successful double-braided eye splice on the first attempt. All admitted total confusion in the final steps before the splices suddenly came together.

Make a braided eye splice soon as practical. Order a splicing kit from *Samson Ocean Systems, Inc., Pleasure Boating Division, 99 High Street, Boston,MA 02110.* OR you can buy 18' of 3/8" double-braided rope, plus a pusher and a 3/8" fid. The rope can be cut into three 6' lengths for six eye splices. The ice pick at first may seem to be a good substitute pusher, though the sharp point under pressure can become dangerous.

201

● **New rope.** This is a major factor to consider since after a double-braided line has been put under tension, the diameter tends to shrink with the core and cover binding together. Wash the line to remove sand, lubricate between the core and cover, and **use a next smaller size fid.**

● **Fid MUST be correct size.** for steps ⓯ to ㉑. The next larger size fid will be almost impossible to pull or push thru the rope...while a smaller diameter fid will hardly provide sufficient opening to PULL the core thru the cover, or visa versa. Choose **metal fids** for smaller rope sizes, which doesn't seem to be as critical for larger diameter rope using plastic fids.

● **Pushing/holding angle step ⓲.** This is the most difficult part of the sequence for most sailors. *A slight angle provides the best leverage* to push, then pull the cover behind the fid and out thru the core. Women, dentists, and medical doctors with good hand dexterity and nimble fingers master it easily.

● **Reserve a full afternoon or evening without interruptions** when making your first braided eye splices...then teach other members of your family or crew to make braided eye splices. You will find numerous uses for your new splicing skill on your boat, in your home, and in the garage.

Jim McGrew is our splicing expert. Request his catalog with unique splicing methods and tools. Order his economical **hour video**, listening to words of our expert while watching his hands perform all kinds of splicing as many times as desired, until you master 3 strand, braided, wire splicing. 8120 Rio Linda Blvd.,Elverta, CA 95626,(916) 991-1142.

---

outer cover | double braided rope

inner core

The double braided eye splice is quite simple **IF you follow the 35 simple steps in exact sequence.** Chances are excellent then that your first braided eye splice will be successful. The next splices will be faster and easier to make as *the splicing sequence starts to make sense...*while you pick up a new skill.

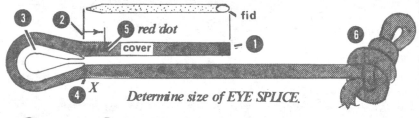

Determine size of EYE SPLICE.

① Tape end. ② Measure back fid length and add a mark.
③ Add thimble to determine size of eye. ④ Mark it *point X.*
⑤ Count seven pairs of threads forward of mark 2 and make a *red dot* on cover. ⑥ Tie SLIP KNOT 4 to 6 feet from eye.

202

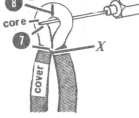

MARK and EXTRACT CORE

⑦ Bend rope at *X,* see right. Separate strands with pusher, and pry out inner core.
⑧ Mark inner core *I* at this point.

If thimble has locking ears, add it now.

MARKING the inner core   X

⑨ Pull out core. ⑩ Tape core end. ⑪ Measure back from *I* amount of fid shown, then mark it *II.* ⑫ Measure a fid length from *II,* add an inch and mark it *III.* ⑬ Cut *to taper both ends* to fit eye in fid. ⑭ Retape with electrical tape, *cut excess tape.*

Powerboating Illustrated

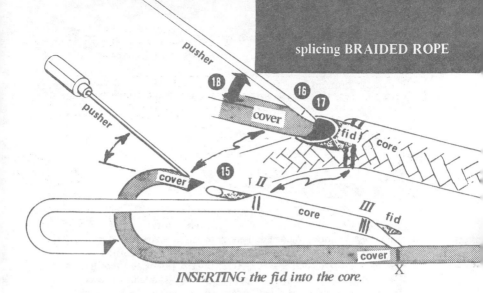

INSERTING the fid into the core.

15 *Insert fid into core at II* and pull out at *III*. **16** Insert taped end of cover into eye of fid. **17** Angle taped end forward to lock cover into fid eye. **Push fid at slight angle BEHIND taped cover end** at **18** until the cover comes out of the core as you see below at step **19**

203

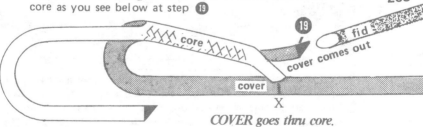

COVER goes thru core.

CORE enters cover.

20 Insert fid 6 pairs of threads *after red dot,* with fid coming out at point *X.* **21** Push core into fid so it comes out at point *X.* **16 17 18** Use the same holding/pushing method only this time it is to pull the *core thru the cover.*

Powerboating Illustrated

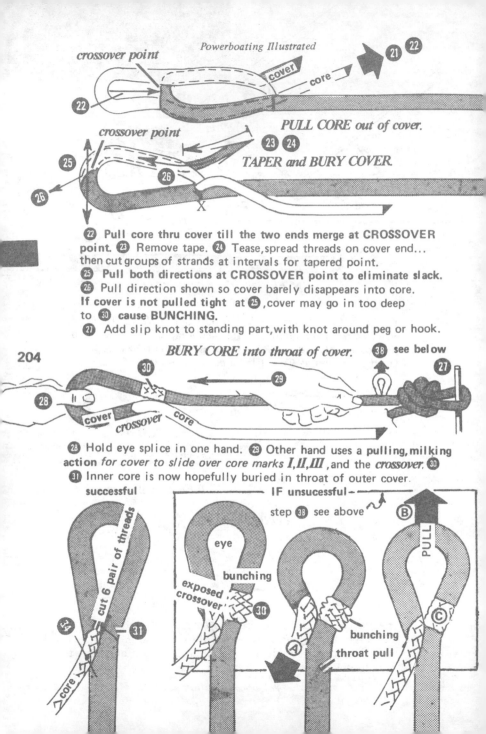

crossover point

cover core

21 **22**

22

PULL CORE out of cover.

crossover point

23 **24**

25

26

26

TAPER and **BURY COVER.**

X

22 Pull core thru cover till the two ends merge at CROSSOVER point. **23** Remove tape. **24** Tease, spread threads on cover end... then cut groups of strands at intervals for tapered point.
25 Pull both directions at CROSSOVER point to eliminate slack.
26 Pull direction shown so cover barely disappears into core.
If cover is not pulled tight at **25**, cover may go in too deep to **30** cause BUNCHING.
27 Add slip knot to standing part, with knot around peg or hook.

204

BURY CORE into throat of cover.   **38** see below

30   **29**   **27**

28

cover   crossover   core

28 Hold eye splice in one hand. **29** Other hand uses a **pulling, milking** action *for cover to slide over core marks I, II, III*, and the *crossover.* **30**
31 Inner core is now hopefully buried in throat of outer cover.

successful

IF unsuccessful—

step **38** see above

B

eye

cut 6 pair of threads

bunching

exposed crossover

30

34

31

PULL

A

bunching

C

core

throat pull

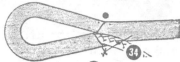

㉜ Open eye splice loop, add thimble.
㉝ Close eye with milking action to lock thimble.

㉞ Rabbit tail. Rigger practice is to cut core tail short enough to disappear just in cover. Author prefers it 3/8'' or even a little longer before cutting... with the *rabbit tail* still showing under pressure outside of cover.

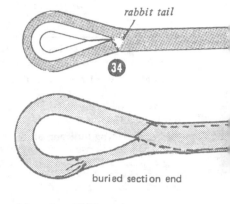

rabbit tail

㉞

Core tail cut too short. Breaking tests indicate double-braid splice usually fails at the ...*end of buried section,* USN term is called ''necking down''.

Buried section flat hollow core space can develop with only cover carrying load under pressure. USN states ''These lines are potential killers and can fail without warning as much as 50% below breaking strength''.

buried section end

205

㉟ Stitch-lock throat. this prevents crossover being pulled out under load. Add whipping thread thru throat with an equal length on both sides of throat. Face up— insert whipping 3 to 4 times pulling snug on each pass.

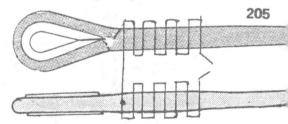

Rotate splice 90 degrees. Use whipping thread on other side 3 to 4 times pulling snug at each pass. Tie both whipping ends with a square knot. Bury knot in throat.

㊱ Lock thimble. Use nylon whipping for nylon dock lines, and Dacron or polyester for halyards and sheets.

㊲ Anchor line chafe. Sand chafes both external AND internal fibers of the line. Tape eye as shown, and at least two or more feet to protect throat and line. Use *duct tape* and retape when chafe begins to show on tape.

㊳ Recover with a martini or double *sarsaparilla*.

Ask a dozen people to define the term safety and you may find a
dozen varied answers, the reason we try to avoid its use when possible.
Safety is a religion or blind belief to some people. It is the safe path
to follow to stay out of harm's way. The totally safe person must avoid
all forms of transportation, avoid exercise as it produces strains and
bruises. He stays home watching TV to precariously live others lives
eating safe, nonsalted potato chips. Their just, deserved award at the
end of the tunnel, is a dull, boring life... and a very early death.

The challenging person enjoys life. He takes good risks operating a
business or profession, choosing active, interesting, spirited sports.

The definition of a sport... *a risk is involved.* Those involved who don't
do their homework and blunder thru on the highway, in the air, and on
the water, will sooner or later make the spectacular evening news, and
the local obituary notices. This is the accident-prone person problem.

Flying a planing hull and an airplane are comparable. For the trained
pilot it is to choose good equipment, then know and stay within the
capabilities and limitations of his craft. He follows periodical maintenance
checks. His takeoffs and landings are uneventful. He maintains adequate
cruising speed and altitude... he doesn't fly low and slow in order to be
safe, comparable to a safe 30 mph speed on a busy freeway.

The operator of small to large planing hulls also has to be well trained
to choose good equipment, know, then stay within its capabilities and
limitations. He makes his own periodic maintenance checks, replacing
parts before failure occurs making the most of his mechanics expertise
so any equipment failures will be minor.. He knows local weather when
to enjoy sloppy weather, and when to run for cover ahead of a storm.

What does *National Safe Boating Week* accomplish, and mean to you?

The emphasis is on boating equipment. Approved equipment is stressed
such as preservers to be safe that usually pass the minimum requirements
of the law. An example is the inexpensive, clumsy AK-i preserver with
organic cloth and cheap metals that soon corrode..

The emphasis should be on the person... can he or she normally swim
100' in protected waters? After this they should test a variety of preservers floating in the water, then swim 200' wearing a variety of Approved preservers. This is often an eyeopener to the new person.

Familiarity is the leading personal problem needing publicity. Few
people give sufficient interest to our greatest hazards most of us face
daily that are the real killers and cripplers. This includes the shower,
bathtub, auto, and bicycle.

A TV news program reported during a 3 day weekend, 56 auto fatalities...
with only 3 fatalities involved wearing seatbelts or shoulder restraints.
If the other 53 wore such restraints... how many would still be alive?

If the purpose of safety is to publicize people hazards, wouldn't more
be accomplished with a *National Safe Bathing in the Bathtub Week?*

He forgot the drain plug again!

Boating Safety?

How dangerous is boating??????

According to a study by U.S. Consumer Product Safety Commission of the top 150 most hazardous consumer products based on the frequency and severity of accidents reported in emergency rooms—

Top of the list was bicycles and related equipment, fishing tackle was 28, water skiing was 102...while boating was NOT on the list. According to the report why don't we change *National Safe Boating Week* which accomplishes little, to the real hazard—*National Safe Bicycling Week?*

I have the safest boat on the bay! It took a lot of planning, but I finally have all the equipment needed to meet any kind of an emergency.

Researcher

The 1972 USCG demand for boat operator licensing soon found USCG leaders with few answers and endless embarrassing questions. From the puzzle developed the *Nationwide Boating Survey* for USCG, made by the National Technical Information Service, Springfield, VA 22161.

While USCG emphasis had been on the small in numbers, visible, slip-berthed boats, the NBS statistics proved the continuously ignored largest segment of the boating world...was the trailerboat.

The survey was a broad-based national sampling of approx. 25,000 homes with USCG leaders finally seeing in their own information what we had been trying to bring to headquarters attention since 1960. And then even the computers with a sense of humor provided figures such as 1000 ferrocement inflatables, 2000 bowrider outboards over 65' long, 7000 *thrill craft* 25' or under had no power, 1000 inboard-powered canoes, etc.

The story behind the Nationwide Boating Survey.

It began in the early 1960's when the new California boating department demanded boat operator licensing, which sounded like a good idea. After analyzing those behind the push with little interest nor expertise in boating, the obvious goal was more control... **to raise more taxes.** I was the primary person stopping 4 out of 5 licensing drives in our state, trying to push the idea that the need was for trailerboating education which was continually ignored—**how could it raise taxes with little effort?**

208

In 1972 USCG Commandant Adm. Chester Bender demanded *mandatory education and licensing*. Was the interest in education...**or to raise more taxes?** I prepared a 24 page booklet defining the need for trailerboating education with 350 copies delivered to USCG Washington, D.C. headquarters.

All bureaucratic battles are nasty. Red faced top USCG leaders had to back off and order the survey, continuing to ignore trailerboating education as the only obvious goal had to be **to raise more taxes with little effort.**

USCG attempted a new end run in 1976-7 by a *mandated boating course* with many obsoleted rules **to raise taxes** ignoring trailerboating education by the same Admiral writing the 1976 Survey *forward.* I enjoyed personally stopping this new bureautic push in Norman, Oklahoma.

Since 1960 I have pushed hard on all levels, the need for specialized, quality trailerboating couses stressing the technical factors of planing hulls, trailers, and powerplants...IF safety is the issue involved, of reducing injury, fatalities and property damage as planing hulls require considerable knowledge and maintenance to operate normally and successfully, while minimizing any hazard in the developing stage.

For over 25 years operator licensing battles on local, state, and federal levels repeat themselves as politicians looking for new revenue sources suddenly discover boating. Licensing is the instant answer for their expertise **to raise taxes** (not mentioned) with little in return to help boaters.

This is YOUR trailerboating world. Endless bureaucrats dream of vast empires supported by your operator licensing taxes. Will you help stop their dreams of grandeur with little in return?

79.7% had outboard motors
9.3% had inboard engines
8.7% had outdrives
.7% had inboard jets
.3% had outboard jets

Powerboating Illustrated

●*The average age of a boat nationwide was 7.6 years old—*

the average outboard boat-8 years old
the average outdrive boat-6.7 years old
the average inboard boat-10.5 years old

> Tremendous complexity is involved in the 200 page 1973 Survey...and the 250 page 1976 Survey.
>
> We can find no better source to define the huge trailerboating world than these Surveys for the USCG.

●*The average trailerboat lengths—*

60.9% of outboard boats are 16' and under
74.1% of outdrive boats are 16' to 25' long
58.0% of inboard boats are 16' to 25' long

● *62.7% of all boats were trailered in 1976.*

29.3% were trailered less than 10 miles.
24.6% were trailered from 11 to 30 miles.
28.4% were trailered 31 to 100 miles.
17.7% were trailered over 100 miles per round trip.

● *Average round trip distance trailered was 72 miles.*

Those boats trailered further per round trip were—

houseboats—200 miles   thrill craft—92 miles
cabin cruisers—144 miles   bowrider runabouts -82 miles
inflatable boats—125 miles   canoes—81 miles
kayaks—118 miles   runabouts—76 miles

● *Boats trailered less than 72 miles per round trip—*

209

dinghies—72 miles   inflatable rafts—51 miles
skiffs—68 miles   non-inflatable rafts—35 miles
jonboats—60 miles   sailboats—27 miles
rowboats—58 miles   pontoon boats—26 miles

● *Average distances trailered by length of boats—*

under 16'   66.0 miles round trip average
16'-25'   81.2 miles round trip average
26'-39'   30.3 miles round trip average
40'-65'   no survey boats trailered this length...?

●*Average outboard boat age nationwide was—*

1973 Survey		1976 Survey	
1. 8-10 years old		1. 11-15 years old	
2. 6-7 years old		2. 9-10 years old	
3. 11-15 years old		3. 5 years old	
4. 4 years old		4. 7-8 years old	
5. 3 years old		5. 3 years old	
6. 2 years old		6. 2 years old	

————— *Trailerboating education is the need—* —————

USCG Survey defines the huge trailerboating field,while we define the complex operation and maintenance technicalities of my friend the outboard motor.Until specialized trailerboating education is available nationwide,a paper license is of ridiculous value to untrained operators.

After quality trailerboating courses are available nationwide, the small group of troublemakers on the water,often causing problems also on the highway and in the air,can be singled out and removed.Who needs layers of bureaucrats trying to **raise more taxes by licensing** to support their lack of interest and expertise,to cripple and legislate the fun out of boating.

Can communications be improved between customers and mechanics ?

Your only product is happy customers...who need your services to provide solutions to their problems. This service requires considerable training, based on your personality and interests to help you reach your highest potentials to be successful in our present economy.

It may be a surprise to find IBM computer manufacturing is really a secondary factor. IBM success is based instead on the idea of defining, then **selling solutions to their customer problems.** This is by continually updating present products to answer the latest customer needs...while developing new products to provide other solutions. Our IBM type-setting machine which is a little larger than a typewriter replaced a huge, complex linotype machine with expensive, highly trained type-setters not many years ago...to do the same job.

Flexibility—a good marine mechanic develops his own following. If it fits his personality, he can later open his own business to sell boats, motors, trailers and equipment, and hiring his mechanics.

210

Or—an outboard mechanic loved ocean fishing. He moved to a nearby island with an endless supply of summer outboard motor customers, while servicing electric motors for local inhabitants, spending the rest of the year...with lots of ocean fishing to fit his personality.

●**Or- do you want to improve communications with your customers?**

This page was added at the last moment due to a friend who found his outboard boat and 50 hp motor sank at its mooring...with repairs that would cost more than what he paid for his 50 hp motor when new. *How would you handle this problem next week, next month, or next year when facing a hostile customer who has no understanding of how to take care of submerged outboard motors.*

If it fits your personality—consider a weekly 2 hour evening course for customers and the public. Cover **basic concepts** requirements for hulls, trailers, plus 2 and 4 cycle engine needs while studiously trying to avoid sales promotions for your special products.

When a student drops a motor overboard, he can contact you to find if you can strip the motor immediately...OR if a time problem is involved, you can tell him to fully submerge the powerhead in a barrel of cold, fresh water. Damage will be minimal, and you will have a cooperative instead of a hostile customer to deal with. Teaching will require extra work, yet the results may soon more than pay for itself.

62.7% of all boats were trailered (page 209) though their owners seldom have a chance to check their rig in a friendly environment to know if their boat, trailer, and rig passes legal requirements.

How will an owner know if his trailerboat rig with endless variables is legal. Does it have *loose ends which could have been recognized easily in a developing stage* that may fail on the highway, or on the water to produce a serious collision. Or will the equipment fail in an isolated area...or when a storm hits your area.

It is up to the local police or highway patrol to pull the owner over for an expensive ticket for trailer lights, tiedowns, or other reasons. **While the CGA may provide a simplistic boat inspection, it is too basic to provide the real need, to the complete trailerboat rig.**

Each trailerboat rig, boat, trailer, powerplant, and equipment, should be inspected as a unit yearly in the early spring.

A team of inspectors from a local boat club could go from town to town with date of arrival listed in local papers. Local owners could tow their rigs to the announced location to have their trailerboat rig on its trailer checked as a unit behind its car, truck, or camper.

211

Three inspectors could rapidly go thru a number of rigs using a standard check list based on our **basic concepts.** While one checks the boat, equipment, and running lights, the second checks the engine, fuel, and steering system. The third inspector can check trailer support, trailer lights, hitch, chain, tire pressure, tongue weight, etc.

● Areas covered should be—*1. legal requirements, 2. potential hazards, 3. recommended equipment such as heaving line, a method to climb back on board*, etc.

This should be a friendly, NOT a mandatory check so an owner is not subject to a fine if his rig doesn't pass all legal requirements. The defects, would have to be corrected before receiving the decals shown which would be recognized by enforcement officials on the water and highway to eliminate most expensive tickets. One decal is placed near the bow, the other on the stern for easy recognition.

Check list requirements and inspections should be made by practicing trailerboat owners with an ample technical background, plus exposure to the endless variables from low to high performance rigs. After such an inspection method is underway, cooperation may come from state and national boating organizations to expand the idea.

courtesy exam decals

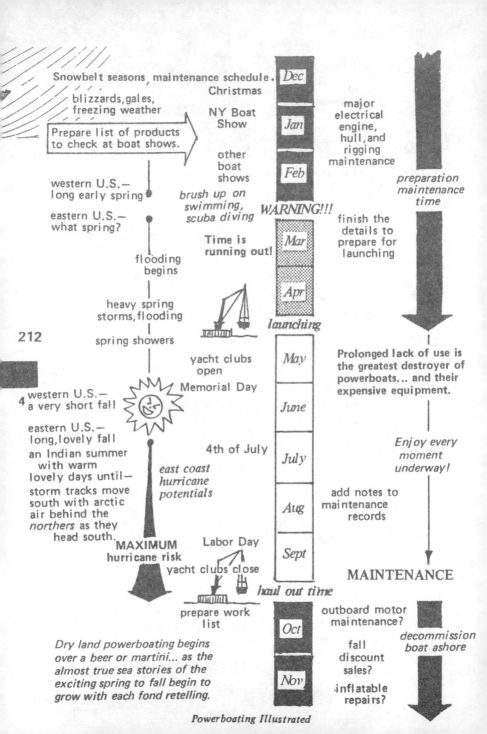

Snowbelt seasons, maintenance schedule.

Christmas

blizzards, gales, freezing weather

Prepare list of products to check at boat shows.

NY Boat Show

other boat shows

western U.S.— long early spring

eastern U.S.— what spring?

brush up on swimming, scuba diving

flooding begins

Time is running out!

heavy spring storms, flooding

spring showers

yacht clubs open

Memorial Day

western U.S.— a very short fall

eastern U.S.— long, lovely fall an Indian summer with warm lovely days until— storm tracks move south with arctic air behind the *northers* as they head south.

4th of July

east coast hurricane potentials

MAXIMUM hurricane risk

Labor Day

yacht clubs close

haul out time

prepare work list

Dry land powerboating begins over a beer or martini... as the almost true sea stories of the exciting spring to fall begin to grow with each fond retelling.

212

4

| Dec |
| Jan |
| Feb |

WARNING!!!

| Mar |
| Apr |

launching

| May |
| June |
| July |
| Aug |
| Sept |

| Oct |
| Nov |

major electrical engine, hull, and rigging maintenance

preparation maintenance time

finish the details to prepare for launching

Prolonged lack of use is the greatest destroyer of powerboats... and their expensive equipment.

Enjoy every moment underway!

add notes to maintenance records

MAINTENANCE

outboard motor maintenance?

fall discount sales?

inflatable repairs?

decommission boat ashore

"I have a little motor problem"

Engine Operation

It is fortunate to be around seventy or so years with exposure to the outboard motor in various time frames and various worlds from displacement to planing operation.

Technology requirements are all important we cover as a rambling story teller. Some basic concepts are continually changing such as the propeller. Some change periodically, while others remain little changed in 40 to 50 years such as hook and rocker.

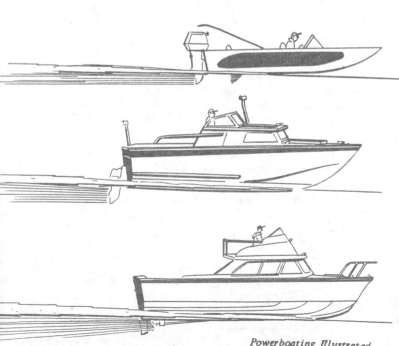

Powerboating Illustrated

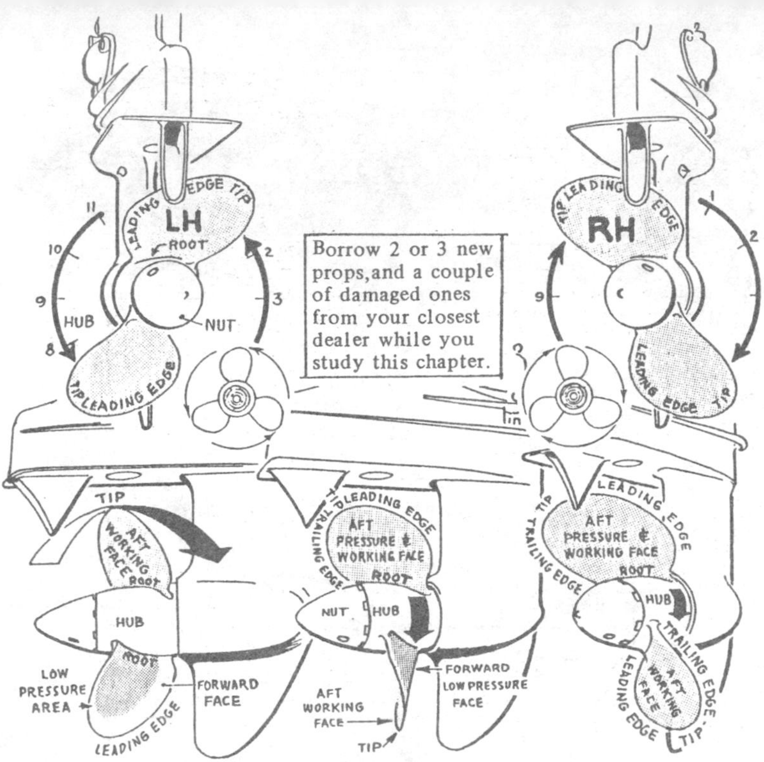

Borrow 2 or 3 new props, and a couple of damaged ones from your closest dealer while you study this chapter.

Controlled powerhead burning rotates the crankshaft, producing lower unit drive shaft torque. This is changed to propeller thrust (*action vs reaction*) pushing the boat. The *positive pressure* aft blade face rotates downward pushing the water aft...while the *negative pressure* forward blade side pulls water into the turning blade.

The *rounded* leading edge of a prop extends from the hub to the tip, cuts into the water it is advancing thru. The *sharper* trailing edge cuts the water from the aft tip to the hub as it leaves the propeller blade.

Efficiency or lift is increased with a waterfoil section across the blade. This lift causes a pressure reduction on the leading edge...with a trailing edge blade thrust pressure increase.

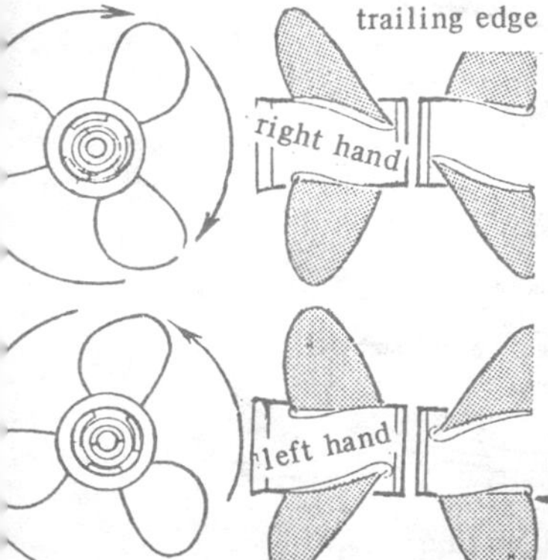

Can you easily put your left or right hand on the hub between the blades of the propellers at left?

An inboard drag boat with prop damage limped into the pits where it was put on its trailer. A passing dealer with a van carrying spare parts installed a new prop. The boat was pushed from the trailer, and the operator gave the throttle a full reverse. The boat took a flying leap to land back on the trailer with a loud splash.

The dealer replaced the LH prop with a RH prop.
If you want a customer with the fastest boat in reverse....

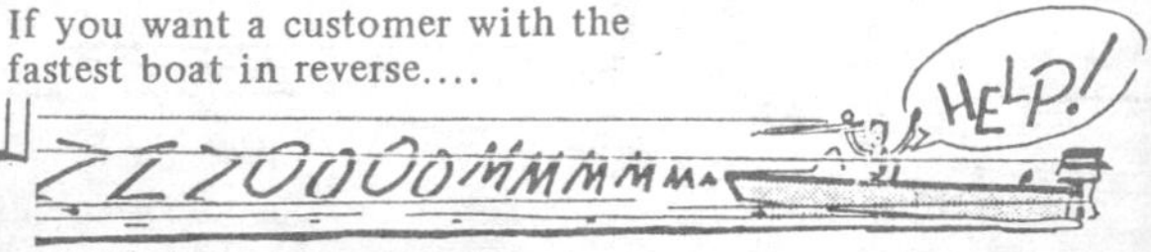

HELP!

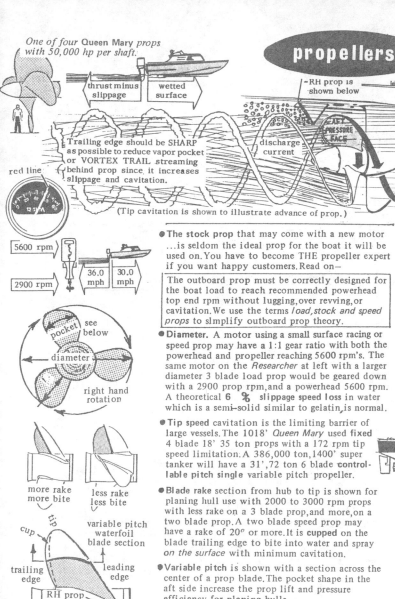

One of four Queen Mary *props with 50,000 hp per shaft.*

thrust minus slippage

wetted surface

RH prop is shown below

AFT PRESSURE FACE

Trailing edge should be SHARP as possible to reduce vapor pocket or VORTEX TRAIL streaming behind prop since it increases slippage and cavitation.

red line

discharge current

(Tip cavitation is shown to illustrate advance of prop.)

5600 rpm

2900 rpm

36.0 mph | 30.0 mph

pocket — see below

diameter

right hand rotation

more rake more bite

less rake less bite

cup

tip

variable pitch waterfoil blade section

trailing edge

leading edge

RH prop

● **The stock prop** that may come with a new motor …is seldom the ideal prop for the boat it will be used on. You have to become THE propeller expert if you want happy customers. Read on—

The outboard prop must be correctly designed for the boat load to reach recommended powerhead top end rpm without lugging, over revving, or cavitation. We use the terms *load, stock* and *speed props* to simplify outboard prop theory.

● **Diameter.** A motor using a small surface racing or speed prop may have a 1:1 gear ratio with both the powerhead and propeller reaching 5600 rpm's. The same motor on the *Researcher* at left with a larger diameter 3 blade load prop would be geared down with a 2900 prop rpm, and a powerhead 5600 rpm. A theoretical 6 **%** **slippage speed loss** in water which is a semi-solid similar to gelatin, is normal.

● **Tip speed** cavitation is the limiting barrier of large vessels. The 1018' *Queen Mary* used **fixed** 4 blade 18' 35 ton props with a 172 rpm tip speed limitation. A 386,000 ton, 1400' super tanker will have a 31', 72 ton 6 blade **controllable pitch single** variable pitch propeller.

● **Blade rake** section from hub to tip is shown for planing hull use with 2000 to 3000 rpm props with less rake on a 3 blade prop, and more, on a two blade prop. A two blade speed prop may have a rake of 20° or more. It is **cupped** on the blade trailing edge to bite into water and spray *on the surface* with minimum cavitation.

● **Variable pitch** is shown with a section across the center of a prop blade. The pocket shape in the aft side increase the prop lift and pressure efficiency for planing hulls.

● *P. S.* — who invented the marine propeller?

A naval architect said the honor goes to a Swiss inventor in the early 1800's. He believed the answer was a long tapered screw... that failed after much testing.

On the return to the dock it hit a submerged rock that broke off most of the screw. The short threads on the remaining stump began biting into the water. Its use for ship propulsion began around 1850.

215

Powerboating Illustrated

The propeller is the most efficient transmission method to transfer powerhead energy into lower unit thrust,is a highly technical field which can make happy customers,and profits for you.Your instructors will be very pleased if students spend considerable time studying our propeller basics so you can move into specific details of their props.

Correct prop? An estimated *HALF of all planing hulls* have the wrong prop for boating use and boat load...with a 5 to 15% top end speed loss.The greater becomes the top end loss,the more your machinery will fight itself with minimum to major damage potentials.

Damaged propellers—*the planing hull needs a spare prop* the way your auto needs a spare tire.I've broken shear pins and aluminum props on rowboats,and a good share of aluminum props on planing hulls...while intentionally damaging a bronze slip clutch prop,pg.218.During 24 years on our sailboat with our aluminum props protected by the keel,we have broken one prop blade,and replaced a slipping,slip clutch prop.Can you repair damaged props...or who will do the repairs for you?(pg.374)

The best advertising? Have a customer tow his boat to your shop.Have him remove his prop doing all the work for familiarity...in ideal conditions.This gives you time to check if his boat has the correct prop, if the prop needs repairs,and if you can convince him he needs a spare prop,a special prop wrench,tachometer,or—

While he then can replace a prop in shallow water...can he change one in deep water if he has no alternative? Discuss anchoring,a flotation jacket for positive buoyancy,lines around props and wrenches so they don't sink,and the hazards involved in wave action.

The outboard motor manufacturer has no idea if his next motor will power an 8' hydro...or a 60' houseboat. Since outboard,outdrive,and inboard boats have direct transmission from powerhead to prop,a *stock prop* on a light hydro is similar to an auto engine operating at 90 mph in low gear,or on a heavy boat,starting a heavy truck in high gear.

Propeller pitch becomes your powerhead to prop transmission method. The goal is to choose a prop that can easily reach and hold the top end recommended rpm on the tach,then check against the speedometer.Repeat with a second prop that may have a higher or lower top end speed at the same top rpm.The customer may want the slower one as a spare prop.

The **variable-pitch waterfoil** is shown compared to a sailboat airfoil. Lift or advance is increased with *less pressure* on the negative side of the blade...increasing the *thrust pressure* on the aft positive side of a prop blade advancing thru the water.

216

Powerboating Illustrated

Prop Dimensions are: Pitch, Diameter, Area, and Number of Blades.

By changing props, one motor can serve many purposes.

The smaller the motor, the less horsepower it has to lose, and the more important it is to have the correct prop.

SPEED PROP
High Gear
Maximum Pitch
Warmer Plugs

For a light load a small quantity of water is moved in a hurry.

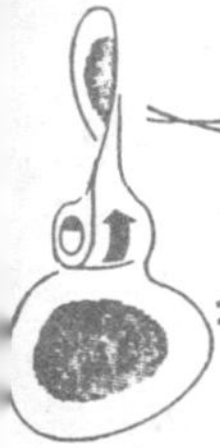

Prop should have lots of cup and perform close to surface as possible without cavitating.

40 hp motor ——

Up to 700 lb. load

OOPS— I drew a LH racing prop.

HP = SPEED x thrust

Speed Prop is for lighter than normal load.

14" Pitch

---

 red line

Propeller pitch is defined as the advance of a screw thread in a single turn thru a semi solid such as gelatin with some slippage. A *tachometer* is necessary to check engine rpm...and secondly, a *speedometer* to check engine speed.

STOCK PROP
Second Gear
Usually comes with motor
Factory Equipped Plugs

40 hp motor ——

14' to 16' boat-for a 700 to 1100 lb. load, 12" Pitch Prop **217**
16' to 18' boat-for a 1100 to 1800 lb. load, 10" Pitch Prop

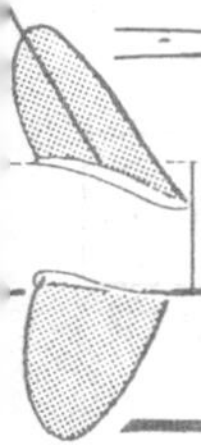

Stock Prop, average use.

11" Pitch

To move a big load it is necessary to move a lot of water slowly. The best comparison is a stream of water coming from a fire hose (Load Prop)compared to a small garden hose (Speed Prop).

LOAD PROP
Low Gear-3 Blades
Colder Plugs

40 hp motor

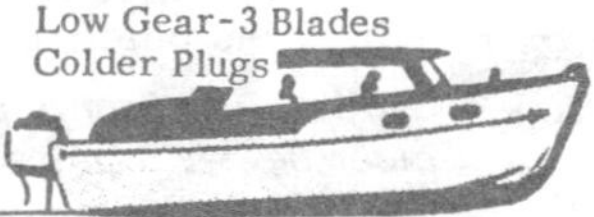

RH props have been shown on this page, LH props turn opposite direction.

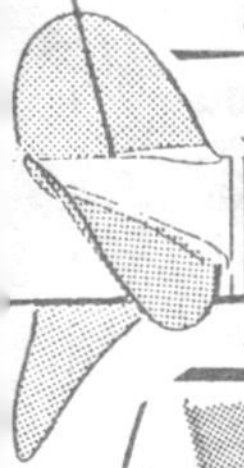

HP = speed x THRUST

Load Prop is for a heavier than normal load.

8"Pitch

less pressure

more pressure

negative pressure

positive pressure

variable pitch waterfoil

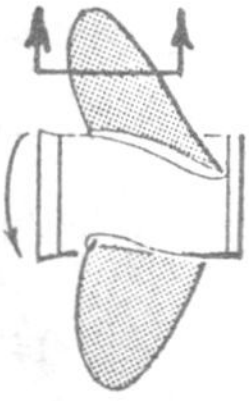

Powerboating Illustrated

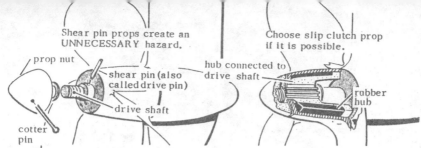

Shear pin props create an
UNNECESSARY hazard.

prop nut

shear pin(also
called drive pin)

drive shaft

cotter
pin

Choose slip clutch prop
if it is possible.

hub connected to
drive shaft

rubber
hub

A friends boat hit a shark 18 miles offshore at 30 mph shearing a
blade off his aluminum prop. His boat drifted the rest of the day, all
night, and the following morning until a passing commercial fisherman
towed the disabled boat back to Long Beach.

An eskimo fractured an aluminum prop 200 miles away from his
camp. He whittled a prop out of a walrus tusk which took his boat
200 miles back to his camp in northern Alaska while dodging icebergs.

A 22' sailboat was underway with outboard power when the shear pin
failed. Only quick action by the owner of a large powerboat saved the
sailboat, drifting into high breakers heading for the beach at Palos Verdes,
as the swirling waters with no wind made anchoring impossible.

⊙Mercury introduced the slip clutch prop in 1952 to replace the shear
pin prop above, though taking several years to be adopted by other
manufacturers. If the shear pin prop had been obsoleted 20 years ago,
it would have eliminated many unnecessary injuries and fatalities...
with the sailboat above, just one of endless examples.

218

A large number of outboard motors using shear pin propellers are still
being used today. They are a *NUISANCE to replace under ideal conditions
...and a serious HAZARD to replace in rough water.*

The early outboard **bronze prop** corroded rapidly with the softer metal
bending under impact, while the slip clutch prop slipped...to protect
the drive shaft and crankshaft. **Stainless outboard props** are stronger,
lighter, and more efficient, have replaced the bronze prop for outboard
motors and outdrives.

Caution—*use bronze props only for inboard boats slip berthed or on
moorings* with props submerged for more than a few days, see pg. 361.

●**Tip speed barriers**- the 18' diameter *Queen Mary* propellers have a
172 rpm limit to avoid cavitation damage. Small raked, outboard and
outdrive 2000 to 3000 **variable pitch** props can develop cavitation
after this prop rpm barrier is exceeded. For 3500 prop rpm and above,
a small *cupped surface prop* is used for racing to bite into water and
spray for thrust with minimum cavitation damage.

●The **hub exhaust propeller** improves engine efficiency...while it
complicates backing as the exhaust and prop want to go opposite
directions. It reduces the noise factor, and instead of the fumes coming
back into the cockpit, the fish below enjoy the carbon monoxide.

We averaged a two day catch of fish while trolling to Catalina on our
sailboat under power using the older cavitation plate exhaust system,
on top of pg. 214. After buying later motors with the hub exhaust
propeller when trolling under power, we rarely have had any hookups.

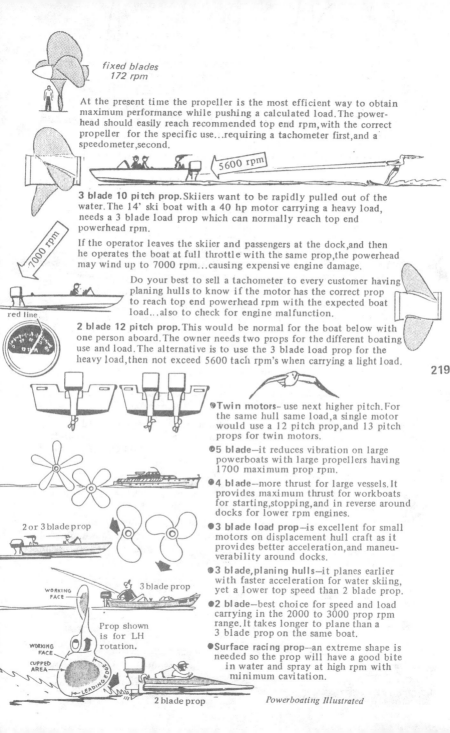

fixed blades
172 rpm

At the present time the propeller is the most efficient way to obtain maximum performance while pushing a calculated load. The powerhead should easily reach recommended top end rpm, with the correct propeller for the specific use...requiring a tachometer first, and a speedometer, second.

5600 rpm

3 blade 10 pitch prop. Skiiers want to be rapidly pulled out of the water. The 14' ski boat with a 40 hp motor carrying a heavy load, needs a 3 blade load prop which can normally reach top end powerhead rpm.

7000 rpm

If the operator leaves the skiier and passengers at the dock, and then he operates the boat at full throttle with the same prop, the powerhead may wind up to 7000 rpm...causing expensive engine damage.

Do your best to sell a tachometer to every customer having planing hulls to know if the motor has the correct prop to reach top end powerhead rpm with the expected boat load...also to check for engine malfunction.

red line

2 blade 12 pitch prop. This would be normal for the boat below with one person aboard. The owner needs two props for the different boating use and load. The alternative is to use the 3 blade load prop for the heavy load, then not exceed 5600 tach rpm's when carrying a light load.

219

◉Twin motors– use next higher pitch. For the same hull same load, a single motor would use a 12 pitch prop, and 13 pitch props for twin motors.

◉5 blade–it reduces vibration on large powerboats with large propellers having 1700 maximum prop rpm.

●4 blade–more thrust for large vessels. It provides maximum thrust for workboats for starting, stopping, and in reverse around docks for lower rpm engines.

●3 blade load prop–is excellent for small motors on displacement hull craft as it provides better acceleration, and maneuverability around docks.

◉3 blade, planing hulls–it planes earlier with faster acceleration for water skiing, yet a lower top speed than 2 blade prop.

●2 blade–best choice for speed and load carrying in the 2000 to 3000 prop rpm range. It takes longer to plane than a 3 blade prop on the same boat.

●Surface racing prop–an extreme shape is needed so the prop will have a good bite in water and spray at high rpm with minimum cavitation.

2 or 3 blade prop

3 blade prop

WORKING FACE

Prop shown is for LH rotation.

WORKING FACE

CUPPED AREA

LEADING EDGE

2 blade prop

Powerboating Illustrated

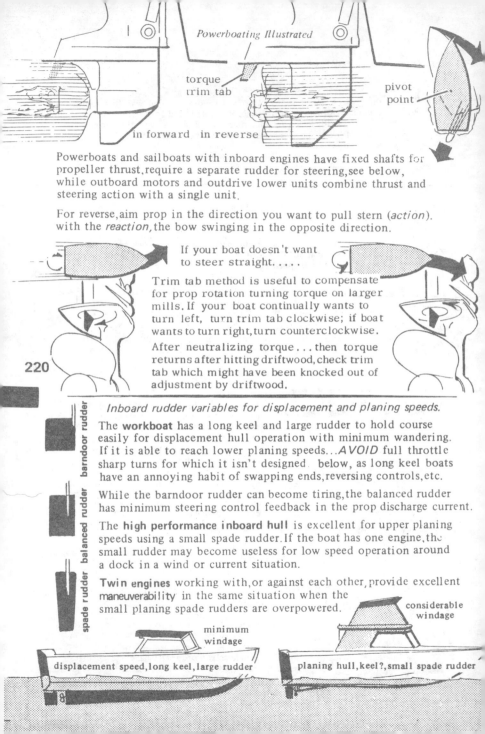

torque trim tab

pivot point

in forward   in reverse

Powerboats and sailboats with inboard engines have fixed shafts for propeller thrust, require a separate rudder for steering, see below, while outboard motors and outdrive lower units combine thrust and steering action with a single unit.

For reverse, aim prop in the direction you want to pull stern (*action*). with the *reaction*, the bow swinging in the opposite direction.

If your boat doesn't want to steer straight.....

Trim tab method is useful to compensate for prop rotation turning torque on larger mills. If your boat continually wants to turn left, turn trim tab clockwise; if boat wants to turn right, turn counterclockwise.

After neutralizing torque...then torque returns after hitting driftwood, check trim tab which might have been knocked out of adjustment by driftwood.

220

Inboard rudder variables for displacement and planing speeds.

barndoor rudder

The **workboat** has a long keel and large rudder to hold course easily for displacement hull operation with minimum wandering. If it is able to reach lower planing speeds...*AVOID* full throttle sharp turns for which it isn't designed. below, as long keel boats have an annoying habit of swapping ends, reversing controls, etc.

balanced rudder

While the barndoor rudder can become tiring, the balanced rudder has minimum steering control feedback in the prop discharge current.

spade rudder

The **high performance inboard hull** is excellent for upper planing speeds using a small spade rudder. If the boat has one engine, the small rudder may become useless for low speed operation around a dock in a wind or current situation.

Twin engines working with, or against each other, provide excellent maneuverability in the same situation when the small planing spade rudders are overpowered.

considerable windage

minimum windage

displacement speed, long keel, large rudder

planing hull, keel?, small spade rudder

All props below are RH rotation.

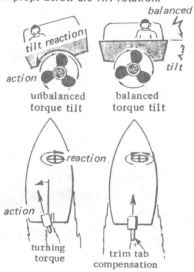

unbalanced torque tilt

balanced torque tilt

turning torque

trim tab compensation

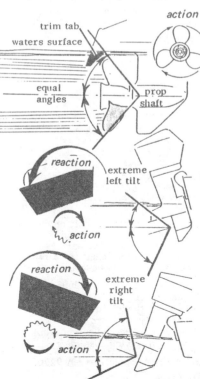

trim tab
waters surface

equal angles

prop shaft

reaction
extreme left tilt

action

reaction
extreme right tilt

action

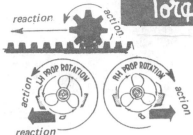

Torque

1950 opened a new outboard world when motors exceeded 50 hp. They passed a barrier with prop torque strong enough to do strange things to hulls and steering controls.

> While inboard torque produced stern walking, the new **outboard prop torque** *action* produced stern walking, hull tilt, and the lower unit turning force *reaction* on the steering wheel.

● Compounding the problem at the time was the stress for LH turns with LH props for counterclockwise racing courses, with the LH torque tilt helping the racing driver.

● A RH rotation prop is needed for right hand controls, pg. 78, for **visibility** **221** of the danger zone to compensate for the hull tilt in all but single purpose racing craft...and twin motors using opposite rotation props. Hull tilt torque for right hand steering controls will be cancelled with a RH prop in forward.

● Normal operation—when the lower unit is almost parallel to the water surface, pg. 62, *the deeper prop blade will have more bite* requiring trim tab compensation on large motors.

● Torque turning factor *action* can be neutralized by adjusting the prop stream trim tab to reduce the torque steering wheel *reaction*.

A torque factor can be owner caused by extreme lower unit tilt.

● Trimmed in excessively—extreme rake of the upper blade providing most thrust will produce maximum counterclockwise tilt torque.

● Trimmed out excessively—the extreme rake of the lower prop blade rake with most thrust will produce maximum clockwise tilt torque.

Powerboating Illustrated

● **A fully submerged prop** though just below the water surface while planing, must dig into solid water pushing it down and aft to move the boat forward. Instead of being considered as a screw moving thru wood... it is closer to a semi solid such as gelatin with approximately 10% slippage.

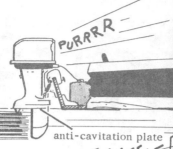

PURRRR

anti-cavitation plate

● **The boat.** The propeller must always have a solid bite in the advancing water as any obstruction in front of the prop causes a disturbance. The prop then no longer under load begins to slip, causing prop cavitation plus excess damaging powerhead rpm.

WHEEEEEE

keel

● **Cavitation OR ventilation plate?** For 30 years I've tried without success to find a better name for the horizontal plate above the prop. We call it a cavitation plate, while comma counters later insisted it is a ventilation plate...while the plate serves both functions.

● It is an **anti-ventilation (aeration?) plate** at planing speed since it must be low enough to prevent air from entering the propeller stream, so the fully submerged prop above without the motor carried too high or trimmed out to far, will have a solid bite in the advancing water.

● Ir is an **anti-cavitation plate** at planing speed to maintain a smooth water stream flow thru the prop blades. We show a straight water flow beneath the hull above, which has to be cut sharp at the transom chine, to help maintain a solid bite for the prop blades without cavitation.

● **Blowout is a racing term.** Outboard and outdrive lower units develop drag as they can't produce lift. Gearcase shapes have to become longer, leaner, and more efficient at upper planing speeds or cavitation begins with expensive damage—*look for burned paint on propellers* in the beginning stage. If the water-hammering pressure increases, the gearcase will explode. When you see burned propeller paint, consider a **nose job**.

Propeller manufacturer/racer Ron Hill* developed various bolt-on **nose-job** extenders to eliminate cavitation blowouts. The crescent shape improves the incoming water flow by separating it more efficiently and evenly. By reducing the drag and cavitation potentials, it increases the top end speed for customers wanting to go 70 mph or faster.

I noticed a little vibration.

Vibration? A few prop nicks may reduce planing hull top speed 10%, static thrust, 30%, and require 20% more fuel to take the boat the same distance...though the powerhead may reach top recommended rpm. *The outboard detective will pay close attention to customer lower units and props with even slight damage IF he wants happy customers.*

*Hill Marine—1431 East Borchard Ave., Santa Ana, CA 92705

Powerboating Illustrated

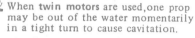

Cavitation

How's that for cavitation!

Taper width and depth of keel for at least 20" forward of transom.

A hull with a **long wide keel**, wants to go straight ahead. In a tight, high speed turn it may *reverse controls, swap ends, broach, and/or flip.*

Check keels before buying planing hulls, especially on aluminum boats. Will the keel need to be tapered to avoid propeller cavitation. Will such a change cause structural hull damage?

When **twin motors** are used, one prop may be out of the water momentarily in a tight turn to cause cavitation.

- The **fin** used on *Blunder* to provide sufficient slippage in a turn could disturb the prop stream, to cause cavitation, note stern tendency to swing in the opposite direction of the bow.

- A **chine** can dig in on a tight turn and disturb water flow to the prop producing *momentary cavitation.*

- **Seaweed or rope** caught on a fin will cause considerable cavitation turbulence when going straight ahead at all but displacement speeds. At planing speed when even a small string of seaweed caught on the fin of *Blunder,* the prop would cavitate immediately.

- **Cavitation erosion** is caused when the prop blade no longer has a good bite in the water, it slips, then begins to wind up which is *the causant.*

The resultant void in the water produces underwater boiling with high pressure steam bubbles collapsing instantly like a hammer in the water with thousands of pounds pressure per square inch.

If your prop shows cavitation tendencies, reduce rpm until the cause is found as the hammering action will pound the prop blades causing metal fatigue failure.

223

For the same outboard motor—

high rake max rpm		low rake low rpm
2 blade	3 blade	4 blade
higher top speed	lower top speed	workboat use good thrust, braking action, and reverse for operation around docks
less blade drag	more blade drag	
less static thrust	more static thrust	

Powerboating Illustrated

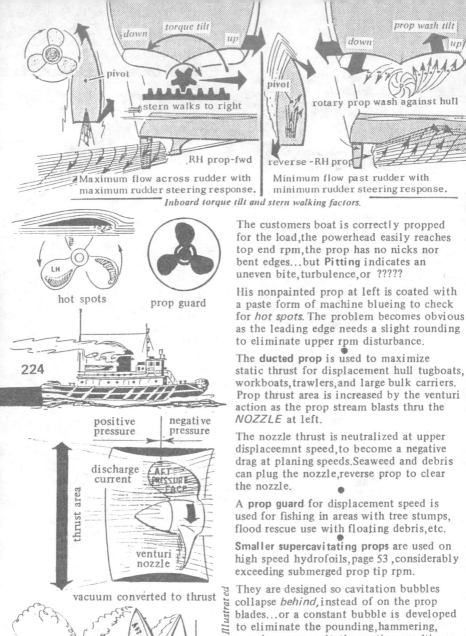

pivot · stern walks to right

pivot · rotary prop wash against hull

RH prop-fwd · reverse-RH prop

| Maximum flow across rudder with maximum rudder steering response. | Minimum flow past rudder with minimum rudder steering response. |

Inboard torque tilt and stern walking factors.

hot spots · prop guard · LH

224

positive pressure · negative pressure

discharge current · AFT PRESSURE FACE

thrust area

venturi nozzle

vacuum converted to thrust · AFT PRESSURE FACE

The customers boat is correctly propped for the load, the powerhead easily reaches top end rpm, the prop has no nicks nor bent edges...but **Pitting** indicates an uneven bite, turbulence, or ?????

His nonpainted prop at left is coated with a paste form of machine blueing to check for *hot spots.* The problem becomes obvious as the leading edge needs a slight rounding to eliminate upper rpm disturbance.

The **ducted prop** is used to maximize static thrust for displacement hull tugboats, workboats, trawlers, and large bulk carriers. Prop thrust area is increased by the venturi action as the prop stream blasts thru the *NOZZLE* at left.

The nozzle thrust is neutralized at upper displaceemnt speed, to become a negative drag at planing speeds. Seaweed and debris can plug the nozzle, reverse prop to clear the nozzle.

A **prop guard** for displacement speed is used for fishing in areas with tree stumps, flood rescue use with floating debris, etc.

Smaller **supercavitating props** are used on high speed hydrofoils, page 53, considerably exceeding submerged prop tip rpm.

They are designed so cavitation bubbles collapse *behind,* instead of on the prop blades...or a constant bubble is developed to eliminate the pounding, hammering, scouring prop cavitation action resulting when bubbles collapse *on* prop blades.

Supercavitating props have poor efficiency at lower speeds when leaving, or returning to their docks while *not cavitating.*

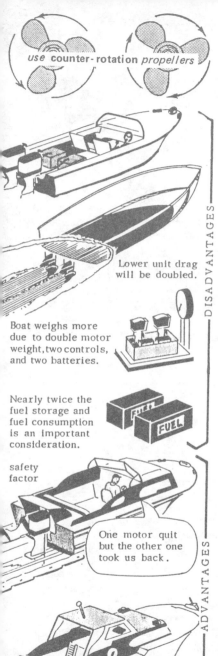

use **counter-rotation** *propellers*

Lower unit drag
will be doubled.

Boat weighs more
due to double motor
weight, two controls,
and two batteries.

Nearly twice the
fuel storage and
fuel consumption
is an important
consideration.

safety
factor

One motor quit
but the other one
took us back.

large outboard
hulls

DISADVANTAGES

ADVANTAGES

Twin Motors

Twin motors are a debators paradise,
and dealers love them as they double
their equipment sales.

Owners who defend twin motors may
spend so much time on the idea that
the other motor will always operate
when the first fails...often ends up
with double motor failure due to their
misguided philosophy. While the debate
continues with aircraft...the final
responsibility is that of the owner.

●

Twin motors are nuisance value on
smaller boats due to doubling all
components while reducing the prime
factor...the passenger space payload.

All propeller lower units develop drag
as they can't develop lift. While drag
is small at lower rpm, the drag will
multiply at upper rpm. If you question
this, try dragging your hand in the
water at 5 mph...then at 30 mph.

*Speed is determined by wetted hull
surface minus lower unit drag, plus
the weight factor of the second motor,
battery, fuel, etc.* As the boat sinks lower,
it takes longer to plane with twin motors.

225

Fuel consumption variables? Expect a
small to larger fuel increase to cover
the same distance than with one motor.

●

The **safety factor** is an advantage on
larger boats covering greater distances.
If you seldom go more than 3 miles
out and 3 miles back for fishing, the
safety factor is questionable if your
motor has proper maintenance.

Will a small hp spare trolling motor
provide a better answer to take you
back at displacement speed if the large
one fails?

●

When powerplant and weight become
secondary factor in larger boats, it is
time to consider outdrives or inboard
engines for planing hulls.

For displacement hulls you may find
the diesel inboard engine has many
more advantages than the gasoline
engine.

Powerboating Illustrated

- Our **engine operation** section provides exposure to various basic concepts. After you understand the various concepts, you can soon put them together to understand the complexity of engine operation.

  We concentrate on earlier concepts with the downdraft carburetor an example.

- *Later carburetors provide the same basic functions.* After studying the older downdraft carb, it becomes easy to explore, analyze, and understand later, more complex, compact carburetors.

- *While we felt a considerable need for this powerboating book going back to 1958,* it has been a puzzle due to the diversity of reader reactions.

  To find an answer, we rented a large RV in 1979 to visit a variety of launching ramps in California, Oregon, and Washington. We had ample time to exchange ideas with mechanics and trailerboat owners finding many of the same old 1960 problems... little changed.

  After returning, a major outboard motor manufacturer's training school requested a training manual for their new mechanics based on our 1960 *Trailerboating Illustrated.* They waited too long to give the order to finish, print, and deliver the books, with the manager soon retiring.

  We used the same foundation requested to which we kept adding thru the years, growing into the present version.

- We asked engineering friends to check our book in the final stage. They found the name had to be changed to stress the highly varied *basic concepts of powerboating* instead of emphasizing trailerboating.

  The second recommendation, was to emphasize what seems to be a smorgasbord of ideas... is easy to understand as it was written in the earthy, working language of mechanics and trailerboat owners.

  Choose any subject from carburetors, spark plugs, electricity, batteries, etc., studying a couple of pages a day. After the subject is understood, repeat the process with other subjects until you can close your eyes to see how the concepts function separately, then work together as a team.

- **Corrosion is the exception.** We found little practical information in this area in 1958. Chemical engineers owning boats seemed to have basic ideas to start with. We made periodic rounds of 2 and 4 cycle mechanics to exchange ideas to develop our present information. We periodically review this information with walks thru trailerboat storage areas, at launching ramps, and parts discarded by marine mechanics.

  You soon find these basic concepts just as practical and useful to apply in other areas from corrosion problems around the home, to troubleshooting balky auto engine problems... and the 2 cycle lawn mower

We detail a basic 4 cycle downdraft automotive carburetor to provide a comparison for the somewhat different marine carburetor.

Oil vapors and blowby enter the breather from the crankcase, valve lifters, and transmission to channel them into the carburetor to eliminate a fire hazard and keep the engine compartment clean.

Five circuits are involved with *float, low speed, high speed, pump and choke*. A double barrel downdraft carburetor has double throats doubling all the circuits.

The *arrestor screen* is darn important. I once saw an engine backfire out the carb, stopped by, and barely penetrating the screen, a horrible memory.

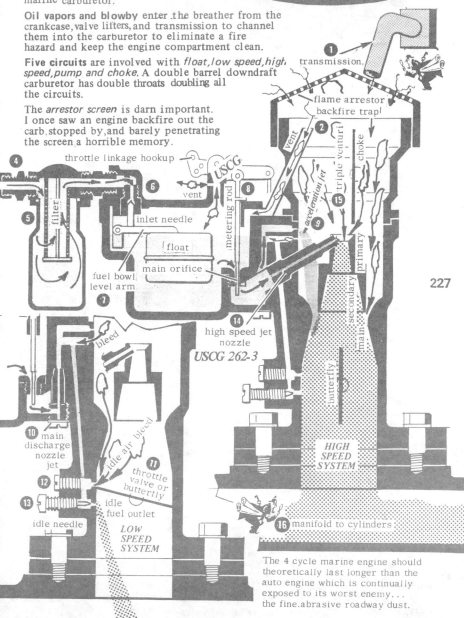

4-cycle

transmission,

flame arrestor
backfire trap

vent

triple venturi

choke

acceleration jet

throttle linkage hookup

USCG

vent

metering rod

inlet needle

filter

float

main orifice

fuel bowl
level arm

bleed

high speed jet
nozzle

USCG 262-3

primary

secondary

main

butterfly

main
discharge
nozzle
jet

idle air bleed

throttle
valve or
butterfly

idle
fuel outlet

idle needle

**LOW
SPEED
SYSTEM**

**HIGH
SPEED
SYSTEM**

manifold to cylinders

227

The 4 cycle marine engine should theoretically last longer than the auto engine which is continually exposed to its worst enemy... the fine abrasive roadway dust.

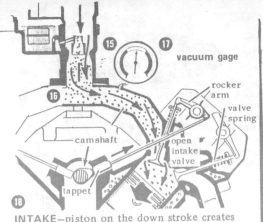

15 **17** vacuum gage

16

rocker arm

valve spring

camshaft

open intake valve

18

tappet

INTAKE—piston on the down stroke creates a low pressure in the cylinder as the inlet valve opens, pulling in the air/fuel mixture from the carburetor, thru the intake manifold.

19 An 8 to 1 COMPRESSION ratio squeezes fuel/air vapors to 1/8 volume, with enough fuel **octane** to resist preignition.

— COMPRESSION—

POWER STROKE—maximum thrust and torque in normal operation may average 600 PSI, and temperature to 4000 degrees. Valves must be leakproof under these normal conditions.

228

ZAP

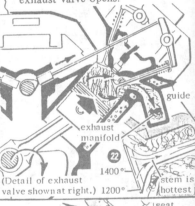

21 **EXHAUST**- temperature drops to 1200 degress and 70 PSI as exhaust valve opens.

guide

exhaust manifold

22 1400°

stem is hottest

(Detail of exhaust valve shown at right.) 1200°

seat

PREIGNITION burns exhaust valves—

Intake valve is cooled by incoming fuel/air mixture, while the *exhaust valve* glows even under ideal conditions.

Protect your valves—warm the engine before putting under load. Stay within normal **vacuum gage** 15-21 inch range, then use **tachometer** according to engine specifications.

Preignition produces excessive pressure and temperature, and boiler scale. Cause is insufficient gasoline octane, the timing is set wrong, engine has wrong size prop.

The exhaust valve is the first to fail as it warps, and leaks, causing blowby with intergranular damage to valve, **23** stem, and seat... the reason **a compression check will be required** before working on a 4 cycle marine engine.

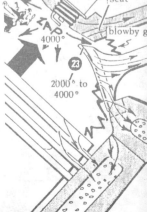

blowby g

ZAP
4000°

23

2000° to 4000°

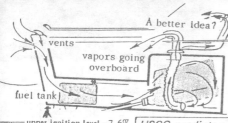

Basic 4 cycle fuel system is shown. Fuel tanks and engines are in separate sealed compartments having intake and exhaust vents. The closed engine compartments considerably reduce cockpit noise.

upper ignition level −7.6% by volume

ignition range

lower ignition level −1.4% by volume

USCG predicts a serious fire or explosion yearly with 1 in 2300 gasoline inboard boats. Our observation—

Most inboard fires and explosions *occur AFTER leaving the dock as bilge fumes are too rich to ignite if a fuel leak exists.* After the blower or the operating engine pulls the fumes down to the UIL range, a soft explosion occurs.

⦿ Before starting engine— sniff bilge by lifting engine hatch to check for a smell indicating a fuel leak. If no fumes are present, start the engine. This procedure should be repeated *every time an engine starts during the day.*

⦿ The bilge blower requires second thoughts. Basic procedure is to turn it on for 3 to 5 minutes to remove gasoline fumes, then start the engine. If a fuel leak exists and *the blower exhaust isn't sniffed,* the air/fuel mixture which was too rich to ignite, it can be taken down to the UIL point when the engine is started. Put your hand next to the overboard exhaust vent...to smell for gasoline fumes on your hand.

Blower face exhaust? The operator would be aware in ½ minute a leak exists in the bilge. USCG doesn't approve this idea wanting all gasoline fumes exhausted overboard, not into the cockpit. A simple valve hooked to the blower exhaust could be turned on and off for a practical compromise to reduce the gasoline leak hazard. **229**

⦿ Automatic Halon 1301 extinguishers used by astronauts in space capsules, bolted to the compartment, could minimize damage by controlling gasoline fires in the initial stage. Blow-trap hatches large enough to release initial explosive force *aft, away from passengers,* should be standard practice. Major damage occurs in a closed compartment at the waterline as the expansion forces hit the incompressible water, and bounces back.

⦿ Filling inboard built-in fuel tanks. Wrap a rag around the nozzle so all vapor fumes go into the tank, and exit the exhaust vent which must be sealed just as thoroughly as the fill pipe. Inspect both pipes regularly...especially after yard work is done on an inboard boat.

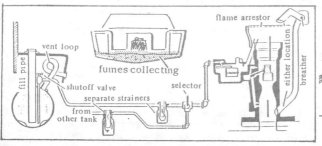

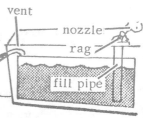

Powerboating Illustrated

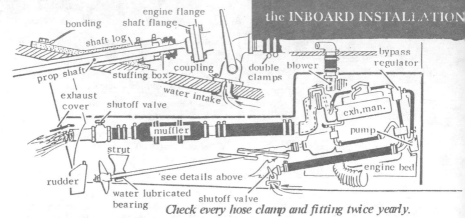

engine flange
shaft flange
bonding
shaft log
engine flange
prop shaft
coupling
stuffing box
double
clamps
blower
bypass
regulator
exhaust
cover
shutoff valve
water intake
exh.man.
muffler
pump
strut
engine bed
rudder
see details above
water lubricated
bearing
shutoff valve

Check every hose clamp and fitting twice yearly.

Inboard installation above is a planing hull with twin 280 hp engines. *See detail above*—the shaft log, stuffing box, and mounting flanges, are used to permit the propeller shaft to rotate freely without water entering the hull. The propeller strut uses a *water lubricated bearing.*

● An **exhaust cover** is required to prevent water from backing into the exhaust system when reversing, slowing down, or stopping. Shutoff valves on raw water intake, and overboard exhaust, should be closed when leaving the boat.

● The **manifold exhaust should bend upwards,** see illustration, coming from the engine, to reduce the chance of water backing thru the exhaust and into the engine. Cooling water discharge bypasses this loop, then is discharged into the exhaust line to cool it. *In rare cases an engine may suddenly develop suction* after reaching the bottom of a fuel tank...to pull outside water thru the exhaust line into and exploding the engine... the reason **for the upward bend loop or trap, and the exhaust cover.**

230

Before buying a boat with an inboard engine, check the following items--

● Can you visually check all fuel tank fittings, hose clamps, vent and fill pipes, and bonding wire hookups.

● Do you have easy access to oil stick, plugs, electrical leads and connectors.

● A simple, well-coded electrical system is required with an easy to reach master switch. We've seen many older powerboats and sailboats with inadequate, poorly planned, and hazardous wiring systems...which for self protection need to be completely rewired. Who will pay for it?

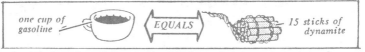

one cup of
gasoline
EQUALS
15 sticks of
dynamite

Statistic from June 1966 pamphlet USCG now feels is exaggerated, but...

A 40' inboard powerboat left a local shipyard after extensive work. The tanks were filled with 180 gallons of gasoline at a fuel dock, with the yard mechanic making a slight (?) mistake. He forgot to install the exhaust vent, see pg. 229, with endless fumes settling in the bilge.

While totalling the boat... it was a **soft blow** due to the rich UIL fuel/air mixture. Maximum explosive force occurs just above the LIL with the fully atomized cup of gasoline being equal to several sticks of dynamite.

UIL— upper level ignition   LIL— lower ignition level

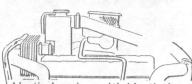

KEEL COOLER can also be flush mounted to reduce parasitic drag.

Identical engines with identical care in an auto, and in a boat with some changes~a marine engine should operate longer as the major auto enemy is missing, the fine abrasive concrete and asphalt dust from pounding tires.

A major inboard enemy is *salting up* with limestone boiler scale occuring in fresh AND salt water, pages 326 and 370. When the raw water exhaust after cooling the engine goes above 160°, boiler scale minerals and salts start to fall out of suspension instead of flowing thru and out the exhaust system. Powerhead temperature increases accelerating boiler scale buildup. The critical exhaust valves no longer able to protect themselves are the first to fail...the reason to make a compression check on 4 cycle engines.

●**Low temperature engines for displacement speed** must operate with a maximum 135° thermostat to retard boiler scale buildup. While we have many powerboat and sailboat examples to choose from, my admiral friend required a new engine yearly for his temperamental barge due to *salting up*.

"I ordered the 180° thermostat removed from my new engine ordering a 135° thermostat replacement", he said grinning. "After all, who can question an admiral? Though we put endless hours on the engine, it kept operating without problems. Four years later we opened the engine as the suspense was too great. The limestone layer was too thin to scrape off, so we added new rings, valves, and a head gasket, and installed the engine back in the barge. Guess I didn't show their company engineers much mercy".

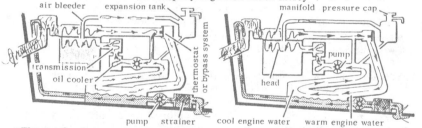

air bleeder   expansion tank   manifold pressure cap

transmission oil cooler   thermostat or bypass system   pump   head

pump   strainer   cool engine water   warm engine water

231

●**The captive heat exchanger cooling unit** *should be considered for low AND high performance 4 cycle engines operated almost daily.*

It is similar to the auto radiator cooling system operating with a pressure cap at 180° or higher temperatures. Both use ethelyene glycol and distilled water as coolant for engine and transmission lubricating oils.

Engine coolant water flow is restricted during warmup to bring the captive system up to operating temperature to eliminate air pockets that cause hot spots...then the full flow begins. Warm engine coolant and raw outside water enter a **keel cooler**, top of page, or a **flush-mounted membrane** above. As both systems flow thru the heat exchanger, excess heat from the captive cooling system, is absorbed and exhausted overboard by the raw water system with a continuous flow for efficient engine operation. *CAUTION*—warm the iron engine block before putting under load, and idle afterwards, otherwise it can cause warping of the head or block, see details on page 268.

●**A fresh water captive system** eliminates repairs of plugged cooling systems.

●**A salt water excursion boat** using a captive cooling system for a 100 hp 4cycle engine operated 10 hours daily, 5 to 6 days a week. After five years it was opened. Rings, valves, and a head gasket were added and it was put back on the 40' boat. *Without the abrasive roadway dust—*

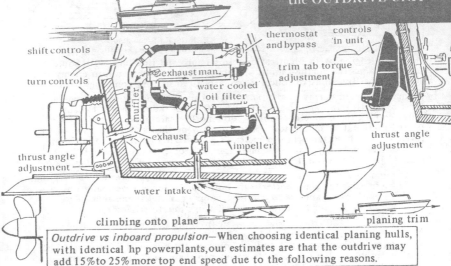

shift controls

turn controls

thrust angle adjustment

thermostat and bypass

controls in unit

exhaust man.

water cooled oil filter

trim tab torque adjustment

muffler

exhaust

impeller

thrust angle adjustment

water intake

232

climbing onto plane

planing trim

> *Outdrive vs inboard propulsion*—When choosing identical planing hulls, with identical hp powerplants, our estimates are that the outdrive may add 15% to 25% more top end speed due to the following reasons.

- **Planing lift**- after passing surfing speed, the outdrive stern rises, with a downward thrust on the bow for planing trim, see above. The inboard prop while planing is dragged at an angle thru the water, with the strut and shaft parasitic drag factors producing a large wasteful wake.

- **Lower unit tilt**--the outdrive permits easy boat launching from a trailer without submerging wheel bearings...while most inboard boats have to be floated off a submerged trailer, or launched with slings.

- **Planing trim**--the outdrive lower unit thrust angle can be changed for different loading and/or weather conditions. As the inboard propeller shaft angle can't be changed, it must be compensated by other factors.

- **Protection underway**—is provided by the outdrive lower unit in forward, tilting when hitting an underwater obstruction...while the inboard shaft, strut, and prop have no protection in an identical situation. **Neither outdrive nor inboard have protection in reverse** when backing into a rock or piling.

- **Backing an outdrive boat is easy.** Providing torque has been compensated for pg. 220, look backwards, then aim the propeller in the direction you want to pull the stern. **Backing** *a twin engine inboard boat* in a clumsy wind or current situation is easy by compensating with different engine rpm's to pull the stern. A *single engine inboard boat* without torque compensation will be clumsy to operate in the same condition.

- After the good news **IF you want to help your outdrive customers**— stress the other side of the story with continuous maintenance and an overhaul **BEFORE it is too late.** Sell your customers our *Powerboating* with major emphasis on corrosion with all the endless kind of underwater emphasis mischief they may face. Invite them to your shop some evening to review the corrosion factors, and let them handle damaged parts. Your personal interest will help pull in more interested outdrive customers.

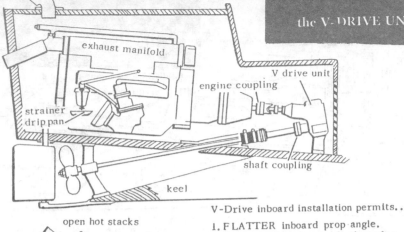

exhaust manifold

V drive unit

engine coupling

strainer
drip pan

shaft coupling

keel

V-Drive inboard installation permits..

open hot stacks

1. FLATTER inboard prop angle.
2. Engine weight carried further aft,a necessity for drag boats.
3. For cruisers it provides a lot more usable space inside cabin normally taken by engine compartment.

water
exhaust

233

When inboard racing speeds increased and DRAG boats became popular, V-Drive unit became standard equipment.

> The V-drive unit was developed for large inboard boats with a quieter ride as the engine is in the after end of the boat. Most owners seemed to prefer noisier engines more than the extra cost of the V-drive unit.

The V-drive unit proved the best answer for drag boat racing acceleration from a stop with full throttle for ¼ mile. These single-purpose racers have reached a high degree of specialization. Every ounce of unnecessary weight is eliminated including water pump and transmission. Before buying a drag boat for general use...take a close look to find how much modification will be required, and what will it cost. *WARNING*—throttle way down before making a tight turn or expect an expensive surprise, see page 74.

The **tunnel drive** was introduced by Penn Yan. It is designed for shallow water operation with prop tips protruding only 2'' below the boat bottom. The propeller bites into solid water flowing into the 5' tunnel, thrusting it out the stern across the rudder. Spray is deflected down and aft by the spray housing.

Bronze family metals provide ample corrosion protection. The inboard engine is mounted lower, with an almost horizontal shaft to provide excellent propeller protection.

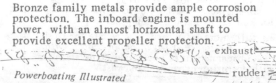

spray housing

tunnel

exhaust

rudder

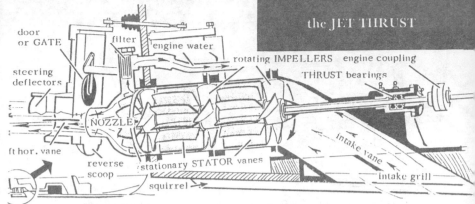

door or GATE

filter

engine water

steering deflectors

rotating IMPELLERS   engine coupling

THRUST bearings

NOZZLE

ft hor. vane

reverse scoop

intake vane

stationary STATOR vanes

intake grill

squirrel

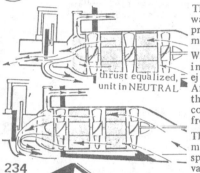

thrust equalized, unit in NEUTRAL

234

The first jet unit mounted to a 4 cycle engine was the three stage Buehler. Competitors later produced lighter, smaller, single stage jets with more usable cockpit space.

Water is pulled thru intake grill into the impeller (internal propeller) and the stream ejected and straightened by stationary vanes. After repeating three times in this installation, the stream is ejected out the nozzle which by compression is accelerated approx. 100 times from intake and out the nozzle.

This *action* thrust energy, with *the reaction,* must be absorbed by **thrust bearings.** Part of the spray is ejected downward by the aft horizontal vane to reduce upward spray volume.

intake grill

quirrel' skeg

Water pump is eliminated for normal operation with sufficient water pressure provided by the nozzle area. A water pump is added for extremely muddy or sandy water operation.

Neutral is obtained by equalizing forward and aft thrust as shown. The gate is lowered with the engine still operating in the same direction. While velocity of ejected water thrust is forward, the boat goes backwards in **reverse.**

Engine rpm is critical. If the engine can't tach out, change impellers up or down as required with a different pitch.

The Buehler jet was the first to conquer the 325 miles of Colorado River from lake Mead to Lee's Ferry...with many engine repairs and holes in boats, with one boat lost. While outboard boats had come down this river, the standing *haystack waves* that were permanent due to bottom upwelling, were barriers to outboard boats going upstream. Dams on the Colorado no longer permit attempting such upstream records.

stamping

Use double clamps for all boat hose systems as both clamps seldom fail at the same time. For salt water. look for stamping— "ALL 300 SS" for 300 series stainless clamp, housing, & screw.

400 series stainless with more magnetism is adequate for fresh water use, less corrosion resistance. *When in doubt--check with an alnico magnet* to avoid magnetism as I've found many stainless clamp mixtures with corrosion expansion and rust.

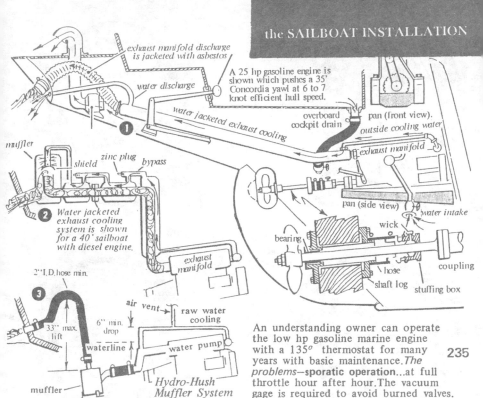

exhaust manifold discharge is jacketed with asbestos

water discharge

A 25 hp gasoline engine is shown which pushes a 35' Concordia yawl at 6 to 7 knot efficient hull speed.

water jacketed exhaust cooling

overboard cockpit drain

pan (front view).

outside cooling water

❶

muffler

shield   zinc plug   bypass

exhaust manifold

❷ Water jacketed exhaust cooling system is shown for a 40' sailboat with diesel engine.

exhaust manifold

pan (side view)   water intake

wick

bearing

water jacketed exhaust cooling

hose   coupling

shaft log   stuffing box

2" I.D. hose min.

❸

33" max. lift

air vent   raw water cooling

6" min. drop

waterline

water pump

Hydro-Hush Muffler System

muffler

An understanding owner can operate the low hp gasoline marine engine with a 135° thermostat for many years with basic maintenance. *The problems—* **sporatic operation**...at full throttle hour after hour. The vacuum gage is required to avoid burned valves.

235

- ● **Study the unique exhaust cooling systems.** Raw water is used to cool all exhaust systems which must be pumped upward with engine using a captive system to cool the diesel engine block.

- ● **Oil changes should be frequent** on gasoline and diesel engines using raw water cooling systems to remove the sulfur and condensation contaminants producing sludge and sulfuric acid. **Warm up iron blocks** before putting under load, and cool off at idle afterwards with raw water cooling systems to prevent the blocks from warping.

The most popular system today is **❸** due to simplicity, it weighs less, minimizes corrosion problems, and the weight is lower in the boat for stability. *Warning—* if the engine won't start, and the operator keeps cranking the engine, cooling water flowing into the muffler without exhaust pressure may back up the exhaust into the cylinders. A major overhaul is required to repair compression AND corrosion damages.

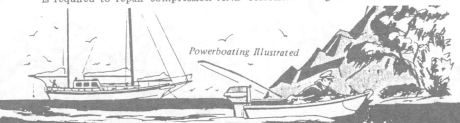

Powerboating Illustrated

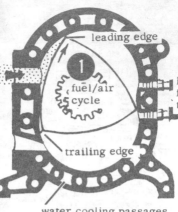

Intake—
Revolving rotor pulls fresh fuel/air through intake port.

No valves or valve mechanisms are required for the Wankel rotary power plant.

leading edge

fuel/air cycle

trailing edge

water cooling passages

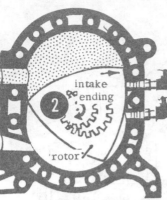

intake ending

rotor

The two plug Mazda rotary engine is detailed.

Compression—
Rotor continues compressing fuel/air mixture by reducing space in chamber.

Triangular rotor follows epitrochoid housing (a figure 8 with fat middle) instead of circle.

compression beginning

236

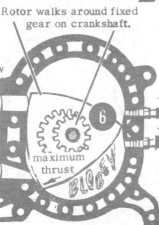

apex seal

compression maximum

trailing plug

leading plug

Rotor walks around fixed gear on crankshaft.

Ignition—
Trailing side of chamber volume is larger before TDC . . . . .

fuel/air mixture is now fully compressed . . . after TDC leading side becomes larger with compressed eddy flow propagating flame front, ignited by leading plug . . .

momentarily followed by second plug firing into upper end of chamber recess to assure maximum combustion.

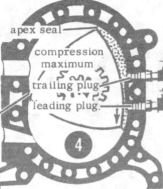

ignition

trailing plug

maximum thrust

Powerboating Illustrated

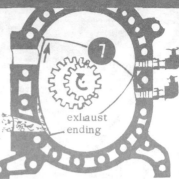

Exhaust—

Burned air/fuel drives rotor clockwise to turn crankshaft.

Rotor then exhausts burned gasses thru exhaust port.

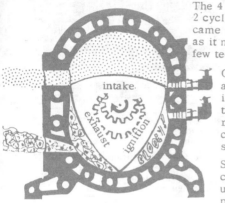

The 4 cycle rotary engine, also with 2 cycle designs had a good start, then came to a grinding halt. Study closely as it may come back to life with a few technical breakthroughs.

Operation is simple, enlarging area for fuel/air intake, reducing it considerably before ignition, then squashing flame front in right direction to speed the combustion, producing crankshaft torque.

237

Sequence shows one phase or cylinder of rotary engine to understand its theory though three phases (3 cylinders) are occurring in one 360° revolution of oil cooled rotor with crankshaft going 3 times speed, or three 360° rotations in same period.

Lubrication of apex seals revolving thru combustion chamber requires engine oil fed to fuel pump or carb to mix with incoming gasoline, or the use of premix in air cooled rotary engines such as those used in snowmobiles.

Advantages of rotary engine.. less space with less weight for equal hp piston engine, and it can operate adequately on 70 octane gasoline without lead additives, items of much interest to the planing trailerboat owner. With less parts such as pistons, rods, valves, camshafts, and lifters, it should run quieter than the piston engine.

The rotary engine may operate at higher continuous rpm than piston engines in which each piston has to stop twice during every 360° crankshaft rotation whether 2 or 4 cycle. What proved fascinating was the differences among research designs made by various manufacturers.

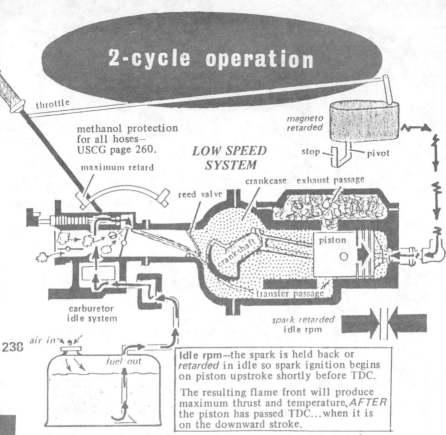

2-cycle operation

throttle

methanol protection for all hoses— USCG page 260.

LOW SPEED SYSTEM

maximum retard

magneto retarded

stop pivot

reed valve

crankcase   exhaust passage

crankshaft

piston

carburetor idle system

transfer passage

spark retarded idle rpm

238   air in

fuel out

Idle rpm—the spark is held back or *retarded* in idle so spark ignition begins on piston upstroke shortly before TDC.

The resulting flame front will produce maximum thrust and temperature,*AFTER* the piston has passed TDC...when it is on the downward stroke.

A piston on the way up will compress the combustible fuel/air vapor into a small area for maximum explosive force. The ignition will not be instantaneous but at a **calculated flame speed which remains constant at all rpm's.**

The flame front must reach its maximum heat, expansion, and thrust AFTER the piston has started the downward stroke...at all rpm's. Since the flame speed cannot be changed, the *rate* at which the spark anticipates firing must be retarded or advanced to compensate for the piston speed powerhead rpm.

When the throttle is advanced

● The butterfly opens to admit more air/fuel vapor thru the carb throat.
● The **spark advance timing** has to be changed to compensate for the increasing powerhead, crankshaft, and piston rpm.

● **Alcohol fuel**—tremendous spark advance is required as alcohol is sluggish and burns slowly, with the carburetor having to be opened approximately 10%. Expect more fuel consumption since three times as much fuel is required when compared to gasoline/air ratio.

The *action*—while *the piston* is on the upstroke when spark ignition begins, the *flame speed reaction* must be adjusted so maximum thrust and temperature occurs from low rpm to high rpm, when the piston is on the down stroke *AFTER* passing TDC (top dead center).

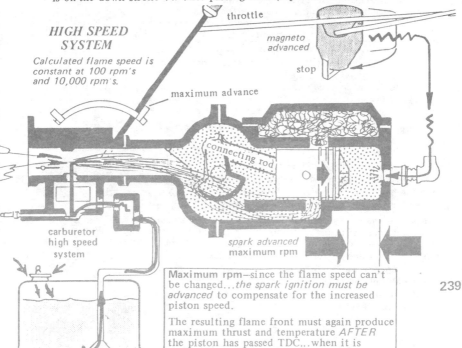

HIGH SPEED SYSTEM

Calculated flame speed is constant at 100 rpm's and 10,000 rpm's.

throttle

magneto advanced

stop

maximum advance

connecting rod

carburetor high speed system

spark advanced maximum rpm

Maximum rpm—since the flame speed can't be changed...*the spark ignition must be advanced* to compensate for the increased piston speed.

The resulting flame front must again produce maximum thrust and temperature *AFTER* the piston has passed TDC...when it is on the downward stroke.

239

When the throttle is moved forward to maximum rpm stop—
● The butterfly is wide open to permit maximum air/fuel carb flow.
● Magneto timing is advanced to anticipate the spark earlier for maximum downward thrust...after the piston has passed TDC.

● Spark advance adjustments are critical. They should be adjusted only by trained mechanics since *IF the calculated flame speed burn* doesn't occur at the precise calculated moment... lost performance and lost rpm will produce expensive repairs.

Curious owners wanting more speed, look at the maximum rpm stop when the throttle is pushed all the way forward...which may be adjusted. If a customer comes in with outboard motor preignition damage...*did he change the maximum rpm stop?*

● Primitive areas with poor quality, low octane, stale gasoline, require *retarding the spark more than normal* to avoid burned plugs and powerhead damage. ALSO—is a specialized 2 cycle oil available to help an engine exist with rust, cockroaches, scorpions. etc.

Show customer timing adjustments needed, and special tools if required. Consider sealed, spare CDI parts, page 303, which may be returned if the container seals haven't been broken.

> Every downward stroke is a power stroke, and every upward stroke is a compression stroke on a two-cycle engine.
>
> Our multi-function two-cycle engine sequence shows the previous generation piston and combustion chamber. This foundation makes it easier to understand a more complex present generation Loop--Charging two-cycle sequence.

We start with the bottom illustration. The piston on the down stroke has opened the **transfer passage port** ❶ Flammable vapors are forced by compression from the crankcase to the combustion chamber, as the piston goes to ❷ BDC (bottom dead center). The piston stops, changes direction, and closes the transfer port on the way up.

Lowered pressure on the bottom side of the piston ❸ opens a *one-way reed valve* ❹ separating carburetor from the crankcase. This pulls in a fresh mixture ❺ of vapors for temporary storage in the crankcase.

The top of the piston going upward ❻ is compressing the trapped flammable vapors. Shortly before TDC ❼ a spark ignites the compressed vapor charge.

After a momentary stop at TDC ❽ , the piston changes to a downward stroke ❾ . Pressure from expanding flame front *produces maximum thrust on the crankshaft from $15°$ to $90°$ when we refer to TDC as vertical or $0°$.*

The combustion chamber downward power stroke thrust- pushes the piston, connecting rod, crankshaft, and drive shaft. This develops **maximum propeller torque thrust** to push your boat thru an approximate $75°$ arc of the power stroke from ❾ to ❿ , see torque def., pg. 279.

Meanwhile the bottom side of the piston on its downward stroke starts compressing vapors in the crankshaft shortly after TDC ❽ closing the one-way reed valve.

The top of the piston on the downward stroke opens the *exhaust port* ⓬ to release burned vapors...then the piston crown ⓭ opens the *transfer passage port* ❶ . The fresh compressed vapors temporarily stored in the crankcase are released again to flow happily into the combustion chamber with a lowered pressure.

The *baffled piston crown* ⓭ controls the incoming vapor flow with a swirling, scouring action to help remove deposits in the combustion chamber.

Fresh new vapors force remaining burned gases ⓮ out the exhaust port. The piston goes down to BDC ❷ stops momentarily, then goes upward closing both transfer AND exhaust ports...with the sequence repeating itself.

●**Timing**- it is fascinating to find how maximum prop torque can be produced thru the $75°$ arc during crankshaft rotation at all rpm's by changing the timing *as flame speed is constant and cannot be changed.*

If the timing is retarded too far the spark ignition arrives too late. It wastes power as the vapors are still burning as they go out the exhaust port. If retarded still further, it may ignite the new vapors coming from the crankcase, thru the transfer passage as they move into the hot combustion chamber.

●**Factory timing recommendations** should be followed closely as the timing curve drops rapidly when either extreme has been passed as shown.

If the timing is advanced too much, preignition damage results with the piston and powerhead fighting, causing damaging temperatures and pressures. Something has to give...especially the customers bankbook when he picks up his overhauled outboard motor.

240

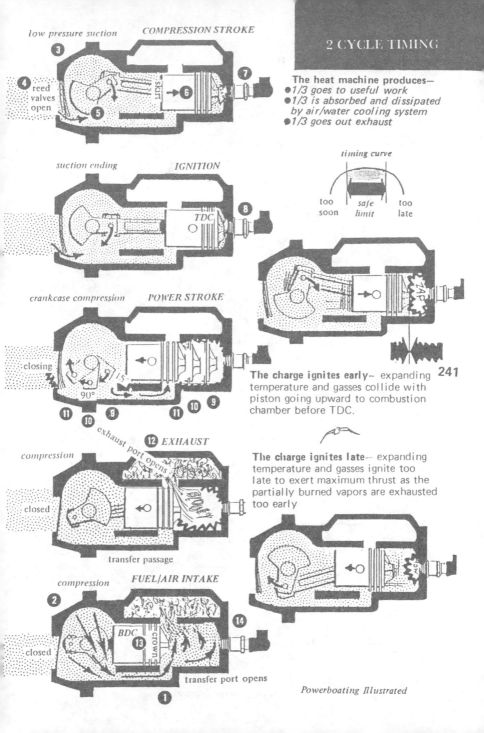

low pressure suction
COMPRESSION STROKE

❸

❹ reed valves open

❺

SKIRT → ❻

❼

The heat machine produces—
● 1/3 goes to useful work
● 1/3 is absorbed and dissipated by air/water cooling system
● 1/3 goes out exhaust

suction ending
IGNITION

TDC

❽

timing curve

too soon | safe limit | too late

crankcase compression
POWER STROKE

closing

15°

90°

❶❶ ❶❶ ❾ ❶❶ ❶❶ ❾

The charge ignites early— expanding 241 temperature and gasses collide with piston going upward to combustion chamber before TDC.

The charge ignites late— expanding temperature and gasses ignite too late to exert maximum thrust as the partially burned vapors are exhausted too early

compression

exhaust port opens

❶❷ **EXHAUST**

closed

BLOOEY

transfer passage

compression
FUEL/AIR INTAKE

❷

closed

BDC ❶❸ CROWN

❶❹

transfer port opens

❶

Powerboating Illustrated

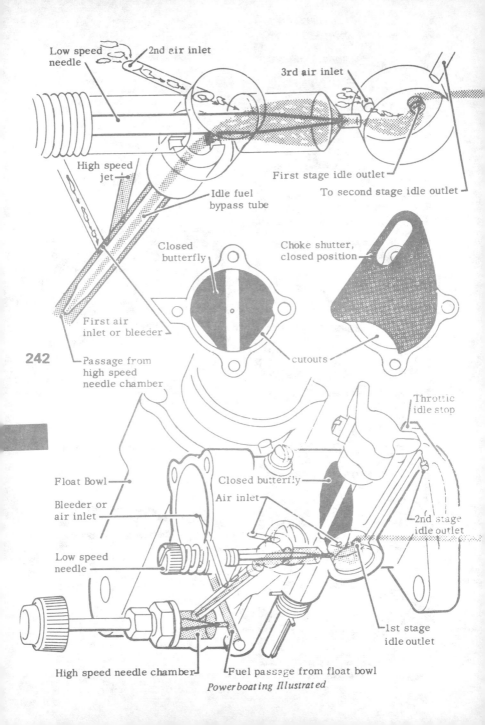

Low speed needle

2nd air inlet

3rd air inlet

First stage idle outlet

To second stage idle outlet

High speed jet

Idle fuel bypass tube

Closed butterfly

Choke shutter, closed position

First air inlet or bleeder

242

Passage from high speed needle chamber

cutouts

Throttle idle stop

Float Bowl

Closed butterfly

Air inlet

2nd stage idle outlet

Bleeder or air inlet

Low speed needle

High speed needle chamber

Fuel passage from float bowl

1st stage idle outlet

Powerboating Illustrated

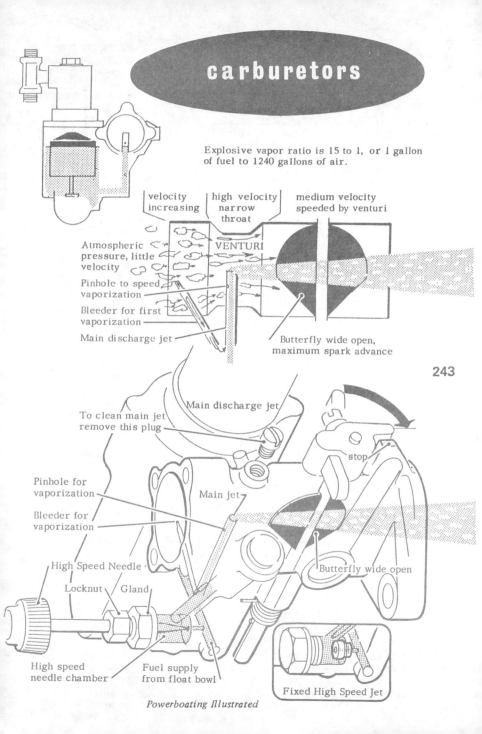

carburetors

Explosive vapor ratio is 15 to 1, or 1 gallon of fuel to 1240 gallons of air.

velocity increasing | high velocity narrow throat | medium velocity speeded by venturi

Atmospheric pressure, little velocity

VENTURI

Pinhole to speed vaporization

Bleeder for first vaporization

Main discharge jet

Butterfly wide open, maximum spark advance

243

Main discharge jet

To clean main jet remove this plug

stop

Pinhole for vaporization

Main jet

Bleeder for vaporization

High Speed Needle

Butterfly wide open

Locknut / Gland

High speed needle chamber

Fuel supply from float bowl

Fixed High Speed Jet

Powerboating Illustrated

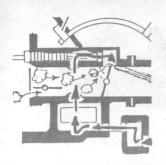
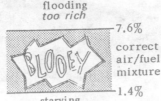

flooding
too rich

7.6%

correct
air/fuel
mixture

1.4%

starving
too lean

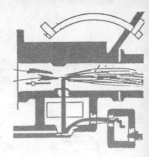

A carburetor mixes fuel and air and meters it in the correct ratio required for the most efficient controlled burning.

The **fuel to air mixture is critical.** Gasoline has a narrow ignition range as shown above for your protection. The purpose of your carburetor is to provide the correct fuel/air flammable mixture for efficient combustion in this narrow ignition range.

Fuel at right is pumped from the tank ❼ by inward and outward diaphragm pulsations ❼ actuated on crankcase pressure produced by the piston movement in the cylinder. Fuel comes through a one way valve ❽ while the changing pulsations forces it out another valve.

Fuel then goes thru a strainer ❾ to keep rust, dirt, paint, varnish, and metal particles from reaching the combustion chamber.

The fuel then goes thru an inlet valve ❿ to the float bowl ⓭ that stores a constant fuel reservoir until needed. When the bowl is full, the float ⓮ rises to contact two levers ⓬ that press upward on the inlet needle ⓫ to stop further flow.

244

- **Starting**--a *choke shutter* is used when starting, not to increase fuel flow, but to speed a very small stream of flammable vapors at hurricane speeds to produce a combustible buildup in the combustion chamber in vapor form instead of falling out of suspension.

  The **side bowl carburetor** shown has a two stage idle system, note jets ⓲ and ⓳ at right.

- The **low speed system** operates on the principle of moving a tiny stream of air and fuel vapor thru a small passage without it falling out of suspension. The **slower a motor idles, the faster must be this flow to keep the vaporized fuel in suspension.**

- The **high speed system** uses a large volume of fuel/air vapor which can travel at a slower rate with the vaporized fuel staying in suspension.

- Fuel is **vaporized** progressively **three times** in the low speed system, and **three times** in the high speed system to insure a well regulated supply of flammable vapors thru a large rpm range.

- **Reed valves**—the vaporized flammable vapor mixture leaves the carburetor to be channeled by reed valves to the correct combustion chamber cylinder in firing sequence.

- **Crankcase**--On the down stroke of the piston after the flammable vapor leaves the one-way reed valves, it is temporarily stored in the crankcase...and then channeled thru a side passage into the combustion chamber for controlled burning.

Powerboating Illustrated

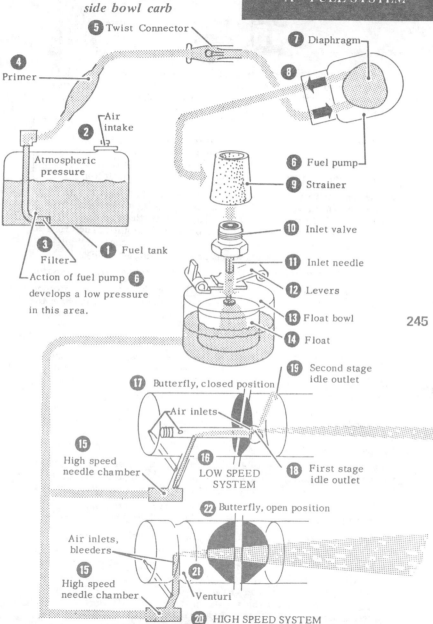

side bowl carb

5 Twist Connector

7 Diaphragm

8

4 Primer

Air intake

2

Atmospheric pressure

6 Fuel pump

9 Strainer

10 Inlet valve

11 Inlet needle

12 Levers

13 Float bowl

14 Float

3 Filter

1 Fuel tank

Action of fuel pump **6** develops a low pressure in this area.

245

19 Second stage idle outlet

17 Butterfly, closed position

Air inlets

15 High speed needle chamber

16 LOW SPEED SYSTEM

18 First stage idle outlet

22 Butterfly, open position

Air inlets, bleeders

15 High speed needle chamber

21

Venturi

20 HIGH SPEED SYSTEM

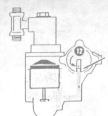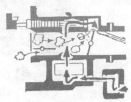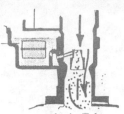

We detail three last generation carburetors for your analysis. Take ample time to study them as this foundation will make it easy to understand present marine carburetors which follow the same theory... with the plumbing juggled for better efficiency.

> *This is the easiest chapter in our book as you are dealing with systematic mechanical operation similar to plumbing.* Other chapters having endless variables require value judgment. While you may find few surprises with hulls and trailers in factory school, our propeller chapter theory is just a foundation instructors can build on.

- **2 cycle carburetors.** Study the *side bowl carburetor* pages 242 to 251, step by step until you can close your eyes to see it functioning from the fuel supply to start, to idle, and to full throttle, as you analyze the physics theories involved from velocity to Bernouilli. Then turn to pages 252 to 254, so you are able to systematically check potential items involved when a carburetor isn't functioning normally.

- Then it is time to repeat the process with the *center bowl carburetor.*

After you have this foundation you will know how to work on older carburetors, and find it easy to adjust to analyzing plumbing changes in later ones. A recent factory manual shows a side bowl carb, a center bowl carb, and a third, a centerbowl carb with the venturi plumbing of a side bowl carb.

- **4 cycle operation.** Analyze the full sequence on pages 227 to 229, covering filling the fuel tank with blower operation, the fuel supply, the carburetor metering device, then follow the vapors down the manifold into the cylinders with the complex valve train.

The 4 cycle engine is excellent for mid range performance operation in a car. Few cars in their lifetime ever operate at full throttle for more than a minute or so before Mr. Chips appears, or the overheated engine with many friction points blows up.

The same person with an inboard engine on a planing hull will want to operate it at full rpm for long periods similar to 2 cycle motors keeping it inside the tachometer limits... *which becomes your problem.*

- **Boiler scale** pg. 231, is a heat problem to prevent *salting up* in salt water AND fresh water using outside cooling water.

- **Burned valves**– always run a compression check before working on 4 cycle engines due to full throttle operation problems.

- **Automotive 4 cycle downdraft carb** is detailed on pages 227 and 228. If you know 4 cycle operation, then you can close your eyes and see the full carburetor operation but never work on one, it will help when explaining 2 cycle operation to customers. If you will work on 4 cycle engines... study the USCG standards for inboard engine installations with changes that become obvious when compared to the automotive carburetor we detail.

246

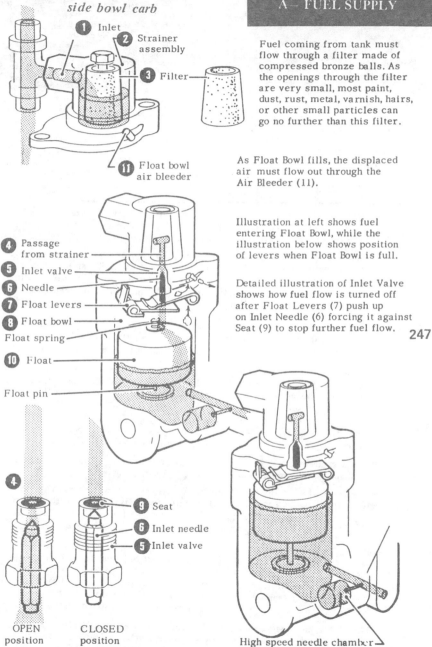

side bowl carb

1 Inlet
2 Strainer assembly
3 Filter
11 Float bowl air bleeder

Fuel coming from tank must flow through a filter made of compressed bronze balls. As the openings through the filter are very small, most paint, dust, rust, metal, varnish, hairs, or other small particles can go no further than this filter.

As Float Bowl fills, the displaced air must flow out through the Air Bleeder (11).

Illustration at left shows fuel entering Float Bowl, while the illustration below shows position of levers when Float Bowl is full.

Detailed illustration of Inlet Valve shows how fuel flow is turned off after Float Levers (7) push up on Inlet Needle (6) forcing it against Seat (9) to stop further fuel flow.

247

4 Passage from strainer
5 Inlet valve
6 Needle
7 Float levers
8 Float bowl
Float spring
10 Float
Float pin

4
9 Seat
6 Inlet needle
5 Inlet valve

OPEN position
CLOSED position

High speed needle chamber

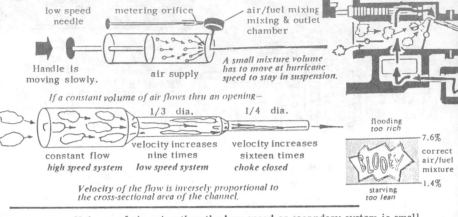

low speed needle · metering orifice · air/fuel mixing mixing & outlet chamber

Handle is moving slowly.

air supply

A small mixture volume has to move at hurricane speed to stay in suspension.

If a constant volume of air flows thru an opening—

1/3 dia.   1/4 dia.

constant flow · velocity increases nine times · velocity increases sixteen times

high speed system · low speed system · choke closed

Velocity of the flow is inversely proportional to the cross-sectional area of the channel.

flooding *too rich*

7.6%

BLOOEY

correct air/fuel mixture

1.4%

starving *too lean*

Volume of air going thru the **low speed** or secondary system is small, while traveling at great velocity so the flammable fuel/air vapors will stay in suspension all the way to the combustion chamber.

●**Starting**— If a motor is hand cranked to 70 rpm or more,or the magneto or alternator takes the crankshaft rpm from 400 to 600 rpm,or the starter motor spins the crankshaft to 200 or more rpm,the idle system is ready to begin operating IF the air/fuel vapors have reached the ignition range in the cylinders by—

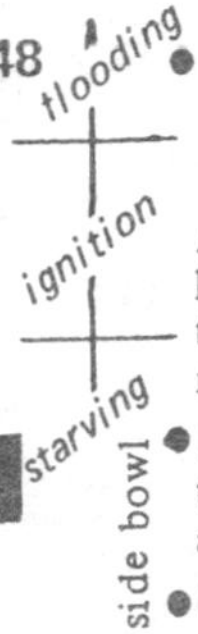

248

flooding

ignition

starving

● The **choke shutter** is closed to restrict and increase air speed flow thru the carb for a cold starting motor.The small,high velocity mixture insures vapors will stay in suspension to combustion chamber.

As the crankshaft starts to rotate and the plugs fire,it develops a lowered pressure in the crankcase to pull in more air/fuel vapors.Then the choke shutter is opened before flooding begins,to maintain the normal vapor mix for combustion.

●**Lower stage idle** -- a slightly larger fuel flow comes up the bypass tube ❸ to the first stage outlet on the side of the carb ❼ with three air bleeders to insure efficient vaporization at this critical stage.

●**Upper stage idle**— as the butterfly barely opens with an increase in idle rpm,the vapors also flow out of the ❽ second outlet.

side bowl

●**One stage idle**-- as the choke shutter opens inside the center bowl carb to maintain correct mixture,fuel is pulled up a bypass ❺ to the upper aft mixing chamber ❿ with two bleeders to speed vaporization. The theory is similar to the inverted spray gun shown above.

● Make **idle adjustments slowly** for the flammable mixture proportion of air to fuel which is *1240 to 1*. If the **mixture is too lean** the motor will have insufficient coolant lubrication and not enough oxygen for efficient combustion.If the **mixture is too rich** the powerhead begins firing on every second or alternate stroke with the vapor falling out of suspension and puddling,followed by drowning the plugs.

The **high speed need adjustment for both carburetors** will affect both low speed and high speed mixtures making both too lean or too rich when out of adjustment.

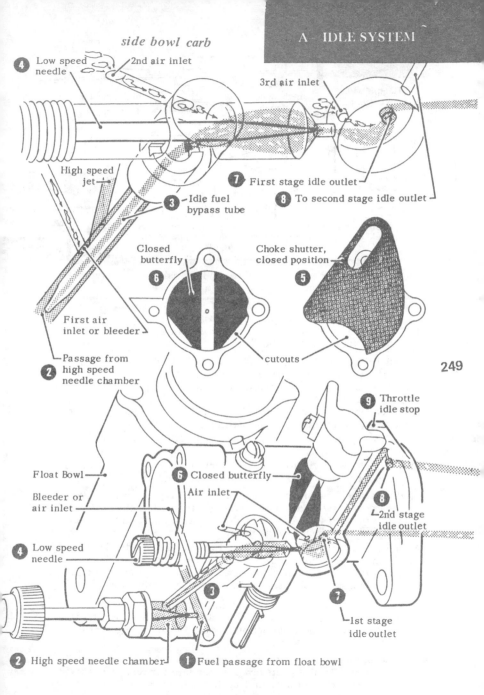

side bowl carb

4 Low speed needle

2nd air inlet

3rd air inlet

High speed jet

7 First stage idle outlet

3 Idle fuel bypass tube

8 To second stage idle outlet

Closed butterfly

6

Choke shutter, closed position

5

First air inlet or bleeder

cutouts

2 Passage from high speed needle chamber

249

9 Throttle idle stop

Float Bowl

6 Closed butterfly

Bleeder or air inlet

Air inlet

8 2nd stage idle outlet

4 Low speed needle

3

7 1st stage idle outlet

2 High speed needle chamber

1 Fuel passage from float bowl

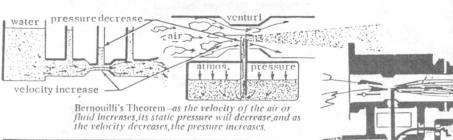

venturi

A larger mixture volume
moves at slower speed.

Handle is
moving fast.

high speed
needle

high speed nozzle

fuel supply

water | pressure decrease

air

venturi

atmos. | pressure

velocity increase

Bernouilli's Theorem—*as the velocity of the air or
fluid increases, its static pressure will decrease, and as
the velocity decreases, the pressure increases.*

The main circuit theory of side bowl and center bowl carburetors
above work on a principle of a spray gun or upright atomizer.

> **The high speed system begins near 1200 rpm's.** *The action-* as the
> butterfly opens sufficiently to increase the air volume flowing thru
> the restriction or **venturi,** *a reaction begins* with a lowered pressure or
> partial vacuum in the float bowl of both carburetors.

250

This pulls fuel up the main jet ❶ where after being vaporized twice
with air bleeders, it combines with the air flowing thru the venturi
restriction, and out the carburetor. The flammable vapors flow thru one-
way reed valves to the crankcase, pg. 238 , where they are stored until the
piston on the downward power stroke opens the bypass passage to the
combustion chamber cylinder selected by the reed valves.

The action- as the throttle is advanced and the butterfly opens wider
to increase the volume and speed of air flowing thru the venturi, it
produces *the reaction* —to pull more fuel out of the float bowl thru
the main jet to be vaporized with the correct air/fuel ratio.

Study the side view of the venturi on the facing page, then compare it
with *Bernouilli's Theorem* above. Though having a technical artist background for several years, I found it difficult to understand the lecture
on carburetion without good illustrations.

After illustrating the two outboard carburetors I began teaching their
operation for familiarity, and to improve the information. They are
seldom detailed in such depth as these carburetors are miserable to
detail, while a side view is ample for our 4 cycle carburetor.

You will find a time lag after giving full throttle before your powerhead
can reach top end rpm. The sudden increase on prop load requires time to
build up the crankcase vapor action to meet full throttle operational
demands.

● **An acceleration jet** is used for immediate acceleration on automobile
carburetors pg. 227 which pours raw gasoline into the venturi of the
4 cycle carb, which isn't used in 2 cycle outboard carburetors.

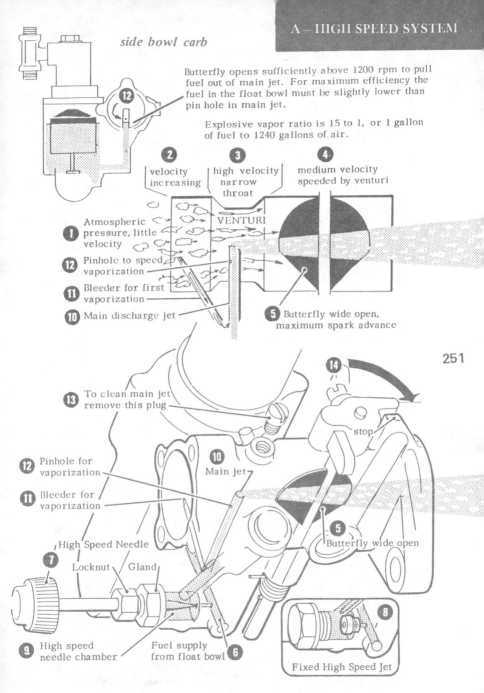

side bowl carb

Butterfly opens sufficiently above 1200 rpm to pull fuel out of main jet. For maximum efficiency the fuel in the float bowl must be slightly lower than pin hole in main jet.

Explosive vapor ratio is 15 to 1, or 1 gallon of fuel to 1240 gallons of air.

2 velocity increasing

3 high velocity narrow throat

4 medium velocity speeded by venturi

VENTURI

1 Atmospheric pressure, little velocity

12 Pinhole to speed vaporization

11 Bleeder for first vaporization

10 Main discharge jet

5 Butterfly wide open, maximum spark advance

251

14

13 To clean main jet remove this plug

stop

10 Main jet

12 Pinhole for vaporization

11 Bleeder for vaporization

High Speed Needle

Locknut   Gland

7

5 Butterfly wide open

9 High speed needle chamber

Fuel supply from float bowl **6**

8

Fixed High Speed Jet

Powerboating Illustrated

CAUTION---REMOVE NUTS WITH WRENCHES--- *NOT PLIERS.*

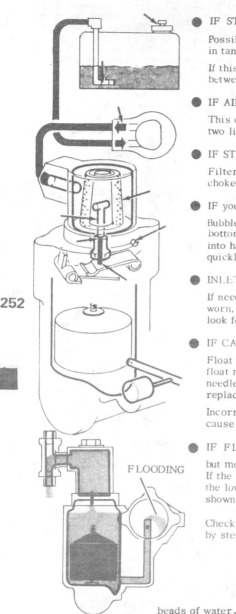

● IF STRAINER IS EMPTY----

Possibility of empty fuel tank, plugged filter in tank, or obstruction in air vent plug.

If this is unsuccessful, check for obstruction between fuel tank and filter assembly.

● IF AIR VENT IS FOAMING----

This can occur on older motors having the two line fuel pressure system due to air leak.

● IF STRAINER IS FULL, float bowl empty---

Filter element, or passage to float bowl is choked with fine hairs, dirt, or moisture.

● IF you think WATER IS PRESENT----

Bubbles or beads of water will be seen on bottom of fuel. To check, pour this fuel into hand or saucer. Gasoline evaporates quickly leaving water behind.

● INLET VALVE TROUBLE----

If needle is worn replace needle; if seat is worn, replace inlet valve. If needle sticks, look for dirt.

● IF CARB IS FLOODING----

Float may be saturated beyond buoyancy, the float may be sticking or out of position, or the needle and inlet valve are worn and need to be replaced.

Incorrect positioning of float levers may also cause trouble with inlet needle.

● IF FLOAT BOWL IS FULL----

but motor won't fire up, check one of the plugs. If the plug is dry, look for an obstruction in the low or high speed passages of carb as shown on the facing page.

Checking for fuel problems is a simple step by step 'plumbing job. '

252

FLOODING

saucer

beads of water

Powerboating Illustrated

side bowl carb

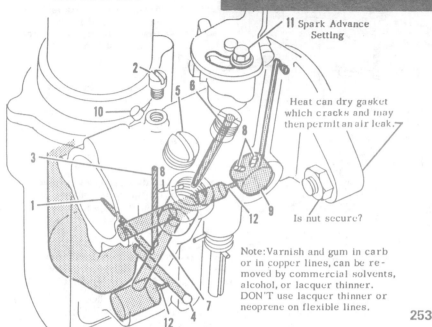

11 Spark Advance Setting

Heat can dry gasket which cracks and may then permit an air leak.

Is nut secure?

Note: Varnish and gum in carb or in copper lines, can be removed by commercial solvents, alcohol, or lacquer thinner. DON'T use lacquer thinner or neoprene on flexible lines.

253

All passages in this carb can be checked visually by using a small penlight or flashlight.

Idle Bleeder Tube (1) seldom plugs up.

To check main jet first remove plug (2), then put penlight into high speed chamber. Now look down main jet (3).

Remove shot (4) to check passage from float bowl into high speed chamber.

Remove bypass screw (5), then idle bypass tube (6), place penlight in high speed chamber, and check for obstruction in bypass channel. Bypass tube (6) can be checked visually after it has been removed.

Next check small idle inlets and outlets visually and with a small dia. wire. If necessary to check further into low speed system, remove plug (9) to check the first idle stage.

Float bowl vent can be checked by running a small dia. wire through opening (10).

Does spark advance (11) have wrong setting?

When adjusting high speed and low speed needles follow 'Owner's Guide' proceedures closely to prevent damage to orifices or seats (12).

● Most carb trouble can be avoided if carbs are run dry before motor is put away after using. Trouble in the fuel lines can be avoided if the owner is careful with his fuel mixing and handling.

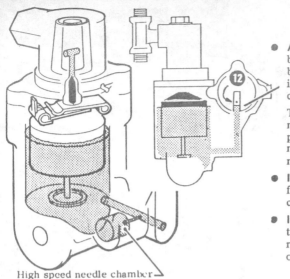

High speed needle chamber

- **Atmospheric pressure** must be maintained in the float bowl as pressure difference is needed to supply the carburetor circuits.

  The side bowl fuel level must be just below the pin hole bleeder...in the main discharge jet when not operating.

- **If the fuel level is higher—** fuel will overflow into the carburetor venturi.

- **If the fuel level is lower—** too much pressure will be required to pull fuel out of the float bowl.

- **High altitude** pg. 278. Since air pressure decreases with altitude, less oxygen is available for burning. It must be compensated for by changing to smaller fuel jets to maintain the same fuel to oxygen ratio.

  When fuel flows into the float bowl from the tank, the float will rise, then the flow begins to taper off as it forces the needle up, closing the inlet when the needle rests against the seat.

- *The action*—the float drops as fuel is used, *the reaction*—to allow more fuel to come into the carburetor in proportion to the fuel consumed. **The higher the engine rpm,** more fuel is consumed. The float drops lower permitting more fuel to flow past the inlet needle.

  When the engine stops, the float rises to close the inlet needle when the bowl is full with the inlet needle stopping further fuel flow.

- **Float bowl problems—** turn the bowl upside down. The float must stay level with the horizontal bowl edge for correct fuel flow supply.

  When the float is *above the horizontal,* the fuel supply will be starving the high speed circuit.

  When the float *falls below the horizontal,* flooding and overflowing will result. Loose fittings, impaired float valve and seat may cause the problem. Older side bowl carburetor floats have been assembled upside down with flooding or pressure variance disturbances.

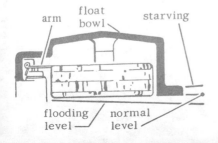

arm | float bowl | starving

flooding level | normal level

Powerboating Illustrated

center bowl carb

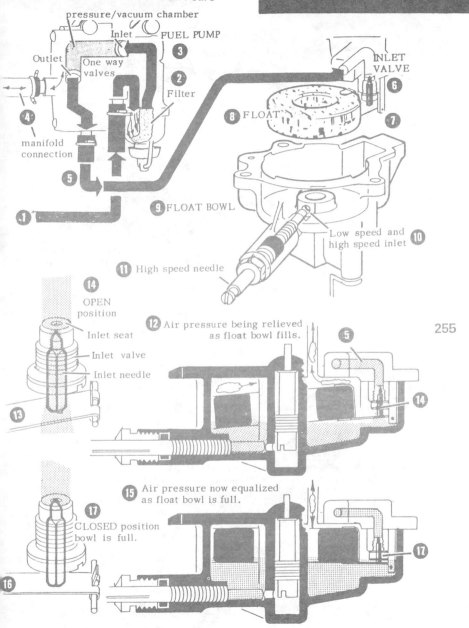

pressure/vacuum chamber

Inlet — FUEL PUMP

Outlet

One way valves

Filter

manifold connection

INLET VALVE

FLOAT

FLOAT BOWL

Low speed and high speed inlet

High speed needle

OPEN position

Inlet seat

Inlet valve

Inlet needle

Air pressure being relieved as float bowl fills.

255

Air pressure now equalized as float bowl is full.

CLOSED position bowl is full.

Powerboating Illustrated

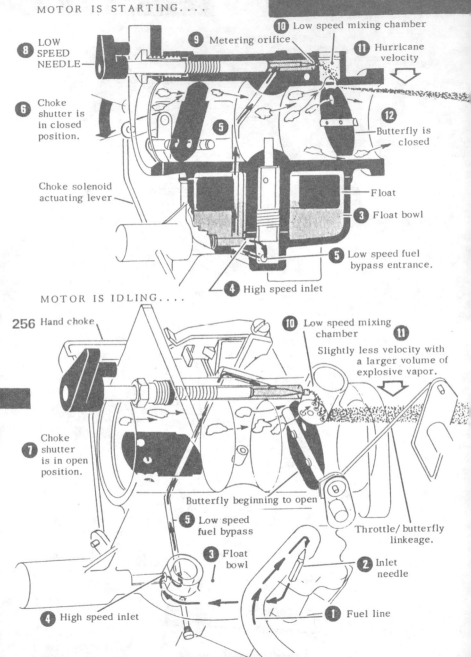

MOTOR IS STARTING....

8 LOW SPEED NEEDLE

9 Metering orifice

10 Low speed mixing chamber

11 Hurricane velocity

6 Choke shutter is in closed position.

12 Butterfly is closed

Choke solenoid actuating lever

5

Float

3 Float bowl

5 Low speed fuel bypass entrance.

4 High speed inlet

MOTOR IS IDLING....

256 Hand choke

10 Low speed mixing chamber

11 Slightly less velocity with a larger volume of explosive vapor.

7 Choke shutter is in open position.

Butterfly beginning to open

5 Low speed fuel bypass

3 Float bowl

Throttle/ butterfly linkage.

2 Inlet needle

4 High speed inlet

1 Fuel line

Powerboating Illustrated

CARB OPERATING AT MAXIMUM RPM

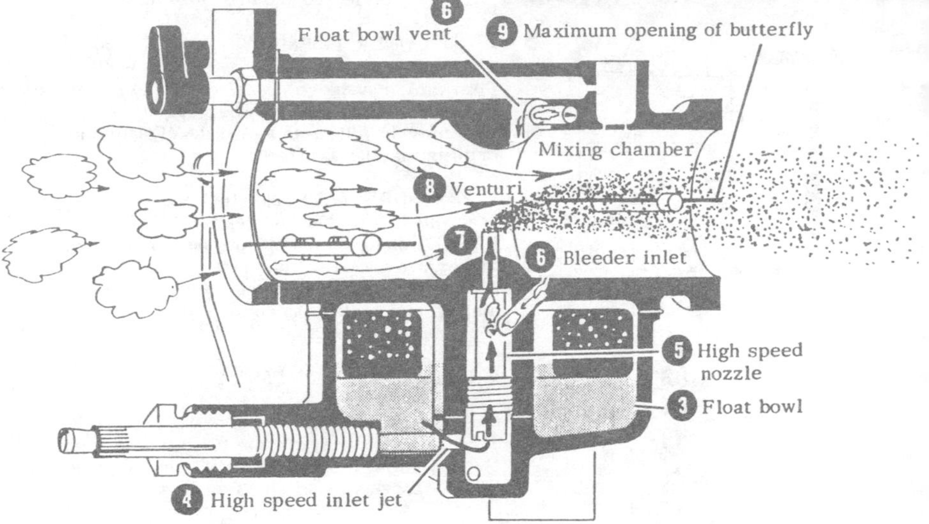

6 Float bowl vent

9 Maximum opening of butterfly

Mixing chamber

8 Venturi

7

6 Bleeder inlet

5 High speed nozzle

3 Float bowl

4 High speed inlet jet

HIGH SPEED NEEDLE

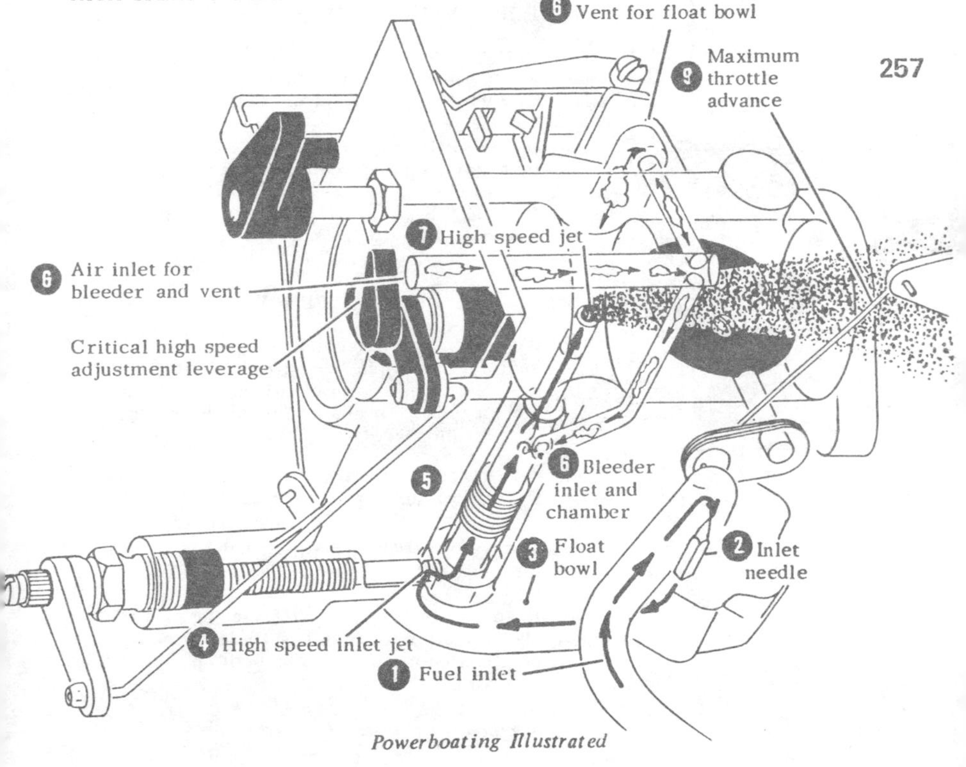

6 Vent for float bowl

9 Maximum throttle advance

257

7 High speed jet

6 Air inlet for bleeder and vent

Critical high speed adjustment leverage

6 Bleeder inlet and chamber

5

3 Float bowl

2 Inlet needle

4 High speed inlet jet

1 Fuel inlet

Powerboating Illustrated

Many fuel problems appear at beginning of boating season due to rust, dust, hairs, lint, etc., collected during storage.

● IF STRAINER IS EMPTY----

Fuel tank may be empty or vent screw closed. Filter screen in tank may be plugged, flexible line may be PINCHED or FRAYED, or fuel primer may be damaged.

If PRESSURE TANK has fuel that isn't reaching filter, check for leaky DIAPHRAGM GASKET on top of tank. It may be worn enough to permit air leak that reduces manifold pressure in tank. Can you carry an extra diaphragm gasket on your boat?

● If FLOAT BOWL is EMPTY----

Check strainer for sediment, rust & hairs. This type of filter seems to soften with age, check tightness of screw as it can compress filter excessively to stop fuel flow.

● INLET VALVE TROUBLE----

STUCK NEEDLE can stop fuel supply while BENT NEEDLE may cause sluggish action with flooding or starving.

If FLOODING, check for FOREIGN OBJECT that may lodge between needle and seat.

If NEEDLE or SEAT IS WORN, an excess quantity of fuel will come through.

● If FUEL REACHES FLOAT BOWL----

But motor doesn't catch, check for water, sediment, varnish, or hairs and lint that may have come down breather. Plug throat and breather as shown during the winter months storage.

● If MOTOR WON'T START----

Check for CHOKE SPRING that is broken or unhooked.

If spring is broken, push finger against the choke shutter to close it sufficiently so that combustion mixture can be built up.

258

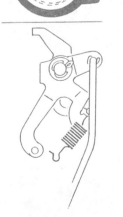

cover this area

Powerboating Illustrated

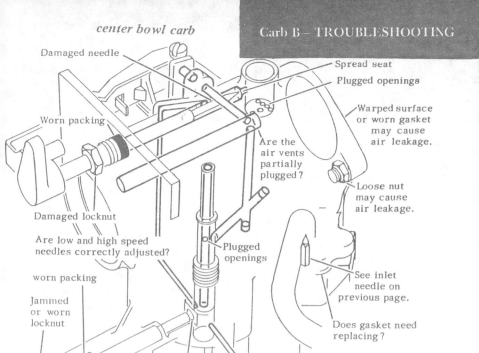

Damaged needle

Spread seat

Plugged openings

Warped surface
or worn gasket
may cause
air leakage.

Worn packing

Are the
air vents
partially
plugged?

Loose nut
may cause
air leakage.

Damaged locknut

Are low and high speed
needles correctly adjusted?

Plugged
openings

worn packing

Jammed
or worn
locknut

See inlet
needle on
previous page.

Does gasket need
replacing?

spread seat

Remove screw to clean
lower bypass line.

259

SEATS can be spread and damaged if needle is turned in too far. If this happens
it will be necessary to replace grooved needle, to have the carb replaced or
pay for expensive repairs. Always replace worn PACKING.

IF MOTOR DOESN'T IDLE CORRECTLY it may be due to air leakage as
shown on the illustration, by incorrectly adjusted choke, or by butterfly that is
worn or improperly adjusted.

Various FUEL and AIR PASSAGES are shown above. If motor STANDS IDLE
for any length of time without draining fuel, gum and varnish deposits can form
a sealant in passages——note locations carefully before attempting to clean any
of these channels. If fuel is drained, but carb is exposed, dust, lint, hairs, etc.,
can enter & plug passages.

Fuel passages may be opened with a long pin, alcohol, or acetone. NEVER boil
out carb as it may remove protective metal coating to aid corrosion. Replace
float bowl GASKET before reassembly if signs of wear are evident.

For several years I've known Stan Holden with an 18 year background as a Boating Standards expert able to provide many difficult to find answers. He operated out of the 11th USCG District Headquarters, Long Beach, California.

His job was to work with boat and engine builders, plus investigating boating accidents. The following discussion defines boat and engine mechanical problems involved with boating injuries and fatalities.

His coverage is to provide an exposure to the **BOATING SAFETY ACT.** *Instead of discussing the regulations...we find it just as important for you to know the REASONS for the regulations.* Some have immediate applications...while others involve developing problems.

1987 Los Angeles Boat Show. We were walking around exchanging various ideas. I mentioned liking an outboard cruiser the size of our old *Researcher.* It was on a trailer a foot shorter than the boat.

260

He replied,"It reminds of several hundreds of boats I checked last year at various boat shows. But all I seem to remember is that the largest boat in one of the shows... had the red and green running lights reversed. Let us begin by answering your questions on the fuel hose regulations".

● **Fuel hoses**—the EPA ordered lead removed from gasoline after 1/1/86.

The problem – *if ethanol or methanol alcohol is added to gasoline,* it attacks rubber fuel hoses, gaskets, seals, and even some metal parts in the fuel system. Rubber hoses and parts deteriorate rapidly and begin leaking with inboard engine fire and explosion potentials, pgs. 227,238.

Explain the reasoning to customers so they know the reason whether you or they update their rubber hoses. Use hoses only clearly marked *U.S.C.G. Type A* or *U.S.C.G. Type B.* These hoses must meet SAE J30R7 or SAE J30R8 spec's without SAE spec's on the hoses.

This chapter started accidentally when two hose manufacturers asked for information on the new regulations... not wanting to contact USCG.

He spent considerable time explaining the reasons and rules. This opened questions in other areas that kept growing, the reason for this chapter.

I finally asked, *"How are mechanics all over the U.S. going to learn the fine points of these rules?"* We agreed a toll-free number was needed for dealers and mechanics to ask technical questions, maintaining anonymity if desired to Wash.,D.C. Headquarters. It is open Monday thru Friday, Eastern Standard Time 8 am to 4 pm, the number... **1-800-368 5647.**

ARE MECHANICS INVOLVED IN THE BOATING SAFETY ACT?

The 1971 Federal Boat Safety Act came into effect in 1972. One of the provisions of the act was that statistical proof of death or injury must be involved before a new regulation can be passed.

Every mechanic should have a copy of USCG Rules and Regulations for Recreational Boats 33 CFR 1-199, Subchapter S.

They are mandatory for boat and engine manufacturers. While they may or may not all be mandatory for mechanics, a liability problem exists when replacing a part that does not meet the 1977 reg's.

If a law suit develops in this situation, the courts have decided the mechanic is the expert... and he should have known better to replace the newer parts to meet the new regulations.

This places the mechanic in an uncomfortable position as he tries to convince the customer that the marine version of the part such as a carburetor may cost twice as much as the 4 cycle auto carb that can be bought from a nearby automotive parts store.

● **Hp ratings**-pg. 261, on boats have been required since 1972. It is a requirement for manufacturers to put on their boats, though only a recommendation for boat owners. Japanese companies rate their hp at the propeller. We have used a powerhead rating though changing to the propeller hp rating method.

261

● **Built-in flotation** has been a requirement for any inboard, outboard, or manually propelled rowboat manufactured after 1972. If the boat is swamped, the boat and its occupants are still supposed to float, page 16.

● **Upsets—** pgs. 47, 52, 73, 75-6, 376. Competition ski boats with flat bottoms slide instead of banking on a curve. If the speed isn't reduced, the hard chine can dig in and trip the boat. The tri-hull with three skegs to hold a straight course with a deep bow entry and a flat stern also has a tendency to trip in a tight turn.

● **Reversed controls**—page 73. The extreme deep V hull with longitudinal strakes, page 49, may be excellent at full throttle in a straightaway course. During a sharp turn at full throttle, the bow may fall off in a left turn, suddenly sheering off into a right turn... with the momentary control reversal also happening with other hulls. When in doubt, ease off from full throttle, then make your turn.

● **Rack and pinion push-pull steering.**—page 72. Cable failures have resulted with engines when a smaller size cable is installed instead of the recommend size. Failure, usually in a tight turn, cannot be predicted... don't cut corners to save money as a collision can result, or the boat capsize.

● **Blisters** have been a common problem on some kinds of larger size, slip-berthed boats in the water for long periods. Catalina Yachts has a five year warranty against blistering. Their hull bottoms are coated with an epoxy at the factory. So far enough boats haven't been in the water for long enough periods to know if the epoxy coating is working.

● **360 degree navigation light**—page 85. While it was previously used only for inland waters, it can now be used for international waters which can eliminate the white light you show forward.

FUEL TANKS

The EPA removed the Tetraethyl Lead from gasoline in 1986 requiring boat owners to take a fresh new look at fuel requirements,see below if alcohol is added to the gasoline.

● **Additives and octane boosters** may have chemicals when added to gasoline that can dissolve the resins in fiberglass fuel tanks.This will plug up the fuel system while exposing the glass fiber reducing its strength.

● **Portable 6 gallon fuel tank**—pgs.271,276, does not have to meet new reg's as it is light enough to be filled on the dock and examined periodically.

● **Fuel tanks over 7 gallons** are not classed as portable.They have to meet the new CG fuel and electrical regulations for permanently installed fuel tanks as the owner isn't going to normally lift the tank out of the boat to fill it and inspect the tank, page 276.

● **Inboard engine hose clamps**– pgs. 234,270. Spring tension hose clamps while used for outboard motors, must be replaced with screw-type clamps on all inboard engine systems.

● **Fuel tanks.** When a boat owner buys an aluminum or stainless fuel tank, it is necessary to have the proper alloy for marine use. Several alloys are not suitable for salt water use as they corrode rapidly.

● **Stainless fuel tanks.** (I have found rapid corrosion problems with built-in stainless tanks due to poor ventilation). Reply—they are suitable if they meet the the burn,shock,and slosh requirements,pressure tests,etc. The only problem as they are welded,the metal tends to become brittle and crack a half,to an inch from the welded seam.

● **Fill pipe**—page 270.No regulation requires it to go to the bottom of the tank...though it is a good practice.

● **Bonding wire**– pg.270. is required between the fuel fill and the tank.The fuel hose requires 4 hose clamps with double clamping at both ends.

The permanently installed fuel tank on page 270 was made for Researcher *in 1959 probably the first installed on an outboard boat.Considerable effort was required for the installation,hose hookup,etc.A screw plug drain was added on the side at the bottom to occasionally drain the tanks of dust and other items settling to the bottom.The drain was removed from the illustration as it does not fit the regulations.*

FUEL SYSTEMS

● **Electrical fuel pump.** Inboard boats built after 1978 must meet the new fuel/electrical regulations.The electrical fuel pump must be wired thru the ignition switch AND the oil pressure sensor on the engine.If the engine quits due to failure...or the ignition switch is turned off, a fire occurs, or a fuel line breaks,the fuel pump will automatically shut off and not continue pumping gasoline.

● **Fuel filter**–pg. 227. It must pass a 2½ minute-burn test and leak requirements to be considered legal for use in a gasoline system. The filter normally has to be made of metal instead of plastic to withstand the burn test.

262

● **Filter drain.** The only place to have an opening permitted between the fuel tank and engine is at the filter. Filter drain plugs require a tapered or a lock type plug in the filter so it can't accidentally unwind.

● **Float bowl vent—pg. 227.** It has been eliminated to prevent gasoline from leaking out the vent in a float failure. The vent from the carburetor throat accomplishes the purpose with any flooding going down the carb throat.

● **High speed carb jet nozzle— pg. 227.** While it pointed upward in the auto carburetor, it now turns downward to prevent gasoline flowing out the carb.

● **Side draft carburetors.** To prevent liquid gasoline from overflowing, a method is required to catch the overflow in the outboard carburetor, also it must have a flame arrestor.

The CG fuel/electrical regulations not only apply to the drive engine, they also apply to auxiliary charging generators, etc., permanently mounted in a boat.

● **Electrolysis?** Industry experts say you don't have an electrolysis problem of a transferral of metal particles between two boats at the same marina, slip to slip, or from the boat to the dock...*it will only occur between dissimilar metals with an inch or so apart.*

Corrosion is the most complex and least understood marine field we've faced in 30 years on the water with all sizes and kinds of powerboats and sailboats. The experts and the author seem to have a slight difference in their opinions.

263

ELECTRICALS

● **CDI electrical systems-pgs. 302-3.** It is extremely susceptible to shorting. Anytime a transistor has a short it causes an almost instant blowout.

● **GFI (ground fault interrupter)**—page 330. The duplex box should have a GFI. If you are using a 12V tool with an internal wiring defect, or working in a damp bilge *it will take less than a second for 1/10th amp 115 AC shoreside current to go thru the heart of a healthy person, then go to ground to kill him.*

The GFI analyzes electrical current going to and from the tool. If a fault difference as small as 0.0005 amp occurs, it will trip an alarm disconnecting the circuit in .0025th of a second.

● **Marina dockside 115v AC outlets.** Most marinas are wired by shoreside electricians using the building code, not used to working in a wet environment. Check every outlet for wiring polarity.

Author—I use a neon tester shown page 330 to check for polarity to show if the dock plug is correctly wired, or the wiring is reversed. This theory was tested on a dock with a dozen newly installed outlets while preparing information for our previous sailing book...with confusing results.

A nearby grinning boat owner asked if he could help. He confirmed that four of the dozen plugs had reversed wiring that could be hazardous.

● **Starter motors**—pg. 320-1. Older ones won't meet the spark proofing or ignition protection regulations A new starter motor must be sealed so it won't have open brushes to cause sparking that could ignite fuel vapors.

● **Alternators,generators,and voltage regulators** and similar items must also meet the spark protection requirements.including the leak and burn tests for normal operation,starting,etc.,to avoid igniting gasoline vapors.

BATTERIES

Author—during the preparation phase of our outboard book in 1958 we had little interest in that black box called the battery.We soon found it was important with considerable complexity if you want reliable equipment. Regular maintenance-free batteries are questionable for boating, pg.351 consider the newer **high-cycle maintenance-free battery,** page 340.

● **Battery lid vent**—page 349. It is a very simple idea to release hydrogen and oxygen vapors to reduce the chance of a battery explosion...which may ignite a larger gasoline explosion.

● **Battery explosions are common** though most are not large,being limited to breaking the battery...again the real concern is to avoid igniting gasoline fumes which can cause a much larger explosion.*Authors note*—page 352 covers the cause of battery explosions.

● **Battery tiedown**—page 349. The battery must be lashed down so with a 90 pound pull it can't move more than an inch in any direction...or the weight of the battery if larger than average size.The battery lid should be snug against the top of the battery to hold it down.

Stan didn't agree with a stout shock cord over the battery top page 349. I question the plastic webbing strap to contain battery cases which are affected by ultraviolet rays of the sun, and battery gassing fumes. page 349.

● **Side mounted terminals.** The battery must be tied down with the same limitations, otherwise it can slide across the deck to contact metal parts. This has resulted in arcing which has caused several fires.

TRAILERBOAT HIGHWAY FIRES

Highway boat fires,pg. 185. Many fires occur on boats trailered with or without cover with cigarettes thrown out of towing car windows.

Information in this regulation chapter is unusual, not indicating our book, nor interpretation of these ideas have USCG Approval . They were provided by sailing friend Stan Holden, USCG Boating Standard expert, and the author discussing problems on the professional level testing mutual ideas to help powerboat mechanics and boat operators.

We all learn from exposure in our business, profession, and sports, the reason for exposure to the USCG regulations, and various listings of collisions, drownings, etc.

Full agreement among professionals is rare, and in our case, it is rigid battery tiedowns, usually plastic that in our experience age rapidly with battery fumes. Again, our only interest is exposure to give you as many options as possible for efficient, happy powerboating.

264

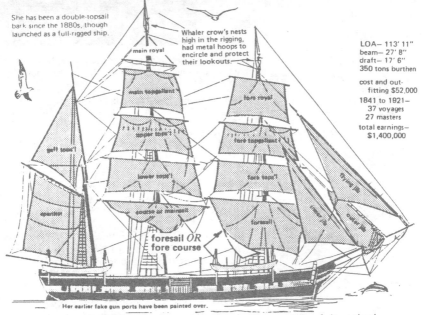

She has been a double-topsail bark since the 1880s, though launched as a full-rigged ship.

main royal

Whaler crow's nests high in the rigging, had metal hoops to encircle and protect their lookouts.

LOA— 113' 11"
beam— 27' 8"
draft— 17' 6"
350 tons burthen

cost and out-
fitting $52,000
1841 to 1921—
37 voyages
27 masters
total earnings—
$1,400,000

main topgallant

fore royal

upper tops'l

fore topgallant

gaff tops'l

lower tops'l

fore tops'l

flying jib

spanker

course or mainsail

foresail

outer jib

foresail OR
fore course

Her earlier fake gun ports have been painted over.

Visit the *Charles W. Morgan* at her Mystic Seaport Wharf, launched in 1841, the only surviving 19th century wooden whaling ship.

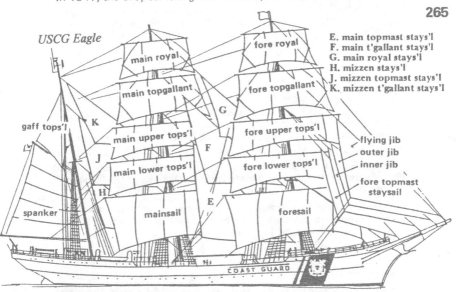

USCG Eagle

fore royal

E. main topmast stays'l
F. main t'gallant stays'l
G. main royal stays'l
H. mizzen stays'l
J. mizzen topmast stays'l
K. mizzen t'gallant stays'l

main royal

main topgallant

fore topgallant

G

gaff tops'l

K

main upper tops'l

fore upper tops'l

flying jib
outer jib
inner jib

J

F

main lower tops'l

fore lower tops'l

fore topmast
staysail

H

E

spanker

mainsail

foresail

COAST GUARD

Additional USCG regulations— *we expect to add more information in future regulations... temporarily adding square rig sailing vessels to save the space.*

Powerboating Illustrated

After a person has once had the experience of touching a firing plug, it is one he will seldom try to repeat.

Suppose the motor is limping or it has conked out. First look for simple things such as empty fuel tanks, loose connections, or frayed wires. Most mechanical failures are simple, that is until an inexperienced person overlooks the cause and starts tearing into something else.

Next check the PLUG... is the ceramic broken or does lead have loose connection?

To check ELECTRICAL SYSTEM, remove plug and turn over slowly so you can see spark jumping to motor as shown at left----hold plug by boot so it grounds through motor, not through you.

If cause of electrical trouble isn't obvious, turn to page 309 for troubleshooting sequence.

●

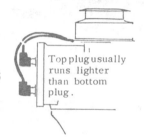

Top plug usually runs lighter than bottom plug.

266

If test shows spark, check FUEL SYSTEM. If it is a 4 or 6 cylinder motor, check to find if any pairs of cylinders are out that might indicate high or low speed needle out of adjustment; or if one plug is out, chances are that bottom of two plugs will run darker and usually foul out first. Check fuel and carb pages for additional details.

●

Can you smell CARBON MONOXIDE from an engine exhaust?

The average adult American has been exposed to more carbon monoxide than he realizes due to high school physics teaching students that *carbon monoxide is tasteless, colorless, and odorless.* This is a half statement that kills people annually in boats, autos, and aircraft.

Develop the positive attitude that you will recognize the smell of exhaust fumes from gasoline engines. *Any time you are able to smell these fumes with partially burned hydrocarbon particles....* **carbon monoxide is also present** inside your garage, car, boat, or aircraft.

Carbon monoxide is a byproduct of combustion in every gasoline engine, along with other partially burned hydrocarbons which must be exhausted and dissipated into the air or water.

Carbon monoxide is a **deoxidizer** which may be absorbed into the blood stream up to 250 times faster than oxygen. It unites with the hemoglobin in the blood ..to prevent oxygen going to skin tissues.

If your boat is underway and you feel you've had a stiff drink, feel drowsy, or become irritable, yet the strongest drink you've had is coffee, or you wake up with a 5 martini hangover without any imbiding, *check immediately for the gentle, numbing, and deadly killer.*

Also see pages 120-1.

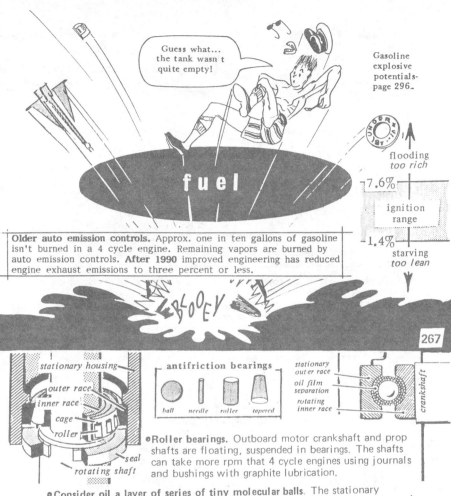

Guess what...
the tank wasn't
quite empty!

Gasoline
explosive
potentials-
page 296.

fuel

flooding
too rich

7.6%

ignition
range

1.4%

starving
too lean

Older auto emission controls. Approx. one in ten gallons of gasoline isn't burned in a 4 cycle engine. Remaining vapors are burned by auto emission controls. **After 1990** improved engineering has reduced engine exhaust emissions to three percent or less.

BLOOEY

stationary housing

outer race
inner race
cage
roller
seal
rotating shaft

antifriction bearings

ball   needle   roller   tapered

stationary
outer race
oil film
separation
rotating
inner race

crankshaft

• **Roller bearings.** Outboard motor crankshaft and prop shafts are floating, suspended in bearings. The shafts can take more rpm that 4 cycle engines using journals and bushings with graphite lubrication.

• **Consider oil a layer of series of tiny molecular balls.** The stationary outer race, and inner race surrounding the rotating crankshaft, are separated by roller bearings. A layer of oil balls adhere to the inner and outer races, while another layer surrounds the rolling ball bearings above.

• **Rolling friction—separation and oil coolant.** The rotating bearings are insulated from the races by an oil layer separation. This thin tough oil film on all three surfaces, and the separation layer between reduces metal to metal contact to 1% or less. This separation layer bleeds any minimal heat buildup for normal upper rpm operation.

• **Sliding friction— bushings and journals** are also used to separate rotating shafts from stationary housings Graphite lubrication reduces sliding wearing, solid friction heat buildup for lower rpm shaft rotation.

bushing
lubrication
groove
journal

friction bearings

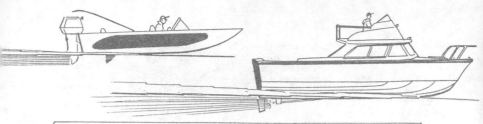

Pg. 14 shows a theoretical comparison of the 2 cycle outboard vs the
4 cycle inboard engine *weighing 4 times as much to push identical
planing hulls the same speed with the same load.* Marine mechanics
have to know the advantages and differences of both engines so your
customers can gain the best performance from their chosen powerplant.

- The **2 cycle outboard motor** *fires on every downward power stroke,*
  with crankshaft and propeller drive shaft supported and suspended in
  bearings when operating under load, page 241. The modern 2 cycle
  engine can operate at factory recommended top rpm continuously
  without damage as bearings eliminate 99% of moving, wearing friction.

  **2 cycle oil must separate moving parts, bleed frictional heat. . then burn
  clean without leaving deposits... pages 269 and 358.**

  2 cycle oil spray-thru lubrication produces a thin, tough, slippery adhesive
  film to *separate bearings and races frictional contact.* Oil next *becomes
  a coolant* to bleed remaining frictional heat. This provides a long healthy
  life for moving metal parts operating at normal working temperature range,
  at top recommended rpm. If this rpm is exceeded, heat buildup becomes
  difficult to dissipate with bearing metals beginning to expand.

268

- **The aluminum powerhead** releases heat so easily and rapidly that a cold
  motor can be given full throttle, then stopped suddenly without metal
  heat fatigue damage.

  WARNING— graphite needed for bushings and journals if squirted into
  a 2 cycle carb *will cause bearings to slide* instead of roll. The sliding,
  wearing, solid friction produces rapid heat buildup metal fatigue.

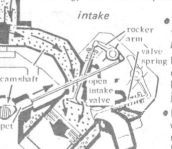

intake

rocker arm

valve spring

camshaft

open intake valve

tappet

- The **4 cycle engine** with weight a secondary
  factor, requires a complex valve train assembly
  that fires on every 2nd power stroke.
  Most are heavyweight weaklings for mid rpm
  operational range. It isn't fully suspended in
  bearings. Frictional areas using bushings and
  journals reduce upper rpm potentials.

- **Iron block heat sink.** If using outside cooling
  water, it needs to be warmed up before putting
  under load. It should be cooled down afterwards
  by idling to minimize block/head warping damage.

- **4 cycle oil separates and cools moving gears and bearings.** *Condensation
  can combine with sulfur blow-by,* developing a weak sulfuric acid in the
  crankcase... change oil often. **During storage**—drain oil, and add oil without
  sulfur content. If additives are needed to compensate for sulfur in the
  oil... will the additives wear off in one, two, or three years?

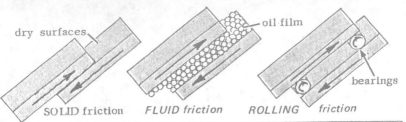

dry surfaces   oil film

SOLID friction   FLUID friction   ROLLING friction   bearings

Lubrication needs are much more critical with boat engines than auto engines operating most of their life in the middle power range. 2 cycle and 4 cycle boat engines operate at *trolling speeds... or full throttle* for many hours between long periods of inactivity.

- **Solid friction**— rub your hands together. Do you feel a heat buildup? Rub two metal surfaces together that seem smooth. A similar heat buildup develops as you will find hills and valleys on their surfaces when examined under a microscope. The dry surfaces similar to sandpaper rubbing against each other, develops a molecular attraction heat buildup.

  Oil and grease are lubricants to limit metal contact. They produce an insulating layer between gears, roller bearings and races, to minimize rubbing, wearing metal surface contact.

  Oil and grease are coolants. They bleed heat from the minimum contact areas so metal moving parts stay within normal heat operating range.

- **Roller bearing friction.** Oil is a lubricant clinging to the bearings plus their inner and outer races to reduce moving metal contact to contact areas. Oil then becomes a coolant to bleed off excess heat to limit heat **269** metal expansion for temperatures to stay in their normal range.

- **When moving metal parts exceed this temperature range** and/or rpm limit, oil coolant protection is reduced. The metal parts expand squeezing out the thin oil film. Contact areas expand rapidly to increase heat buildup producing *metal fatigue intergranular corrosion,* pg. 358.

- **Fluid friction— the outboard lower unit.** Periodically check the lower unit grease level before operating your outdrive, or outboard motor. If the lower unit is warm from exposure to the sun... then suddenly lowered into the water, a drop or two of water may be sucked past the seal. *Change lower unit grease yearly* to remove small abrasive metal particles, and moisture resulting from the breathing process.

- **Washers must absorb engine vibration** between lower unit housing seals and vent screws... **to prevent them from vibrating loose.** When these washers are overlooked and the screws vibrate loose during operation, pressure will force the grease out. Suction will pull water in after cooling down... sealing the water inside the lower unit housing.

- **Water and grease emulsify like adding sugar to coffee...** reducing the grease cooling protection. As the trapped heat can't escape during operation, *solid friction potentials increase.* Metal heat expansion develops with *metal fatigue corrosion* following, page 373.

bushing
lubrication groove
journal

- **Sliding friction.** Bushings and journals use graphite for lubrication. If graphite is squirted into a 2 cycle outboard carb, bearings begin to slide. The heat will soon cause *metal fatigue corrosion.*

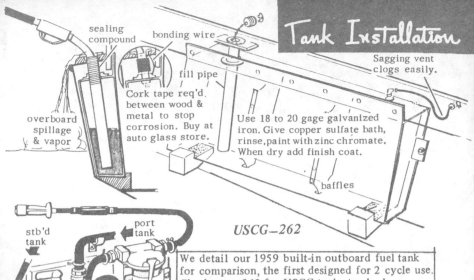

sealing compound

bonding wire

fill pipe

Cork tape req'd. between wood & metal to stop corrosion. Buy at auto glass store.

overboard spillage & vapor

Sagging vent clogs easily.

Use 18 to 20 gage galvanized iron. Give copper sulfate bath, rinse, paint with zinc chromate. When dry add finish coat.

baffles

stb'd tank

port tank

USCG–262

One method of installing fuel selector valve and strainer.

270

inexpensive overboard vent

We detail our 1959 built-in outboard fuel tank for comparison, the first designed for 2 cycle use. Check page 262 for USCG tank standards.

6 gallon tanks can be filled on a dock. Due to weight, larger ones must be filled on the boat and unless spillage & fumes go overboard they collect in the bilge. This hazard cannot be overstressed.

●

Study the illustrations closely for solutions to most installation problems. Hulls come in all shapes and sizes, so have a sheet metal specialist who makes tanks, measure & fabricate one for your boat with desired gallonage. Most if not all of the installation can be done by you with basic tools. Price of our 18 gallon custom made tanks was about the same as many ready made tanks that were clumsy to lash down and had questionable safety features.

FILL PIPE must be straight. Regulations call for fill pipe going almost to bottom of tank to localize fire when filling. Plugged vent can make slow filling, overhand loop for drainage is suggested. If neoprene fill hose is used, metal parts must be BONDED with copper wire to prevent static spark explosion.

SPILLAGE & FUMES must go overboard! Tanks filled inside of boat can be compared to sitting on a keg of lighted dynamite.

●

Mix metals little as possible. Copper tubing ages fuel, so neoprene even though it may be pinched or cut, may be better. Air circulation is very important to reduce corrosion; wood must be insulated from the metal by CORK. STRAINER must be serviceable, note extra loop in hose permitting it to be lifted out without removing wing nuts, etc. As elbows, tees, etc., are usually brass, replace periodically around salt water.

For assembly, slip clamp on hose, add fitting, adjust clamp.

Spring tension clamps may only be used on outboards...NOT for inboard engine use!

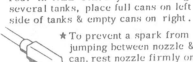

*Check bottoms of portable metal
fuel tanks for corrosion, pg. 276.
Additives can dissolve resin in
fiberglass fuel tanks,USCG pg. 262.*

All filling and mixing should be done ashore or on the dock.

6 gallon tank

1 Pour ONE GALLON of gasoline into empty fuel tank.

2 Pour in ALL OIL. If you are filling several tanks, place full cans on left side of tanks & empty cans on right.

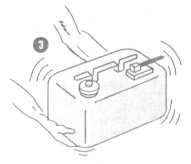

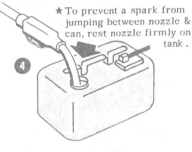

★ To prevent a spark from jumping between nozzle & can, rest nozzle firmly on tank.

3 Replace cap and SHAKE THOROUGHLY in partially full tank----can you shake a full tank?

4 Pour in rest of gasoline as fast as possible then replace cap and wipe tank clean. Wait a moment or so to permit fumes to dissipate on the dock before stowing.

271

Portable fuel tanks must be constrained in a collision—

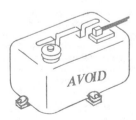

AVOID

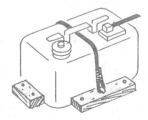

A full portable fuel tank weighing approx. 42 lbs. needs more restraint in rough weather or a collision than just the clamps shown.

Are the wood blocks bolted in place? Tank must be restrained from going forward, aft, or sideway, with a strong strap over top, limiting movement to less than an inch in any direction.

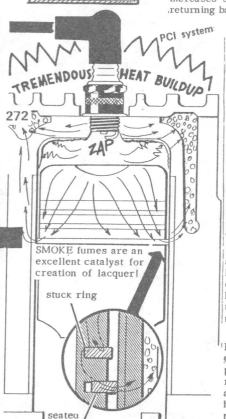

FUEL NEEDS OXYGEN for combustion. Unburned gases and smoke coming from barrel are going through carb, choking from lack of oxygen.

Barrel has INSUFFICIENT WATER to DISSIPATE HEAT from cylinder. Water has increased proportion of smoke. What kind of a coolant is hot water and smoke going through motor powerhead?

Cylinder temperature must go up; result, serious overheating with abnormal pressure. As PROP is biting into mixture of smoke and spray, it develops excessive RPM due to cavitation.

Plugs must burn clean. TOO MUCH OIL is hard to burn off, resulting in partially burned carbon that increases smoke pouring into water from motor, returning back into carb and cylinders.

•

Due to PREIGNITION from heat buildup, unburned gasoline begins to form a sticky surface over all areas. This'll stick the piston rings and cling to the cylinder walls like flypaper to act as an insulator to collect unburned carbon.

STUCK RINGS. The only method for heat transference from piston to water jacket is through skinny rings needing solid contact by spring action with the water cooled cylinder walls.

Before rings had chance to set, varnish and gum sealed the rings to piston. Top of piston grows progressively warmer as it can't dissipate heat until or unless heat is transferred to the cylinder walls and water jacket.

PREIGNITION which is seldom heard as a 'ping' in outboard motors (look for burned plugs/heat symptoms) creating excessively high temperatures with very high pressures inside cylinder. As the temperature rises piston and rings may start burning and melting.

•

If motor was idled for long periods, unburned fuel residue may freeze pistons to cylinder walls, or at higher rpm cause the kind of damage shown at left. There was little doubt helping hand our friend above had given to his motor, killed the poor thing before it had a chance to leave the barrel.

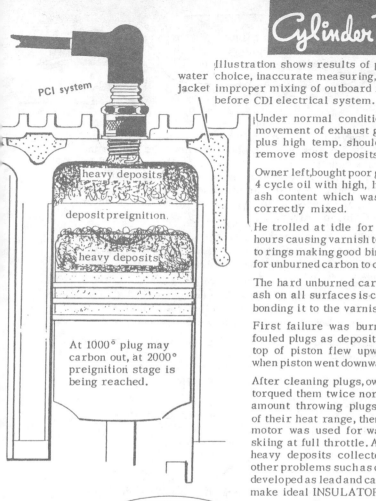

PCI system

water jacket

Illustration shows results of poor choice, inaccurate measuring, and improper mixing of outboard fuel before CDI electrical system.

heavy deposits

deposit preignition.

heavy deposits

At 1000° plug may carbon out, at 2000° preignition stage is being reached.

Deposit throw off can foul burned plug.

PCI system

white ceramic (heat)

lead deposits

melted, eroded electrodes

Under normal conditions movement of exhaust gases plus high temp. should help remove most deposits.

Owner left, bought poor grade 4 cycle oil with high, hard ash content which was not correctly mixed.

He trolled at idle for ten hours causing varnish to freeze to rings making good binder for unburned carbon to cling.

The hard unburned carbon ash on all surfaces is cooked bonding it to the varnish.

First failure was burned / fouled plugs as deposits on top of piston flew upward when piston went downward.

273

After cleaning plugs, owner torqued them twice normal amount throwing plugs out of their heat range, then the motor was used for water skiing at full throttle. As the heavy deposits collected, other problems such as cooling developed as lead and carbon make ideal INSULATOR.

Since heat cannot flow to water jacket, the cylinder temperature rises rapidly. Preignition begins with chronic condition of burned plugs, or burn a hole through top of piston...indicated by aluminum deposits on plugs.

Considerable scraping was required to remove the owner caused deposits, plus replacing damaged parts, an expensive unnecessary job.

He said he can't figure what's wrong with the motor------it worked good two years ago!!!!

Before leaving your boat after a weekend, run the fuel out of the motors. For the short moment the fuel is in the crankcase, the oxidation can change it to gum and to varnish very shortly. As an example let's consider a John D. who paid $3500 for his new rig, used it a couple of times, and stored it for a vacation three months later on the Colorado River.

After 500 miles of hard trailering John and three of his friends launched the boat in a swift current. Then he tried to start the motor up which had fuel sitting in it for over three months.

One carb eventually fired up, the second worked spotty, the third was dead. Even though the boat could easily go 30 mph it was now lucky to make 8 mph upstream.

We had lectured him on stale gasoline so he had dumped the old fuel out of his tanks, and refilled them in a small out of the way service station. Since it had a small turn-over, the gasoline was overage or stale.

A 'well meaning' fellow outboarder came to the rescue with a trusty screwdriver, to kill the poor, tortured creature. We hope the owner soon chooses bird watching as a hobby... but should we warn the birds ahead of time?

Breathing gasoline fumes can produce MECHANICAL PNEUMONIA.

A friend towed his houseboat home for the first time in 10 years. The next morning he smelled gasoline due to a rupture in the houseboat fuel tank. Instead of calling the fire department he handled the problem himself... breathing in a lot of gasoline fumes.

He became very ill on a vacation to Sweden, with a diagnosis as mechanical pneumonia at a local hospital. As they couldn't treat the illness with their technology he returned to the U.S.

The gasoline fumes dried the moisture in his lungs to produce a result similar to pneumonia... which wouldn't respond to pneumonia drugs. After a lengthy hospital stay he requested, "I can't leave the U.S. again as the gasoline fumes have damaged my health. Please pass this information along to your readers".

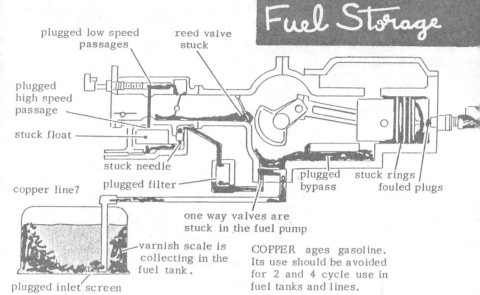

Fuel Storage

plugged low speed passages

reed valve stuck

plugged high speed passage

stuck float

stuck needle

copper line?

plugged filter

plugged bypass

stuck rings

fouled plugs

one way valves are stuck in the fuel pump

varnish scale is collecting in the fuel tank.

plugged inlet screen

COPPER ages gasoline. Its use should be avoided for 2 and 4 cycle use in fuel tanks and lines.

Mix oil and automotive gasoline, pour into container, seal, let it stand 6 to 8 months ... producing a sticky mess due to aging or instability of gasoline. The INHIBITORS have lost their strength and unstable or OLEFINIC compounds break loose leaving gum formation, eventually changing to a hard varnish like deposit. While part is due to evaporation of VOLATILE parts evaporating at room temperature or a LOW boiling point, most STALE gasoline is due to aging.

275

- 2 CYCLE TANKS. Owner should run his tanks <u>dry</u> before refilling or storing. If tanks are left out in sun, increased temperature speeds aging of fuel. If fresh fuel is added to stale fuel, life expectancy of new fuel is considerably reduced. The advantage, 2 cycle oil reduces corrosion potentials <u>inside</u> tank, major corrosion will be on bottom and outside of tank.

- 4 CYCLE TANKS. They are seldom emptied. Owners keep adding gasoline to reduce condensation during storage since without oil mix, 4 cycle tanks may corrode internally and externally. Again, avoid copper fuel tanks and copper lines which rapidly age gasoline storage life.

Suppose you have a powered trailerboat with 20 to 30 gallons of fuel stored in built-in tanks, and your rig is stored in a garage, prohibited in some states. Also check to see if your insurance policy prohibits this type of storage.

If you have a few gallons of fuel left over, consider pouring it into your car. What type of a pump transfer method will you use, also do transfer in open air away from any kind of ignition source.

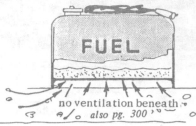

Portable outboard fuel tank bottoms require air flow!

no ventilation beneath
also pg. 300

We stored a new jeep can in our garage having outboard mix. A year later we smelled gasoline as the bottom corroded out... yet the sides and top were still in new condition.

As gasoline evaporates, it cools which causes condensation on the tank ... especially under the tank placed on concrete. This draws alkali and other hygroscopic salts from the cement up into the bottom surface of the tank starting a 24 hour rusting action. Continually check bottoms of fuel tanks because of this dead air space needing ventilation, as metal may be paper thin yet other surfaces look new.

OUTBOARD fuel tank storage. While we recommend storing them full, if empty they will have little corrosion from the inside due to interior oil coating. Yet they must be stored on a board, tilted up to prevent condensation on the bottom.

4 cycle inboard tank corrosion—

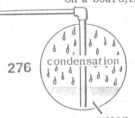

condensation

water

276

The 4 cycle fuel tank must face corrosion on both inner and outer surfaces. If tank is only partly full during storage period, condensation may be major problem causing inner corrosion which is often hard to detect.

As water is heavier than gasoline, water will sink to bottom of tank. In one inboard boat that hadn't been used for six months, the engine promptly quit as so much condensation collected it overflowed both the water trap and filter... requiring cleaning three times until all the condensation was removed.

Four cycle tanks should be filled before storage to reduce chance of condensation to reduce internal surface corrosion, or empty the tanks and fill with CO_2 and oil mist.

AVOID!!!!

Location of built-in fuel tanks on planing trailerboats under 20' may be very critical. Though it required considerable time to find the answer, it proved basic.

If center of built-in tanks were over trailer axle, it would equalize weight distribution at displacement AND planing speeds. Avoid extreme locations as your hull balance at planing speed is VERY critical for best performance with maximum speed, yet minimum fuel consumption.

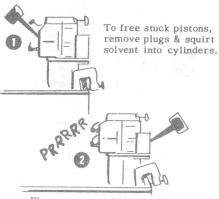

To free stuck pistons, remove plugs & squirt solvent into cylinders.

Use a good two cycle solvent.

Warm motor up in test tank or on boat. After running at 2/3 to full throttle start adding heavy loads of solvent through carburetor or carburetors.

After five to ten minutes operation flood motor with solvent and choke it out. Let motor sit about twenty minutes so solvent can work into all corners and tight spots.

277

Start motor up to begin burning out the solvent, then add more solvent. Keep motor running until all cleaner has been burned up in the cylinders.

Now is time to retire old plugs that have probably taken quite a beating and are probably well fouled from solvent action.

CAUTION... don't add acetone solvent into fuel tank that has flexible fuel lines as acetone has a damaging effect on neoprene hose.

If a boat has permanently installed fuel tanks that have COPPER fuel lines, NEVER squirt solvent into tank. First gasoline flowing through lines forms a barrier to pacify or cover and neutralize copper action.

IF COPPER SUPPLY LINES are used from fuel tank, shutoff valves should be installed at tank connection so gasoline will not be standing and aging in the copper lines.

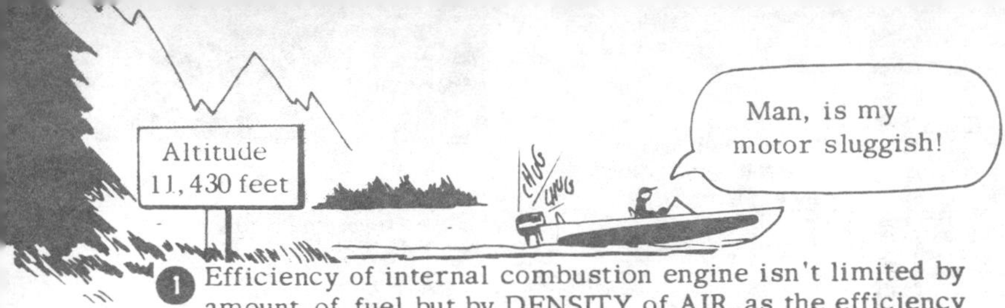

Altitude
11,430 feet

Man, is my
motor sluggish!

1 Efficiency of internal combustion engine isn't limited by amount of fuel but by DENSITY of AIR, as the efficiency or hp increases when more oxygen is available. There are several factors involved to increase or decrease the air density with resulting engine efficiency.

2 Maximum hp LOSS can occur with following combination: hot weather•high humidity•low barometer•high altitude

3 Maximum hp GAIN can occur with following combination: cool weather• low humidity•high barometer•sea level

4 SAE specs. applied to horsepower, are corrected to sea level at 60°f with a barometer reading of 29.92 in a fairly dry atmosphere. These are conditions used for both OBC and SAE ratings in which outboard motors develop maximum continuous hp. (To a purist the term may be outboard engine, but we use the term motor as it is more commonly applied by the outboarding industry.)

278

5 TEMPERATURE is important as a 10° rise can mean a 1% hp loss. As an example, blow up a balloon and seal the opening. As the balloon is heated its volume expands over a larger area... without increasing quantity of oxygen available for combustion.

6 As ALTITUDE is increased the amount of oxygen will decrease. To keep the fuel/oxygen ratio constant, it is necessary to DECREASE quantity of fuel going into the carb. The engines don't work harder at high altitude, they can't work as hard. Adding more oil for altitude increases plug fouling. SPARK may also be retarded for high altitude.

7 If HUMIDITY is 100% but other factors are ideal, every molecule of moisture displaces a molecule of oxygen. The resulting moisture content doesn't burn as efficiently and hp is reduced.

8 Since these are conditions that we have little control over, the outboarder can compensate for any noticeable losses by changing to a prop that has less bite or less pitch to match power loss, yet still be able to reach and maintain manufacturers recommended rpm. In extreme cases power loss may be as great as 20% whether the internal combustion engine is on your boat or in your car.

Powerboating Illustrated

Top Dead Center

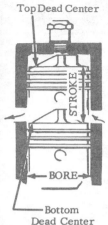

STROKE

BORE

Bottom
Dead Center

pivot

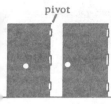

pivot or fulcrum

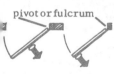

more	less
force	force
LESS	MORE
torque	torque

boat race
vs
motor race

What is
horsepower?

HP– USCG page 261

BORE is diameter of cylinder while STROKE is distance piston moves in inches between top and bottom dead center.

DISPLACEMENT is the cubic volume compressed during one upward stroke of the piston. The piston displacement of the entire engine is found with the following formula:

COMPRESSION RATIO is the ratio between the total volume of interior of cylinder, with piston at bottom dead center, to the volume at top dead center.

Let's take these terms and see how they apply to the 70hp Mercury that displaces about 66 cubic inches while an inboard with comparable power weighs 600 lbs., or three times as much and displaces about 150 cubic inches.

The 70 hp (SAE) is developed in a powerhead that has a bore of 2 9/16" with a 2 1/8" stroke, hp measured at 5500 rpm for continuous duty. The 75 hp (OBC) Johnson or Evinrude has a bore of 3 3/8" with a 2 1/2" stroke. It displaces 89. 46 cubic inches and develops the 75 hp at 4500 rpm.

•

Engineers glibly talk about TORQUE in terms of formula, but **279** what does it mean to the rest of us?

All other factors equal, which of the two doors shown at left is easier to open? It is very obvious that the one having a knob on the outside is easier to open and close than the door having a knob in the center.

It is the MOMENT or TORQUE measured in pounds to produce necessary twist or rotation that force alone cannot achieve.

To make FORCE effective in producing rotary motion, the FORCE and its DISTANCE should be as far away from the PIVOT as possible: moving force closer reduces the leverage, increasing amount of force required for the same job.

•

Outboard motor races are run on a DYNO while hull races are run with the motor on a boat. The unit of power is the — ONE FOOT-POUND per SECOND that is measured in torque or brake horsepower at a certain rpm. As a result:

1 horsepower = 550 ft-lb/sec. or 33,000 ft-lb/min.

A 10 hp engine operated at continuous recommended rpm should develop 330,000 ft-lb during each minute of operation. In one second engine can lift 550 pounds 10 feet, or 55 pounds 100 feet, or 5.5 pounds 1,000 feet.

Powerboating Illustrated

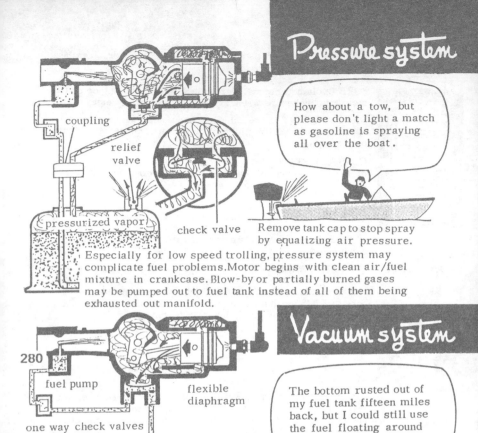

Pressure system

coupling

relief valve

pressurized vapor

check valve

How about a tow, but please don't light a match as gasoline is spraying all over the boat.

Remove tank cap to stop spray
by equalizing air pressure.

Especially for low speed trolling, pressure system may
complicate fuel problems. Motor begins with clean air/fuel
mixture in crankcase. Blow-by or partially burned gases
may be pumped out to fuel tank instead of all of them being
exhausted out manifold.

Vacuum system

280

fuel pump

flexible diaphragm

one way check valves

atmospheric pressure

PRRRR

The bottom rusted out of my fuel tank fifteen miles back, but I could still use the fuel floating around in the boat.

After motor starts, on SUCTION or up stroke in crankcase,
plastic diaphragm is pulled towards crankshaft. This forms
partial vacuum pulling fuel out of tank into pump. Air must
go into fuel tank to displace outgoing fuel ... is air vent open?

Downward stroke crankcase compression forces diaphragm
outward, and fuel trapped in fuel pump, forced out into strainer.
Fuel cannot return to tank or pump due to action of one way
check valves.

After operating motors with this type system since 1957
we have found it safe and foolproof. If your motor still uses
pressure system, we highly recommend it be changed to
the much safer and more practical vacuum system.

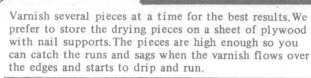

drying board

Varnish several pieces at a time for the best results. We prefer to store the drying pieces on a sheet of plywood with nail supports. The pieces are high enough so you can catch the runs and sags when the varnish flows over the edges and starts to drip and run.

> Varnish should NOT be stirred, shaken, nor agitated as it will produce harmful air bubbles.

Pour sufficient varnish for the job into a large paper cup. Put the top rapidly back and on firmly *to avoid starting a chemical drying action skin on top inside the can*...the reason we use two small cans of varnish instead of a large one.

store
upside
down

●**Varnish brushes are expensive**...as they have to flow the varnish on without leaving varnish dandruff behind. avoid brushes used for painting. Varnish brushes can last a lifetime, or be destroyed the first time if not cared for.

hole   nail

While the brush is being used, we prefer to store it in a plastic container with turpentine or linseed oil covering the hairs. The plastic top has a hole just large enough to slip the brush handle up and thru. The nail will hold the brush upright for indefinite storage without the hairs touching the bottom of the container.

281

Varnish brush and container are stored outside in a paint locker away from garage ignition sources such as dryers, etc.

When the brush is to be used, brush out the turpentine on an old newspaper sheet. The brush is ready for revarnishing or drying out for storage.

●**Revarnishing?** Try to do it before a crack in the varnish surface permits water to leak into the wood below making a stain. It is then necessary to remove the varnish, let the wood dry, then revarnish. We try to have 9 to 10 layers of varnish for our boat nameplates exposed most of the year for yearly revarnishing without cracks and wood stains.

●**Rapid drying varnish** can be used for the first 3 coats or so, with each layer drying in 8 hours...while the outer *Polyurethane and Durathane* strong protective layers require 24 hour drying per layer.

●**Aluminum ocean dinghies?** I asked my retired admiral friend, pg. 231, why he had such a horribly corroded aluminum skiff for his 37' *Igdrasil*. He grinned, "I took an afternoon off from our Caribbean base to go fishing. I was drifting 200 yards offshore at dusk when it was time to return, but my motor wouldn't start. My hollering was ignored, the wind came up and blew me 9 to 10 miles offshore, and the wind stopped.

"After three days and nights the wind came up and blew me back into the entrance of our navy base. I've tried to replace the skiff and my battered outboard...but for the first time I must admit, have you ever heard of a sentimental admiral?"

How often should
I change plugs?

Spark plugs are the most often replaced items on outboard motors. They should be changed at least once a year or when motor begins to run ragged.

If plug electrodes have burned away to half of their original diameter it will be hard for them to maintain correct gap. A heat problem is indicated, what is the cause.

If plugs have a heavy oil/carbon deposit that can't be wiped off easily, they should be replaced after you know whether a plug problem is indicated or if it is symptom of trouble elsewhere in motor.

●

2 cycle plugs are often damaged by incorrect sandblast preparation.

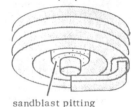

sandblast pitting

"Why does sandblasting work good on my auto plugs, yet they seem to foul up my outboard motor plugs?"

Most people are used to handling auto plugs without an oily coating. All 2 cycle plugs have to first be degreased with solvent such as acetone (fingernail polish remover) or carburetor cleaner.

If oily coating isn't removed, the sandblasting breaks oil film in spots to roughen or pit the ceramic. As insulator is roughened up, oils and carbonaceous materials find it easy to stick to rough surface so plug fouls out faster than before.

After degreasing, 2 cycle plugs can be blasted just as efficiently as 4 cycle plugs. Next file gap in order to remove roughness on electrodes, then check and set the correct gap.

●

It was middle of June in Florida when a fisherman came in with burned plugs that had only been used a few hours in an almost new motor.

He had bought the motor during October and spent a five day vacation trolling in northern Minnesota. The dealer had installed J-12J plugs to burn off the excess fuel in his motor that was idling under extreme conditions.

He was now on a vacation in Florida with the fishing holes five miles away from the dock—at full throttle in the middle of the summer. About two miles out his plugs died a sudden fiery death.

After plugs were replaced with J-5J's our fisherman was on his way to that new fishing hole at full speed. P.S. His tackle box now included a spare set of plugs and a deep-throated plug wrench.

282

The heart of your outboard motor is its spark plugs. Before replacing any plugs, find WHY they need replacement.

spark plugs

J-6 JM

Plug condition can indicate any of the following symptoms to a trained mechanic:

PCI systems

1 VARNISH
stale fuel

2 CARBON
deposits

3 NOT ENOUGH OIL
poor lubrication

4 TOO MUCH OIL
fouled plugs

5 EXCESSIVE HEAT

WATER pump
STUCK rings
GASKET set wrong
poor lubrication
excess spark advance
LEAD buildup
wrong prop

6 MISHANDLING
broken porcelain

7 ELECTRICAL PROBLEMS
condenser, points, coil,
broken insulation

8 RESTRICTION or SITTING
on fuel line

9 IMPROPER MIXING
burn hot, burn cold

10 INCORRECT GAP SETTING

11 PUDDLING

12 WRONG HEAT RANGE
too hot
too cold

Powerboating Illustrated

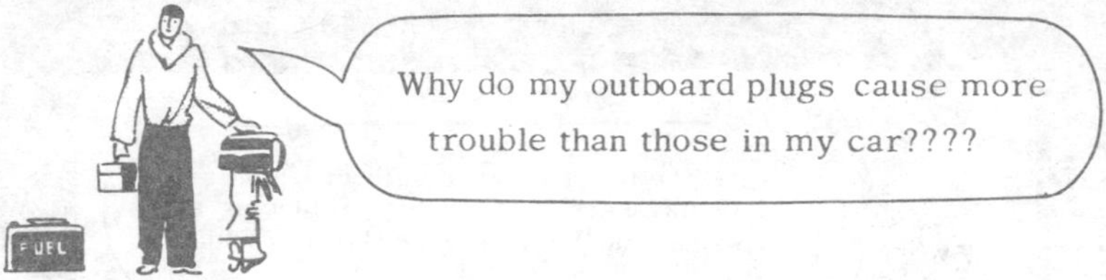

> Why do my outboard plugs cause more trouble than those in my car????

At trolling speeds, cylinder temperatures are low & the swirling scouring action of gases at minimum, so plug must fight carbonaceous buildup or foul out. As full throttle is other speed, the tremendous temperatures & pressures generated at the tip must burn plug clean without burning itself up.

A plug in an outboard motor operating at top rpm for 50 hours will usually fire more times than a plug in an auto traveling 10,000 miles due to:

● Without dead stroke 2 cycle plug fires twice as many times as 4 cycle engine plug operating at same rpm.
● Powerhead operates continuously at 4000-5500 rpm, car engine rpm is usually 1/2 to 1/3 as much.
● A 2 cycle plug fires THREE to EIGHT times as often as a 4 cycle plug under varying heat conditions yet it has to swallow oil and burn itself clean or foul out.
● When an outboard plug quits, remember it was doing double duty. It will be the same as two plugs quitting in your auto at the same time.
● They have considerably more handling problems such as bouncing around in the back of a car or truck and being subjected to occasional or continuous spray.

●

The outboard plugs do a tremendous job while taking a horrible beating. They may be expensive at a dollar each, but look what they have to accomplish... a person should think of spark plugs as being expendable.

Before discarding plugs you should first find the trouble source. A MECHANIC is an ANALYST who realizes that the plug is just a method of getting the energy across the gap inside a combustion chamber. He knows a plug is the heart of your motor and its failure is a symptom and aid to locating and finding a remedy for the trouble source. With our coverage you may be able to become your own plug doctor.

Always carry spare plugs in sealed containers so they are protected from corrosion and various objects in your toolkit. Without this airtight container, spare plugs can soon be in worse condition than if they were being used in your motor.

284

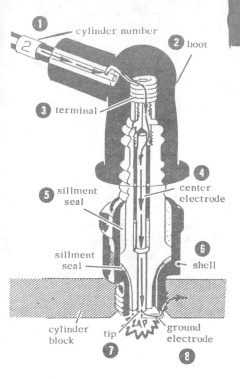

1 cylinder number
2 boot
3 terminal
4 center electrode
5 sillment seal
sillment seal
6 shell
cylinder block
7 tip
ZAP
8 ground electrode

The spark plug is just a means by which a spark can be triggered off in the combustion chamber.

Electrical charge caused by collapse of secondary must flow through plug lead, down center electrode, to jump gap at precise moment igniting the air/fuel mixture. It jumps across to the ground electrode where it flows out the threads & into the block.

Tremendous voltage is required to jump the gap. As high voltage will take the path of least resistance, it will do anything it can to avoid jumping the gap if it has a chance.

As many outboard motors are portable there is a constant chance of ceramic insulators being cracked or damaged, or if stored in a shed where oily soot can collect, this may become the unwelcome conductor so charge can bypass gap and go to ground.

285

A rubber boot is recommended for all motors as overnight condensation can collect on ceramic. Resulting flashover can cause misfiring until ceramic is dry.

insulator and ribs reduce flashover

11
12 ZAP

9 normal operation
10 chipped insulator
broken ceramic
flashover or external short

Powerboating Illustrated

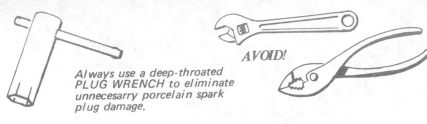

Always use a deep-throated
PLUG WRENCH to eliminate
unnecesarry porcelain spark
plug damage.

AVOID!

What type of plug wrench do you carry on your boat?
Every outboarder should become familiar with plugs if
he is going to understand his motor.

If you can get at the plugs with a deep-throated wrench
shown at upper left, there will be considerably less
chance of damaging ceramic. With other type wrenches
or pliers a person applies pressure and plug suddenly
starts unwinding. The handle of either instrument will
have a good chance to hit and break ceramic insulator
on other plugs that are in its way.

When you have time, practice changing plugs with one arm
while leaning over the end of your boat. It's a trick that
may come in handy some day.

●

When putting plugs back into a motor it is necessary to
pay close attention to the plug gasket to see that it is
clean & has a good solid contact between plug and block
for heat transference.

The older copper gaskets corroded surrounding metals
and crushed easily. The corrosion deposits reduced
efficiency of heat transfer and gasket need replacing
every time plug was removed and checked.

The newer steel gaskets reduce corrosion deposits
and do not lose tension as easily. They crush but will
still have enough tension to be reseated several times
if they are clean.

In a 4 cycle high compression engine, peak firing temp.
goes to 4000° with pressures of 1250 psi. It is lower
than this at present with smaller 2 cycle motors, but
with larger motors there won't be much difference.

As for TORQUING down a plug, put it in finger tight and
give a half turn with a wrench to seat it. This is very
important in a 2 cycle motor as there is practically no
period when the combustion chamber isn't cooling off.

As the plug gasket has to transfer a lot of heat in a short
space of time it has to be correctly seated or the plug
will be thrown out of its heat range.

Powerboating Illustrated

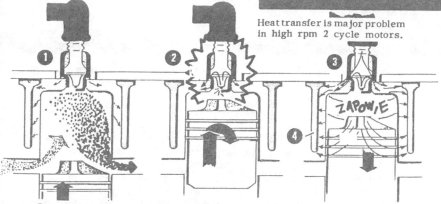

Heat transfer is major problem in high rpm 2 cycle motors.

② Peak firing temperature up to 4000° with 1200 pounds per square inch pressure may be generated.

③ Plug heat must be dissipated by way of threads and gasket to water jacket. Piston heat must go through rings to water jacket.

④ With motor in good condition and operating at upper rpm, temperature of water flowing through jacket rises 80-100°. Heat transference isn't as effective if water jacket is plugged with silt or boiler scale. As a result cylinder runs at higher temperature, plugs start to burn, power output is reduced and preignition may begin.

287

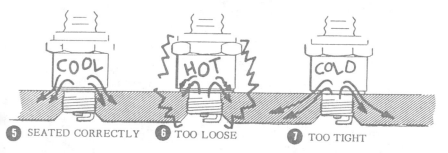

⑤ SEATED CORRECTLY   **⑥** TOO LOOSE   **⑦** TOO TIGHT

⑤ Gasket needs firm clean contact for normal heat transference. Torque plugs from 15-20 lbs. maximum, or put in HAND TIGHT, give HALF TURN with wrench. If gasket is correctly seated both sides are a good conductor.

⑥ If gasket isn't torqued down tight enough, heat transference is reduced and plug, thrown out of heat range, begins burning.

⑦ If gasket is crushed by torquing too tight or too many times, heat transference difficulty throws plug out of range. If there is question of gasket being crushed, replace with new gasket. Gasket must have CLEAN surfaces without any sand, salt or rust to raise part of it as this can throw plug out of heat range.

3 A plug must BURN CLEAN without burning itself up.

•

In most situations outboarder should use manufacturer's plug recommendations. It is based on an average set of conditions for a plug being able to run warm enough to burn off carbon & oil deposits efficiently at lower rpm. At maximum rpm, plug temperature should be well under point of preignition whether at rated speed, under speed, or over speed condition. If plug runs cooler, it will not retain sufficient heat to burn off deposits. Fouling will soon result.

•

2 COLD PLUG/hot motor, J-58R (formerly J-2). For full throttle operation such as racing with water temp. 90° and air temp. over 100°.

1 HOT PLUG/cold motor, J-14J. For other extreme such as trolling with water temperature near freezing where it is difficult to retain heat long enough to prevent fouling from carbonaceous buildup.

288

•

When CHANGING ALTITUDE such as going from sea level to 8000', carb fuel adjustments must be leaned out to compensate for oxygen deficiency. Some rather change plugs such as going from J-6J to J-8J to burn excess fuel. Practice is questionable.

If you like to troll in the early spring or late fall with water temperatures near freezing warmer than normal plugs are required.

If you then take the same boat on a hot summer day for continuous full throttle skiing, the standard plugs will be running too hot and burn out. Plugs with colder than average heat range may be required.

Electrode temperature on firing end should be warm enough to prevent fouling, yet have minimum gap erosion from continuous heat of explosions. If electrode temp. goes above safe level, oxidation erosion or corrosion will destroy electrodes and increase gap.

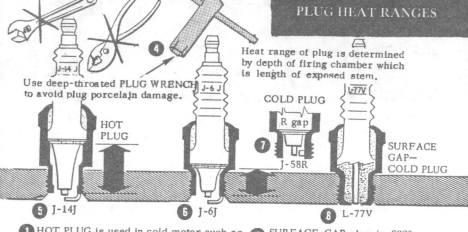

Use deep-throated PLUG WRENCH to avoid plug porcelain damage.

Heat range of plug is determined by depth of firing chamber which is length of exposed stem.

HOT PLUG

COLD PLUG
R gap
J-58R

SURFACE GAP— COLD PLUG

❺ J-14J **❻ J-6J** **❽ L-77V**

❶ HOT PLUG is used in cold motor such as trolling, retaining heat to prevent buildup of carbon and oil deposits. As Champion number increases plug will be hotter.

❷ COLD PLUG is used in hard working, warm racing motor which rapidly burns average plug electrodes. Small chamber dissipates heat rapidly as possible.

❸ SURFACE GAP plug is 800° to 1000° colder than average plug heat range. Gap wear and fouling are at minimum and the plugs don't overheat or burn at full throttle.

Though they have a long life, it is better to be replaced yearly.

289

❾ TYPE J **❿** AUTOMOTIVE **⓫** SURFACE GAP

PCI system CDI system

Plug must burn clean at all rpm's. Main advantage of 'J' over automotive plug is that it leaves more exposed spark so flame front can clean a little better instead of being localized. Flame front also has a better chance to get in and burn carbonaceous material that wants to bridge gap in stem of plug.

Outboard motors with Capacitor Discharge systems are able to use circle-gap plugs which are self cleaning due to much higher peak spark voltage.

● Plugs may foul out on older electrical system by—

⓬ GAP BRIDGING, materials collecting between electrodes causing direct short.
⓭ INSULATOR BRIDGING where deposits collect in stem or insulator nose and bore of shell that cause it to be bridged and shorted.
⓮ DEPOSIT SHUNTING when deposits on top of the piston break loose as piston changes direction.

PCI systems

Powerboating Illustrated

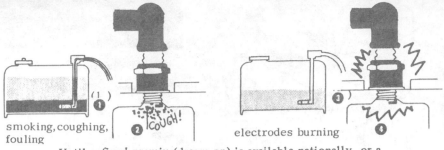

smoking, coughing, fouling

electrodes burning

Until *refined premix* (dream on) is available nationally, or a new fuel appears, many two cycle motors will have to burn their way thru fuel which the owner may have partially mixed falling out of suspension.

As fuel comes from bottom of tank (above) first part of the fuel mixture will have an excessively high oil content. Motor is very hard to start up and may foul even at high speed until it has burned through oil layer.

If motor can choke its way through oil barrier, it next runs on a mixture with insufficient oil coolant. When operated at low rpm gasoline may act as temporary lubricant but loses this property at high rpm. Result is damaging heat buildup from metal to metal contact.

We've seen plugs used 500 hours that were regapped & used again. Such unusual performance shows operator was well aware of fuel, fuel mixtures & motor care. With others it is considerably different & plugs take a beating so severe they have to be discarded in a few hours use.

Much has been said and will continue to be said about fuel deposits & deturgents to aid their removal, a special problem of 2 cycle motors burning oil and gasoline.

There are many kinds of deposits such as METALLIC deposits building up in cylinder to make a good type of insulator restricting heat dissipation both burning AND fouling plugs. There are SOFT ASH deposits from incomplete combustion that are easy to sluff out the exhaust manifold. There are PHOSPHOROUS additives to make deposits that keep temp. of existing deposits to below that of deposit preignition. They work efficiently on 4 cycle engines not having the added carbon burning problems from lubricating oil.

Plug deposits range from heavy carbonaceous with a hard or soft ash content, to those with high carbon and LEAD mixture. The refiners say it isn't the amount of deposit that causes the trouble but the kind of deposit. Most outboard distributors and mechanics we contacted felt that all 2 cycle fuel should be CLEAN burning with deposits kept to minimum regardless of rpm.

290

PCI systems

1980 basics?

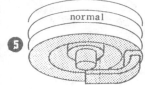

⑤ normal

●If motor was tested at factory for 20 minutes it will have a light gray or coffee tan color. If plug still looks like this after weeks or months operation, check gap and reuse.

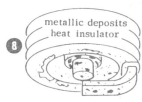

⑥ mass deposits- fouling

● NOT ENOUGH HEAT (incomplete combustion). Motor smokes excessively, plug misses & fouls out. It may indicate more care is needed in fuel proportion and mixture or plug that burns warmer is required. This may also indicate use of 4 cycle oil with additives not meant for combustion.

●PHOSPHOROUS ADDITIVE used in automotive gasoline to modify deposits and increase plug life by reducing deposit preignition. Some deposits may glow at 650° in cylinder, phosphorous alters deposits chemically to reduce glowing until above 1000°.

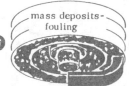

⑦ phosphorous additives

Without phosphorous in high compression 4 cycle engine serious fouling problems might develop. In 2 cycle motors having to burn gasoline & oil the quantity of deposits increases sharply. If not exhausted, a deposit throw off or shunting may compound problem..

●Metallic LEAD deposits have much better chance to collect onto unburned carbon particles and stay in cylinder building up a glowing lead insulated deposit that has chronic case of burned or burned and fouled plugs. Look for flat specs, colored odd shapes, flat smears. Change from automotive fuels (high lead content) to white (non leaded) or to 80/87 (low lead content) should be considered.

291

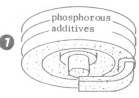

⑧ metallic deposits heat insulator

●TOO MUCH HEAT (plug damaged). Note WHITE ceramic and eroded electrodes. Too much spark advance may be indicated causing excessive heat & pressure in cylinder. Water pump impeller 371, may have become worn or bonding between impeller & shaft has failed needing replacement. Gasket may be incorrectly seated or TWO gaskets used reducing heat transfer. Lack of cooling, lubrication, plug with wrong heat range, or heat dissipation problem can be indicated. Rings may be stuck 272, requiring solvent 277, or stripdown to scrub away deposits 273, that glow, cause preignition. Replace plugs AFTER finding source of trouble.

Round magnetic balls come from melted electrode.

⑨ excess heat

●TOO MUCH HEAT (plug not yet damaged). Plug looks normal at first glance, however WHITE ceramic will indicate heat trouble such as wrong plug heat range, or plug incorrectly torqued down.

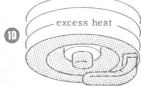

⑩ excess heat

●SUDDEN RAPID BURNING. May be due to water from condensation in fuel tanks. Since gasoline and oil float on water, the first part of mixture to reach plug will be water. Ceramic filter OUTSIDE motor is suggested. Have accessible, easy to service, page 270.

PCI systems

SHUNTING—deposits build up on top of piston and are flung upwards when piston suddenly changes direction of travel.

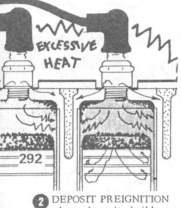

292

② DEPOSIT PREIGNITION where deposits build up to retard heat transfer.

Water JACKET deposits reduce volume of water flow; result, loss of heat transfer burns plugs.

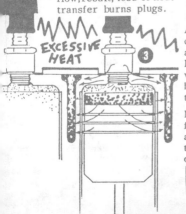

"I put new plugs in the motor last time out so I know they were in good condition. I haven't touched the rig for three months. Yesterday we went skiing and when I gave motor full throttle BOTH cylinders quit at the same time. When I checked the new plugs they were loaded with junk... what happened?"

During storage some of the deposits on top of the piston became soft. He gave sudden full throttle and as piston hit top of travel and suddenly reversed, the deposits on piston crown broke loose and flew up to foul out plug. This is called deposit 'shunting'. After plugs were cleaned they worked perfectly. Stripdown and cleaning to remove deposits is eventually answer if problem becomes chronic.

●

"I've used a 25 hp ------on my 17' outboard cruiser for the last three years and it has always worked good until recently. Now it runs for a while then slows up considerably. After I let it sit for a while, I can start it up, and momentarily give it full throttle but it soon begins to slow up. And man does it eat up plugs. Is it necessary to have my carb boiled or change boats?"

This is a classic. Chronic plug burning was due to DEPOSIT PREIGNITION acting as insulator to retard dissipation of heat after explosion in cylinder. Motor operates normally until deposits start glowing. This preignites fuel before plug fires, intense uncontrolled heat burns plugs power loss and/or damage results. After cylinders cool off, motor starts normally yet cycle will be repeated until deposits are removed by stripdown and cleaning.

●

Motor lower left was operated three times in period of six months---and burned two sets of plugs even though motor was new.

After being opened up, small shellfish almost the size of a fingernail had attached themselves in the cooling passages and had grown until they restricted flow of water through cylinder head. To avoid this salt water growth, occasionally flush with fresh water as it kills barnacles and other shellfish.

●

After continuous use for a year the motor developed chronic case of burned plugs. Cylinder deposits were at a minimum but cooling passages were plugged. Mechanic said, "If you'd flush this motor with fresh water after using it on the ocean this buildup would have been avoided. You have to flush the salts out of these motors... see how they collect."

Motor had only been used on fresh water aqueduct system for a large city, it had never seen salt water! It was a boiler scale or LIMESTONE deposit not salt that had to be removed. Boiler scale buildup can happen in salt or in fresh water,

Powerboating Illustrated

LESS OXYGEN -----
LESS HORSEPOWER
at 7,000 feet
altitude.

SEA LEVEL

Maximum oxygen content
maximum horsepower
efficiency and output.

"Man did you sell me a lemon!It took more time
to get the skiiers out of the water than with my
old motor . . .and it couldn't even reach within
1200 rpm's of what you guys brag about. Now a
guy with another brand motor was telling me
that your motors------"

Questioning revealed old boat towed one skiier
at sea level. New rig was taken on a vacation
to 7,000' altitude. This dropped efficiency 20%,
hot weather took another 4%, he bought stale
gasoline, and the boat was overloaded while
carrying three skiiers.

Altitude is an oxygen deficiency common to all
internal combustion engines. After it was brought
to owner's attention, he realized the new car was
overheated and pinged on climb to same lake.

Carb adjustments needed to be leaned out and
prop changed for one with less pitch so motor
could still reach recommended rpm ... with
less horsepower.

●

"Your motor is misrepresented, all I could get
out of it is 4000 rpm's while you rate it at
5000 rpm's. Is that how you sell------"

293

It is obvious customer was upset. After plugs
were checked they showed no motor troubles.
When tank tested motor was able to turn up
rated rpm so customer could see it;what next?

After his tack was 'adjusted' to correct reading,
his motor ran much better.

●

"My motor starts hard, runs ragged and fades
at high speed. I get sore at the motor, my wife
gets sore at me & the dog bites the kid. Could
you please straighten out this 2 cycle monster?"

Before further questioning dealer checks plugs
to find they are a healthy light brown, motor is
operating in top condition. Possibility of intermittent mechanical trouble is remote. It looks
as though customer must have been sitting on
flexible fuel line, or line has a kink in it.

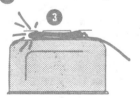

Incorrect reading?

Watch out for kinks
in flexible fuel lines.

Questioning revealed customer wanted to get
excess fuel line out of way so it wouldn't be
tripped over. After wrapping it several times
around handle on tank, the line was squeezed
restricting fuel flow.

Powerboating Illustrated

⑤ What is operating RPM?

Examine all plugs
very closely- - - - - -

is the plug below fouled
or burned, or both?

⑥

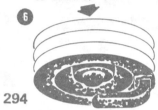

294

PCI system

To maintain the same
PEAK operating RPM,
always change props
⑦ when motor is put on a
heavier or lighter boat.

12' planing hull

18' planing cruiser

"I have the plugs you recommended for water skiing
but they keep burning out. Did you give me plugs with
the wrong heat range?"

Owner bought the boat with intentions of lugging two
or three skiiers at at time while carrying two people
besides himself on the boat.

Questioning revealed after buying the boat he liked to
take it out alone most of the time & did a lot of racing.
As he had a load prop, motor developed excessive rpm
which he didn't realize without tach.

While racing around with his light load he should have
used colder plugs, used a prop with more pitch while
keeping a check on rpm with no tachometer.

●

"You gave me hot plugs because I told you I wanted
to do a lot of trolling- - - - - -but they always foul out!
I picked up a hotter set at another dealer but they
fouled sooner. Should I still get warmer plugs?"

The dealer was busy when he sold this boat & failed
to ask customer many questions. As plugs were taken
out, dealer notice a layer of black carbon but - - - wait,
what are those specs or particles in the oil?

The owner bought the boat at sea level and used it at
Lake Mead alt. 3000', water temp. 95°, air temp. 110°
yet he was interested in trolling--AFTER running his
motor wide open for 1/2 hour to reach fishing hole.

Plugs were burned out... not fouled out as appeared
at first glance. Plug trouble must be THOROUGHLY
investigated to eliminate the REAL problem.

●

"My motor keeps burning plugs on my new boat–this
never happened on my old boat. "

Questioning revealed previous boat was a light 12'
planing hull powered by a 35 hp motor.

He built a new heavy 18' cabin cruiser and loaded it
with a lot of heavy gear.

The owner overlooked changing props when installing
the new prop on his boat. As the old prop carried too
much pitch it was lugging and couldn't reach rpm. As
it had spark advance without the rpm flame front was
triggered off too soon. Changing props cured his plug
problems.

Powerboating Illustrated

oxidation
corrosion

 flammable
vapors

 vapor
explosion

slow ◄──────── **FORMS OF COMBUSTION** ──────► rapid

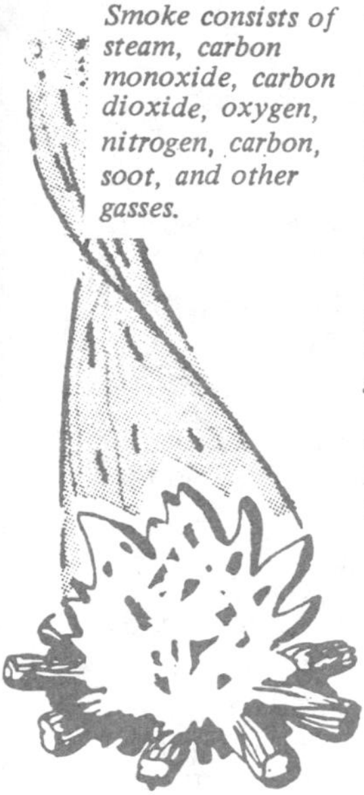

Smoke consists of steam, carbon monoxide, carbon dioxide, oxygen, nitrogen, carbon, soot, and other gasses.

Man has been fascinated with the mysterious source of power since cave man days called fire.

A chain-reaction fire begins when the temperature of any item— wood, paint, cloth, etc., reaches its self-ignition point IF three basic factors exist— fuel, heat, and oxygen.

Self-ignition point— when wood has been heated to reach this temperature, flammable vapors and gasses rise in sufficient quantity above the wood surface to combine with oxygen. The result will be *spontaneous combustion.*

Flash Point— is the lowest temperature wood or other materials, will provide sufficient vapors that are flammable... to temporarily ignite.

oxygen Below this temperature not enough vapors are present to cause normal ignition.

295

If you look closely at a wood fire such as shown at left, you will find the vapor flames in the beginning stage will be above its surface. The flames eventually drop closer to the wood surface, then into the wood pores in the final stage.

Fahrenheit **self-ignition temperatures** have variables.Sources— National Bureau of Standards, *National Fire Protection Guide on Hazardous Materials.* **Lighted cigarette range** is from 550 on the surface... to 1,350 in its center with drafts.

wood— 378-428	paraffin wax— 473
wood fiberboard— 421	turpentine— 488
wood shavings— 442-507	fuel oil— 444-765
newspapers— 446	jet fuel— 435-475
wool— 401	gasoline— 536-853
cotton— 446-551	olive oil— 650
rubber— 320-590	grain alcohol— 793
rubber solvent— 450	denatured alcohol— 750
acetone— 1000	butane— 723
	propane— 871

● *Everything will burn IF temperatures are high enough!*

Class D metal fires. Magnesium, titanium, zirconium, even aluminum, have extremely high self-ignition temperatures. They are the most hazardous fires to control and extinguish.

one cup of gasoline **EQUALS** *15 sticks of dynamite*

USCG pamphlet CG-395 stated, *"A cup of gasoline spilled in the bilges has the explosive potential power of 15 sticks of dynamite"*. It was a starting point for 20 years... USCG now questions.

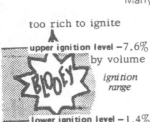

fumes dissipating

If your auto has a fuel leak— gasoline and gasoline fumes *being heavier than air* fall to the road. They evaporate and/ or are blown away. Gasoline fumes do not rise like natural gas used in our kitchen stoves.

fumes collecting

Enclosed 4 cycle engine with a similar fuel leak. Gasoline falls to the bilge where it vaporizes and fumes collect.

Boat operator with fuel leak not checking bilge is heading for trouble. *Without bilge blower* boat explosions seldom occur at dock as gasoline fumes are too rich to ignite.

Many boat explosions occur **after leaving the dock.** The carburetor pulls in a tremendous volume of air. This reduces the too rich mixture down to the upper ignition level followed by a soft blow. If the fuel air mixture is ignited near the lower ignition level it would be a stronger explosion.

too rich to ignite

upper ignition level −7.6% by volume

ignition range

lower ignition level −1.4% by volume

296

too weak to ignite

Fumes may be ignited by starter motor, charging generator, regulator, loose electrical connections. Fuel spills are caused by fuel hose break, stuck carb float, fuel pump failure, loose or aging fuel lines and connections.

Periodically check your engine or engines, tank fittings and fuel lines regardless how normal engine is operating, to eliminate developing problems. If engine starts cranky, suddenly runs ragged, a fuel leak is indicated.

Sniff inboard engine bilges before starting your engine.

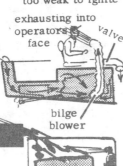

exhausting into operators face

valve

bilge blower

Bilge blower may be hazardous... if you don't sniff blower exhaust. If a gasoline spill exists, the blower can remove enough air to reduce fumes to the UIL level to explode boat at dock. If blower exhausted into operators face he would have a warning under 30 seconds he has a spill problem. USCG doesn't agree with idea.

Automatic Halon 1301 is triggered at rising temperature to smother fire and eliminate reignition potentials. If engine hatch opens aft in explosion, it reduces cockpit damage to operator and passengers.

gasoline, water???

filler cap

Standardized colors of filler caps with gasoline, diesel, and water printed on caps reduce chance of gasoline poured into water tank at busy fuel dock. Explosion potentials seem to occur more often with rented houseboats as operators have little familiarity to supervise fuel dock practices.

fuel

heat   oxygen

fuel

~~heat~~   oxygen

fuel

heat   ~~oxygen~~

~~fuel~~

heat   oxygen

fuel?
(turn off valve)

heat?   oxygen ?
(water)(smothering)

lip

shutoff
valve

DON'T USE
on LPG fire !!!

The three basics of a fire are fuel, heat, and oxygen.
Remove any of these three to stop a fire.

- **Flash point**— wood heated to this temperature will release enough flammable vapors to temporarily ignite.

- **Ignition point**— wood heated to this temperature produces sufficient quantities of *flammable vapors and gasses above its surface* combining with oxygen for self ignition or *spontaneous combustion.*

wood......cloth......drapes......rugs......sofa

- **Class A fires**— COOL THEM. Water is a coolant to penetrate the pores to extinguish this class fire by reducing temperature below flash point.

liquid fuel – gasoline..oil..paint..grease..cooking fats

- **Class B fires**— SMOTHER THEM. These are HOT fast moving surface fires that must be stopped immediately to bring under control. A smothering blanketing action is required to *seal out oxygen.* **Water will spread Class B fires!**

solid fuel fires— rubber....plastic....urethane, etc.,

They *burn, melt, and flow.* Smother and cool with combination Class A and B extinguishers.

Kitchen stove fires— TURN OFF GAS. Then put lid on stove top pan to seal out oxygen. *Inside oven—* put cover over pan...or throw handful of *baking soda (NOT baking powder)* to smother fire.

electrical equipment in shops, offices homes,
autos, RVs, powerboats, sailboats, aircraft

- **Class C fires**— BREAK the CIRCUIT *to remove the electrical fire source.* Extinguishers are only a temporary aid to retard electrical fires while removing the source such as pulling plug in TV fires. For auto fires— *remove negative battery clamp.*

- **Alcohol stove fires— gravity-feed recommended.** Build a *drip pan with a 1" metal lip* under stove to contain alcohol fire spilling and spreading. Put a teakettle of cold water on stove. If alcohol spill fire results when lighting stove, pour water into fire to cool alcohol below flash point.

- **Pressurized alcohol stoves—replace gaskets under pressure often.** Remote fuel tank requires easy to reach *shutoff valve* to stop flammable vapor spray Use dry chemical extinguisher, smother fire.

- **LPG— liquid petroleum gas, butane & propane**

  TURN OFF VALVE— don't use extinguisher!!!!! Raw LPG under pressure hitting hot end of pipe where fire was... can explode with tremendous force.

297

Powerboating Illustrated

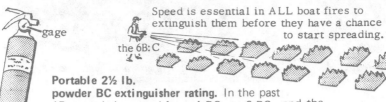

Speed is essential in ALL boat fires to extinguish them before they have a chance to start spreading.

the 6B:C

Portable 2½ lb. powder BC extinguisher rating. In the past 15 years it increased from 4 BC, to 6 BC, and the recent one checked had a 10 BC rating. Weight is 2½ to 2¾ pounds. This is a disposable extinguisher with pressure gage.

Check Approval and rating. It needs USCG approval for boat use. Then check for Underwriters Laboratory, Inc., classification, an older 6 -B:C.

Obtaining the 6-B:C rating. It has to consistently extinguish 14 square foot pans of lighted naptha in controlled conditions.

UL reduces the coverage of its testing by 60% due to stress, and other factors in a sudden fire. The 6 B:C extinguisher in trained hands may extinguish a 14 square foot gasoline spill fire. Portable *CO_2 extinguisher* with a 1-B:C rating is useless to put out same spill fire. The *B:C* extinguisher has a baking soda base with CO_2 under pressure. The *A:B:C* extinguisher agent is ammonium phosphate using nitrogen under pressure.

Aim extinguisher at base of fire is recommended to keep fire away from you, and seal out oxygen. In some conditions we prefer to shoot first spray ABOVE flame. As it falls down... then hit base of fire.

298

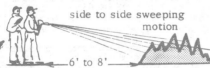

side to side sweeping motion

6' to 8'

The best way to know how to operate a dry chemical extinguisher is to use one though it may be hazardous.

Backup man should be standard practice for all extinguisher practice exhibitions. Backup man has extinguisher aimed at you for protection in case of a sudden wind shift, reversing the fire towards you.

This is USN practice I was taught by 'Louie', a retired aircraft carrier firefighter, after 20 years fighting the most hazardous fires imagineable.

shake hard!

Extinguisher location. It should be easy to reach and use in boat, auto, camper, RV, and home near kitchen stove. We've seen several in, or next to engine compartment. It would be too hot to hold in a fire when you need maximum protection for your family and yourself.

hit bottom!

Dry powder can compact in boats, campers, and cars due to pounding underway. Periodically turn upside down and shake to minimize problem. If caught in a fire and the fully charged extinguisher doesn't spray... hit bottom hard on solid object to break baking soda compaction.

Powerboating Illustrated

powder residue vs no residue gas

CO₂ built-in extinguishers. They were used in commercial aircraft and larger boats in our early 1950 boating days, the advantage, no residue.

Halon extinguishers were developed to protect our astronauts. They lead sales today with their flexibility, especially with electrical equipment, no powder mess.

Portable Halon 1211 extinguisher. The coolant is a liquified gas, with a gas vapor smothering action. It is not permitted in total flooding systems in occupied areas with same toxicity as CO_2.

bilge
water ...
corrosion???

Automatic Halon 1301 extinguisher is used in engine and other closed compartments with ratings listed in square feet. The heavy gas flooding system smothers fire to eliminate reignition.

metal horn?

Older portable CO₂ extinguishers metal horns rapidly cooled to stick to operators hand sometimes removing skin.

Later portable CO_2 extinguishers still have the same cooling characteristics with a plastic horn insulation for your protection when used. It still needs a warning for operator— *do not touch the metal pipe between extinguisher and horn as it is metal....* with the potential to freeze to your hand during operation.

metal pipe

299

Check extinguisher gage— don't test with a slight squeeze of trigger. This can break seal causing a leak to slowly discharge the extinguisher... and who wants a dead extinguisher?

minimum cone
of effectiveness

larger cone of effectiveness
minimizes fire hazards

hazardous

backup man   splatter?

Cone of effectiveness. Extinguisher effectiveness increases when farther from a fire, and less effective as you are closer to a fuel spill fire.

Auto fires are excellent for practice as you can stand farther from the fire for effectiveness, standing behind another auto for protection.

Know extinguisher capabilities and limitations for boat use. You may have to move close to a fuel spill fire in a small area... but not close enough for discharge to splatter fire, expanding your problem.

Flammable liquids. While gasoline may be stored in a sealed saftey can aboard underway, other liquids such as paint, varnish, thinner, solvent, resins, and similar flammable liquids should be left ashore, not in your garage... but in an outside paint locker.

Corroding cans— varnish, paint, etc., corrode rapidly in the ocean environment. The contents may drain into the bilge with vapors easy to ignite. *Pressurized paint cans* being used near an open flame can explode as a bomb if the spray is ignited.

A container of paint thinner to ignite charcoal, and pressurized cans of spray-on lubricants to loosen corroded bolts, will be found on most cabin boats. Replace before leakage potentials exist and carry in a well-ventilated location.

Cigars and cigarettes are a double hazard. While serving as an ignition source, they reduce smelling potentials to recognize a fuel leak... and carbon monoxide below in the cabin.

All ignition sources must be extinguished before refueling. This includes cigars, cigarettes, hibachi charcoal fires, pilot lights, etc.

Simple wind telltale mounted on bow. Though tanks are filled correctly with fumes going overboard, tricky winds may blow gasoline fumes into cockpit.

300

The telltale will help warn of such a potential. It is also useful for docking and undocking by indicating whether the wind is blowing your boat into... or away from the dock.

also pg. 276

Periodically check bottoms of safety cans. Condensation builds up as bottom can't breathe with the bottom the first area to rust out and leak fuel. *Storing on concrete in a garage*-- in less than a year a new jeep can with some gasoline inside rusted out though the sides and top looked new. Corrosion action of the concrete plus trapped condensation speeded corrosion process.

Our 6 gallon jeep can when filled with outboard mix weighs about 37 pounds. Store spout in a sealed plastic bag to keep dust away and reduce corrosion rust going into fuel tank.

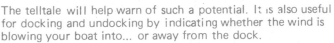

● **Spontaneous heat combustion.** Flammable vapors are released in the curing stage so paint can dry rapidly in open areas.

Paint rags, and solvent rags used to clean brushes also liberate a similar volume of flammable vapors when trapped in a container with little ventilation. The trapped vapors in the rags cause rapidly rising temperatures until starting its own fire when reaching the self ignition point.

Flammable vapor liberated during this oxidation curing process occurs also with oily rags, cut grass, hay, grain, soft coal, wood shavings, etc.

Powerboating Illustrated

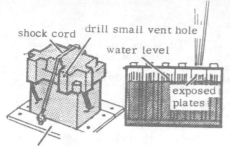

shock cord   drill small vent hole

water level

exposed plates

tray

Battery needs positive restraint in its own tray with a stout tie-down, without moving an inch any direction. Plastic case collects spilled battery electrolyte.

Battery terminals must be tight enough to prevent arcing. Drill small hole in plastic case lid to release hydrogen and oxygen gasses.

USCG records numerous battery explosions though damage seems minor. *Distilled water must be added when required...* to prevent arcing across exposed tops of plates. When ignited gasses expand many diameters... it is called an explosion.

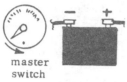

master switch

Electrical fires may be knocked down temporarily with extinguishers. They won't normally be put out until negative battery clamp is removed, or by turning off master switch... then check for cause of fire. For an inexpensive battery switch for small boats, check trailer equipment stores.

Fuse every system on open trailerboats subjected to spray and corrosion, with in-line fuses, and carry spares. Consider a *master switch* on cabin trailerboats. Mount master switch high as practical inside cabin so it can be reached   from cockpit. A low switch panel shorts out rapidly **301** if a boat is sinking or awash wiping out the radio telephone... while battery posts are too far apart to short out when submerged fully.

Portable gasoline and butane stoves are excellent for outdoor picnics. As their fumes are heavier than air collecting in a cabin boat bilge... use inside a cabin boat is hazardous .

Hibachi charcoal cooking on a boat. If wake of passing boat upsets the hibachi, have a bucket of water handy to stop fire!

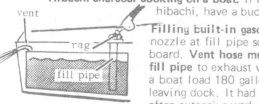

vent

rag

fill pipe

Filling built-in gasoline tanks. Wrap rag around nozzle at fill pipe so fumes go into tank or overboard. **Vent hose must be sealed as thoroughly as fill pipe** to exhaust vapors as tanks fill. I watched a boat load 180 gallons of gasoline, exploding AFTER leaving dock. It had just come from the boatyard after extensive work. A mechanic forgot to reinstall the overboard vent hose with all the fumes going to the bilge... booom.

Most fires start small in a well-maintained boat. Automatic built-in Halon extinguishers set to go off at a predetermined temperature is recommended for gasoline engine compartments. In case of an engine fire *plug both air vents* to help smother fire.

Powerboating Illustrated

Fifty five years of outboard motors.

The new mechanic will have excellent factory training with the present capacitor discharge ignition system. We provide considerable exposure to the previous generation points condenser ignition system. Hundreds of thousands of the PCI units are used daily worldwide which you may also service with information difficult to find.

While the numbers are dwindling I've seen outboard motors in Ensenada, Mazatlan, and other areas of Mexico 40 to 50 years old, made before the spark plug boot and the Alnico magnet...that were cranky but still operating. Let us begin with a short history of the outboard ignition system.

Before the Alnico magnet.

Dad bought an outboard motor for fishing in 1932. It would only start 25 miles away from the reservoir giving me lots of rowing practice.

We bought a new 1.7 hp motor in 1947. While good for a small dinghy, it provided some propulsion for a rowboat but was underpowered for steering, pg. 32.

● AVOID one-cylinder outboard motors as they are cranky to start and operate. Two weeks later we traded the 1.7 hp for a used 5 hp 1940 motor with two cylinders. It had at least five times the dependability especially for starting. If one plug was tired, the second would fire coaxing the first to operate.

302

The 5 hp motor proved excellent for propulsion AND steering for an 8 to 10' rowboat...IF stored inside overnight, otherwise it would sleep soundly until noon. The weak magnets available at the time required a lot of heat to cook the humidity off the magnets. Since the plugs didn't have boots, pg.285, a spark could leak to ground the easy way down the outside ceramic bypassing the plug gap... inspiring my cartoon.

● **The Alnico magnet.** It was introduced to the outboard motor world in the early 1950's. We needed dependable equipment as almost all of our research was on the ocean. We had excellent results with the Alnico magnet on the flywheel magneto system, the 4-cylinder magneto system, and the alternator rectifier system.

PCI systems

● **Points, condenser ignition systems.** A 50,000 mile warranty was introduced by auto manufacturers in the mid 50's. Problems soon developed with the PCI systems involving the warranty when shade-tree mechanics and fumbling owners tried to make periodic adjustments.

CDI systems

● **Capacitor discharge ignition system.** The answer was to develop an electrical system with sealed components with the CDI system introduced in 1967 under various brand names. As the components could not be adusted and only replaced, it eliminated questionable claims.

build up ▲ tail off

points/condenser spark

The previous Alnico magnet PCI system required considerable time for the spark going to the plug *to build up to its peak...followed by a long tapering tail off.*

The CDI system uses the same amount of energy which is built up for storage in a capacitor.

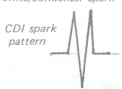

CDI spark pattern

Then by the use of an electronic gate, the charge is delivered from the capacitor to jump the plug gap. The full impulse is delivered with a much shorter timespan insuring a healthy spark without the wasteful buildup and tail off of the older PCI system, also eliminating periodic adjustment.

*Old problems are supposed to
disappear when a new technology
is introduced. Then begins a new
educational process to find answers
to the baffling new problems
that it introduces.*

electricity

● **Points, condenser, ignition system.** We concentrate on plug problems of the previous generation PCI system since as rpm increases, power available at the plug gap begins to decrease. The first sign of trouble is a motor running ragged and/or quitting due to plug failure. A few years later it proved a blessing in disguise.

> **Capacitor discharge ignition system.** Plug fouling disappeared with up to 40,000 volts in 4 micro seconds, approximately 1/12 the time period of the magneto spark taking 50 micro seconds.
>
> With the changing technology plugs with ample power could fire happily caring little if insufficient or the wrong lubrication is used. Without the CDI system plug warning, damage may occur elsewhere. On the smaller hp hand-cranked outboard motors I found a harder pull was required to start the motor, with an easier pull for the PCi magneto system.

● **An owner has to know his sealed CDI system connections and leads.**

The short timespan CDI spark delivery with ample voltage for all speeds has many advantages for an owner knowing the system. It is sealed and water resistant which may last for the life of your 2 or 4 cycle engine.

The CDI system must be periodically checked for loose connections and chafed leads. This preventive maintenance is the responsibility of the owner...and the mechanic when it is in for repairs.

Battery leads are important. Connections must be tight and clean as corroded or loose connections can cause an electrical imbalance.

303

● **Low or dead batteries may cause expensive problems.**

If you can hand crank a large motor with a CDI system having a low battery, luck is with you. But...*DON'T hook a charger to a battery then try to start a 2 or 4 cycle engine.* The powerful shore current in an opposite direction to diodes and rectifiers can overpower and burn them up.

This situation requiring an expensive repair bill to put the powerplant back in operation was more common in past years than it is today.

> *Always unhook the motor harness before you turn on shore power to the battery charger.*

If shore current can leak thru the powerhead to ground in the water, it can cause all kinds of mischief to lower units and to the PCI system, see page 368.

● **Pacemaker warning.** The CDI system will be so powerful, that if it is malfunctioning in an outboard motor, an inboard engine, or auto... any person wearing a Pacemaker should stay at a considerable distance for self protection.

● *If a customer is going to take his outboard motor with a CDI system into primitive areas for a prolonged period...provide him with a sealed kit of spare parts that may need replacement. Also recommend periodic checks for chafed leads and loose connections.*

electrical energy
changing to
chemical energy

chemical energy
changing to
electrical energy

①
*Conventional
current flow
is shown,
see pg. 308.*

②
charging
battery
flow

③
discharging
battery
flow

④ the basic magnet—
pgs. 306, 314, 322, 416.

304

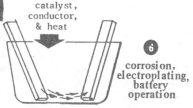

magnetic field

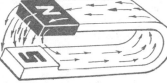

electrical
current

⑤

an electro-
magnetic field

catalyst,
conductor,
& heat

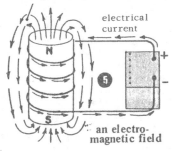

⑥
corrosion,
electroplating,
battery
operation

● The wet cell lead-acid storage battery is a temporary reservoir of chemical energy, which is converted to electrical energy when required.

● A battery is charging when excess current from a generator flows to the battery for storage.

● A battery is discharging when the stored chemical energy is released by the chemical action of an electrolyte which weakens as the water percentage increases...and the lead sulfate of the positive plate, and the spongy lead of the negative plate change to lead sulfate.

● A magnetic current begins when a conductor is moved at right angles to the *magnetic lines of force* supposedly flowing from the north pole of a magnet to its south pole, page 314.

The voltage induced starts current flowing thru a conductor core of a magneto primary coil which is broken.

The current goes to a condenser to build up enough voltage in the coil secondary to jump the plug gap to ground. This turns the crankshaft for engine operation with excess current charging the battery.

● When an electric current flows thru a wire coil—a magnetic field surrounds the coil becoming an electromagnet.

When a soft iron bar is put into the coil, the current will shorten the electro-magnetic field. This magnetic energy is changed to mechanical energy by moving the soft iron bar becoming a solenoid.

When the current is turned off the electromagnetic field collapses and the soft iron bar is rapidly demagnetized.

● An EMF electron flow, pgs. 308, 360, occurs between dissimilar metals in an electrolyte. The flow is from a metal which is more active electrically to one with less energy.

The electrolytic process, page 359, is called corrosion in an uncontrollable form.

In a controlled form electrolysis can produce electroplating, and when the current flow is reversible, it can charge a lead-acid storage battery.

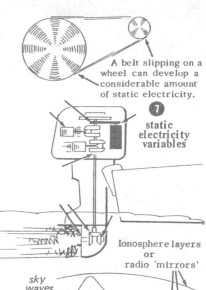

A belt slipping on a wheel can develop a considerable amount of static electricity.

7 static electricity variables

Ionosphere layers or radio 'mirrors'

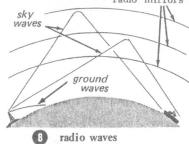

sky waves

ground waves

8 radio waves

9

line-of-sight waves

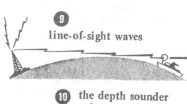

10 the depth sounder

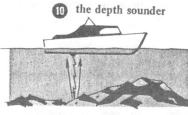

Powerboating Illustrated

● Consider an electric current flow a huge army of electrons. When the circuit is completed, the army moves thru the wire and ground at fantastic speeds.

When the current is broken the electrons are disorganized as they wander aimlessly thru the wire and ground.

● Static electricity is an uncontrolled flow of electrons developing in moving, slipping parts of an engine. When friction develops, an accumulation and dissipation of potentials plus heat buildup puts some of the electrons on the move.

We were curious in our early research if this uncontrolled flow buildup was a corrosion factor.

Besides causing static on AM radios and heat buildup with the friction of a slipping belt, it didn't cause corrosion.

● Crystals used in microphones and record player pickups will generate a small electrical flow.

These crystals under mechanical stress form a positive charge on one face... while the other face forms a negative charge starting an electron flow.

305

● Radio waves travel outward and upward from a transmitting antenna.

● Sky waves are reflected back to earth after they bounce off layers of the ionosphere...while the shorter ground waves are usually restricted to a shorter radius.

● Other waves follow the line of sight path directly from the transmitter to the receiver.

Examples of these are Radio Direction Finders, radar, VHF, UHF, SHF, FM, and TV. Their transmitters must be placed high as possible, otherwise their signals can only be picked up for short distances from the transmitters.

● A depth sounder uses an ultrasonic "ping" directed vertically into the water. The time measurement to bounce off an underwater object then returned to the receiver, is calibrated as the depth of the water.

Also see page 322.

① dipoles in unmagnetized metal

② magnetizing by induction

small magnets

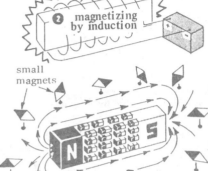

③ magnetized iron or steel

306

④ LIKE poles repel

⑤ UNLIKE poles attract

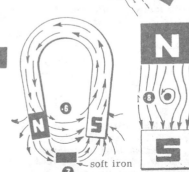

soft iron

● **Dipole theory of magnetism.** We prefer this simple idea with tiny, unorganized magnetic dipole particles floating in an unmagnetized metal bar.

This soft metal bar is placed in a solenoid, pg. 316. When a current is turned on, it induces or excites the little dipoles to pull together in one direction to form a large magnet.

We show the electrical field surrounding the large magnet...made by pulling all the small dipole magnets into alignment.

● **Natural magnets** such as lodestone are bodies with a peculiar form of polarity being capable of exerting on...and acted upon by a magnetic force.

● **Temporary magnets** are made using a copper coil with a current turning it into an electromagnet such as a solenoid. around a *soft iron bar* which is activated with the current flow. The soft iron bar must lose its magnetic force immediately after the starter button has been released, see page 317.

● **A permanent Alnico magnet.** It is made of hard steel which will retain its force of magnetism long after it has been taken out of an electromagnetic field. If all Alnico magnets were suddenly demagnetized, all forms of transportation in the air, on the road, and on the water would come to a screeching halt.

● *Like poles repel—*
and unlike poles attract—

forming the basis for all kinds of electrical operation covered in the pages of this chapter.

● **Soft iron**—when the starter button is released and a solenoid bar is no longer excited, it has little magnetic retention. with the dipoles rapidly returning to their disorganized wandering state.

● **Hard magnetic material**—after the tiny dipoles have been placed in a definite alignment, they become a **permanent magnet** maintaining their alignment.

Powerboating Illustrated

Amperes (flow) against ohms (resistance)...
induced by voltage (pressure) is measured
in watts or horsepower.

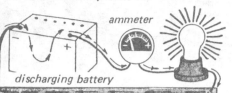

ammeter

discharging battery

$$VOLTS \times AMPS = WATTS$$
$$\frac{VOLTS}{OHMS} = AMPS$$
$$AMPS \times OHMS = VOLTS$$
$$\frac{VOLTS}{AMPS} = OHMS$$

- Direct current is continuous, unidirectional, and non-pulsating as it comes from a battery, requiring alternating current to be rectified for battery storage. While DC current is carried thru much of the cross-section depth of a copper wire...AC current is carried on the outer skin of the wire due to high frequency.

- Ampere (flow)—is the quantity of electrons moving past a given point in a circuit measured by an *ammeter.* If a reader wants a comparison, it is similar to so many gallons of water flow per minute thru a pipe.

$amps = \frac{volts}{ohms}$

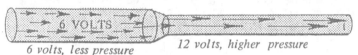

6 VOLTS

6 volts, less pressure   *12 volts, higher pressure*

- Voltage (pressure)—is a measurement of EMF force, page 360, which is measured by a *voltmeter.* Voltage is equal to the resistance to be overcome, which cannot exceed the maximum resistance of the circuit. For a similar comparison...it is the amount of pressure required to force water thru a certain diameter pipe.

$volts = amps \times ohms$

307

six feet   one foot

- Ohms (resistance)—it depends on the wire metal, the diameter and length of the wire which opposes the current flow causing a heat buildup. A six foot length of copper wire will have six times the resistance of the identical copper wire that is only one foot long.

$ohms = \frac{volts}{amps}$

- Watts (power)—is the work output unit obtained by multiplying the amperes flowing...and by the voltage required to force it to flow. For an example—a 6 volt 10 amp hour motor...and a 12 volt 5 amp motor would both consume 60 watts.

$watts = volts \times amps$

- Watt-hour— *is the unit of electrical energy* measured by multiplying the ampere-hour output with the average voltage during discharge in a specified time period measured in *watt-hours.*

- One kilowatt equals 100 watts.

- One horsepower equals 746 watts. The horsepower of an electric motor is determined by dividing the wattage by 746.

- The 6 hp electric motor at right according to this formula would have a work output of 4476 watt hours.

6 HP

Powerboating Illustrated

I assure you that we hire only the best of factory qualified mechanics to diagnose your motor problems.

The temperamental outboard motor provides as much fun today as 30 years ago. When an owner claims he has one, ask the reasons... and you soon find it has a temperamental owner.

Owners and mechanics must know the theoretical operation of their equipment if it is to be dependable. When it doesn't work, a systematic search begins to find the problem. After it has been diagnosed, repair or replacement becomes a minor item and the outboard motor is operational and happy again.

For the owners of temperamental outboard motors who think otherwise, we show our witchdoctor friend to convince them of their opinions.

Current flow proved an interesting problem for our electrical, battery, and corrosion chapters. The history of "electrics" or substances which could be charged by friction appeared around 1600 A.D., then--

- **Conventional flow.** Benjamin Franklin proposed that an excess amount of fluid developed at the positive... with an opposing deficiency at the negative. It persists today with "current" often said *to be passing from the positive to negative terminal of a battery or generator*, page 374.

308
- **Electron flow.** Prof. J. J. Thomson discovered the basic sub-atomic particle of negative electricity in 1897 called the **electron**. During electrification it became obvious that *the negative rather than the positive charge was transferred*, pg. 374.

- **Alternating current.** When magnetic current flux flows are developed in the primary, and broken across the secondary windings of a magneto coil, alternating current is produced.

- **The alternator** is an AC generator that converts mechanical energy into electrical energy. While DC generators were used in autos to the early sixties, more output was needed beginning with a 12 volt battery producing ¼ more energy than a same size 6 volt battery. The alternator replaced the DC generator as it was smaller and lighter, and it could produce some output with an engine at idle as it could be geared for higher rpm.

- **Rectification.** As everything used in the operation of an auto or boat uses DC, AC alternator output must be changed to DC with a *silicone semiconductor rectifier*. It is mounted inside the alternator housing to rectify AC into one-way DC current for battery storage. We show the previous generation **alternator rectifier** on pages 318-9.

During metallic wire conduction flow, no material is transported or deposited on the circuit terminals... which is different in an electrolyte.

- **Ions** are electrically charged particles that change a liquid to an electrolyte *(a solution having salts, acids, or bases, page 359)* which can conduct a current flow. The current transports atoms from an underwater anode to a cathode producing corrosion. In a controlled form it can produce electroplating, pg. 357, and when reversed, it can charge a battery, pg. 339.

With all this excellent but confusing technical background, it becomes obvious why we chose the simple conventional flow for your use, pg. 374.

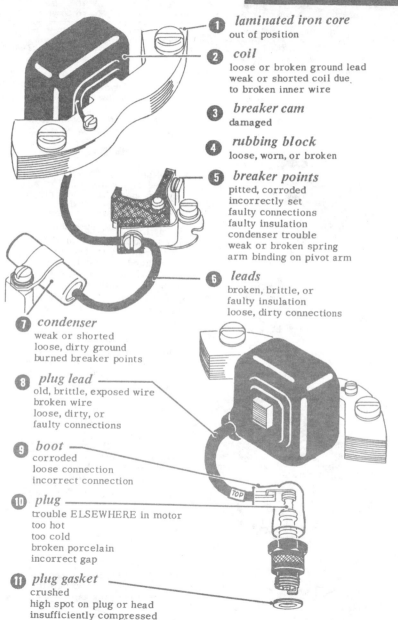

1 *laminated iron core*
out of position

2 *coil*
loose or broken ground lead
weak or shorted coil due
to broken inner wire

3 *breaker cam*
damaged

4 *rubbing block*
loose, worn, or broken

5 *breaker points*
pitted, corroded
incorrectly set
faulty connections
faulty insulation
condenser trouble
weak or broken spring
arm binding on pivot arm

6 *leads*
broken, brittle, or
faulty insulation
loose, dirty connections

309

7 *condenser*
weak or shorted
loose, dirty ground
burned breaker points

8 *plug lead*
old, brittle, exposed wire
broken wire
loose, dirty, or
faulty connections

9 *boot*
corroded
loose connection
incorrect connection

10 *plug*
trouble ELSEWHERE in motor
too hot
too cold
broken porcelain
incorrect gap

11 *plug gasket*
crushed
high spot on plug or head
insufficiently compressed

Powerboating Illustrated

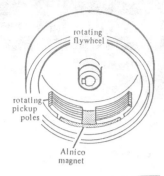

rotating flywheel

rotating pickup poles

Alnico magnet

> *The self-contained magneto generates its own ignition energy.* It has to be built up, timed, and delivered with enough high voltage to jump across the spark plug gap to go to ground.

● Three types of magnetos— **revolving powerhead magneto, revolving core, and induction magneto.** We show a one-cylinder flywheel magneto with coil, points, and condenser... which are doubled for a two-cylinder outboard motor.

Voltage is induced or built up in a laminated iron core to develop a magnetic flux in the primary coil. It is interrupted by the points opening to stop then reverse the flux direction to build up voltage in the coil secondary.

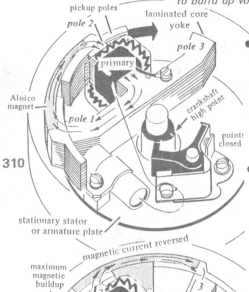

pickup poles
pole 2
laminated core
yoke
pole 3
primary
Alnico magnet
pole 1
crankshaft high point
points closed

310

stationary stator or armature plate

magnetic current reversed

maximum magnetic buildup
2
3
1
points opening
charging condenser

● An aluminum flywheel is located on the upper end of a rotating crankshaft containing an Alnico magnet with two pickup poles.

Inside the revolving flywheel is a stationary aluminum stator or armature plate. On top of it is mounted a laminated 3 pole core yoke, with a coil mounted around the center yoke.

● A current begins to flow when the rotating pickup poles in the flywheel start to touch the core poles 1 and 2. The current or flux keeps building until 200 to 300 volts are built up in the primary windings shown at left with closed breaker points.

A high point on the crankshaft opens the breaker points to interrupt the primary field with the current at maximum.

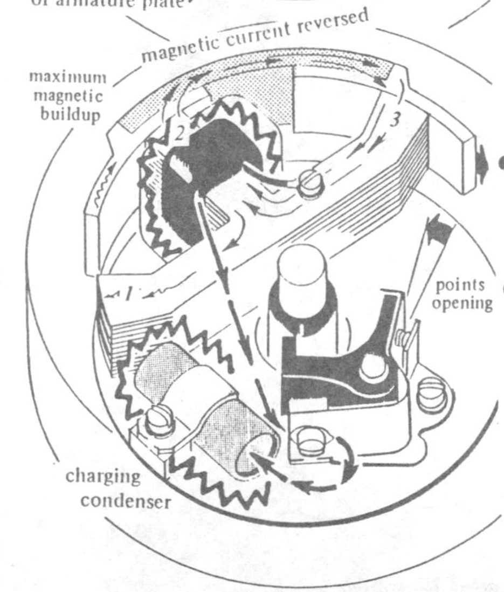

● The current wants to go to ground across the opening points, but is detoured into a condenser to build up and break the primary current.

● The rotating pickup poles meanwhile contact coil poles 2 and 3. This reverses the current or flux thru the coil with the magnetic lines of force dropping to zero.

The collapse of the primary at right angles to the secondary induces a high voltage buildup to jump the plug gap.

Powerboating Illustrated

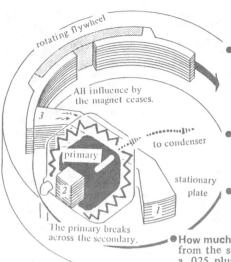

rotating flywheel

All influence by the magnet ceases.

3

to condenser

primary

stationary plate

2

1

The primary breaks across the secondary.

Flywheel magneto

Let us review the sequence—

- The opening points pull the primary current to go to ground...which is shunted instead to the condenser.

  The current flux going thru the center core pole with the coil is reversed. The magnetic lines of force shrink inwardly dropping to zero.

- The primary magnetic field which is interrupted at its peak, collapses at right angles across 87.5 times as many strands of fine copper wiring in the secondary.

- This collapse induces a high voltage buildup with the amps dropping to zilch to discharge thru a spark plug gap for ignition.

- **How much voltage?** 20,000 volts (pressure) from the secondary coil is required to jump a .025 plug gap.

- **Step-up transformer.** The magneto is a transformer with primary and secondary wire coils magnetically coupled with a laminated iron core. While transformers are made to step up or step down alternating voltages, the magneto is a step-up transformer.

311

- **Breaker points.** While they open fast, they can't snap open fast enough to fully prevent arcing. This becomes critical for 2 cycle operation firing 60 times a second at 4000 rpm. Considerable information is provided on the next page covering breaker points.

All outboard motors have recommended breaker point opening, timing angle, and dwell, specified by the manufacturer.

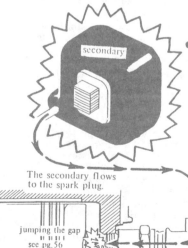

secondary

The secondary flows to the spark plug.

jumping the gap
see pg.56

piston

20,000 volts
for a .025 gap

water jacket

Powerboating Illustrated

- **Dwell plates** are used for timing. They provide angular measurements of point opening as well as angular measurement when the points are in contact. This provides the time required to charge the coil.

  Dwell ends the moment the breaker points open.

  This reverses the magnetization process, causing the collapse to induce the high voltage required to jump the plug gap.

  We hope you are as fascinated with the simple, yet highly complex magneto as I am. The information will have many applications.

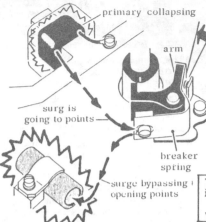

primary collapsing

arm

surg is
going to points

breaker
spring

surge bypassing
opening points

laminated
iron core   coil ground

secondary

to points &
condenser

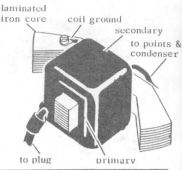

to plug   primary

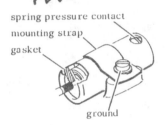

spring pressure contact

mounting strap

gasket

ground

312

alternate tinfoil
conductor layers

alternate layers of
paper insulation

frayed insulation

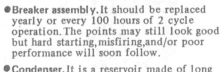

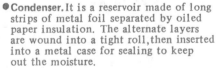

corroded or loose connections

> The 3 pole iron coil must be laminated. If it were solid iron, stray internal currents would cause a heat buildup interfering with a magnetic field buildup & collapse.

● An ignition coil may consist of 200 to 300 primary windings of coarse No. 20 copper wire, and 20,000 fine turns of No. 38 copper wire...with a ratio of 87.5 turns between the primary and secondary in the coil.

One end of the primary goes to ground, the other goes to the breaker. In the secondary, one end goes to the ground, the other to the spark plug.

The condenser is a spark arrestor. It reduces arcing to a minimum when the points are snapped open, helping to build up voltage for the secondary windings.

● **Breaker assembly.** It should be replaced yearly or every 100 hours of 2 cycle operation. The points may still look good but hard starting, misfiring, and/or poor performance will soon follow.

● **Condenser.** It is a reservoir made of long strips of metal foil separated by oiled paper insulation. The alternate layers are wound into a tight roll, then inserted into a metal case for sealing to keep out the moisture.

Condensers are tested with surges to 350 volts. The needle clings as the surge goes to the condenser. The voltage drops immediately as the current can't leak out the condenser insulation to ground.

● *Moisture is the enemy.* A dry condenser can last hundreds of times longer than one slightly moist. If a condenser has loose or corroded connections, resistance will cause arcing across the points.

> Replace points and condensers after a dump job, and when any malfunction begins.

Points & Condensers

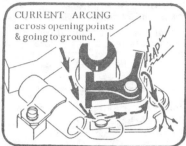

CURRENT ARCING
across opening points
& going to ground.

.018 or
.020

Correcting
alignment

NEVER
FILE
POINTS!

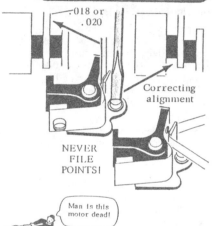

Man is this
motor dead!

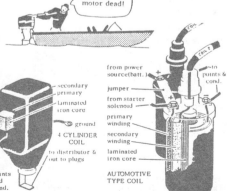

secondary
primary

laminated
iron core

ground

4 CYLINDER
COIL

to distributor &
out to plugs

from power
source(batt.)

jumper

from starter
solenoid

primary
winding

secondary
winding

laminated
iron core

AUTOMOTIVE
TYPE COIL

to
points &
cond.

- **Coil problems?** Check for loose, worn, or frayed connections.

Powerboating Illustrated

A breaker assembly consists of two tungsten coated points, one on the stationary bracket, the other on the breaker arm.

As primary current reaches maximum, the field is broken by the opening points. The current wanting to go to ground, is sidetracked by the condenser acting as a spark arrestor.

By the time the condenser is charged, the breaker contacts are far enough apart to prevent arcing. The current surge thru the core is then stopped collapsing the primary field at its peak.

- *The coil discharge and plug firing may occur more than 60 times per second. The points must be set with care and checked carefully as the points wear at every contact, get out of adjustment, and become dirty.*

2 and 4 cycle engine breaker points require a break-in period...followed by a check after ten hours operation. Also check the breaker points every 12 to 18 months of normal operation. **313**

- **Cleaning breaker points.** Dirt and other deposits are removed with a cleaning solvent. Wipe the points clean and dry with linen tape or bond paper to avoid leaving a lint deposit.

Avoid filing points as the thin, hard tungsten coating can be damaged to soon cause stuck or burned points.

- **Can you replace a condenser**...and do you have a sealed container to carry one in your tool kit?

If a leaky condenser kills your motor and a spare isn't available, cut the condenser lead to permit arcing across the opening points. This will burn the points, but they may last long enough to take your boat back to the launching ramp.

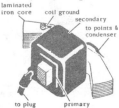

laminated
iron core   coil ground

secondary
to points &
condenser

to plug   primary

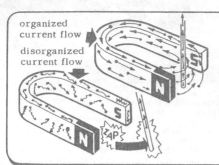

The circuit is completed—and a current flow begins when moving a conductor between poles of a magnet.

The current flow must be built up, broken, and channeled off for use.

Current developed from this humble beginning is increased by developing more lines of force, plus speeding collapse of the magnetic flux.

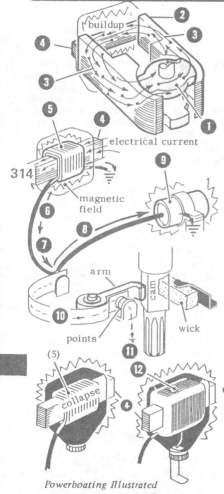

organized current flow

disorganized current flow

buildup

electrical current

314

magnetic field

arm

cam

points

wick

(5)

collapse

Powerboating Illustrated

● A four pole magnetic rotor revolves inside a U-shaped laminated core with a coil. The magnetic lines of force are broken every 90 degrees of the shaft driven rotating magnet.

The current surges thru the magnet and laminated core at left to develop a magnetic field flowing thru the coil primary with the 200 to 300 windings of coarse copper wire. The cam lobe on the rotor opens the points to speed collapse of the primary.

At the same time the primary surges to the opening points but is side-tracked into the condenser becoming a "brick wall" to stop the buildup.

The primary collapses at right angles across 20,000 turns of fine wire to produce 18,000 to 20,000 volts in the secondary to jump the plug gap.

The goal for the 4 cylinder magneto magnet revolving inside the core... or the flywheel magneto revolving around the stationary three pole core is identical, to produce a spark correctly timed for spark plug ignition in the cylinder.

● Tachometer. It is critical to obtain maximum performance for the four cylinder outboard motor using self-contained magneto ignition.

Attach the tachometer as shown on the facing page. It records the current surge changes in the magneto... which are recorded as powerhead rpm.

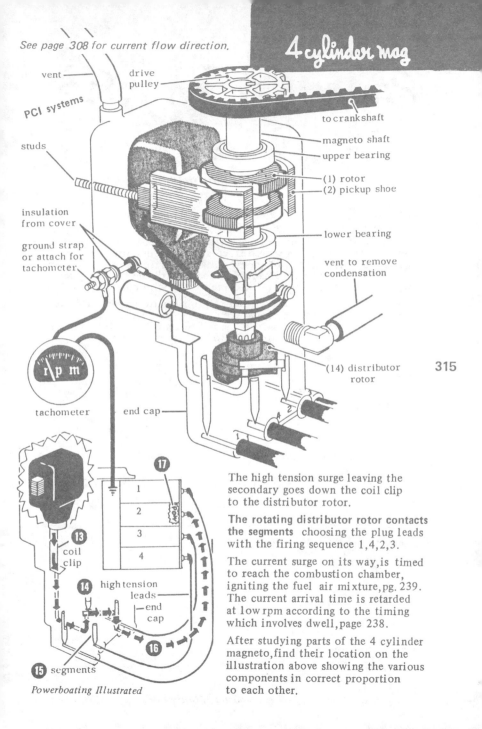

See page 308 for current flow direction.

4 cylinder mag

vent

drive pulley

PCI systems

studs

insulation from cover

ground strap or attach for tachometer

to crankshaft

magneto shaft

upper bearing

(1) rotor
(2) pickup shoe

lower bearing

vent to remove condensation

(14) distributor rotor

315

tachometer

end cap

r p m

17

1

2

3

4

13 coil clip

14 high tension leads
end cap

15 segments

16

Powerboating Illustrated

The high tension surge leaving the secondary goes down the coil clip to the distributor rotor.

The rotating distributor rotor contacts the segments choosing the plug leads with the firing sequence 1,4,2,3.

The current surge on its way,is timed to reach the combustion chamber, igniting the fuel air mixture,pg. 239. The current arrival time is retarded at low rpm according to the timing which involves dwell,page 238.

After studying parts of the 4 cylinder magneto,find their location on the illustration above showing the various components in correct proportion to each other.

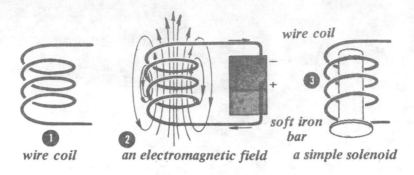

| ① wire coil | ② an electromagnetic field | ③ a simple solenoid |

An electromagnet becomes a solenoid when it performs a mechanical task such as operating a starter motor.

We begin with several turns of copper wire to form a loop. When a current flows thru this loop, each wire turn combines to develop a continuous single field. This creates a temporary magnetic field having north and south poles similar to a permanent magnet... with the lines of force going the same direction thru the center of the wire coil.

A soft iron bar is put into the center of this electromagnet with the current flowing thru the coil and iron bar. As the magnetic lines of force shorten the electromagnetic field, the iron bar is pulled into the wire coil with the current flow transformed into mechanical energy.

The magnetic field collapses when the current thru the coil is turned off. The soft iron bar in the center rapidly loses its magnetism, is returned by a spring to its original position.

If the iron bar sticks though the ignition key is turned off, the battery current will keep flowing thru the solenoid. A master switch is the best way to stop such a current flow on a powerboat, pages 301, 335, using a hammer to ''unstick it'' on an auto. When you check for solenoid problems on a starter motor or switch, take a jumper from the battery bypassing the solenoid.

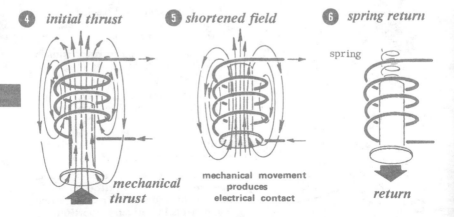

④ *initial thrust* ⑤ *shortened field* ⑥ *spring return*

mechanical thrust

mechanical movement produces electrical contact

spring   *return*

the Solenoid

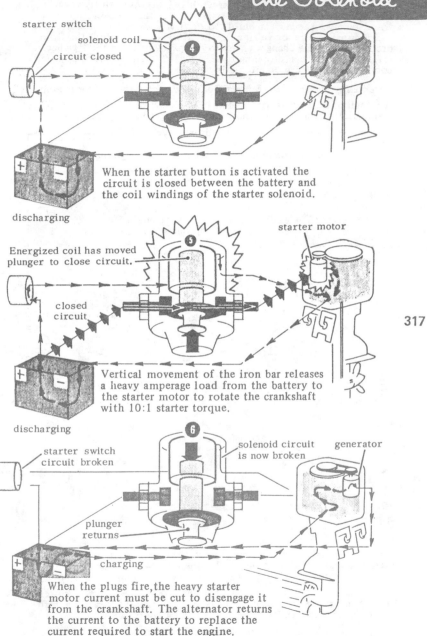

starter switch
solenoid coil
circuit closed

④

When the starter button is activated the circuit is closed between the battery and the coil windings of the starter solenoid.

discharging

starter motor

Energized coil has moved plunger to close circuit.

⑤

closed circuit

Vertical movement of the iron bar releases a heavy amperage load from the battery to the starter motor to rotate the crankshaft with 10:1 starter torque.

discharging

⑥

starter switch circuit broken

solenoid circuit is now broken

generator

plunger returns

charging

When the plugs fire, the heavy starter motor current must be cut to disengage it from the crankshaft. The alternator returns the current to the battery to replace the current required to start the engine.

317

Powerboating Illustrated

The **alternator rectifier system** shown below begins with flywheel magnets revolving around a stator or stationary core with windings. As the flywheel revolves, the current builds to *positive maximum* when the magnets and laminated core are in line. As the flywheel rotates 90° the flow drops to zero. This changes to *negative maximum* when the flywheel rotates to 180°, then dropping to zero at 270°. This cycle is repeated continuously to develop alternating current.

Alternating current must be rectified for direct current battery storage.

A selenium rectifier is used which is an electrical check valve or policeman directing the positive and negative charges to the battery.

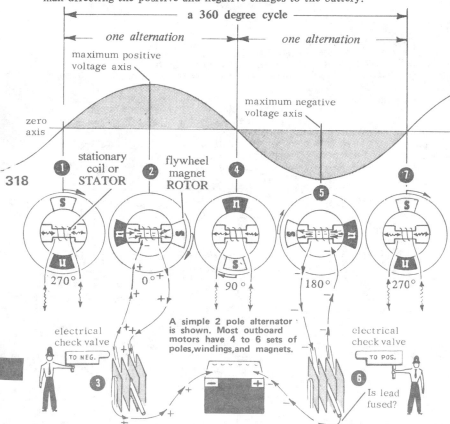

One rectifier is used to change alternating current to direct current for battery charge. We show a **one-cycle sine wave** with the positive and the negative particles flowing to two rectifiers to simplify the concept.

The battery charger is a rectifier changing alternating to direct current sending positive particles to the negative terminal, and visa versa, with the leads changed inside the charger to avoid confusion.

Powerboating Illustrated

8

NORMAL 9 BURNED OUT

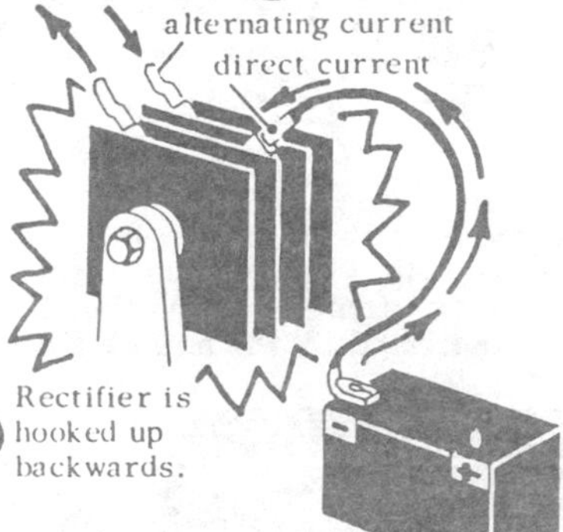

alternating current
direct current

Rectifier is
10 hooked up
backwards.

Corroded or
11 loose connections

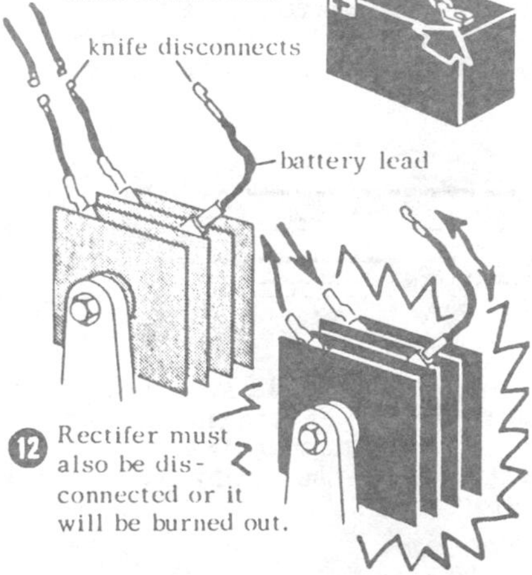

knife disconnects

battery lead

Rectifier must
12 also be dis-
connected or it
will be burned out.

Scorched or bubbled paint.

• **Burned out.** Outboard rectifiers range from dull red to gray. Whey they are damaged or burned out it will be easy to recognized with the dark color.

• If the battery is **hooked up backwards,** current will be sent back to the rectifier...while current from the battery meets it coming from the other direction. As the conflicting currents build up, the rectifier becomes hot.

Sparks start to arc across the negative ground plates burning the selenium coatimg. The coating becomes darker while the ability to transfer current diminishes,it becomes more difficult for the battery to hold a full charge.

Current coming from the alternator must reach the battery...or it will start backing up with the increasing heat burning the rectifier plates.

• Terminals—if they are corroded or have poor connections...or if the battery case has insufficient ventilation,any of the three methods can cause a current leakage.

319

If the rectifier has **loose connections** to the battery, the magneto or the alternator keeps sending the same current volume having no place to go but cause a heat buildup burning the selenium on the plates.

●

• *A rectifier can be unhooked in some magneto systems to operate without a battery.*

Unhook the battery and rectifier leads...then tape the leads to the alternator so they are separated and insulated from each other.

If only the battery leads are unhooked, current from the alternator will be pumped to the rectifier.A rapid heat buildup will result burning the selenium coating on the plates.

Powerboating Illustrated

A starter motor has to operate under a high amp load to develop 50 to 150 rpm cranking torque to start an engine. It should be operated for 10 seconds at the most, followed with a short cooling period before another attempt. If cranked for longer periods, excess heat develops and electrical transmission becomes difficult...which will run down the battery and/or burn out the starter motor.

L H motor rule

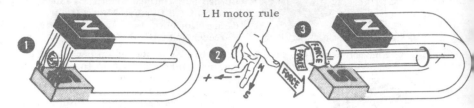

L.H. motor rule—magnetic current flows from north to south. When a conductor is placed between two poles, a magnetic field surrounds it tending to—1.rotate the conductor, 2.move it in direction of the thumb, and, 3.develop a current flow in direction indicated by the middle finger.

320

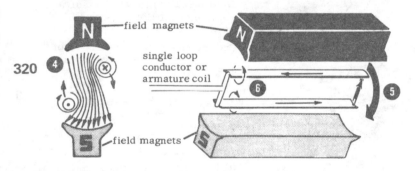

field magnets

single loop conductor or armature coil

field magnets

Armature. The conductor becomes an armature free to rotate according to the pull of the magnetic field. Magnetic poles have maximum attraction when the armature bars are lined up as shown above. When the armature rotates 90°, the magnetic pull becomes neutralized and the armature stops.

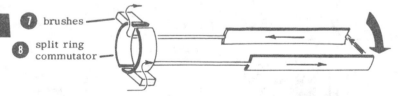

brushes

split ring commutator

Commutator. When the armature rotates to 90° to the field magnets a commutator is added to change the polarity. Instead of being neutralized the current in the armature is *suddenly reversed* . This permits the armature to rotate another 180° before polarity is again changed by the commutator to produce continuous rotation.

Powerboating Illustrated

Starter motor

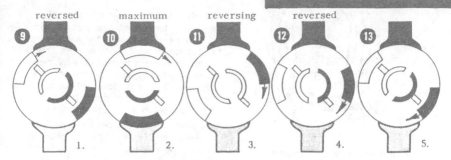

reversed   maximum   reversing   reversed

9   **10**   **11**   **12**   **13**

1.   2.   3.   4.   5.

Polarity and change of current direction within the starter armature is controlled by the commutator... while the outside current tends to flow in one direction, see current flow schematic below.

A coil mounted on the shaft is governed by the **force rotating it in a clockwise direction.** 1. Polarity has been reversed by the commutator as the armature has gone thru neutral position. The sudden change forces the armature to 3., where opposite poles in line **develop maximum force or torque.** As the torque force dissipates at 3., polarity suddenly reverses to send the coil segments again into position of maximum force (torque).

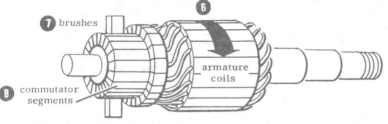

6

7 brushes

8 commutator segments

armature coils

321

Numerous coils are used as one coil would not have uniform torque or speed since maximum force only develops when the opposite poles are in line. As one coil is forced out from the magnetic field...another coil moves into place. This provides continuous torque to start an engine until battery current flow is broken at the solenoid.

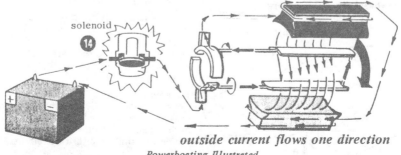

solenoid

14

outside current flows one direction
Powerboating Illustrated

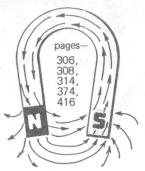

pages—
306,
308,
314,
374,
416

*The two-wire system is shown below
using the conventional current flow.*

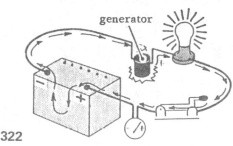

generator

the charging battery

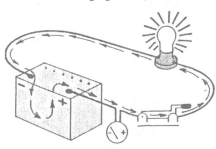

the discharging battery

an incomplete circuit

Unified field theory? For 200 years
scientists have been unsuccessful to
define a simple theory for magnetism
and electricity. The ideas work, but
confusion exists to explain why they
work beginning with the magnet.
Whether it does or doesn t have a
flow. and the proper name for the
flow, we leave to debating professors.

● **Magnetic current** is the term we use,
while others prefer the *lines of force.*
Our purpose is to show flow around
the entire magnet from N to S poles
that may be continuous for millions
of times. With this happy confusion
we begin your wiring chapter.

●**Conventional current flow.** We show
the older current flow theory thru
our book for consistency. We **emphasize
the completed circuit flow...** though
the flow direction in most situations
becomes of minor importance.

> *The exception-* locate fuses on the
> positive or ' hot side" of the 6v
> and 12v lead-acid storage battery.

●**The charging battery.** Current flows
from the − side of the battery,
thru the generator,light,and ammeter,
returning to the + battery terminal.

● **The discharging battery.** Current
flows from the + side of the
battery,thru the ammeter,the light,
and back to the − side of the
battery.

If the current flows too long,the
light grows dim,then goes out.The
battery then has to be recharged
as discussed on page 339.

● **Voltage** is the invisible pressure or
force driving the current or gale of
electrons moving at thousands of
miles per second thru a wire with
the individual atoms spaced at
relatively great distances.

●**Incomplete circuit.** When the wire
freeway or circuit of electrons is
broken or interrupted,the billions
of disorganized electrons will be
wandering aimlessly thru the circuit.

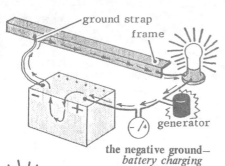

ground strap
frame

generator

the negative ground—
battery charging

After covering the two wire system, we discuss the single wire system for an auto using the auto frame ground to complete the other half of the circuit.

American autos used the negative ground system for many decades, while English autos used to have a positive ground with equal efficiency.

● **Negative marine ground system.** It has been standard for 25 years to reduce underwater corrosion damage discussed on page 326.

● **Positive marine ground system.** While it is practical for cold northern waters, underwater damage is rapid from corrosion in warm waters.

● **Electricity is lazy.** It always takes the least line of resistance or the shortest practical distance. We show the shortened electrical current flow due to a frayed wire exposed to and rubbing against the frame.

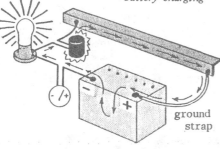

ground strap

the positive ground—
battery charging

323

● **Short circuit.** The circuit has been accidentally shortened with the current taking the shortened path.

The short circuit is the most difficult kind to contend with as it is on the "hot side" before the fuses requiring the battery to be disconnected immediately.

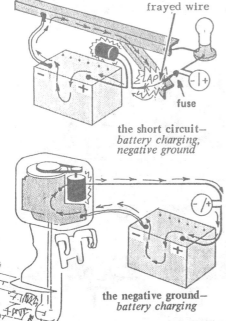

frayed wire

fuse

the short circuit—
battery charging,
negative ground

the negative ground—
battery charging

● **A new engine.** Negative ground flow is excellent for 2 cycle and 4 cycle engines. Tight bolt and screw connections on clean metal surfaces provide an efficient ground completing the circuit.

Efficiency of the ground decreases with age as rust and grime collect, while connections become corroded and/or loose.

● Current flow resistance grows at these points with friction causing a voltage drop. Less voltage is available to start and operate an engine.

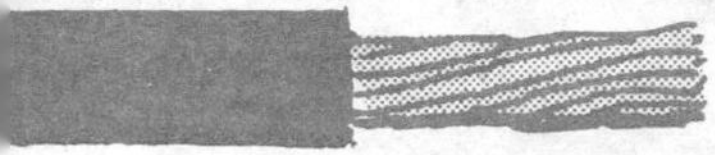

- **Multi-stranded copper wire.** Choose it for boating use with a tough Hypalon covering as the wiring has to take considerable pounding, flexing, vibration, and chafe.

- **Solid copper wire.** It rapidly age hardens and fractures in boating use. *Exception—* solid uncovered copper wire is used on wooden sailboat masts for lightning protection.

- **Aluminum wire.** It was introduce shortly after World War II due to the shortage of available copper wire.

  Avoid aluminum wiring for shoreside use with corrosion potentials at connectors, and if chafe exists, developing heat buildup and fire potentials. Avoid it on boats, especially those used in the salt water environment as hygroscopic salts can accelerate connector corrosion and heat buildup.

▲ **Dockside electrical outlets.** Our 24' sailboat now 26 years old, has faced probably half of the various outlets in local marinas, Long Beach, San Diego, Oceanside, and other ports.

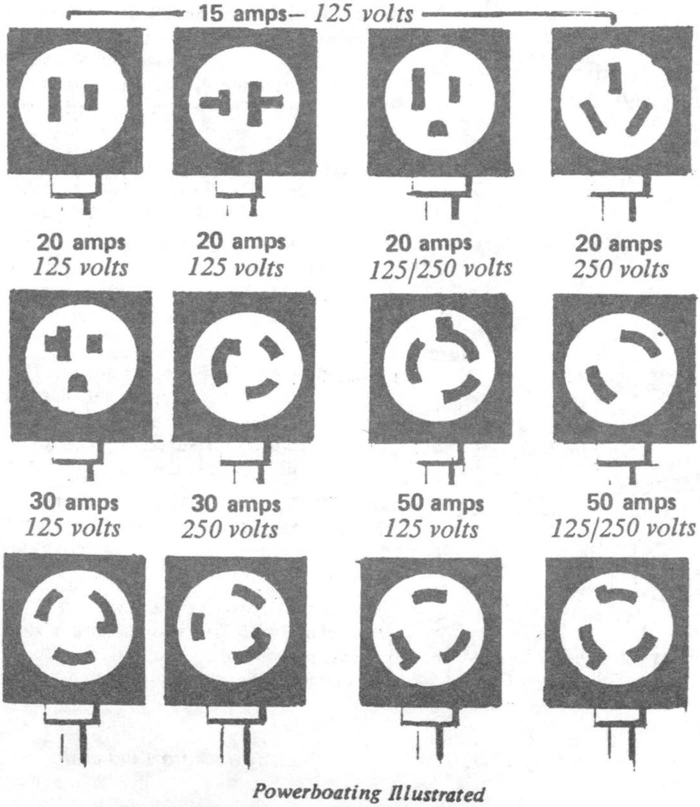

324

━━━━━━ **15 amps—** *125 volts* ━━━━━━

| **20 amps** *125 volts* | **20 amps** *125 volts* | **20 amps** *125/250 volts* | **20 amps** *250 volts* |
| **30 amps** *125 volts* | **30 amps** *250 volts* | **50 amps** *125 volts* | **50 amps** *125/250 volts* |

Powerboating Illustrated

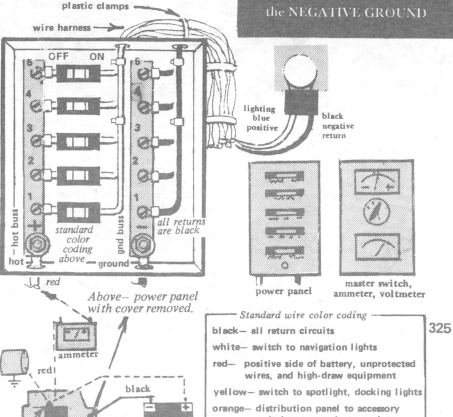

plastic clamps
wire harness

OFF   ON

lighting
blue
positive

black
negative
return

hot buss   gnd buss

standard
color
coding
above

all returns
are black

hot — + — ground

red

*Above— power panel
with cover removed.*

power panel

master switch,
ammeter, voltmeter

ammeter

red

black

engine
ground

hot solenoid junction stud

Wiring harness support. This
requires non-conductor plastic
clamps, the maximum distance
between of 14″ throughout its
entire length.

Clamps cannot be tight enough
to cut nor crush insulation.

— Standard wire color coding —

black— all return circuits

white— switch to navigation lights

red— positive side of battery, unprotected
wires, and high-draw equipment

yellow— switch to spotlight, docking lights

orange— distribution panel to accessory
switches, convenience outlets

pink— switch to fuel level indicator

light green— switch to ventilaton blowers

dark green— bonding system, hull ground
plate, non-current carrying

dark blue— switch to cabin & panel lights

purple— switches instrumentation common
feed to electrical instruments

brown— switch to pumps

325

Negative ground system, page 323. Power distribution panel is the
takeoff point to control, protect, and distribute various circuits.

Since, theoretically, flow comes first thru positive side of circuits, this
is the side that blows fuses or trips circuit breakers when abnormal
current flow problems develop. For the other side, the **positive ground
system** for comparison, see pages 323 and 326.

The positive ground gives no warning of an electrical leak.

positive ground   negative ground

GIVER   TAKER

> Many older sailboats have operated successfully in the North Atlantic from England to Norway and Sweden with positive electrical ground systems in water temperature close to freezing...BUT—

Rapid underwater corrosion develops when these boats are sailed to our waters to tie up in marinas from Santa Barbara to San Diego with water temperature from 58 to 75° which speeds current flow in our ocean water electrolyte.

● A wooden boat with a **positive ground electrical system** has a bad wire splice in its watery bilge. The battery current leaks to the engine, out the prop shaft, thru the water, and up the keel bolts *or a partially submerged outdrive unit,* The current continues into the bilge, and thru the bad wire splice it returns to the battery without a warning of the rapidly corroding keel bolts. The only indication of a problem is the battery which is having a difficult time to hold a charge.

● **Negative ground electrical system.** An identical boat has an identical bad splice in its watery bilge. When the owner coming aboard turns on the master switch, then the problem circuit with a leakage...a fuse should blow or a circuit breaker trip to alert the owner that he has a problem developing in the initial stage.

● **Can it also be a fresh water problem?** In east coast areas of North and South Carolina with low mineral content, underwater current flow is retarded in colder fresh water. which can often be used in a battery.

The *underwater demolition team* of warm water/ high mineral content in the Colorado River from Lake Mead to Hoover Dam, and south to the Mexican border, is almost as efficient for underwater corrosion as our local Pacific Ocean electrolyte. Owners of slip-berthed boats in this area and their electricians, need a similar understanding of corrosion as owners and marine electricians in nearby ocean marinas.

● The captain of the large, two masted metal sailboat *Roland von Bremen* was discussing how stray electrolysis currents can speed the corrosion process, almost sinking his boat at the dock except for—

"I dropped by the boat to check it out for a race later in the week. I noticed big bubbles coming up alongside our hull, then a new powerboat in the slip next to ours. That boat, and two boats on the other side of us were charging batteries...with our metal hull caught in the middle of a current exchange between negative and positive grounds.. I had to move our boat out of the slip immediately...then later work out the details with the other boat owners to eliminate future problems"

We were finishing supper with our autopilot inventor Art Hill when his phone rang. With a smirk he asked, "Would you like to join me on a house call to help a sick autopilot?"

"The sailboat around 48' long, was made in England probably 40 years ago. It was sailed to the U.S. arriving in the Long Beach Marina four months ago. The underwater metals are having a rapid corrosion attack with the warm water conductivity, stray currents, and his batteries.

"I told the owner the major cause, was his *positive ground system.* He would have to change to a negative ground which would be a complex operation on his boat with the 200V/ 50 Hz English shoreside system, to our 115V/ 60 Hz standards... but I strongly suspect he just changed the battery terminal leads. *All DC systems are now LIVE* making the situation worse". (All information comes from a recording made by Art).

Art told me he had to hold a screwdriver (insulated handle) to touch his autopilot drive unit, to ground it. He had to prove it was electrically alive ... followed by a loud zap and a blue flash. His momentary problem was to hold position since if he jumped up he would bang his head on the low overhead above the pilot.

The situation was exactly as Art had predicted with the battery leads... over the hilarious protests of innocence by the highly educated British scientist owner.

327

"My wife must have changed the battery leads last weekend when I was in London on business"... with his wife staring at him wondering if the sentence for murder would be less in the U.S., or London at Old Bailey.

1. Turn off ALL electrical equipment, and disconnect generators.

2. Disconnect battery cables and turn batteries 180 degrees.

3. Reconnect battery cables so their polarity is reversed (which had been accomplished). New cable clamps may be necessary as the 11/16" positive battery post is 1/16" larger than the negative battery post.

4. Reverse ammeter connections.

5. Remove regulator and replace with a negative ground unit.

6. Replace generator with one having a negative ground, or change to an ·alternator with more output.

7. Reverse low tension leads on ignition coils.

8 Hire an electronic specialist to make changes on electronic gear.

9. Have final check by a marine electrician of all leads, connections, etc., that needed changing before firing up negative ground.

10. Be ready for a quick disconnect when he fires up the engine... in case something had been overlooked.

Heat shrink tubing?

ring-end terminal lug

Terminal lug metals are important in the corrosive, vibrating ocean world for continuity with minimum resistance—*seal connection with heat-shrink tubing.*

Ring-end terminal lug remains captive even if the stud or nut loosens, while spade and forked terminal lugs may loosen and disconnect.

Provide a close fit. Ring-end terminal lug should match the wire size to which it is crimped, with a close fit around the stud terminal.

Soldering is required for heavy storage battery terminal lugs. They should match the wire size they are crimped to, with a close fit around terminal post. No terminal post should have more than four terminal lugs.

Crimped terminal lugs. We've seen good crimed connections on various boats, and others with poor mechanical connections. *Use crimping hand tools made by those manufacturing the terminal lugs you are working with* as the poor ones were often crimped with pliers.

Boats under 30′ long in the 1960's with high humidity and corrosion potentials preferred fuses to protect from overloads, and circuit breakers used on larger craft with better ventilation and less spray below. Excellent sealed trip-free circuit breakers emerged in the 1970's that were able to live in high humidity world of boats under 30′ long.

328

Dockside 115V plug polarity. After the plugs were rewired on our dock, I faced total confusion when checking them with a neon polarity tester. A marine electrician on a nearby boat came by to help. "Nothing makes sense with my neon tester instructions," with the tester in his hands finding 4 of the 12 having reversed polarity. *Check every dock plug with a well-insulated neon tester before use that is new to you.*

Dockside circuit breakers. I asked, "What is the major factor in electrical fires on well-found sailboats I've known thru the years with the breakers tripping one to three minutes late?"

"Dockside wiring is usually by electricians following the land wiring code with minimum knowledge of the marine world. A slow response may result from corrosion and lack of occasionally turning it off and on".

Dielectric lubricants are nonconductors. WD 40® is relatively dry, which soaks into the metal pores for circuit breakers on dock plugs".

On/off switches. Use marine approved switches only. Avoid household, auto, and RV switches made for the land environment that corrode, restricting flow, causing heat buildup. *Mounted vertically*— on is up position and off, down. *Mounted horizontally*— on, to the right, off, to the left.

Garden hose. For electrical wiring that must go thru damp and/or oily bilges on larger craft, thread wiring thru a hose for insulation thru the bilges with both ends high and dry.

12 v AWG (American Wire Gage)

Electrical wiring is an insulated metal conductor. It provides a flow path for electrons coming from an electrical source to electrical equipment or lighting source... and return.

Electricity must flow from its source through the circuit to do its job and return, with sufficient cross section size area (in circular mills) without diminishing along the way, nor taking another path, as it returns back to its source.

● **3% voltage drop** in first chart below is for critical circuits, navigation lights, electronic gear, etc. 12v AWG gage is provided with length of conductor, from current source, to the most distant fixture in the circuit, and return to source (battery?).

total amp draw	distance in feet								
	20	30	40	50	60	70	80	90	100
5	14	12	12	10	10	8	8	8	8
10	12	10	8	8	6	6	6	5	5
15	10	8	6	6	5	5	5	4	3
20	8	6	6	5	4	3	2	2	2
25	8	6	5	4	3	3	2	1	1

● **10% voltage drop** in second chart below is for cabin lights and other circuits that aren't as critical. 12v AWG gage is provided for length of conductor from current source, to most distant fixture, and return .

total amp draw	distance in feet								
	20	30	40	50	60	70	80	90	100
5	14	14	14	14	14	14	14	14	12
10	14	14	14	12	12	12	10	10	10
15	14	14	12	10	10	10	8	8	8
20	12	12	10	10	8	8	8	6	6
25	10	10	10	8	8	8	6	6	6

NFPA insulation and application spec's are--- -

For general use except machinery spaces		
RW	moisture and oil resistant	140°f
RH-RW	moisture, heat, oil resistant	140°f
TW	moisture resistant, flame retardant	140°f

for general use		
RHW	moisture, heat, oil resistant	167°f
THW	moisture, heat resistant, flame retardant	167°f
temperatures listed are for maximum operating temp.		

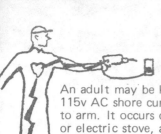

An adult may be killed in less than a second if a tenth of an amp 115v AC shore current goes thru the heart from arm to foot or arm to arm. It occurs on boats with damp bilges, incorrectly wired tools or electric stove, and on land with damp cement or moist ground

Are dockside female plugs wired correctly? While most large powerboats have polarity testers built in to their systems for test purposes, this is a problem facing owners of smaller boats. We tested newly installed wiring in a nearby marina. *We found 4 of 12 female plugs in one group had reversed wiring* to be used by boat owners. Such incompetence is inexcusable. Your next assignment is to check dock-plug wiring.

Use a neon circuit tester. *Warning— both rubberized holders must be well insulated to protect user as 115v AC current flows thru tester.*

Check dockside female plug for polarity. Standard land practice is—
black—hot...... green—ground...... white—neutral.

330

dead-correct

1 and 2. *Bulb lights on both indicating circuit complete from hot to ground.* **3. Final check—** *neutral to ground... NO light.*

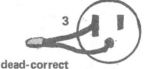

4. Reversed wiring— *neutral to ground... expect bright neon light.*

reversed-danger!

4. Soft fluctuating light... slight load imbalance, shoreside wiring is o.k.

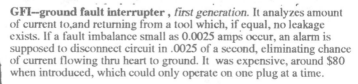

GFI--ground fault interrupter , *first generation.* It analyzes amount of current to,and returning from a tool which, if equal, no leakage exists. If a fault imbalance small as 0.0025 amps occur, an alarm is supposed to disconnect circuit in .0025 of a second, eliminating chance of current flowing thru heart to ground. It was expensive, around $80 when introduced, which could only operate on one plug at a time.

GFCI--ground fault current interruptor became required use within five years. All new hotels and motels required GFCI plugs for bathroom protection while shaving, etc., with water on the floor. Our office has several GFIC power strips,   each with 5 to 6 inlets. They also protect sensitive electronic equipment in a sudden power surge.

Powerboating Illustrated

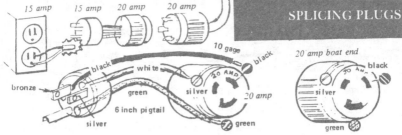

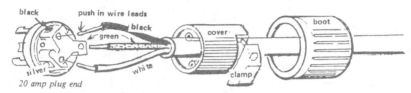

Short pigtail connectors can be made by you for use on your camper, boat, and/ or recreational vehicle. .. 20 and 30 amp pigtals are shown.

20 amp plug end

Larger size 20 and 30 amp plugs are easier to splice. Take the plugs apart, pull 3 strand cord thru, strip wire ends, solder the ends, and assemble.

Black – hot wire...stick end into hole with *black screw.*
Green – ground wire... stick end into hole with *green screw.*
White – neutral wire... stick end into hole with *silver screw.*

Tighten colored screws. An option before assembly, is to fill the cover above with a non-conductor *dielectric* silicone sealant. Boot is not usually required for pigtails having temporary use.

331

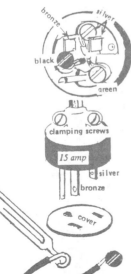

At left— *15 amp straight blade 3 wire plug with black/green/white screw terminal coding.* If the terminal has a different coding

Black – hot wire...goes to *brass*
Green wire – ground... goes to *green*
White – neutral wire... goes to *silver*

Strip wire ends. Solder ends clockwise lower left to fit screw top. Pull back cord, fill spaces with sealant if desired. Slip cover at left over prongs, then push tight for a snug fit. Tighten *clamping screws* and your plug is ready for use.

Plugs with clamping screws don't require the *Underwriter's knot* required for home plugs without clamps. Add boot over clamps if used outdoor year round to reduce clamp corrosion.

Buying plug end at right requires less effort. *Stagger splices and wrap splices separately.*

Wire end at left must be covered by screw.

Powerboating Illustrated

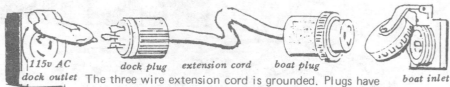

115v AC dock outlet   *dock plug*   *extension cord*   *boat plug*   *boat inlet*

The three wire extension cord is grounded. Plugs have twist-lock connectors with good waterproof protection.

The ideal electrical hookup? They were impossible to find in the 1960's, beginning to appear in marinas and trailer parks in the 1970's. If you do even a minimum of moving around in your boat or RV, choose a quality extension cord... making three or so pigtail adapters to plug the extension cord into various electrical outlet configurations.

Extension cord— will it be 10', 20', 30', 40', or 50' long from dock plug to your boat. You will be fortunate if you can buy the extension cord to meet the shoreside female outlet, to the one installed in your boat, or the one you want to install if doing your own wiring.

Powerboat inlet hookup. Install a 115v AC grounded 20, 25, or 30 amp twist lock power inlet. Check carefully for the best out of the way location. Probably half are easy to step on or trip over in most installations which greatly increase fire risk.

Female dock plug configurations Check to find the amp rating which should fit the blade hookup patterns on page 324. then splice the matching male plug to the dock end of your extension cord.

332

Our first extension cord— We installed a 20 amp twist-lock inlet in the cockpit. On the other end of a 25' extension cord we spliced a rare 15 amp plug to match the 115v AC dock outlet which was hard to find.

Our second extension cord was longer for our next permanent slip Use **ten gage twisted copper wire** for 30' to 50' boat extension cords Seven years later we moved to our present marina. The 20 amp dockside plug was changed to another 15 amp oddball plug sold in only one store.

Information in this electrical chapter will prove useful for RV and camper owners.

We were tired and it was late at night when parking our 20' RV shown right, in a trailer park near Ensenada, Mexico. We added our two blade to three blade pigtail to our extension cord, plugging it into the park plug.

When returning to the RV and turning on the lights... something was wrong. I grabbed the metal door handle to swing to the damp ground, wearing rubber thongs.

The realization came as I zoomed skyward, I should have used the neon tester. Our metal RV shell was alive with electrical current due to the park plug with reversed wiring. Suddenly I was no longer sleepy.

Powerboating Illustrated

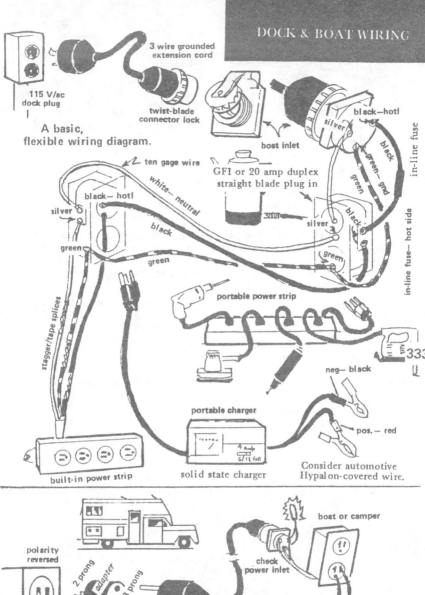

3 wire grounded extension cord

115 V/ac dock plug

twist-blade connector lock

A basic, flexible wiring diagram.

boat inlet

black—hotl

silver

black

green—gnd

green

in-line fuse

ten gage wire

GFI or 20 amp duplex straight blade plug in

white— neutral

black— hotl

silver

black

black

silver

black

green

green

green

in-line fuse— hot side

stagger/tape splices

portable power strip

333

neg— black

pos. — red

built-in power strip

portable charger

solid state charger

4 Amp

Consider automotive Hypalon-covered wire.

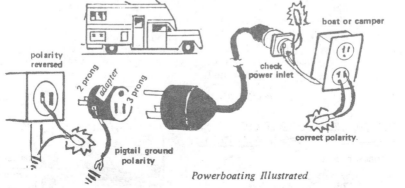

boat or camper

polarity reversed

2 prong

adapter

3 prong

check power inlet

correct polarity

pigtail ground polarity

Powerboating Illustrated

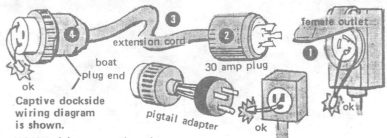

female outlet

extension cord

boat plug end

ok

30 amp plug

pigtail adapter

ok

ok

Captive dockside wiring diagram is shown.

While wiring our outboard
cruiser *Researcher,* our new 24' sailboat proved a challenge as we could find no practical wiring diagram in 1964. Sailing friend David Clark came to the rescue with a Rolls Royce, antique car mechanical background. He wired our boat as shown at right. It is undergoing its 3rd rewiring in 26 years following the same pattern, with better conduits shown below.

Captive boat wiring system, page 335, is used in our 24' sailboat. It is an insulated fiberglass shell without wiring grounded to an engine or the water. Current comes from, and returns to dock plug. It might work as well with a positive ground if computers, etc., aren't used, to avoid expensive semiconductor and other electronic current flow damage.

This system, using a 12v deep-cycle battery, operated adequately thru the years with ample dockside charging time, which was sufficient for a ten day Catalina vacation. Our handcranked 7½ hp motor is isolated from the boat wiring system to eliminate electrolysis problems.

334

Many cabin sailboats to 26', 8 to 10 years or older, may have poor wiring which can be updated and expanded with the closed system shown. Any powerboat mechanic who knows electrical wiring, can make an excellent installation for sailboat owners wanting to improve their wiring system.

Battery installations are horrible on some sailboats. Many 12 v batteries on a popular 25' class, are often installed in the sump shown lower right. I continually warn owners the sump is for collecting water in wave action or a heavy rain... mount the 12v battery elsewhere.

We were at a party exchanging ideas with a mechanic, mentioning an owner had strange corrosion problems inside his 25' sailboat. During a heavy rain the sump filled covering the battery. Battery acid mingled with the rain water filling and overflowing the sump on the cabin floor. We grinned as I said, "I think I know the owner"

Wiring conduit. The best one we could find is below left. Install high as possible with excellent ventilation for long life. The snap-on cover is easy to remove to check wiring circuits, and to add new systems. Make two wire color code references, one for the boat, and keep the other home.

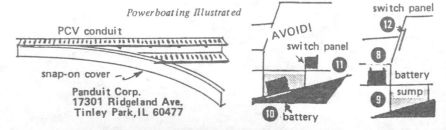

Powerboating Illustrated

PCV conduit

snap-on cover

**Panduit Corp.
17301 Ridgeland Ave.
Tinley Park, IL 60477**

AVOID!

switch panel

battery

switch panel

battery

sump

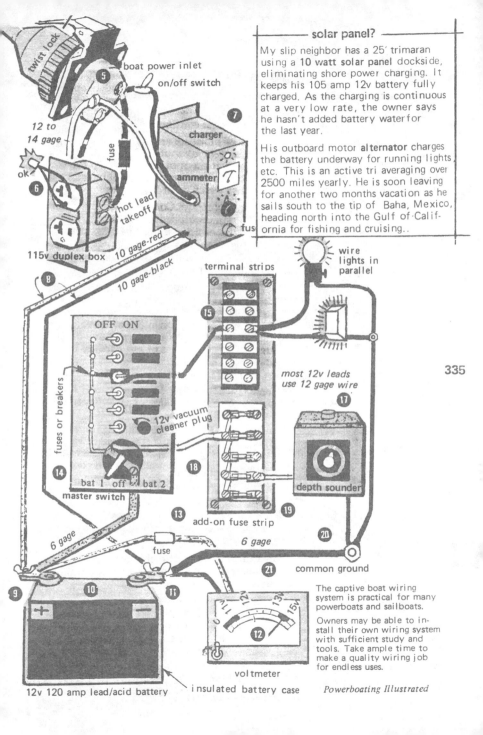

twist lock

boat power inlet
on/off switch

5

12 to
14 gage

fuse

ok

6

hot lead takeoff

115v duplex box   10 gage-red

10 gage-black

8

solar panel?

My slip neighbor has a 25' trimaran using a **10 watt solar panel** dockside, eliminating shore power charging. It keeps his 105 amp 12v battery fully charged. As the charging is continuous at a very low rate, the owner says he hasn't added battery water for the last year.

His outboard motor **alternator** charges the battery underway for running lights, etc. This is an active tri averaging over 2500 miles yearly. He is soon leaving for another two months vacation as he sails south to the tip of Baha, Mexico, heading north into the Gulf of California for fishing and cruising..

charger

7

ammeter

fuse

terminal strips

wire lights in parallel

15

335

OFF   ON

fuses or breakers

12v vacuum cleaner plug

14

bat 1 off bat 2
master switch

13

add-on fuse strip

18

19

most 12v leads use 12 gage wire

17

depth sounder

20

6 gage

fuse

6 gage

21   common ground

9

10

11

12v 120 amp lead/acid battery

voltmeter   insulated battery case

12

The captive boat wiring system is practical for many powerboats and sailboats.

Owners may be able to install their own wiring system with sufficient study and tools. Take ample time to make a quality wiring job for endless uses.

Powerboating Illustrated

bright, smooth, silvery, edges feathered	dull and lumpy
strong physical, electrical connection	high resistance, low conductivity

Soldering information taught thru apprenticeship, is difficult to find. Solder a few connections on a piece of wood as an insulator in ideal conditions before attempting it on a boat, often in awkward locations.

Flux. Solder wire has a soft tube or hollow core filled with flux to remove and absorb oxides from metals to be joined. Solder adds a binding to make the wire joint stronger physically and electrically. The lower solder surface tension will spread and penetrate more easily while without the flux, hot molten solder rolls off the wire.

Use **rosin flux** for electrical connections. The stronger 60% tin/ 40% lead content, mixes together at a lower temperature than tin or lead. *Acid flux* is used only for nonelectrical connections.... which are corrosive to electrical copper wire joints.

Wire stripping. While some people prefer the simple cutter/stripper, the stripper/cutter/crimper serves more purposes. Since it corrodes easily around salt water dulling the cutting surfaces... clean often with demineralized steam iron water, spray with *WD-40* which we prefer, or dry, and add an oil coating. ®

336

Western Union splice below. Strip two to three inches of insulation off both wire ends to be joined; less splice length is required for smaller diameter wires. Cross bare wire ends shown using pliers to twist 5 to 8 turns for a strong mechanical link. Scrape wire surfaces with a knife as solder won't stick to dirty surfaces. One of the worst problems to a good solder joint is *body oil from your fingertips.*

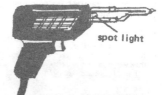

Remove oxid coating from used soldering tip by sanding or grinding until copper has a shiny surface.

Tinning. Plug in heat, give tip a thin solder coating to speed heat transfer, also reducing pitting and corrosive oxides.

Heat until solder just melts. Wipe excess if tip overheats with coating turning black. Joint needs to be retinned.

spot light

Solder gun— 100 to 400 watts. It heats and cools rapidly, tips last a long time, are easy to replace. Tips can be bent to reach awkward areas. Gun is ready to operate in 10 seconds with 100 amps at 3 volt surge from primary coil when trigger is pulled. Trigger actuates a spot light for area you are working on.

Warm the wire not the solder. Apply flat side of tip to wire strands or joint to provide enough heat to melt the solder.

Slowly turn joint on wood surface so solder will flow into and over the strands. Successful soldering requires just enough heat to melt the solder. Too much heat makes a bad connection with high resistance and low conductivity. If the connection is too hot, solder balls up as it won't spread.

Slide tip away for a smooth soldered joint after the rosin is boiled out... before releasing trigger. *If tip becomes cold or is pulled away rapidly,* a poor connection may result with a dull, lumpy, rough surface.

Unsolder. Use the hot solder tip to melt the solder. Separate the copper wires, resolder with new solder.

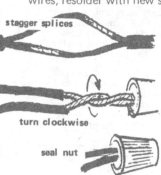

stagger splices

turn clockwise

seal nut

Splice double leads **staggering splices** far enough apart to eliminate overlap with shorting potentials.

Tape splices separately, then together... or use *heat shrink tubing* which can make a smooth, tight cover with a cigarette lighter.

Wire nuts are commonly used with home wiring. Twist leads in clockwise spiral, put into nut, then **337** continue to screw in same direction. If tension isn't involved, wire nuts can be filled with hot glue, while silicone sealant will seal out ocean corrosive hygroscopic salts.

Crimp nuts. Twist same way, add sealant, then squeeze nut with a crimping tool.

Screw terminal wire end. Turn the bare wire in a tight right hand direction tight enough so it won't extend beyond screw head... then solder. If wire end is soldered when straight, it may be too stiff, with a poor fit around screw terminal.

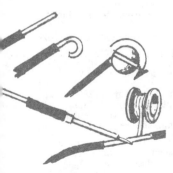

Provide ample time for your first soldering adventure!

Soldering pencil— 20 to 40 watts. If it had been used, use sandpaper to remove oxide from copper tip until shiny, then tin area.

Pencil iron may require ten minutes to warm sufficiently for larger wire sizes used for lighting in boats, homes, and shop.

Electronic components— a minute or two warming may be sufficient with wires of smaller diameter.

Many boating hazards begin quietly with battery problems.

It was a lazy summer afternoon with a lifeguard boat two weeks old drifting outside the huge breaker line. When the breakers were too close, it was time to start the engine and move farther out... but the engine wouldn't start. A nearby rescue boat responded to the call for help. It was a hazardous rescue with both boats inside the huge breaker line.

Dull battery posts were the culprit with a thin lead/oxide insulation coating, the battery was fully charged. Use the **wire brush terminal cleaner** so posts and connectors are always shiny and clean.

for connectors

3.7% of the lead-acid storage battery production goes to the marine field with the choice of maintenance free... or deep-cycle batteries.

● **Cranking power.** Maintenance-free batteries were introduced in the early 1970's rated in *Cold-Cranking Amps (CCA)* to start auto engines. They had a long shelf life, and the lead-calcium grids reduced terminal corrosion. They were not designed for a deep discharge. If you forgot to turn off your auto lights, the ability to regain a full charge seemed questionable.

● **High Cycle.** This is a new catagory for lead-calcium maintenance-free batteries. They have a CCA rating for police, taxi, and RV use having frequent discharge and recharge cycles..."where electrical loads occasionally exceed charging system capability, or where long periods of engine idle are common". They have come a long way in the last decade!

● **Deep-cycle batteries** are rated with a *20 amp-hour capacity.* "They provide a service where deep-discharge is common for which auto and truck batteries aren't intended", such as larger powerboats and sailboats plus golf carts. They have thicker, denser, and more active materials for starting AND lighting using lead-antimony plate grids. We emphasize the deep-cycle battery technology with its little reported complexity.

338

positive   insulator   negative

(orange)   (grey)

lead peroxide   separator   sponge / lead

DISSIMILAR METALS

container   ammeter   voltmeter

An AMMETER is used in series while a VOLTMETER is used in parallel.

30% acid, 70% water
Electrolyte solution is made of:

LIQUID and CONDUCTOR

36.8% sulfuric acid by weight for 1.280, or 34.4% for 1.260 reading, the rest being distilled water.

electrolyte

We begin the basics with a miniature 2 volt outboard motor operating on a one cell lead-acid battery.

● **Positive plate meshes** on an electrically conducting grid framework are filled with active lead peroxide paste. The color ranges from orange to dark brown.

● **Negative plate meshes** grid framework are gray in color. They are filled with a porous mass of lead in a spongy form.

● **Thin insulating separators** are inserted between the plates with ribs facing the positive plates to improve circulation and flow within the cell.

The two plates with different EMF ratings are placed in a container and immersed in an electrolyte.

The battery electrolyte is a conductive solution that carries a current from one metal to the other until the current ceases.

The electrolyte flow is then reversed by a charging current, while the corrosion electrolyte flow is one direction, page 359.

lead-antimony battery grids

● Charging—the magneto,alternator,or generator is supplying more current than required to operate the engine and boat electrical equipment.

A chemical change *electrolysis,*takes place when a current passes thru an electrolyte with arrows showing the directional flow of the charging current, using the *Franklin Theory,*page 308.

● Discharging—the motor is idling while trolling requiring more current to operate than the generator supplies. The current flow direction is reversed as the battery discharges.

The acid solution is weakening as the water percentage increases...as the sulfate combines with the active materials on the + and − plates.

The lead peroxide on the + plate is changing to lead sulfate...while the spongy lead on the − plate is changing to lead sulfate.

● Discharged—after excess idling,stopping, and starting,the battery is discharged. While the battery is classed as *dead* in a boat or auto...it can't supply enough current to start the engine though carrying a 60% to 80% charge.

The acid solution is very weak.Both positive and negative battery plates are coated with *lead sulfate called sulfation.* As EMF differences cease,the chemical action also ceases.

● *The SULFATION coating must be broken away from the plates by FORCE-FEEDING a stronger charging current.*

The sulfate is broken away from the lead sulfate on both plates so it can combine with the hydrogen in the water to again build up the acid specific gravity to 1.280 or 1.260.

The oxygen goes to the + plate to form lead peroxide,while the − plate changes to spongy lead after the lead sulfate has been removed.

The electrical charger continues force-feeding current thru the battery until all sulfation or lead sulfate disappears.

batteries

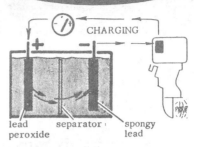

CHARGING

lead peroxide   separator   spongy lead

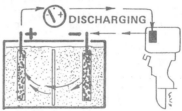

DISCHARGING

Acid percentage is decreasing, sulfation percentage is increasing.

339

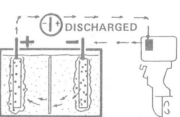

DISCHARGED

Plates are covered with SULFATION, a white lead sulfate powder.

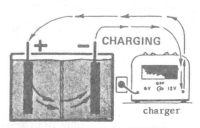

CHARGING

charger

Eliminating sulfation by FORCED-FEEDING with a battery charger.

- The ELEMENT is made of a positive plate group welded to a post strap...and a negative plate group welded to a post strap.

  They are assembled with separators between the grooved faces of separators next to the positive plates to improve efficiency.

  When the plate groups and separators are assembled, it becomes an element.

- Voltage is basic as a fully-charged one-cell battery can only produce a little over 2.2 volts regardless the size.

  The **6 volt 3 cell battery** was standard for auto use to the 1950's. It was then replaced with the 6-cell 12 volt battery with more cranking power.

- **SAE BATTERY CAPACITY RATINGS**

  We bought a maintenance-free battery, a DELCO 70-60S for our 1979 Pontiac. Displayed on the top are—525 CCA, and 260 load test amps.

- **DELCO 70-60S** is the catalog number while 70 is a BCI (Battery Council International) group size battery.

- **525 CCA**--is 525 Cold-Cranking Amps. It specifies the number of amps available a new, fully-charged battery will deliver for 30 seconds of engine cranking corrected to 0°F for a 12 volt battery maintaining a minimum of 7.2 volts.

  The SAE CCA battery starting power rating replaces the former high-rate discharge voltage, and ampere hour rating.

- **260 load test amps is a Reserve Capacity Rating** is listed as 80 Reserve Minutes in the DELCO catalog.

  This is the number of minutes a new fully-charged battery at 80°F can be discharged at a constant current of 25 amps while maintaining a terminal voltage of 10.5 volts. It represents the electrical load which must be supplied in an engine-off operation or charging-system failure.

  The RC Rating on High-Cycle batteries is an approximation of continuous operating time between recharges.

- **100 AH (ampere-hour) battery,** the older rate, would be 12.5 amps for 8 hours, or 5 amps for a 20 hour discharge rate before voltage drops below usable 10.5v level. This capacity is more for lighting and other equipment than cranking a heavy engine.

Plates and separators must be porous and thin to allow free flow of current thru plates in starting battery cells.

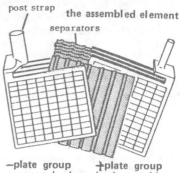

post strap   the assembled element

separators

−plate group   ╋plate group
spongy lead   *lead peroxide*

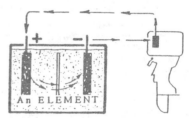

An ELEMENT

One cell 2 volt
lead-acid storage battery.

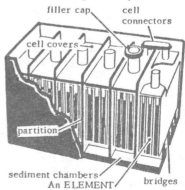

filler cap   cell connectors

cell covers

partition

sediment chambers
An ELEMENT   bridges

Six cell 12 volt
lead-acid storage battery.

Send for excellent **Delco Battery** catalog 7A-98—DELCO REMY, Box 2439, Anderson, IN 46018-9986

340

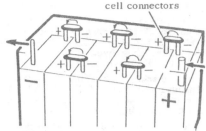

When the cells are assembled in the battery case—the positive plate groups of one cell are welded to the negative plate groups of its adjoining cell in series *using connectors or straps.*

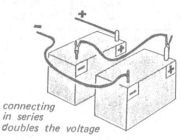

*connecting
in series
doubles the voltage*

Connecting batteries **in parallel** will double the amperage.This is the method used to start an engine with a weak or low battery.

Connecting batteries **in series** will double the voltage.If a full discharge 12v battery is needed but not locally available,*two 6v golf cart batteries* connected in series will be excellent.

Our battery is dead, can you help us?

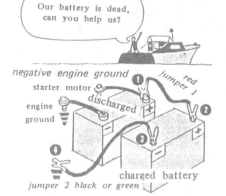

negative engine ground
starter motor
engine ground
discharged
red jumper 1
charged battery
jumper 2 black or green

341

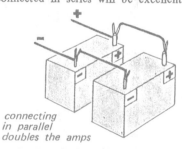

*connecting
in parallel
doubles the amps*

Passengers on a new 34' powerboat at Catalina frantically waved to us passing by on *Jewel.*We changed course to tie alongside their anchored boat,"Our bait tank drained our batteries,can you help us?"

First question—"Are they 6 volt or 12 volt batteries?"
The second—"Does the engine have a negative or positive ground?"

Disconnect the battery terminals on your outboard boat and loan them the battery...if you have a large powerboat or sailboat,**turn off the master switch** to protect the CDI diodes and rectifiers.

● **Connect batteries in parallel,negative ground.**Hook up the jumpers in the sequence shown with clamp ❹ attached to a solid metal part on the engine away from moving parts *and 18" from the discharged battery.*After the engine starts and is operating,remove the jumper cable clamps *by reversing the sequence exactly as shown above.*

If the negative jumper clamp instead goes to the − terminal of the discharged battery,a spark may occur when disconnecting the jumpers igniting the battery hydrogen and oxygen gasses—**leave caps on!**

● **Positive battery ground.**Hook the positive instead of the negative jumper cable to ground.The positive ground is used successfully on many autos while few boats use a positive ground,see pgs. 323, 326.

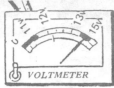

VOLTMETER

The battery has a full charge.

Sulfuric acid is 1.835 times as heavy as water.

hydrometer or dip stick —

float —

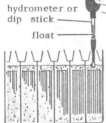

- A **voltmeter** is used on larger power and sailboats to show the condition of fully charged 1.260 and 1.280 batteries at 13.5 to 13.7 volts. The smaller outboard boat is limited to a **hydrometer** to check the health of a lead-acid storage battery.

- **Plate groups** of a lead-acid battery must be covered while charging. Distilled water is added AFTERWARDS so the electrolyte is 3/16" above the plates replacing water vaporized during gassing, page 350.

If water is needed but not added, acid concentration increases to reduce battery lifespan. When the plates become exposed and an internal spark occurs it can cause a battery explosion, page 352.

- A **hydrometer** measures the weight or specific gravity of acid concentration in an electrolyte with water having the value of 1...it continues at right.

Automotive **starting batteries** have a 'twelve eighty' reading for maximum torque to crank starter motors. **Larger deep cycle batteries** have the same quantity of sulfuric acid with an extra water reservoir capacity above the plates with a 'twelve sixty' reading.

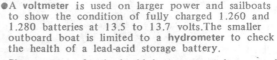

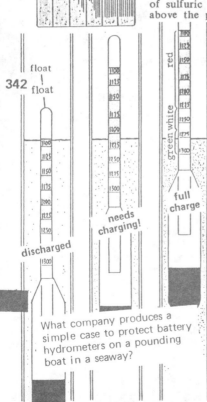

342

float | float

discharged

needs charging!

— weight

What company produces a simple case to protect battery hydrometers on a pounding boat in a seaway?

red | green white

full charge

lead-antimony battery grids

• charge state—	1.280	1.260	1.225
fully charged	1.280	1.260	1.225
75% charged	1.230	1.220	1.180
50% charged	1.180	1.170	1.135
25% charged	1.130	1.120	1.090
discharged	1.080	1.070	1.045

lead-calcium battery grids

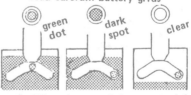

green dot   dark spot   clear

over 65%   *charge needed*   *water needed*

Built-in indicator shows state of charge and electrolyte level of maintenance-free battery.

The green ball floats to the top of the rod where it is visible in the round window on the battery top indicating it has a 65% or more charge.

The ball sinks causing the window to become dark. It indicates the battery has enough fluid...but requires a charge.

When the window is clear...water must be added or battery discarded.

Full charge? Check with voltmeter, the reading should be 13.5 or more volts.

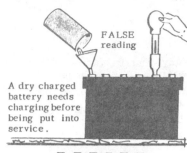

FALSE reading

A dry charged battery needs charging before being put into service.

An idle battery slowly discharges itself, and the rate will be rapidly increased if placed on concrete... store on wood which will be an insulator.

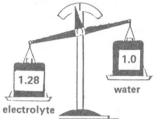

1.28 electrolyte

1.0 water

The electrolyte specific gravity of a fully charged battery is 'twelve eighty', or 1.28 times as heavy as an equal volume of water.

temp. 100°

lead-antimony battery grids

The hydrometer float temperature is calibrated to only be accurate if the temperature is 80 degrees f.

When the electrolyte is warmer—it produces a **lower reading** as the expanding acid volume isn't as dense.

When the electrolyte is cooler—it produces a **higher reading** as the shrinking acid volume is denser.

Many boat batteries with a 3 year life potential may be dead in a year due to mishandling and/or neglect.

● **Dry-charged batteries** are shipped with dry porous separators, and charged plates delivering 75% of capacity at time of manufacture, then dried. Both battery and electrolyte should be from 60-90°f. when adding electrolyte and charged to reach capacity.

Dry-charged batteries in the dry state must be stored in a dry atmosphere with the vent plugs sealed to maintain dry-charged capacity during storage. The seals must be removed when the battery is put into service.

● **Take a hydrometer reading** before you buy a lead-antimony battery. Due to the nature, it will be discharging when sitting idle in a charged condition with a new, discharged lead-antimony battery a rather poor investment.

● **sun belt/snow belt regions—**

● **The self-discharge rate of a lead-acid battery increases as the temperature increases.** A fully-charged battery at—

343

60°f.—may lose 15 points of specific gravity in 30 days.

80°f.—may lose 30 points of specific gravity in 30 days.

100°f.— may lose 60 points of specific gravity in 30 days.

A fully-exposed, fully-charged 1.280 battery at Lake Mead, Nevada in the 100°f. summer may easily drop to 1.220 or less in a month of inactivity.

● **tropical heat variables**

The definition is a climate where water never freezes... having a 1.225 specific gravity with a milder strength acid. It is less deteriorating for batteries operating at high temperatures.

● **If the temperature decreases—**

80°f.—a hydrometer reading is 1.270 being close to 100% capacity. Due to viscosity though having a 1.270 reading—

32°f.—capacity is down to 65%.

20°f.—hydrometer registers 1.270, is corrected to 1.246, dropping to 40% of capacity.

The dependable lead-acid storage battery friend has served us well on the ocean for over 30 years in all kinds ot vessels.Know him thoroughly to help him become and stay your friend,also that of your customers...**as he becomes an overpowering enemy when ignored.**

> *Information for charging outboard motor, and outdrive 12 v battery variables has been moved to the corrosion chapter pages 368, 369. Study closely to avoid electrolysis damage in ocean water AND fresh water.*

●**Sealed,solid-state circuitry** has made more of a contribution to boating than most people realize.Mechanical chargers were used in the 1950's which were excellent for a protected garage.Failure was rapid and unpredictable on a boat when they were exposed to hygroscopic salts and the pounding action when underway.

My worst battery experience recorded on page 22 was in an upper force 6 storm on *Jewel* with a 60 hp no-neutral motor.We bailed with everything but our toes to keep bilge water from reaching the battery terminals to avoid shorting out the battery.This was later disproved as the terminals of a 12 volt lead-acid battery are far enough apart to minimize chance of shorting out.

Mount a **master switch panel**,page 334, high as possible on larger cabin powerboats to help in an emergency situation to summon help as a low mounted panel with leads close together can rapidly short out with water coming aboard.

●**Electrolyte temperature is the secret to charging small,medium,and**
344 **large lead-acid storage batteries.**An auto battery can be put on a high or fast charger for a few minutes without damage if the electrolyte temperature stays below 110 degrees.

●**The 4-amp solid-state battery charger** is excellent for SLI auto starting batteries.It should take an auto battery to full charge for 12 hours or overnight, then tapering off with electrolyte staying in a safe range.

●**The 6-amp battery charger will recharge a battery 33% faster than a 4-amp charger** with the electrolyte temperature too close to,or exceeding the limit to cause buckling and internal plate damage... for many automotive starting batteries.

●**The 6-amp battery charger** is excellent for larger physical side deep-cycle powerboat and sailboat batteries. They have a larger electrolyte reservoir capacity with a 'twelve sixty' reading so the electrolyte will stay well below the 110 degree limit.

Overnight charging is ample for new automotive starting batteries and deep-cycle batteries. While the time period is ample for our 120 amp hour deep-cycle sailboat battery...a longer charge is required after 3 to 4 years of normal operation to bring it back to full capacity.

> **During charging the vent caps must be on,pg. 352, and the plates covered with electrolyte to prevent internal arcing...but don't top off or add distilled water to** *full level until AFTER the battery is fully charged.*Otherwise the electrolyte may overflow in the final gassing plugging vents and threads.As the pressure of the trapped gasses keeps building,an explosion may result to relieve the pressure.

Charge a 1.280 battery when it has a
1.250 reading. Charge immediately with
a 1.220 hydrometer reading as damage
may result in an auto starter battery
if left in this condition for a week.

Battery charging

Hooking charger to battery--

Attach + to + or *RED to RED* clip
lead to battery post, and GREEN to
GREEN. Plug charger into AC current
outlet. Finally.... turn on charger.

After charging-- turn off charger and
remove clips from terminals.

EXPLOSIONS-- if clips are *reversed*,
or connected to battery posts with
AC current on, a spark near battery
vents can ignite hydrogen and oxygen
gasses—VROOOOOOM.

? volt battery
arging rate is
.8 to 15 volts.

GREEN
negative
RED *positive*

Vent cap holes
must NOT be
plugged.

6&12v.   4 AMP

off
6v ⟷ 12v

rubber or wood *insulator*

Built-in Lewco 1220 battery charger is charging a
110 to 120 amp hour deep-cycle 12v battery. It can
charge three batteries separately at different times
with separate switches and fuses.

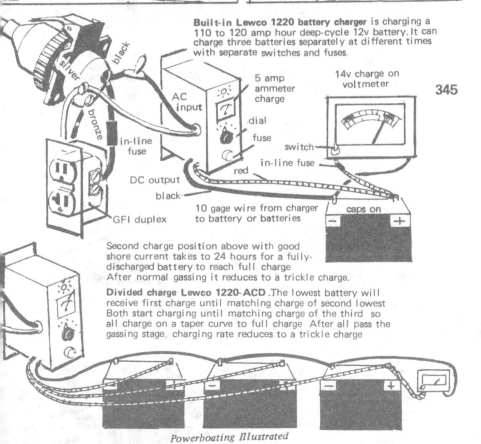

5 amp
ammeter
charge

14v charge on
voltmeter

AC
input

dial

fuse

switch

in-line fuse

in-line
fuse

DC output

red

black

GFI duplex

10 gage wire from charger
to battery or batteries

caps on

−   +

Second charge position above with good
shore current takes to 24 hours for a fully-
discharged battery to reach full charge
After normal gassing it reduces to a trickle charge.

Divided charge Lewco 1220-ACD. The lowest battery will
receive first charge until matching charge of second lowest
Both start charging until matching charge of the third so
all charge on a taper curve to full charge After all pass the
gassing stage, charging rate reduces to a trickle charge

Powerboating Illustrated

The lead-acid storage battery surrounded by endless myths,exists in a unique world of its own.A marine battery has a fascinating complexity requiring eight pages of basic information to help you help your customers choose the right battery...then keep it well maintained.

Batteries are perishable.A person buys one with a certain productive current rate for a limited lifespan whether on the road,in the air,or on the water.Battery life can be terminated early due to neglect and/or mishandling for the reasons listed on this page.To this we also have to add the major boating problem...occasional use.

heat fatigue—
- Overcharging at excessive rates.
- Excess heat from the sun's rays, or too close to a hot engine.

Exposed plates—
- Owner forgetting to add water.
- Spillage or overflow while gassing in last stage of charging.
- Plates are exposed due to over-charging.Warping,buckling,acid concentration buildup,or a spark can cause an internal explosion.

Premature old age—
- Overcharging causing sluffing of active particles at an excessive rate reducing cranking capacity while shorting out the bottom areas of the ─┼─and ── plates.
- Arthritis due to sitting idle with low charge.The hard sulfation insulation stops battery plates from taking...or giving a charge.

Normal old age—
- The active positive particles will gradually sluff off the plates during normal use in a battery predicted lifespan—
- After a lead-acid battery drops to 80% to 85% of cranking capacity due to sluffing,the battery is not able to crank over starter motor.
- Sediment collects in the bottom of the cell chambers.It continually grows until the sluffing is high enough to become a conductor.
- If it shorts out **only one cell** of the positive and negative plate groups,it interferes with both the charging,and retention charge.
- If only one cell shorts out—so does the entire battery.
- **Planing hull pounding accelerates sluffing action.**Locate battery at fulcrum point,pg.**349**,add padding beneath battery box to extend life.

346

I have a terrible fever.

Heat stroke, loss of energy.

Water, water everywhere, but not a drop to drink.

Exposed plates can kill a battery.

Old age home for neglected batteries.

A battery can't holler when it is hurt. You pay for it however when you buy your next battery!

JUNK PILE

A battery is dead for practical purposes when one cell shorts out...or it is no longer able to turn over a starter motor.

● **Cell 1**—normal sediment deposit of a lead-acid battery cell 2/3 thru normal lifespan.Sediment can be drained with battery still used to operate lights and accessories,not able to provide enough cranking surge.

● **Cell 2**—active material sluffing from the positive plates builds up in the sediment chamber of one cell.It shorts out the bottom of the plates interfering with charging,and charge retention of the battery.

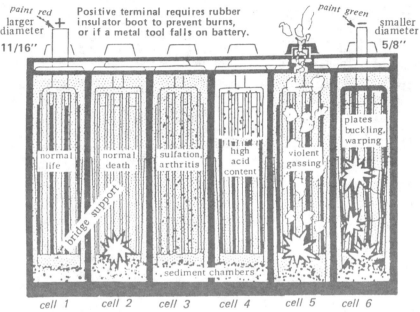

paint red
larger
diameter **+** Positive terminal requires rubber insulator boot to prevent burns, or if a metal tool falls on battery.
11/16″

paint green **−** smaller diameter
5/8″

normal life — bridge support — cell 1

normal death — cell 2

sulfation, arthritis — cell 3

high acid content — cell 4

violent gassing — cell 5

plates buckling, warping — cell 6

sediment chambers

347

● **Cell 3**—sulfation or arthritis has developed in the battery with a low charge for a long time.Sulfation begins as a light powder which if left in this state begins to harden.The longer a battery is left in this condition the more difficult it is to take or give a charge.

● **Cell 4**—extreme sulfation occurs on the exposed areas of the plates above the electrolyte.As the water in .the electrolyte disappears,the acid concentration becomes too high causing resistance with an excessive heat buildup in the remaining electrolyte.

● **Cell 5**—shows an excess charging rate while gassing.The violent gas bubbles dislodge active particles from the positive plates which will reduce the useful lifespan of the battery.

● **Cell 6**—shows premature death by insufficient water and overcharging causing the positive plates to warp and buckle.Damaged areas of the buckling plates rub against,and break thru the separators to short circuit the plates.The crumbling chips from the damaged plates fall to the sediment chamber where they build up and short out the negative and positive plate groups...*farewell cruel world.*

deep-discharge cycling

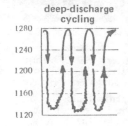

1280
1240
1200
1160
1120

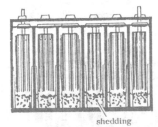

shedding

When a fully charged battery passes 2/3 normal life,the electrolyte and shedding particles can be drained,and new electrolyte added.This will increase the useful life without shedding shorting out the plate bottoms.

348

starting vs deep-cycle batteries

●**Automotive 1.280 starting batteries** use thin, very active porous materials to crank a starter motor with a 40 to 60 amp surge of 3 to 7 seconds.The alternator operating at 13.5 to 15v returns the charge to the battery.

When providing long power periods requiring repeated charging,the active material erodes or falls from the plate grids rapidly destroying the auto battery cranking power ability.

●**Deep-cycle 1.260 batteries** are designed for RV's and boats with long power periods for lights,radios,discharging engines while trolling, with endless discharge and charging cycles.

●**The deep-cycle marine battery** with thicker plates and denser active materials will cost more,but easily outlast many auto batteries designed for starting only,not deep-discharge.

●**Golf cart and industrial batteries** require cycling three times to soften the hard,active positive particles to reach full capacity.

These are deep-cycle batteries fully discharged at the end of the day.An overnight charge takes them up to full capacity the following morning.
●

●**Dumped batteries**—they may be revived after recovery if all liquid is emptied,filled with fresh water,dumped and refilled several times to remove the ocean water.

●**Desalting**—overfill with distilled water and charge at a normal rate.Keep flooding the battery with distilled water until no more *sudsy foam* appears.

After desalting empty the distilled water.Add a weak electrolyte solution,and charge at a slow rate until no change in reading is shown for three successive hours.Empty,then add the electrolyte obtained from automotive stores, mix with required amount of distilled water, and charge the battery.

●**Distilled or pure water** should be added to the lead-antimony battery as tap water in many areas has a high mineral content upsetting the chemical process charging action.While the minerals are good for your health...they can reduce useful battery life.

There are isolated areas across the U.S. with mineral-free water excellent for battery use. If local water quality is unknown and distilled water isn't available...look for drinking water without sediment that is crystal clear,odorless, and tasteless.

Powerboating Illustrated

choose

Λ fulcrum point

Battery location is critical for a long life without being a hazard.

AVOID

Drill a small vent hole to release hydrogen and oxygen gasses so they can be diluted into the atmosphere.

vent

A 4% hydrogen concentration in an enclosed compartment or area becomes explosive.

shock cord

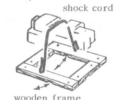

wooden frame

metal case

Avoid metal battery boxes as they may cause a battery short.

SULFURIC ACID is HAZARDOUS!

Sulfuric acid from an exploding/upset battery causes SERIOUS burns!

The plastic insulated battery case is a trailerboat owners best friend to keep a battery clean,and to contain sulfuric fumes combining with condensation to produce a weak electrolyte solution in the bottom of the case.

- **The fulcrum**—is the preferred mounting location for a battery with the least up and down hull movement.The life of a battery mounted near the bow is greatly reduced due to the pounding which sheds an excessive amount of active material.

- **The 12 volt lead-acid battery can become an explosive bomb** which is backed up with USCG Boating Statistic Records.

- **Drill a small vent hole on the top of the battery case** as shown to release and dissipate the lighter than air charging gases.Raw hydrogen and oxygen may otherwise be trapped with a spark from a loose connection causing an explosion.

- An internal explosion can result when the tops of the plates are exposed which produces a spark,see page 352.

- **USCG rules require a positive restraint** to prevent a battery upsetting in a turn, so a battery cannot move more than an inch in any direction.It also contains one in a collision which might fly forward hitting anything in the way...or break to spray battery parts and electrolyte over the passengers and boat.

- **A restraining frame** is needed around the bottom of the plastic case.We prefer a **stout shock cord** over the top of the case which is within the USCG one inch restraint rules in an explosion,page 352.

- **Plastic webbing restraint is questionable** as the ultraviolet rays of the sun react on the material.I've had three webbing restraints crumble in my hands on my sailboat as they reacted to the gassing fumes and condensation inside my boat.

349

Strip completely,take a shower,or jump in the water as THE FIRST MINUTE SAFETY FACTOR IS VERY CRITICAL.

Wash 10-15 minutes with fresh water to remove ALL traces of electrolyte...then seek medical help immediately afterwards.

Neutralize all clothing,boat areas,etc.,with baking SODA and ample fresh water.

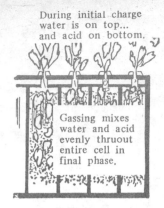

During initial charge
water is on top...
and acid on bottom.

Gassing mixes
water and acid
evenly thruout
entire cell in
final phase.

*Prying connections
with screwdriver or
hammer causes internal
battery damage.*

Clean,and coat with
continuous film Silicone
Grease or Vasoline to
reduce corrosion.

350

post

clamp
connector

baking soda
NOT
baking powder

Corroded terminals
impede current flow,
also causing leakage.

*What would
you do with
a hot ring???*

●Why can't a battery be topped off before it is
charged instead of just covering the plates?

The battery level should be kept low enough
to avoid overflowing during liquid expansion
by gasses liberated in last 20% of charge.

Before gassing in the final part of charging,
heavier parts of sulfuric acid are on the bottom,
with water on the top. Gassing is required to
mix water and acid evenly to provide an even
electrolyte throughout the cells.

●*A battery is fully charged* when all cells are
gassing freely with no hydrometer reading
change for three successive hours. Then after
charger is disconnected, fill all battery cells to
proper level with distilled water, page 348.

●What causes battery terminal deposits ?

To find an answer we checked our five lead
acid batteries, all having different kinds of
deposits caused during gassing *due to less than
perfect sealing around battery terminals.*

Wash terminals with fresh water and baking
soda, but don't let this fluid enter the battery
cells as it will combine with the electrolyte.
Scrub with wire brush to remove all traces of
deposits and baking soda. Any particles left will
form conductor trails between battery terminals
to increase self discharge rate of battery.

●*The insulator*—add light silicone grease or
Vasoline to clean battery terminals to reduce
current leakage...*then* store *and keep a battery
clean in a well vented fiberglass battery case.*

●Remove NEGATIVE battery clamp first...
only after removing wrist watches and rings.

A lifeguard was removing the positive battery
terminal clamp first on his jeep battery, when
the wrench accidentally touched engine metal.
A completed circuit drained the battery current
thru the wrench to the ring on his finger which
glowed brightly...producing severe burns.

When the negative battery clamp is removed
first, and the wrench accidentally touches the
engine or frame, the circuit isn't completed...
eliminating current going thru your body to
ground. When installing terminals **add positive
clamp first** as circuit isn't completed...THEN
add negative battery clamp.

Both are lead-acid batteries.

plates
bridge

plates

lead-antimony grids   lead-calcium grids

sediment chamber shedding

The maintenance-free,no-fuss, no-fill battery. The goal was to produce *auto starting batteries* without adding water for 5 years that would not lose charge when idle.This was a major challenge with steadily rising underhood temperatures plus smog equipment.

● **Lead-antimony battery grids** used an antimony alloy as a stiffener as the lead grids would otherwise be flexible as wet noodles.

Antimony caused problems leaching out to deposit on the negative plates during charging,lowering the voltage while increasing the charging current. This caused gassing by breaking the electrolyte into hydrogen and oxygen speeding water loss corroding battery posts and clamps.

Antimony in the battery grids was 11% in the 1930's, down to 7% by 1947. The antimony alloy was 4.5% in the 1960's, dropping to 2.5% in the 1970's with batteries losing water at a much slower rate for charging and normal operation. The reduced antimony content reduced terminal and clamp corrosion plus increasing battery life.

Lead-antimony grids are supported by *bridges* upon which the plate elements rest,with sediment chambers beneath.Flaking from the lead-peroxide positive plates gradually falls off during charging going to the sediment chambers.The particles keep collecting so by the time the cells are spent,the flakes are almost high enough to short out the bottom of the plates...though they can be drained,see page 347.

351

● **Lead-calcium grids for maintenance-free batteries.** Designers wanted to eliminate ALL antimony. Lead-calcium grids used for 50 years as telephone exchange standby use seemed to have the potentials.

Lead-calcium grids proved difficult to adapt to high-volume production for autos with plates only 28% as thick,now having to resist vibration.

The plates are sealed in plastic microporus envelopes to prevent shorting, by holding falling flakes,eliminating separators and sediment chambers.

● **As the plates are lower in the case** the electrolyte volume above the plates can provide 5 years of starting auto engines. The factory filled electrolyte with correct volume and strength cannot be contaminated. A major advantage--*self-discharge is eliminated when not in use* having a long shelf life.Battery terminal corrosion which was so common with lead-antimony batteries a few years ago has been almost eliminated.A disadvantage haunting the new auto battery in the early years.if the battery was drained by forgetting to turn off the lights.   it seemed to have less ability to regain a full charge.

● **Gelled electrolyte batteries.** After slow technology advances going back to 1950, the sealed, immobilized *gelled- electrolyte maintenance-free batteries* quietly entered the critical marine market. These batteries have airworthiness testing since 1978 with the super-sonic *Concorde* to USN and other fighter aircraft.

The sealed gel construction eliminates hydrogen and oxygen gasses, sloshing acid, and corroding terminals. If properly supported, it can be mounted on its side for normal operation. It can operate upside down, also totally submerged in water.

For 30 years we've faced a controversy whether to charge a battery with the caps on or off. If the caps are removed a spark can go into the cells igniting hydrogen and oxygen gasses. *Leave the caps on as—*

Battery caps are one-way flame arrestors. Cap threads should be clean and vent holes unplugged. Charge at normal rate with plates covered but not topped off. If either or both are ignored, expanding electrolyte overflows plugging cap vents and threads building internal pressure.

●A charging battery produces explosive hydrogen and oxygen gasses. They are easy to ignite if an open flame is near from a match, cigarette, or sparks from an electric drill motor.

If the battery caps are removed while charging— an open flame can go into the cells. This will ignite concentrated hydrogen and oxygen gasses expanding many diameters for a huge explosion.

●The vent caps become one-way valves while charging as hydrogen and oxygen gasses come out the pin hole on the top of the battery cap. If the gasses are accidentally ignited, the flame should stop at the vent cap hole as it becomes a one--way valve due to greater internal cell pressure.

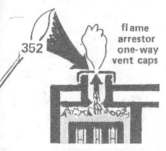

flame
arrestor
one-way
vent caps

*For a parallel—*when you light the gas on top of a stove in your kitchen, pressure of the gas coming out of the pipe thru a small hole, also makes it a one-way valve. The flame stays at this stove jet acting as a flame arrestor instead of backing thru the pipe to explode the gas plant stowage tank.

The **battery case pinhole vent** is of major importance, pg. 349, to release charging gasses. The pin hole in the cap, see left should be open, yet if plugged, gasses may leak out cap threads.

●**USCG records include many battery explosions.** We avoided adding water to an outboard battery for eight months to see what would happen. It exploded when starting our motor, with a possible spark arcing across the top of exposed plates. The battery case top lifted sufficiently releasing the pressure, restrained by a stout shock cord, with electrolyte and parts contained in the case. **When exposed to battery electrolyte— strip at once, washing ALL electrolyte from your skin within that FIRST minute.**

●**The electrical auto future?** Considerable advances have been made with solar panels, the problem— *battery storage.* The inexpensive lead-acid battery is our standard, though better batteries appeared 30 years ago.

Nickel-iron batteries store 30% more energy. Nickel-cadmium batteries are almost ready, but cadmium makes them too expensive. A 700 degree molten salt battery has good potentials, with problems. Others being tested with more promise, are 10 to 20 years away. The auto battery has come a long way... but is another, better answer required?

Read— *Is the Hydrogen Car in Our Future,* by Dr. Roger Billings, The American Academy of Science, Independence, Missouri.

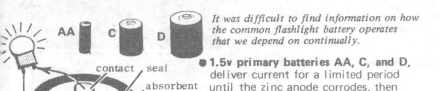

It was difficult to find information on how the common flashlight battery operates that we depend on continually.

contact
seal
absorbent liner
carbon rod collector
positive chemicals
electrolyte paste
zinc container

replace!

● **1.5v primary batteries AA, C, and D,** deliver current for a limited period until the zinc anode corrodes, then the current ceases.

Though all three have same voltage, larger capacity C and D with lower internal resistance maintain current flow for a longer period.

● **These aren't dry-cell batteries,** but nonspillable sealed wet cells, with a heavy liquid paste so that they are able to operate in any position.

● **One-discharge carbon/zinc 1.5v battery** converts chemical energy into electrical energy, in an insulated steel case separating ＋ top cathode contact from sacrificial − zinc anode case. Current flows from top ＋ contact thru bulb, then returns to bottom of the steel-coated zinc case *a one-way, nonreversible process.*

Current flows by chemical action up thru negative electrolyte paste, to positive particles packed around the porous carbon collector rod. Current continues up and out top ＋ contact point thru the bulb.

353

● **Insulated container** separating chemicals from interaction, is eventually corroded by the inner zinc. Pin holes develop for corrosive electrolyte chemicals to leak out.

● **One-discharge 1.5v alkaline batteries.** While more expensive, we prefer them in various sizes with up to ten times the operational life. Not only do they provide economical savings, their longer life reduces corrosion damage potentials to 1/10th of the carbon/zinc 1.5v batteries.

● **6v alkaline and carbon/zinc batteries** follow similar one-way patterns before corroding. **9v electronic batteries** protect equipment without seeming to have leaking corrosive chemicals after discharge.

● **Recharging nickel-cadmium (Ni-Cad) batteries.** Their advantage is their continuous **1.25v** delivery until sudden death, then it is time to recharge.

● **These batteries have a normal year life cycle.** Use the tester shown to eliminate your dying batteries. Test all new batteries before buying to avoid those on the shelf too long that are new, and almost dead. When these batteries aren't being used for a week or longer, remove and store in a refrigerator for longer life, or in a clean, dry, cool, insulated case away from sunlight and salt spray.

● **Baggies?** Separate your batteries in storage. A barrier is needed to contain electrolyte chemicals from a corroding dry cell battery that would otherwise leave a mess, damaging nearby batteries.

Current restrictions— Federal law prohibits the use of bottom paint containing TBT on vessels less than 82 feet (or 25 meters) long, *except for aluminum hulls and aluminum outdrives and outboard motors* as of March 1, 1990.

Only certified applicators will be able to purchase and apply these paints except 16 oz. spray containers registered for use on aluminum motors or lower drive units of vessels, which may be used by non-certified persons.

Page 8 describes the new outboard motor that wouldn't fit our engine compartment. We started a search for the long-shaft Mercury little changed in 17 years. We stumbled over one as a dealer was walking with me thru his boatyard. It was a 1976 model lost in a warehouse for several years. After 20 hours operation it was sold to the dealer. It disappeared in inventory until we tripped over the new? 76 model.

My mechanic changed plugs, lubed it, added lots of WD-40® and it fired happily for 3 months. It quit, the carb full of water, traced to the service station where I bought the gasoline. As it can't be tilted out of the water it needed TBT bottom paint... no longer available.

As dealers and mechanics had no idea of the new law, we called the USCG 800 number with the pamphlet arriving two days later delivering copies to local mechanics.

354

TBT pesticide regulation? The reason was high pesticide content in marinas wanting us to only use copper-bottom paints, except for boats and lower units of aluminum. What is puzzling, that any vessel over 82' can use TBT made of glass or wood when copper-bottom paints are still excellent? What insider has a 82' powerboat?

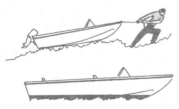

Copper bottom paint?????

We've seen more than our share of outboard motor lower units painted with copper bottom paint. For results, turn to page 372.

Don't pull aluminum boat across a rocky or gravel beach as it scrapes off the protective oxide coating, exposing bare aluminum.

Aluminum hulls, outboard motor lower units— *copper-bottom paints rapidly corrode aluminum!*

Aluminum boat, salt water use. Bottom must be clean. Apply etch solution for aluminum, use stiff brush to work it into corners & pores. Etch recommended time, flush surfaces with fresh water, dry with clean cloth.

Brush on three *zinc chromate coats—* don t sand between coats.

Machine shake TBT bottom paint soon before using to mix heavy particles evenly!

Use roller to add TBT bottom paint so it will have an even thickness for protection.

surface damage   major damage   total damage

● *Corrosion is your lifetime enemy with endless faces.* After 35 years
studying its various forms on outboard boats, inboard boats, and sailboats,
corrosion still has surprises. The first corrosion experts we contacted
had formulas...with little of practical use.

I began making the rounds of marine mechanics picking up ideas and
problems one place, then exchanging these ideas with other mechanics
who provided answers, and new problems with vague patterns developing.
When exchanging ideas with chemical engineers, one with a powerboat
background and the other sailing, I found my corrosion experts...a good
idea for you to consider when unusual problems develop.

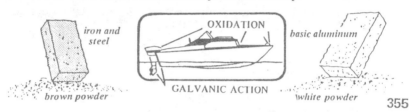

iron and steel

OXIDATION

basic aluminum

brown powder   GALVANIC ACTION   white powder

355

● We start with *the reaction or resultant* of the two most common forms
of corrosion facing marine mechanics...which is **oxidation** above the
water, and **galvanic action**, below the water. While the methods are
considerably different, the resultant is the same—to hasten your metals
involved to return to more stable chemical forms that are no longer
of practical use to you.

● **Steel** — is iron mixed with up to 2% carbon hardening to form the alloy
steel, which is excellent for tools. If more carbon is added it becomes
cast iron or pig iron. The cast iron is a pushover for ocean hygroscopic
salts pg. 364, *if not protected continuously.* A brown oxide surface
powder develops with brown stains as the oxide particles flake off. The
part becomes weaker as the process continues, see above, until it fails.

● **Stainless steel** — with nickel and chromium added, is highly corrosion
resistant in the ocean air. Stainless steel *galvanic corrosion* can be rapid
for underwater props struts, shafts, etc., for slip-berthed powerboats .

● **Aluminum** — is the 3rd largest element in the world. We begin with a
warning to **AVOID surplus aircraft aluminum parts**, bolts, nuts, etc.,
as they rapidly self destruct in ocean use for which they aren't designed
unless you have a good knowledge of the various grades of aluminum.

● *Oxygen is the enemy AND friend of aluminum.* The surface of a sailboat
untreated aluminum mast corrodes rapidly with a **white rust** leaving a
dark gray stain on a sail rubbing against the mast. The best way to protect
an aluminum mast is to corrode it electrochemically called **anodizing**
with many kinds, as the better ones will become more expensive.

Powerboating Illustrated

Seagoing metals—birth...life...death

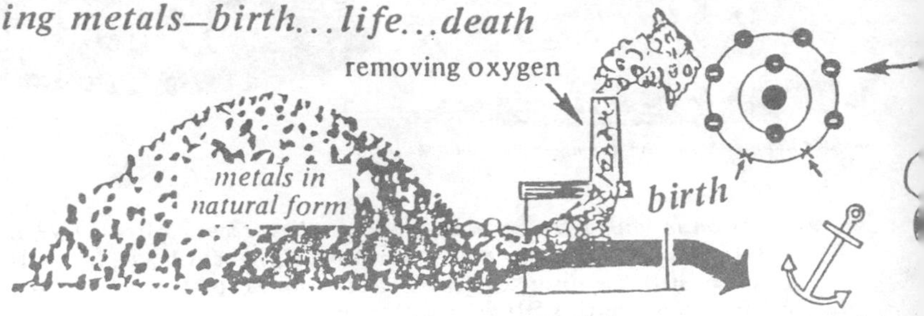

removing oxygen

metals in natural form

birth

stable chemical compounds   refining   useful re

HEMATITE (red iron-oxide ore) ...becomes pig iron...changes to iro

BAUXITE is refined to Alumina (aluminum oxide)..to become alumin

● **The full cycle**—after considerable corrosion research without finding basic patterns,I finally realized I had been looking at *the reaction* side of the problem only.It caused us to reverse our thinking to find *the action* side of the story...with the full cycle shown above.

――――― *Birth,life,and destruction of seagoing metals* ―――――

Most seagoing metals exist temporarily in their refined condition. They begin as stable compounds of nature.The oxygen is removed or "cooked out" at the refinery so the raw metals can be refined into alloys or compounds **in a temporary form for seagoing use.**

356

The red ore **hematite** is refined to iron after the oxygen is removed.It becomes a *mild steel* when 0.2% to under 2% carbon is added to become our workhorse for tools and structural supports.If more carbon is added, the iron becomes hard and brittle for cast iron engine blocks.

There are endless kinds of stainless steel made specifically for engine use.When 18% chrome and 8% nickel are added to iron,302 and 304 stainless alloys are produced for sailboat rigging with minimum stretch, maximum strength,flexibility,and fatigue resistance.*The tiny rust spots on stainless rigging comes from a small carbon content.*

Your responsibility is to know and choose stable metal compounds or alloys for specific uses. Then use the best corrosion prevention methods *to extend their useful life before they return to more stable oxides which are no longer of use to us.*

Study the full range of corrosion forms so you can recognize corrosion in the early stages for your customers so it can be stopped,or at least slowed down to an acceptable rate.

● **The ocean operator** faces a relentless 24 hour a day attack on his underwater metals especially in warm weather,and to the hygroscopic salts above the water on his boat,car,exposed plumbing,TV antenna,etc.

● **If you only operate on fresh water**—you may be surprised.The worst corrosion in our outboard research was with *Jewel* in Nevada on Lake Mead behind Hoover Dam.We were alongside a metal boat with a charging generator for 3 nights.Our lower unit not raised out of the water...tried to electroplate the side of the 26' steel powerboat.

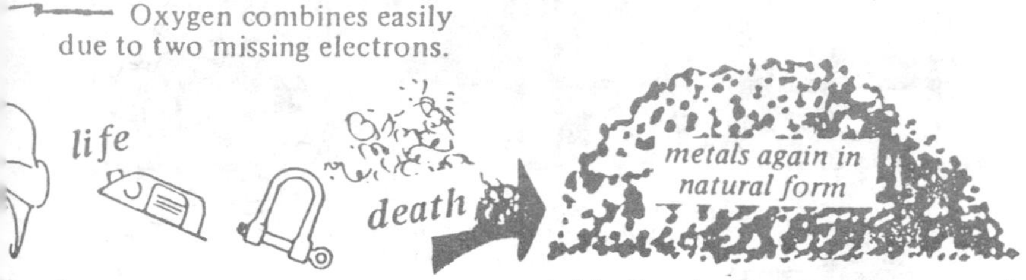

Oxygen combines easily
due to two missing electrons.

life

death

*metals again in
natural form*

...ined metal products

stable chemical oxides & compounds

...steel compounds & alloys...corrodes to a brown powder (iron oxide)

...m compounds and alloys...corrodes to a white powder (aluminum oxide)

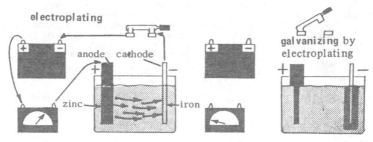

electroplating

anode   cathode

zinc   iron

galvanizing by
electroplating

An **ion** of one metal placed at the *positive anode* is carried thru an
electrolyte solution and deposited on the *negative cathode* terminal.
The amount deposited is directly proportional to the quantity of the
charge carried thru the electrolyte. *The stronger the electrical charge...
the faster will be the plating action.*

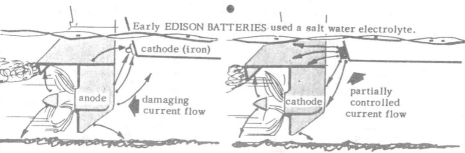

Early EDISON BATTERIES used a salt water electrolyte.

cathode (iron)

anode   damaging
            current flow

partially
controlled
current flow

cathode

In a **salt water electrolyte**—corrosion results when an outward current
flow takes with it flakes or molecules of metal.

Galvanic action or galvanic corrosion is similar to electroplating. with
a current going thru an electrolyte...though *the metal flakes go into
solution* instead of electroplating. The waster metal **zinc** with a higher
EMF rating,protects surrounding metals by being soluable and by
dissolving ...instead of the metals the zinc is protecting.

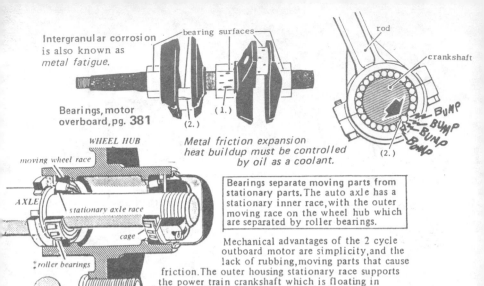

Intergranular corrosion
is also known as
metal fatigue.

bearing surfaces

rod

crankshaft

Bearings, motor
overboard, pg. **381**

(1.)

(2.)

BUMP
BUMP
BUMP
BUMP

(2.)

WHEEL HUB

*Metal friction expansion
heat buildup must be controlled
by oil as a coolant.*

moving wheel race

AXLE

stationary axle race

cage

roller bearings

ball

Bearings separate moving parts from
stationary parts. The auto axle has a
stationary inner race, with the outer
moving race on the wheel hub which
are separated by roller bearings.

Mechanical advantages of the 2 cycle
outboard motor are simplicity, and the
lack of rubbing, moving parts that cause
friction. The outer housing stationary race supports
the power train crankshaft which is floating in
bearings... which is similar to an electric motor.

Do you have to *break in* an electric motor which
has all moving parts floating in bearings?

358

2 cycle spray-thru lubrication requires endless testing to protect drive-
train bearings. It has a *thin, tough, adhesive film* to limit frictional area
contact to reduce heat buildup... with oil a coolant to remove heat
from bearings and races rotating under load. When motors without tach-
ometers operate above top end rpm, frictional heat causes metal expansion.
The thin oil film disappears as the metals expand and rub against
each other beyond capabilities of oil to act as a coolant.

roller

● Almost friction free—the contact areas remaining between stationary and
moving races are small ball tips, or roller edges. These parts are made of
a hard alloy steel for long life, and to minimize contact between races and
bearings under load. The bearings are locked into a cage between the races,
with the cage made of a softer metal; *pages 267-9.*

tapered

● Lifetime is based on load with probably 90% of bearings in normal use
able to turn more than a million revolutions. It is the *small contact areas*
between bearings and races under load and rotation that eventually produce
metal fatigue pitting. Bearing contact areas enlarge and become noisy with
a heat buildup to speed bearing failure.

needle

● Gravity begins when an engine stops with auto weight increasing on
the upper and lower wheel bearing areas. This increases the metal to
metal contact areas, squeezing out the oil film. If your auto or boat
trailer will not be operated for two or more months, use jacks to take
unnecessary weight off wheel bearings to avoid gravity damage.

● A poor grade, or incorrectly mixed 2 cycle oil causes a heat buildup as
the oil can't efficiently bleed off the heat. Contact areas enlarge to speed
heat buildup with metal expansion and metal fatigue underway.

● Submerged outboard motors need emergency care to reach, clean, and
seal bearings and races still in good condition. Oxygen, hygroscopic salts,
and heat otherwise cause these moving parts to expand and rust with a
heat buildup and metal fatigue failure, see page 381 for care sequence.

Underwater electrolyte corrosion flow is a one-way process...while battery electrolyte flow is reversed with a charging current.

the ELECTROLYTE PROCESS

1. dissimilar metals

Galvometer

NO current flow

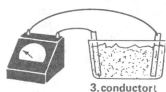

2. liquid (solvent)

NO current flow

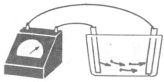

3. conductor

NO current flow

4. electrolyte solution liquid and conductors

CURRENT FLOW

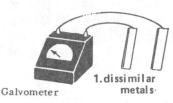

5. battery current

6. heat

Major CURRENT FLOW, major DESTRUCTION

> *Many factors are involved to produce a major, complex boating problem called* **galvanic corrosion.**
>
> **The answer—eliminate one of the factors involved to reduce the destruction rate.**

● An atom corrosion flow will result between two dissimilar metals with different EMF potentials, but many factors are needed to support this flow.

● For our purpose—water is a **liquid** that dissolves acids, bases, and salts to form an electrolyte.

When we use distilled water without salt or minerals, corrosion can't start as the water can't support a current.

● **Conductors or ions such as minerals, salts, alkali, and soda** cannot support a corrosion current flow. *But if you add distilled or tap water you have—*

● An **electrolyte** with a **liquid** (water) and **conductors** (salts, minerals, soda, etc.) *will support an ionic flow or* current. Atoms can then flow from metals having a higher EMF voltage to metals with a lower EMF voltage.

359

● **Electrolysis** occurs when **battery, shoreside, or generator currents** are added to accelerate the corrosion destruction even in fresh water with mineral content, an example, Lake Mead, pg. 326.

> *Consider* galvanic corrosion *with these 6 basic steps. You will soon begin to find the cause...and the solution for most underwater metal problems.*

For a basic example—the corrosion rate with variables is reduced considerably in fresh water due to the smaller volume of conductors (see variables pg. 326).

The use—wash salt water hygroscopic salts, page 364, to greatly reduce the number of salt spray conductors.

Remove one of these basic factors and the galvanic corrosion rate is reduced, especially if it is caused by current leakage electrolysis. If you can remove an additional factor—

The lower a metal element is placed on the *giver end* of the EMF scale, the greater becomes its electrical potential, instability and willingness...such as zinc, to combine with metals on the *taker end* of the scale.

This ion exchange and metal destruction process is speeded with exposure to oxygen, salt spray, heat, and escaping electrical currents.

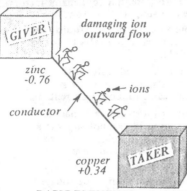

damaging ion outward flow

zinc
-0.76

conductor

← *ions*

copper
+0.34

BASIC ELEMENTS only—
the electromotive series

360

ANODIC end, least stable, least noble		
Magnesium	-1.86 (active)	
Aluminum	-1.70	
Manganese	-1.10	
Zinc	-0.76	
Chromium	-0.557	
Iron	-0.44	
Nickel	-0.23	
Tin	-0.14	
Lead	-0.12 (lazy)	
● Hydrogen	-0.00	
Copper	+0.34	
Silver	+0.80	
Platinum	+0.92	
Chlorine, Gold	+1.36	
Flourine	+2.85	
CATHODIC, noble, or protected end		

givers / losers — *corrosive*

takers / gainers — *protective*

Every boat owner should have a working knowledge of the EMF Series to have a sufficient foundation to begin understanding **element** corrosion potentials.

The next step is to consider the activity of various **alloys** which may be similar... or considerably different in action when compared to the basic elements.

Electricity can be classed as a current flow thru a conductor, pgs. 322-3, or thru an electrolyte, pgs. 339,357, requiring a potential or difference (Franklin vs electron flow) to cause a directional flow, pgs. 308,374.

A primary cause of corrosion is *the potential difference between different metals being subjected to electrolytic action.* The difference of the amount between dissimilar elements is measured in VOLTS according to the EMF Series activity.

EMF current flow is from − to +. The elements on the negative side corrode easily...while those on the positive side such as GOLD remains unaffected by corrosion such as gold bars recovered from shipwrecks hundreds of years later.

The EMF Series listing is only for basic elements. Though pure aluminum on the listing is more active than zinc...a zinc block is used to protect aluminum alloys which become less active and more stable than the pure zinc element block.

We provide a brief discussion on the facing page of the reactions of the various compounds and metal alloys subjected to the salt water corrosive environment. This is just a basic pattern to start with for your analysis, so expect variables, and occasionally, reversals...which may occur if too large a zinc anode is used may speed corrosion of nearby metals.

- Zinc—unstable,corrodes easily,it is an excellent sacrificial metal.
- Aluminum—it has many refined forms.Owners must be on constant guard for corrosion evidence as half of an outboard motor is made of aluminum.*All aluminum surfaces should be covered with a firm, continuous coating* to minimize corrosion potentials.
- Anodized aluminum—it is a thick,hard,aluminum oxide coating put on by electrically corroding the surface.*Corrosion will begin if it is scratched,scraped,or perforated* when aluminum is exposed beneath the anodizing;heavy black anodizing is the excellent exception.
- Wrought iron is thousands of years old,seldom found on recreational boats...while it is used in various alloys such as steel,an iron carbon alloy which is excellent for tools though corrodes rapidly in an ocean environment.
- Galvanizing—a zinc coating over iron or steel is added by dipping the part into a tub of hot molten zinc,by spraying on,or electroplating. The zinc acts as a protector corroding,instead of the metal beneath.
- Stainless steel—there are numerous grades of *low carbon content,*high nickel content steel.Stainless steel is the beautiful protecting metal above the water as it has to breathe *as its chromium ions are programmed to corrode at a programmed rate* above water.Don't tape nor seal off stainless as *oxygen starvation* (crevice corrosion may begin) also look for stress cracks indicating intergranular corrosion with metal failure.DON'T use stainless parts underwater for inboard installations due to crevice corrosion resulting from oxygen starvation.
- Chrome plating—is a thin tough exterior plating,but what does it hide or cover? New chrome plating has fine cracks under a microscope that become increasing larger as the metal beneath will shrink or stretch more than the chrome exterior....with nickel,or nickel/copper buffer zones used between the two as chrome won't adhere to steel.AVOID chrome fittings on powerboats as it can be the master,and you the slave.

361

- Copper— use with caution! Copper fuel lines are easy to bend,and resistant to fatigue or becoming brittle,though *corroding and aging gasoline.* Stable copper parts speed corrosion of nearby metals when combined with numerous more electrically active metal parts.
- Brass—a zinc/copper mixture found in home improvement stores has thousands of varieties ..while marine stores often class many bronze self-protective fittings as brass.AVOID the zinc/copper accidental mixture *because of DEZINCIFICATION in which the zinc flows out, leaving behind a weak salmon pink metallic copper.Even if sealed in a deck,or below in a cabin,the zinc/copper mixture may dezinc due to resin and moisture electrolyte conductor in wood.*
- Bronze,a copper tin alloy—is excellent for inboard installations underwater with many varieties,with silicone bronzes having the greatest resistance to corrosion.
- Magnesium bronze was preferred in the late 1960's,early 1970's for outboard motor propellers.While aluminum propellers would fracture and break,these props would bend blades upon impact though they corroded rapidly.Stainless steel propellers were later introduced with better performance due to stronger,thinner blades,with impact stresses hopefully being absorbed by the *slip clutch propeller hub.*

For more information on seagoing metals...read our Sailing Illustrated HOMESTUDY GUIDE *covering metals for sailboat use.*

CORRODING end
(anodic)

magnesium
magnesium alloys

zinc

aluminum 2 S

cadmium

aluminum 17 ST

steel or iron
cast iron

chromium-iron*

Ni-Resist

18-8 stainless*
18-8-3 stainless*

lead-tin solders
lead
tin

362 nickel*
Inconel*

brasses
copper
bronzes
copper-nickel alloys
Monel

silver solder

nickel**
Inconel**

chromium-iron**
18-8 stainless**
18-8-3 stainless**

silver

graphite
gold
platinum

PROTECTED end
(cathodic)

* active
** passive

If you plan to work on larger slip-berthed powerboats and sailboats, take a quick glance at this page, then study it later. If you only intend to work on outboard powerplants, this page is of minimum importance to you.

When you mix metals in an electrolyte.... will the mixture **increase the corrosion rate,** or will it be a healthy mixture to **minimize the corrosion rate?**

●*The first item to consider—is* **the distance apart of the different metals in the galvanic series.**

Note the groupings of metals at the left.

If you mix metals in the marine brasses to Monel grouping *of similar size—* in an electrolyte where they have direct contact for EMF flow, the corrosion rate should be minimum...if other factors aren't added to upset the balance.

● *The second item to consider—is* **the electrical contact of the metals.**

If the metal parts are separated by wood or an insulator, or if they are far enough apart from each other on a boat...the chance of developing corrosion currents become minimal without external help.

●*The third item to consider—is* **relative areas** covered in greater depth on the facing page. Unless used to force zinc cathodic protection, avoid combinations where the smaller part is higher on the galvanic series than the larger size metal part.

Example— we bought several Monel washers on sale which we used in various locations on our Jewel. Within six months we had several unusual metal failures caused by the Monel washers...that drained the electrical content from surrounding metals producing severe, rapid corrosion failure.

The highly protective Monel washers were still in shiny new condition.

● *The fourth item to consider—is* **the thickness** of the metal as to thick or thin parts.

Example– a thin sheet of zinc will corrode more rapidly than a square block if the weight of both parts are identical.

Powerboating Illustrated

● *The fifth item to consider*—is forced protection or forced corrosion using relative areas of metals of differing sizes...and in extreme cases, where a small and a large part of the same metal are mixed.Unless a zinc anode is used for forced corrosion protection...avoid combinations where the *active ANODE metal part is smaller.*

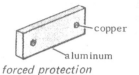

copper

aluminum

forced protection

If copper screws are used in an aluminum plate,they are balanced because—

the copper screws will be protected though they are lower on the Galvanic Series.

We reverse the situation using aluminum screws in a copper plate with the screws corroding rapidly...as they are the more active metal with their electrical content flowing out to protect the copper plate.

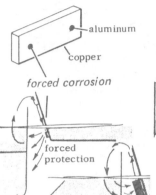

aluminum

copper

forced corrosion

We discussed metals existing in harmony with each other at left.We now reverse the process to turn this peculiar metal interaction to your advantage.

> A small zinc block is designed to corrode at a rapid rate to protect surrounding useful metals in an electrolyte.The outward atom flow will *intentionally corrode the sacrificial zinc block.*

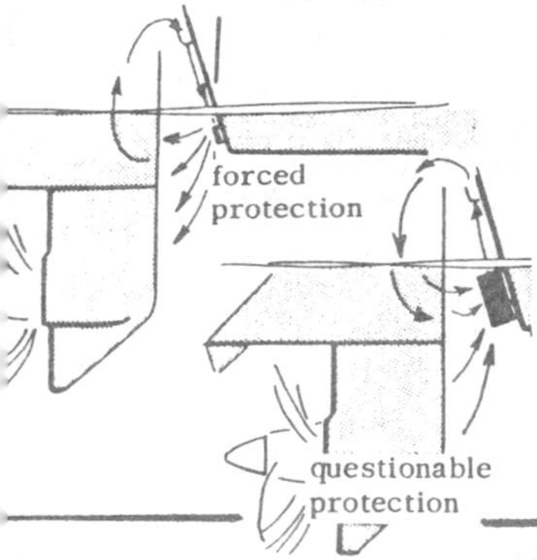

forced
protection

Example—when a zinc block corrodes rapidly, replace with the **same size OR smaller block** until finding the source of the corrosion,or—

363

A large zinc block or series of blocks will provide LESS protection...or in an extreme situation reverse the process to corrode the nearby parts you want to protect.If you paint a zinc block with bottom paint...it is neutralized and will not be able to protect surrounding metals.

questionable
protection

Large sailboats/outside cooling water— a boat yard owner said,"60% of engine failures were water jacket failures due to small isolated hose clamps.Most of the problem was cured by bonding all metal parts in the cooling system"

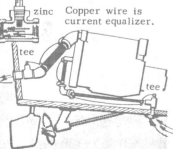

zinc   Copper wire is
current equalizer.

tee

tee

The reasoning—most corrosion is caused by a voltage difference between metals.**Bonding** the metal parts reduce the corrosive action to help equalize the potentials of the small, isolated hose clamps.

Zinc plugs were installed on the water intake and outlet tees as shown at left have bonding from one zinc tee plug,thru the system,to the other zinc tee plug.A 40' sailboat with chronic water jacket failure needed both zinc plugs replaced every 4 to 6 months.They absorbed the strong corrosion currents...also use double clamps as they seldom fail at the same time.

Powerboating Illustrated

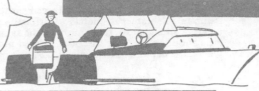

I can't see why the metal parts are moist. Just an hour ago I wiped off all the salt water with a dry cloth.

It isn't common table salt...but calcium,iodine,and magnesium salts that are responsible for corrosion because of *their ability to pull moisture from the air due to* **hygroscopic water seeking action.**

When we moved to Newport Beach we rented an apartment a block from the beach with corrosion on TV antennas,outside plumbing, autos not garaged,etc.The patterns became obvious,but a major clue was missing until examining the aluminum mast on the 54' *Good News* soon to sail around the world.The mast,made in 1940 wasn't anodized, with heavy corrosion up to 12' above the deck,where it disappeared... due to the **heavy**,always-thirsty ocean salts.

Drainage over eons of time has carried tremendous mineral and salt deposits down to the ocean.As they aren't light enough to float nor heavy enough to sink to the bottom... they remain in suspension.

Salt spray guarantees your boat metals will be moist.The sun may burn off the daytime moisture.As evening moves in,temperature drops and humidity increases,the **thirsty salts** pull moisture out of the air guaranteeing the electolytic corrosion process discussed on pg. 369.

364

These are **heavy salts** that except in a major storm wave action seldom go higher than 15' above the ocean surface.They fall out of the air when crossing the beach causing corrosion in the first two blocks.The heavy salts corrosion rate rapidly disappear further inland.

I'm thirsty!   water   Ahhhhhhhhh, that's better!

*If you want to test the idea—*put calcium chloride crystals on a plate. The crystals will soon be surrounded by a pool of water pulled out of the air by these hygroscopic salts which are corrosive because—

⊚ They are **conductors** providing excellent current flow paths,but—

● They need a **liquid** to complete a corrosive current flow between metals...which hygroscopic salts pull out of the air.

These heavy salts wouldn't be much of a trailerboating problem in the cold waters around Iceland.Since we enjoy warm weather boating, ● an ample supply of **heat and oxygen** will always be available to help the electrolytic current corrosion speeding metal destruction.

*To summarize—*wash your metals thoroughly with fresh water after returning to minimize the thirsty salts,choose corrosion-resistant metals,and/or add protective paint and zinc barriers.It is a complex skill requiring many years for motor manufacturers to perfect.

Direction of corrosion current flow can be reversed under certain conditions.

1. Flow direction due to NATURAL EMF because of different metals with a liquid and a conductor.

2. BATTERY DISCHARGING, motor idling, battery current leakage.

3. BATTERY CHARGING above idle, with battery current leakage.

salt water electrolyte

normal EMF flow

1. Corrosion current flow due to voltage difference (EMF) between metals.

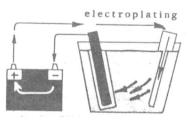

electroplating

battery DISCHARGING
(Franklin Theory)

2. Battery leakage imposes stronger current than natural EMF, direction of electroplating flow or corrosion is reversed.

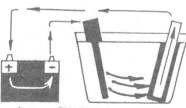

battery CHARGING

3. Battery leakage may speed disintegration of zinc block instead of lower unit.

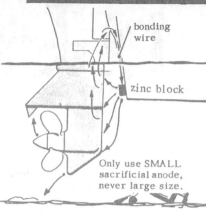

bonding wire

zinc block

Only use SMALL sacrificial anode, never large size.

To complete circuit block must be wired or bonded to motor.

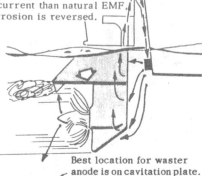

galvanic action

365

Best location for waster anode is on cavitation plate.

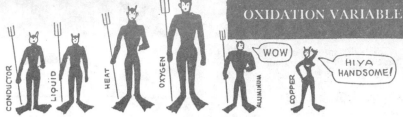
● Our major oxidation enemies are **oxygen...heat...** and **hygroscopic salts.**

If you are to wage a successful war against corrosion...you must know how the enemy thinks. Until then they can often make many end runs.

After a lot of technical theory we introduce your enemies as cartoon characters. While all six enemies are involved, **heat and oxygen** are available in endless supply ABOVE the water...while BELOW the water the **mineral and salt content** to carry electrolytic currents, pg. 368-9. are the major enemies to cause galvanic corrosion.

The nasty characters above cause oxidation metal corrosion affecting hardware, lights, etc., especially metals with minimum corrosion resistance. Stainless is the exception which protects itself by corroding at a programmed rate, pg. 361, which is a beautiful topside metal.

● Chrome is a beautiful surface coating which is good for auto bumpers. For salt water boating always ask, "What metal does it cover?"

366

sealer

SEALER—paint, wax, plastic, oil.

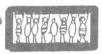

molecule slaves

Separate metals with different EMF ratings. If you used hardware store brass fittings with a zinc/copper mixture with aluminum, it invites rapid oxidation corrosion. The rate will be accelerated when salt spray dries on metal parts under a hot, humid sun.

Keep similar metals together...and seal their surfaces to keep out oxygen, liquid, and the thirsty hygroscopic salt spray.

Metal molecules are slaves...don't let them escape! Once the metal surface is broken they escape, and their usefulness is gone. The part they are escaping from will leave stains, lose strength, and eventually fail.

Zinc is your friend. If a part wants to corrode but can't be replaced for various reasons, cover it with zinc chromate and let the paint corrode while protecting the part beneath.

Salt Spray hygroscopic salts speed metal corrosion, especially when the parts are drying under a hot sun. Wash off the always-thirsty salts with fresh water to minimize stray oxidation corrosion current flows.

To summarize— above the water keep metal surfaces clean and sealed, wash off hygroscopic salts, and separate metals with different EMF ratings.

Your boat should have an open weave cover at night that can breathe to keep the dust and hygroscopic salts off your boat and motor.

Underwater galvanic corrosion has the same nasty characters, but the proportions involving underwater metals are different.

Manufacturers spend tremendous time and effort to provide protection in depth for their outboard motors and outdrives to minimize corrosion potentials....which is added to your cost.

You are responsible when these protective layers in depth are broken to expose the raw aluminum beneath.

Every owner and mechanic has to become his own aluminum *anti-corrosion expert*. Aluminum will probably be used for many decades for outboard motors and outdrives due to strength, light weight, rapid heat transfer, and nominal cost. The problem, exposed aluminum in an electrolyte corrodes easily if not protected continuously.

Early aluminum outboard motors without zinc paint or anodizing protection crumbled rapidly in salt water. Aluminum protection had improved considerably by 1958 with a better choice of aluminum, zinc primer, and a hard continuous paint film. Aluminum had little protection under the cowling which if left off a night or two next to the ocean, the powerhead had noticeable corrosion.

367

In our active research I often broke the outer white paint surface requiring the area to be washed with **distilled water** to remove the conductors, add zinc chromate, and seal with a white enamel paint. The white paint was a continual cosmetic problem, so—

I used black enamel spray paint on all white surfaces ...a practice soon followed by motor manufacturers. They also used black enamel under the cowling making it difficult to make adjustments under poor lighting when installing remote controls, etc.

When you break thru the paint barriers, cover the exposed aluminum right away, even with oil or grease to seal out the oxygen. Otherwise the galvanic and oxidation corrosion will undermine a much larger area than appears on the surface.

When you have time, scrub off the chipped paint and metal oxides with emery cloth and a soft brush so you don't remove excess aluminum. Wash the area with distilled water, and add at least two coats of zinc chromate for protection.

Spray on at least two or three coats of enamel paint to seal the aluminum surface.

Avoid tight plastic covering !

exposed battery

DIS IS A .CINCH!

HIYA FELLAS!

368 Outward current flow is causing pitting and loss of strength in lower unit.

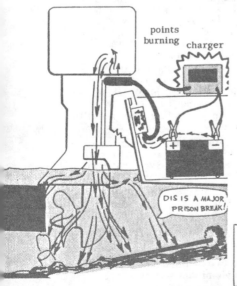

points burning charger

DIS IS A MAJOR PRISON BREAK!

There are many variables that will increase or decrease corrosion damage. We show at left a common condition that rapidly depreciates an expensive outboard motor investment.

A discharge current potential exists as the battery is hooked up to the motor with the lower unit in the water. Lower unit metals slowly corrode with the thin walls crumbling under normal stress a few months later.

The tight plastic cover traps heat during the daytime, producing condensation in the evening when the temperature drops producing oxidation corrosion.

The exposed battery—if one terminal has been unhooked, a thin salt film can begin a leakage across the top of the battery causing a rapid self discharge ...thru the lower unit in the water.

The owner turned on his battery charger then he left for breakfast. Something was different when he returned an hour later.

He kept staring at the lower unit housings of his twin 35 hp motors which ended at the waterline...only the vertical stainless drive shafts remained in the water.

The 115 volt battery charger current drained thru the batteries, to the motors, and out the lower units...to the shallow bay bottom with metal parts nearby. This **electrolysis** disaster occurred two blocks from our beach apartment.

Stray electrical currents can raise havoc— pg. 326, the 94' (?)*Roland von Bremen,* with nearby metals boats always posing a hazard. Electrically started outboard motors should always be tilted out of the water when not being used, and/or the battery unhooked in a marina to prevent interaction with stray currents on nearby boats with charging batteries.

Water temperature is a major factor! Galvanic current flow is minimum in 30°. Iceland water. It is rapid in 70° local water...doubling in 80° Mazatlan ocean water for outboard motors.

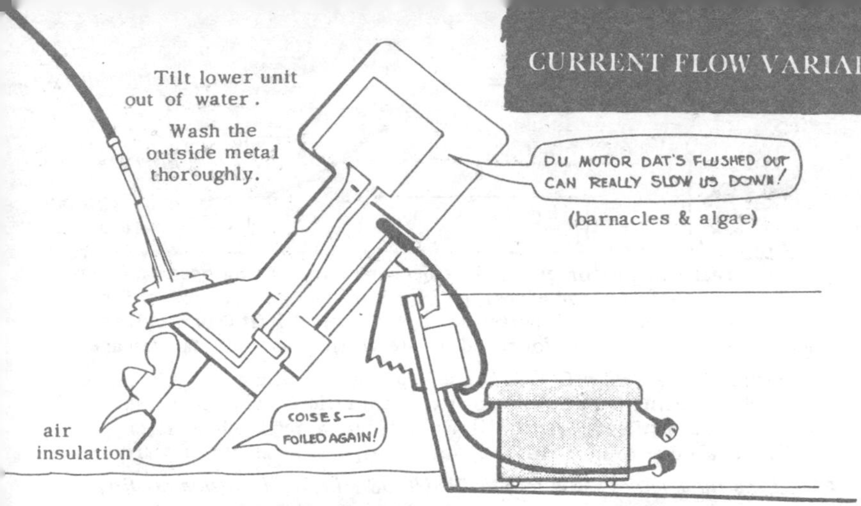

Tilt lower unit out of water.

Wash the outside metal thoroughly.

DU MOTOR DAT'S FLUSHED OUT CAN REALLY SLOW US DOWN!

(barnacles & algae)

air insulation

COISES— FOILED AGAIN!

Corrosion damage potentials can be eliminated or considerably reduced by **breaking all circuits** to disorganize galvanic and oxygen EMF current flows, and disconnect the battery to prevent electrolysis damage.

● **Air insulation barrier.** Tilt the lower unit up and out of the water to eliminate galvanic action corrosion potentials.

● **Remove hygroscopic salts** by washing outboard motor surfaces with fresh water. Wash bare aluminum areas with distilled water, dry with a cloth, and cover with a zinc chromate barrier, or a temporary oil film.

369

● **Eliminate electrolysis** by unhooking battery leads from the motor even if you will use the rig tomorrow. It eliminates battery self discharge and a fire hazard from a wiring short when your boat is unattended. All larger boats need a **master switch** to disconnect all battery circuits when leaving the boat, *see pocket cruiser electrical system*, page 335.

● **Open weave canvas ventilation** permits good circulation while keeping out dust and rain, pg.185. Tight weave synthetic cloth restricts air flow, while a plastic cover eliminates air flow. As temperature, humidity, and condensation develop, even the *fungi growth* can cause corrosion.

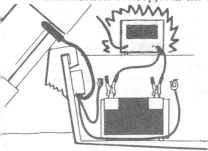

Before charging DISCONNECT motor!

When you have to charge a battery on an outboard boat—

● Tilt lower unit out of water and disconnect battery leads.

● Will the electrical cord dangle in the water causing a short, or be chafed by float or dock movement?

● **An aluminum boat**—charger and battery need an insulation barrier from the metal hull.

● Can children play with the charger?

Failure to observe these basic precautions has caused electrocution to curious swimmers.

Powerboating Illustrated

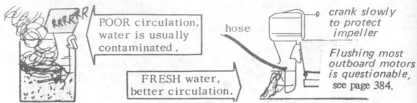

POOR circulation, water is usually contaminated.

hose

FRESH water, better circulation.

crank slowly to protect impeller

Flushing most outboard motors is questionable, see page 384.

The internal combustion engine is a heat machine with a *heat exchanger* cooling system to remove excess heat for normal operation. When the cooling system plugs with boiler scale, the trapped heat causes cylinder head temperatures to rise, followed by preignition and internal damage.

● *The auto engine with a CLOSED cooling system* using a pressure cap, has high operating temperature for excellent efficiency. When a leak develops, add **distilled water** until fixed. If tap water is added, salts and minerals due to heat will fall out of suspension as boiler scale.

● *Most marine engines using a CONTINUOUS FLOW of outside cooling water,* must operate at lower temperatures to avoid boiler scale buildup. The best example is the Admirals Barge discussed on page 231.

Salt water is hard water with high mineral content which comes out of a marine cooling system 70° to 100° warmer than at intake. The salts and minerals will stay in suspension while flowing thru the heat exchanger cooling system if it exits under 160°.

> **Boiler scale.** After this temperature barrier is exceeded, the insoluble **calcium and magnesium salts** fall out of suspension to produce a *limestone compound.* This forms a stone coating insulator on the inside surfaces of the heat exchanger cooling system.

370

Temperature and boiler scale buildup may start slowly. As the heat buildup increases, the trapped heat rapidly accelerates in 2 cycle and 4 cycle marine engines. *Warning*– an outboard motor less than a year old used only on our water aqueduct system... had the cooling system plugged solid with boiler scale, it had never operated in salt water. Boiler scale is also a fresh water problem,

● **Marine growth.** A new motor operated the second time in 4 months burned plugs. The dealer provided new plugs which burned within an hour. The dealer opened the motor to find shell fish the size of your fingernail which had grown in a trapped water pocket stopping flow. Our motors have a **yearly** fresh water flushing to kill barnacles in our cooling system by our mechanic adding the new annual waterpump.

● Your dealers **test tank** is excellent to flush outboard motors with an ample supply of air and cooling water. Flushing should be avoided in small barrels as shown above as water and junk in the barrel are often worse than the ocean water. Boiler scale buildup may start as the barrel doesn't have enough clean air or water to cool the motor.

● **Cylinder deposits.** pg. 273, 4 cycle oil can produce helpful deposits for 4 cycle engines... which become glowing insulators when used in a 2 cycle motor. The cylinder head temperature causes boiler scale. TEL (lead) pg. 273, used to cause cylinder deposits in earlier PCI electrical system outboard motors fouling plugs and reducing the efficiency of the outboard motor heat exchanger cooling systems.

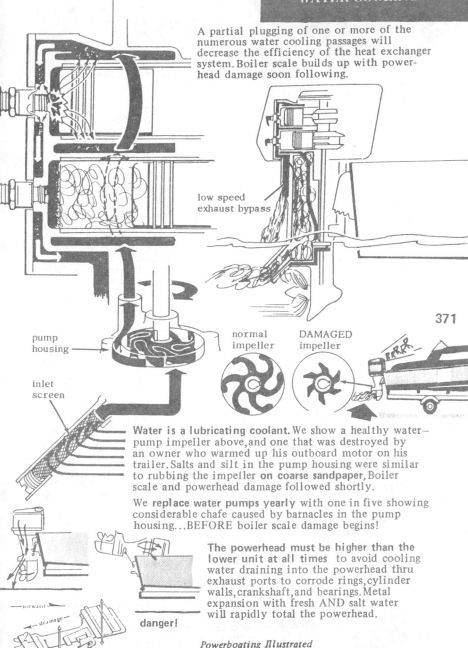

A partial plugging of one or more of the numerous water cooling passages will decrease the efficiency of the heat exchanger system. Boiler scale builds up with power-head damage soon following.

low speed
exhaust bypass

pump
housing

inlet
screen

normal
impeller

DAMAGED
impeller

Water is a lubricating coolant. We show a healthy water–pump impeller above, and one that was destroyed by an owner who warmed up his outboard motor on his trailer. Salts and silt in the pump housing were similar to rubbing the impeller **on coarse sandpaper.** Boiler scale and powerhead damage followed shortly.

We **replace water pumps yearly** with one in five showing considerable chafe caused by barnacles in the pump housing...BEFORE boiler scale damage begins!

The powerhead must be higher than the lower unit at all times to avoid cooling water draining into the powerhead thru exhaust ports to corrode rings, cylinder walls, crankshaft, and bearings. Metal expansion with fresh AND salt water will rapidly total the powerhead.

forward

drainage

danger!

Powerboating Illustrated

My keys were in my swim trunks when I had a swim yesterday. What caused their rapid corrosion?

The water was warm for you to go swimming. You had all the items needed for rapid corrosion with dissimilar metals, hygroscopic salts, plus oxygen and heat when you let the keys dry in the warm air.

● What corroded the inside of my motor?

The tight, form-fitting plastic cover is a heat trap during the day...that doesn't permit overnight condensation to evaporate.

Both you and your motor powerhead have to breathe to stay healthy.

● I live 800 miles from the ocean. Why should my outboard motor, auto, and household paint corrode so rapidly?

The electrolyte solution in your lead acid battery with a 1280 reading has a 36.8% sulfuric acid content by weight, with the rest being distilled water.

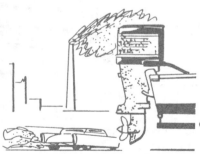

High school chemistry defines sulfuric acid as the chemical compound H_2SO_4, composed of hydrogen, sulfur, and oxygen.

Sulfur in the air comes from auto exhausts, refinery, and industrial plants, with sulfur and other corrosive exhausts.

● Hydrogen and oxygen in the atmosphere produce condensation, which combines with sulfur in the air to produce an electrolyte out of the water. This airborn electrolyte corrodes auto and boat metals, and exterior paint. Marine paint is much more corrosive resistant for painting house exteriors.

● "My idea is so obvious I can't understand why it hasn't been used before", confides the owner, dealer, or mechanic, as I am escorted to the new invention.

My first clue, the outboard motor lower unit is in the water. The second, is a smug grin as the lower unit is raised out of the water painted four to five months earlier with corrosive copper-bottom paint.

Two or three areas where copper was in contact with bare aluminum is paper thin. The crumbling lower unit will explode when throttle is applied... *farewell cruel world.*

Aluminum antifouling bottom paint— *turn to page 354!*

372

See page 269.

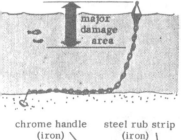

grease vent

flush plug

VIBRATION WASHERS!

grease filler

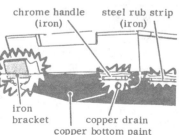

Lubricate prop shaft thoroughly to prevent prop, nut, & shaft from welding themselves together by corrosion.

major damage area

chrome handle (iron)   steel rub strip (iron)

iron bracket   copper drain
copper bottom paint

● *What caused my expensive lower unit repairs...I lubricate it regularly?*

It is easy to overlook vibration washers after checking the lower unit grease level. The screws without their insulators have metal to metal contact vibration with the lower unit to begin unwinding.

Internal operating pressure forces grease out,then when cooling,the suction pulls water in past the threads.The water and grease emulsify reducing heat potential transfer.The heat buildup with metal expansion seizes the lower unit.

Remove propeller shaft periodically and grease the prop shaft.This is important as outboard and outdrive lower units with various metal combinations surrounded by an electrolyte trying to enter...which can weld the parts together with corrosion.

● *Why is the most corroded part of my mooring chain near the surface?*

The warmer water is close to the surface. More oxygen is available as the boat bobs up and down with the most corrosion in the first 6 to 8 feet below the water.

373

To this we add electrolyte contamination from sewage and industrial plant discharges which have been reduced in many areas.

● *I thought copper bottom paint would protect my motor lower unit...but???????*

Lower left—if the paint surface barriers have been broken exposing bare aluminum, cathodic copper bottom paint can rapidly corrode aluminum which is high on the anodic end,*see the galvanic series,* pg. 362.

A few months later the gear housing looks like swiss cheeze,suddenly disintergrating when full power is applied.

● *Another example is the outboard boat transom at left* having various mixed metals at or below the waterline...to which copper bottom paint is added.

The outboard motor without zinc block protection and seldom tilted out of the water required a new lower unit due to the strong galvanic corrosion currents.

With a little care, the useful life
span of batteries & flashlights
can be increased.

*flashlight
batteries—
page 353*

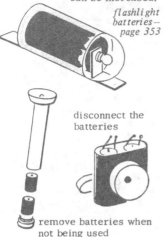

disconnect the
batteries

remove batteries when
not being used

374

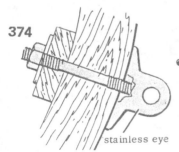

stainless eye

●**Break the circuits.** Disconnect and separate dry
cell batteries when not in use to reduce their
self discharge...and store in a cool dry area.
Use PLASTIC not metal flashlights, as the
metal surfaces only need a few specs of hygroscopic salts to speed battery self discharge.

●*What caused the towing eye failure in our
dinghy towed in rough seas last week?*

**Before buying chromed fittings for structural
use**--what metal does the plating cover?

Underneath the chrome plating on the dinghy
bow part remaining, was a salmon pink cover.
This indicated a cheap zinc/copper hardware
brass which *dezinced,* see pg. 361 definition.

●**Pot metal warning**—it is term used in the
printing field where all kinds of metals are
dumped into a boiling pot to make molten
metal type. We've seen similar *pot metals*
of questionable backgrounds sold for trailerboating use with fancy names. *Question metals
for corrosion resistance with unproven track
records...especially having fancy names.*

_____ **Current flow direction????** _____

Current flow for electrical, battery, and corrosion chapters proved an
interesting problem. We began with the Franklin theory, then changed
to the electron theory. After trying to show the complex ion exchange
we decided the traditional Franklin theory was more practical to
communicate with readers in a simple, direct manner , **page 308.**

The **Franklin theory** proposed an excess of fluids developed at the
positive terminal, with an opposing deficiency at the negative.

The **electron theory** discovered in 1897 by Thomson, proposed that
the negative rather than the positive charge was transferred during
the movement of particles to produce an electrical current.

Ions are electrically charged particles conducting an electrical current
in a solution with acids, salts, or bases, the negatively charged particles
being the only free charges capable of motion.

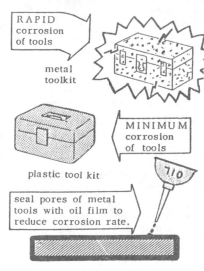

RAPID corrosion of tools

metal toolkit

plastic tool kit

MINIMUM corrosion of tools

seal pores of metal tools with oil film to reduce corrosion rate.

Handle metal items as little as possible.

Rifles, door handles, etc., show rapid corrosion due to handling.

My trailer looks terrible --------what happened?

DIS JOINT'S A CINCH TO BLOW!

Painted surfaces need a PRIMER coating, chrome needs a strong plastic coating.

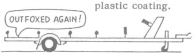

OUTFOXED AGAIN!

Powerboating Illustrated

● *What causes tool box corrosion?*

Metal tool boxes are always a problem around salt water.as the paint surface easily scratches to expose the steel beneath. With help from moisture, heat, hygroscopic salts and oxygen... the tool box becomes a battery with emf flows surging thru the box having mixed metal parts. The corroding, expanding rusting metal parts become useless.

● **Plastic tool and tackle boxes** provide insulation against corrosive current flows which are confined to individual compartments to reduce the problem.

Wash conductors from your tools after use near salt water, and store the metals in separate groups. Cover tools with a **thin oil insulation film**. It is a barrier to keep out oxygen, moisture, and heat, reducing localized emf current flows.

● *Why should a person avoid touching a gun barrel?*

It is impossible not to deposit body salts and oils on the metal surface... which increases with perspiration. So even your fingerprints may be corrosive to unprotected metal surfaces.

375

While stainless and bronze parts are self protective, other trailerboat metals may need to be sealed off soon as possible for salt water use to extend their useful life with varnish, zinc chromate, paint, or-

● *Before buying a trailer, was the metal surfaces protected with a zinc coating by electroplating or hot dip... before the outer paint coating was added?*

The other method is to buy an unpainted trailer, have the mill scale sandblasted and the metals surfaces etched with vinegar for ½ hour, followed by a water rinse.

Paint two layers of zinc chromate with a brush to protect the metal, then add two layers of enamel.

While black enamel will cover rust spots, the black trailer can become hazardous at night requiring reflective tape for trailering without a boat.

> The motor would have gone to the bottom
> if it wasn't bolted on when the boat flipped.

Galvanic action is the enemy below the water...but the major damage occurs **after the motor comes out of the water due to oxygen and heat.**

To this we add the minerals and salts in varying degrees in fresh water, and the always thirsty hygroscopic ocean salts combining with the oxygen and heat to accelerate the corrosion process. *Keep the motor submerged until you know what procedure to follow.*

● **Hand cranked motor**—if it went overboard shorting out the electrical system before water reaches the crankcase or combustion chamber—

1. After the motor surfaces, submerge the powerhead completely in a barrel or tub of cold fresh water for delivery to your mechanic. Phone him so he knows it is an emergency, hopefully starting to strip the powerhead as soon as you deliver the motor.

2. If you have the tools, know how, and help available to strip a motor immediately after a salt water dump—turn to page 381.

● 3. *First aid*—follow procedures on page 379. Flush motor with fresh cold water after it comes out to wash off hygroscopic ocean salts, and in fresh water, minerals, salts, soda, and alkali, before oxygen and heat can start current flows. **Use an alcohol rinse to mix with water so both evaporate harmlessly,** using rubbing, grain, or wood alcohol.

376

Remove moisture from the critical lower bearing by running the motor at full throttle for 2 to 3 hours. Older motors with bleeder drains to drain excess fuel will help to remove the moisture, which hasn't been permitted in outboard motors since 1970.

● **Overboard, not operating in fresh water.** Powerhead surface corrosion is involved with minimum chance for water to enter carburetor. Run at full throttle to remove any internal moisture, then hose off the powerhead, or preferably, used distilled water to protect bare metal.

● **Electrically started motors** have more complexity. Though the electrical system may work temporarily after being submerged...take the motor to your mechanic soon as possible as some of the parts or even assemblies will have to be replaced.

● **Following spray damage,** page 385, with a motor mounted on a bracket, or a boat long enough to require a 20" transom, having a 15" transom instead, is little understood by owners. A little salt spray periodically is atomized by the carburetor spraying salts and minerals over all internal surfaces, plus heat and oxygen...seldom provides warning. The corroding metals expand, sieze up and the powerhead may be totalled. *The answer*—after you realize the damage of following spray and the boats prone to cause this damage...buy boats without this problem.

● **Hydraulic damage** is always terminal...and unnecessary. After studying page 383 you soon begin to realize why the motor must be kept on the transom to eliminate over 95% of this type damage.

motor overboard

short, tight chain

motor bolted to transom

AVOID all long chains!

I have a little motor problem-----

A chemical *action* has started when an outboard motor is submerged... which requires a chemical *reaction* to stop the rapid corrosion damage.

The submerged motor known as a *dump job* by mechanics, was reported with much detail in our 1960 *TrailerBoating Illustrated,* though it is still the least understood of all trailerboating fields.

We have been involved with many dump jobs thru the years to help others. Most are difficult as the owners emotions cloud their rationality during this period.

The most important item is a question I've asked many times, even last month with an owner complaining the repairs for his submerged motor were more than the new motor cost 10 years ago.

377

"How could you have prevented this from happening?" The unpleasant truth slowly sinks in, since except for an unexpected upset or an Act of God, it could and should have been prevented.

Vibration is always at work. We've only had one motor in which the clamps didn't want to unwind. It was a 40 hp used motor with the steel clamps and aluminum bracket firmly corroded together.

A lock across the clamps can stop them from unwinding, though a short cable, chain or rope is a better answer to keep the motor on the boat. Larger motors should be bolted to the transom.

If a chain is long enough for the motor to fall off the transom— which has worked loose with the boat underway, what will happen when the motor hits the end of the chain and bounces back?

Powerboating Illustrated

A TOTAL LOSS!!! But my motor was only in the water for FIVE MINUTES.

The damage happened after it came out of the water. Didn't it stay in your garage for two weeks before taking it in to us for repairs?

Study the corrosion chapter a little at a time to feel the full range of basic factors involved,then test your ideas with other classmates. This is necessary to develop flexibility as no two dumped motors have identical patterns.

Outboard racing mechanics are the experts in this unusual field... especially in the sun belt areas with year round competition.Racing mechanics I've known sometimes operate on more dumped motors in a month than other outboard mechanics do in five years.

Have a beer party inviting a couple of outboard racing drivers and/or mechanics...with plenty of spare cassette tape to record their ideas. Most racing mechanics I've known are very generous to exchange ideas AFTER working hours.

These mechanics have an ample exposure to an unpleasant problem— how to help your customers if you are the bearer of bad news such as their motor being overhauled needs a new crankshaft and bearings.

●*Example*—a racing motor was dumped and recovered just before a race on a fresh water reservoir.The water was pumped out by hand cranking, compressed air blew moisture out of the magneto,the plugs were cleaned. Alcohol was then poured thru the carburetor and cylinders.

378

The motor started easily with the first pull,and the boat won the race. When the motor was started for the second race,operation was ragged due to **condensation** in the magneto.After compressed air was forced thru the magneto,the motor operated good enough to take a second place in the next race.

Shortly afterwards the motor was stripped down.After running 15 miles at full throttle...**enough water drops were in the lower bearings** to corrode the crankshaft and bearings at a slow rate after the motor had been submerged in fresh water,not salt water.

●**First aid,salt water**—fresh water with an inner and outer alcohol rinse will remove most of the hygroscopic salts,sand,and silt.Afterwards try operating the motor.

●**First aid,fresh water**—use fresh water to wash out the sand,silt,and minerals.Use an inner and outer alcohol rinse,then operate the motor.

Unexpected help came from our autopilot manufacturer when discussing how to care for his pilot when submerged.

"We strip our drive units completely, giving all shaft bearing surfaces and bearings a water and alcohol rinse. If we don't strip the units, the lower unit will freeze up within a week, as we can't get the bearing warm enough in normal operation to boil out the water. That lower bearing is as much of a problem to us as it is in a submerged outboard motor".

Powerboating Illustrated

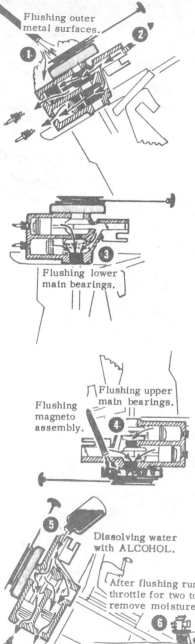

Flushing outer metal surfaces.

Flushing lower main bearings.

Flushing upper main bearings.

Flushing magneto assembly.

Dissolving water with ALCOHOL.

The hand-cranked motor stopped operating before water reached the combustion chamber. The inner surfaces will be warm, but cool soon. An **oil film** from the fuel mixture will cover most bearing surfaces...but expect only temporary protection.

> After the motor comes out of the water, heat and oxygen are available to speed inner corrosion. **First aid must be given right away** to stop the major corrosion potentials.

● **Salt water submerging**— pull cowling, covers, etc., ❶ to wash sand, silt, and conductors with fresh water.

Remove the spark plugs, and run fresh water ❷ thru the carburetors. Pull motor by hand, put plugs in loosely.

Put the motor in an upright position ❸ , then pull over a couple of times. *Turn the motor upside down* ❹ and crank by hand, then pull the plugs to drain water in powerhead.

379

Next pour alcohol ❺ into carburetor. Add plugs, repeat sequence ❸ and ❹ then pull plugs to drain powerhead.

It is time to decide to run the motor ❻ or strip the powerhead, page 381.

● **Fresh water submerging**—if salt, soda, and alkali conductors are minimum, repeat alcohol sequence ❸ ❹ ❺ .

The outboard motor has temporary protection. The next decision is to operate it near top rpm to remove condensation from lower bearing and powerhead...or strip powerhead to protect crankshaft surfaces, pg. 381, before etch marks cause terminal damage.

After flushing run motor at full throttle for two to three hours to remove moisture still in powerhead.

Powerboating Illustrated

Submerged motors don't
operate very efficiently.

● A galvanic corrosion *action* is started chemically which can be stopped by a chemical *reaction*.

The submerged outboard motor powerhead is made of active,dissimilar metals. It is surrounded by a salt water electrolyte with efficient conductors,plus heat buildup as the motor was operating. **Water temperature** will be important as cold water retards galvanic corrosion,and warm water speeds galvanic corrosion.

● *First—separate dissimilar metals*

Strip the powerhead completely and fast as possible. Major attention must be given to **crankshaft bearing surfaces,** starter motor and other shafts, plus **bearings and races** which are critical to maximum power-head rpm. Even a slight layer of rust on bearings or bearing surfaces at maximum rpm may develop too much heat buildup to be compensated for by the cooling properties of 2 cycle oil.

380

● *Second--remove the conductors*

Salts and minerals are soluble in fresh water. All metal surfaces must be flushed thoroughly with fresh water which will not stop corrosive action *but slow it down.*

● *Third- remove the liquids*

For salt water and fresh water submerged motors— **give all metal surfaces an alcohol rinse** as water is soluble in alcohol. Alcohol and water form a mechanical compound so the mixture evaporates quickly. The following kind of alcohol under various names may be used—
Isopropanol—rubbing alcohol; Methanol—wood alcohol; and
Ethanol—grain alcohol

● *Fourth- seal the surfaces*

Apply a light oil film to all dry metal surfaces. This forms a barrier to stop oxidation corrosion, then separate the metals into various groups.

● **Warning-** water and salts are not completely soluble in petroleum products.

If an outboard motor after being taken to the surface and the power-head taken apart... **don't take shortcuts.**

If the parts are submerged in a barrel of oil or petroleum base solvents, the corrosion rate has been slowed down by removing the oxygen. *The corrosion has not been stopped* as the electrolytic liquid and conductors have not been removed.

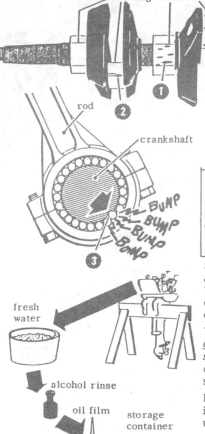

bearing surfaces

rod

crankshaft

fresh
water

alcohol rinse

oil film

storage
container

When storing, separate
parts into different
metal groups to reduce
EMF corrosion flow.

Does your tool box have enough
tools to strip an outboard motor
if it is suddenly required?

The powerhead should
be stripped immediately
after surfacing from
salt water...to separate
dissimilar metals to
reduce corrosion damage.

The sealed lower unit doesn't
require disassembly.

Connecting rod bearings must ride on
high, smooth, crankshaft surfaces...
any variation that causes pounding
requires a new crankshaft. *Speed is
essential* to minimize crankshaft etch
marks that may develop in 5 minutes,
5 hours, or 2 days.

Saved ❶—etch marks *go part way
across the crankshaft bearing surface.*
The crankshaft can operate at top
end rpm as roller bearings can ride
on the high outer surface.

381

Too late ❷—a single etch mark
*goes the full length across the crank-
shaft bearing surface...* so tiny it
can hardly be felt with your finger
spells trouble because—

Every roller bearing must roll down
into the groove, and come pounding
up the other side.

❸ The pounding will be harder and
faster as rpm increases **knocking the
roundness out of the roller bearings.**
The answer—replace the crankshaft.

Replace bearings and races showing
corrosion signs as rusty bearings
rolling over rusty surfaces develops
heat buildup, friction, metal fatigue.

Battery started motors—the same
procedure is followed with starter
motor shafts to minimize etch marks
on bearing surfaces so the bearings
can ride on high smooth surfaces
without pounding.

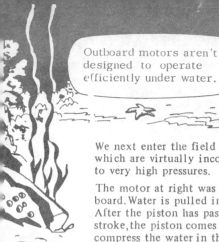

Outboard motors aren't designed to operate efficiently under water.

We next enter the field of hydraulics involving liquids which are virtually incompressible, even when subjected to very high pressures.

The motor at right was operating when it went overboard. Water is pulled into the carburetor and crankcase. After the piston has passed TDC and starts the downward stroke, the piston comes to a shuddering stop as it can't compress the water in the crankcase. Expressed in physics terms *when pressure is applied to an enclosed liquid, the pressure is transmitted with undiminished force in all directions.*

The hydraulic pressure of the water tries to push the block one way, and the crankshaft the other. The answer, a new powerhead.

Our first exposure to a motor overboard was on Catalina at midnight after a beach campfire. The timing was off when the owner took his dinghy thru the breakers to his anchored 40' sailboat. The dinghy went under, and the submerged motor wouldn't start.

We rowed to the sailboat. I tied a dock line around the motor, and before the horrified eyes of the owner, dropping it overboard to stay fully submerged for 17 hours. When our disassembly line was formed, the motor was hauled up on deck. I held the motor on the moving sailboat telling the owner how to take it apart as he was a surgeon with excellent finger dexterity. After following the procedure pg. 381, *only one new part was required...the cost, 56 cents.*

Every submerged outboard motor you work on will be different... the reason we try to cover it from many angles. We have to consider another important variable when a customer calls you telling that his motor went overboard, but due to your work schedule or other reasons, it can't be worked on for two days or so.

The same procedure will also apply to an expensive camera, a portable generator and other kinds of equipment.

Submerge the powerhead (or camera) fully in a tub or barrel of cold fresh water, distilled water if possible, the moment it surfaces. Add chunks of ice and ice cubes to take the temperature down to 40°. For practical purposes galvanic corrosion action has been stopped.

Warn each customer that *his main enemies are oxygen and heat, the reason the powerhead must be fully submerged* until you are able to strip the powerhead. A plastic or wooden barrel is preferred to a metal tub or barrel.

Powerboating Illustrated

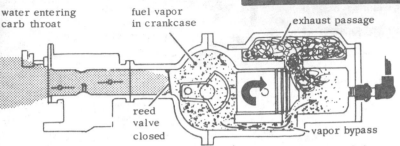

water entering
carb throat

fuel vapor
in crankcase

exhaust passage

reed
valve
closed

vapor bypass

Motor has gone under while operating. Since water has not grounded out
electrical system, water is entering through the carburetor, and in this
case it enters crankcase on up stroke of piston.

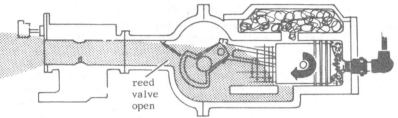

reed
valve
open

383

Vacuum pressure of piston on up stroke fills crankcase until piston
reaches top dead center, then begins downward stroke against water
that REFUSES TO COMPRESS.

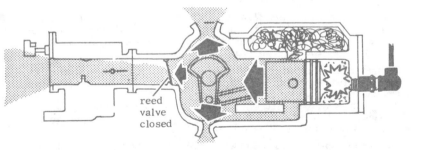

reed
valve
closed

The extreme pressures involved have to act upon some surface. In this case
parting line between crankcase and cylinder is weakest area. Hydraulic force
of water opens it up like a watermelon.

Sometimes water may first reach top of piston which tries to compress it
on up stroke. If top of cylinder doesn't blow, the connecting rod may twist.
If neither fail, the extreme pressures react on the crankshaft, trying to
push it out the side of crankcase.

Powerboating Illustrated

> $348 FOR REPAIRS---
> But it worked perfectly
> two weeks ago!!!!!!!

> Undetected spray may
> cause extensive internal
> corrosion-----check these
> damaged parts which came
> from your motor.

The most conniving type of corrosion begins with a boat underway with salt spray splashing into the cowling, which is atomized by the carburetor producing a thin hygroscopic salt layer over all inner powerhead surfaces...to which we add oxygen and heat.

The owner isn't aware he has a problem as he hoses down his boat and trailers it home. The following weekend the corroding, expanding metals have frozen together so the motor won't turn over. It soon becomes your unpleasant task to tell him of the major damage to his motor...with the parts neatly boxed for him to examine. Then open our book so we may help provide his answers to help you.

- **Short shaft, long shaft protection?** Our 14' *Blunder* had a short shaft motor, while 15½' *Jewel* had a long shaft motor. At a private club dock on Catalina, *Blunder* when tied alongside in wave action, recovered for two hours without spray coming into the boat, nor into the cowling, though it was close to the top of the transom continually. *Jewel*, next to the same dock in identical wave action, had occasional spray coming over the transom into the boat, and into the cowling, motor not operating.

A friend bought an 18' outboard cruiser I only saw for a moment before it was shipped to Canada...with twin short shaft motors. His mechanic confided that salt spray required one or both motors to be worked on an average of three times yearly.

- **Flushing outboard motors???** We found it an old wives tale for ocean operation...with agreement among those actively involved with outboard racing and maintenance. The real enemy is **boiler scale in fresh and salt water**...not just the ocean hygroscopic salts.

- **Cooling system problems.** In the 1960s I enjoyed consulting work with troubleshooters for two outboard manufacturers when unusual problems developed. Three large motors were returned, still under warranty, with severe cooling system corrosion pitting damage. After a phone discussion I provided questions to ask the three owners, which is the expertise of top factory mechanics making the final decisions.

Two motors were only used for water skiing, one on the ocean, the other in fresh water. Questioning found both owners came into the beach at full throttle. At the last moment they turned the motors off, pulling large amounts of sand into the cooling system. This sandblasted the cooling system heat exchanger when the boats left the beach at full throttle. I felt both were operator caused not covered by warrantee.

The third large motor was used on a cruiser only for ocean cruising and fishing. I had a good idea, but to verify it I contacted the expert for the other motor manufacturer. He began laughing. "I had the same problem last week finding it was a bookkeeping snafu. During lunch it had somehow passed our cooling system 'pickling vat'... which also happened in this case to our competitor." The motor was replaced without more questions.

384

FOLLOWING SEA

inboard well

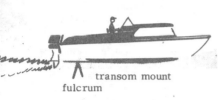

transom mount
fulcrum

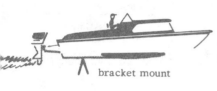

bracket mount

bracket
mount

Since an operator must be aware at all times to protect his motor from being swamped, we show different kinds of motor mounts responding to a large following wave.

● The long shaft, transom mounted motor usually lifts in time to protect the motor from a following wave though time is close...the short shaft transom is questionable.

● The bracket mounted motor responds slower in following waves with greater chance of being swamped, or spray entering carburetor.

● When climbing to a plane, or coming down from a plane, the bracket mounted motor is carried lower than normal. This greatly increases the chance of spray entering and being atomized by the carburetor...which is seldom noticed by the operator.

385

While the bracket mounted motor is quieter...is it worth the extra hazards in stormy weather?

──── **Anything going thru a carburetor must be atomized.** ────

The operator took his boat into the beach for a flying stop. When he suddenly turned off the ignition, a following wave came up to hit the transom, splashing upwards into the cowling.

Enough spray entered the carburetor throat to spray all inner surfaces with a film of salt spray. If the owner had realized what had happened, he would have operated his motor for an hour or more at near full throttle to burn off the corrosive salt spray film.

Instead he drove his rig home with the motor not operating for five days. 1960 prices—$486 worth of repairs were require for a motor that cost $600 when new.

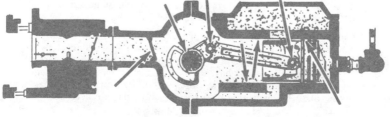

Powerboating Illustrated

I have the quietest motor and the longest bracket on the lake. It is so quiet... do we still have our motor?

The outboard motor is the most unique and versatile internal combustion powerplant, the little romanticized workhorse of the world. My background is a researcher, reporter, artist, and writer to report the story of my friend the outboard motor.

After you can overhaul, and take boats and motors to peak performance, take another look at the outboard motor. Can it do a better job for your potential customers? Can you help our mutual friend do a better job with a few changes in motor design, hull design, or a combination. Important basic breakthru ideas come from individuals such as you... they seldom come from behind the walls of large corporations.

- **Bracket mounting.** We questioned it then, but we still see advertising today with bracket mounted large twin motors on a large offshore fishing boat where they could be subjected to salt spray and swamping in storm wave action. I enjoy sailing, with the same situation becoming spirited, yet normal operation when powerboats are having problems. If perfect weather could be guaranteed, it would be another matter.

It is quite effective for huge motors on high performance hulls today in protected areas. As the lower unit is farther from the transom, the motor can be raised higher to reduce drag with a higher top speed.

- **Catamarans.** I met catamaran designer Rudy Choy in 1960 who was interested in outboard motors. Due to light weight and excellent thrust, an extra long shaft 35 to 40 hp motor can easily push a 43' sailing catamaran at 7 to 8 knots in smooth or lumpy seas.

- **Reverse transom sailboats.** For 10 years these have been popular for a longer waterline with better sailing speed, pg. 28...with a small motor carried on a bracket. This installation can prove the best of both worlds if the motor can be removed and stored below in wave action... if not, it is subject to spray and swamping, the worst of both worlds.

- **Cruising cabin sailboats.** The small diesel engine is ideal for sailboats 28' and longer. While heavy, it provides good mileage for monohull displacement speed operation.

- **Motor compartment.** The first I saw was long after the illustration was made, is popular for sailboats under 26' without reverse transoms, for outboard motors with most installations made by the owners. Can the lower unit be tilted out of the water when not in use?

- **Closed compartment.** It is shown on page 28, with better protection for an outboard motor in heavy wave action. We found in unusual wave action that the combination of sail and power could provide an easier ride while other sailboats were having a rougher ride. The disadvantage— *the motor can't be tilted out of the water when not being used.* It has to be hand cranked to minimize electrolysis and galvanic action.

386

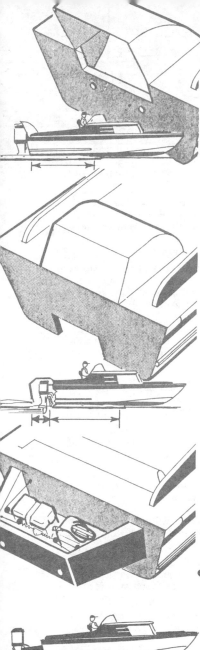

This illustration made in 1959 shows
the three basic ways to mount the
same outboard motor on similar hulls
with the major factors of safety
and speed. The first recommendation
is a long shaft motor on a 20'' transom
for protection in a following sea.

● **Transom mount** is used on most boats
will permit maximum speed with
minimum wetted surface support.

The self-draining well is required
for all ocean going outboard boats
so drainage from an overtaking wave
will drain overboard instead of coming
into the boat. Motor noise can be
reduced with a hood which can fold
if the motor has to suddenly tilt
when hitting driftwood, etc.

● **Compartment mounting.** The motor
is mounted forward of the transom
increasing the wetted bottom surface
area, with a loss in top speed.

387

This kind of a mounting in a small
open boat was very noisy with smoke
problems, and engine vibrations
bouncing inside the boat.

The advantage, it is a good compromise
for ocean fishermen as the speed
loss is less important with the motor
being protected in following waves
breaking over the stern.

It has proven very successful for
cabin sailboats operating at displacement speed, protecting the motor in
rough water.

● **Bracket mounting.** This installation
had much promotion at time of
illustration to reduce the noise, and
increase cockpit space with battery
and fuel tank carried in bracket.

Even in a protected lake following
spray can cause problems discussed
page 385 if the water has any
mineral content.

Powerboating Illustrated

Excess water in engine
compartment drains
to cabin sump.

convection currents
take out moisture

—high humidity areas

sailing illustrated

overboard
pump

2'' vent

sump

A good idea that
doesn't work!!!!

Few trailerboats face the exposure of our sailboat living continuously
in the ocean environment since 1964. Study our black spore and ventilation
problem sequence so you can apply this information to problems in the
developing stages on your customers small boats to large boats.

Our outboard boats were seldom in the water for more than three
months when they had to be hauled out on a trailer for maintenance.
Our 24 sailboat launched in 1964 provides a different view of the
marine story as it has been in the water continuously except for a
yearly weekend haulout for bottom paint and minor repairs.

It was the first practical fiberglass, pocket cruising sailboat we had been
looking for. We made most of the installations to explore the new sailing
world of fiberglass, Dacron sails, and new seagoing metals. Our boat was
very active in the first nine years as we taught over 1600 sailing students
on the water with full day sailing lessons.

● **Mildew problems** developed two weeks after launching. We drilled 22
two inch vents thruout the boat and its compartments, plus adding an
air scoop for ventilation. All cushions had to be turned on their sides
when leaving the boat to minimize condensation potentials.

388

● **Wind pressure.** Our vertical bow vent was pointed into the prevailing
westerlies in August when a storm moved in. We returned on a hot, humid
morning after three days of heavy rain to find tremendous fungi growth.
Many hours of scrubbing and ventilation were needed to remove the spores.

● **Suction flow.** A month later the bow vent was turned aft as we left
Catalina to prevent large waves breaking aboard, from going into the vent
and draining below. Two days of heavy rain and two hot summer days
later we returned to our boat expecting a black fungi mess, but—

We found few traces of fungi spores. **Our forward air vent facing aft,
developed a suction flow** so the hot, moist convection currents will
rise to go overboard, pulling in cooler, drier air. This idea worked quite
well until the Pacific *El Nino* winter-storms hit which overwhelmed
our boat, with the second heaviest rain in local recorded history.

● **The horizontal vent** was introduced at the next sailboat show that
could work thru a 360 degree arc which we installed. Guess what, NO
rain that year, but thru the following years fungi growth was minimal.
Present models operating on solar cells do a much better vent job.

● **New fiberglass hulls** have smooth shiny surfaces to the eye, while under a
microscope you will find **small pores.** These small pores grow progressively
larger to provide good footholds for fungi spores to collect and grow
in rainy, high humidity periods. When our boat was 18 years old the
local boatyard added a $1600 **linear polyurethane paint** to the sides
of our hull to plug the pores above the waterline. It was an excellent
investment. The red shows little fading, and the smooth surface keeps the
spores away. Wash the LP surface with soap and water... DON'T use wax.

hull care

vertical vent   *360 degree horizontal vent*

By the end of the 1950's, fiberglass had been accepted as the most practical and popular material for small trailerboats. It is still important to know the specialized problems of wooden powerboats and sailboats especially in larger sizes that will be operating worldwide for many more years.

- **Snow-belt boating.** The first 36 to 48 hours after a wooden boat is launched in the spring is critical as the planks are dry. Water leaks thru the seams filled with caulking, until the planks swell together, during which time water coming aboard thru the seams will finally cease.

- **Sun-belt boating.** We face a different problem in the southwestern states with low humidity and more sun tending to *overdry wooden hulls,* especially those spending most of their time on trailers. In the early days aluminum boats, pg. 354, provided better answers for fresh water use. By the late 1950's the emerging fiberglass planing hulls with outboard motors in a horsepower race became the best trailerboat choice for both areas.

Many excellent large wooden powerboats and sailboats will still be operating worldwide after the turn of the century. One of my favorites is the 36' *Sunda* built in Seattle in 1940, on which I enjoyed three races to Ensenada, Mexico. The airline pilot owner asked how to protect his boat. "The boat builder chose excellent resistant woods. He eliminated small compartment air traps, minimizing short butt ends.

389

"A good quality wooden boat can last many years when an owner realizes the need for a continuous suction air flow to keep the moisture below the 18% moisture danger zone in the beginning stage."

While we had a better supply and choice of woods in the past, It wasn't until 1965 that an ample choice of excellent corrosion-resistance metals moved into the expanding sailing and powerboating markets.

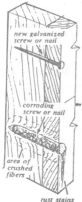

new galvanized screw or nail

corroding screw or nail

area of crushed fibers

rust stains

Rust stains down the hull of a wooden boat spell trouble. The steel nail at left fastening a plank to a frame, didn't have a zinc coating... *or it had dezinced thru the years.* Rust breaking thru the paint indicates a corroding and expanding bolt, screw, or nail.

Steel fastenings can expand 3, 4, or more diameters as they corrode to iron oxide failing sooner or later. The expansion causes tremendous pressure, crushing the surrounding wood fibers, to be replaced by a much larger diameter fastening... a warning especially for wooden planing hulls.

Bronze family bolts, nails, and screws should be recommended to your customers, especially for salt water use on wooden hulls as they can be sealed indefinitely... *AVOID brass fastenings.*

mycelium

hypha

> Now there's a tasty morsel !

"Us **fungi** are the scavengers of the plant world being microscopic plant life with a large, varied, and enormous appetite...any contributions?"

"There are many kinds of us with appetites for one or more of the products above. All of us have the same basic needs...**oxygen, fresh water, food, and a favorable temperature** so we can survive, grow, and reproduce. If you remove one of these items...*it will stop us, or kill us*".

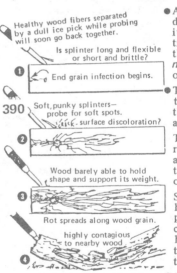

Healthy wood fibers separated by a dull ice pick while probing will soon go back together.

Is splinter long and flexible or short and brittle?

❶ End grain infection begins.

390

Soft, punky splinters— probe for soft spots.

surface discoloration?

❷

Wood barely able to hold shape and support its weight.

❸

Rot spreads along wood grain.

highly contagious to nearby wood

❹

Earth to earth...dust to dust...

- A baby **spore**, reproduced by fungi, lands on a damp piece of wood, usually the end grain, where it follows a damp, wet wood grain path. It sends tiny threads called **hypha** which begin eating the cellulose, changing it to sugar...*do you notice the sweet telltale smell?* It is invisible on the outer surface in the developing stage.

- The **hypha threads** are becoming so numerous that the visible form of the fungi plant called the **mycelium** develops, continuously eating away in the damp wood grain paths.

The fungi plant is visible on the wood surface reproducing more baby **spores** that awaken with a healthy appetite. The timber, no longer able to take stress, is reduced to an empty shell capable only of supporting its own weight.

Since 60% of the wood content, the cellulose, has been eaten, with the rest being 28% lignum, plus 12% organic compounds, the decaying wood crumbles into small chunks. The fungi scavengers have completed the routine of nature by returning the dead wood and vegitation nutrients back to the soil...for the next generation of plants and trees.

- **Light color permeable paints** have small holes to aid ventilation and drainage for immunity to ever-present contagious spores in the air.

- **Enamel** produces a glossy, waterproof coating reducing wood breathing. A thick outer paint layer increases the problem **especially with dark, heat absorbing enamel**. Wood heat expansion squeezes caulking from between the planks, increasing humidity and moisture content inside the planks. The problem escalates if the wood was painted when damp, and/or the wood wasn't fully seasoned before use.

Fungi hibernates during the winter, to awaken with a huge appetite for anything organic when the weather warms up.

Powerboating Illustrated

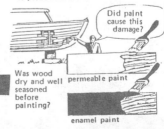

Is paint beneficial.. or a hazard?

> Did paint cause this damage?

Was wood dry and well seasoned before painting?

permeable paint

enamel paint

stabilized wood —15%	moisture content	20% — deteriorating wood
dead and healthy		active and sick

A tree is cut down and hauled to the mill to be cut into timbers and planks. It begins as *green wood* with a sap and moisture content above 18% which to minimize warping and rot potentials, has to be reduced below 15%. While 3 years outside drying time was adequate in the past, a week of kiln drying is more commonly used today.

● **Fungi awakens at 18% moisture content** by weight... with the maximum growth between 20% to 35%. Above that, growth is retarded to become dormant at 75% due to insufficient oxygen. Rot will cease when wood is. submerged due to lack of oxygen... *as marine borers move in for a feast.*

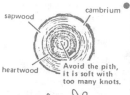

sapwood

cambrium

heartwood

Avoid the pith, it is soft with too many knots.

● **Heat sensitivity** rot growth ceases below 40°when the fungi becomes dormant. Maximum fungi growth occurs between 70° to 90°, then decreasing above 100°. If the wood temperature reaches 150° this. will kill the fungi... but it can be reinfected later.

Consider wood as a tightly bound bundle of drinking straws. It is the passages running with the grain into which water can enter that are most prone to rot... as the side of a plank has minimum absorption.

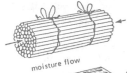

moisture flow

● **Butt ends of a timber** are most vulnerable to absorb moisture, especially short timbers with end-cut angles. The *wet rot growth* begins at the timber ends, then moves into and along the wood grains.

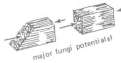

● **Heartwood vs sapwood.** Approximately 1% of a tree, the outer thin *cambrium layer* of cells beneath the bark surface, is alive... which is a major area of rot due to a *high sap content.* As we go deeper into the center of a tree, we enter the **heartwood area** having more rot resistance without the sap content.

391

major fungi potentials!

● **Salt and salt water** have a preservative effect on wood, while fresh water is the enemy... especially with deck and window leaks becoming the problem when hosing down a wooden boat... to wake up the fungi.

I was washing the deck teak of a sailboat with salt water, little realizing the owner of a new 40' powerboat nearby followed my idea, his deck having a thin teak veneer. Two years later I heard in no uncertain terms—

"We are going to wash our boat with fresh water to protect our metals", suddenly realizing why all his vents, etc., on his 2 year old boat had to be rechromed.

Squirt fungacide twice yearly into all end joints.

The damage was too late as I suddenly smelled the sweet fungi blowing from his boat as he didn't know how to ask questions. How could we protect our boat from his spores downwind? How would you handle this problem if you were involved.

● Exterior vs marine plywood. We've had excellent luck with exterior plywood having small internal voids. Use a primer, permeable paints and fungacides. Marine plywood is more expensive with all internal voids filled.

Protecting metals or irrigating fungi?????

Dry rot is a confusing term referring to decayed wood which was dry by the time the damage was discovered. The decay was instead caused by *wet rot* due to poor ventilation, sapwood, or unseasoned wood with wood moisture content above 18% activating the fungi growth.

Rot is not an unseen enemy that swoops down on a beautiful boat without warning... leaving a decayed rotting hull behind. Wooden boats have been used for many centuries with some today 50, 75, and 100 years old still having little appreciable fungi growth while others develop it in a short time period involving *action and reaction.*

●Wooden boats also have powerplants. If they interest you, study these pages, plus the information in our *Sailing Illustrated Homestudy Guide* to analyze wood variables. Then spend time studying wooden boats being worked on in a boatyard handling large powerboats and sailboats.

After a few boatyard walks you begin to pick up patterns as to the kinds of boats most prone to rot, the areas, and the reasons. Excellent ideas can be provided by helping a marine surveyor check out a wooden boat for insurance or damage claims.... and you soon find wood has no secrets.

●An excellent 18' wooden skiff was 18 months old.. The dad put it on a sandy beach on Long Island to buy bait. The son then pushed the boat out, jumping in the boat with his foot going thru the bow planking. The cause--a piece of *unseasoned wood* with a very embarrassed boat builder.

●Check every piece of wood you buy. I ordered several 2 x 4 planks with three having severe rot stains on the surface indicating internal problems before being kiln dried. The lumber yard ''expert'' was very indignant when I said the three had to be replaced. What was his wood background?

392

While mahogany will take a beautiful finish, we have many chuckles when watching **teak and similar kinds of wood** being varnished. Teak and its oddball friends are self-protecting woods with high oil content, the oil continually seeping out to protect the surface.

●If teak is varnished it becomes a never-ending job. Raw teak decks will corrode from a rich brown to a dull gray which doesn't hurt the wood. The best answer for teak trim is to sand off the gray surface and oil it every few weeks for a good cosmetics appearance. Our teak floor board in the cabin below always looks good if oiled yearly.

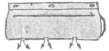

Fungi spores are always in the air looking for any kind of organic product. While they enjoy feasting on structural members that sink boats, the black spores also collect on smooth, synthetic vinyl surfaces.

During our *El Nino* period, we had a very wet and spirited sail after which we stored our soaking foul weather gear in our main cabin bulkhead bag. I forgot it till a week later with the outer vinyl surface having many black spores ... while inside the bag the foul weather gear was dry and clean without mildew. We had installed three grommet drains on the bottom of the bags which had drained the moisture and condensation.

●Canned foods should be periodically examined when stored aboard any boat, especially tight quarters with minimum ventilation such as on a trailerboat. Any cans with tomato should be removed every 4 months or examined closely as canned ravioli, puree, and tomato soup corrode easily producing an instant fungi spore population explosion.

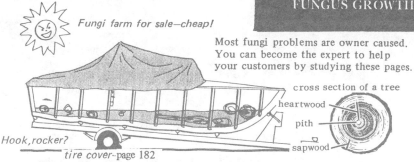

Fungi farm for sale—cheap!

Most fungi problems are owner caused. You can become the expert to help your customers by studying these pages.

cross section of a tree

heartwood

pith

Hook, rocker?

sapwood

tire cover-page 182

We provide an example above of a full-fledged *fungi farm* to analyze as it may apply in varying degrees to some of your customers.

Air temperature is an ideal 70° to 90° range for maximum fungi growth in a wooden boat above. The hot sun is cracking paint with moisture seeping thru cracks on the bow, also making little water traps on the sides to aid outside fungi growth. The hot sun by day produces condensation by night, added to the rainwater in the bilge.

100% humidity is maintained without ventilation. The synthetic tight-weave cover keeps the condensation inside the locked boat. The rain water in the bilge which cannot drain is warping the bottom.

Wood has fungi variables. It can be unseasoned wood, sapwood, short timbers with end-cut angles, plus condensation trapped in wood pockets, which is escalated with high humidity and ideal temperatures.

393

A fungi smorgasbord feast above is well underway. It is the ideal situation with high humidity, ideal temperature and an endless supply of fresh water and an endless supply of organic products.

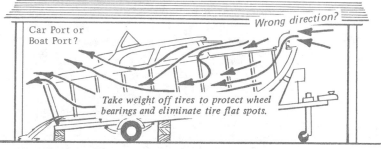

Car Port or Boat Port?

Wrong direction?

Take weight off tires to protect wheel bearings and eliminate tire flat spots.

Preventing fungi growth begins by taking all unnecessary items off the boat in storage, then providing a good air flow to remove the nasty air by reversing the vent above to develop a suction air flow, page 388.

Raise the bow and pull the drain plugs so any rainwater or condensation will drain immediately. Even if fungi growth has started, it will slow down, and stop when fresh water is removed with the wood moisture content dropping below 18%. Drain holes in the frames must be periodically checked so wood shavings, dog hairs, etc., are removed to prevent puddles of fresh water than can start the rot process.

Hydroids

Annelids or tube worms

Gooseneck Barnacle

Blue Mussel

Rock Barnacle

Algae or Grass

body

matrix or resin

+

poison

394 copper oxide

———— Can a boat slide on coarse sandpaper?————
Our sensitive high-performance *Blunder* after easily reaching
30 mph, was left at a local marina without bottom paint. In a
week the speed had dropped to 25 mph, and in two weeks the
speed had dropped to 20 mph. By the end of the month the
bottom growth was so thick on *Blunder* it couldn't even plane.

The only boating group seldom affected by bottom growth is
the trailerboat fleet in the water for an afternoon or weekend.
If your boat is left in salt water for a week, antifouling paint
isn't necessary if the bottom is cleaned with a coarse *gunny sack*.
Fresh water growth is limited to algae while our underwater
garden friends are barnacles, mussels, tube worms... and algae.

Our local underwater garden awakens in the spring when ocean
temperature rises above 60° with a healthy summer appetite
with 72° harbor water temperature. In November it is replaced by
deep offshore upwelling returning to 60° stopping their growth.

The British Admiralty kept accurate records of their bottom
paints going back 700 years, said USN bottom-paint expert.

Copper plating provided the best protection for bottoms of
wooden warships, cargo vessels, and clipper ships with several
years between haulouts. Copper plates corroded new *iron and
steel hulls*, requiring bottom paint with an anoidic barrier.

New glass hull — use solvent to remove wax and mold-parting
compounds. Sand with waterproof 220 paper, then hose off.

Late 1950's— soft copper bottom paint was standard.

1965— hard, copper-based bottom paints are available for
fiberglass and wooden hulls. **Machine-shake expensive bottom
paints as heavy particles rapidly fall out of suspension.** Use
roller to apply two coats, the first using a lot of paint, the
second, a fraction of the amount. Use a brush only in small
touchup areas to minimize breathing bottom paint fumes.

Commercial vessels since 1960, use a thick, professionally
applied bottom paint. Captain of cruiser *Long Beach*, said it
was underway 4 years, with only two small areas of growth.
It was ordered into drydock for a $20,000 bottom paint job (1965).

**Copper-based bottom paints corrode aluminum outdrives, out-
board motor lower units, aluminum hulls,...** *use only TBT.*
See pages 354, 372.

Considerable paint mixing is required as the heavier poisons rapidly
fall out of suspension. Before buying a trailerboat bottom paint—*will it
be just as effective if the boat is launched a month later, then in and out*
without developing an oxide coating sealing the poisons making it useless?

Poison compounds must be dissolved at a *steady rate* to stop plant and animal growth until the poisons are fully dissolved.

Growth only on waterline.

② Sudden growth, old paint.

③ ④ Sudden growth, new paint.
⑤

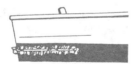

⑥ Sudden spotty growth.

⑦ Growth around metal strip.

⑧

Severe corrosion on aluminum boats is usually caused by their owners.

Our *Jewel* spent more time in the water than our other planing hulls finding the best hard bottom antifouling paints had erratic behavior under extreme conditions.

Warning— study bottom paint instructions, then machine mix expensive copper bottom paint for best efficiency.

① **Oil makes a continuous film.** It seals the bottom paint at the waterline attracting our underwater friends. A partially filled oil can fell off a nearby dock...or the boat went thru an oil slick underway on the water.

② New bottom paint—rapid bottom growth developed 3 months later. The bottom paint was partially mixed and the poison disappeared, or we've seen too much thinner added to make the paint easier to apply to brush on. **Roll on bottom paint only!**

New bottom paint—rapid bottom growth began a month later with various causes.

③ *Weak bottom paint* was used, or the paint poorly mixed.

④ The boat was put in the water several days after the bottom was painted. *What is the best bottom paint locally for the trailerboat going in, out, and back in the water?* Avoid bottom paints that can develop an oxide film retarding and stopping poison release.

⑤ Warm, stagnant ocean water—the boat with little use is surrounded in an active mating season with decaying wooden hulls and docks with an active plant and animal life. After these creatures have made a beachhead, it is difficult to retard further assault.

⑥ The boat had a good bottom paint. The boat was often taken up on a beach after towing water skiiers. Sand and gravel rubbed off the antifouling bottom paint.

⑦ *Jewel* had an excellent aft wooden bumper with metal trim for fresh water use which was underwater or below the waterline at an ocean dock...with the copper bottom paints pitting and helping marine growth.

⑧ **Aluminum planing hulls are excellent, but they need special attention on the ocean.**

Occasional salt water use—apply a thin and continuous film of varnish or lacquer to all surfaces, and hose off after use. For much use in salt water, turn to page 354.

395

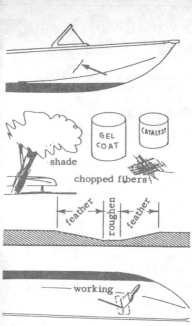

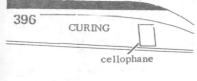

396

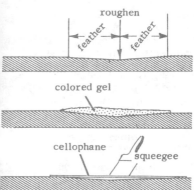

● for DEEP SURFACE repair

If has gone through the gel coating and glass cloth but has not broken through hull —

Area must be dry and clean without oil or wax.

Roughen side and bottom of damaged area shown, then feather from 2'4" on either side.

Mix an equal quantity of gel coat & chopped fibers. Use an eye dropper to add two drops of catalyst. Work catalyst thoroughly into gel coat and mix completely. Use only enough mixture for job as it can't be reused after it mixes and sets.

Work mixture into the damaged area with wedge such as knife. This will help to puncture any air bubbles as well as pressing mixture firmly into place.

Fill to 1/16" above damaged area. Cover with wax paper or cellophane to seal off from the air. This begins the cure.

In 10-15 minutes it will be partially cured. Remove covering and use a knife or razor to trim excess flush with the surface.

Replace cover for final curing for 30 minutes. Patch will now shrink slightly below surface. Then it is time to repair outer hull surface.

●

● for OUTER SURFACE repair

If outer surface has been scratched, or surface has been damaged and repaired in the sequence discussed above —

Roughen bottom and edges of hole, then feather hole into surrounding gel coating.

Mix a small amount of gel coat and pigment. Add a couple of drops of catalyst and mix thoroughly.

Fill hole to about 1/16" above surrounding surface with mixture. Cover with cellophane to start cure.

When partially cured, remove cover and use sharp knife or razor to trim flush with surface.

After trimming, place small layer of gel, cover with cellophane, then squeegee it level with area around patch. Leave cellophane on for an hour or two for final curing.

After, use wet sandpaper & buff with fine rubbing compound.

Powerboating Illustrated

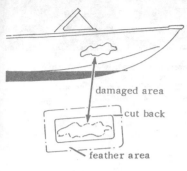

damaged area

cut back

feather area

● THROUGH-HULL PUNCTURES

Same materials are required as for previous jobs plus addition of fiber glass mat and back up materials.

Area must be clean & dry, work in a shaded area as sun will speed curing of resin.

Cut back to firm material by enlarging hole as shown at left.

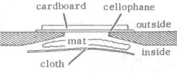

cardboard   cellophane

outside

mat

inside

cloth

The FEATHERING, about 2" on all sides should be done INSIDE boat. Use a rough dry sandpaper to improve bonding between patch and hull.

On outside of hull, cover with cellophane and back up with cardboard. Tape to outside of hull.

Cut a patch of fiber glass cloth and mat that will be 2" larger than hole. Mix resin and catalyst, soak mat and cloth thoroughly by stippling, not by brushing as it can tear mat material.

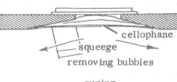

cellophane

squeege

removing bubbles

Apply soaked mat & cloth, cover with cellophane and squeegee from center to outside to remove air bubbles. Let patch cure for 1-2 hours.

397

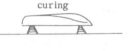

curing

After patch has been completely cured, remove cardboard from outside. Use rough sandpaper on center of patch to edge of hole.

remove backing

Feather edge of hole 2-3" to outside of area. Mask off surrounding area.

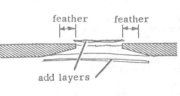

feather   feather

add layers

Cut a patch of fiber glass mat about 1" larger than hole. Cut a layer or two of fiber glass cloth to a slightly larger size. This is to build the patch slightly above surrounding area. Apply the soaked layers and work out air bubbles with squeegee or knife. Work from center to outer edges to remove all bubbles.

After 15-20 minutes of curing, cut away excess mat and cloth with sharp razor or knife. Cure overnight.

On following morning use rough dry sandpaper to blend surfaces & smooth patch. Look for bubbles, puncture them and fill with catalyzed resin. Let it cure for 1-2 hours and sand again.

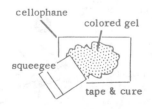

cellophane

colored gel

squeegee

tape & cure

Mix gel, pigment and catalyst, then work into patch. Cover with cellophane and squeegee down to a smooth surface. Tape cellophane, don't remove until curing has been completed.

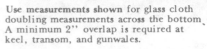

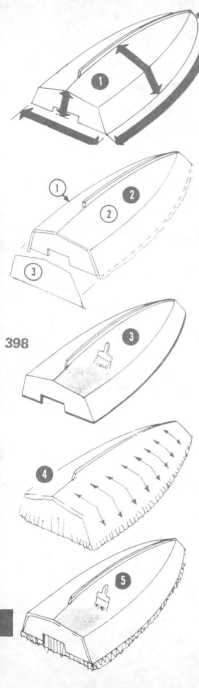

398

Use measurements shown for glass cloth doubling measurements across the bottom. A minimum 2'' overlap is required at keel, transom, and gunwales.

Remove chine strips so continuous area of glass cloth extends on either side of keel all the way up to the gunwale.

Glass cloth will adhere to an outside radius than to an inside angle or curve.

Fiberglass cloth adheres better to a radius than a sharp edge that might cut the cloth. This is your challenge to keep the transom chine SHARP as possible to prevent a secondary rocker at planing speeds, pages 56-7.

Lay cloth on hull, cut with scissors to conform to the bottom, sides, and transom. Tack or staple cloth to transom then stretch it to the bow. *As compound curves and wrinkles develop that cannot be stretched... slit cloth there.*

Glass cloth strips used to cover keel, splash rails, and chine strips, are available in 2'', 4'', and 6'' widths.

Apply generous layer of resin with brush to spread evenly without sagging or running. Clean your brush immediately.

Apply cloth by hand before wet resin becomes tacky. Smooth glass cloth on wood from keel to gunwale following arrow directions shown. Tack or staple glass cloth to the hull during this operation.

Keel strip if removed, is added any time before final resin coat. *Before resin has hardened, apply second coat.* Saturate cloth thoroughly so no air spaces or pin holes remain as resin penetration must be complete. Let hull dry.

Apply first and second coats early in morning so sun can aid drying. When second coat is dry (*resin will not clog sandpaper*) then sand to a smooth finish. Remove the fine white powder after the sanding protecting skin and eyes and nose, breathing thru a mask

Apply 3rd, 4th, and 5th resin coats that can have a little thinner added. Cure thoroughly. *Sand, wax, and polish* fiberglass surfaces.

Bolt or nail rails and chine strips to hull. Add antifouling paint if required after boat has set and been cured for several days.

Powerboating Illustrated

Bill Tritt

Shortly after moving to Newport Beach in 1958, I met **Bill Tritt** living a short walking distance from our apartment the Glasspar designer responsible for our three trailerboats above. A short outboard boat ride away was designer **Dick Reineman,** designer of the 130' *Andromeda* series below. I was fortunate to know two of what I feel the most important fiberglass designers on a personal basis. Let us return to our new fiberglass miracle product in the early 1950s.

Reineman *Andromedian* Series—
60' to 130', 110 footer shown

The new fiberglass boatbuilding world began with many splashes. The new, flexible, low-performance bathtubs became faster as the wobbly hulls age hardened. The day came when the bottom became too rigid cracking with a loud splash... with many builders rapidly closing shop.

Naval architects designed glass planing hulls. As displacement hulls were their expertise, planing performance was questionable, and looks???? The first good glass outboard racing hulls I remember came from Arizona. The secret, bottom bracing rigidity for planing lift. But looks????

399

Bill Tritt, an auto designer, began building fiberglass outboard hulls in his garage, expanding so rapidly three years later, into **Glasspar,** the largest builder in the field at the time. Bill was the planing hull pioneer relying on native intelligence, he wasn't a naval architect. He designed three of our outboard trailerboats *Researcher, Little Jewel, and Thumper.*

Bill designed good performing, comfortable planing hulls with customer appeal. 30 years later after endless fleets of flashy tinsel toys, his designs are still the best outboard hulls in the harbor. We enjoyed an endless flow of ideas in 1960 when he checked our *Trailerboating Illustrated,* before printing. Engineering genius made Glasspar the U.S. leader.

Financiers moved into the expanding business with *accounting engineering.* Bill bought a hotel. In 3 years Glasspar stock dropped from $80 to a few cents. Glasspar still knew the exact number of paperclips used yearly.

Tritt designed his planing hulls for new, larger hp outboard motors, with Richard Bertram taking the lead with larger outdrive and inboard power-plants for ocean operation on his deep V stepped hulls. Dick Reineman was a quiet leader for large, comfortable yachts worldwide. Planing hulls today have a considerable mix beginning with these three designers.

1980-1990 technology moved rapidly many ways Thanks go to expert Jack Wells for his help and patience such as the blister page rewritten 8 times Thanks also go to friend patternmaker Floyd Humeston working with fiberglass for over 30 years from museum exhibits to the most advanced aerospace composites. Thanks team!

> *Fiberglass boatbuilding is a highly skilled craft, a complexity involving 20 key factors that must occur within precise tolerances. Molds, labor, tooling, materials, production, and advertising costs must be kept under control for the competitive market.*

- **FRP or fiberglass.** American slang shortcuts produce half answers. The term FRP, Fiber Reinforced Plastic is more accurate. The basic FRP concept continues to evolve and improve thru the years with endless new FRP materials and methods. **Quality control** is the key factor with constant supervision required for the complex production steps that are involved, requiring numerous workers.

- **Female mold.** Wood works best with flat surfaces, while fiberglass fabric and resin combine inside a female mold to build complex compound curves for stiffness with a flexible hull shell. This FRP method eliminates wooden hull caulking, wood rot, and yearly painting of wooden hulls.

- **Late 1950s.** It began with E-glass, resin, and wood structure support pg. 59. *Sandwich construction* followed using E-glass, mat, and woven roving fibers improving stiffness with less weight. Early boatbuilders cooked plastic flake resins. These were dissolved in styrene to become liquid, then catalysts were added with boatbuilders using their own mix ratios. The next step was pre-mixed resins for some catalysts.

- **Mid 1960.** Production was slow with resin mixing in small batches. The spray gun was adapted to spray resin, and later also shoot chopped fibers reducing cost, increasing production. Control problems developed in the early stages with hulls thick in some areas, and thin in others.

400
- **Late 1970.** An industry wide problem was developing with blisters called the pox... ranging from cosmetics to disaster. Ten years research were required with warranty costs multiplying, to find practical answers to endless baffling details. One cause was poor maintenance and use of resin spray equipment. *Since woven roving, mat, and orthopolyester were involved with the pox... new methods had to be found.*

- **Enter the Composites.** FRP boatbuilding complexity increased in the early 1980s with new materials and technical skills. Builders now had to hire engineers to specify, manage, and provide quality controls beyond previous methods. Unidirectionals, bidirectionals, S-2 glass, Kevlar, carbon fiber, honeycomb, PVC foam, and balsa core, isopolyester, vinyl ester, and epoxies entered the new world of composite boatbuilding.

- **Prepregs** emerged in the aerospace industry for composite-built bomber structures, radar dome protection, etc. Fabric impregnated with resin is frozen for delivery to builders requiring baking over 350 degrees F for several hours in an autoclave. Low temperature prepregs, not frozen, are cured in an oven at 140 degrees F for an hour. They were used to build decks and hulls for American Cup sailboats.

- *Knight & Carver* **One Off, Male Mold, Advanced Composite** concept pages 404-7, is used for single, light, performance oriented custom built designs, with a one-off wooden station frame.

Limp fiberglass cloth becomes a
rigid reinforcement for structural
strength when bonding with resin.

fg cloth reinforcement

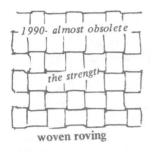

woven roving

mat

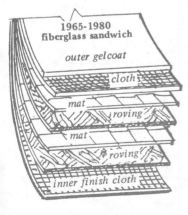

- **Polyester resin** is used on many production boats, **vinylester resin** on some custom boats. Military boats use fire-retardant resins.

- **Hand layup.** A gel coat layer is sprayed into a female mold. Alternate layers of fabric, roving, and mat, squeegeed by hand, layer by layer, follows until desired strength and thickness are reached. *Glass to resin content is the key for strength to weight ratio... 30-4 to 60-70 ratios.*

- **Woven roving** is used for a heavy hull, playground slides, etc. It is seldom used today for lighter, stronger hulls.

- **The chopper gun** is less labor intensive, more cost effective. Before standardized controls it eliminated many boatbuilders. Color is added to liquid activator to spray on evenly.

- **Sandwich construction** uses layers of wood blocks, or foam between layers of reinforcement. Balsa is the most common core to produce strong, light hulls. Balsa grain blocks are laid perpendicular to fiberglass so if the skin is punctured, water damage is minimized.

- **Nomex honeycomb,** excellent bulkhead nylon fiber core material, is lighter than balsa block sandwich construction. Use above water only to avoid cells filling with water.

- **Vacuum bagging.** All laminates are placed in mold before resin is cured. A plastic sheet covers the full laminates, the sheet sealed, and air withdrawn. Atmospheric pressure compresses the laminates for lighter, high glass to resin ratio.

- **S-glass** is finer than E-glass so greater glass volume can occupy same space for more strength. for use with any resin if applied with correct coupling agent. Vinylester resin must be used with Kevlar, not polyester unless Kevlar fibers contain approx. 10% S-glass inserted.

- **Unidirectional fibers** add approx. ten times more strength to structure. Structural mat or veil is inserted between uni-fabric plies for bonding,

- **Novalac epoxies** are used with prepregs including carbon fibers, stored frozen. Oven cure is 350-450 degrees for several hours under autoclave pressure.

- **Composites** replaced the older, heavier sandwich method at left for boatbuilding to reduce blister potentials, page 403..

_____ The fiberglass evolution process is continuous. _____

Old problems are supposed to disappear when a new technology is introduced. Then begins a new educational process to find answers to new baffling problems the miracle technology introduces.

● **1958 outboard planing hulls.** While fiberglass had flexing, the boxing method page 59 with frames and stringers, provided ample support. Sailboat builders waited for outboard boatbuilders to work out most of the bugs with customer testing... factory testing came much later.

● **1962 sailboat technology.** Columbia Yachts in Costa Mesa, was the first to introduce several sizes of quality semi-production sailboat lines. So many orders came a second shift started four months later.

We bought our 24' Columbia sailboat in 1964. The hull was a sandwich of several fiberglass and resin layers with rigidity less important for displacement speed operation. More practical room was below decks as structural frames and stringers were eliminated, which were required for a wooden sailboat of similar length and comparable design.

● **Fiberglass boatbuilding is a highly skilled craft** not lending itself to Detroit mass-production methods. Workers need the best training, knowhow and dedication using the latest methods available. Supervision must be continuous to keep everything under control ... as problems still surface

● **Cal 25 technology** in 1965 was the benchmark, the first hull fully designed before leaving the drawing board. Mat and roving were introduced for lighter, stronger hulls reducing fiberglass cloth layers. It was a financial success with all factors- cloth, resin, ballast, amortization of molds, and production costs fully known. Weight of the hulls were probably 12 pounds more or less than predicted on the drawing board.

● **Fiberglass blisters** surfaced over 20 years ago in fiberglass hot tubs, a warning ignored by boatbuilders, almost bankrupting the builder until finding *polyester resin was semipermeable.* Blisters seem more common in warm fresh water which is several times more reactive than salt water.

● **Hull laminate chemical reaction.** Complexity is involved *as 20 key factors must occur within precise tolerances.* Resin and catalyst must be mixed thoroughly and in the correct proportion. Temperature must be between 60 to 90 degrees F. Air conditioning is needed for low humidity to keep moisture below the critical point, which if above can severely reduce structural strength. Ample time is needed to complete the curing process, but won't fill existing voids. If the laminate isn't stable, it becomes worse.

● **Incomplete chemical reaction** permits water penetration into the laminate membrane. Excess acid left in the building stage of resin or expired catalyst, can leave resin undercured. Chemical action continues causing internal pressure and blistering. Damage may appear two to three years later.

● **Gel coat** with a maximum .030" thickness, isn't sufficient to provide an impenetrable barrier *requiring an epoxy coating.* A sunbelt advantage is to take monthly walks thru boatyards. A three-step hydro approx 30' long with a dull gel coat had minute cracks stem to stern. Was it an incomplete chemical reaction; was the gel coat too thick chosen without enough flexibility. Twin rudders showed tremendous cavitation damage from the athwartship steps. The expensive boat was an owners nightmare.

Underwater blister damage— cosmetics or disaster?

Hairline cracks and star crazing can occur above the water due to brittle, overcured gel coat laminate that isn't stable. *We soon found that the hull damage blisters also called pox, occur underwater beneath bottom paint thru a semipermeable gel coat membrane. The process is called osmosis.*

Curing time limit. Fiberglass technology has advanced so far it requires highly trained technicians to build boat hulls and stealth bomber composite wings without blisters. It begins with a time limit working with fiber glass fabric on a gel coat before the resin 'kicks off' and curing begins. This critical curing time limit can be shortened or lengthened.

Bridging may develop when working with large sheets of fabric against gel coat, developing valleys and voids while curing For a 3° model, cut 3″ x 3″ squares of cloth, and 2′ x 2′ sheets of cloth for a 100′ hull Individual sheets are rolled down for total resin penetration, the squares rotated various directions for maximum strength before the resin kicks off

Regardless the curing time for complete bonding, if molecular voids, not pinholes are in the laminate... curing won't eliminate these voids.

Osmosis is a law of nature defying rationalization that occurs in many man and animal body systems. *When two solutions with different concentrations are separated by a permeable membrane (polyester gel coat), the less concentrated outside water passes thru the membrane to the more concentrated one in the hull laminate, attempting to equalize the concentration with the one-way membrane valve-action law of nature.*

403

You can run your hand over a *smooth gel coat that seems impervious* before adding bottom paint. If any molecular voids exist in the laminate, they pull less concentrated outside water thru a semi-permeable gel coat by molecular movement. Fresh water is a more powerful osmosis blister producer than sea water.

As less concentrated outside water migrates thru the gel coat membrane to fill voids and dilute the stronger solution, pressure cells develop with pressures to 5 times the outside air. They expand and merge seeping into mat and roving by capillary action and reverse osmosis. The laminate may continue to deteriorate due to hydrolysis (water breakdown) with delamination.

Bilge-water blisters. Paint bilge with epoxy... and keep bilge dry!

Minor blisters. Open all blisters to drain moisture, small areas can be opened with a disc sander. After fully dry, fill and fair the voids until the bottom is smooth. Build a well-bonded epoxy barrier over the bottom.

Structural damage is a concern. Use a gel-coat peeler for large areas. Three months drying time should follow in a moderate climate before repairs begin. Then starts a time-consuming job working from the laminate outward using vinylester resin to build a layer ¼″ or more with unidirectional fabrics. Fill and fair bottom till smooth. Apply 2 to 10 epoxy coats, finally bottom paint. This is the present answer... for tomorrow?????????

When blisters appear— repair soon as practical to minimize potential damage. Otherwise the repairs later as the hull strength deteriorates, will be more expensive and time consuming.

Boatbuilding 1990 and beyond. *Information comes from designer Dick Reineman and son-in-law Hugo Carver, a partner in Knight and Carver Custom Yachts, Inc, with two locations and over 100 employees. The company has built over 80 custom-designed vessels since opening in 1973. Inside information indicates it is one of few, if not the leader in the 'state of the art' builder of custom fiberglass vessels.*

Many construction materials are available today for the naval architect and builder, to professional, and skilled amateurs with a blending of both in kit boat construction.

The major factor in boatbuilding is time. Much more time is required than an amateur initially estimates compared to building a house... which doesn't face the test of surviving storm wave and wind action.

● **Wood** retains its charm for carvel-built displacement hulls. while *cold molding* is used in the building of dinghies to sailboats and power-boats 100' and larger. Thin wood veneer strips saturated in an epoxy are glued together, sometimes in combination with carbon fibers.

● **Steel** is used for displacement hulls above 35', and planing hulls 60' and longer. It has the lowest cost when using flat plates, and the most expensive when using compound curves. Steel is a heavy material requiring more hp and larger engines to match speeds of vessels using lighter materials.

Much information is available, steel is inexpensive, produced in high quality sheets. New rust coating protection eliminates most past problems. Good engineering and welding are required with careful detailing and coating.

● **Ferrocement.** While many vessels have been made worldwide with this material, I've only been on one properly built using lines of a time tested sailboat hull. Many I've seen were built to questionable designs by backyard builders in too much of a hurry, with many not finished.

As they worried about structural strength, they often added 2 to 3 times the necessary cement with the clumsy, overweight, poorly-faired hulls fighting normal wave action. How can an owner predict the mechanical strength of the steel skeleton imbedded in cement?

● **Aluminum** is popular for dinghies to high speed vessels 150' and longer. It is light weight and price is moderate. Aluminum is easy to work with clean construction methods. Much engineering information is available, with corrosion controlled by modern paint systems. Welding is difficult which requires attention to avoid structural flexing at welds.

Insulation that doesn't retain moisture, is needed to separate aluminum from other metals.

Since aluminum is an excellent electrical conductor, the owner has to be continually aware of electrolytic attack potentials from within the hull, and at the dock where stray underwater currents mav develop. pg. 326.

● **Glass fibers** on a pound-for-pound basis, combined into FRP with resin and composites, become stiffer and stronger than steel. Even with all the technical problems, it has the best promise for your boatbuilding future.

The **88 footer weighed 104,000 lbs.** only, at launching. A similar length hull from a female mold, shell only, may be twice the weight with half the speed using similar hp engines.

The massive 88' *Newmar* at launching held 30 knots in sea trials, built with present K & C technology. It is listed in the 100 best designs for past 5 years including European designs in *Power and Motor Yachts*.

The future goal of boatbuilding is performance using stronger, lighter composite materials, reducing weight where possible.

A boat with solid fiberglass construction will weigh 30% more than an identical design with cored construction, with the extra cost of unnecessary layers of fiberglass. The heavier boat will require larger, heavier engines with larger and heavier fuel tanks, requiring more fuel to maintain the same speed.

Traditional teak decking requires ¾'' solid teak planking. A 1/10'' teak deck veneer with epoxy-carbon seams for longer life, reduces deck weight on a 50 footer by 350 to 420 pounds.

405

Gas turbine? A strong, light weight 70' Sportsfisher under construction can reach 24 knots with modern diesels. An 8000 hp gas turbine main drive, can develop speeds to 60 knots. The gas turbine with 1/10 weight of a comparable diesel, has about the same cost per horsepower.

Cored fiberglass sandwich construction boatbuilding is the 'state-of-the-art' for stronger, lighter hulls. It can be expensive with carbon-fiber skin at $70 a pound, and steel, 30 cents a pound. The goal is to make it cost effective with a stronger, lighter hull using less fiberglass and resin.

The interior designer is responsible to reduce interior weight in new construction. Thin, laser-cut counter tops are glued to space-age honeycomb core panels, developed for aircraft floors 40 years ago. Solid hardwood paneling is replaced with thin wood veneers bonded to cored panels to save weight. They look identical to wood paneling. They are often more stable bonded to cored panels, at a fraction of the weight.

Fiberglass hull female molds produce majority of production hulls today from dinghies to 150' long, an efficient, easy production method. Good engineering and quality are needed for long lasting quality hulls.

OOMMAC— *One Off, Male Mold, Advanced Composite* is the fiberglass boat construction method used by Knight & Carver. It is a superior method to build large hulls to fit the needs of individual owners with considerable flexibility and specialization. The One Off construction costs are comparable to that of the female mold for mass production, which doesn't have the flexibility of the OOMMAC boatbuilding method that follows.

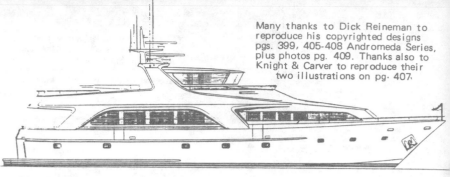

Many thanks to Dick Reineman to reproduce his copyrighted designs pgs. 399, 405-408 Andromeda Series, plus photos pg. 409. Thanks also to Knight & Carver to reproduce their two illustrations on pg. 407.

The recently launched 94' design *Hawkeye III*, was the cover boat for *Sea Magazine* April 1990, and *The Yacht* cover also for 1990.

Knight & Carver **One Off, Male Mold, Advanced Composite** concept.

One Off. Each design from 50 feet plus is a unique expression of its owner, with only one vessel built from that plug. It will be destroyed after serving its singular purpose eliminating the high cost of building female molds, then storing and maintaining the molds.

Male mold begins the construction process to which the foam core panels are secured. The male mold must be completed and faired accurately to exact shape of the naval architects plans before hull building begins.

Advanced Composite is the process developed by K & C to produce strong, lightweight hulls using the most advanced fiberglass cloth and resins to **406** eliminate problems of blistering and incomplete chemical reactions.

Gravitational forces continually aid OOMMAC building process. The laminations are applied a layer at a time until appropriate skin thickness and fiber orientation are achieved with various fiberglass reinforcements.

OOMMAC quality control is provided at every step with the male mold. Glass laminations are applied to the foam core panels in a "down hand" manner with resins correctly machine mixed, then squeegeed by hand.

Monocoque structural process begins after the hull is turned right-side-up. The frames are removed in stages while being used for interior scaffolding. Inner skin laminations are applied with interior stringers, beams, tanks, and other structures completing the structural frame, taped and resined into an integral unit.

Composite hull construction provides insulation reducing condensation with cooler living areas in warm weather, and warmer areas in cold weather. Insulation effect reduces engine noise and dampens vibration.

OOMMAC weight savings are 30% compared to similar aluminum and solid fiberglass hulls. OOMMAC hulls cubic capacity volume are increased 10% to 15% compared to a similar aluminum hull due to elimination of aluminum frames.

The new light, strong composite materials increase performance, to reduce maintenance and down time, producing a considerable fuel savings.

Knight & Carver Custom Yachts, Inc., 3550 Hancock St., San Diego CA 92110

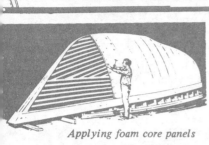

110' Andromeda

Construction plug is a **male form** with fir frames mounted on upright timbers. They are joined together with battens running fore and aft. The plug usually requires a week to build.

The plug is faired by hand to the exact contour lines from dimensions and shapes provided in naval architects plans.

Applying foam core panels

Foam core panel sheets are screwed to the completed male plug. Glass and resin are applied directly to the foam sheets for maximum bond.

The lamination process begins with fiberglass reinforcement layers applied one at a time always "glassing down" on the foam core with four to five laminations applied, each providing continuous unidirectional fibers to retain maximum high-tensile strength. *Isopthalic polyester and vinylester resins* of highest quality are used in the lamination process. Proportional mixing machines insure proper catalyst/resin ratio. **407**

Resin is hand squeegeed thru the glass cloth with desired 50/50 ratio, while typical fiberglass production is 40/60. The "wet on wet" feature on a one-at-a-time layer, is scheduled to achieve overlapping cure times, providing a continuous bond of layers on the outer hull skin.

The **gel coat** applied first in female boat molds, is less controllable than the OOMMAC final outside fairing operation. Polyester resin is used with glass bubbles and amorphous fumed silica powder as fillers.

The fairing coating is encapsulated in two part *solid-epoxy resin* to stop moisture penetration. A gray epoxy primer is then applied to prevent sanding thru the epoxy coat surface, to add a top coat **high gloss LP finish.** Bottom paint can be added, then the hull turned upright.

Typical Composite Layup (Varies with size & design of each hull)

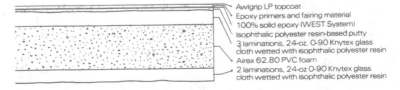

Awlgrip LP topcoat
Epoxy primers and fairing material
100% solid epoxy (WEST System)
Isophthalic polyester resin-based putty
3 laminations, 24-oz, 0-90 Knytex glass cloth wetted with isophthalic polyester resin
Airex 62.80 PVC foam
2 laminations, 24-oz 0-90 Knytex glass cloth wetted with isophthalic polyester resin

Dick Reineman* is a unique designer, one of the best U.S. model makers producing large pre-construction scale models at the time he develops the plans on his drawing board. Dick invited me to see his Newmar *model just finished, the hull made of FRP. He took it apart deck by deck, fully completed inside. A few days later he gave me photos of this model in the water, floating on its lines.*

The 88'.*Newmar* is one of his *Andromeda* series of yachts 60' and longer. We show the 130' *Andromeda* series below with a 26' beam. It is a fast, general-purpose ship with 9' headroom in the salon.

The *Andromeda* series is his present project involving the latest advances in technology and performance, plus economic factors reducing its maintenance and down time. It begins with eliminating outside varnish.

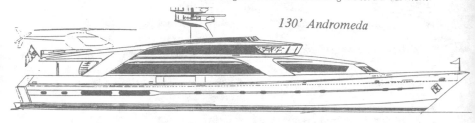

130' Andromeda

408 I studied photos of his 36'' *Newmar* model, and the 44'' model of the 130' *Andromeda.* I kept staring, unable to find one photo detail to prove whether they were full size yachts in the water floating on their lines... or models made and photographed by a master craftsman.

When Dick invited me to see his 130' pre-construction model, I mentally walked the flying bridge analyzing controls, and the upper aft deck with room for a small helicopter. He removed the flying bridge so I could walk thru the enclosed pilot house with console, electronics, etc.

The upper deck was removed as I entered the main deck unbroken stem to stern, walking thru the salon area, bar, fireplace, dining room, and galley. I walked forward to enter a split-level area with spa-pool, guest lounge and bar with tape deck, plus a library, recreational area.

The main deck was removed. I started from the bow examining quarters for 6 crew members, captains cabin, guest cabins, master suite & engine room. Stern wash deck with garage-door opener permits one-man launch and retrieval of two 20' boats stored inside in various conditions.

Port and starboard outfolding control stations permit single-handed docking visibility requiring minimum crew for anchoring and docking.

Reineman has produced powerboat designs for 40 years. He designed production models for Bristol ski boats, Owens, Pacifica, Brunswick, etc. He designed custom yachts for Willard Boat Works, Ted Elliot, Admiral Marine, Knight & Carver, and others. We show the latest from his drawing board for the next generation of large yachts. His emphasis is performance to increase top speed with stronger, lighter designs, that will be more sea kindly in the whole range of ocean conditions.

**Richard Reineman, Industrial Design, 3698 Zola Street, San Diego, CA 92106*

A 36'' pre-construction model of the *Newmar* page 405.

Large powerboat designs limited to top, side, and sectional views in style' with popular trends, produce attractive advertising brochures. As time wasn't taken to test the designs by building accurate scale models, small to large unforseen problems may surface later.

A major builder distributed brochures of his new 40 footer looking like a 50 footer below in the cabin. He asked me to be the first to see the new hull. He introduced me topside to the interior designer, then he left.

The designer panicked below. He had taken the upper deck level outline instead of the much smaller floor level outline below on the plans which reduced capacity to 70% shown in the full-color brochure. Many more tragic and hilarious design stories can be added, yet space is limited.

Future of large powerboats— we need better visibility from the helm in all directions as we go faster, with single handed skipper docking. Smaller crews have to be more efficient handling dock lines, anchor lines, and mooring pickups. For speeds 50 knots and above, we need seat belts, kidney supports, back support, and hand holds with Dick building several High Performance seats. Every inch topside and enclosed cabin space areas must be fully engineered with the latest style trends, comfort, and roominess.

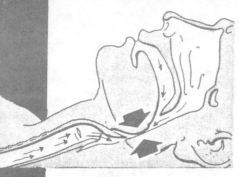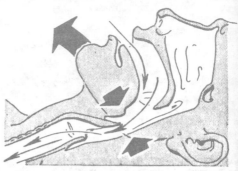

Drowning is the third major cause of accidental U.S. fatalities with nonswimmers who fall overboard, a major boating contribution. Panic is immediate followed by trying to holler for help underwater.

- **The throat is a one-way valve** with the back of the tongue pressing against and blocking the upper air passageway involved in suffocation, drownings, and heart attacks. Many auto deaths are caused by an airway obstruction, shock, or respiratory arrest, NOT primary injuries.

- **The throat must be opened immediately** by pulling or pushing the jaw so air can be inhaled...and exhaled from the lungs.

410

- **Air must be forced into the lungs** by mouth to mouth, or mouth to nose.

  Few people seem interested in artificial respiration which is simple to understand and apply. Then with startling swiftness a drowning victim's life is in your hands, or the situation reversed with you the victim. Will your sailing friends or family be able to help you?

- **The timing cycle is critical.** Adults may have irreversible brain damage in 4 to 6 minutes from oxygen starvation, while damage occurs much more rapidly with small children and **infants** with smaller lungs.

- **Before you start—** clear victims mouth and air passage, then force air into an adults lungs. Give an adult victim **four quick breaths** without an interruption. Take a deep breath (twice normal), then open the **victim's** mouth and begin forcing air into his lungs.

- **If the heart has stopped—** which is determined after the artificial respiration procedure has started, CPR is required.

- **CPR** (cardiopulmonary resuscitation) **training?** Are CPR classes offered by hospitals or other organizations in your area? Please take a course which will not require much time so you are able to act immediately if required to help a heart attack, or drowning victim.

Emergency Care— Robert J. Brady Company, Bowie, MD 20715. It is used to teach police, firemen, and rescue units. A copy protected in a zip-lock bag should be aboard sailboats and powerboats going offshore, and a second in the home library as you never know when it is needed.

Sailing Illustrated

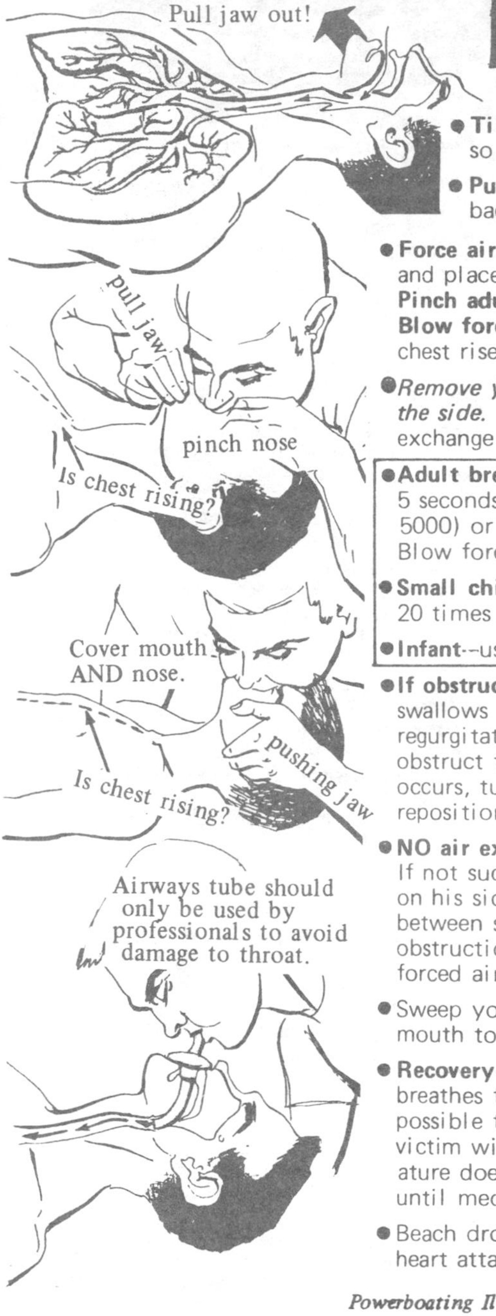

Pull jaw out!

pull jaw

pinch nose

Is chest rising?

Cover mouth AND nose.

Is chest rising?

pushing jaw

Airways tube should only be used by professionals to avoid damage to throat.

- **Tilt head to break the air block** so chin points 45 degrees upward.

- **Push/pull jaw** to lift tongue from back of throat to open throat.

- **Force air in** by opening your mouth and place it tightly over victims mouth. **Pinch adult's nose** to make a tight seal. **Blow forcefully** to make the victim's chest rise.

- *Remove your mouth, turn your head to the side.* Can you hear or feel an air exchange with an **outward rush of air?**

- **Adult breathing cycle—** is once every 5 seconds (count 1000 2000 3000 4000 5000) or approximately 12 per minute. Blow forcefully and vigorously.

- **Small child--** use normal breath pressure 20 times per minute or every 3 seconds.

- **Infant--**use small puffs from your cheeks. **411**

- **If obstruction exists--** drowning victim swallows some **water** and if **food** is regurgitated from the stomach, it will obstruct the air passage. If vomiting occurs, turn victim on side, wipe mouth, reposition victim, continue blowing.

- **NO air exchange?** Check head and jaw. If not successful—turn victim quickly on his side. Hit several sharp blows between shoulder blades to dislodge obstruction, reposition, and continue forced air cycle. Occasionally—

- Sweep your fingers through victim's mouth to remove any foreign matter.

- **Recovery--** continue **cycle** till victim breathes freely. Keep him quiet as possible till breathing regularly. Cover victim with blanket so body temperature doesn't go down. Treat for shock until medical help arrives.

- Beach drownings also occur from heart attacks and sun strokes.

Powerboating Illustrated

INDEX

trailerboats-5
classroom use-6
our background-7
mechanic's goals-8
trailerboating?-9
sunbelt, snowbelt-10,11

● **basic concepts**
outboard/inboard 12-15
hull basics-16,17
accident prone-18-9,116-7,206-8
semi-planing-20,21
seaworthiness-22,23
wet or dry ride-24,25
G force durability-26,27

● **displacement hulls**
sailboat outboards-28
varied basics-29-31
hull strength/speed-32
the rocker-33 34
plowing/planing-35

● **planing hulls**
412   planing theory 36,37
trailerboats-38,39
Blunder planing-40-43
1,2 3 point hulls-44,45
bow entry-46
hull efficiency-47,48,49
planing aids-50,51
hull air lift-52
hydrofoil-53
your exam-54

● **planing problems**
transom chine-56,57
the hook-58,59
rocker, porpoise-60,61
thrust angle-62,63
transom mounting-64,65
basic problems-66,67
overloading-68,69
directional stability-70,71
steering-72

● **broach, flip**
the basics-73
turning flip-74,75 261
broach, chine flip-76,77

water, fuel weight-115

● **regulations, lights**
collision basics-78,79
powerboat rules-80,81
sailboat rules-82,83
operating lights-84-87
large vessels-88,89
large vessel charts-90,91
fog signals-92,93
fog cause, prediction-94,95
Radar Flag-94,95

● **powerboat operation**
basic factors-96,97
USCG statistics-98,99
prop torque-100-103
twin props-103
buoyage-104,105
tides-106,107
magnetic compass-108,109
wind force-110,111
currents-112
rdf-113
towing, cleats-114,115
liquor -116
fishermen,hunters-117
open zipper hazard-117
equipment problems-118,119
narrow channels-119
CO poisoning-120,121,266
seasick?-122
preservers-123,206
exposure-dehydration,
        hypothermia-124-127
swim,SCUBA lessons-126
drownproof, overboard-128,129
George & Charlie- 130-136
Courageous—130,131
planning survival-132,133
large vessel lookouts?-134
the EPIRB-135
water still-136
inflatables-137
canoe, kayak-138
surface anchor-139,140
bottom anchors-140-143

● **weather patterns**
square rig sailing-144
Cutty Sark-145
weather proverbs-146,147
cloud formations-148,149
world patterns-150
U.S. storm patterns-151-153
barometer-153
thunderstorms-154,155
lightning-156,157
sea breeze-158 159
air funnels-159
devil winds-160
CAT-161
dusters-clear air-154

● **boat trailers**
regulation terminology-162
front bumper hitch-162
support, coupler-163
handling ease-164,165
short haul long haul-166,167
trailer support-168,169
adjustments-170
tiedowns-171
towing vehicle-172
trailer wiring-173
the hitch-174
surge brakes-175
sailboat trailers-176,177
auto hub bearings-178,358
marine hub bearings-179
packing hubs, brakes-180,181
slings, pad eyes-180
tires-182,183
boat cover-184 185
water, fuel weight-115
boat cover fires-185

● **Rope-knots splices**
size/strength-186
knots vs strength-186
terms, hockle-187
braided rope-188 189
new rope-190
joining rope-191
cleats, hitches-192
heaving line-194
coiling rope-195
bowline, square-196
whipping ends-197
3 strand eye splice-198
short splice-199

end or back splice-199
togboat hitch-200
towing bridle-200
braided rope splice-201-205

● **boating safety**
definition-206
boating risks-207
licensing?-208
Nationwide Boating
Survey statistics-208,209
teach boating-210
boat inspection-211

● **propellers**
LH vs RH props-214
prop terms-215
prop choice-216,217
shear pin,slip clutch-218
2,3,4,5 blade prop-219
prop torque-220,221
inboard rudders-220
cavitation-222,223
cavitation blowout-222
high vs low rake-223
stern walking-224
venturi nozzle-224
supercavitation-224
twin motors-225

● **4-cycle engines**
downdraft carb-227,263
combustion-228
fuel handling-229
ignition range-229,248,267,296
inboard engine-230
inboard cooling-231
boiler scale-231,370
the outdrive-232
V drive/tunnel drive-233
jet drive-234
double hose clamps-234
sailboat engines-235
rotary engine-236,237

● **2-cycle engine**
operation theory

● **2-cycle carburetors**
side bowl carb-242-254
center bowl carb-255-259
ignition range-229,248,267,296

413

27 easy ways to enter powerboating...

Royce's
Powerboating Illustrated
ISBN 0-911284-02-8
416 pages, 5 1/4 x 7 1/2
$15.00 retail, paperback
plus $1.50 postage
*"The best of ALL
Powerboating Worlds"*

Royce's **Powerboating
Illustrated Workbook**
ISBN 0-911284-03-6
48 pages 7 1/2 x 10
$5.00 retail, $1.00 postage
Volume discounts?
The most efficient teaching
method for industry & owners

● **USCG standards**
fuel hoses,hp ratings-260,261
upsets,steering problems-261
fuel tanks,filters,jet nozzle-262-3
electricals,GFI,,battery,vent-264
highway fires-264

414 *USCG EAGLE-265*

● **fuel basics**
CO engine exhaust-120-1,266
ignition range-229,248,267,296
oil coolant-268,269
bearing lubrication-268
1960 fuel tank-270,276
fuel hose clamps-234,270, USCG 262
2 cycle mixing-271
tank/battery restraint-271,301,349,352
stuck rings-272
cylinder deposits-273
mechanical pneumonia 274
stale fuel-274 275
tank corrosion-276
built-in tanks-262,270,276 301
troll/solvents-277
hp variables-261 278,279
4 alcohol in gasoline- 262
pressure/vacuum systems 280

● **spark plugs**
12 problems-283
plug basics-282,283
plug boot-285

plug wrench-286
heat dissipation-287
heat ranges-288
poor mixing-290
plug diagnosis-291
foul/shunting-293
plug gap-293
plug problems-294,295

● **fire cause/prevention**
fuel ignition range
fire classes-297
LPG warning-297
cooking alcohol-297
extinguishers-298,299
flammable liquids-300
spontaneous combustion-300
electrical fires-297,301
gas, butane stoves-301
fueling/vent hose-301

● **electricity**
PCI,CDI systems-302
CDI system variables-303
forms of electricity-304,305
magnetism-306,308,314,320,416
measuring current-307
ions, **current flow-308,374**
troubleshooting-309
flywheel magneto-310,311
points & condensers-312,313
4 cylinder magneto-314,315